FRENCH NOW! Level 1

Fourth Edition

by

Christopher Kendris, Ph.D.

Former Assistant Professor
Department of French and Spanish
State University of New York
Albany, New York

and

Theodore Kendris, Ph.D.

Former Adjunct Instructor
Penn State University
Hazleton Campus

BARRON'S

To St. Sophia Greek Orthodox Church
of Albany, New York, our parish
and
to the eternal memory of our beloved
YOLANDA FENYO KENDRIS
who is always by our side
with love

Cover Photo: *Notre Dame gargoyle with the Paris skyline in the background.*
Telegraph Colour Lib/FPG International Corp.

All inquiries should be addressed to:
Barron's Educational Series, Inc.
250 Wireless Boulevard
Hauppauge, New York   11788
www.barronseduc.com

ISBN-13: 978-0-7641-3560-6 (book)
ISBN-10: 0-7641-3560-0 (book)
ISBN-13: 978-0-7641-7958-7 (book/CD-ROM package)
ISBN-10: 0-7641-7958-6 (book/CD-ROM package)

Library of Congress Catalog Card No. 2006026220

Library of Congress Cataloging-in-Publication Data

Kendris, Christopher.
    French now! level one / by Christopher Kendris and Theodore Kendris.—4th ed.
        p. cm.—(Barron's educational series)
    English and French.
    Includes index.
    ISBN-13: 978-0-7641-3560-6
    ISBN-10: 0-7641-3560-0
    ISBN-13: 978-0-7641-7958-7
    ISBN-10: 0-7641-7958-6
    1. French language—Textbooks for foreign speakers—English.   I. Kendris, Theodore.   II. Title.

PC2129.E5K429   2007
448.2'421—dc22   2006026220

PRINTED IN THE UNITED STATES OF AMERICA

Table of Contents

Part 2: Vocabulary   377

Part 3: Idioms, Verbal Expressions, and Dialogues 415

Part 4: Skill in Listening Comprehension 435

Part 5: Skill in Reading Comprehension 451

Part 6: Skill in Writing 469

About the Authors

Christopher Kendris has taught French at Northwestern University, at the College of the University of Chicago, at Rutgers University, at the State University of New York at Albany, and at Schenectady County Community College. For several years he also taught French and Spanish at Farmingdale High School, Farmingdale, New York, where he was chairman of the Department of Foreign Languages.

Dr. Kendris received his B.S. and M.S. degrees at Columbia University in the City of New York and his M.A. and Ph.D. degrees at Northwestern University in Evanston, Illinois. He also earned two certificates with *Mention très Honorable* at the École Supérieure de Préparation et de Perfectionnement des Professeurs de Français à l'Étranger, Faculté des Lettres, Université de Paris.

He is the author of numerous school and college books, workbooks, and other language guides. Among his most popular works are *501 French Verbs* and *501 Spanish Verbs Fully Conjugated in All the Tenses, with special new features* (both books in a Sixth Edition), *French the Easy Way*, Fourth Edition (with answers), *Spanish Grammar, French Grammar, French Vocabulary, Write It in French, Write It in Spanish* (both composition workbooks with answers), *Master the Basics: French* (Second Edition), *Master the Basics: Spanish* (Second Edition), *Pronounce It Perfectly in French* (Second Edition, with three CDs), *Spanish Now! Level 2*, Second Edition (with two audiocassettes), and many others, all of which have been published by Barron's. He is listed in *Contemporary Authors* and the *Directory of American Scholars*.

Theodore Kendris earned his B.A. degree in modern languages at Union College, Schenectady, New York, where he received the Thomas J. Judson Memorial Award for modern language study. He went on to earn his M.A. degree in French language and literature at Northwestern University, Evanston, Illinois, where he held a teaching assistantship. He earned his Ph.D. degree in French Literature at Université Laval in Quebec City, where he studied the Middle Ages and Renaissance. While at Université Laval he taught French writing skills as *chargé de cours* in the French as a Second Language program and, in 1997, he was awarded a doctoral scholarship by the Fondation de l'Université Laval. He has also taught in the Department of English and Foreign Languages at the University of St. Francis in Joliet, Illinois, as well as at the Hazleton campus of Penn State University.

Abbreviations used in this book

adj.	adjective	*fam.*	familiar	*par.*	paragraph
adv.	adverb	*i.e.*	that is, that is to say	*part.*	participle
advl.	adverbial	*illus.*	illustration	*per.*	personal
art.	article	*indef.*	indefinite	*pers.*	person
conj.	conjunction	*indic.*	indicative	*pl.*	plural
def.	definite	*indir.*	indirect	*poss.*	possessive
dem.	demonstrative	*inf.*	infinitive	*prep.*	preposition
dir.	direct	*interj.*	interjection	*pres.*	present
disj.	disjunctive	*interrog.*	interrogative	*pron.*	pronoun
e.g.	for example	*m.* or *masc.*	masculine	*refl.*	reflexive
etc.	et cetera, and so on	*n.*	noun	*rel.*	relative
exclam.	exclamation	*no.*	number	*s.* or *sing.*	singular
expr.	expression	*obj.*	object	*subj.*	subject
f. or *fem.*	feminine	*p.*	page	*v.*	verb

Preface to the Fourth Edition

FRENCH NOW! Level 1 is intended for students of elementary French in schools and colleges. This book makes the study of French stimulating for the student of any age because it is infused with enthusiasm, life, and vigor.

The book can also be used for self-instruction. It is suitable for review if you have already studied French and would like to refresh your memory of the basics of the language.

The book also features evidence of French as a living language. There are clippings from French newspapers and magazines, photographs of famous places, maps, the words and music of French songs, two easy poems, crossword puzzles and other word games, simple riddles, proverbs, even a recipe in French for a delicious stew, announcements, and many other features. The stories and dialogues in this book, for the most part, tell of the adventures of an imaginary French family— Claire and François Paquet, their two children, Janine and Pierre, and their dog, Coco.

The traditional exercises in this book provide you with a solid foundation in the basic structures of the French language, including a thorough presentation of a wide range of vocabulary, idiomatic expressions, grammar, and verbs.

This book focuses on French for communication. The primary objective is to help you communicate freely in French by providing exercises that encourage you to participate in speaking, listening, reading, and writing to achieve proficiency.

The exercises in this book focus on practical situations that are functional, such as meeting people, socializing, providing and obtaining information, talking about what you see in pictures, expressing personal feelings, asking for help, giving advice, helping others, shopping, sports, educational and cultural topics, an appreciation of French art, and much more.

Other new features include verb tables, in the back pages of the book, for easy and quick reference, and a section on definitions of basic grammatical terms with examples in French and English to help you achieve a better understanding of the different parts of speech and elements of sentence structure. There is also a comprehensive index.

The language content in this book meets the minimum standards and sequence of an introductory course of study in French.

We want to thank Françoise Lapouille, friend and colleague of Christopher Kendris. Mme Lapouille was born and educated in France and has been a teacher of French for many years. She holds the degree of *Licence ès Lettres* from the Université de Paris (La Sorbonne). She read the draft of this book to make certain that the French is *juste et comme il faut*, correct and as it should be.

We hope you find the stories, dialogues, situations for speaking and writing, artwork, photographs, the variety of exercises, word games, and puzzles interesting and fun to do.

Finally, we are grateful for the assistance provided by the Service de Presse et d'Information of the Ambassade de France and the French Government Tourist Office, both offices in New York.

In order to help students acquire skill in conversational French, this book is also available with a set of three audio CDs available from Barron's and at bookstores.

Christopher Kendris, Ph.D.
Theodore Kendris, Ph.D.

Interesting Facts

Did you know that the population of France is almost 63 million? Did you know that French is spoken in many other places besides France? French is spoken in Belgium, Cameroon, Canada (chiefly in the provinces of Québec and New Brunswick as well as some parts of Ontario), Djibouti, French Guiana, the French West Indies, Gabon, Haiti, the Ivory Coast, Laos, Lebanon, Luxembourg, Mali, Senegal, Switzerland, and Chad, just to name a few! French is also spoken in Morocco and Tunisia, which are in the North African region known as the Maghreb.

Did you know that an estimated 160 million people speak French, either as their native language or second language? In fact, some estimates are as high as 180 million! On top of that, there are approximately 250 million people in the world who can conduct their everyday activities in French. In the United States alone there are almost 500,000 French immigrants; over 11 million people in North America are native French speakers, mainly in Canada.

You are one of millions of students all over the world who are studying the French language!

Simple Guide to the Basics of French Pronunciation

The purpose of this guide is to help you pronounce French words as correctly as possible so you can communicate effectively when speaking and to help you recognize French words when you hear them spoken. It is not intended to perfect your pronunciation of French; that is accomplished by imitating spoken French that you must hear from the lips of persons who pronounce French accurately. If you want to improve your pronunciation of French, we recommend *Pronounce It Perfectly in French*, also published by Barron's. The book comes in a case with three CDs. You can listen to the beautiful French language spoken by professional French radio commentators and imitate what you hear during the pauses.

The column headed *French single letters, doubles,* and *clusters* has an alphabetical list of vowels, semi-vowels, clusters or groups of semi-vowels and vowels, nasal vowels, and consonants. When you see a French word in this book, try to pronounce it aloud after you look up the French letters in the alphabetical listing. There are some exceptions, but these will not matter significantly, as long as you pronounce the word accurately enough to make yourself understood. When in doubt, ask someone who speaks French well to pronounce the word or words for you. In the column next to the French spellings there are English words that contain similar sounds. The letters in the English words are printed in *italics* to indicate that those sounds are something like the French sounds.

Here are a few tips to keep in mind:

1. Never pronounce the t in the word **et**, meaning *and*. Pronounce the word *ay*, as in the English word *may*.

2. If a word ends in a consonant, do not pronounce that consonant. There are many exceptions to this rule, but here are a few examples when you do pronounce the final consonant: **le parc, le chef, l'oeuf, le fils** (*feess*). Be aware that pronunciation affects meaning. Generally, when you encounter **est**, it is a verb form meaning *is*, and the three letters are pronounced like the *e* in the English word *egg*. If you pronounce the **st** in **est**, it means *east*.

3. If a word ends in **z**, pronounce it as **z** only if the word right after it begins with a vowel or silent **h**. Do the same if the word ends in **s** or **x**. The following sentence illustrates this.

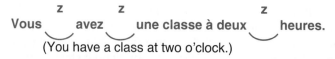

(You have a class at two o'clock.)

4. When **e** is the last letter of a French word or verb form, it is pronounced ever so slightly with no stress, like the *e* in *the* when you say *the book*. That **e** is called a mute **e** because it is barely pronounced.

5. In French, there are several spellings for the same sound. Here is one typical example where the different spellings are all pronounced *ay*, as in the English word *may*.

   et   (j')ai   (parl)é   (av)ez   (all)er   (l)es

6. When speaking French, stress is evenly distributed on the vowels, but you must raise your voice slightly on the last sound when more than one is in a given word or group of words; for example, in pronouncing **s'il vous plaît** (please), raise your voice a bit on **plaît**. Consult the alphabetical list for the sounds.

7. There are only four nasal vowel sounds in French. They are expressed in the following catchy phrase, which means a *good white wine*: **un bon vin blanc**. How do you nasalize

a vowel in French? Instead of letting your breath (air) out through your mouth, you must push it up your nose so that it does not come out through your mouth. For the various spellings of nasal vowels, consult the alphabetical list.

8. In French there are only three accent marks that are written over certain vowels. They are **accent aigu (´)**, **accent grave (`)**, and **accent circonflexe (^)**. For the pronunciation of vowels with these accent marks, consult the alphabetical list.

9. Now study the following list of French single letters, doubles, and clusters found in French words. It is not exhaustive or encyclopedic. These are merely the sounds most commonly used in French words. Also study the second column of English words with similar sounds. Remember that the sounds represented by the *italicized* letters in the English words are only approximate. As long as you pronounce French well enough to make yourself understood when speaking, that is all that really matters. Improvement in French pronunciation comes with practice, experience, and imitation of people who pronounce French accurately. The best way to accomplish that is to take a trip to a place where French is spoken. **Bon voyage!**

French single letters, doubles, clusters	English words with similar sounds	French single letters, doubles, clusters	English words with similar sounds
a, à	*lo*lly pop, T*o*m	eau, eaux	*oh!*
â, as	*ah!*	ei, eil, eille	m*a*y
ai, ay, aye	m*a*y	eim, ein	s*a*ng (nasal vowel)
ail, aille, âille	*eye*	elle, elles	*Ell*en
aile	*Ell*en	em, en	y*on*der (nasal vowel)
aim, ain	s*a*ng (nasal vowel)	-ent	As a verb ending, do not pronounce.
ais, ait, aît	*e*gg	ère	*air*
am, an	y*on*der (nasal vowel)	est-ce	bl*ess*
aou, aoû	t*oo*	-et	*e*gg (ending of a word)
au, aud, ault, aut, aux }	*oh!*	eu, eue	c*u*te
aude	*o*de	-eu, -eue, eux	p*u*dding (ending of a word)
aune	*ow*n	euil, euille	*loya*l
b	*b*un	eul	h*ull*
c + a, o, u	*c*at, *c*op, *c*ut	eur, eure	*pur*ple
c + e, i, y	*c*ent, *c*ity, *c*ylinder	ey, ez	m*a*y
ç	*s*it	f	*if*
ch	*sh*ip; rarely *k* as in echo	g + a, o, u	*g*as, *g*o, *g*um
d	*d*og	g + e, i, y	mea*s*ure
dj	bri*dge*	gn	ca*ny*on
e	th*e*	gua	*Gua*m
é, ée, ées, er, ey ez, et }	m*a*y	gue	*gue*rilla
è, ê	*e*gg	gui	*ge*ese

xi

French single letters, doubles, clusters	English words with similar sounds	French single letters, doubles, clusters	English words with similar sounds
h	Not pronounced as a single letter; see ph, sh, th in this list.	oui	*we*
		p	*p*ark; at times not pronounced, as in **sept** (set)
i, î, id, ie, ies, is, it, iz	s*ee*		
		ph	*ph*iloso*ph*y
ia	*ya*rd	q, qu	*k*it
ied, ier, iers	*yea*	qua	*ca*t
ieu	*yu*ppy, *yu*ppie	que	*ke*rchief
il, ils	*eel*	qui	*k*ey
im, in	s*ang* (nasal vowel)	r	ga*r*gle
ique	s*eek*	rr	pu*rr*
j	mea*s*ure	s	*s*it; at times ro*s*e
k	*k*it	sc + a, o, u	*sc*andal, *sc*old, *sc*um
l	*l*et	sc + e, i, y	*sc*ene, *sc*ience, *sc*ythe
ll	*l*et; at times, like *y* in *y*et, as in **fille**	sh	*sh*ampoo
		squa	*squa*nder
m	*m*e	ss	ki*ss*
n	*n*o	t, tt	*t*o
o	*u*p; at times, s*o*	tch	*ch*urch
ô, ot	s*o*	th	*t*ea
oeil	l*oya*l	u, û, ue	*cu*te
oeu, oeud, oeufs	p*u*dding	ueil, ueille	l*oya*l
oeur	p*ur*ple	ui, uie, uis, uit, uy	f*ew ea*t
oi, oid, oids, oie, oigt, ois, oix, oua, oy	*wa*sh	um, un	s*ung* (nasal vowel)
		v, w	*v*erb
oim, oin	*wang*le (nasal vowel)	x	e*x*cuse, e*x*ample, gee*s*e
om, on, ons, ont	s*ong* (nasal vowel)		
ou, où, oud, oue, oup, ous, out, oût, oux	t*oo*	y	s*ee*; at times, *y* as in *y*et
		z	*z*ero
oué	*wa*y		

Leçons Préliminaires
Preliminary Lessons

I. La famille Paquet: Présentation

Salut! *Hi!*
Nous sommes la famille Paquet.
We are the Paquet family.

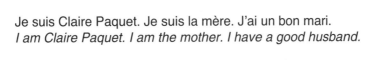

Je suis Claire Paquet. Je suis la mère. J'ai un bon mari.
I am Claire Paquet. I am the mother. I have a good husband.

Je suis François Paquet. Je suis le père. J'ai une bonne épouse.
I am François Paquet. I am the father. I have a good wife.

Je suis Janine. Je suis la fille. J'ai un bon frère.
I am Janine. I am the daughter. I have a good brother.

Je suis Pierre. Je suis le fils. J'ai une bonne soeur.
I am Pierre. I am the son. I have a good sister.

Je suis Coco. Je suis le chien. J'ai une bonne famille.
I am Coco. I am the dog. I have a good family.

Present Tense		Present Tense	
être *(to be)*		**avoir** *(to have)*	
je suis	I am	j'ai	I have
tu es	you are	tu as	you have
il est	he *or* it is	il a	he *or* it has
elle est	she *or* it is	elle a	she *or* it has
nous sommes	we are	nous avons	we have
vous êtes	you are	vous avez	you have
ils sont	they are	ils ont	they have
elles sont	they are	elles ont	they have

EXERCISES

I. Fill in the missing French words on the blank lines. Refer to the preceding page if you have to.

1. Je suis François Paquet. Je suis ____le____ ____père____ . J'ai ____une____ ____bonne____ ____épouse____ .

2. Je suis Claire Paquet. Je ____suis____ la ____mère____ . J'ai _____ un ____bon____ mari.

3. Je suis Pierre. Je ____suis____ le fils. J'ai ____une____ bonne ____soeur____ .

4. Je suis Janine. Je suis ____la____ ____fille____ . J'ai un ____bon____ frère.

5. Je suis Coco. Je ____suis____ ____le____ chien. ____J'ai____ une bonne ____famille____ .

II. Match the following.

1. I am the daughter.   __3__   Je suis le fils.
2. I am the father.   __4__   Je suis la mère.
3. I am the son.   __1__   Je suis la fille.
4. I am the mother.   __5__   Je suis le chien.
5. I am the dog.   __2__   Je suis le père.

III. Write five short sentences telling who's who in the Paquet family.

1. __François est le père__
2. __Claire est la mère__
3. __Janine est la fille__
4. __Pierre est le fils__
5. __Coco est le chien__

IV. Description. Proficiency in Writing.

A. Write two adjectives to describe a boy you know.

    1. _____   2. _____

B. Write two adjectives to describe a girl you know.

    1. _____   2. _____

V. Qui est-ce? (Who is it?) On the blank line write in French the name of the person described. **C'est . . .** (It's . . .)

1. Je suis la fille. J'ai un bon frère.

   Qui est-ce? C'est_____Janine_____.

2. Je suis la mère. J'ai un bon mari.

   Qui est-ce? C'est_____Clair_____.

3. Je suis le père. J'ai une bonne épouse.

   Qui est-ce? C'est_____François_____.

4. Je suis le chien. J'ai une bonne famille.

   Qui est-ce? C'est_____Coco_____.

5. Je suis le fils. J'ai une bonne soeur.

   Qui est-ce? C'est_____Pierre_____.

VI. Choose the correct answer and write the letter on the blank line.

1. Janine est
   (a) la mère.   (b) le père.   (c) la fille.   (d) le fils.   _____c_____

2. Pierre est
   (a) le père.   (b) la mère.   (c) la soeur.   (d) le frère.   _____d_____

3. Claire Paquet est
   (a) le père.   (b) la mère.   (c) la fille.   (d) le fils.   _____b_____

4. Coco est
   (a) le fils.   (b) la fille.   (c) la soeur.   (d) le chien.   _____d_____

5. François Paquet est
   (a) le frère.   (b) le fils.   (c) le père.   (d) la mère.   _____c_____

c'est - say

II. Choses (Things)

The pictures are arranged alphabetically by word.

l'arbre — Est-ce un arbre? — Oui, c'est un arbre. Il est grand.

le ballon — Est-ce un ballon? — Oui, c'est un ballon. Il est rond.

la banane — Est-ce une orange? — Non, ce n'est pas une orange.
Est-ce une banane? — Oui, c'est une banane. Elle est bonne.

la chaise — Est-ce une table? — Non, ce n'est pas une table.
Est-ce une chaise? — Oui, c'est une chaise. Elle est petite.

5

EXERCISES

I. Fill in the missing words (adjectives). Refer to the statements next to the pictures on the previous page.

1. L'arbre est _grande_ .
2. Le ballon est _rond_ .
3. La banane est _bonne_ .
4. La chaise est _petite_ .

II. Choose the correct adjective. Refer to the statements on the previous page.

1. La chaise est (a) petite. (b) ronde. (c) grande. (d) bonne. _a_
2. La banane est (a) ronde. (b) grande. (c) petite. (d) bonne. _d_
3. Le ballon est (a) rond. (b) grand. (c) bon. (d) petit. _a_
4. L'arbre est (a) grand. (b) petit. (c) rond. (d) bon. _a_

III. Match the following.

1. the chair
2. the ball
3. the tree
4. the banana

_4_ la banane
_3_ l'arbre
_1_ la chaise
_2_ le ballon

le chapeau	Est-ce un chapeau?	Oui, c'est un chapeau. Il est joli.
la commode	Est-ce une chaise? Est-ce une commode?	Non, ce n'est pas une chaise. Oui, c'est une commode. Elle est belle.
le crayon	Est-ce un stylo? Est-ce un crayon?	Non, ce n'est pas un stylo. Oui, c'est un crayon. Il est long.
la fleur	Est-ce une fleur?	Oui, c'est une fleur. Elle est jolie.

nice lovely pretty

beautiful

long

EXERCISES

I. Fill in the missing words (adjectives). Refer to the statements next to the pictures above.

1. Le chapeau est _joli_ .
2. La commode est _~~beau~~ belle_ .
3. Le crayon est _long_ .
4. La fleur est _jolie_ .

II. Match the following. Refer to the statements on the previous page.

1. the pencil   _____3_____ la fleur
2. the hat   _____1_____ le crayon
3. the flower   _____4_____ la commode
4. the dresser   _____2_____ le chapeau

III. Choose the correct adjective. Refer to the statements on the previous page.

1. Le chapeau est
   (a) joli.   (b) long.   (c) bon.   (d) petit.   _____a_____

2. La commode est
   (a) belle.   (b) ronde.   (c) longue.   (d) bonne.   _____a_____

3. Le crayon est
   (a) joli.   (b) rond.   (c) bon.   (d) long.   _____d_____

4. La fleur est
   (a) jolie.   (b) ronde.   (c) grande.   (d) longue.   _____a_____

le garage	Est-ce un garage?	Oui, c'est un garage. Il est <u>grand</u>. *big*	
le gâteau	Est-ce un chapeau? Est-ce un gâteau?	Non, ce n'est pas un <u>chapeau</u>. *hat?* Oui, c'est un gâteau. Il est <u>délicieux</u>.	
le jambon	Est-ce un jambon?	Oui, c'est un jambon. Il est <u>beau</u>. *beautiful* *delicious*	
le journal	Est-ce un journal?	Oui, c'est un journal. Il est <u>intéressant</u>. *interesting*	

EXERCISES

I. Fill in the missing words (adjectives). Refer to the statements next to the pictures above.

1. Le garage est _____grand_____.
2. Le gâteau est _____délicieux_____.
3. Le jambon est _____beau_____.
4. Le journal est _____intéressant_____.

II. **Choose the correct adjective. Refer to the statements on the previous page.**

1. Le garage est
   (a) intéressant.   (b) délicieux.   (c) grand.   _____c_____

2. Le gâteau est
   (a) long.   (b) intéressant.   (c) délicieux.   _____c_____

3. Le jambon est
   (a) beau.   (b) grand.   (c) intéressant.   _____a_____

4. Le journal est
   (a) rond.   (b) intéressant.   (c) beau.   _____b_____

III. **Fill in the missing words. Refer to the statements next to the pictures on the previous page.**

1. Est-ce un garage? Oui __c'est__ __un__ __garage__ . Il __est__ grand.

2. Est-ce un chapeau? Non, ce __n'est__ __pas__ un chapeau. C'est __un__ gâteau.

3. Est-ce un jambon? Oui, __c'est__ un jambon. Il est __beau__ .

4. Est-ce un journal? Oui, __c'est__ un journal. Il __est__ intéressant.

une – Feminine
un – masculine

une lampe   Est-ce une lampe?   Oui, c'est une lampe. Elle est splendide.
  ouröu   splendid

un lit   Est-ce une commode?   Non, ce n'est pas une commode.
  lee   Est-ce un lit?   Oui, c'est un lit. Il est confortable.
                                                        comfortable

une maison   Est-ce un garage?   Non, ce n'est pas un garage.
                  Est-ce une maison?   Oui, c'est une maison. Elle est charmante.
                                                        charming

un oeuf   Est-ce un ballon?   Non, ce n'est pas un ballon.
  uff   Est-ce un oeuf?   Oui, c'est un oeuf. Il est blanc.
                                                        white

EXERCISES

I. **Choose the correct adjective. Refer to the statements next to the pictures above.**

1. Le lit est
   (a) blanc.   (b) délicieux.   (c) intéressant.   (d) confortable.   _____d_____

2. La lampe est
   (a) confortable. (b) splendide.   (c) bonne.   (d) longue.   _____b_____

3. La maison est
   (a) délicieuse.   (b) bonne.   (c) charmante.   (d) ronde.   _____c_____

4. L'oeuf est
   (a) blanc.   (b) charmant.   (c) confortable.   (d) beau.   _____a_____

II. Match the following.

1. a house
2. a lamp
3. a bed
4. an egg

_4_ un oeuf
_3_ un lit
_1_ une maison
_2_ une lampe

un parapluie Est-ce un parapluie? Oui, c'est un parapluie. Il est ouvert. *open*

une pomme Est-ce une banane? Non, ce n'est pas une banane. *beautiful*
Est-ce une pomme? Oui, c'est une pomme. Elle est magnifique. *apple*

une robe Est-ce un chapeau? Non, ce n'est pas un chapeau.
Est-ce une robe? Oui, c'est une robe. Elle est mignonne.

un sandwich Est-ce un gâteau? Non, ce n'est pas un gâteau.
Est-ce un sandwich? Oui, c'est un sandwich. Il est délicieux.

EXERCISES

I. Fill in the missing words (adjectives). Refer to the sentences next to the pictures above.

1. Le parapluie est _ouvert_. 3. La robe est _mignonne_.
2. La pomme est _magnifique_. 4. Le sandwich est _délicieux_.

II. Fill in the missing words. Refer to the sentences above.

1. Est-ce un parapluie? Oui, c'est _un_ _parapluie_. Il _est_ ouvert.
2. Est-ce une banane? Non, ce _n'est_ _pas_ une banane. C'_est_ un pomme.
3. Est-ce un chapeau? Non, _ce_ _n'est_ _pas_ un chapeau. C'est _une_ robe.
4. Est-ce un sandwich? Oui, c'est _un_ sandwich. Il est _délicieux_

un stylo
on la écrit

Est-ce un crayon?
Est-ce un stylo?

Non, ce n'est pas un crayon.
Oui, c'est un stylo. Il est <u>long</u>.

un téléphone

Est-ce une radio?
Est-ce un téléphone?

Non, ce n'est pas une radio. *black*
Oui, c'est un téléphone. Il est <u>noir</u>.

un téléviseur

Est-ce un téléviseur?

Oui, c'est un téléviseur. Il est beau.

un tele ← common word

un ordinateur

Est-ce un ordinateur?

Oui, c'est un ordinateur. Il est grand.

un ordi ← common word

EXERCISES

I. Choose the correct adjective. Refer to the sentences next to the pictures above.

1. Le stylo est
   (a) blanc.   (b) délicieux.   (c) ouvert.   (d) long.   _____d_____

2. Le téléphone est
   (a) confortable.   (b) joli.   (c) rond.   (d) noir.   _____d_____

3. Le téléviseur est
   (a) délicieux.   (b) beau.   (c) charmant.   (d) confortable.   _____b_____

4. L'ordinateur est
   (a) long.   (b) grand.   (c) noir.   (d) délicieux.   _____b_____

II. Match the following.

1. a television set   ____4____ un stylo
2. a chair   ____5____ un téléphone
3. a flower   ____1____ un téléviseur
4. a pen   ____6____ un oeuf
5. a telephone   ____2____ une chaise
6. an egg   ____3____ une fleur

III. **Personnes** (People)

க் தெரிவில்	க தெரிபில்	க் தெரிவில்
Que fait-il?	Que fait-elle?	Que font-ils?
(What is he doing?)	(What is she doing?)	(What are they doing?)

	Le garçon boit du lait. *wa milk*	Que fait-il?	Il boit du lait. *He drinks milk*
	La petite fille danse. *dance*	Que fait-elle?	Elle danse.
	Le garçon lit un livre. *read*	Que fait-il?	Il lit un livre.
	La petite fille et le garçon courent.	Que font-ils?	Ils courent.

EXERCISES

I.   **Fill in the missing words. Refer to the sentences next to the pictures above.**

1. Le garçon boit du lait. Que fait-il? Il ___boit___ du ___lait___ .

2. La petite fille danse. Que fait-elle? Elle ___danse___ .

3. Le garçon lit un livre. Que fait-il? Il lit ___un livre___ .

4. La petite fille et le garçon courent. Que font-ils? Ils ___courent___.

II.   **The following sentences are scrambled. Write them in the correct word order. Refer to the sentences next to the pictures above.**

1. Le / lait / du / garçon / boit / ___Le garçon boit du lait___ .

2. La / danse / jeune / fille / ___La ~~pe~~ jeune fille danse___ .

3. Le / livre / un / garçon / lit / ___Le garçon lit un livre___ .

4. La / fille / jeune / et / garçon / le / courent / ___La jeune fille et le garçon courent___

11

young woman sings

La jeune femme chante.
C'est une chanteuse. Que fait-elle? Elle chante.

La femme écrit une lettre. Que fait-elle? Elle écrit une lettre.

L'agent de police arrête les autos. Que fait-il? Il arrête les autos.

EXERCISES

I. Fill in the missing words. Refer to the sentences next to the pictures above.

1. La jeune femme chante. Que fait-elle? Elle _chante_ .

2. La femme écrit une lettre. Que fait-elle? Elle _écrit_ une lettre.

3. L'agent de police arrête les autos. Que fait-il? Il _arrête_ les _autos_ .

II. Choose the correct answer. Refer to the sentences next to the pictures above.

1. La jeune femme
   (a) arrête les autos. (b) chante. (c) écrit une lettre. _b_

2. La femme
   (a) écrit une lettre. (b) arrête les autos. (c) danse. _a_

3. L'agent de police
   (a) boit du lait. (b) lit un livre. (c) arrête les autos. _c_

IV. **L'École: la salle de classe** (The School: the classroom)

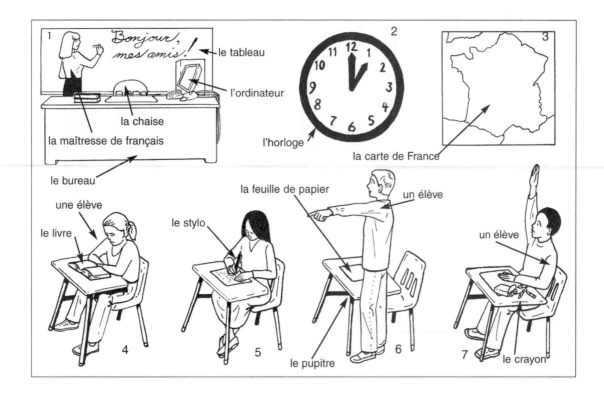

EXERCISES

I. Choose the sentence in Column A that corresponds to the picture and write it on the line next to the number of the picture in Column B. If you have to, look up the French words in the vocabulary at the end of the book.

Column A

Le garçon est debout. *Standing*

✓ La jeune fille lit un livre.

✓ Il y a une carte de France sur le mur.

✓ Madame Duval est derrière le bureau.

Le garçon lève la main.

✓ La jeune fille écrit une composition.

✓ Il est une heure.

Column B

1. _Madam Duval est derrière le bureau_

2. _Il est une heure_

3. _Il y a une carte de France sur le mur_

4. _La jeune fille Lit un livre_

5. _La jeune fille écrit une Composition_

6. _Le garçon est debout_

7. _Le garçon lève la main_

II. **Answer each question following the example in the box.**

Non, madame (mademoiselle, monsieur), ce n'est pas la table. C'est le bureau.

Est-ce la table?

1. Est-ce le stylo?   2. Est-ce la feuille de papier?   3. Est-ce l'ordinateur?

1. _Oui madame, c'est un stylo_
2. _Non madame, ce n'est pas la feuille de papier. C'est un livre_
3. _Non madame, ce n'est pas l'ordinateur. C'est un horloge_

4. Est-ce un élève?   5. Est-ce la chaise?   6. Est-ce une élève?

4. _Oui madame, c'est une élève_
5. _Non madame, ce n'est pas la chaise. C'est un table_
6. _Non madame, ce n'est pas une élève. C'est un élève_

14

7. Est-ce le petit banc?   8. Est-ce l'horloge?   9. Est-ce le tableau?

7. _____

8. _____

9. _____

The Louvre Museum with its façades by Francis I and Louis XIII contrasts with the modern crystal Pyramid entry by the celebrated architect I. M. Pei. This view juxtaposes the old and new faces of Paris.

V. **La Maison: la salle à manger** (The House: the dining room)

EXERCISES

I. **Answer each question following the example in the box.**

C'est une table.

C'est un vase.

Qu'est-ce que c'est?

Qu'est-ce que c'est?

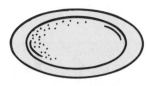

1. Qu'est-ce que c'est?

2. Qu'est-ce que c'est?

3. Qu'est-ce que c'est?

4. Qu'est-ce que c'est?

5. Qu'est-ce que c'est?

6. Qu'est-ce que c'est?

1. _____

2. _____

3. _____

4. _____

5. _____

6. _____

II. Fill in the missing letters of these French words.

1. UNE CHA_I_SE

2. UNE ASS_S_IET_T_E

3. UN TAPI_S_

4. UNE FO_R_RCHET_T_E

5. UN COU_T_EAU

6. UNE NAP_P_E

7. UN VER_R_E

8. UN_E_ TAS_S_E

9. UNE CU_I_LLER

10. UN_E_ FL_EU_R

17

VI. **La Ville: dans la rue** (The City: in the street)

EXERCISES

I.   Answer each question following the example in the box.

1. Qui est-ce? 2. Qui est-ce? 3. Qui est-ce? 4. Qui est-ce? 5. Qui est-ce?

1. _____
2. _____
3. _____
4. _____
5. _____

6. Qu'est-ce que c'est? 7. Qu'est-ce que c'est? 8. Qu'est-ce que c'est?

6. _____
7. _____
8._____

II. Fill in the missing letters of these French words.

1. UNE VALISE
2. UN PETIT CHIEN
3. LE TROTTOIR
4. LE MÉTRO

VII. Summary of two very common irregular verbs: **avoir** and **être** in the present tense, affirmative, and negative.

For speaking practice, say aloud the verb forms, with the subject pronouns, of avoir and être in the present tense, affirmative, and negative.

avoir (to have)

affirmative		negative	
j'ai	I have	**je n'ai pas**	I don't have
tu as	you have *(familiar)*	**tu n'as pas**	you don't have
il a	he *or* it has	**il n'a pas**	he *or* it doesn't have
elle a	she *or* it has	**elle n'a pas**	she *or* it doesn't have
nous avons	we have	**nous n'avons pas**	we don't have
vous avez	you have	**vous n'avez pas**	you don't have
ils ont	they have	**ils n'ont pas**	they don't have
elles ont	they have	**elles n'ont pas**	they don't have

être (to be)

affirmative		negative	
je suis	I am	**je ne suis pas**	I am not
tu es	you are *(familiar)*	**tu n'es pas**	you are not
il est	he *or* it is	**il n'est pas**	he *or* it isn't
elle est	she *or* it is	**elle n'est pas**	she *or* it isn't
nous sommes	we are	**nous ne sommes pas**	we are not
vous êtes	you are	**vous n'êtes pas**	you are not
ils sont	they are	**ils ne sont pas**	they are not
elles sont	they are	**elles ne sont pas**	they are not

Note that the subject pronoun **vous** is singular or plural. Use it when speaking to an adult you do not know or, if you do know the person, use it for courtesy, politeness, and respect. Examples:

Singular	*Plural*
Vous êtes Monsieur Paquet?	**Vous êtes Monsieur et Madame Paquet?**
You are Mr. Paquet?	*You are Mr. and Mrs. Paquet?*

Note also that the subject **tu**, which also means *you*, is used in the singular when speaking to a child, a relative, a friend, or an animal. The plural of **tu** is **vous**. Examples:

Singular	*Plural*
Tu es Janine? Tu es Pierre?	**Vous êtes Janine et Pierre?**
You are Janine? You are Pierre?	*You are Janine and Pierre?*

Saint-Tropez. French city on the Mediterranean Sea.

Part 1: Structures and Verbs

Madame Paquet cherche dans l'armoire, Janine cherche dans la commode, et Pierre cherche sous le lit.
(Mrs. Paquet is searching in the closet, Janine is searching in the dresser, and Pierre is searching under the bed.)

Work Unit 1
The Noun and the Definite and Indefinite Articles (Singular)

Have you ever looked high and low
for something you lost?

Le chapeau échappé

Monsieur Paquet cherche son chapeau. Madame Paquet cherche le chapeau dans l'armoire. [*cherche = search, chapeau = hat*]
Janine cherche dans la commode, et Pierre cherche sous le lit. Le chien est sous le lit.

Monsieur Paquet:	Où est mon chapeau? [*where is my hat?*]
Janine:	Je cherche dans la commode, papa. Tiens! J'ai trouvé mon télé-phone portable.
Pierre:	Nous cherchons partout, papa. Je cherche sous le lit maintenant. [*under bed, now*] Hé! J'ai trouvé mon iPod!
Madame Paquet:	Je cherche aussi, François. Je cherche dans l'armoire. Oh! Je suis fatiguée de chercher le chapeau!
Monsieur Paquet:	Je cherche sous la chaise maintenant. Cherchons dans la cuisine, dans le salon, dans la salle de bains, dans la cave, sous le lit, sous la commode, dans l'armoire, dans le garage. Partout dans la maison!
Janine:	[*Hey!*] Tiens! Papa! Coco mange le chapeau. Il est sous la commode maintenant!
Monsieur Paquet:	Ah, non! Quelle horreur!
	(Monsieur Paquet quitte la chambre vite.)
Madame Paquet:	Où vas-tu, François?
Monsieur Paquet:	Je vais en ville acheter un nouveau chapeau. Zut, alors!
Madame Paquet:	Attends, attends! Je vais avec toi. J'aimerais acheter une nouvelle robe.

VOCABULAIRE

acheter *v.,* to buy
aimer *v.,* to like, to love
l'armoire *n. f.,* the closet
aussi *adv.,* also, too
avec *prep.,* with
la cave *n.,* the cellar
la chaise *n.,* the chair
la chambre *n.,* the room
le chapeau *n.,* the hat
chercher *v.,* to look for, to search for
le chien *m.,* **la chienne** *f., n.,* the dog
la commode *n.,* the dresser, the chest of drawers
la cuisine *n.,* the kitchen
dans *prep.,* in

de *prep.,* of
échappé *m.,* **échappée** *f., adj.* escaped
elle *pron.,* she, it
en *prep.,* in, into
et *conj.,* and
être *v.,* to be
la famille *n.,* the family
fatigué *m.,* **fatiguée** *f., adj,* tired
la fille *n.,* the daughter
le fils *n.,* the son
le garage *n.,* the garage
l'horreur *n. f.,* the horror
il *pron.,* he, it
iPod *m.,* iPod
je *pron.,* I
le *m.,* **la** *f., def. art.,* the

le lit *n.,* the bed
madame *n.,* Mrs., madam
maintenant *adv.,* now
la maison *n.,* the house
manger *v.,* to eat
la mère *n.,* the mother
mon *m.,* **ma** *f., poss. adj.,* my
monsieur *n.,* Mr., sir
nous *pron.,* we, us
nouveau *m.,* **nouvelle** *f., adj.,* new
où *adv.,* where
partout *adv.,* everywhere
le père *n.,* the father
petit *m.,* **petite** *f., adj.,* small
placard *n. m.,* closet
quel *m.,* **quelle** *f., adj.,* what

qui *pron.,* who
quitter *v.,* to leave
la robe *n.,* the dress
la salle de bains *n.,* the bathroom
le salon *n.,* the living room
son *m.,* sa *f., poss. adj.,* his, her
sous *prep.,* under
le téléphone portable *n.,* cell phone
tiens! *exclam.,* look!
toi *pron.,* you
un *m.,* une *f., indef. art.,* a, an
la ville *n.,* the town, the city
vite *adv.,* quickly

le vocabulaire *n.,* the vocabulary
zut alors! *exclam.,* darn it!

Verb forms used in this dialogue:

j'aimerais I'd like, I'd love
attends wait
je cherche I look (for), I am looking (for)
il cherche, elle cherche he is looking (for), she is looking (for)

qui cherche who is looking (for)
nous cherchons we are looking (for)
cherchons let's look (for)
est is
il est he is, it is
il mange he eats, he is eating
il quitte he leaves, he is leaving
J'ai trouvé ... I found ...
je suis I am
je vais I am going
vas-tu? are you going?

EXERCISES

Review the dialogue and vocabulary before starting these exercises.

I. Choose the correct answer based on the dialogue in this unit.

1. Monsieur Paquet cherche

    (a) dans la commode.   (b) sous le lit.   (c) le chapeau.   (d) dans l'armoire.   *c*

2. Janine cherche

    (a) sous le lit. (b) dans le salon. (c) sous la commode. (d) dans la commode.   *d*

3. Pierre cherche

    (a) sous la chaise. (b) dans le garage. (c) dans la salle de bains. (d) sous le lit.   *d*

4. Le chapeau est

    (a) dans la commode. (b) sous la commode. (c) sous le lit. (d) dans la cuisine.   *b*

5. Coco mange le chapeau sous

    (a) le lit.   (b) la chaise.   (c) l'armoire.   (d) la commode.   *d*

II. Answer the following questions in complete sentences.

   Model: Qui cherche sous le lit?   Answer: **Pierre cherche sous le lit.**
   (Who is searching under the bed?)   (Pierre is searching under the bed.)

1. Qui cherche dans la commode?

    Janine cherche dans la commode

2. Qui cherche dans l'armoire?

    Madame Paquet cherche dan l'armoire

3. Qui cherche sous la chaise?

    _____

III. Looking for Something. Proficiency in Speaking and Writing.

Situation: You are looking for a letter you received from a friend. Janine is helping you. You are **Vous.**

1. Janine: **Tu as la lettre?**

2. Vous: *Non, je n'est pas la lettre*

3. Janine: **Où cherches-tu?**

4. Vous: *Je ~~sais~~ cherche sur la commode*

5. Janine: **Je vais chercher sous le lit.**

IV. Un acrostiche (an acrostic). Complete the French words in the squares across.

1. definite article (*fem. sing.*)

2. and

3. to search, to look for

4. horror

5. closet

6. father

7. she

8. to love, to like

9. indefinite article (*masc. sing.*)

STRUCTURES DE LA LANGUE

A. The definite articles
"The"

MASCULINE NOUNS			
le père	the father	l'homme *ouló*	the man
le garçon	the boy	l'ami *ouól*	the friend (boy)
le frère	the brother	le fils *ou oflóu* "f"	the son

FEMININE NOUNS			
la mère	the mother	la femme	the woman, wife
la jeune fille	the girl	l'amie	the friend (girl)
la soeur	the sister	la fille	the daughter

RULES AND OBSERVATIONS:

1. Nouns are classified by gender, which means that they are either masculine or feminine. A noun is a word that refers to a person, thing, place, or quality; *e.g.*, **la mère, la chaise, le salon, la beauté** (beauty).

2. Nouns denoting persons of the male sex are naturally of the masculine gender.

3. Nouns denoting persons of the female sex are naturally of the feminine gender.

4. Animals that are male or female are naturally of the masculine or feminine gender; *e.g.*, **le chat, la chatte** (the cat).

5. Things are also either masculine or feminine, but there is no easy way to determine their gender. You must learn the gender of a noun when you learn the noun by putting **le** or **la** in front of it! **Le** is masculine, **la** is feminine.

6. Some nouns, whether masculine or feminine, take **l'** in front, if they begin with a vowel or a silent **h**. The **e** in **le** drops and the **a** in **la** drops. You're left with **l'**.

7. Some nouns are sometimes masculine, sometimes feminine, in which case the meaning changes; *e.g., **le livre** (the book), **la livre** (the pound).

8. To sum it up, French has three forms for the definite article in the singular: **le, la, l'**—they all mean **the**.

A FEW MORE COMMON MASCULINE NOUNS	
l'arbre the tree	**le fils** the son
le beurre the butter	**le garage** the garage
le café the coffee, the café	**le mari** the husband
le chapeau the hat	**le nom** the name
le chef the chief, the chef	**l'ordinateur** the computer
l'enfant the child (boy)	**le téléphone portable** the cell phone

A FEW MORE COMMON FEMININE NOUNS	
la bouche the mouth	**l'heure** the hour
la calculatrice the calculator	**la maison** the house
la campagne the countryside	**la montre** the watch
la chaise the chair	**la porte** the door
l'enfant the child (girl)	**la souris** the mouse
la famille the family	**la table** the table

EXERCISES

Review the preceding material before starting these exercises.

I. Use the appropriate definite article in the singular: le, la, or l'.

1. __le__ garçon
2. __la__ mère
3. __le__ père
4. __la__ jeune fille
5. __l'__ ami

6. __l'__ homme
7. __le__ café
8. __le__ chapeau
9 __l'__ enfant
10. __la__ commode

11. _____ nom
12. __l'__ arbre
13. __le__ lit
14. __la__ porte
15. __l'__ amie

II. Word Hunt. Can you find these 10 words in French in this puzzle?

1. the woman
2. the man
3. the boy
4. the girl
5. the sister
6. the tree
7. the child
8. the brother
9. the book
10. the mother

L	A	M	L	E	L	I	V	R	E	P	L
O	L	E	G	A	R	Ç	O	N	F	G	A
J	H	I	L	A	M	È	R	E	A	E	S
A	U	O	I	L	H	O	M	M	E	E	O
L	A	J	E	U	N	E	F	I	L	L	E
E	B	L	E	F	R	È	R	E	A	E	U
L	E	J	O	U	R	L	A	I	R	O	R
A	L	A	F	E	M	M	E	M	B	O	Y
L	E	L	E	N	F	A	N	T	R	U	E
Z	Y	L	E	L	A	M	O	I	E	N	A

III. Food and Drink. Proficiency in Speaking, Reading, and Writing.

Situation: You are at a table in a restaurant deciding what to eat and drink. You are talking with the waitress/**la serveuse**.

In this guided conversation, you are playing the role of **Vous**. You may use your own words and ideas or those suggested below. Review the vocabulary in the **Leçons Préliminaires**. You must read the statements the waitress makes in order to say something related to what she says. Before writing your words, say them aloud.

La serveuse: **Bonjour. Vous désirez?**

Vous: _Je désirez un sandwich_

Tell her you want **(Je désire)** a sandwich.

La serveuse: **Un sandwich? Bon! Un sandwich au jambon?**

Vous: _Oui. Un jambon sandwich au jambon_

Yes. A ham sandwich.

La serveuse: Et avec le sandwich? Une tasse de café? Avec crème? Sucre?

Vous: _____

And with the ham sandwich a cup of coffee with cream and sugar.

La serveuse: Vous désirez un fruit?

Vous: _____

Tell her you want an apple and a banana.

IV. Shopping. Proficiency in Speaking, Reading, and Writing.

Situation: You are shopping for a few things in a furniture store because you are moving into a new apartment. You are talking with the salesman/**le vendeur.**

You are playing the role of **Vous.** You may use your own words and ideas or those suggested below. Review the vocabulary under the dialogue in this unit. Before writing your words, say them aloud.

Le vendeur: Bonjour. Vous désirez?

Vous: _____

Tell him you want to buy (acheter) a chair.

Le vendeur: Nous avons de belles chaises. Les voici/Here they are.

Vous: _____

Yes, they are beautiful.

Le vendeur: Vous désirez une table aussi?

Vous: _____

Tell him you also want to buy a bed, an armoire, a lamp, and a table.

V. Planning a Trip to France. Proficiency in Speaking, Reading, and Writing.

Situation: You and your family are planning a trip to France. You are looking for the passports.

In this guided conversation, you are playing the role of **Vous.** You may use your own words and ideas or those suggested below. Review the vocabulary under the dialogue at the beginning of this unit. Before writing your words, say them aloud.

Le père: Où sont les passeports?

La mère: Je cherche dans l'armoire, François.

Vous: _____

I'm looking under the bed, Dad.

Janine: Je cherche dans la commode, papa.

Vous: _____

Now I'm looking under the chair, Dad.

La mère: Nous cherchons partout, François. Oh! Je suis fatiguée de chercher les passeports!

Vous: _____

_____

Let's look in the kitchen, in the living room, in the bathroom, in the cellar, under the dresser, in the garage. Everywhere in the house!

VI. Write the answers to the question in complete French sentences. Use the noun in parentheses with the appropriate definite article: **le, la,** or **l'**.

Question: **Où est le chapeau?**
(Where is the hat?)

Model answer: **(salon) Le chapeau est dans le salon.**
(The hat is in the living room.)

1. (cuisine)

_____

2. (armoire)

_____

3. (maison)

_____

4. (commode)

_____

5. (garage)

_____

B. The indefinite articles

MASCULINE NOUNS		FEMININE NOUNS	
un père	a father	**une mère**	a mother
un garçon	a boy	**une jeune fille**	a girl
un frère	a brother	**une soeur**	a sister
un homme	a man	**une femme**	a woman
un ami	a friend (boy)	**une amie**	a friend (girl)
un parapluie	an umbrella	**une orange**	an orange

RULES AND OBSERVATIONS:

1. The indefinite article has two forms: **un** and **une**. The first is masculine and the second is feminine. Each means **a** or **an**. e.g., **un père, une mère**.

2. **Un** is used with a masculine noun whether it begins with a consonant, a vowel, or a silent **h**; e.g., **un garçon, un ami, un homme**.

3. **Une** is used with a feminine noun whether it begins with a consonant, a vowel, or a silent **h**; e.g., **une femme, une orange, une horreur**.

EXERCISES

Review the preceding material before starting these exercises.

I.   Use the appropriate indefinite article in the singular: un or une.

1. _____ garçon

2. _____ mère

3. _____ père

4. _____ ami

5. _____ amie

6. _____ homme

7. _____ café

8. _____ chat

9. _____ chatte

10. _____ nom

11. _____ arbre

12. _____ orange

13. _____ porte

14. _____ famille

15. _____ parapluie

II.   Word Hunt. Can you find these five words in French in this puzzle?

1. a tree

2. an orange

3. a boy

4. an umbrella

5. a girl

U	N	E	J	E	U	N	E	F	I	L	L	E	A
N	E	F	I	L	M	O	A	U	V	O	U	S	S
A	R	B	E	A	U	N	G	A	R	Ç	O	N	S
R	O	U	G	E	P	L	U	S	E	R	S	T	U
B	L	U	N	P	A	R	A	P	L	U	I	E	R
R	J	O	I	N	D	R	E	E	T	R	E	S	E
E	U	N	E	O	R	A	N	G	E	U	N	A	N

III. Picture Interpretation. Proficiency in Speaking and Writing.

Situation: Study the picture below and complete the dialogue. You are talking with a friend about what the woman in the picture is doing. Review the vocabulary in this work unit and the preliminary lessons. You may use words of your own or any of the following: **la femme**, **ma mère** (my mother), **une nouvelle robe**, **pourquoi** (why), **elle va** (she is going).

Une femme cherche dans l'armoire.

1.	**Richard:**	**Qui est la femme?**
2.	**Vous:**	_____
3.	**Richard:**	**Que fait-elle?**
4.	**Vous:**	_____
5.	**Richard:**	**Que cherche-t-elle?**
6.	**Vous:**	_____
7.	**Richard:**	**Pourquoi?**
8.	**Vous:**	_____

IV. **Comment dit-on en français...?** (How do you say in French...?)

Find the following statements in the dialogue at the beginning of this work unit and write them in French.

1. Mr. Paquet is looking for his hat.

_____

2. The dog is under the bed.

_____

3. We are searching everywhere.

_____

4. I'm going downtown to buy a new hat.

_____

5. Coco is eating the hat.

_____

V. Fill in the blanks with an appropriate singular definite or indefinite article.

Coco, _____ chien, est sous _____ commode. Madame Paquet, _____ mère,
         1   2   3

cherche dans _____ armoire. Janine cherche dans _____ commode, et Pierre cherche
                4   5

sous _____ lit. Madame Paquet est fatiguée de chercher _____ chapeau. Monsieur
      6   7

Paquet, _____ père, va en ville acheter _____ nouveau chapeau et Madame Paquet va
        8   9

acheter _____ nouvelle robe.
       10

VI. Activities. Proficiency in Writing.

A. Write the French words for five foods you would take on a picnic.

1. _____ 3. _____ 5. _____

2. _____ 4. _____

B. Write the French words for six things usually placed on a table for a meal.

1. _____ 3. _____ 5. _____

2. _____ 4. _____ 6. _____

C. Write eight French verbs that indicate what a person is doing.

1. _____ 3. _____ 5. _____ 7. _____

2. _____ 4. _____ 6. _____ 8. _____

AU CLAIR DE LA LUNE

Au clair de la lu — ne Mon a — mi Pier — rot

Prê — te — moi ta plu — me Pour é — crir' un mot

Ma chan — dell' est mor — te, Je n'ai plus de feu;

Ou — vre moi ta por — te Pour l'a—mour de Dieu.

Au clair de la lune.
Pierrot répondit :
Je n'ai pas de plume,
Je suis dans mon lit.
Va chez la voisine,
Je crois qu'elle y est,
Car, dans sa cuisine,
On bat le briquet.

Au clair de la lune.
On n'y voit qu'un pen.
On chercha la plume.
On chercha le feu.
En cherchant d' la sorte,
Je n' sais ce qu'on trouva.
Mais je sais qu' la porte,
Sur eux se ferma.

Courtesy of French Cultural Services, New York.

Quel déjeuner! (What a lunch!)

Work Unit 2
The Noun and the Definite and Indefinite Articles (Plural)

In this scene, Claire and François Paquet are with their friends from Martinique, Joséphine and Alphonse Banluc, who are living in Paris. They are all with their children at the Bois de Boulogne, a park near Paris, to celebrate La Fête Nationale on July 14.

Vive le quatorze juillet!

Claire Paquet:	Venez, tout le monde. Venez! Nous pouvons déjeuner sur l'herbe maintenant. Nous allons commencer par la viande. Janine, as-tu les sandwichs?
Janine:	Les sandwichs? Quels sandwichs? Je n'ai pas les sandwichs. J'ai seulement les gâteaux et les petits fours glacés. C'est pour le dessert.
Claire Paquet:	Tu n'as pas les sandwichs? Bon, bon. Pierre, tu as apporté les sandwichs, j'espère.
Pierre:	Mais non! J'ai seulement les éclairs.
Claire Paquet:	François, tu as sûrement apporté la viande: le rosbif, le veau, le porc, le jambon, et le poulet.
François Paquet:	Mais non, ma chérie. J'ai apporté la glace.
Claire Paquet:	Joséphine, tu as sûrement apporté la viande, j'espère.
Joséphine Banluc:	Mais non. J'ai apporté un gâteau!
Claire Paquet:	Alphonse, tu as les saucisses et les saucissons, j'espère.
Alphonse Banluc:	Mais non, Claire. J'ai apporté un grand gâteau et les brioches au chocolat! C'est pour le dessert. J'ai apporté aussi une bouteille d'eau minérale pour notre santé.
Claire Paquet:	Quel déjeuner!
Tous les enfants:	C'est merveilleux! Nous aimons mieux les desserts!
Claire Paquet:	Eh, bien! C'est la Fête Nationale et, dans l'esprit de ce grand jour de fête, moi, je dis: Mangeons les brioches—et les gâteaux!

VOCABULAIRE

l'an *n. m.*, the year
apporter *v.*, to bring
bien *adv.*, well
le bois *n.*, the woods
bon *m.*, **bonne** *f.*, *adj.*, good
la bouteille *n.*, the bottle
la brioche *n.*, bread with a slightly sweet taste
ce *dem. adj.*, this
chéri *m.*, **chérie** *f.*, *adj.*, darling, dearest
le chocolat *n.*, the chocolate; **au chocolat**

(with) chocolate; **un gâteau au chocolat** *n.*, a chocolate cake
commencer *v.*, to begin
déjeuner *v.*, to have lunch
le déjeuner *n.*, the lunch
le dessert *n.*, the dessert
dire *v.*, to say
l'eau *n. f.*, the water; **l'eau minérale** *n.*, mineral water
l'éclair *n. m.*, the eclair
eh bien! *exclam.*, oh, well!
espérer *v.*, to hope

l'esprit *n. m.*, the spirit
la femme *n.*, the wife
la fête *n.*, the holiday
le gâteau *n.*, the cake
la glace *n.*, the ice cream
glacé *m.*, **glacée** *f.*, *adj.*, glazed, frosted
l'herbe *n. f.*, the grass
le jambon *n.*, the ham
le jour *n.*, the day
juillet *n. m.*, July
les *def. art., pl.*, the
mais non! *exclam.*, why no!

35

le mari *n.*, the husband
merveilleux *m.*, merveilleuse *f.*, *adj.*, marvelous, wonderful
mieux *adv.*, better
moi *pron.*, me
non *adv.*, no
ou *conj.*, or
oui *adv.*, yes
le parc *n.*, the park
la pâtisserie *n.*, the pastry
le petit four *n.*, the little cake
le porc *n.*, the pork
le poulet *n.*, the chicken
pour *prep.*, for
pouvoir *v.*, to be able
près (de) *adv.*, near (to)
quatorze *adj.*, fourteen
le quatorze juillet *n.*, July 14; La Fête Nationale the French national holiday
quel *m.*, quelle *f.*, *adj.*, what; quel déjeuner! what a lunch!

le rosbif *n.*, the roast beef
le sandwich *n.*, the sandwich
la santé *n.*, health
la saucisse *n.*, the sausage
le saucisson *n.*, bologna
seulement *adv.*, only
sur *prep.*, on
sûrement *adv.*, surely
tous *m.*, toutes *f.*, *adj.*, *pl.*, all, every
tous les enfants all the children
tout *m.*, toute *f.*, *adj. sing.*, all, every
tout le monde everybody
tu *per. pron.*, you
le veau *n.*, the veal
venir *v.*, to come
la viande *n.*, the meat
vivre *v.*, to live

Verb forms used in this dialogue:
j'ai I have
je n'ai pas I do not have
tu as you have
tu n'as pas you do not have
as-tu? have you?
nous aimons we like, we love
nous allons we are going
j'ai apporté I brought
il a apporté, elle a apporté he brought, she brought
je dis I say
j'espère I hope
c'est it is
mangeons! let's eat!
nous pouvons we can, we are able
il va, elle va he goes, she goes (is going)
venez! come!
ils viennent (de) they come (from)
vive —! long live —!

EXERCISES

Review the dialogue and vocabulary before starting these exercises.

I. Choose the correct answer based on the dialogue in this unit.

1. Le déjeuner dans le parc est sur

    (a) les gâteaux.   (b) le dessert.   (c) les petits fours glacés.   (d) l'herbe.   _d_

2. Joséphine et Alphonse Banluc viennent

    (a) du Bois de Boulogne.   (b) de la Bastille.   (c) de la Martinique.   (d) du parc.   _c_

3. Le rosbif et le porc sont des

    (a) viandes.   (b) gâteaux.   (c) desserts.   (d) sandwichs.   _a_

4. Tout le monde a apporté

    (a) de la viande.   (b) des sandwichs.   (c) de l'eau minérale.   (d) de la pâtisserie.   _d_

5. Tout le monde mange

    (a) du gâteau et de la glace.   (b) des saucisses.   (c) du veau.   (d) des sandwichs.   _a_

II. Picnic in the Park. Proficiency in Writing.

Situation: You and your friends are planning a picnic in the park. You call your friend to discuss what you will each bring. In three sentences tell your friend what food you would like to have at the picnic. Then ask your friend which of these he or she would like to bring. You may use your own ideas or ideas suggested by the following: **avoir, apporter, les sandwichs, les desserts, les éclairs, la glace, le gâteau, le poulet, la viande, le veau, le jambon, la saucisse.**

1. _____

2. _____

3. _____

III. In a Fast-Food Restaurant. Proficiency in Writing.

Situation: You and a friend are in a fast-food restaurant/**dans un restaurant cuisine rapide**. Your friend asks you why you like mineral water/**Pourquoi aimes-tu l'eau minérale?** Begin your response with: **Pour moi**/For me. In three sentences tell why you like it. You may use your own words and ideas or those suggested by the following: **c'est bon, la santé, aimer mieux, le café.**

1. _____

2. _____

3. _____

IV. **Mots croisés** (crossword puzzle). Give the French words for the English clues.

Horizontalement

1. I
4. good (*masc. sing.*)
6. also
8. the (*pl.*)
9. definite article (*fem. sing.*)
11. the sandwiches
13. with
16. definite article (*masc. sing.*)
17. to bring
18. you (*fam. sing.*)
19. at, to
20. my (*fem. sing.*)
21. and

Verticalement

2. the ice cream
3. is
5. only
7. the cakes
10. year
12. on
14. she
15. for

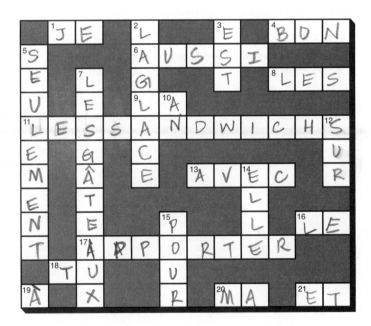

STRUCTURES DE LA LANGUE

A. Formation of regular plural of nouns

MASCULINE AND FEMININE NOUNS			
Singular		*pronounced lay* *Plural*	
la mère	the mother	**les mères**	the mothers
le père	the father	**les pères**	the fathers
la jeune fille	the girl	**les jeunes filles**	the girls
la fille	the daughter	**les filles**	the daughters
l'homme	the man	**les hommes**	the men
l'arbre	the tree	**les arbres**	the trees

RULES AND OBSERVATIONS:

1. To form the plural of a noun, whether masculine or feminine, ordinarily just add **s** to the singular form.

2. Change the definite article **the** from **le** to **les**, **la** to **les**, and **l'** to **les**.

3. In sum, French has only one form for the definite article in the plural: **les**.

B. Formation of irregular plural of nouns

RULES AND OBSERVATIONS:

1. Nouns that end in **-s**, **-x**, **-z** in the singular, whether masculine or feminine, do not normally change in the plural. They remain the same. See examples in the box below. You can tell the noun is singular or plural from **le** or **la**, or **les**.

Singular		*Plural*	
le fils	the son	**les fils**	the sons
la voix	the voice	**les voix**	the voices
le nez	the nose	**les nez**	the noses

2. Nouns that end in **-au**, **-eu**, **-ou** in the singular, whether masculine or feminine, ordinarily add **-x** to form the plural. See examples in the box below.

Singular		*Plural*	
le gâteau	the cake	**les gâteaux**	the cakes
le jeu	the game	**les jeux**	the games
le genou	the knee	**les genoux**	the knees

3. Nouns that end in **-al** or **-ail** in the singular ordinarily drop that ending and add **-aux** to form the plural. See examples in the box below.

Singular		Plural	
le journal	the newspaper	**les journaux**	the newspapers
le travail	the work	**les travaux**	the works

4. There are other irregular plurals of nouns. Study the examples in the box below.

Singular		Plural	
le ciel	the sky, heaven	**les cieux**	the skies, heavens
l'oeil	the eye	**les yeux**	the eyes
madame	Mrs., madam	**mesdames**	ladies
mademoiselle	miss	**mesdemoiselles**	misses
monsieur	mister, sir, gentleman	**messieurs**	sirs, gentlemen

(handwritten note near mesdames: P. "may")

EXERCISES

Review the preceding material before starting these exercises.

I.   Write the plural form for each noun.

1. le garçon _____les garçons_____
2. le fils _____les fils_____
3. le chapeau _____les chapeaux_____
4. le journal _____les journaux_____
5. le ciel _____les cieux_____

6. l'oeil _____les yeux_____
7. le père _____les pères_____
8. la voix _____les voix_____
9. la mère _____les mères_____
10. le chat _____les chats_____

II.   Write the singular form for each noun.

1. les tables _____la table_____
2. les nez _____le nez_____
3. les genoux _____le genou_____
4. les voix _____la voix_____
5. les yeux _____l'oeil_____

6. les messieurs _____le monsieur_____
7. les hommes _____l'homme_____
8. les jeunes filles _____la jeune fille_____
9. les enfants _____l'enfant_____
10. les arbres _____l'arbre_____

III. Change to the singular or to the plural, depending on which is given.

1. les pères ___le père___
2. les hommes ___l'homme___
3. l'eau ___les eaux___
4. le fils ___les fils___
5. la table ___les tables___

6. les journaux ___le journal___
7. le cheval ___les chevaux___
8. l'oiseau ___les oiseaux___
9. les élèves ___le élève___
10. le pays ___les pays___

C. Contraction of the definite article with **à** and **de**

à + **le** *changes to* **au**	de + **le** *changes to* **du**
à + **les** *changes to* **aux**	de + **les** *changes to* **des**

RULES AND OBSERVATIONS:

1. When the preposition **à** (*at, to*) is in front of the definite article **le** or **les**, it changes to the forms given in the box above.

2. When the preposition **de** (*from, of*) is in front of the definite article **le** or **les**, it changes to the forms given in the box above.

3. There is no contraction of **à** followed by **l'** or **la**. It remains **à l'** or **à la**.

4. There is no contraction of **de** followed by **l'** or **la**. It remains **de l'** or **de la**.

Janine va au café.

Madame Paquet va aux grands magasins.

Janine va à la gare.

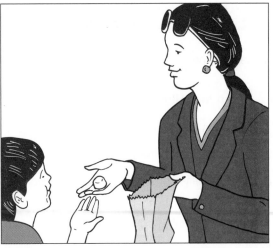

Madame Paquet donne un bonbon à l'enfant.

Pierre vient du restaurant.

Madame Paquet vient des grands magasins.

Pierre vient de l'école.

Janine vient de la bibliothèque.

EXERCISES

Review the preceding material before starting these exercises.

I. Match the following.

1. Janine is going to the station.

2. Pierre is coming from the restaurant.

3. Mr. Paquet is coming from the department stores.

4. Janine is coming from the library.

5. Pierre is coming from the school.

6. Mrs. Paquet is giving candy to the child.

7. Janine is going to the café.

8. Mrs. Paquet is going to the department stores.

_____ Janine va au café.

_____ Madame Paquet va aux grands magasins.

_____ Pierre vient de l'école.

_____ Monsieur Paquet vient des grands magasins.

_____ Madame Paquet donne un bonbon à l'enfant.

_____ Pierre vient du restaurant.

_____ Janine va à la gare.

_____ Janine vient de la bibliothèque.

II. Fill in the missing words. Choose au, aux, à l', or à la.

1. Janine va _____ café.

2. Pierre va _____ gare.

3. Madame Paquet va _____ grands magasins.

4. Hélène va _____ école.

III. Fill in the missing words. Choose du, de l', de la, or des.

1. Pierre vient _____ restaurant.

2. Janine vient _____ école.

3. Monique vient _____ bibliothèque.

4. Marie vient _____ grands magasins.

D. Use of the definite article with **de** for possession

le livre **du** maître	the teacher's book
le livre **de la** maîtresse	the teacher's book
les livres **des** garçons	the boys' books
le livre **de** Janine	Janine's book
le livre **de l'**élève	the pupil's book

RULES AND OBSERVATIONS:

1. The preposition **de** is used to express possession, as shown in the examples in the box on the previous page.

2. The preposition **de** changes to **du** or **des**, as shown in the examples in the box on the previous page.

EXERCISES

Review the preceding material before starting the exercises.

I. **Match the following.**

1. le parapluie de Pierre   _____ the boy's hat

2. les robes des jeunes filles   _____ the boys' dogs

3. les cheveux de Janine   _____ the girl's skirt

4. le chapeau du garçon   _____ the girls' dresses

5. le journal de Pierre   _____ the pupil's pencil

6. les chiens des garçons   _____ the pupils' pens

7. la jupe de la jeune fille   _____ Janine's eyes

8. les yeux de Janine   _____ Janine's hair

9. les stylos des élèves   _____ Pierre's newspaper

10. le crayon de l'élève   _____ Pierre's umbrella

II. **Fill in the missing words. Use du, des, de, de l', or de la.**

1. J'ai les crayons _____ jeunes filles.   6. J'ai le chapeau _____ homme.

2. J'ai le journal _____ femme.   7. J'ai le jeu _____ Janine.

3. J'ai les livres _____ Pierre.   8. J'ai les journaux _____ père.

4. J'ai les cahiers _____ garçon.   9. J'ai les bonbons _____ enfant.

5. J'ai le stylo _____ élève.   10. J'ai le parapluie _____ mère.

III. Obtaining and Providing Information. Proficiency in Speaking and Writing.

Situation: Your friend Janine is visiting you in your house. She is always asking questions. Provide answers for her.

Your role is **Vous**. You may vary and extend this dialogue with your own words and ideas. Later, after you have written what you said on the lines, you may exchange roles with Janine for more practice in speaking and writing. Use any or all of the following: **dis-moi**/*tell me*; **dans cette photo**/*in this photo*; **qui mange**/*who is eating*; **ce parapluie**/*this umbrella*; **ma tante**/*my aunt*; **ma mère**/*my mother*; **mon père**/*my father*; **tout le temps**/*all the time*; **les gants**/*the gloves*; **c'est ...**/*it's ...*; **ce sont**/*they are ...*

Janine: **Dis-moi, dans cette photo, qui est la femme qui mange?**

Vous: _____

Tell her: It's my Aunt Sophie. She eats all the time.

Janine: **Et ce parapluie sur le lit?**

Vous: _____

Tell her: It's my mother's umbrella.

Janine: **Et les gants sous la chaise?**

Vous: _____

Tell her: They are my father's gloves.

Avignon, France

Avez-vous de la viande? Avez-vous des saucisses? Avez-vous du café?
(Do you have any meat? Do you have any sausages? Do you have any coffee?)

Work Unit 3
The Noun and the Definite and Indefinite Articles
(Conclusion)

*Some people always know what to
order in a restaurant and some
don't. Have you ever done what
Pierre does in this scene?*

La grande décision

Le Serveur:	**Bonjour. Vous désirez?**
Pierre:	**Bonjour. Avez-vous de la viande?**
Le Serveur:	**Oui. Nous avons de la viande.**
Pierre:	**Avez-vous des saucisses?**
Le Serveur:	**Oui. Nous avons de belles saucisses.**
Pierre:	**Non, je ne veux pas de viande. Je ne veux pas de saucisses.**
Le Serveur:	**Nous avons du poisson.**
Pierre:	**Je ne veux pas de poisson … Avez-vous de l'eau minérale?**
Le Serveur:	**Oui. Nous avons de l'eau minérale.**
Pierre:	**Non, je ne veux pas d'eau minérale … Avez-vous du café?**
Le Serveur:	**Oui. Nous avons du café.**
Pierre:	**Non, je ne veux pas de café.**
Le Serveur:	**Aimez-vous les éclairs et les tartes?**
Pierre:	**Oui, oui. J'aime les éclairs et les tartes.**
Le Serveur:	**Je regrette. Nous n'avons ni éclairs, ni tartes.**

VOCABULAIRE

aimer *v.*, to like, to love;
  aimez-vous? do you like?
  j'aime I like
avoir *v.*, to have; **avez-vous?** do you have? **nous avons** we have; **nous n'avons ni éclairs, ni tartes** we have neither eclairs nor tarts
beau *m.*, **belle** *f., adj.*, beautiful
bonjour *salutation,* good day

la décision *n.*, decision
désirer *v.*, to wish, to desire; **vous désirez?** you wish?
l'école *n. f.*, the school
grand *m.*, **grande** *f., adj.*, great, big
ni … ni *conj.*, neither … nor
parle *v.*, form of **parler** (to talk, to speak); **Pierre parle** Peter is talking
le poisson *n.*, the fish

regretter *v.*, to regret, to be sorry; **je regrette** I'm sorry
le restaurant *n.*, restaurant
le serveur *n.*, server, waiter
la serveuse *n.*, server, waitress
veux *v.* form of **vouloir** (to want); **je ne veux pas** I do not want; **Pierre veut** Peter wants
vous *pron.*, you

EXERCISES

Review the dialogue and vocabulary before starting these exercises.

I.   Choose the correct answer based on the dialogue in this unit.

1. Pierre est dans

    (a) une école.   (b) un parc.   (c) la maison.   (d) un restaurant.   _____

2. Pierre parle avec

    (a) un ami.   (b) une amie.   (c) une femme.   (d) un serveur de restaurant.   _____

3. Pierre aime

    (a) la viande.   (b) le poisson.   (c) les éclairs et les tartes.   (d) les saucisses.   _____

II.   Lists. Write a list of words for each situation.

A. You are in a restaurant. Write a list of four things that are on the table.

    1. _____   2. _____   3. _____   4. _____

B. You are in a pastry shop **(une pâtisserie)**. Write a list of four things you would like to buy.

    1. _____   2. _____   3. _____   4. _____

III.   Word Hunt. Can you find these words in French in this puzzle? Circle them.

1. I like
2. some fish
3. we have
4. the meat
5. some coffee
6. sir
7. some water

D	U	C	A	F	É	D	E	S
U	M	O	N	S	I	E	U	R
P	D	U	O	D	E	L	A	O
O	C	A	U	J	A	I	M	E
I	D	C	S	P	O	I	D	U
S	E	L	A	V	O	S	N	E
S	L	A	V	I	A	N	D	E
O	E	D	O	E	L	A	E	A
N	A	E	N	A	U	E	A	E
D	U	L	S	O	M	O	N	S

STRUCTURES DE LA LANGUE

A. The Partitive

Essentially, the plural of the indefinite articles **un** and **une** is **des**. The partitive denotes a part of a whole; or in other words, *some*. It can be plural or singular in form.

1. SIMPLE AFFIRMATIVE	
J'ai **du** café.	I have *some* coffee.
J'ai **de la** viande.	I have *some* meat.
J'ai **de l'**eau.	I have *some* water.
J'ai **des** bonbons.	I have *some* candies.

2. SIMPLE NEGATIVE	
Je n'ai pas **de** café.	I don't have *any* coffee.
Je n'ai pas **de** viande.	I don't have *any* meat.
Je n'ai pas **d'**eau.	I don't have *any* water.
Je n'ai pas **de** bonbons.	I don't have *any* candies.

3. WITH AN ADJECTIVE	
J'ai **du** bon café.	I have *some* good coffee.
J'ai **de** jolis chapeaux.	I have *some* pretty hats.
J'ai **de** jolies jupes.	I have *some* pretty skirts.

OBSERVATIONS BASED ON THE EXAMPLES GIVEN IN THE THREE BOXES ABOVE:

1. Use **du**, **de la**, **de l'**, or **des** in front of the noun, depending on whether the noun is masculine or feminine, singular or plural. Study the examples in the first box above.

2. The form **du** is used in front of a masculine singular noun beginning with a consonant, as in **j'ai du café**. See the first box above.

3. The form **de la** is used in front of a feminine singular noun beginning with a consonant, as in **j'ai de la viande**. See the first box above.

4. The form **de l'** is used in front of a feminine or masculine singular noun beginning with a vowel or a silent *h*, as in **j'ai de l'eau**. See the first box above.

5. The form **des** is used in front of all plural nouns.

6. To express *any* in front of a noun, when the verb is negative, use **de** in front of the noun. The noun can be feminine or masculine, singular or plural, but it *must* begin with a consonant, as in **je n'ai pas de café**. See the second box.

7. To express *any* in front of a noun, when the verb is negative, use **d'** in front of the noun. The noun can be feminine or masculine, singular or plural, but it *must* begin with a vowel or silent *h*, as in **je n'ai pas d'eau**. See the second box.

8. When the noun is preceded by an adjective, use **de**, as in **j'ai de jolis chapeaux**. See the third box.

9. When the noun is preceded by an adverb or noun of quantity or measure, use **de**, as in **j'ai beaucoup de choses**/I have many things.

10. When the noun is modified by another noun, use **de**, as in **une école de filles** / a girls' school.

11. The partitive is not used with **sans** or **ne ... ni ... ni**.

   Examples: Je quitte la maison **sans argent**.
   (I'm leaving the house *without any money*.)

   Nous **n'**avons **ni** éclairs, **ni** tartes.
   (We have *neither* eclairs *nor* tarts.)

EXERCISES

Review the preceding material before starting these exercises.

I.   **Answer the following questions in the affirmative.**

   Model: **Avez-vous du café?**   **Answer:**   **Oui, j'ai du café.**
   (Do you have any coffee?)   (Yes, I have some coffee.)

1. Avez-vous du pain?

_____

2. Avez-vous de la viande?

_____

3. Avez-vous de l'eau?

_____

4. Avez-vous des bonbons?

_____

5. Avez-vous du beurre?

_____

Avez-vous des bonbons?

II. **Answer the following questions in the negative.**

Model: **Avez-vous du café?**   Answer: **Non, je n'ai pas de café.**
       (Have you any coffee?)   (No, I haven't any coffee.)

1. Avez-vous du café?

_____

2. Avez-vous de la viande?

_____

3. Avez-vous de l'eau?

_____

4. Avez-vous des bonbons?

_____

5. Avez-vous du beurre?

_____

III. Notes. Proficiency in Writing.

Situation: On your way to school this morning, you lost a few things. Using at least eight words, write a note to your friend who sits near you in French class asking if he/she has any of those things for you today; for example, candies, money, paper, a pen, a pencil.

_____

_____

_____

IV. Answer the following questions in the negative.

Model:	**Avez-vous du bon café?**	Answer:	**Non, je n'ai pas de bon café.**
	(Do you have [any] good coffee?)		(No, I don't have any good coffee.)

1. Avez-vous du bon café?

_____

2. Avez-vous de jolis chapeaux?

_____

3. Avez-vous de jolies jupes?

_____

4. Avez-vous du bon vin?

_____

5. Avez-vous de jolies cravates?

_____

B. The definite article with parts of body and clothing

J'ai **les** mains sales.	My hands are dirty.
J'ai **les** yeux bruns.	My eyes are brown.
J'ai **les** cheveux noirs.	My hair is black.
J'ai **le** chapeau sur **la** tête.	I have my hat on my head.

Rule: Use the definite article instead of the possessive adjective when you know without a doubt who the possessor is.

EXERCISES

I.   Answer the following questions in the affirmative.

Model: **Avez-vous les mains sales?**   Answer: **Oui, j'ai les mains sales.**
(Are your hands dirty?)   (Yes, my hands are dirty.)

1. Avez-vous les mains sales?

_____

2. Avez-vous le visage sale?

_____

3. Avez-vous le nez long?

_____

4. Avez-vous les yeux bruns?

_____

5. Avez-vous les cheveux noirs?

_____

II.   Answer the following questions in the negative.

Model: **Avez-vous les pieds grands?**   Answer: **Non, je n'ai pas les**
(Are your feet big?)   **pieds grands.**
                                                    (No, my feet are not big.)

1. Avez-vous les pieds grands?

_____

2. Avez-vous le visage sale?

_____

3. Avez-vous les mains sales?

_____

4. Avez-vous le chapeau sur la tête?

_____

5. Avez-vous les cheveux noirs?

_____

C. The definite article with parts of the day

Je vais à l'école **les** matins.	I go to school *in the* mornings.
Je joue **les** après-midi.	I play *in the* afternoons.
J'étudie **les** soirs.	I study *in the* evenings.

Rule: Use the definite article with parts of the day. It can also be used in the singular. In English it means *in the*.

Je vais à l'école le matin. **Je joue l'après-midi.** **J'étudie le soir.**

EXERCISES

I. **Answer the following questions in the affirmative.**

 Model: **Allez-vous à l'école les matins?** **Answer:** **Oui, je vais à l'école les**
 (Do you go to school in the mornings?) **matins.** (Yes, I go to
 school in the mornings.)

1. Allez-vous à l'école les matins?

_____

2. Allez-vous à la bibliothèque les après-midi?

_____

3. Allez-vous au restaurant les soirs?

_____

4. Allez-vous au parc les après-midi?

_____

5. Allez-vous au café les soirs?

_____

II. **Answer the following questions in the negative.**

> Model: **Allez-vous au cinéma les soirs?**   Answer: **Non, je ne vais pas au**
> (Do you go to the movies in the   **cinéma les soirs.**
> evenings.)   (No, I don't go to the movies
>   in the evenings?)

1. Allez-vous au cinéma les soirs?

_____

2. Allez-vous à l'école les matins?

_____

3. Allez-vous à la bibliothèque les soirs?

_____

D. Omission of the definite article with **parler**, **de**, and **en**

Janine est **de** France.	Elle **parle** français.	Elle **prononce** bien **le français**.
Janine is from France.	She speaks French.	She pronounces French well.
Julie **répond en** français dans la classe **de** français. Julie answers in French in the French class.			

RULES AND OBSERVATIONS:

1. Do not use the definite article in front of the name of a language if the verb **parler** directly precedes it.

2. Do not use the definite article in front of the name of a language if the preposition **de** or **en** directly precedes it.

3. **De** indicates *concerned with* in expressions such as the following:
   la classe de français (the French class), **la leçon de français** (the French lesson), **le professeur d'anglais** (the English teacher), **le maître de musique** (the music teacher).

4. Change **de** to **d'** if the word that follows starts with a vowel or a silent *h*. Example: **le professeur d'anglais**.

E. Omission of the indefinite article with **cent** and **mille**

J'ai **cent dollars**.	I have *one hundred dollars*.
J'ai **mille dollars**.	I have *one thousand dollars*.

Rule: Do not use the indefinite article **un** or **une** in front of **cent** (100) or **mille** (1,000).

EXERCISES

Review the preceding material before starting these exercises.

I. Write two sentences using the word (language name) given in italics. Begin the first sentence with **il** (he) or **elle** (she) and use the verb **parle** (speaks). Begin the second sentence with the appropriate subject pronoun (**il** or **elle**) and use the verb **prononce** (pronounces) and the adverb **bien** (well).

Model: **Pierre est de France.**   You write: **Il parle français.**
        (Peter is from France.)   **Il prononce bien le français.**
                                                     (He speaks French.)
                                                     (He pronounces French well.)

1. Louis est de France.

    le français _____

2. María est d'Espagne.

    l'espagnol _____

3. Madame Belini est d'Italie.

    l'italien _____

4. Monsieur Armstrong est d'Angleterre.

    l'anglais _____

5. Hilda est d'Allemagne.

    l'allemand _____

II. Answer the following questions in the affirmative.

Model: **Avez-vous cent dollars?**   Answer: **Oui, j'ai cent dollars.**
        (Have you 100 dollars?)   (Yes, I have 100 dollars.)

1. Avez-vous cent dollars?

    _____

2. Avez-vous mille euros?

    _____

3. Avez-vous cent livres?

    _____

4. Avez-vous mille amis?

    _____

III. Complete with an appropriate selection: **le, la, l', or les.** Use a dash (—) if no definite article is required.

Le maître de _____ musique à _____ école est aussi professeur de _____ français. Il parle
                  1   2   3

_____ français dans _____ classe de français, et il prononce bien _____ français. Il a
    4   5   6

_____ yeux bleus et _____ cheveux noirs.
    7   8

55

IV. Change the words in italics to either the singular or plural, depending on which is given.

> **Model:** J'ai le gâteau.   **Answer:** J'ai les gâteaux.
> (I have the cake.)   (I have the cakes.)

1. J'ai *le sandwich.* _____

2. J'ai *l'éclair.* _____

3. J'ai *les saucisses.* _____

4. J'ai *un dollar.* _____

5. J'ai *des jupes.* _____

6. J'ai *le chapeau.* _____

7. J'ai *les desserts.* _____

8. J'ai *des gâteaux.* _____

V. Jeu de mots (Word game) Translate these 14 words into French to fill in the squares.

1. the newspapers
2. water
3. health
4. dress
5. children
6. on
7. works (*noun*)
8. afternoon
9. indefinite article (*fem. sing.*)
10. roast beef
11. tree
12. nose
13. head
14. evening

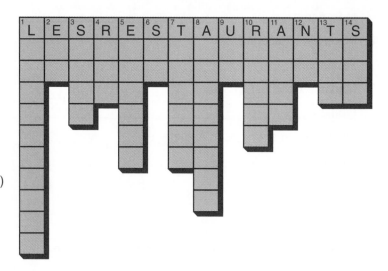

VI. Physical Characteristics. Proficiency in Writing.

Situation: You are filling in an application for a job with a modeling agency in Montreal. You are asked to write a short paragraph in French containing four or five sentences stating a few of your physical characteristics.

Before you begin, you may want to review this topic and the exercises in section **B** in this work unit.

You may use your own ideas and words or the following: *I have blue (brown, gray, green) eyes/***J'ai les yeux bleus (bruns, gris, verts).** *I have black (brown, blond, red) hair/***J'ai les cheveux noirs (bruns, blonds, roux).** *I have big (small) feet/***J'ai les pieds grands (petits).** *I have a round (long) face/***J'ai le visage rond (long).** *I have big (small) hands/***J'ai les mains grandes (petites).**

Practice writing the paragraph here:

_____

_____

_____

_____

VII. Dining Out. Proficiency in Speaking and Writing.

Situation: You are in a small café-restaurant **(un bistro)** in Paris. In this guided dialogue, you are playing the role of **Vous**. You may address the waiter **(le serveur)** as **Monsieur**/*Sir*.

You may use your own words and ideas or those suggested below. After you say the words aloud, write them on the lines. Before you start you may want to review the dialogue and vocabulary at the beginning of this lesson. Make use of the words the waiter says before and after what you want to say. You may also want to use the vocabulary and verb forms at the end of the book.

Le serveur: Bonjour, madame (mademoiselle, monsieur). Vous désirez?

Vous: _____

Respond with a greeting and ask: Have you any fish today?

Le serveur: Oui, nous avons du poisson aujourd'hui.

Vous: _____

Do you have any meat?

Le serveur: Oui, nous avons de la viande. Nous avons du bifteck et du rosbif aux pommes frites/*steak and roast beef with French fries.*

Vous: _____

Do you have any mashed potatoes?

Le serveur: Oui, nous avons de la purée de pommes de terre.

Vous: _____

Do you have any sausages?

Le serveur: Oui, nous avons de belles saucisses.

Vous: _____

No, sir. I'm sorry. I don't want any meat. I don't want any sausages.

Le serveur: Vous désirez du poisson?

Vous: _____

No, sir, I don't want any fish. I'm sorry.

Le serveur: Vous désirez du café?

Vous: _____

No, sir, I don't want any coffee.

Le serveur: Aimez-vous les éclairs et les tartes?

Vous: _____

Yes, yes. I like eclairs and tarts.

Le serveur: Je regrette. Nous n'avons ni éclairs, ni tartes.

VIII. Shopping. Proficiency in Speaking and Writing.

Situation: You are in a pastry shop **(une pâtisserie)** in Paris. In this guided dialogue, you're playing the role of **Vous**. When you greet the clerk, use **Madame**.

You may use your own words and ideas or those suggested below. After you say the words aloud, write them on the lines. Say **J'aimerais** for *I would like*. Before you start, review the dialogue and vocabulary at the beginning of Work Units 2 and 3.

Madame: **Bonjour, madame (mademoiselle, monsieur). Vous désirez?**

Vous: _____

I would like a big chocolate cake **(un grand gâteau au chocolat).**

Madame: **Et avec ceci?/And with this?**

Vous: _____

I would like two eclairs and two apple tarts **(deux tartes aux pommes).**

Madame: **C'est tout?**

Vous: _____

Yes, that's all, thank you.

Madame: **Vous pouvez payer à la caisse. Merci.** (You may pay at the cash register. Thank you.)

IX. Socializing. Proficiency in Speaking and Writing.

Situation: You are at a party with five new foreign exchange students. Janine and Pierre Paquet are there. You are introducing them to the new students.

On the lines below, write three short statements in French about each of the new students. You may use your own words and ideas or those under the lines. First, you may need to review Exercise I under section **E** in this lesson.

1. _____

   Jacques is from France. He speaks French. He pronounces French well.

2. _____

   María is from Spain. She speaks Spanish. She pronounces Spanish well.

3. _____

   Rosa is from Italy. She speaks Italian. She pronounces Italian well.

4. _____

   Ian is from England. He speaks English. He pronounces English well.

5. _____

   Marlena is from Germany. She speaks German. She pronounces German well.

X. Obtaining and Providing Information. Proficiency in Speaking and Writing.

Situation: You are spending an afternoon shopping at La Trifluvienne, a beautiful department store **(un beau grand magasin)**. You are talking with a receptionist to obtain some information about the location of certain departments.

You may use your own words and ideas or those suggested below. After you say the words aloud, write them on the lines. Say **J'aimerais savoir** for *I would like to know*; **où se trouve le restaurant?**/where is the restaurant located? **à gauche**/on the left; **à droite**/on the right; **tout droit**/straight ahead; **au fond**/in the rear; **au rez-de-chaussée**/on the ground (main) floor; **au deuxième étage**/on the second floor; **l'escalier mécanique**/the escalator; **les toilettes**/the rest rooms.

Review the English words and terms with their French translations in the ad on the following page.

Vous: _____

_____

Greet the receptionist, using **Madame**. Tell her you would like to know where the restaurant is located.

Madame: **Le restaurant se trouve au troisième étage.**

Vous: _____

And where is the travel agency located, please?/(s'il vous plaît)

Madame: **L'Agence de voyages se trouve au rez-de-chaussée, au fond.**

Vous: _____

Ask her at what time the store closes./(le magasin ferme)

Madame: **Nous fermons à sept heures du soir.**

Vous: _____

Tell her you would also like to know where the snack bar is located.

Madame: **Le bar rapide se trouve ici sur le rez-de-chaussée, tout droit, au fond.**

Vous: _____

And the rest rooms?

Madame: **Les toilettes se trouvent au sous-sol. L'escalier mécanique est à gauche.**

Vous: _____

Thank her, then ask her where the interpreters are located.

Madame: **Les interprètes se trouvent au premier étage. Mais vous parlez français extraordinairement bien!**

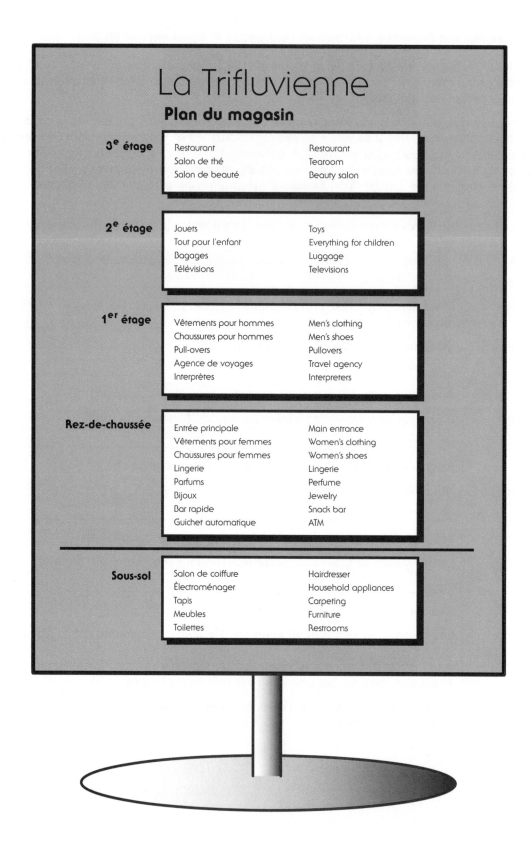

Maman, papa, notre téléviseur ne marche pas!
(Mother, Dad, the television doesn't work!)

Work Unit 4
Present Indicative Tense of Regular Verbs Ending in *-er*

Can Janine and Pierre live without violence on television for one evening?

La beauté ou la violence?

Janine et Pierre allument le téléviseur, mais il ne marche pas. Tous les deux sont inquiets parce que l'émission ce soir est "La violence triomphe!" La mère et le père entrent dans le salon et Pierre et Janine s'exclament:

—Maman, papa, notre téléviseur ne marche pas!
—Bon! Vous regardez trop de violence à la télévision, vous deux, dit la mère.
—Mais l'émission ce soir est très importante! C'est "La violence triomphe!" s'exclament Janine et Pierre.
—La violence ne triomphe pas dans cette maison! Je regrette, dit le père.
—Est-ce que nous allons faire réparer le téléviseur? demandent Janine et Pierre.
—Allons-nous faire réparer le téléviseur?! répètent la mère et le père. Oh! s'exclament-ils. Oh, non! Aujourd'hui, non!

Pierre et Janine regardent dans les journaux. L'émission "Les oeuvres d'art du Louvre" est à la télévision ce soir avant l'émission "La violence triomphe!" Alors, ils s'exclament:

—Papa, maman, c'est l'émission "Les oeuvres d'art du Louvre" à la télévision ce soir!
—Quoi?! Vite! Allons au magasin! Nous allons acheter un téléviseur à écran plasma!

VOCABULAIRE

aller *v.,* to go; **nous allons** we are going; **Allons au magasin!** Let's go to the store!

allumer *v.,* to turn on (a machine or device)

alors *adv.,* then

après *prep.,* after

aujourd'hui *adv.,* today

avant *prep.,* before

la beauté *n.,* beauty

cet *m.,* **cette** *f., adj.,* this

demander *v.,* to ask

deux *adj.,* two; **tous les deux** both

dire *v.,* to say, to tell; **dit la mère** says the mother

un écran *n.* **plasma** plasma screen, plasma display

l'émission *n. f.,* the show, the television program

entrer *v.,* to enter

s'exclamer *v., refl.,* to exclaim

faire *v.,* to do, to make

inquiet *m.,* **inquiète** *f., adj.,* upset, worried

mais *conj.,* but

marcher *v.,* to walk; to run, to work (a machine or device)

l'oeuvre *n. f.,* **d'art** *n. m.,* the work of art

parce que *conj.,* because

quoi *interr. pron.,* what

regarder *v.,* to look (at), to watch

réparer *v.,* to repair; **faire réparer** to have (something) repaired

répéter *v.,* to repeat

le soir *n.,* the evening

le téléphone *n.,* the telephone

le téléviseur *n.,* the television set

un téléviseur *n.,* **à écran** *n.,* **plasma** *n.,* a plasma screen television set

la télévision, la télé *n.,* television

tout de suite *adv.,* right away, immediately, at once

très *adv.,* very

triompher *v.,* to triumph

trop (de) *adv.,* too much (of)

la violence *n.,* violence

EXERCISES

Review the story and vocabulary before starting these exercises.

I. Answer the following questions in complete sentences. They are based on the story "La beauté ou la violence?"

1. Qui allume le téléviseur?

_____

2. Qui entre dans le salon?

_____

3. Qui regarde dans les journaux?

_____

II. Expressing Personal Feelings. Proficiency in Speaking and Writing.

Situation: Your friend Pierre wants to know your personal feelings about watching television on Saturday nights. Make three statements; then write them on the lines.

1. _____
2. _____
3. _____

III. Choose the correct answer based on the story in this unit.

1. Janine et Pierre allument

   (a) la radio.   (b) le téléviseur.   (c) l'émission.   _____

2. Janine et Pierre regardent dans

   (a) le téléviseur.   (b) le téléphone.   (c) les journaux.   _____

3. Madame et Monsieur Paquet entrent dans

   (a) la cuisine.   (b) le salon.   (c) le garage.   _____

IV. Complete by writing the missing French words. Find them in the story in this unit.

Janine et Pierre _allument_ le téléviseur mais il ne _marche_ pas. La mère et le père _entrent_ dans le salon et Pierre et Janine s' _exclament_.

—Maman, papa, notre téléviseur ne _marche_ pas!

La mère dit: Bon! Vous _regardez_ trop de violence à la télévision, vous deux.

—Est-ce que nous allons faire réparer le téléviseur? _demandent_ Janine et Pierre.

—Oh! Oh, non! Aujourd'hui, non! s'exclament la _mère_ et le _père_.

STRUCTURES DE LA LANGUE

A. Introduction

A verb is a word that expresses an action *(to dance)* or a state of being *(to think)*. Tense means time. French and English verb tenses are divided into three main groups of time: past, present, and future. A verb tense shows if an action took place (past), is taking place (present), or will take place (future). Here we will study the present tense.

French verbs are divided into three main conjugations (types) according to the infinitive ending, which can be either **-er**, **-ir**, or **-re**. You might say that these endings mean *to* in English; for example, **danser** means "to dance." In this unit, we will concentrate on the first conjugation (**-er** ending).

You must memorize the personal endings for the **-er** verbs because they indicate the subject. You must also memorize the personal subject pronouns in French because each one is used with its own personal ending on the verb. These are all given in boldface letters in the following chart.

FIRST CONJUGATION

	-er
Infinitive →	**danser** *to dance*
	I dance, *or* I do dance, *or* I am dancing; you dance, etc.

Required subject pronouns

PERSON	SINGULAR	
1. **je**	I	danse
2. **tu**	you *(familiar only)*	dans**es**
3. **il** **elle**	he *or* it she *or* it	danse

	PLURAL	
1. **nous**	we	dans**ons**
2. **vous**	you	dans**ez**
3. **ils** **elles**	they	dans**ent**

RULES AND OBSERVATIONS:

1. To form the present tense of a regular verb ending in **-er**, drop the **-er**. What remains is called the *stem*. Add to the stem the correct personal ending: **-e**, **-es**, **-e**, **-ons**, **-ez**, or **-ent**.

2. Note that *do, am, are, does, is* (which are used in English in the present tense) are *not translated* into French. Therefore, **je danse** can mean *I dance*, or *I do dance*, or *I am dancing*. The same applies to the rest of the conjugation, for example, *you dance*, or *you do dance*, or *you are dancing*, etc.

SINGULAR	
With noun	With pronoun
Janine danse tous les soirs. (Janine dances every night.)	**Elle danse tous les soirs.** (She dances every night.)
L'ours danse. (The bear is dancing.)	**Il danse.** (It (or he) is dancing.)

PLURAL	
Janine et Marie dansent souvent. (Janine and Mary dance often.)	**Elles dansent souvent.** (They dance often.)
Janine et Pierre dansent beaucoup. (Janine and Peter dance a lot.)	**Ils dansent beaucoup.** (They dance a lot.)
Les ours dansent. (The bears are dancing.)	**Ils dansent.** (They are dancing.)

B. The subject pronouns

1. Study the subject pronouns in the first conjugation chart.

2. The subject pronoun is placed in front of the verb in an affirmative statement: **Je danse tous les soirs**. I dance every night.

3. The subject pronoun is always used with the verb.

4. In French, there are two subject pronouns that mean *you*:

    (a) **tu** is used when you are speaking to a member of your family, a close friend, a classmate, someone younger than you, or an animal.

    (b) **vous** is the polite form of *you*; it is used at all other times.

    (c) **vous** is also the plural of **tu**; when you are speaking to two or more members of your family at the same time, or two or more close friends at the same time, use **vous**.

5. If the first letter of a verb is a vowel, drop the **e** in **je** and add an apostrophe: **j'aime la glace**. I like ice cream.

6. The subject pronouns **il**, **elle**, **ils**, and **elles** are used to take the place of a noun, whether it is a person, place, thing, or animal.

7. The subject pronoun **il** is used to take the place of a masculine singular noun.

8. The subject pronoun **elle** is used to take the place of a feminine singular noun.

9. The subject pronoun **ils** is used to take the place of two or more masculine nouns. It is also used to take the place of one masculine and one feminine noun. Any number of feminine nouns could be subjects, but as long as at least one masculine noun is mixed in with the subjects, the pronoun must be **ils**.

10. The subject pronoun **elles** is used to take the place of two or more feminine nouns *only*.

C. Some common regular verbs of the first conjugation

aimer	to love, to like	**fermer**	to close
apporter	to bring	**jouer**	to play
chanter	to sing	**montrer**	to show
chercher	to look for	**oublier**	to forget
demander	to ask (for)	**parler**	to talk, to speak
désirer	to desire, to wish	**porter**	to carry, to wear
donner	to give	**regarder**	to look (at), to watch
écouter	to listen (to)	**réparer**	to fix, to repair
étudier	to study	**trouver**	to find

D. The uses of the present tense

This tense is used much of the time in both French and English. It indicates:

(a) An action or a state of being at the present time.

Examples:
1. **Je vais** à l'école maintenant. *I am going* to school now.
2. **Je pense**; donc, **je suis**. *I think;* therefore, *I am*.

(b) Habitual action.

Example:
1. **Je vais** à la bibliothèque tous les jours. *I go* to the library every day.

Voir c'est croire. *(Seeing is believing.)*

(c)   A general truth, something that is permanently true.

Example:
1.   Deux et deux **font** quatre. Two and two *are* four.

(d)   Vividness when talking or writing about past events. This is called the *historical present*.

Example:
1.   Marie-Antoinette **est** condamnée à mort. Elle **entre** dans la charrette et **est** en route pour la guillotine. Marie-Antoinette *is* condemned to die. She *goes* into the cart and *is* on her way to the guillotine.

(e)   The near future.

Example:
1.   Il **arrive** demain. He *arrives* tomorrow.

(f)   An action or state of being that occurred in the past and *continues up to the present*. In English, this tense is the *present perfect*.

Examples:
1.   Je **suis** ici depuis dix minutes. I *have been* here for ten minutes. (meaning: I am still here.)
2.   Elle **est** malade depuis trois jours. She *has been* sick for three days. (meaning: She is still sick.)

E. The verb in the negative

1.   To use a verb in the negative, place **ne** in front of the verb and **pas** after it:

Je **ne** danse **pas**.	I do not dance (or, I am not dancing).

2.   If the first letter of a verb is a vowel, drop the **e** in **ne** and add an apostrophe:

Je **n'**aime **pas** le café.	I do not like coffee.

F. The verb in the interrogative

1.   To use a verb in a question, put **est-ce que** in front of the subject:

Est-ce que vous dansez?	Do you dance?
Est-ce que Janine danse?	Is Janine dancing?

2.   If the first letter of the subject is a *vowel* or *silent h*, drop the **e** in **que** and add an apostrophe:

Est-ce qu'Albert danse? Is Albert dancing?	**Est-ce qu'**il danse? Is he dancing?
Est-ce qu'Hélène danse? Is Helen dancing?	**Est-ce qu'**elle danse? Is she dancing?

67

3. To use a verb in a question, there is something else you can do instead of using the **est-ce que** form. You can use the *inverted form*. Move the subject pronoun and put it after the verb, joining it with a hyphen:

Dansez-vous?	Do you dance?

4. If the subject pronoun is **je**, do not use the inverted form. Use the **est-ce que** form. The inverted form with **je** is used only with certain verbs.

5. In the inverted form, when the last letter of the verb is a vowel in the third person singular, insert -t- in front of **il** or **elle**:

Danse-t-il?	Does he dance?
	Is he dancing?
Danse-t-elle?	Does she dance?
	Is she dancing?

6. In the inverted form, if the subject is a noun, mention the noun first and use the pronoun of the noun:

Pierre danse-t-il?	Does Peter dance?
Janine danse-t-elle?	Does Janine dance?
Le garçon danse-t-il?	Is the boy dancing?
La jeune fille danse-t-elle?	Is the girl dancing?

G. The verb in the negative interrogative

1. To use a verb in a question that is negative, first use the interrogative form you learned above (section **F**).

2. Put **ne** in front of the verb.

3. Put **pas** after the verb if you use the **est-ce que** form.

4. Or, if you use the inverted form, put **pas** after the subject pronoun:

Est-ce que vous ne dansez pas?	Don't you dance?
Est-ce qu'Albert ne danse pas?	Doesn't Albert dance?
Est-ce qu'elle ne danse pas?	Doesn't she dance?
Ne dansez-vous pas?	Don't you dance?
Ne danse-t-il pas?	Doesn't he dance?
Janine ne danse-t-elle pas?	Doesn't Janine dance?
Le garçon ne danse-t-il pas?	Doesn't the boy dance?

EXERCISES

I.   Obtaining and Providing Information. Proficiency in Speaking and Writing.

Situation: You are talking with a friend while standing in line for tickets to a basketball game. Your friend wants to know where and when you work **(travailler)**, when you watch **(regarder)** television, and if you speak **(parler)** French all the time.

After you make three statements, write them on the lines for practice.

1. _____

2. _____

3. _____

II. Substitute only one appropriate subject pronoun for the word or words in italics and rewrite the entire sentence in French.

Model: **Janine allume le téléviseur.**   You write: **Elle allume le téléviseur.**
        (Janine turns on the television set.)   (She turns on the television set.)

1. *Madame Paquet* entre dans le salon.

_____

2. *Pierre* cherche le journal.

_____

3. *Marie et Alice* chantent bien.

_____

4. *Robert et Georges* jouent à la balle.

_____

5. *Janine et Pierre* regardent trop de violence à la télévision.

_____

Janine et Pierre regardent trop de violence à la télévision.

III. Vocabulary Building. Proficiency in Writing.

Write a list of four French verbs you would need to use to talk to a clerk in a store while buying a TV set. The verbs must be of the **-er** type. They are all in this work unit.

1. _____ 2. _____ 3. _____ 4. _____

IV. Meeting People. Proficiency in Speaking and Writing.

Situation: Five parents are visiting the school where you are the French teacher. They all speak French. They obtained permission from the principal to visit classes because they want to see if the students use the language. Their children are shy and they would like to see them encouraged to speak French.

Of the above list of commonly used regular **-er** verbs in section **C**, select three and use them in brief sentences. You may use your own words and ideas and/or the following: **Désirez-vous parler français avec moi? Parlez-vous français à la maison? Est-ce que vous chantez en français avec les enfants?**

After the parents leave the classroom, write what you said on the lines for practice. Begin your statements with a greeting, such as **Bonjour, madame/monsieur. Comment allez-vous?**

1. _____

2. _____

3. _____

V. Answer the following questions in the affirmative in complete French sentences. In answer (a) use **oui**. In answer (b) use **aussi** (also). Study the models. Use subject pronouns in your answers.

Models: (a) **Chantez-vous les matins?** You write: (a) **Oui, je chante les matins.**
(Do you sing in the mornings?) (Yes, I sing in the mornings.)

(b) **Et Simone?** You write: (b) **Elle chante aussi.**
(And Simone?) (She sings also.)

1. (a) Dansez-vous les matins?

_____

(b) Et François?

_____

2. (a) Pierre cherche-t-il le chapeau?

_____

(b) Et Janine?

_____

3. (a) Hélène étudie-t-elle la leçon?

_____

(b) Et vous?

_____

VI. Answer the following questions in the negative in complete French sentences. In answer (a) use non. In answer (b) use non plus (either). Study the models carefully. Use subject pronouns in your answers.

Models: (a) **Est-ce que vous dansez?** You write: (a) **Non, je ne danse pas.**
(Do you dance?)   (No, I don't dance.)

(b) **Et Charles?**   You write: (b) **Il ne danse pas non plus.**
(And Charles?)   (He doesn't dance either.)

1. (a) Est-ce que vous dansez?

_____

(b) Et Paul?

_____

2. (a) Est-ce qu'il étudie?

_____

(b) Et Monique?

_____

3. (a) Est-ce que Paul cherche la balle?

_____

(b) Et les enfants?

_____

4. (a) Est-ce que la femme écoute la musique?

_____

(b) Et vous?

_____

5. (a) Est-ce que tu fermes la fenêtre?

_____

(b) Et nous?

_____

VII. Choose the correct verb form and write it with its subject on the blank line.

1. Je (fermes, ferme, fermons) la porte.   _____*Je ferme*_____

2. Tu (apportes, apportez, apportent) le gâteau.   _____

3. Il (étudient, étudions, étudie) les devoirs.   _____

4. Elle (parlent, parle, parlez) bien.   _____

5. Nous (marche, marchez, marchons) lentement.   _____

6. Vous (donner, donnez, donnons) des fleurs à la maîtresse. _____

7. Ils (joue, jouent, jouons) dans la rue.   _____

8. Elles (chante, chantent, chantes) doucement.   _____

9. Vous (cherchez, cherches, cherchent) le chapeau.   _____

10. J' (aimes, aime, aimons) la glace.   _____

VIII. Word Search. Can you find these verb forms with their subject pronouns *in French* in this puzzle? Circle them.

1. I dance.

2. You (*familiar form*) study.

3. She plays.

4. We love.

5. They (*m.*) are singing.

6. I love.

7. He arrives.

8. He talks.

9. He forgets.

J	E	D	A	N	S	E	N	T	C	O
A	J	A	I	M	E	J	I	U	N	I
I	L	P	A	R	L	E	O	É	O	E
I	L	O	U	B	L	I	E	T	U	A
E	L	L	E	J	O	U	E	U	S	U
J	E	J	O	U	E	A	L	D	A	O
I	L	A	R	R	I	V	E	I	I	I
E	L	L	E	A	R	R	I	E	M	E
N	O	U	S	J	O	U	O	S	O	A
I	L	S	C	H	A	N	T	E	N	T
A	E	I	O	U	I	L	S	P	S	L

IX. Activities. Proficiency in Speaking and Writing.

A. Situation: You are at home. Your mother and father want to watch a TV show about French art. You and your brother (or sister) want to watch **Le Tour de France** on TV. In three short sentences tell your mother and father why you prefer to watch the sports program. You may use your own words, those in this lesson, or any or all of the following: **allumer le téléviseur, regarder mon émission préférée, je préfère, nous préférons, j'aime, nous aimons, les sports, les cyclistes, la télé, la télévision.**

B. Situation: You and your friend cannot decide on what to do this Saturday night. You want to go dancing but your friend wants to go to a concert. In four sentences tell what you want to do and why. You may use your own words, those in this unit, or the following: **préférer, aimer mieux, danser, aller, écouter la musique, au concert.**

C. Now, write what you said on the lines below for practice.

_____

_____

_____

X. Entertainment. Proficiency in Speaking and Writing.

Situation: Michel and Michelle are talking about what to do this evening. Michel wants to dance but Michelle wants to see a movie.

You are playing both roles. What would he say? What would she say? After you say the words aloud, write them on the lines for practice. You may want to review the vocabulary in this lesson, in the back pages, and in the verb tables. Use **Je désire** for *I want* or **J'aimerais** for *I would like.*

Michel: _____

Michelle: _____

XI.   Daily Activities. Proficiency in Writing.

Situation: You are corresponding with Maryse, a pen pal in Guadeloupe. She wants to know about your daily activities.

Write a note telling her three activities that you do every day. You may use your own words and ideas or the following: **Je vais à la bibliothèque tous les jours/**I go to the library every day. **Je regarde la télé tous les soirs/** I watch TV every evening. **J'étudie mes leçons de français/**I study my French lessons.

Before you write the note, pretend you are talking to her. Then write your three sentences.

le premier janvier, 2007

Chère Maryse,

_____

_____

_____

Ton ami(e),

_____

XII.   Dining Out. Proficiency in Speaking and Writing.

Situation: You and Janine are looking for a good French restaurant to have lunch. You look at the menu and prices on the window and you decide to go in. You talk to the waiter/**le serveur**.

You may use your own words and ideas or the suggested words under the lines. Later, after you have written what you said on the lines, you may play the roles of Janine and the waiter for more practice in speaking and writing.

Janine:	**Aimes-tu le menu? Les prix sont bons/**The prices are good. **Nous entrons?/**Shall we go in?
Vous:	_____
	Yes, the menu is good. And the prices are good. Let's go in!/**Entrons!**
Janine:	**D'accord!/**Okay! **Entrons!**
Le serveur:	**Bonjour. Vous désirez?**
Vous:	_____
	We are looking for a good French restaurant.
Le serveur:	**Ce restaurant est le meilleur!/**This restaurant is the best! **Voici une bonne table/**Here is a good table. **Asseyez-vous, s'il vous plaît/**Sit down, please.
Janine:	**Merci.**
Vous:	_____
	Bring us the soup of the day/**Apportez-nous la soupe du jour.**
Le serveur:	**Excellent! J'apporte deux soupes du jour tout de suite/**right away.
	(You have been waiting fifteen minutes for the waiter to return with the soup.)
Vous:	_____
	What a restaurant!/**Quel restaurant!** What a waiter! Where is he?!
Janine:	**Mon Dieu!/**My God! **Le service est très mauvais ici.**
	(The waiter finally returns with the two soups.)

Vous: _____

There are flies in the soup!/Il y a des mouches dans la soupe!

Janine: **Sortons d'ici tout de suite!**

Vous: _____

Yes, Janine. Let's get out of here right away! What a restaurant!

XIII. Appreciating French Art. Proficiency in Speaking and Writing.

Situation: You and a friend are visiting an art museum. You are admiring a painting by Pierre Auguste Renoir, a great French artist, **un grand artiste français**. It is entitled *Madame Georges Charpentier et ses enfants.*

Look at the picture below and answer the questions in French in complete sentences.

1. Qui est la femme?

_____

2. Combien d'enfants y a-t-il dans ce tableau/*in this painting?*

_____

3. Est-ce que le chien est grand ou petit?

_____

4. Que voyez-vous sur la table? Un vase de fleurs? Des fruits? Une carafe?

_____

5. Aimez-vous ce tableau? Est-il beau? Magnifique? Splendide?

_____

Madame Georges Charpentier et ses enfants / Madame Charpentier and her children (1878) by Pierre Auguste Renoir (1841–1919). The Granger Collection, New York.

Au revoir, Monsieur! (Good-bye, Sir!)

Work Unit 5
Present Indicative Tense of Regular Verbs Ending in *-ir*

Have you ever received a note from a boy or girl in class at school? If you are an adult using this book, do you remember your school days when notes were passed from one student to another? In this episode, Pierre is reading a note that was just passed to him.

Tout est bien qui finit bien

Pierre est en classe de mathématiques. Il lit un petit mot caché dans les pages de son livre. Voici le mot:

Pierre, mon chéri:
Je déteste ce cours et je déteste le professeur. Il est très mauvais prof. Il choisit des leçons difficiles et il punit les élèves quand ils ne finissent pas leurs devoirs.
Je t'aime et je t'adore.
Anne-Marie

Le professeur dit à Pierre:

—Tu ne finis pas tes devoirs! Tu as un mot caché dans les pages de ton livre! De qui est ce mot? Donne-moi le mot!

Pierre rougit. Il regarde la belle Anne-Marie et elle lui dit tendrement de ses beaux yeux bleus de ne pas révéler leur amour secret et de ne pas donner le petit mot au professeur.

A ce moment-là, le signal retentit. Le cours est fini! Tous les élèves quittent la salle de classe immédiatement et Pierre aussi, avec le petit mot caché dans les pages de son livre.

Quand il est à la porte, Pierre s'exclame:

—Au revoir, monsieur!

Dans le couloir, Anne-Marie dit à Pierre:

—Chéri, tu es formidable! Tu es vraiment un homme.

Pierre dit:

—Ouf! Je l'ai échappé belle! Tout est bien qui finit bien!

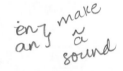

VOCABULAIRE

à *prep.*, to, at
adorer *v.*, to adore
aimer *v.*, to love, to like; **je t'aime** I love you
au revoir *salutation*, goodbye
cacher *v.*, to hide; **caché** hidden
la calculatrice *n.*, calculator

choisir *v.*, to choose; **il choisit** he chooses
le cours *n.*, the course
détester *v.*, to detest
les devoirs *n. m. pl.*, the homework, the assignments
dit *v.* form of **dire** (to say, to tell); **le professeur dit** the teacher says

donner *v.*, to give; **donne-moi** give me
échapper *v.*, to escape; **je l'ai échappé belle!** I had a narrow escape!
l'élève *n. m. f.*, the student, the pupil; **tous les élèves** all the students

fini, finis, finit, finissent *v.* forms of **finir** (to finish); **fini** finished; **tu ne finis pas** you are not finishing; **ils ne finissent pas** they do not finish; **tout est bien qui finit bien!** all's well that ends well!

formidable *adj.*, terrific

ils *subject pron. m.*, **elles** *subject pron. f.*, they

immédiatement *adv.*, immediately

la leçon *n.*, the lesson

leur, leurs *poss adj.*, their

lit *v. form of* **lire** (to read); **il lit** he is reading

le livre *n.*, the book

lui *indir. obj. pron.*, to him, to her; **elle lui dit** she says to him

mauvais *adj. m. s.*, bad

le moment *n.*, moment; **à ce moment-là** at that moment

le mot *n.*, the word, the note; **un petit mot** a note

ne pas révéler not to reveal; **ne pas donner** not to give

ouf! *interj.*, whew!

la porte *n.*, the door

le professeur *n.*, the teacher

punit *v. form of* **punir** (to punish); **il punit** he punishes

quand *adv.*, when

qui *pron.*, who, whom, which; **de qui** from whom

quittent *v. form of* **quitter** (to leave); **tous les élèves quittent la salle de classe** all the students leave the classroom

retentit *v. form of* **retentir** (to resound, to ring); **le signal retentit** the signal sounds, the bell rings

rougit *v. form of* **rougir** (to blush); **Pierre rougit** Pierre blushes

la salle *n.*, the room; **la salle de classe** the classroom

son *poss. adj. m. sing.*, his

ton *poss. adj. m. sing.*, your

voici here is

EXERCISES

Review the story and vocabulary before starting these exercises.

I.   **Choose the correct answer based on the story in this unit.**

1. Pierre est dans

    (a) le restaurant.   (b) le garage.   (c) l'école.   (d) la bibliothèque.   *c*

2. Pierre lit

    (a) un journal.   (b) un livre.   (c) un menu.   (d) un petit mot.   *d*

3. Le petit mot est caché dans les pages du livre

    (a) du professeur.   (b) de son ami.   (c) de Pierre.   (d) de son amie.   *c*

II. **Activities. Proficiency in Speaking.**

A. Situation: You are in French class. All the students have finished an exercise in writing except you. The teacher approaches and asks why you are not finishing the assignment: **Pourquoi ne finis-tu pas le devoir?** In two sentences tell your teacher why. You may use your own words, those in this lesson, or the following: **finir, accomplir, choisir, la leçon, l'exercice, parce que, difficile.**

B. Situation: You and a friend are in the school cafeteria talking about homework. In three sentences tell your friend about an assignment one of your teachers gave your class. Explain why the assignment was given. You may use your own words, those in this lesson, or the following: **punir, choisir, les exercices, faciles, difficiles, parce que.**

III. **Choose the appropriate French word and write it on the blank line. Base your choice only on the content of the story in this unit.**

| **rougit** | **finit** | **retentit** | **choisit** | **finissent** |

1. Le professeur _choisit_ des leçons difficiles.
2. Pierre _rougit_ .
3. Tout est bien qui _finit_ bien.
4. Les élèves ne _finissent_ pas les devoirs.
5. Le signal _retentit_ .

STRUCTURES DE LA LANGUE

Here are the personal endings for verbs of the second conjugation (**-ir**).

SECOND CONJUGATION

			-ir
Infinitive		→	**finir** *to finish*
			I finish, *or* I do finish, *or* I am finishing; you finish, etc.
Required subject pronouns			
PERSON	SINGULAR		
1. **je**	I		fin**is**
2. **tu**	you (*familiar only*)		fin**is**
3. **il**	he *or* it		
elle	she *or* it		fin**it**
	PLURAL		
1. **nous**	we		fin**issons**
2. **vous**	you		fin**issez**
3. **ils**	they		fin**issent**
elles			

Note that **vous** is also formal singular.

RULES AND OBSERVATIONS:

1. To form the present tense of a regular verb ending in **-ir**, drop the **-ir**. What remains is called the *stem*. Add to the stem the personal endings shown in the above chart: **-is, -is, -it, -issons, -issez, -issent.**

2. Note that *do, am, are, does, is* (which are used in English in the present tense) are *not translated* into French. Therefore, **je finis** can mean *I finish,* or *I do finish,* or *I am finishing*. The same applies to the rest of the conjugation, for example, *you finish*, or *you do finish*, or *you are finishing*, etc.

Some Common Regular Verbs of the Second Conjugation

accomplir	to accomplish	**punir**	to punish
bâtir	to build	**remplir**	to fill
bénir	to bless	**réussir (à)**	to succeed (in)
choisir	to choose	**rougir**	to blush
désobéir (à)	to disobey	**saisir**	to seize
obéir (à)	to obey	**salir**	to soil, to dirty

EXERCISES

Review the preceding material before starting these exercises.

I.   Expressing Personal Feelings. Proficiency in Speaking and Writing.

Situation: You are on the phone telling a classmate your personal feelings about the new biology teacher.

You may use your own words and ideas and/or any of the following: **J'aime la biologie mais je n'aime pas le maître (la maîtresse)**/*I like biology but I don't like the teacher;* **il (elle) punit les élèves quand ils ne finissent pas les devoirs**/*he (she) punishes the students when they don't finish their homework;* **quand il (elle) explique la leçon, je ne saisis rien**/*when he (she) explains the lesson, I don't grasp anything;* **il (elle) choisit des questions très difficiles**/*he (she) chooses very difficult questions.*

There is a lot of static on the telephone and your friend is not sure what you are saying. Write a note containing at least three statements about your feelings. Practice writing on the lines below.

La date: _____

Cher ami Paul (Chère amie Janine),

_____

_____

_____

Ton ami (Ton amie),

_____

II. **Expressing Personal Feelings. Proficiency in Speaking and Writing.**

Situation: Take a minute to study the picture shown below. Pretend that you are either the boy or girl. Make two statements in French expressing your personal feelings in response to what the woman is saying to you.

After you make two statements aloud, write them on the lines under the picture for practice.

Madame Berty punit les élèves.

1. _____

2. _____

III. **Use the subject pronoun in parentheses to take the place of the subject pronoun in italics. Rewrite each sentence in French, making the required changes in the verb forms.**

    Model: *Nous* finissons la leçon.   (Je)   You write: Je finis la leçon.
              (We are finishing the lesson.)   (I am finishing the lesson.)

1. (Ils) _____ *finisent* _____   4. (Elle) _____ *finit* _____

2. (Tu) _____ *finis* _____   5. (Vous) _____ *finissez* _____

3. (Il) _____ *finit* _____   6. (Elles) _____ *finnissent* _____

IV. **Use the subject pronoun in parentheses to take the place of the subject pronoun in italics. Rewrite each sentence in French, making the required changes in the verb forms. Keep them all in the negative.**

   Model: *Elle* ne finit pas le dîner.   (Je)   You write: Je ne finis pas le dîner.
            (She is not finishing the dinner.)   (I am not finishing the dinner.)

   1. (Vous) _ne finnisez pas_   4. (Elles) _ne Finnisent pas_
   2. (Il) _ne finit pas_   5. (Ils) _____
   3. (Tu) _ne finis pas_   6. (Nous) _ne finissent pas_

V. **Answer the following questions in the affirmative in complete French sentences, using subject pronouns in your answers. In answer (a) use Oui. In answer (b) use aussi.**

   Models: (a) **Henri finit-il la leçon?**   You write: (a) **Oui, il finit la leçon.**
                 (Is Henry finishing the lesson?)   (Yes, he is finishing the lesson.)

             (b) **Et vous?**   You write: (b) **Je finis la leçon aussi.**
                 (And you?)   (I am finishing the lesson also.)

1. (a) Henri finit-il le livre?

   _____

   (b) Et vous?

   _____

2. (a) Les professeurs punissent-ils les mauvais élèves?

   _____

   (b) Et Monsieur Fouchy?

   _____

3. (a) Monsieur Banluc choisit-il une nouvelle automobile?

   _____

   (b) Et Madame et Monsieur Paquet?

   _____

4. (a) Le chien obéit-il au garçon?

   _____

   (b) Et les chats?

   _____

5. (a) Finissez-vous la leçon aujourd'hui?

   _____

   (b) Et Janine?

   _____

VI. Answer the following questions in the negative in complete sentences in French, using subject pronouns in your answers. In answer (a) use Non. In answer (b) use non plus (either).

Models: (a) **Est-ce que vous finissez la leçon?** (Are you finishing the lesson?)

(b) **Et Charles?** (And Charles?)

You write: (a) **Non, je ne finis pas la leçon.** (No, I am not finishing the lesson.)

You write: (b) **Il ne finit pas la leçon non plus.** (He isn't finishing the lesson either.)

1. (a) Est-ce qu'Henri désobéit?

   _____

   (b) Et vous?

   _____

2. (a) Est-ce que tu finis la leçon?

   _____

   (b) Et Pierre?

   _____

3. (a) Est-ce que Monsieur Paquet choisit une auto?

   _____

   (b) Et Madame Paquet?

   _____

4. (a) Est-ce que nous bâtissons une maison?

   _____

   (b) Et Monsieur et Madame Banluc?

   _____

5. (a) Est-ce que vous rougissez?

   _____

   (b) Et les jeunes filles?

   _____

VII. Choose the correct verb form and write it with its subject on the blank line.

1. Je (finissons, finis, finissez) la leçon.   _____

2. Tu (saisis, saisit, saisissons) la balle.   _____

3. Il (accomplis, accomplit, accomplissez) les devoirs.   _____

4. Elle (bâtit, bâtissons, bâtissent) une maison.   _____

5. Nous (choisissons, choisissez, choisissent) un dessert.   _____

6. Vous (punis, punit, punissez) le chien.   _____

7. Ils (rougit, rougissez, rougissent) facilement. _____

8. Elles (désobéissent, désobéit, désobéissez) à leurs parents. _____

9. Je (remplis, remplit, remplissons) le vase. _____

10. Vous (finis, finissons, finissez) les devoirs. _____

VIII. Word Search. Can you find these verb forms with their subject pronouns *in French* in this puzzle? Circle them.

1. We finish.

2. You (*polite form*) succeed.

3. I choose.

4. You (*familiar form*) obey.

5. He seizes.

6. I finish.

7. She punishes.

8. He blesses.

9. I build.

A	E	I	O	J	E	C	H	O	I	S	I	S	J
E	A	E	L	L	E	P	U	N	I	T	A	E	O
I	L	B	É	N	I	T	A	E	O	U	I	F	B
V	O	U	S	R	É	U	S	S	I	S	S	E	Z
F	O	T	N	Z	Z	S	S	I	L	F	I	N	I
N	O	U	S	F	I	N	I	S	S	O	N	S	E
J	E	O	E	L	J	E	L	L	A	N	O	U	S
E	L	B	S	J	E	B	Â	T	I	S	F	I	N
I	S	É	S	S	F	O	N	S	S	I	T	S	T
V	O	I	U	R	I	U	E	S	I	S	E	Z	S
J	E	S	F	O	N	L	M	O	T	N	L	L	E
I	L	C	H	O	I	M	N	A	E	I	U	A	N
B	N	E	I	T	S	N	O	U	S	P	A	L	R

IX. Appreciating French Sculpture. Proficiency in Writing.

Situation: Last year when you were in Paris, you visited **Le Musée Rodin** and were overwhelmed as you looked at Auguste Rodin's many sculptures, in particular, *Le Penseur*/*The Thinker*. This year you are visiting the Rodin Museum in Philadelphia where there are many bronze casts of his works.

Look at the photo below of *Le Penseur.* Write at least three sentences telling us your impressions. You may use your own words and ideas and/or any of the following: **C'est une oeuvre d'art magnifique**/*It's a magnificent work of art.* **Je pense que cette statue est la plus belle de toutes les oeuvres de Rodin**/*I think that this statue is the most beautiful of all the works of Rodin.* **C'est une grande joie de regarder cette statue**/*It's a great joy to look at this statue.*

1. _____

2. _____

3. _____

Le Penseur *(The Thinker)* by Auguste Rodin, French sculptor. A bronze cast of this magnificent statue is in front of Philosophy Hall on the Columbia University campus in New York City. Photograph reprinted courtesy of Nikolay Misharev, Shutterstock, Inc.

X. Appreciating French Art. Proficiency in Speaking and Writing.

Situation: During a field trip with your French teacher and classmates, you visit a museum where you admire a painting of a young woman by Jean-Jacques (*dit* James) Tissot.

It's your turn to say a few words in French about the painting. Look at the picture on the following page. You may use your own words and ideas or the following.

A few verbs you may want to use: **voir** / to see; **regarder** / to look at; **admirer** / to admire; **avoir** / to have; **être** / to be; **porter** / to carry, to wear; **être assis(e)** / to be seated.

A few nouns: **le tableau** / painting; **la jeune femme** / young woman; **le livre** / book; **le chapeau** / hat; **l'arbre** / tree; **les feuilles** / leaves; **le visage** / face; **les yeux** / eyes; **le nez** / nose; **la bouche** / mouth; **les lèvres** / lips; **la robe** / dress; **les cheveux** / hair; **l'oreille** / ear; **le manteau** / coat; **le col** / collar; **les fleurs** / flowers.

A few adjectives: **beau, beaux, belle, belles** / beautiful; **grand, grande** / big; **joli, jolie** / pretty; **élégant, élégante** / elegant; **impressionnant** / impressive; **splendide**/ splendid; **superbe** / superb. Use the vocabulary and verb tables in the back pages of this book.

After you have jotted down a few words in French that you plan to use, say them aloud. Then, pretending that you are talking to a friend, use them in at least ten short sentences for practice on the lines below. All you need is a subject and a verb and you have a sentence. Try these, just for starters: **Le tableau de Tissot, artiste français, est superbe** / The painting by Tissot, French artist, is superb. **La jeune femme est belle** / The young woman is beautiful. **Elle a de beaux yeux** / She has beautiful eyes. **Elle porte une jolie robe** / She is wearing a pretty dress. **Elle est chez elle** / She is at home. **Elle est assise** / She is sitting.

1. _____

2. _____

3. _____

4. _____

5. _____

6. _____

7. _____

8. _____

9. _____

10. _____

Type of Beauty, Mrs. Newton by Jean-Jacques (dit James) Tissot (1836–1902).
Christie's Images / The Corbis Collection.

Test 1

This test is based on Work Units 1 to 5. Review them before starting this test.

PART ONE   SPEAKING PROFICIENCY

Directions: Read the ten situations given below. Take a few minutes to organize your thoughts about the words you are going to speak. Select five of them.

1. **Situation:** You are looking for a letter you received from a friend. Janine is helping you. Imagine a brief conversation between you and Janine. Make five statements in all, two that you would make and three that Janine would make. You are playing both roles.

2. **Situation:** You are at a table in a restaurant deciding what to eat and drink. You are talking to the waiter or waitress. Make at least four statements.

3. **Situation:** You are in a furniture store shopping for a few things because you are moving into a new apartment. You are talking with the salesman. Make six statements in all, three that you would make and three that the salesman would make. You are playing both roles.

4. **Situation:** You and your family are planning a trip to France. You are looking for the passports. Make at least three statements.

5. **Situation:** You and a friend are in a fast-food restaurant/**dans un restaurant cuisine rapide**. Your friend wants to know why you like mineral water. Make three statements telling why you like it.

6. **Situation:** Your friend Catherine is visiting you in your house. She wants to know whose umbrella is on the bed. Tell her it's your mother's umbrella. She also wants to know whose gloves are under the chair. Tell her they are your father's gloves. Catherine is looking at a picture in your photo album. She wants to know who the woman is who is eating. Tell her it's your aunt Sophie who eats all the time.

7. **Situation:** You are in a small café-restaurant in Paris. Ask the waiter if he has any fish today, any mashed potatoes, any sausages. Tell him you don't want any roast beef with French fries.

8. **Situation:** You are at a party introducing three foreign exchange students to a friend. Say that Jacques is from France, he speaks French, he pronounces French well. María is from Spain, she speaks Spanish, she pronounces Spanish well. Rosa is from Italy, she speaks Italian, she pronounces Italian well.

9. **Situation:** Your friend Pierre wants to know your personal feelings about watching television on Saturday nights. Make three statements.

10. **Situation:** You are at the Musée Rodin in Paris admiring the sculpture *Le Penseur.* Make three statements about it.

PART TWO   LISTENING PROFICIENCY

Directions: Your teacher will read aloud four short paragraphs. Each one will contain only a few sentences. You will hear each paragraph twice. Then you will hear one question based on each. You will hear the question only once. It is printed below. Choose the best suggested answer and check the letter of your choice.

Selection Number 1

1. Qui cherche sous le lit?

   A. Monsieur Paquet
   B. Madame Paquet
   C. Pierre
   D. Janine

Selection Number 2

2. Qui a apporté la glace?

   A. Monsieur Paquet
   B. Janine
   C. Pierre
   D. Monsieur Banluc

Selection Number 3

3. Qui a de grands pieds?

   A. François
   B. Françoise
   C. Raymond
   D. Janine

Selection Number 4

4. Où sont Janine et Pierre?

   A. dans le salon
   B. dans la cuisine
   C. dans le garage
   D. dans la cave

PART THREE   READING PROFICIENCY

Directions: In the following passage there are five blank spaces numbered 1 through 5. Each blank space represents a missing word. For each blank space, four possible completions are provided. Only one of them makes sense in the context of the passage.

First, read the passage in its entirety to determine its general meaning. Then read it a second time. For each blank space choose the completion that makes the best sense and is grammatically correct. Then write its letter in the space provided.

Pierre _____ en classe de mathématiques. Il lit un petit mot caché dans les pages de

1. A. sont
   B. est
   C. a
   D. ont

son livre. Voici le mot:

Pierre, mon chéri:

Je déteste ce cours et je déteste le professeur. Il est

_____ mauvais. Il _____ des leçons difficiles

2. A. beaucoup
   B. tendrement
   C. très
   D. formidable

3. A. choisissons
   B. choisissez
   C. choisit
   D. choisis

et il punit les élèves quand ils ne finissent pas leurs devoirs.

Je t'aime et je t'adore.

Anne-Marie

Le professeur dit à Pierre:

—Tu ne _____ pas tes devoirs! Tu as un mot caché dans les pages

4. A. finis
   B. finit
   C. finissez
   D. finissent

de ton livre! De _____ est ce mot? Donne-moi le mot!

5. A. que
   B. quoi
   C. qui
   D. qu'

PART FOUR   WRITING PROFICIENCY

Directions: Of the ten situations in Part One (Speaking Proficiency) in this test, select five and write what you said on the lines below.

Situation No. __ _____

_____

_____

Situation No. __ _____

_____

_____

Situation No. __ _____

_____

_____

Situation No. __ _____

_____

_____

Situation No. __ _____

_____

_____

Pour combien vendez-vous ce vase, madame?
(For how much are you selling this vase, Madam?)

Work Unit 6
Present Indicative Tense of Regular Verbs Ending in -re

Have you ever bought anything at a flea market? Sometimes you can pick up something interesting.

Le vase extraordinaire

Aujourd'hui Janine est au marché aux puces avec son amie Monique. Elles passent la journée au marché parce que c'est un endroit très intéressant.

—Oh, Monique! Regarde! Un joli vase. Il est superbe! s'exclame Janine.

—Pour combien vendez-vous ce vase, madame? demande Monique.

—Je vends ce vase pour dix euros, mademoiselle, répond la marchande. Il est vraiment très joli.

—Il est d'une beauté très rare! dit Janine. Mais je n'ai pas dix euros sur moi. J'ai deux euros. Monique, as-tu huit euros?

—Non, Janine, je n'ai pas huit euros, répond Monique.

—Je vais retourner à la maison pour demander à ma mère les huit euros. Je veux avoir ce vase. Il est extraordinaire, dit Janine à la femme. Viens, Monique!

Après une heure, Janine et Monique reviennent avec l'argent. Quand elles arrivent à la boutique où la femme vend le vase, Janine s'exclame:

—Oh! Le vase n'est pas ici! Où est le vase extraordinaire, madame? Le vase rare! Le joli vase!

—Je regrette, mademoiselle, mais il est vendu, répond la femme.

Janine et Monique vont partir et après un moment, la femme ajoute:

—Attendez! Attendez! Attendez, mesdemoiselles! J'ai beaucoup de vases exactement comme l'autre.

La marchande ouvre une grande boîte et elle met sur la table quinze vases exactement comme l'autre.

—Choisissez, mademoiselle! dit la femme.

VOCABULAIRE

ai, as *v. forms of* **avoir** (to have); **j'ai** I have; **je n'ai pas** I don't have; **as-tu?** do you have?

ajoute *v. form of* **ajouter** (to add); **la femme ajoute** the woman adds

l'argent *n. m.,* money

arrivent *v. form of* **arriver** (to arrive); **elles arrivent** they arrive

attendez *v. form of* **attendre** (to wait); **attendez!** wait!

aujourd'hui *adv.,* today

autre *adj., pron.,* other; **l'autre** the other one

la boîte *n.,* the box

la boutique *n.,* the shop

c'est it's, it is

choisissez *v. form of* **choisir** (to choose); **choisissez!** choose!

combien *adv.,* how much

comme *adv.,* like, as

dix *adj.,* ten

l'endroit *n. m.,* the place

un euro euro, eurodollar

exactement *adv.,* exactly

extraordinaire *adj.,* extraordinary, unusual

huit *adj.,* eight

ici *adv.,* here

intéressant *adj.,* interesting

joli *m.,* **jolie** *f., adj.,* pretty

la journée *n.,* the day

le marchand *n.,* **la marchande** *n.,* the merchant, shopkeeper

le marché *n.,* the market; **au marché aux puces** at the flea market

met *v. form of* **mettre** (to put); **elle met** she puts

ouvre *v. form of* **ouvrir** (to open); **elle ouvre** she opens

partir *v.,* to leave

passent *v. form of* **passer** (to spend time); **elles passent** they are spending

la puce *n.,* the flea

quinze *adj.,* fifteen

rare *adj.,* rare

regarde *v. form of* **regarder** (to look, to look at); **regarde!** look!

répond *v. form of* **répondre** (to reply, to answer); **répond la marchande** answers the shopkeeper

retourner *v.,* to return, to go back

reviennent *v. form of* **revenir** (to return, to come back); **elles reviennent** they return

vais *v. form of* **aller** (to go); **je vais** I'm going

le vase *n.,* the vase

vend, vendez, vends, vendu *v. forms of* **vendre** (to sell); **la femme vend** the woman is selling; **vendez-vous?** are you selling?; **je vends** I am selling; **vendu** sold

veux *v. form of* **vouloir** (to want); **je veux** I want

viens *v. form of* **venir** (to come); **viens!** come!

vont *v. form of* **aller** (to go); **elles vont** they are going

vraiment *adv.,* really

EXERCISES

Review the story and vocabulary before starting these exercises.

I. Oui ou Non?

1. Aujourd'hui Janine est au marché aux puces.   _____

2. La marchande vend le vase pour quinze euros.   _____

3. Monique n'a pas huit euros.   _____

4. Janine et Monique retournent à la maison.   _____

5. Quand elles retournent à la boutique avec l'argent, le vase est vendu.   _____

II. Complete the dialogue between Janine and the merchant. Refer to the dialogue in this unit if you have to.

1. Janine: Pour combien _____-vous ce vase, madame?

2. La Marchande: Je _____ ce vase pour _____ euros, mademoiselle.

3. Janine: Oh! Il est _____ très rare!

4. La Marchande: Oui, et il est très _____ aussi.

III. The words in the following boxes are scrambled. Unscramble them to find a meaningful sentence. Write the sentences on the lines provided.

Model:

combien	pour	madame?
vase	ce	vendez-vous

You write: *Pour combien vendez-vous ce vase, madame?*

(For how much are you selling this vase, madam?)

1.

vends	vase	pour
dix euros	ce	je

You write: _____

2.

marchande	de	la
vend	beaucoup	vases

You write: _____

3.

moment	un	après	Attendez!
ajoute	femme	la	Attendez!

You write: _____

STRUCTURES DE LA LANGUE

Here are the personal endings for verbs of the third conjunction **(-re).**

THIRD CONJUGATION

		-re
Infinitive →		**vendre** *to sell*
		I sell, *or* I do sell, *or* I am selling; you sell, etc.
Required subject pronouns		
PERSON **SINGULAR**		
1. **je** I		vend**s**
2. **tu** you (*familiar only*)		vend**s**
3. **il** he *or* it **elle** she *or* it		vend
PLURAL		
1. **nous** we		vend**ons**
2. **vous** you		vend**ez**
3. **ils** they **elles**		vend**ent**

Note that **vous** is also formal singular.

RULES AND OBSERVATIONS:

1. To form the present tense of a regular verb ending in **-re**, drop the **-re**. What remains is called the *stem*. Add to the stem the personal endings shown in the chart on the previous page: **-s, -s, -, -ons, -ez, -ent.**

2. Note that for an **-re** verb there is normally no ending to add in the third person singular. The last letter of the stem is often **d**, so the verb form remains the same as the stem, for example, **il** or **elle vend**. However, there are some **-re** verbs whose last letter in the stem is not **d**. In that case, you have to add **t**:

interrompre	*to interrupt*	**rompre**	*to break*
il, elle interrompt		il, elle rompt	

3. In the plural, note that the personal endings for an **-re** verb are the same as those for an **-er** verb.

4. Finally, note also that *do, am, are, does, is* (which are used in English in the present tense) *are not translated* into French. Therefore, **je vends** can mean *I sell*, or *I do sell*, or *I am selling*. The same applies to the rest of the persons, for example, *you sell*, or *you do sell*, or *you are selling*, etc.

Some Common Regular Verbs of the Third Conjugation

attendre	to wait (for)	**interrompre**	to interrupt
défendre	to defend, to forbid	**perdre**	to lose
descendre	to go (come) down, to descend	**rendre**	to give back, to return
		répondre (à)	to answer, to reply
entendre	to hear	**rompre**	to break

EXERCISES

Review the preceding material before starting these exercises.

I. Substitute only one appropriate subject pronoun for the word or words in italics and rewrite the entire sentence in French.

> Model: ***La dame* répond au téléphone.** You write: **Elle répond au téléphone.**
> (The lady is answering the phone.) (She is answering the telephone.)

1. *Le soldat* défend sa patrie.

_____

2. *La marchande* vend des vases.

_____

3. *Anne et Georges* entendent la musique.

_____

4. *L'homme et la femme* vendent leur maison.

_____

5. *Le grand chien* rompt la petite barrière.

_____

II.   Helping a Friend. Proficiency in Writing.

Situation: You are helping a friend use French verbs. Ask your friend to follow the directions in each situation below.

A. Write three French verbs that you would use while shopping in a department store. They must be of the **-re** type.

1. _____   2. _____   3. _____

B. Write three French verbs that you would use when talking on a telephone. They must be of the **-re** type.

1. _____   2. _____   3. _____

C. Write three French verbs that you would use to describe the picture of Anne and Georges. They must be **-er, -ir,** or **-re** types.

1. _____

2. _____

3. _____

Anne et Georges entendent la musique.
(Anne and George hear the music.)

III.   Shopping. Proficiency in Speaking and Writing.

Situation: You are in an antique shop in Paris. You like a vase and you want to buy it.

Complete the following dialogue. The saleswoman is **la vendeuse**. You are **Vous**. You may use your own words and ideas and/or the words under the lines. Use **Je désire** for *I want.*

La vendeuse: **Bonjour, monsieur (madame, mademoiselle). Vous désirez?**

Vous: _____

Greet her and say you want to buy this vase/**ce vase**.

La vendeuse: **Il est joli, n'est-ce pas?**/*isn't it?*

Vous: _____

Ask her for how much she is selling this vase.

La vendeuse: **Je vends le vase pour cent euros.**

Vous: _____

Ask her if it is rare.

La vendeuse: **Oui, il est rare.**

Vous: _____

Ask her if she accepts credit cards.

La vendeuse: Oui, nous acceptons les cartes de crédit.

Vous: _____

Here is my credit card/**Voici ma carte de crédit.**

La vendeuse: Et votre passeport, s'il vous plaît.

Vous: _____

Here is my passport.

IV. Answer the following questions in the affirmative in complete French sentences, using subject pronouns in your answers. In answer (a) use **oui**. In answer (b) use **aussi** (also). Make the required changes in the verb forms.

Models: (a) **La dame répond-elle au téléphone?**
(Is the lady answering the phone?)

You write: (a) **Oui, elle répond au téléphone.**
(Yes, she is answering the phone.)

(b) **Et les dames?**
(And the ladies?)

You write: (b) **Elles répondent au téléphone aussi.**
(They're answering the phone too.)

1. (a) Pierre répond-il à la lettre?

_____

(b) Et vous?

_____

2. (a) Monsieur Coty vend-il la maison?

_____

(b) Et Monsieur Dupont?

_____

3. (a) Le soldat défend-il la patrie?

_____

(b) Et vous?

_____

4. (a) Le vase est-il joli?

_____

(b) Et le parapluie?

_____

5. (a) Janine est-elle au marché aux puces?

_____

(b) Et Monique?

_____

V. Change the following affirmative statements to interrogative sentences. Use the inverted form only.

Model: **Pierre danse tous les soirs.** You write: **Pierre danse-t-il tous les soirs?**
(Pierre dances every evening.) (Does Pierre dance every evening?)

1. Janine étudie dans la bibliothèque.

_____

2. Elle cherche le chapeau.

_____

3. Il finit la leçon.

_____

4. Elle choisit une jolie robe.

_____

5. Nous répondons à la lettre.

_____

6. Ils vendent la maison.

_____

VI. Change to the plural or singular, according to what is given.

Models: **Il vend.** (He sells.) You write: **Ils vendent.** (They sell.)
Elles chantent. (They sing.) **Elle chante.** (She sings.)

1. Elle attend. _____ 4. Il écoute. _____

2. Je vends. _____ 5. Tu finis. _____

3. Nous dansons. _____ 6. Ils répondent. _____

VII. Change the following affirmative statements to interrogative sentences. Use the **est-ce que** form only.

Model: **Pierre étudie.** You write: **Est-ce que Pierre étudie?**
(Pierre is studying.) (Is Pierre studying?)

1. Elle finit le livre.

_____

2. Monsieur Berty vend la voiture.

_____

3. Elle choisit un joli chapeau.

_____

4. Il défend la patrie.

_____

5. Hélène ouvre la boîte.

_____

97

VIII. Write the French word opposite each picture. Use the definite article with the word.

1. _____

2. _____

3. _____

4. _____

5. _____

6. _____

IX. Complete each verb form in the present indicative by writing the correct letter or letters on the blank lines.

1. J'aim _____ le français.

2. Vous chant _____ bien.

3. Janine étudi _____ beaucoup.

4. Je chois _____ un chapeau.

5. Ils attend _____ l'autobus.

6. Je vend _____ l'automobile.

7. Vous chois _____ une leçon facile.

8. Nous fin _____ les devoirs.

X. Give the three English translations for each of the following French verb forms in the present indicative.

1. Je danse. _____ _____ _____

2. Vous finissez. _____ _____ _____

3. Nous vendons. _____ _____ _____

XI. Word Search. Can you find these verb forms with their subject pronouns *in French* in this puzzle? Circle them.

1. He sells.

2. She waits.

3. We answer.

4. They (*m.*) lose.

5. You (*familiar*) forbid.

6. They (*f.*) lose.

7. I give back.

8. You answer.

N	N	O	I	L	V	E	N	D	O	U	I	N
I	L	S	P	E	R	D	E	N	T	I	C	I
E	L	L	E	S	I	M	P	O	R	T	A	N
L	U	I	E	L	L	E	A	T	T	E	N	D
E	L	L	E	S	P	E	R	D	E	N	T	O
E	J	E	R	E	N	D	S	A	L	O	R	S
V	O	S	S	E	T	M	O	I	S	O	N	T
N	O	U	S	R	É	P	O	N	D	O	N	S
U	E	A	I	P	N	A	C	E	G	L	I	L
A	E	I	T	U	D	É	F	E	N	D	S	T
V	O	U	S	R	É	P	O	N	D	E	Z	U

Paris market.

99

XII. Appreciating French Art. Proficiency in Writing.

Situation: You are in a museum of French impressionist art admiring the painting **Le Bateau-Atelier**/*The Studio Boat* by the French artist Claude Monet.

Write at least four short sentences about the picture below. You may use your own words and ideas or tell us who is in the boat, what he or she is doing, and something about the scenery outside the boat.

1. _____

2. _____

3. _____

4. _____

Monet's Le Bateau-Atelier *(Monet's Studio Boat)* 1874 by Claude Monet.
Francis G. Mayer / The Corbis Collection.

XIII. Educational Tour. Proficiency in Speaking and Writing.

Situation: You are on an educational tour in Paris with a group of students from your school. Your guide is **Madame Durand,** who is a professor at the **Université de Paris**. You have been asking her questions about Paris. Now she has a few questions to ask you because she is impressed with your ability to speak French.

Participate in this conversation. You are playing the role of **Vous**. Later, for more practice, switch roles with her and do the conversation with a friend.

Madame Durand:	Vous parlez français extraordinairement bien!
Vous:	_____
	Thank her.
Madame Durand:	Depuis combien de temps étudiez-vous le français?/*How long have you been studying French?*
Vous:	_____
	Tell her you have been studying French for one year/**J'étudie le français depuis un an.**
Madame Durand:	Vous êtes extraordinaire! Où habitez-vous?
Vous:	_____
	Tell her in what city and country you live.
Madame Durand:	Aimez-vous mon pays?/*my country*
Vous:	_____
	_____
	Tell her you like the country, the French language/**la langue française**, the French people/**les Français**, the culture/**la culture**, music/**la musique**, and French art/**l'art français**.
Madame Durand:	Merci. Bon. Maintenant, nous allons au marché aux puces/*Now we are going to the flea market.* Venez, tout le monde!/*Come, everybody.*
Raymond:	Où allons-nous?
Vous:	_____
	We are going to the flea market.
Madame Durand:	C'est ça!/*That's right!* Bravo!
Vous:	_____
	Ask her what the word for "flea" is in French: **Quel est le mot pour** *flea* **en français?**
Madame Durand:	Le mot est "la puce." Allons!/*Let's go!* Attention aux puces!/*Watch out for the fleas!*

XIV. Shopping. Proficiency in Speaking and Writing.

Situation: After your conversation with **Madame Durand**, you and the other students in the group go to **le marché aux puces.** You are still playing the role of yourself—**Vous.**

You may use your own ideas and words or those under the lines. Later, for more practice, switch roles with her and do the conversation with a friend.

Madame Durand:	Le voici!/*Here it is!* C'est le marché aux puces! Désirez-vous acheter quelque chose?/*something?*
Vous:	_____
	Tell her yes, you want to buy something.
Madame Durand:	Qu'est-ce que vous désirez acheter? Avez-vous assez d'argent?/*Have you enough money?*
Vous:	_____
	Tell her you have enough money and you want to buy a pillow/**un oreiller.**

Madame Durand:	**Un oreiller?! Pourquoi?**
Vous:	_____
	Tell her the pillow on your bed at the hotel is not good. Or, give another reason.
Madame Durand:	**D'accord**/*Okay,* **si vous insistez.**
Vous:	_____
	Say there are many articles at good prices here/**Il y a beaucoup d'articles à bons prix ici.** Then ask her where the pillows are.
Madame Durand:	**Les oreillers sont là-bas**/*over there.* **Tout droit**/*straight ahead.*
Vous:	_____
	Ask the saleswoman for how much she is selling the pillows. Address her as **Madame.**
La vendeuse:	**Un euro pour chaque oreiller**/*One euro for each pillow.* **Ce n'est pas beaucoup. Cet**/*this* **oreiller est très joli. Il n'y a pas beaucoup de puces dedans**/*There aren't many fleas inside it.*
Vous:	_____
	Tell her you'll take it/**Je le prends.** Then tell her: "Here's one euro."
La vendeuse:	**Attention aux puces!**
Vous:	_____
	Thank her and say good-bye. Also say, "Have a nice day!"/**Passez une bonne journée!**

Pierre aime les sports. Son sport favori est le football.
(Pierre loves sports. His favorite sport is soccer.)

Work Unit 7
Formation and Use of Reflexive Verbs in the Present Indicative

*Are you as eager as Pierre to play
in a soccer game?*

Surprise! Surprise!

Pierre aime les sports. Son sport favori est le football. Il veut être toujours en forme parce qu'il est gardien de but dans son équipe à l'école. Il veut être toujours prêt à bien jouer. Il est au régime. Il mange seulement des aliments qui sont bons pour la santé. Pendant la saison de football, il évite les glaces, les pommes frites, et les pâtisseries. C'est un brave garçon.

Il se couche de bonne heure, il se lève avec le soleil, il se lave soigneusement, il s'habille vite, et il prend le petit déjeuner.

Il annonce à ses parents:

—C'est le grand match de football aujourd'hui! C'est après les classes.

Pierre dit à Janine:

—Janine, tu vas jouer dans l'équipe avec les garçons et les jeunes filles aussi, n'est-ce pas?

—Oui, répond Janine. Les jeunes filles aiment les sports aussi. Je vais être au stade pour jouer avec les garçons et les jeunes filles cet après-midi.

Pierre se dépêche pour arriver tôt dans la grande cour de l'école. Il court un kilomètre sur la piste avant d'entrer dans l'école.

Pour Pierre, le football est tout. Il se rappelle les bons conseils de son entraîneur de football:

—Attention au filet, Pierre! Attention au filet! Garde le but! Le but!

Pierre joue extrêmement bien. C'est un très bon garçon, bon étudiant, bon joueur. Ses camarades aiment beaucoup Pierre.

Après la dernière classe, Pierre va au gymnase. Il se prépare pour le grand match. Il met sa tenue d'exercice. Il fait de la gymnastique avant de commencer le match.

Pierre fait de la gymnastique pendant quelques heures. Maintenant il est prêt pour le grand match!

Pierre court à toute vitesse au stade. Quand il arrive au stade, il voit que tout le monde est là.

—Pierre! Pourquoi es-tu en retard? demande l'entraîneur.

Pierre ne répond pas. Il est à bout de souffle.

—Le match commence tout de suite, dit l'entraîneur.

—Je ne peux pas jouer au football aujourd'hui, s'exclame Pierre.

—Pourquoi pas? demande l'entraîneur.

—Je suis trop fatigué!

VOCABULAIRE

l'aliment   *n. m.,* food

annoncer   *v.,* to announce

l'après-midi   *n. m.,* the afternoon

attention à   watch out for

à bout de souffle   out of breath

brave   *adj., m. f.,* good, fine, honest (when **brave** follows a noun, it means *brave;* **une femme brave, un homme brave** a brave woman, a brave man)

le but   *n.,* the goal; **gardien de but** goalie

c'est …   it's (*sometimes* he's … (or) she's …)

le conseil   *n.,* advice

se coucher   *refl. v.,* to go to bed

la cour   *n.,* the yard

court   *v. form of* **courir** (to run); **Pierre court** Peter runs

se dépêcher   *refl. v.,* to hurry

dernier   *m.,* **dernière** *f., adj.,* last

l'entraîneur   *n. m.,* the coach, sports instructor

l'équipe   *n. f.,* the team

éviter   *v.,* to avoid

fais, fait   *v. forms of* **faire** (to do, to make); **il fait de la gymnastique** he does gymnastics

fatigué   *adj., m. s.,* tired

le filet   *n.,* the net

le football   *n.,* soccer (in the U.S.A.)

la forme   *n.,* the shape, the form; **en forme** in good shape

garder   *v.,* to guard; **gardien de but** goalie

le gymnase   *n.,* the gymnasium; **la gymnastique** *n.,* gymnastics

s'habiller   *refl. v.,* to get dressed

jouer   *v.,* to play; **le joueur** *m.,* **la joueuse** *f., n.,* the player

le kilomètre   *n.,* kilometer (about 0.62 miles)

là   *adv.,* there

se laver   *refl. v.,* to wash oneself

se lever   *refl. v.,* to get up

le match   *n.,* the game, the match (sport)

mettre   *v.,* to put, to put on (wear); **il met** he puts on

n'est-ce pas?   isn't it so? aren't you?

le petit déjeuner   *n.,* breakfast

peux   *v. form of* **pouvoir** to be able; **Je ne peux pas …** I can't …

la piste   *n.,* the track

les pommes frites   *n. f.,* fried potatoes, French fries (You can also say **les frites** for French fries.)

prendre   *v.,* to take; **prendre le petit déjeuner** to have breakfast

se préparer   *refl. v.,* to prepare oneself, to get ready

prêt *m.,* **prête** *f., adj.,* ready, prepared

que   *interrog. pron.,* what; *as a conj.,* that

que   *adj., m. s.,* what (which); **quel sport?** what (which) sport?

se rappeler   *refl. v.,* to remember, to recall

le régime   *n.,* diet; **au régime** on a diet

se   *refl. pron.,* himself, herself, oneself, itself, themselves

soigneusement   *adv.,* carefully

le soleil   *n.,* the sun

son   *poss. adj., m. s.,* **ses** *pl.,* his

le stade   *n.,* the stadium

tard   *adv.,* late

la tenue d'exercice   gym suit

tôt   *adv.,* early

toujours   *adv.,* always

tout de suite   *adv.,* immediately, right away

trop   *adv.,* too

veut   *v. form of* **vouloir** (to want); **il veut** he wants

la vitesse   *n.,* speed; **à toute vitesse** very fast

voit   *v. form of* **voir** (to see); **il voit** he sees

EXERCISES

Review the story and vocabulary before starting these exercises.

I. **Answer the following questions in complete sentences. They are based on the story, "Surprise! Surprise!"**

1. Quel est le sport favori de Pierre?

_____

2. Pourquoi veut-il être toujours en forme?

_____

3. Quels aliments mange-t-il?

_____

4. Se lève-t-il tôt ou tard?

_____

5. Est-ce que Janine va jouer dans le match aussi?

_____

II. **Answer the following questions in complete sentences. They are personal questions and require answers of your own.**

1. Aimez-vous les sports?

_____

2. Est-ce que vous vous couchez tôt ou tard?

_____

3. Vous dépêchez-vous pour arriver à l'école?

_____

4. Est-ce que vous vous lavez soigneusement?

_____

5. Vous habillez-vous vite?

_____

III. **Vocabulary Building. Proficiency in Writing.**

A. Write four foods that you would take with you on your way to see a soccer game.

1. _____ 2. _____ 3. _____ 4. _____

B. Write four words related to any game or sport.

1. _____ 2. _____ 3. _____ 4. _____

IV. Un acrostiche. Complete the French words in the squares across.

1. slowly
2. to avoid
3. to go to bed
4. to get up
5. for
6. or
7. to answer
8. late
9. to wash oneself

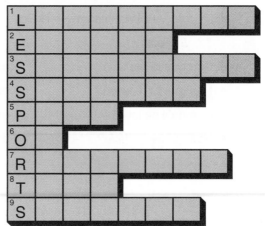

STRUCTURES DE LA LANGUE

A. Formation and use of reflexive verbs in the present indicative; all four forms: Affirmative, Negative, Interrogative, and Negative Interrogative

se laver   *to wash oneself*

AFFIRMATIVE

I wash myself, I am washing myself, I do wash myself, etc.			
Singular		*Plural*	
je	**me lave**	nous	**nous lavons**
tu	**te laves**	vous	**vous lavez**
il	**se lave**	ils	**se lavent**
elle	**se lave**	elles	**se lavent**

NEGATIVE

I am not washing myself, I do not wash myself, etc.			
Singular		*Plural*	
je	**ne me lave pas**	nous	**ne nous lavons pas**
tu	**ne te laves pas**	vous	**ne vous lavez pas**
il	**ne se lave pas**	ils	**ne se lavent pas**
elle	**ne se lave pas**	elles	**ne se lavent pas**

107

INTERROGATIVE WITH **est-ce que** FORM

Am I washing myself? Do I wash myself? etc.	
Singular	*Plural*
est-ce que je me lave?	**est-ce que** nous nous lavons?
est-ce que tu te laves?	**est-ce que** vous vous lavez?
est-ce qu'il se lave?	**est-ce qu'**ils se lavent?
est-ce qu'elle se lave?	**est-ce qu'**elles se lavent?

INTERROGATIVE WITH *INVERTED FORM*

Am I washing myself? Do I wash myself? etc.	
Singular	*Plural*
*****est-ce que** je me lave?	**nous** lavons-nous?
te laves-tu?	**vous** lavez-vous?
se lave-t-il?	**se** lavent-ils?
se lave-t-elle?	**se** lavent-elles?

*The inverted form is ordinarily used in the first person singular *only* with certain verbs.

Observe that the subject pronoun shifts in the interrogative when using the inverted form; it is joined to the verb with a hyphen:

Affirmative:	Tu te laves.	Nous nous lavons.
Interrogative:	Te laves-tu?	Nous lavons-nous?

Est-ce que je ne me lave pas?

NEGATIVE INTERROGATIVE WITH **est-ce que** FORM

Am I not washing myself? Don't I wash myself? etc.

Singular	*Plural*
est-ce que je **ne** me lave **pas**?	**est-ce que** nous **ne** nous lavons **pas**?
est-ce que tu **ne** te laves **pas**?	**est-ce que** vous **ne** vous lavez **pas**?
est-ce qu'il **ne** se lave **pas**?	**est-ce qu'**ils **ne** se lavent **pas**?
est-ce qu'elle **ne** se lave **pas**?	**est-ce qu'**elles **ne** se lavent **pas**?

NEGATIVE INTERROGATIVE WITH *INVERTED FORM*

Am I not washing myself? Don't I wash myself? etc.

Singular	*Plural*
***est-ce que** je **ne** me lave **pas**?	**ne** nous lavons-nous **pas**?
ne te laves-tu **pas**?	**ne** vous lavez-vous **pas**?
ne se lave-t-il **pas**?	**ne** se lavent-ils **pas**?
ne se lave-t-elle **pas**?	**ne** se lavent-elles **pas**?

*The inverted form is ordinarily used in the first person singular *only* with certain verbs.

Observe that the subject pronoun shifts in the negative interrogative when using the inverted form; it is joined to the verb with a hyphen:

Negative:	Tu ne te laves pas.	Nous ne nous lavons pas.
Negative Interrogative:	Ne te laves-tu pas?	Ne nous lavons-nous pas?

RULES AND OBSERVATIONS:

1. To form the present tense of a reflexive verb in a simple affirmative sentence, put the reflexive pronoun in front of the verb. Study the first box (Affirmative).

2. A reflexive verb expresses an action that is turned back upon the subject; for example, I wash *myself* (je **me** lave). The reflexive pronoun in the English sentence is *myself*; in the French sentence it is **me**.

3. The reflexive pronouns in French are **me**, **te**, **se**, **nous**, and **vous**.

4. The reflexive pronouns in English are **myself**, **yourself**, **herself**, **himself**, **itself**, **ourselves**, **yourselves**, and **themselves**.

REFLEXIVE PRONOUNS

Singular		*Plural*	
me	myself	**nous**	ourselves
te	yourself	**vous**	yourselves (yourself)
se	himself, herself, itself	**se**	themselves

5. Be careful to use the appropriate reflexive pronoun, the one that matches the subject pronoun. You already know the subject pronouns, but here they are again, next to the reflexive pronouns.

	Singular		*Plural*
1.	**je me…**	1.	**nous nous…**
2.	**tu te…**	2.	**vous vous…**
3.	**il se…**	3.	**ils se…**
	elle se…		**elles se…**

6. Note that in the third person singular and third person plural, the reflexive pronoun is the same: **se** (himself, herself, itself, themselves).

7. Note that in the first person plural, the reflexive pronoun is the same as the subject pronoun: **nous** (ourselves).

8. Note that in the second person plural, the reflexive pronoun is the same as the subject pronoun: **vous** (yourself, yourselves).

9. Most of the time, a verb that is reflexive in French is also reflexive in English. Here's one example of a verb that is not reflexive in English but is in French.

se dépêcher   to hurry

je me dépêche   I hurry, *or* I do hurry, *or* I am hurrying

10. Note the position of the reflexive pronouns and the **ne** and **pas** in the boxes above.

11. The reflexive pronouns **me**, **te**, and **se** become **m'**, **t'**, and **s'** when they are in front of a verb beginning with a vowel or silent *h*, as in the following example:

s'appeler   to be called, named

je m'appelle Marie.	My name is Mary.
tu t'appelles Hélène.	Your name is Helen.
il s'appelle Henri.	His name is Henry.
elle s'appelle Jeanne.	Her name is Jeanne.

B.   Formation of some irregular reflexive verbs

s'asseoir *to sit down*	
je m'**assieds**	nous **nous asseyons**
tu t'**assieds**	vous **vous asseyez**
il s'**assied**	ils s'**asseyent**
elle s'**assied**	elles s'**asseyent**

s'endormir *to fall asleep*	
je m'**endors**	nous **nous endormons**
tu t'**endors**	vous **vous endormez**
il s'**endort**	ils s'**endorment**
elle s'**endort**	elles s'**endorment**

se servir *to use*	
je **me sers**	nous **nous servons**
tu **te sers**	vous **vous servez**
il **se sert**	ils **se servent**
elle **se sert**	elles **se servent**

se souvenir *to remember*	
je **me souviens**	nous **nous souvenons**
tu **te souviens**	vous **vous souvenez**
il **se souvient**	ils **se souviennent**
elle **se souvient**	elles **se souviennent**

Some Other Common Reflexive Verbs			
s'amuser	to enjoy oneself, to have a good time	**se rappeler**	to remember, to recall
se coucher	to go to bed, to lie down	**se regarder**	to look at oneself
s'habiller	to get dressed, to dress oneself	**se reposer**	to rest
se lever	to get up	**se trouver**	to be situated, to be located

EXERCISES

Review the preceding material before starting these exercises.

I.   Fill in the missing reflexive pronouns.

1. Je _____ lave.

2. Je ne _____ dépêche pas.

3. Tu _____ amuses.

4. Il _____ couche.

5. Elle _____ habille.

6. Nous _____ levons.

7. Vous _____ rappelez.

8. Ils _____ amusent.

9. Elles _____ reposent.

10. Il _____ regarde.

II.   Match the following.

1. Je me dépêche.   _____ She is falling asleep.

2. Je m'appelle Yves.   _____ You are having a good time here.

3. Vous vous couchez de bonne heure.   _____ Are you washing yourself?

4. Tu t'amuses ici.   _____ Aren't I washing myself?

5. Il s'habille.   _____ My name is Yves.

6. Est-ce que je ne me lave pas?   _____ I sit down.

7. Je m'assieds.   _____ I hurry.

8. Elle s'endort.   _____ You go to bed early.

9. Te laves-tu?   _____ He is getting dressed.

10. Vous ne vous lavez pas.   _____ You don't wash yourself.

III. Word Search. Can you find the following five verb forms in French with their subject pronouns in this puzzle?

1. I am getting dressed.

2. You are washing yourself.

3. He is hurrying.

4. They (*m.*) are enjoying themselves.

5. I am resting.

D	E	I	P	T	E	C	H	E	J
J	E	L	A	U	L	A	V	R	E
D	I	S	D	T	E	J	A	U	M
I	L	S	U	E	L	O	I	N	E
A	S	A	I	L	M	A	N	G	R
J	E	M	H	A	B	I	L	L	E
I	D	U	O	V	E	E	O	A	P
I	É	S	S	E	M	E	T	S	O
O	P	E	I	S	S	E	L	V	S
J	Ê	N	A	P	P	E	L	E	E
U	C	T	I	L	S	E	M	E	L
A	H	J	E	I	U	O	I	L	T
J	E	M	E	R	E	G	A	R	E

IV. Fill in the missing subject pronouns.

1. _____ m'amuse.

2. _____ t'habilles.

3. _____ vous regardez.

4. _____ (or) _____ se servent.

5. _____ (or) _____ se souvient.

6. _____ nous couchons.

7. _____ vous levez.

8. _____ (or) _____ s'assied.

9. _____ (or) _____ se reposent.

10. _____ m'endors.

V. Answer the following questions in the affirmative.

> Model: **Vous lavez-vous?**   You write: **Oui, je me lave.**
> (Do you wash yourself?)   (Yes, I wash myself.)

1. Vous amusez-vous?

_____

2. Vous couchez-vous?

_____

3. Vous reposez-vous?

_____

4. Vous habillez-vous?

_____

5. Vous asseyez-vous?

_____

VI. Answer the following questions in the negative.

> Model: **Vous lavez-vous tous les jours?**   You write: **Non, je ne me lave**
> (Do you wash yourself every day?)   **pas tous les jours.**
> (No, I do not wash myself
> every day.)

1. Vous amusez-vous ici?

_____

2. Vous couchez-vous de bonne heure tous les soirs?

_____

3. Vous habillez-vous vite tous les matins?

_____

4. Vous appelez-vous Jean-Jacques?

_____

5. Vous asseyez-vous ici?

_____

VII. **Change each sentence by replacing the verb in italics with the proper form of the verb in parentheses. Keep the same subject. Rewrite the entire sentence in French.**

Model: **Se dépêche-t-il tous les matins? (s'habiller)**
(Does he hurry every morning [to get dressed]?)

You write: S'habille-t-il tous les matins?
(Does he get dressed every morning?)

1. *Se lave*-t-il tous les soirs? (se dépêcher)

_____

2. Je *m'assieds* sur cette chaise. (s'endormir)

_____

3. Nous *nous couchons* de bonne heure. (se lever)

_____

4. Il *s'habille* vite. (se laver)

_____

5. Je *me lave* tous les jours. (s'amuser)

_____

VIII. **The words in the following boxes are scrambled. Unscramble them to find a meaningful sentence. Write the complete sentences on the lines provided.**

Model:

nous	café	maintenant
servons	du	nous

You write: ___ **Nous nous servons du café maintenant.** ___

(We are serving ourselves coffee now.)

1.

m'	ma	habille
dans	je	chambre

2.

ils	samedis	théâtre
au	tous les	s'amusent

3.

tu	reposes	te
dîner	après	le

4.

me	heure	bonne
couche	je	de

5.

dépêchons	pour	à l'école
nous	aller	nous

6.

je	tous	matins
les	lave	me

1. _____

2. _____

3. _____

4. _____

5. _____

6. _____

IX. Daily Activities. Proficiency in Writing.

Situation: You are studying French in a summer session at the Alliance Française Institute in Paris. Before you left for France, you promised your friend Donald that you would write a postcard about your daily activities.

On the lines below, write a note telling him at least five things you do every day. Use the reflexive verbs you studied in this lesson. For example, you may want to say that you go to bed early, you fall asleep easily, you get up with the sun, you wash yourself carefully, you dress quickly, and you are enjoying yourself in Paris. You may add other words and ideas of your own.

le trois avril, 2007

Cher ami Donald,

_____

_____

Ton ami (Ton amie),

_____

X. Change the following statements into questions. Use the inverted form only.

Model: Il se lave avant de manger. You write: **Se lave-t-il avant de manger?**
(He washes himself before (Does he wash himself before
eating.) eating?)

1. Elle se repose.

_____

2. Vous vous levez très tard le matin.

_____

3. Elle s'assied devant la porte.

_____

4. Nous nous dépêchons.

_____

5. Ils se couchent tard.

_____

XI. **Change the following statements into negative interrogative sentences. Use the est-ce que form or the inverted form.**

Model: **Pierre se lève avec le soleil.**
(Pierre gets up with the sun.)

You write: **Pierre ne se lève-t-il pas avec le soleil?**

Or: **Est-ce que Pierre ne se lève pas avec le soleil?**
(Doesn't Pierre get up with the sun?)

1. Pierre se couche de bonne heure.

_____

2. Il se lave soigneusement.

_____

3. Il s'habille vite.

_____

4. Il se dépêche.

_____

5. Il se prépare à jouer au football.

_____

XII. **Choose the correct form and write it on the blank line. Write the verb form with the subject.**

1. Je (me lave, vous lavez, se lavent) tous les matins.

_____

2. Vous (vous amusez, s'amusent, nous amusons) tout le temps.

_____

3. Il (s'endorment, s'endort, vous endormez) vite.

_____

4. Elle (s'habille, s'habillent, nous habillons) dans la chambre.

_____

5. Nous (me couche, vous couchez, nous couchons) de bonne heure.

_____

6. Tu (t'amuses, s'amuse, s'amusent) tous les jours!

_____

7. Ils (se sert, se servent, nous servons) du café noir.

_____

8. Elles (s'endort, vous endormez, s'endorment) tranquillement.

_____

9. Je (s'amuse, m'amuse, nous amusons) tous les soirs au café.

_____

10. Madame Paquet (se dépêche, nous dépêchons, vous dépêchez) pour sortir.

XIII. Activities. Proficiency in Writing.

Situation: You are writing a letter to a pen pal in Martinique but first you want to practice a few French words you plan to use.

A. Write four reflexive verbs that you would use when talking about yourself and what you do in the mornings and evenings.

1. _____ 2. _____ 3. _____ 4. _____

B. Write three foods that a person avoids eating when trying to lose weight to be in shape for a sport.

1. _____ 2. _____ 3. _____

XIV. Obtaining Information. Proficiency in Writing.

Situation: You also promised to write to Diane during your summer studies in Paris. This time you are going to ask her questions using reflexive verbs with **est-ce que** or the inverted form. Use the familiar **tu** form (2nd pers., sing.) because she is your friend. Ask at least three questions.

You may use your own ideas and words and/or the following: **Est-ce que tu t'amuses tous les jours?**/*Are you enjoying yourself every day, Are you having a good time every day?* **Moi, je m'a-muse beaucoup ici**/*As for me, I am enjoying myself a lot here.* **Te couches-tu tard ou tôt?**/*Do you go to bed late or early?* **T'endors-tu facilement?**/*Do you fall asleep easily?* **Moi, je m'endors facilement**/*As for me, I fall asleep easily.* **Te reposes-tu quand tu es fatiguée?**/*Do you rest when you're tired?* **Je me repose quand je suis fatigué(e)**/*I rest when I'm tired.*

La date: _____

Chère amie Diane,

_____

_____

_____

_____

_____

Ton ami (Ton amie),

_____

XV. Sports. Proficiency in Speaking and Writing.

Situation: You spent a wonderful afternoon at an indoor swimming pool in Paris. A picture of the pool is shown on the following page. It's something to write home about.

Write at least four sentences. You may use your own ideas and words and/or the following: **j'aime nager**/*I like to swim;* **je nage tous les jours dans cette belle piscine**/*I swim every day in this beautiful pool;* **j'aime la natation**/*I like swimming;* **c'est mon sport favori**/*it's my favorite sport;* **voici une photo de la piscine**/*here is a photo of the swimming pool.*

After you state your sentences, practice writing them on these lines:

_____

_____

_____

117

XVI. Sharing Information. Proficiency in Speaking, Reading, and Writing.

Situation: Today you are serving as an interpreter. A conference of school principals is being held in your school. One of the visitors is **Monsieur Dufy,** who is principal of a school in Montpellier. Mrs. Johnson, your school principal, does not speak French and the visitor speaks very little English.

In this dialogue the three of you are in Mrs. Johnson's office. Your role is **Vous.** Don't forget to use the **vous** form when talking to **Monsieur Dufy** because he is an acquaintance. After **Monsieur Dufy** makes a statement, tell Mrs. Johnson in English what he is saying. You can express yourself easily in French by using words that **Monsieur Dufy** says in French.

You may vary and extend the conversation with your own ideas and words. Later, switch roles with a friend for more practice.

Mrs. Johnson:	Ask him if he wants to have lunch with us in school.
Vous:	Monsieur, _____
	_____
Monsieur Dufy:	Oui, je désire déjeuner avec vous à l'école. Avec plaisir.
Mrs. Johnson:	That's good. Now ask him if he wants to eat meat or fish.
Vous:	Monsieur, _____
	_____
Monsieur Dufy:	Je préfère manger de la viande. Je n'aime pas le poisson.
Mrs. Johnson:	That's fine. Now ask him if he is going to speak in French to the students of the French Club at three o'clock in room 312.
Vous:	Monsieur, _____
	_____
Monsieur Dufy:	Oui, oui, certainement. Je vais parler en français aux étudiants du Cercle Français à trois heures dans la salle 312. Avec grand plaisir.

118

Mrs. Johnson:	Ask him at what time he is going to leave in a taxi to go to the airport.
Vous:	Monsieur, _____
	_____
Monsieur Dufy:	**Je vais partir en taxi pour aller à l'aéroport à quatre heures.**
Mrs. Johnson:	Please thank him. Tell him to have a good trip!/**Bon voyage!**
Vous:	_____, Monsieur. _____

XVII. Appreciating French Art. Proficiency in Speaking and Writing.

Situation: You are in Paris at **Le Moulin Rouge**/The Red Mill. It's a place of entertainment where you can have dinner and see musical shows.

Look at the picture below and tell us what is happening. Use your own words and ideas or the following in three short sentences. First, say them aloud, then write them on the lines. **Le Moulin Rouge est un endroit de divertissement à Paris**/The Moulin Rouge is a place of entertainment in Paris. **Les femmes portent de beaux manteaux longs, de belles robes longues, et de beaux chapeaux**/The women are wearing beautiful long coats, beautiful long dresses, and beautiful hats. **Les hommes et les femmes parlent pendant qu'ils dînent**/The men and women are talking while dining. **Ils s'amusent**/They are enjoying themselves. **Dans quelques minutes la chanteuse Jane Avril va chanter dans un nouveau spectacle à minuit**/In a few minutes the singer Jane Avril is going to sing in a new show at midnight.

1. _____
2. _____
3. _____

Au Moulin Rouge / At the Moulin Rouge, oil on canvas, 1893–1895, 123 x 141 cm, by Henri de Toulouse-Lautrec, French, (1864–1901). The Granger Collection, New York.

—Ch! Ch! Filez! Filez! Oh, ces mouches! s'exclame Madame Paquet.
("Shoo! Shoo! Go away! Oh, these flies!" exclaims Mrs. Paquet.)

Work Unit 8
Cardinal and Ordinal Numbers

Have you ever been at a public auction? Let's see what happens to Madame Paquet.

Ch! Ch! Filez! Filez!

Madame et Monsieur Paquet quittent la maison pour aller à une vente aux enchères. Madame Paquet aime beaucoup les ventes aux enchères. Elle veut acheter une petite table ronde pour le salon de sa maison.

Ils arrivent et ils entrent dans la salle des ventes. Ils entendent le commissaire-priseur qui parle à un groupe de personnes:

Le Commissaire-priseur: **Mesdames, Messieurs, attention! S'il vous plaît!**

(Monsieur et Madame Paquet prennent deux places au cinquième rang près de la porte.)

Le Commissaire-priseur: **J'ai ici, mesdames et messieurs, un très, très beau fauteuil. Qui offre cinquante euros?**

(Monsieur Paquet parle à sa femme à voix basse: —Tout est si élégant ici. Très élégant.)
(Madame Paquet répond à voix basse: —Oui, mais je n'aime pas les mouches! Et le fauteuil est très laid!)

Le Commissaire-priseur: **Merci, monsieur! J'ai cinquante euros pour ce beau fauteuil. Qui offre soixante euros?**
… Soixante euros, ce n'est pas beaucoup pour ce beau fauteuil! Qui offre soixante euros?

(Madame Paquet dit à son mari à voix basse: —Les mouches dans cette salle sont terribles!)

Le Commissaire-priseur: **Merci, madame! Merci! J'ai soixante euros de la dame au premier rang. Qui offre soixante-dix euros?**

(Madame Paquet demande à son mari à voix basse: —François, qui est la dame au premier rang qui offre soixante euros pour ce fauteuil monstrueux? Elle doit être folle!)
(Monsieur Paquet répond: —Je ne sais pas, ma chérie.)

Le Commissaire-priseur: **Merci encore, madame! J'ai une offre de soixante-dix euros! Qui offre quatre-vingts?… Merci, monsieur! J'ai une offre de quatre-vingts euros. Qui offre quatre-vingt-dix euros? … Merci, madame! J'ai quatre-vingt-dix euros de la dame là-bas au troisième rang. Qui offre cent euros? Cent euros? Qui offre cent euros?**

(Madame Paquet lève la main pour chasser les mouches de son nez. —Ch! Ch! Filez! Filez! Oh, ces mouches!)

Le Commissaire-priseur: **Merci, madame! J'ai cent euros de la dame au cinquième rang près de la porte! J'ai cent euros! C'est la dernière mise! Une fois, deux fois, trois fois. C'est fini! Vendu à la charmante dame avec son mari au cinquième rang près de la porte! Vous pouvez payer à la caisse, s'il vous plaît, madame.**

(Tout le monde regarde Madame Paquet.)

Madame Paquet: **Qui? Moi?**

VOCABULAIRE

ai *v. form of* **avoir** (to have); **j'ai** I have

assister à *v.,* to be present at, to attend

beau *m.,* **belle** *f., adj.,* beautiful, handsome

la caisse *n.,* the cash box; **à la caisse** at the cash desk

Ch! Ch! *interj.,* Shoo! Shoo!

charmant *m.,* **charmante** *f., adj.,* charming

chasser *v.,* to chase away

le commissaire-priseur *n.,* the auctioneer

doit *v. form of* **devoir** (to owe, ought to, must); **elle doit être folle** she must be crazy

l'enchère *n. f.,* the bid, the bidding

l'euro *n. m.,* the euro; unit of money used by several countries in Europe

le fauteuil *n.,* the armchair

filez! *exclam.,* go away!

fois *n. f.,* time; **une fois** one time, once; **deux fois** two times, twice

folle *f.,* **fou, fol** *m., adj.,* crazy

le franc *n.,* the franc, the former French unit of money

là-bas *adv.,* over there

laid *m.,* **laide** *f., adj.,* ugly

lève *v. form of* **lever** (to raise, to lift); **elle lève la main** she raises her hand

la mise *n.,* the bid; **la dernière mise** the last bid

moi *pron.,* me

monstrueux *m.,* **monstrueuse** *f., adj.,* monstrous

la mouche *n.,* the fly

le nez *n.,* the nose

offre *v. form of* **offrir** (to offer); **une offre** an offer; **qui offre?** who offers?

payer *v.,* to pay

la place *n.,* the seat, the place

pouvez *v. form of* **pouvoir** (to be able, can, may);

vous pouvez you can, you may

prennent *v., form of* **prendre** (to take); **ils prennent** they take

le rang *n.,* the row

rond *m.,* **ronde** *f., adj.,* round

sais *v. form of* **savoir** (to know); **je sais** I know; **je ne sais pas** I don't know

la salle *n.,* the (large) room; **la salle des ventes** the auction sales room

si *adv.,* so; *conj.,* if

s'il vous plaît please

tout *pron.,* everything, all; **tout le monde** everybody

vendu *v. form of* **vendre** (to sell) sold

la vente *n.,* the sale; **la vente aux enchères** the auction

la voix *n.,* the voice; **à voix basse** in a low voice

EXERCISES

Review the story and vocabulary before starting these exercises.

I. **Answer the following questions in complete sentences. They are based on the story in this unit.**

1. Qui aime beaucoup les ventes aux enchères?

_____

2. Qui entre dans la salle des ventes?

_____

3. Pourquoi Madame Paquet lève-t-elle la main?

_____

4. Qui offre cent euros pour le fauteuil?

_____

5. Qui regarde Madame Paquet?

_____

II. **Answer the following questions in complete sentences. They are personal questions and require answers of your own.**

1. Aimez-vous les ventes aux enchères?

_____

2. Avez-vous un salon dans votre maison?

_____

3. Avez-vous une jolie petite table ronde dans votre maison?

_____

III. **Comment dit-on en français ...?** (How do you say in French ...?) Find these statements in the story and write them in French.

1. Mr. Paquet talks to his wife in a low voice.

_____

2. Mrs. Paquet raises her hand to chase away the flies from her nose.

_____

3. I have one hundred euros.

_____

IV. **The words in the following boxes are scrambled. Unscramble them to find a meaningful sentence. Write the sentence in French on the line provided.**

Model:

de	ils	maison
la	bonne heure	quittent

You write: **Ils quittent la maison de bonne heure.**

                (They leave the house early.)

1.

salle	ils	la
dans	des ventes	entrent

3.

est	élégant	dans
cette salle	si	tout

2.

n'aime	je	ce
fauteuil	pas	monstrueux

4.

veux	une	je
ronde	table	jolie petite

1. _____

2. _____

3. _____

4. _____

123

STRUCTURES DE LA LANGUE

A. Cardinal Numbers 1 to 1,000

0	zéro	31	trente et un	201	deux cent un
1	un, une	32	trente-deux, etc.	202	deux cent deux, etc.
2	deux	**40**	**quarante**	**300**	**trois cents**
3	trois	41	quarante et un	301	trois cent un
4	quatre *— cat*	42	quarante-deux, etc.	302	trois cent deux, etc.
5	cinq	**50**	**cinquante**	**400**	**quatre cents**
6	six	51	cinquante et un	401	quatre cent un
7	sept *set*	52	cinquante-deux, etc.	402	quatre cent deux, etc.
8	huit *wit*	**60**	**soixante**	**500**	**cinq cents**
9	neuf	61	soixante et un	501	cinq cent un
10	**dix**	62	soixante-deux, etc.	502	cinq cent deux, etc.
11	onze	**70**	**soixante-dix**	**600**	**six cents**
12	douze	71	soixante et **onze**	601	six cent un
13	treize	72	soixante-douze, etc.	602	six cent deux, etc.
14	quatorze	**80**	**quatre-vingts**	**700**	**sept cents**
15	quinze *— canz*	81	quatre-vingt-un	701	sept cent un
16	seize *— sayz*	82	quatre-vingt-deux, etc.	702	sept cent deux, etc.
17	dix-sept *— di*	**90**	**quatre-vingt-dix**	**800**	**huit cents**
18	dix-huit	91	quatre-vingt-onze	801	huit cent un
19	dix-neuf	92	quatre-vingt-douze, etc.	802	huit cent deux, etc.
20	**vingt** *— van*	**100**	**cent**	**900**	**neuf cents**
21	vingt et un	101	cent un	901	neuf cent un
22	vingt-deux, etc.	102	cent deux, etc.	902	neuf cent deux, etc.
30	**trente**	**200**	**deux cents**	**1,000**	**mille**

RULES AND OBSERVATIONS:

1. Learning numbers in French is easy. It's very much like the way we form numbers in English.

2. From 0 to 16 it's a matter of learning new vocabulary because there is, naturally, a word for each number. Study the simple words in French from 0 to 16 in the table.

3. Next, notice that numbers 17, 18, and 19 are based on 10 plus 7, 8, and 9. The word for 10 (**dix**) is joined with a hyphen to the word for 7 (**sept**), 8 (**huit**), and 9 (**neuf**). Examine these three numbers in the table.

4. The compound numbers actually start with 20. From 20 to 29, just state the word for 20 (**vingt**) and add to that word the cardinal numbers from 1 to 9. This is how we form the numbers in English too. There is one exception: You are supposed to use the word **et** (*and*) with **un** (*one*). The **et** is omitted after one: vingt-deux, vingt-trois, etc. Don't forget to join the added word with a hyphen.

5. Next, it's a matter of learning new vocabulary after 20: **vingt** (20), **trente** (30), **quarante** (40), and so on. To each whole number add **un** through **neuf**. Don't forget to use **et** (*and*) with **un** only and drop it from **deux** to **neuf**. Study these numbers in the table.

6. The word 100 is also new vocabulary for you: **cent**, with no **un** in front of it for one hundred. It's just plain **cent**.

7. From 200 to 900, you're using words you have already learned: 200 is **deux cents**, 300 is **trois cents**, just as in English. Notice the **s** on **cents**. The **s** drops with compound numbers in the hundreds; **deux cent un** (201), **trois cent un** (301), and so on. In brief, there is an **s** on **cents** only in the round whole number in the hundreds: 200 (**deux cents**), 300 (**trois cents**), 400 (**quatre cents**), and so on. In the hundreds, never use **et** (*and*). Any multiple, any other number added to the round whole number drops the **s** on **cents**: **cent un** (101), **cent deux** (102), and so on.

B. Simple arithmetical expressions

deux **et** deux **font** quatre	$2 + 2 = 4$
trois **fois** cinq **font** quinze	$3 \times 5 = 15$
douze **moins** dix **font** deux	$12 - 10 = 2$
dix **divisés par** deux **font** cinq	$10 \div 2 = 5$

RULES AND OBSERVATIONS:

1. In French you need to state **et** (*and*) as we do in English when adding. Besides saying two *and* two are four, we can say two *plus* two are four. In French, we say **et** (*and*).

2. The symbol × (meaning *times*) is expressed by **fois** in French.

3. In French, we use the word **moins** to express *minus* or *less*.

4. In French, we say **divisés par** to express *divided by*.

5. In French, we use the word **font** (meaning *make*) to express *are* or *make*.

C. Fractions

½	**un demi**	a (one) half
⅓	**un tiers**	a (one) third
¼	**un quart**	a (one) fourth
⅕	**un cinquième**	a (one) fifth

D. Approximate amounts

une dizaine	about ten
une quinzaine	about fifteen
une vingtaine	about twenty
une trentaine	about thirty
une quarantaine	about forty
une cinquantaine	about fifty
une soixantaine	about sixty
une centaine	about a hundred
un millier	about a thousand

125

OBSERVATIONS:

1. Notice that each of the approximate amounts listed above is based on a cardinal number.

2. Did you notice that **une quarantaine** (*about forty*) is related to the English word *quarantine*, which means a period of *forty* days?

E. Ordinal numbers: first to twentieth

first	**premier, première**	1st	**1ᵉʳ, 1ʳᵉ**
second	**deuxième (second, seconde)**	2nd	**2ᵉ**
third	**troisième**	3rd	**3ᵉ**
fourth	**quatrième**	4th	**4ᵉ**
fifth	**cinquième**	5th	**5ᵉ**
sixth	**sixième**	6th	**6ᵉ**
seventh	**septième**	7th	**7ᵉ**
eighth	**huitième**	8th	**8ᵉ**
ninth	**neuvième**	9th	**9ᵉ**
tenth	**dixième**	10th	**10ᵉ**
eleventh	**onzième**	11th	**11ᵉ**
twelfth	**douzième**	12th	**12ᵉ**
thirteenth	**treizième**	13th	**13ᵉ**
fourteenth	**quatorzième**	14th	**14ᵉ**
fifteenth	**quinzième**	15th	**15ᵉ**
sixteenth	**seizième**	16th	**16ᵉ**
seventeenth	**dix-septième**	17th	**17ᵉ**
eighteenth	**dix-huitième**	18th	**18ᵉ**
nineteenth	**dix-neuvième**	19th	**19ᵉ**
twentieth	**vingtième**	20th	**20ᵉ**

RULES AND OBSERVATIONS:

1. You must learn the difference between a **cardinal** number and an **ordinal** number. If you have trouble distinguishing between the two, just remember that we use the cardinal numbers most of the time: **un**, **deux**, **trois** (one, two, three), and so on.

2. Use the *ordinal* numbers to express a certain *order*: premier (première, if the noun following is feminine), deuxième, troisième (first, second, third), and so on.

3. **Premier** is the masculine singular form and **première** is the feminine singular form. Examples: **le premier homme** (*the first man*), **la première femme** (*the first woman*).

4. The masculine singular form **second**, or the feminine singular form **seconde**, is used to mean *second* when there are only two. When there are more than two, **deuxième** is used. Examples: **le Second Empire** because there were only two empires in France; however, **la Deuxième République** because there have been more than two republics in France.

5. The superscript letters in **1er** are the last two letters in the word **premier**; it is equivalent to our *st* in *1st*. The superscript letters in **1re** are the last two letters in the word **première**, which is the *feminine* singular form of *first*.

6. The superscript letter **e** after an ordinal number (for example, **2e**) stands for the **ième** ending of a French ordinal number.

7. When referring to sovereigns or rulers, the only ordinal number used is **Premier**. For all other designations, the cardinal numbers are used. The definite article (*the*) is used in English but not in French. Examples:

but:	François Ier	François Premier	Francis the First
	Louis XIV	Louis Quatorze	Louis the Fourteenth

EXERCISES

A. Cardinal numbers

I.   Complete the following by writing in the French word or words.

1. Deux et deux font _____

2. Trois et quatre font _____

3. Cinq et sept font _____

4. Six et quatre font _____

5. Huit et neuf font _____

6. Neuf et trois font _____

II.   Write the French word or words for the following cardinal numbers.

1. 2 _____

2. 4 _____

3. 6 _____

4. 8 _____

5. 10 _____

6. 20 _____

7. 21 _____

8. 22 _____

9. 30 _____

10. 37 _____

11. 61 _____

12. 69 _____

13. 70 _____

14. 80 _____

15. 100 _____

III. Activities. Proficiency in Speaking.

A. Take a good look at the picture at the beginning of this work unit. Describe the scene to a friend in at least ten words in French.

B. Tell your friend that you are going to a used furniture store to buy a few things for your room.

C. How many students are there in each of the rows in your French class? Begin by saying that there are **(il y a)** so many students in the first row **(dans le premier rang)**, so many in the second row, and so on.

IV. Choose the correct answer and write the word on the line.

1. Deux et cinq font   (a) quatre   (b) six   (c) sept   (d) neuf.   _____

2. Trois fois cinq font   (a) quinze   (b) vingt   (c) dix-sept   (d) huit.   _____

3. Douze moins dix font   (a) vingt-deux   (b) cent vingt   (c) deux   (d) vingt.   _____

4. Dix divisés par deux font   (a) douze   (b) cinquante   (c) six   (d) cinq.   _____

5. Douze divisés par six font   (a) douze   (b) dix-huit   (c) deux   (d) dix.   _____

B. Ordinal numbers

I.   Match the following.

1. troisième   _____ first

2. cinquième   _____ second

3. premier   _____ third

4. deuxième   _____ fourth

5. quatrième   _____ fifth

6. vingtième   _____ fifteenth

7. quinzième   _____ seventeenth

8. dix-neuvième   _____ twentieth

9. seizième   _____ nineteenth

10. dix-septième   _____ sixteenth

II. Activities. Proficiency in Speaking.

Situation: Your neighbors have a child who is about six years old. The parents have asked you to teach their child how to count in French from one to thirty. You have agreed to do this in exchange for a big piece of chocolate cake! It will be fun! Now, begin.

III. Match the following.

1. Henri Quatre   _____ Francis I

2. Louis Seize   _____ Louis XIV

3. François Premier   _____ Henry V

4. Henri Cinq   _____ Louis XVI

5. Louis Quatorze   _____ Henry IV

C. Cardinals, fractions, approximate amounts, ordinals, simple arithmetical expressions, weights and measures

I. Complete the following by writing in the French word or words.

1. Six moins quatre font

_____

2. Vingt et quarante font

_____

3. Cinquante divisés par deux font

_____

4. Trois cents moins cent font

_____

5. Mille moins deux cents font

_____

II. Word Search. Find these seven words *in French* in this puzzle and circle them.

1. one hundred
2. thirty
3. third
4. one thousand
5. fifty
6. five
7. twelve

U	N	M	I	C	T	R	E	N	T	E	X
N	D	E	C	I	N	Q	U	A	N	T	E
M	T	R	C	C	E	N	T	A	I	N	E
T	R	O	I	S	I	È	M	E	U	N	E
O	M	I	N	L	D	O	U	Z	E	L	L
Q	C	I	Q	N	T	R	M	I	L	L	E

III. Match the following.

1. four	_____ un quart
2. about a thousand	_____ une centaine
3. eighty	_____ quatorze
4. one half	_____ quatre
5. fourteenth	_____ soixante-neuf
6. about a hundred	_____ quatre-vingts
7. one fourth	_____ quatorzième
8. fourteen	_____ un demi
9. ninety	_____ quatre-vingt-dix
10. sixty-nine	_____ un millier

IV. Transcribe the following into French words.

Model: $2 \times 5 = 10$ You write: **Deux fois cinq font dix.**

1. $3 \times 9 = 27$

_____

2. $8 - 6 = 2$

_____

3. $20 \div 5 = 4$

_____

4. $7 \times 100 = 700$

_____

5. $80 \text{ et } 10 = 90$

_____

Trois fois cinq font quinze.

V. Picture Interpretation. Proficiency in Speaking and Writing.

Situation: Look at the picture shown above. Write at least ten words in French, saying something about the teacher, the pupils, and the subject being taught. You may use your own ideas and words or any of the following: **une classe de mathématiques, l'élève, la maîtresse, intelligent, difficile, facile.**

VI. Transcribe the following French words into simple arithmetical expressions using symbols and figures.

Model: Deux fois dix font vingt. **You write:** $2 \times 10 = 20$.

1. Trois fois cinq font quinze.

_____

2. Douze moins dix font deux.

_____

3. Dix divisés par deux font cinq.

_____

4. Deux et deux font quatre.

_____

5. Neuf fois dix font quatre-vingt-dix.

_____

VII. Shopping. Proficiency in Speaking and Writing.

Situation: You go with a friend to an auction because you want to buy a small round table for your bedroom.

In this conversation you are speaking for yourself as **Vous.** Select one of your friends to talk with you. Let's say her name is Catherine. You may use your own ideas and words, those under the lines, or those that Catherine uses. Review the story at the beginning of this work unit. After the dialogue is completed, write what you said on the lines. Later, you may switch roles with your friend for more practice.

Catherine: **Aimes-tu la petite table ronde?**

Vous: _____

Tell her you like the small round table but you don't like the flies in this salesroom.

Catherine: **Oui. Les mouches dans cette salle des ventes sont terribles.**

Vous: _____

_____

Ask Catherine who the lady is in the first row who is offering sixty euros for the monstrous armchair.

Catherine: **Je ne sais pas. Elle doit être folle!**

Vous: _____

Surely (**sûrement**), she must be crazy!

Catherine: **Alors/**_so,_ **tu désires acheter la petite table ronde?**

Vous: _____

Yes, it is perfect for my room/**Oui, elle est parfaite pour ma chambre.**

Catherine: **As-tu assez d'argent?**

Vous: _____

Yes, I have enough money. I am going to offer two hundred euros.

Catherine: **Tu vas offrir deux cents euros?! C'est trop!/**_It's too much!_

Vous: _____

Oh, these flies! Shoo! Shoo! Go away!

Catherine: **Si tu offres deux cents euros, tu es folle/*fou aussi/**_also._

Vous: _____

No matter/**N'importe.** The small round table is perfect for my room.

***fou,** _masc. sing.;_ **folle,** _fem. sing._

Monsieur Paquet dit: L'avion va partir sans nous!
(Mr. Paquet says, "The plane is going to leave without us!")

Work Unit 9
Time Expressions, Telling Time, Dates, Age, Months, Days, Seasons

In this scene, Monsieur and Madame Paquet, Janine, and Pierre are going through security at Charles de Gaulle Airport. What an experience!

Bon voyage! Bon retour!

La famille Paquet fait des préparations pour un voyage par avion aux États-Unis. Madame Paquet a une soeur qui habite à La Nouvelle-Orléans avec son mari et ses trois enfants. Maintenant, ils font les valises et dans quelques minutes ils vont quitter la maison pour aller à l'aéroport Charles de Gaulle.

—Quelle heure est-il? demande Monsieur Paquet.

—Il est huit heures, répond sa femme.

—Il faut se dépêcher, dit Pierre. L'avion va partir dans deux heures.

Madame Paquet est très heureuse parce qu'elle va revoir sa soeur. Janine et Pierre sont heureux aussi parce qu'ils vont voir leurs cousins pour la première fois. Monsieur Paquet est heureux parce qu'il va voir la Louisiane.

Ils montent dans le taxi et dans quelques minutes ils arrivent à l'aéroport. Ils ont acheté leurs billets électroniques en ligne. Ils vont au guichet pour l'enregistrement.

—Votre nom, s'il vous plaît, demande la jeune dame au guichet.

—Paquet. Nous allons aux États-Unis pour quelques semaines, à La Nouvelle-Orléans, en Louisiane.

—Vous êtes sûr que c'est pour aujourd'hui, monsieur? demande la jeune dame.

—Oui, oui. Quelle est la date aujourd'hui? C'est le premier juillet, n'est-ce pas? demande Monsieur Paquet.

—Oui, c'est bien ça, répond-elle. Voilà! Quel âge ont les deux enfants?

—Janine, dis à la dame ton âge, dit la mère.

—J'ai quinze ans, répond Janine.

—Pierre, dis ton âge à la dame.

—J'ai dix ans, répond Pierre.

—Bien, dit la dame. Vos passeports, s'il vous plaît.

Monsieur Paquet donne les passeports à la dame.

—Parfait. C'est parfait, dit la dame au guichet. Voici vos cartes d'embarquement. L'avion va partir dans quelques minutes. Veuillez passer par le contrôle de sécurité. Bon voyage et bon retour!

—Merci, merci, merci, merci, répondent-ils.

Ils passent au contrôle de sécurité où il y a un détecteur de métal et une machine à rayons X. Quand le sac de vol de Monsieur Paquet passe par la machine à rayons X, ils entendent un signal d'alarme assourdissant. Un agent arrive vite.

—Halte! crie-t-il. Il faut chercher dans le sac, dit l'agent.

—Quel embarras! C'est très ennuyeux, dit monsieur Paquet. L'avion va partir sans nous. Il est dix heures moins deux!

—Je regrette, monsieur, mais les règles sont les règles.

L'agent de police cherche dans le sac de Monsieur Paquet.

—Ah! Ha! Un pistolet! Vous êtes arrêté! s'exclame l'agent.

—Mais ce n'est pas une arme! s'exclame Pierre. C'est mon pistolet à eau!

L'agent ferme le sac.

—Vous pouvez passer. Mais nous gardons le pistolet à eau, le coupe-ongles, et les allumettes, dit l'agent.

—Ils nous volent toutes nos affaires, dit Monsieur Paquet à Madame Paquet.

—Notre vol! Vite! crie Madame Paquet. L'avion va partir sans nous!

VOCABULAIRE

l'aéroport *n. m.*, the airport

les allumettes *f.*, matches

l'arme *n. f.*, the weapon

arrêter *v.*, to stop; **l'arrêt** *n. m.*, the stop, the arrest; **vous êtes arrêté** you are under arrest

assourdir *v.*, to deafen; **assourdissant** *adj.*, deafening

avez *v. form of* avoir (to have); **vous avez** you have

l'avion *n. m.*, the airplane

le billet *n.*, the ticket; **le billet électronique** electronic ticket, e-ticket

bon retour! *exclam.*, have a good return (trip)!

bon voyage! *exclam.*, have a good trip!

la carte d'embarquement boarding pass

cela *dem. pron.*, that (ça is short for **cela**); **c'est ça** that's it; **c'est bien ça** that's quite right

le contrôle de sécurité security check (travel)

le coupe-ongles nail clippers

crie *v. form of* crier (to shout, to cry out); **crie-t-il** he shouts

déjà *adv.*, already

dis *v. form of* dire (to tell, to say); **dis à la dame …** tell the lady …

la douane *n.*, customs

en ligne online

ennuyer *v.*, to annoy; **ennuyeux** annoying

l'enregistrement *m.*, check-in

Les États-Unis *n. m.*, the United States; **aux États-Unis** to (in) the United States

fait, font *v. forms of* faire (to do, to make); **faire un voyage** to take a trip

falloir *v.*, to be necessary; **il faut** it is necessary

le guichet *n.*, the ticket window

habiter *v.*, to live, to reside

l'heure *n. f.*, the hour (used in telling time); **quelle heure est-il?** what time is it?

heureux *m.*, **heureuse** *f.*, *adj.*, happy

il est dix heures moins deux it's two minutes to ten

il y a there is, there are

j'ai quinze ans I'm fifteen years old; **j'ai dix ans** I'm ten years old

leurs *poss. adj. pl.*, their

la Louisiane *n.*, Louisiana

la machine à rayons X X-ray machine (travel)

merci thank you

monter *v.*, to climb up or into, to ascend, to get into; **ils montent dans le taxi** they get into the taxi

le nom *n.*, the name

La Nouvelle-Orléans *n.*, New Orleans

l'objet *n. m.*, the object

par *prep.*, by

parfait *adj.*, perfect

passent *v. form of* passer (to pass, to go by); **ils passent à la douane** they go to customs

le pistolet à eau water pistol

quel âge ont les deux enfants? how old are the two children? **quelle est la date aujourd'hui?** what's the date today? **quelle heure est-il?** what time is it?

quelque *adj.*, some, any; **quelque chose** something

le sac de vol carry-on bag

le signal *n.*, the signal; **le signal d'alarme** the alarm

sûr *adj.*, sure, certain; **bien sûr** of course, certainly

ton *poss. adj. m. s.*, your

va, vont *v. forms of* aller (to go); **elle va** she is going; **ils vont** they are going

voir *v.*, to see

le vol the flight

voler to fly; also to steal **Ils nous volent toutes nos affaires!** They're stealing all our things!

le voyage *n.*, the trip

135

EXERCISES

Review the story and vocabulary before starting these exercises.

I. Choose the correct answer based on the story.

1. La famille Paquet va faire un voyage à

   (a) Paris.   (b) Chicago.   (c) La Nouvelle-Orléans.   (d) New York.   _____

2. Madame Paquet est heureuse parce qu'elle va revoir

   (a) son frère.   (b) sa mère.   (c) ses cousins.   (d) sa soeur.   _____

3. Janine et Pierre sont heureux parce qu'ils vont voir

   (a) leur chien.   (b) leurs amis.   (c) leurs cousins.   (d) l'aéroport.   _____

4. Janine a

   (a) douze ans.   (b) treize ans.   (c) quatorze ans.   (d) quinze ans.   _____

5. Pierre a

   (a) treize ans.   (b) douze ans.   (c) onze ans.   (d) dix ans.   _____

II. Expressing Personal Feelings. Proficiency in Speaking and Writing.

Situation: You have just arrived at the **Aéroport Charles de Gaulle.** A representative of the airline is talking to you. Say four words in French to describe your flight; then write them on the lines.

1. _____   2. _____   3. _____   4. _____

III. Scrambled sentences. Unscramble each sentence so that it is meaningful. Write them in the proper word order. Look for them in the story.

1. Quinze ans j'ai.

_____

2. Heure est quelle il?

_____

3. Aujourd'hui date la est quelle?

_____

IV. Answer the following questions in complete sentences. They are personal questions and require answers of your own.

1. Aimez-vous faire des voyages?

_____

2. Aimez-vous les avions ou les trains?

_____

3. Aimez-vous regarder un avion dans le ciel?

_____

STRUCTURES DE LA LANGUE

A. Telling Time

TIME EXPRESSIONS

Quelle heure est-il?	What time is it?
Il est une heure.	It is one o'clock.
Il est une heure dix.	It is ten minutes after one.
Il est une heure et quart.	It is a quarter after one.
Il est deux heures et demie.	It is half past two; it is two-thirty.
Il est trois heures moins vingt.	It is twenty minutes to three.
Il est trois heures moins le quart.	It is a quarter to three.
Il est midi.	It is noon.
Il est minuit.	It is midnight.
à quelle heure?	at what time?
à une heure	at one o'clock
à une heure précise	at exactly one o'clock
à trois heures précises	at exactly three o'clock
à neuf heures du matin	at nine in the morning
à trois heures de l'après-midi	at three in the afternoon
à dix heures du soir	at ten in the evening
à l'heure	on time
à temps	in time
vers trois heures	around three o'clock
un quart d'heure	a quarter of an hour
une demi-heure	a half hour
Il est midi et demi.	It is twelve-thirty.

Il est une heure.

Il est une heure dix.

Il est une heure et quart.

Il est deux heures et demie.   Il est trois heures moins vingt.   Il est trois heures moins le quart.

RULES AND OBSERVATIONS:

1. In telling time, **Il est** is used plus the hour, whether it is one or more than one (e.g., **Il est une heure**, **Il est deux heures**).

2. If the time is *after* the hour, state the hour, then the minutes (e.g., **Il est une heure dix**).

3. The conjunction **et** is used with **quart** after the hour and with **demi** or **demie** (e.g., **Il est une heure et quart**, **Il est une heure et demie**, **Il est midi et demi**).

4. The masculine form **demi** is used after a masculine noun (e.g., **Il est midi et demi**). The feminine form **demie** is used after a feminine noun (e.g., **Il est deux heures et demie**).

5. **Demi** remains **demi** when *before* a feminine or masculine noun, and it is joined to the noun with a hyphen (e.g., **une demi-heure**).

6. If the time expressed is *before* the hour, **moins** is used (e.g., **Il est trois heures moins vingt**).

7. A quarter *after* the hour is **et quart**; a quarter *to* the hour is **moins le quart**.

8. To express A.M. use **du matin**; to express P.M. use **de l'après-midi** if it is the afternoon or **du soir** if it is the evening.

B. Asking the date, giving the date

Quelle est la date aujourd'hui?	
Quel jour du mois est-ce aujourd'hui?	What's the date today?
Quel jour du mois sommes-nous aujourd'hui?	
C'est aujourd'hui le premier mai.	Today is May first.
C'est aujourd'hui le deux mai.	Today is May second.

RULE:

In giving the date, use the cardinal numbers except for the first of the month, which is always **le premier**.

C. Asking your age, giving your age

Quel âge avez-vous?	How old are you?
J'ai quinze ans.	I am fifteen (years old).

RULES:

1. In giving your age, use the cardinal numbers.

2. The verb **avoir** is used in French; the verb *to be* is used in English.

D. Months of the year

Les mois de l'année sont **janvier**, **février**, **mars**, **avril**, **mai**, **juin**, **juillet**, **août**, **septembre**, **octobre**, **novembre**, **décembre**.

The months of the year are January, February, March, April, May, June, July, August, September, October, November, December.

RULES:

1. The months are not ordinarily capitalized.

2. They are all masculine in gender.

E. Days of the week

Les jours de la semaine sont **dimanche**, **lundi**, **mardi**, **mercredi**, **jeudi**, **vendredi**, **samedi**.

The days of the week are Sunday, Monday, Tuesday, Wednesday, Thursday, Friday, Saturday.

Le samedi nous faisons des achats.   (On Saturdays we go shopping.)

Quel jour est-ce aujourd'hui?	**C'est aujourd'hui lundi.**
(What day is it today?)	(Today is Monday.)

RULES:

1. The days are not capitalized.

2. They are also all masculine in gender.

F. Seasons of the year

Les saisons de l'année sont **le printemps**, **l'été**, **l'automne**, **l'hiver**.

The seasons of the year are spring, summer, fall, winter.

RULES:

1. The seasons are not capitalized.

2. They are masculine in gender.

139

EXERCISES

Review the preceding material before starting these exercises.

I.   Match the following.

1. Quelle heure est-il?

2. Est-il deux heures?

3. Il est neuf heures.

4. Il est midi.

5. Il est minuit.

6. Il est une heure.

_____ It is 9 o'clock.

_____ It is noon.

_____ Is it 2 o'clock?

_____ What time is it?

_____ It is midnight.

_____ It is 1 o'clock.

II.   Quelle heure est-il? Write the answer in a complete sentence (in French) on the line provided under each clock.

Model:

You write: **Il est dix heures moins deux.**
              (It is two minutes to ten.)

1.

3.

_____

2.

4.

_____

140

III. **Quelle est la date aujourd'hui?** Write the answer in a complete sentence on the line provided under each calendar.

Model:

SEPTEMBRE
D	L	M	M	J	V	S
	1	2	3	4	5	6
7	8	9	10	11	12	13
14	15	⑯	17	18	19	20
21	22	23	24	25	26	27
28	29	30				

You write: **C'est aujourd'hui le seize septembre.**
(Today is September 16.)

1.

OCTOBRE
D	L	M	M	J	V	S
			①	2	3	4
5	6	7	8	9	10	11
12	13	14	15	16	17	18
19	20	21	22	23	24	25
26	27	28	29	30	31	

_____

2.

NOVEMBRE
D	L	M	M	J	V	S
						1
2	3	4	5	6	7	8
9	⑩	11	12	13	14	15
16	17	18	19	20	21	22
23/30	24	25	26	27	28	29

_____

IV. **À quelle heure?** (At what time?) Answer the following questions in complete sentences (in French) using the time given in parentheses. Be sure to use one of the following with each time stated: **du matin, de l'après-midi, du soir.**

Model: **À quelle heure étudiez-vous?** (8 P.M.)
(At what time do you study?)

You write: **J'étudie à huit heures du soir.**
(I study at 8 o'clock in the evening.)

1. À quelle heure vous levez-vous? (6:30 A.M.)

_____

2. À quelle heure allez-vous à l'école? (8 A.M.)

_____

3. À quelle heure regardez-vous la télévision? (4 P.M.)

_____

4. À quelle heure dînez-vous? (6 P.M.)

_____

5. À quelle heure vous couchez-vous? (10:30 P.M.)

_____

141

V. Persuasion. Proficiency in Speaking and Writing.

Situation: You are at home. Your mother and father want to watch a soap opera on television. You and your brother (or sister) were planning on watching a program of French art. Both shows are at the same time.

In three sentences try to persuade your parents to let you watch the program on French art. You may use your own ideas and words and/or the following: **Nous désirons regarder l'art français à la télé**/*We want to watch French art on TV.* **Nous aimons l'art français**/*We like French art.* **Si nous avons la permission de regarder notre émission, nous promettons de laver la voiture et nettoyer la salle de bains**/*If we have permission to watch our show, we promise to wash the car and clean the bathroom.* **Nous promettons, aussi, de nettoyer nos chambres**/*We promise, also, to clean our rooms.*

First, say your sentences aloud; then write them on the lines.

1. _____

2. _____

3. _____

VI. Answer the following questions in complete sentences. You will write two sentences. In your first sentence (a) answer the question in the negative. In your second sentence (b) give the day that precedes the day asked in the question.

Model: **Est-ce dimanche aujourd'hui?**
(Is today Sunday?)

You write: (a) **Non, ce n'est pas dimanche.**
(No, it's not Sunday.)

(b) **C'est aujourd'hui samedi.**
(Today is Saturday.)

1. Est-ce lundi aujourd'hui?

    (a) _____   (b) _____

2. Est-ce mardi aujourd'hui?

    (a) _____   (b) _____

3. Est-ce mercredi aujourd'hui?

    (a) _____   (b) _____

4. Est-ce vendredi aujourd'hui?

    (a) _____   (b) _____

5. Est-ce jeudi aujourd'hui?

    (a) _____   (b) _____

VII. Write in French the questions that would have been asked.

Model: **Elle a vingt-huit ans.**   You write: **Quel âge a-t-elle?**
(She is twenty-eight years old.)   (How old is she?)

1. Il a cinquante ans.

_____

2. Il est trois heures.

_____

3. Elle a trente ans.

_____

4. C'est aujourd'hui le premier mai.

_____

5. Il est minuit.

_____

VIII. **Planning a Trip to France. Proficiency in Speaking and Writing.**

Situation: You and your family are planning a trip to France. Select one of your friends to talk with you. Let's say his name is Luc. You may use your own ideas and words, those under the lines, or those that Luc uses. After the conversation is completed, write what you said on the lines. Later, you may switch roles with your friend for more practice in speaking and writing.

Vous: _____

Greet your friend and ask him how he is/**Salut, Luc! Comment vas-tu?**

Luc: **Pas mal. Et toi?**/*Not bad. And you?* **Quoi de neuf?**/*What's new?*

Vous: _____

Very well, thank you. I am going to take a trip to France with my family/**Très bien, merci. Je vais faire un voyage en France avec ma famille.**

Luc: **C'est formidable!**/*That's great!* **Quand allez-vous partir?**

Vous: _____

Tell him the day and date.

Luc: **En avion ou en bateau?**/*By plane or boat?*

Vous: _____

By plane.

Luc: **À quelle heure allez-vous partir?**

Vous: _____

Tell him at what time you are going to leave.

Luc: **Quelles villes allez-vous visiter en France?**

Vous: _____

Tell him what cities you are going to visit in France.

Luc: **C'est formidable! Quels endroits intéressants** _(what interesting places)_ **allez-vous visiter à Paris?**

Vous: _____

The Louvre Museum/**Le Musée du Louvre,** the Eiffel Tower/**La Tour Eiffel,** and **L'Arc de Triomphe.**

Luc: **Tu as de la chance!**/_You're lucky!_ **Bon voyage!**

Le Train à Grande Vitesse (TGV)/high-speed train.

IX. L'aéroport. Proficiency in Writing.

Situation: You have just arrived at Charles de Gaulle Airport and you have taken the following picture with your cell phone. You want to send the photo to your best friend. What do you say to him or her? Some words that you may want to use: **arriver** / to arrive; **venir** / to come; **énorme** / enormous; **le plafond** / ceiling; **la porte** / (airport) gate; **le terminal** or **l'aérogare** / terminal.

_____

_____

_____

Terminal at Charles de Gaulle Airport. The Corbis Collection

X. La Corse. Proficiency in Writing.

Situation: You are visiting the island of Corsica in the Mediterranean Sea (la mer Méditerranée). You are writing an instant message to a friend to describe the view in the harbor. Here are a few words that you may want to use: **les bateaux**/boats; **le port**/harbor; **les palmiers**/palm trees; **pittoresque**/scenic; **il fait beau**/the weather is good; **il fait du soleil**/it is sunny; **je m'amuse bien**/I'm having a lot of fun.

La Corse (Corsica, France), Ajacco, boats near harbour.
Reprinted with permision of Iconotec.

LA CARTE DE FRANCE

Tout d'un coup, Coco arrive en courant dans la grande salle. Sur la tête, il a le chapeau haut de forme, dans la gueule le bâton et la cape, et sur le dos le lapin!
(All of a sudden, Coco arrives running into the auditorium. On his head he has the black silk top hat, in his mouth the wand, and on his back the rabbit.)

Work Unit 10
Formation and Use of the Imperative (Command)

*Who do you suppose wins the big
talent show prize?*

Le concours de talents à l'école

C'est aujourd'hui vendredi. C'est le grand jour du concours de talents dans la grande salle de l'école. Il y a des étudiants qui vont chanter, danser, faire des tours de force et des tours de main, jouer d'un instrument de musique, et raconter des contes drôles. Janine et Pierre sont dans le concours de talents aussi. Pierre est le magicien et Janine l'assistante. Ils préparent leur représentation.

—Donne-moi mon chapeau haut de forme, dit Pierre à Janine.

—Je n'ai pas ton chapeau haut de forme, répond Janine.

—Apporte-moi mon bâton, dit Pierre à Janine.

—Je n'ai pas ton bâton, répond Janine.

—Donne-moi ma cape, dit Pierre.

—Je n'ai pas ta cape, répond Janine.

—Apporte-moi le lapin, dit Pierre.

—Je n'ai pas le lapin, répond Janine.

A ce moment-là, quelques spectateurs dans la grande salle s'écrient:

—Dansez! Chantez! Faites quelque chose!

Ce sont les étudiants et les professeurs.

—Zut, alors! Ne finissons pas, Janine. Nous n'avons ni chapeau haut de forme, ni bâton, ni cape, ni lapin.

—Ne choisis pas cette alternative, dit Janine à Pierre.

—Alors, restons-nous ou partons-nous? demande Pierre. Il faut faire quelque chose!

—Allez-vous faire quelque chose, enfin?! demandent tous les spectateurs.

—Ne réponds pas, Janine, dit Pierre.

Tout d'un coup, Coco arrive en courant dans la grande salle. Sur la tête il a le chapeau haut de forme, dans la gueule le bâton et la cape, et sur le dos le lapin!

—Viens ici, Coco! s'exclame Pierre.

—Assieds-toi, Coco! s'exclame Janine.

—C'est merveilleux! dit Pierre. Maintenant, finissons la représentation.

Janine et Pierre finissent leur représentation. Les autres étudiants finissent leurs représentations aussi. Et qui gagne le grand prix? Coco, naturellement! Parce qu'il a beaucoup de talent!

VOCABULAIRE

apporte! bring!; **apporte-moi** bring me

assieds-toi! sit down!

le bâton *n.,* the wand, stick, baton

ce sont … they are …, it's …

le chapeau haut de forme *n.,* the top hat

la chose *n.,* thing; **quelque chose** something

le concours de talents the talent show

le conte *n.,* the story, tale

courant *pres. part. of* **courir; en courant** (while) running

donne-moi give me

le dos *n.,* the back

drôle *adj.,* funny, droll, odd

faites *v. form of* faire (to do, to make); **faites quelque chose!** do something!

finissons! let's finish!; **ne finissons pas!** let's not finish!

gagne *v.,* to win

la grande salle *n.,* the auditorium

la gueule *n.,* the mouth of an animal

le lapin *n.,* the rabbit

le magicien, la magicienne *n.,* the magician

le maître, la maîtresse *n.,* the teacher

naturellement *adv.,* naturally

partons-nous? are we leaving?

le prix *n.,* the price, the prize; **le grand prix** the grand prize

raconter *v.,* to tell, to relate

la représentation *n.,* the presentation, performance, show

restons-nous? are we staying?

le spectateur, la spectatrice *n.,* the spectator

la tête *n.,* the head

tour de force feat of strength; **tour de main** sleight of hand, hand trick

tous *adj. m. pl.,* all

tout d'un coup all of a sudden

viens ici! come here!

zut, alors! darn it!

Note that **ne** + verb + **ni** + noun + **ni** + noun = neither … nor

EXERCISES

Review the story and vocabulary before starting these exercises.

I.   Answer the following questions in complete sentences. They are based on the story.

1. Quel jour est-ce aujourd'hui?

_____

2. Dans le concours de talents, qui va jouer le rôle de magicien?

_____

3. Qui est l'assistante de Pierre?

_____

4. Est-ce que Pierre et Janine ont le chapeau haut de forme, le bâton, la cape, et le lapin?

_____

5. Qui arrive dans la grande salle avec le chapeau, le bâton, la cape, et le lapin?

_____

6. Qui gagne le grand prix?

_____

II. **Answer the following questions in complete sentences. They are personal questions that require answers of your own.**

1. Avez-vous du talent? Dansez-vous? Chantez-vous?

    _____

2. Est-ce que vous jouez d'un instrument de musique?

    _____

3. Aimez-vous le français?

    _____

4. Quel jour de la semaine allez-vous au cinéma?

    _____

III. **Comment dit-on en français ...?**

Find these statements in the story and write them in French.

1. Today is Friday.

    _____

2. It's the big day of the talent show.

    _____

3. Bring me my wand; bring me the rabbit.

    _____

IV. **Picture Interpretation. Proficiency in Speaking.**

Situation: It is your turn in French class to look at a picture and say a few words about it.

Look at the picture at the beginning of this work unit. In a brief oral report, about two minutes, tell your classmates what is going on in the scene. You may begin with: **Aujourd'hui c'est le grand jour du concours de talents dans la grande salle de l'école. Janine et Pierre sont ...**

STRUCTURES DE LA LANGUE

A. Formation and use of the imperative (command) in the three regular conjugations (**-er, -ir, -re**)

AFFIRMATIVE

	2nd person singular (**tu**)	2nd person plural (**vous**)	1st person plural (**nous**)
DANSER	**danse!**	**dansez!**	**dansons!**
to dance	*dance!*	*dance!*	*let's dance!*
FINIR	**finis!**	**finissez!**	**finissons!**
to finish	*finish!*	*finish!*	*let's finish!*
VENDRE	**vends!**	**vendez!**	**vendons!**
to sell	*sell!*	*sell!*	*let's sell!*

NEGATIVE

DANSER	ne danse pas!	ne dansez pas!	ne dansons pas!
	don't dance!	*don't dance!*	*let's not dance!*
FINIR	ne finis pas!	ne finissez pas!	ne finissons pas!
	don't finish!	*don't finish!*	*let's not finish!*
VENDRE	ne vends pas!	ne vendez pas!	ne vendons pas!
	don't sell!	*don't sell!*	*let's not sell!*

RULES AND OBSERVATIONS:

1. In the two boxes above, the second person singular and the second person plural are right next to each other so that you can compare the forms. The first person plural stands alone at the right.

2. To form the *imperative* in the affirmative, use the same verb form as in the present indicative, which you have already learned. Drop the subject pronoun **tu**, **vous**, or **nous**.

3. There is one exception. You must drop the final **s** in the second person singular of an **-er** verb. This is done in the affirmative and negative, as shown on the previous page, as in **danse!** For more about this, see Work Unit 11.

4. To form the negative of the imperative, place **ne** in front of the verb and **pas** after it, as you learned to do when forming the negative of the present indicative.

EXERCISES

Review the preceding material before starting these exercises.

I.   Write the three forms of the imperative in the affirmative.

      Model: **danser**   You write: **danse**   **dansez**   **dansons**

                                         (2nd pers., sing.)   (2nd pers., pl.)   (1st pers., pl.)

A. -ER verbs

    1. donner   _____ _____ _____

    2. apporter   _____ _____ _____

    3. chercher   _____ _____ _____

    4. aider   _____ _____ _____

    5. chanter   _____ _____ _____

B. -IR verbs

    1. finir   _____ _____ _____

    2. choisir   _____ _____ _____

    3. bâtir   _____ _____ _____

    4. punir   _____ _____ _____

    5. obéir   _____ _____ _____

C.   -RE verbs

1. vendre   _____   _____   _____

2. attendre   _____   _____   _____

3. descendre   _____   _____   _____

4. répondre   _____   _____   _____

5. rendre   _____   _____   _____

II.   Change the following imperative sentences to the negative.

Model: **Danse, mon enfant!**   You write: **Ne danse pas, mon enfant!**
(Dance, my child!)   (Don't dance, my child!)

1. Chante, Janine!

_____

2. Finissons le travail maintenant!

_____

3. Vendez la maison, Monsieur Paquet!

_____

4. Écoute la musique, Pierre!

_____

5. Attendez l'autobus!

_____

III.   Friendly Persuasion. Proficiency in Speaking.

Look at this picture. Imagine a conversation between the mother and the child according to one of the situations described. Use verbs in the imperative in the **tu** form.

Situation: The mother tells her daughter to eat her spinach **(Mange tes épinards)** but the girl refuses **(Je refuse).** Or the mother tells the girl to finish her homework **(Finis tes devoirs),** and the girl says she doesn't want to **(Je ne veux pas).** These are two suggestions to get you started, or you may use your own ideas. Choose a classmate to do the dialogue with you. Later, write the conversation for intensive practice.

B. Formation and use of reflexive verbs in the imperative

AFFIRMATIVE

	2nd person singular (tu)	2nd person plural (vous)	1st person plural (nous)
S'ASSEOIR	**assieds-toi!**	**asseyez-vous!**	**asseyons-nous!**
to sit down	*sit down!*	*sit down!*	*let's sit down!*
SE LEVER	**lève-toi!**	**levez-vous!**	**levons-nous!**
to get up	*get up!*	*get up!*	*let's get up!*
SE LAVER	**lave-toi!**	**lavez-vous!**	**lavons-nous!**
to wash oneself	*wash yourself!*	*wash yourself! or wash yourselves!*	*let's wash ourselves!*

NEGATIVE

	2nd person singular (tu)	2nd person plural (vous)	1st person plural (nous)
S'ASSEOIR	**ne** t'assieds **pas!**	**ne** vous asseyez **pas!**	**ne** nous asseyons **pas!**
	don't sit down!	*don't sit down!*	*let's not sit down!*
SE LEVER	**ne** te lève **pas!**	**ne** vous levez **pas!**	**ne** nous levons **pas!**
	don't get up!	*don't get up!*	*let's not get up!*
SE LAVER	**ne** te lave **pas!**	**ne** vous lavez **pas!**	**ne** nous lavons **pas!**
	don't wash yourself!	*don't wash yourself! or don't wash yourselves!*	*let's not wash ourselves!*

RULES AND OBSERVATIONS:

1. To form the negative of a reflexive verb in the affirmative, use the same verb as in the present indicative, unless the form is irregular in the imperative.

2. Drop the subject pronouns **tu**, **vous**, and **nous**.

3. You must drop the **s** in the second person singular of an **-er** verb. This is done in the affirmative and negative, as shown. See **se lever** and **se laver** in the second person singular.

4. Keep the reflexive pronouns **te**, **vous**, and **nous**. They serve as direct object pronouns. **Vous** and **nous** are reflexive pronouns as well as subject pronouns.

5. The reflexive pronoun is placed *after* the verb in the affirmative of the imperative. The verb and pronoun are joined with a hyphen. **Te** becomes **toi** when it is placed *after* the verb with a hyphen. This happens only in the affirmative.

6. To form the imperative of a reflexive verb in the negative, keep the reflexive pronoun *in front of* the verb form. **Te** becomes **t'** in the negative imperative when the verb right after it starts with a vowel or a silent *h*, as in **ne t'assieds pas**.

7. To form the negative imperative, place **ne** before the reflexive pronoun and **pas** after the verb.

EXERCISES

Review the preceding material before starting these exercises.

I. Choose the correct verb form and write it on the line.

1. Wash yourself! (lavez-vous, lavons-nous, vous vous lavez)

_____

2. Sit down! (asseyons-nous, assieds-toi, vous vous asseyez)

_____

3. Get up! (levons-nous, nous nous levons, levez-vous)

_____

4. Sit down! (asseyez-vous, asseyons-nous, levez-vous)

_____

5. Let's wash ourselves! (lavez-vous, vous vous lavez, lavons-nous)

_____

6. Get up! (lève-toi, levons-nous, lave-toi)

_____

7. Don't wash yourself! (ne te lave pas, ne te lève pas, lave-toi)

_____

8. Let's not get up! (ne nous levons pas, ne vous levez pas, levez-vous)

_____

9. Don't sit down! (ne nous asseyons pas, ne vous levez pas, ne vous asseyez pas)

_____

10. Wash yourself! (lave-toi, lève-toi, lavons-nous)

_____

II. Change the following affirmative imperatives to the negative imperative.

Model: **Levez-vous!**   You write: **Ne vous levez pas!**
       (Get up!)   (Don't get up!)

1. Lavons-nous! _____
2. Asseyez-vous! _____
3. Lave-toi! _____
4. Assieds-toi! _____
5. Lavez-vous! _____
6. Lève-toi! _____

III. Telling Someone What to Do. Proficiency in Speaking and Writing.

Situations A and B.

A. You are a surgeon talking to a nurse in an operating room. Write a list of three verbs in the imperative using the **vous** form telling the nurse to give you something, bring you this, look for that, and any other verbs in this lesson that would make sense in this situation; for example, to get you started, you can say **donnez-moi** (give me). Don't forget to add **s'il vous plaît!**

1. _____ 2. _____ 3. _____

B. Review the scene at the beginning of this work unit, **Le concours de talents à l'école.** Write a list of three verbs in the imperative using the **tu** form that you can find in that scene.

1. _____ 2. _____ 3. _____

IV. Fill in the missing letters to form the imperative.

Model: Dance!   **Answer: DANSE _Z_ !**

1. Listen!   ÉCOUTE ___ !
2. Give!   DONN ___ ___ !
3. Sing!   CHANTE ___ !
4. Finish!   FIN ___ ___ ___ EZ !
5. Choose!   CHOISISS ___ ___ !
6. Let's not sell! NE VEND ___ ___ ___ PAS!
7. Don't wait   N'ATTEN ___ ___ ___ PAS!
8. Answer!   RÉ ___ ___ N ___ ___ Z!
9. Wait!   ATT ___ ___ D ___ ___ !
10. Sit down!   A ___ ___ EY ___ ___ -VOUS!
11. Get up!   LEV ___ ___ -VOUS!
12. Wash yourself! L ___ VE ___ -VOUS!

V. Storytelling. Proficiency in Speaking and Writing.

Situation: Judy, one of your classmates, was absent when this lesson was covered in class. She wants you to tell her what is going on in the picture at the beginning of this work unit about the talent show in your school. It was summarized in class.

You may use your own words and the vocabulary words on the pages following the picture. When you tell her, make at least five statements. Then practice writing them here:

1. _____

2. _____

3. _____

4. _____

5. _____

VI. Health. Proficiency in Speaking and Writing.

Situation: Pretend that you are a dentist (**le, la dentiste**), telling your patient what to do.

Use the imperative (command) in the polite **vous** form as practiced in this lesson. For example, you may want to say: **Asseyez-vous**/*Sit down*; **ouvrez la bouche**/*open your mouth*; **fermez les yeux**/*close your eyes*; **fermez la bouche**/*close your mouth*; **ouvrez les yeux**/*open your eyes*; **levez-vous**/*get up*. Don't forget to add **s'il vous plaît** (*please*) after each command!

Say aloud at least six statements in the imperative that you would say to your patient. Then practice writing them here:

1. _____

2. _____

3. _____

4. _____

5. _____

6. _____

VII. Girl Talk. Proficiency in Speaking, Reading, and Writing.

Situation: Look at the picture of the three French girls talking. From left to right, they are Claudette, Yvette, and Odette. The picture is on the next page.

Let's imagine what they are saying. You may use your own ideas and words or those in the following guided conversation. Say and write the words on the blank lines. Use the *tu* form of a verb (2nd pers., sing.) because they are friends.

A note of cultural interest: the young women are wearing the typical Pont-Aven costume of Bretagne, a region of France located in the northwest. Original features of the Breton costume include the headdress/**la coiffe** and the large collar made of starched lace.

Claudette: **Moi? Oh, non, je ne chante pas bien!**

Yvette: _____
But you dance very well.

Odette: **Claudette danse très bien quand elle danse avec son ami Roger. N'est-ce pas, Claudette?**/*Isn't that so, Claudette?*

Claudette: _____
Yes. It's true.

Yvette: _____
Are you going to the big dance in town with Roger tonight?

Claudette: **Oui, je vais au grand bal en ville avec Roger ce soir. Viens avec nous, Yvette/***Come with us, Yvette.*

Yvette: _____
With my friend Pierre?

Claudette: **Bien sûr, avec ton ami Pierre. Et toi, Odette, tu viens avec nous? Avec Gérard?**

Odette: **Gérard et moi nous allons au cinéma ce soir. Nous allons voir le film *Les Parapluies de Cherbourg. / The Umbrellas of Cherbourg.* C'est un vieux film, mais excellent.**

Claudette: _____
*It's a fascinating film!/*C'est un film passionnant!*

*Cherbourg is a French seaport located in the northwest on the English Channel/**La Manche.**

157

VIII. Appreciating French Art. Proficiency in Speaking and Writing.

Situation: You and your classmates are on a field trip to the Philadelphia Museum of Art. You are admiring a painting by Pierre-Auguste Renoir, a great French artist/**un grand artiste français.** It is entitled *Les Grands Boulevards.*

Look at the picture below. Say aloud a few words in French that come to mind while you appreciate looking at the painting. You may use your own words or, for starters, you may use the following:

Ce tableau de Renoir est magnifique/*This painting by Renoir is magnificent.* How about a few more adjectives? For example, **impressionnant/***impressive;* **intéressant/***interesting;* **splendide/***splendid;* **beau/***beautiful.* A few nouns: **les gens/***the people;* **les beaux arbres/***the beautiful trees;* **le grand boulevard/***the big boulevard.* A few verbs: **Je regarde/***I'm looking at;* **je vois/***I see;* **les gens se promènent/***the people are taking a walk;* **j'admire/***I admire.* If you want to use other verbs, check them out in the verb tables beginning on page 510. Now, practice writing what you said on these lines:

_____

_____

_____

Les Grands Boulevards by Pierre-Auguste Renoir (1841–1919).
Reprinted with permission of the Philadelphia Museum of Art / The Corbis Collection.

Test 2

This test is based on Work Units 6 to 10. Review them before starting this test.

PART ONE   SPEAKING PROFICIENCY

Directions: Read the eleven situations given below. Take a few minutes to organize your thoughts about the words you are going to speak. Select seven of them.

1. **Situation:** You are helping a friend use French verbs. Say three French verbs that you would use while shopping in a department store. They must be of the **-re** type. Also say three French verbs that you would use when talking on a telephone. They must also be of the **-re** type.

2. **Situation:** You are in an antique shop in Paris. You like a vase and you want to buy it. Make four statements that you would use while talking with the saleswoman.

3. **Situation:** You are in a museum of French impressionist art admiring the painting **Le Bateau-Atelier**/*The Studio Boat* by the French artist Claude Monet. Make at least three statements about the painting. It is in Work Unit 6.

4. **Situation:** You are on an educational tour in Paris with a group of students from your school. Your guide is Madame Durand. She is impressed with your ability to speak French. She wants to know how long you have been studying French, in what city and country you live, and if you like the French language, the people, culture, music, and art of France. Answer her.

5. **Situation:** You are a tourist shopping at the **marché aux puces.** Make at least three statements about a used pillow you want to buy because you don't like the one in your hotel room.

6. **Situation:** Say aloud four reflexive verbs that you would use when talking about yourself and what you do in the mornings and evenings.

7. **Situation:** State three foods that a person avoids eating when trying to lose weight.

8. **Situation:** You spent a wonderful afternoon at an indoor swimming pool. A picture of it is in Work Unit 7. Make at least four statements.

9. **Situation:** Your neighbors have a child who is about six years old. The parents have asked you to teach their child how to count in French from one to fifty. You agree to do this in exchange for a pleasant surprise.

10. **Situation:** You have just arrived at the Aéroport Charles de Gaulle. A representative of the airline is talking to you. Say four adjectives to describe your flight.

11. **Situation:** You are at the Philadelphia Museum of Art admiring the painting *Les Grands Boulevards* by the French artist Renoir. Make at least three statements about the painting. It is in Work Unit 10.

PART TWO   LISTENING PROFICIENCY

Directions: Your teacher will read aloud four short paragraphs. Each one will contain only a few sentences. You will hear each paragraph twice. Then you will hear one question based on each. You will hear the question only once. It is printed below. Choose the best suggested answer and check the letter of your choice.

Selection Number 1

1. Pourquoi Pierre désire-t-il être toujours en bonne forme?
   A. parce qu'il aime manger
   B. parce qu'il est gardien de but
   C. parce qu'il est à l'école
   D. parce que son sport favori est le tennis

Selection Number 2

2. Où va Pierre après la dernière classe?

   A. à la piscine
   B. à l'école
   C. au gymnase
   D. à la maison

Selection Number 3

3. Qu'est-ce que Madame Paquet désire acheter?
   A. une maison
   B. une vente aux enchères
   C. un foyer
   D. une petite table ronde

Selection Number 4

4. Combien d'enfants a la soeur de Madame Paquet?
   A. cinq
   B. quatre
   C. trois
   D. deux

PART THREE   READING PROFICIENCY

Directions: In the following passage there are five blank spaces numbered 1 through 5. Each blank space represents a missing word. For each blank space, four possible completions are provided. Only one of them makes sense in the context of the passage.

First, read the passage in its entirety to determine its general meaning. Then read it a second time. For each blank space choose the completion that makes the best sense and is grammatically correct. Then write its letter in the space provided.

Madame Paquet est très _____ parce qu'elle va revoir sa soeur.
1. A. heureux
   B. heureuse
   C. heureuses
   D. content

Janine et Pierre sont heureux aussi parce qu'ils vont _____ leurs cousins
2. A. vois
   B. voit
   C. voir
   D. voient

pour la première fois. Monsieur Paquet est heureux parce qu'il _____ voir
3. A. vais
   B. vas
   C. va
   D. vont

La Louisiane. Ils _____ dans le taxi et dans quelques minutes ils

    4. A. monte
        B. montons
        C. montez
        D. montent

arrivent à l'aéroport. Ils cherchent les billets, _____ sont déjà payés.

    5. A. qui
        B. que
        C. quel
        D. quels

PART FOUR   WRITING PROFICIENCY

Directions: Of the eleven situations in Part One (Speaking Proficiency) in this test, select seven and write what you said on the lines below.

Situation No. __ _____

_____

_____

Situation No. __ _____

_____

_____

Situation No. __ _____

_____

_____

Situation No. __ _____

_____

_____

Situation No. __ _____

_____

_____

Situation No. __ _____

_____

_____

Situation No. __ _____

_____

_____

Qu'est-ce que c'est?

Qu'est-ce que c'est?

Qu'est-ce que c'est?

Qu'est-ce que c'est?

Qu'est-ce que c'est?

163

Work Unit 11
Irregular Verbs in the Present Indicative and Imperative

Have you ever played guessing games in English? In French? Here are some in French.

Qu'est-ce que c'est?

A brief description is given of something and then you are asked, "Qu'est-ce que c'est?" (What is it?) See how many you can do. The answers are upside down following the descriptions.

1. C'est quelque chose à boire. Il peut avoir le goût d'orange, ananas, pamplemousse, raisin, ou tomate. Il peut être en boîte ou en bouteille. C'est toujours délicieux. Qu'est-ce que c'est?

2. C'est un meuble. Vous vous asseyez sur ce meuble. Qu'est-ce que c'est?

3. C'est quelque chose à manger. Elle est toujours froide et crémeuse. Elle peut être au chocolat, à la vanille, aux fraises. Elle est toujours délicieuse. Qu'est-ce que c'est?

4. C'est un fruit. Il a la couleur rouge ou jaune ou verte. Qu'est-ce c'est?

5. C'est une machine qui a un moteur et quatre roues. Elle peut aller vite ou lentement. Elle est dangereuse si le conducteur ne fait pas attention. Elle ne peut pas marcher sans essence. Qu'est-ce que c'est?

6. C'est un appareil. Une personne peut parler dans cet appareil et peut entendre une autre personne parler. Quand une personne veut parler, cet appareil sonne. Qu'est-ce que c'est?

7. C'est un animal qui a des plumes et des ailes. Il vole comme un avion. Qu'est-ce que c'est?

8. C'est un appareil que vous utilisez pour travailler et pour surfer. Il a une souris. Qu'est-ce que c'est?

9. C'est un appareil. Il sonne tous les matins quand vous dormez, et vous vous levez. Qu'est-ce que c'est?

10. C'est une partie du corps humain. Elle a cinq doigts. Qu'est-ce que c'est?

11. C'est un objet d'habillement. C'est pour la tête. Qu'est-ce que c'est?

	11. un chapeau	10. une main	9. un réveille-matin
8. un ordinateur	7. un oiseau	6. un téléphone	5. une automobile ou une voiture
4. une pomme	3. une glace	2. une chaise	1. un jus de fruit

VOCABULAIRE

l'aile *n. f.,* the wing

l'ananas *n. m.,* the pineapple

l'appareil *n. m.,* the apparatus, the instrument

boire *v.,* to drink

la boîte *n.,* the box, tin can

la bouteille *n.,* the bottle

le conducteur, la conductrice *n.,* the driver

le corps *n.,* body; **le corps humain** the human body

crémeux *m.,* **crémeuse** *f., adj.,* creamy

dangereux *m.,* **dangereuse** *f., adj.,* dangerous

délicieux *m.,* **délicieuse** *f., adj.,* delicious

le doigt *n.,* the finger

entendre *v.,* to hear

l'essence *n. f.,* gasoline

faire attention *v.,* to pay attention, to be careful

la fraise *n.,* the strawberry

froid *m.,* **froide** *f., adj.,* cold
le goût *n.,* the taste, flavor
l'habillement *n. m.,* clothing
jaune *adj.,* yellow
le jus *n.,* juice; **jus d'orange** orange juice
le meuble *n.,* piece of furniture
le moteur *n.,* motor, engine
le pamplemousse *n.,* the grapefruit
la partie *n.,* the part (of a whole)

la personne *n.,* the individual, person
peut *v. form of* **pouvoir** (can, be able to); **elle peut aller** it can go; **il peut avoir** it can have; **il peut être** it can be
qu'est-ce que c'est? what is it?
le raisin *n.,* the grape
la roue *n.,* the wheel
rouge *adj.,* red
sans *prep.,* without
sonner *v.,* to ring

la souris *n.,* the mouse
surfer *v.,* to surf (the Internet); you can also use **naviguer** to navigate, to surf (the Internet)
la tomate *n.,* the tomato
la vanille *n.,* vanilla
veut *v. form of* **vouloir** (to want); **une personne veut** a person wants
la voiture *n.,* the car, automobile
voler *v.,* to fly

EXERCISES

Review the preceding material before starting these exercises.

I. Choose the correct answer based on the guessing game at the beginning of this unit.

1. Un jus de fruit est quelque chose à

   (a) manger.   (b) boire.   (c) conduire.   (d) pouvoir. _____

2. La glace est toujours

   (a) charmante.   (b) froide.   (c) ennuyeuse.   (d) ronde. _____

3. Une voiture peut être dangereuse si le conducteur ou la conductrice ne fait pas

   (a) sa leçon.   (b) ses devoirs.   (c) son stylo.   (d) attention. _____

II. Answer the following questions in complete sentences. They are personal questions and require answers of your own.

   Model: **Mon fruit favori est l'orange.**   (My favorite fruit is the orange.)

1. Quel est votre fruit favori?

   _____

2. Quel est votre dessert favori?

   _____

3. Quel est votre sport favori?

   _____

III. **Un acrostiche.** Complete the French words in this puzzle.

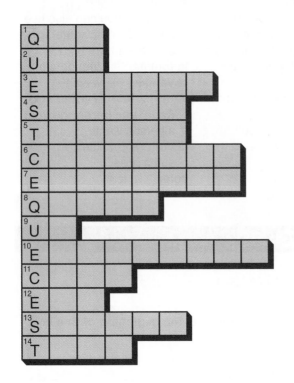

1. who
2. indefinite article (*f., sing.*)
3. gasoline
4. to ring
5. tomato
6. creamy (*f.*)
7. annoying (*m.*)
8. when
9. indefinite article (*m., sing.*)
10. United States
11. key
12. water
13. mouse
14. head

IV. Guessing Games. Proficiency in Speaking.

Situation: Your French teacher asks you to face all the students in the classroom and describe a few objects in French. Describe the object and then ask what it is: **Qu'est-ce que c'est?** Describe at least four. You may use your own ideas or those suggested in this lesson.

V. More Guessing Games. Proficiency in Speaking.

Situations:

A. Look at the five things in the picture at the beginning of this work unit. In French, ask a friend what each thing is. If you don't get an answer, give a response.

B. Select three items in your French classroom and ask a student who sits near you to answer your question. "**Qu'est-ce que c'est?**"

STRUCTURES DE LA LANGUE

A. Irregular verbs in the present indicative tense

1. aller *to go* je vais tu vas il, elle va nous allons vous allez ils, elles vont	**2. apprendre** *to learn* j'apprends tu apprends il, elle apprend nous apprenons vous apprenez ils, elles apprennent	**3. avoir** *to have* j'ai tu as il, elle a nous avons vous avez ils, elles ont
4. boire *to drink* je bois tu bois il, elle boit nous buvons vous buvez ils, elles boivent	**5. comprendre** *to understand* je comprends tu comprends il, elle comprend nous comprenons vous comprenez ils, elles comprennent	**6. courir** *to run* je cours tu cours il, elle court nous courons vous courez ils, elles courent
7. devenir *to become* je deviens tu deviens il, elle devient nous devenons vous devenez ils, elles deviennent	**8. devoir** *have to, must, should* je dois tu dois il, elle doit nous devons vous devez ils, elles doivent	**9. dire** *to say, tell* je dis tu dis il, elle dit nous disons vous dites ils, elles disent
10. écrire *to write* j'écris tu écris il, elle écrit nous écrivons vous écrivez ils, elles écrivent	**11. être** *to be* je suis tu es il, elle est nous sommes vous êtes ils, elles sont	**12. faire** *to do, make* je fais tu fais il, elle fait nous faisons vous faites ils, elles font
13. lire *to read* je lis tu lis il, elle lit nous lisons vous lisez ils, elles lisent	**14. mettre** *to put, place, put on* je mets tu mets il, elle met nous mettons vous mettez ils, elles mettent	**15. ouvrir** *to open* j'ouvre tu ouvres il, elle ouvre nous ouvrons vous ouvrez ils, elles ouvrent

16. **partir** *to leave, depart*	17. **pouvoir** *can, to be able*	18. **prendre** *to take*
je pars tu pars il, elle part nous partons vous partez ils, elles partent	je peux *or* puis tu peux il, elle peut nous pouvons vous pouvez ils, elles peuvent	je prends tu prends il, elle prend nous prenons vous prenez ils, elles prennent
19. **revenir** *to come back*	20. **savoir** *to know (how)*	21. **sortir** *to go out, leave*
je reviens tu reviens il, elle revient nous revenons vous revenez ils, elles reviennent	je sais tu sais il, elle sait nous savons vous savez ils, elles savent	je sors tu sors il, elle sort nous sortons vous sortez ils, elles sortent
22. **venir** *to come*	23. **voir** *to see*	24. **vouloir** *to want*
je viens tu viens il, elle vient nous venons vous venez ils, elles viennent	je vois tu vois il, elle voit nous voyons vous voyez ils, elles voient	je veux tu veux il, elle veut nous voulons vous voulez ils, elles veulent

EXERCISES

I. **Answer the following questions in the affirmative in complete sentences. In answer (a) use oui; in answer (b) use aussi. Study the models.**

Models: (a) **Allez-vous au cinéma?**   You write: (a) **Oui, je vais au cinéma.**
(a) Are you going to the movies?   (a) Yes, I am going to the movies.

(b) **Et Pierre?**   (b) **Il va au cinéma aussi.**
(b) And Pierre?   (b) He is going to the movies also.

1. (a) Lisez-vous beaucoup?

_____

(b) Et Janine?

_____

2. (a) Apprenez-vous le français?

_____

(b) Et Pauline?

_____

3. (a) Avez-vous de la glace?

_____

(b) Et Dominique?

_____

4. (a) Buvez-vous du jus d'orange?

_____

(b) Et Robert?

_____

5. (a) Comprenez-vous la leçon?

_____

(b) Et Joséphine?

_____

II. Answer the following statements in the negative in complete sentences. In answer (a) use **non**. In answer (b) use **non plus**. Study the models.

Models: (a) **Est-ce que Pierre fait attention en classe?**
(a) Does Peter pay attention in class?

(b) **Et vous?**
(b) And you?

You write: (a) **Non, il ne fait pas attention en classe.**
(a) No, he does not pay attention in class.

(b) **Je ne fais pas attention en classe non plus.**
(b) I do not pay attention in class either.

1. (a) Est-ce que Robert lit beaucoup?

_____

(b) Et vous?

_____

2. (a) Est-ce que Monique met le vase sur la table?

_____

(b) Et Jacques?

_____

3. (a) Est-ce que vous ouvrez la porte?

_____

(b) Et Charles?

_____

4. (a) Est-ce que Marie part à huit heures?

_____

(b) Et l'avion?

_____

5. (a) Pouvez-vous aller au cinéma ce soir?

_____

(b) Et Madame et Monsieur Paquet?

_____

III. **Change each sentence by replacing the verb in the sentence with the proper form of the verb in parentheses. Keep the same subject, of course. Rewrite the entire sentence in French.**

Model: **Ouvre-t-il la fenêtre? (fermer)**   You write: **Ferme-t-il la fenêtre?**
(Does he open the window?)   (Does he close the window?)

1. _Ferme_-t-il la porte?   (ouvrir)

_____

2. Est-ce qu'elle _écrit_ la lettre?   (lire)

_____

3. _Buvez_-vous du café?   (prendre)

_____

4. Il ne _comprend_ pas la leçon.   (faire)

_____

5. _Savez_-vous la date?   (écrire)

_____

IV. **Socializing. Proficiency in Speaking and Writing.**

Situation: A new student was transferred to your French class today. Her name is Debbie. Greet her and introduce yourself. Then tell her about the French guessing games you are playing in class.

Try to use some irregular verbs in the present tense on the preceding pages; for example, **aller, apprendre, devoir.** You may use your own ideas and words and/or the following for starters: **Dans la classe de français nous jouons un jeu très intéressant/**_In French class we are playing a very interesting game;_ **je vais donner la description d'une chose et tu dois deviner ce que c'est/**_I am going to give the description of a thing and you must (are supposed to) guess what it is;_ **puis, je demande, "Qu'est-ce que c'est?"/**_then, I ask, "What is it?";_ **tu vas deviner la réponse/**_you are going to guess the answer._

After you make your statements, write them on the following lines for practice.

_____

_____

_____

V. **Choose the correct verb form.**

1. Nous (vois, voyons, voient) la mer.   _____

2. Je (savez, savent, sais) la réponse.   _____

3. Ils (fait, faisons, font) leur travail.   _____

4. Ils (part, partent, partez) maintenant.   _____

5. Tu (bois, buvez, boivent) du lait.   _____

170

VI. Answer the following questions in complete sentences in the affirmative, substituting the subject pronoun **ils** or **elles** for the noun **frères** or **soeurs**. Add **aussi**.

Model: **François apprend bien. Et vos frères?**
(François learns well. And your brothers?)

You write: **Ils apprennent bien aussi.**
(They learn well also.)

1. Pierre comprend bien. Et vos frères?

_____

2. Guillaume écrit bien. Et vos soeurs?

_____

3. Michel va bien. Et vos frères?

_____

4. Guy lit bien. Et vos soeurs?

_____

5. Alfred voit bien. Et vos frères?

_____

B. The imperative of some common irregular verbs

Infinitive	2nd pers. sing. (tu)	2nd pers. pl. (vous)	1st pers. pl. (nous)
aller	va *go!*	allez *go!*	allons *let's go!*
apprendre	apprends *learn!*	apprenez *learn!*	apprenons *let's learn!*
avoir	aie* *have ...!*	ayez* *have ...!*	ayons* *let's have...!*
boire	bois *drink!*	buvez *drink!*	buvons *let's drink!*
dire	dis *say!*	dites *say!*	disons *let's say!*
écrire	écris *write!*	écrivez *write!*	écrivons *let's write!*
être	sois* *be ...!*	soyez* *be ...!*	soyons* *let's be ...!*
faire	fais *do!* (or) *make!*	faites *do!* (or) *make!*	faisons *let's do!* (or) *let's make!*

* These forms are present subjunctive.

171

lire	lis	lisez	lisons
	read!	*read!*	*let's read!*
mettre	mets	mettez	mettons
	put …!	*put …!*	*let's put …!*
ouvrir	ouvre	ouvrez	ouvrons
	open …!	*open …!*	*let's open …!*
partir	pars	partez	partons
	leave!	*leave!*	*let's leave!*
prendre	prends	prenez	prenons
	take!	*take!*	*let's take!*
revenir	reviens	revenez	revenons
	come back!	*come back!*	*let's come back!*
sortir	sors	sortez	sortons
	go out!	*go out!*	*let's go out!*
venir	viens	venez	venons
	come!	*come!*	*let's come!*
voir	vois	voyez	voyons
	see!	*see!*	*let's see!*

RULES AND OBSERVATIONS:

1. In the boxes, the second person singular (**tu**) and the second person plural (**vous**) are right next to each other so you can compare the forms of the second persons. The first person plural (**nous**) stands alone at the right.

2. It was pointed out previously that the final **s** drops in the second person singular on an -**ER** verb in the imperative. However, when the pronouns **y** and **en** are linked to it, the **s** is retained in all regular -**ER** verbs and in the verb **aller**. Examples: **donnes-en** (*give some!*); **manges-en** (*eat some!*); **vas-y** (*go there!*). The reason for this is that it makes it easier to link the two elements by pronouncing the **s** as a **z**.

EXERCISES

Review the preceding material before starting these exercises.

I. Choose the correct verb form in the imperative.

1. Drink! (buvez, partez, faites) _____

2. Come! (pars, viens, vois) _____

3. Say! (dites, faites, voyez) _____

4. Write! (mettez, ayez, écrivez) _____

5. Read! (soyez, sortez, lisez) _____

6. Open! (ouvrons, ouvre, écris) _____

7. Let's go out! (sortez, sortons, voyons) _____

8. Let's be …! (soyez, soyons, ayons) _____

9. Let's drink! (allons, buvons, buvez) _____

10. Come back! (revenez, sortez, venez) _____

Dis la vérité. (Tell the truth.)

II. **Change each sentence by replacing the verb in the sentence with the proper form of the verb in parentheses. Keep the imperative form, of course. Rewrite the entire sentence in French. The verb form you write must be in the same person as the one you are replacing.**

Model: **Dites la vérité.**　　　　You write: **Ecrivez la vérité.**
(Tell the truth. [Write])　　　　　　　　　(Write the truth.)

1. *Ecrivez* la phrase.　(dire)

_____

2. *Prends* le lait.　(boire)

_____

3. *Venez* tout de suite.　(partir)

_____

4. *Ouvre* la fenêtre.　(fermer)

_____

5. *Mets* la valise là-bas.　(prendre)

_____

6. *Lisons* la lettre.　(écrire)

_____

7. *Apprenez* le poème.　(lire)

_____

8. *Partons* maintenant.　(sortir)

_____

9. *Soyez* à l'heure.　(revenir)

_____

10. *Voyons* la leçon.　(faire)

_____

III. **Match the following.**

1. Close the door.　　　　　　　　　_____ Donnes-en au garçon.

2. Take your time.　　　　　　　　　_____ Manges-en si tu veux.

3. Let's open the windows.　　　　　_____ Mettez les valises ici.

4. Eat some if you want.　　　　　　_____ Vas-y.

5. Leave right away.　　　　　　　　_____ Ouvrons les fenêtres.

6. Put the suitcases here.　　　　　_____ Revenez demain.

7. Give some to the boy.　　　　　　_____ Ferme la porte.

8. Go there.　　　　　　　　　　　　_____ Dis la vérité.

9. Come back tomorrow.　　　　　　_____ Pars tout de suite.

10. Tell the truth.　　　　　　　　　_____ Prenez votre temps.

IV. For each sentence write a response in the imperative.

A. Model: **Je veux manger maintenant.**   You write: **Bon! Alors, mangez**
(I want to eat now.)   **maintenant!**
                                            (Good! Then eat now!)

Je veux partir maintenant. (I want to leave now.)

1. Je veux partir maintenant.

_____

2. Je dois ouvrir la fenêtre.

_____

3. Je désire faire la leçon.

_____

4. Je vais écrire une lettre.

_____

5. Je vais lire le journal.

_____

B. Model: **Nous voulons boire de l'eau**   You write: **Bon! Alors, buvez de**
maintenant.   **l'eau maintenant!**
(We want to drink water now.)   (Good! Then drink water now!)

1. Nous désirons sortir maintenant.

_____

2. Nous voulons être ici à dix heures.

_____

3. Nous allons faire le travail ce soir.

_____

4. Nous désirons apprendre l'anglais.

5. Nous voulons parler français.

The following is a summary of **avoir** and **être** in the present indicative affirmative and negative, and in the interrogative and negative interrogative with **est-ce que** and the inverted form.

AVOIR		ÊTRE	
Affirmative		**Affirmative**	
j'ai	nous avons	je suis	nous sommes
tu as	vous avez	tu es	vous êtes
il *or* elle a	ils *or* elles ont	il *or* elle est	ils *or* elles sont
Negative		**Negative**	
je n'ai pas	nous n'avons pas	je ne suis pas	nous ne sommes pas
tu n'as pas	vous n'avez pas	tu n'es pas	vous n'êtes pas
il n'a pas	ils n'ont pas	il n'est pas	ils ne sont pas
elle n'a pas	elles n'ont pas	elle n'est pas	elles ne sont pas

AVOIR	ÊTRE
Interrogative	**Interrogative**
(a) with **est-ce que**	(a) with **est-ce que**
Est-ce que j'ai?	Est-ce que je suis?
Est-ce que tu as?	Est-ce que tu es?
Est ce qu'il a?	Est-ce qu'il est?
Est-ce qu'elle a?	Est-ce qu'elle est?
Est-ce que nous avons?	Est-ce que nous sommes?
Est-ce que vous avez?	Est-ce que vous êtes?
Est-ce qu'ils ont?	Est-ce qu'ils sont?
Est-ce qu'elles ont?	Est-ce qu'elles sont?
(b) **Inverted form**	(b) **Inverted form**
ai-je?	suis-je?
as-tu?	es-tu?
a-t-il?	est-il?
a-t-elle?	est-elle?
avons-nous?	sommes-nous?
avez-vous?	êtes-vous?
ont-ils?	sont-ils?
ont-elles?	sont-elles?

AVOIR	ÊTRE
Negative interrogative	**Negative interrogative**
(a) with **est-ce que**	(a) with **est-ce que**
Est-ce que je n'ai pas?	Est-ce que je ne suis pas?
Est-ce que tu n'as pas?	Est-ce que tu n'es pas?
Est-ce qu'il n'a pas?	Est-ce qu'il n'est pas?
Est-ce qu'elle n'a pas?	Est-ce qu'elle n'est pas?
Est-ce que nous n'avons pas?	Est-ce que nous ne sommes pas?
Est-ce que vous n'avez pas?	Est-ce que vous n'êtes pas?
Est-ce qu'ils n'ont pas?	Est-ce qu'ils ne sont pas?
Est-ce qu'elles n'ont pas?	Est-ce qu'elles ne sont pas?
(b) **Inverted form**	(b) **Inverted form**
n'ai-je pas?	ne suis-je pas?
n'as-tu pas?	n'es-tu pas?
n'a-t-il pas?	n'est-il pas?
n'a-t-elle pas?	n'est-elle pas?
n'avons-nous pas?	ne sommes-nous pas?
n'avez-vous pas?	n'êtes-vous pas?
n'ont-ils pas?	ne sont-ils pas?
n'ont-elles pas?	ne sont-elles pas?

EXERCISES

I. Newspaper Advertisement. Proficiency in Reading and Writing.

Situation: You are looking for an apartment in the classified ads of a French newspaper. Read the following ad and answer the questions in complete sentences.

> **BEL APPARTEMENT**
> belle vue
> 2 pièces, salle de bains
> cuisine moderne, petit balcon
> à Montparnasse
> tél. 45-04-55-14

1. Combien de pièces y a-t-il dans l'appartement?

_____

2. Est-ce que l'appartement est grand ou petit?

_____

3. Quel est le numéro de téléphone?

_____

II.   Sharing. Proficiency in Reading and Writing.

Situation: Look at the picture below of two children playing together. Answer the questions in complete sentences on the lines provided.

1. **Combien d'enfants y a-t-il dans cette photo?**

_____

2. **Qu'est-ce qu'ils font ensemble/together? Jouent-ils? Étudient-ils? Mangent-ils?**

_____

3. **Où sont-ils? Dans un parc? Dans une chambre?**

_____

4. **Quel âge a le garçon à gauche? Quatre ans? Six ans?**

_____

5. **Et le garçon à droite? A-t-il quatre ans? Cinq ans?**

_____

III. Home for the Holidays. Proficiency in Speaking and Writing.

Situation: You are home from college for the holidays. It's Christmas!/**C'est Noël!** Your friend Anne is visiting you. You are talking about how to spend the day together.

Your role is **Vous.** You may vary and extend this guided conversation with your own words and ideas. Later, after you have written on the lines what you said, you may exchange roles with Anne for more practice in speaking and writing. Here, you are going to use some of the irregular verbs in the present indicative tense that are in this work unit. Use the **tu** form of verbs because you and Anne are friends. Feel free to use some of the words that Anne uses when you make your statements.

Anne: Que veux-tu faire aujourd'hui?

Vous: _____

           _____

           I want to buy a few presents. It's Christmas, you know! Do you have to buy some pre-
           sents too?

Anne: **Oui, je sais que c'est Noël. Oui, je dois acheter quelques cadeaux aussi.**

Vous: _____

           We can go to the department stores together.

Anne: **Quelle bonne idée! Nous pouvons aller au grand magasin Les Galeries
           Lafayette.**

Vous: _____

           I have a lot of money! I can buy presents for all my friends.

Anne: **Moi, aussi. J'ai beaucoup d'argent. Je peux acheter des cadeaux pour tous mes
           amis.**

Vous: _____

           I see in the newspapers that Santa Claus is at the Galeries Lafayette.

Anne: **Que dis-tu? Le Père Noël est aux Galeries Lafayette aujourd'hui?!**

Vous: _____

           I'm saying that Santa Claus is at the Galeries Lafayette today.

Anne: **Allons en ville tout de suite.**

Vous: _____

           Okay. Let's go downtown right away.

Anne: **Veux-tu prendre le métro ou le bus?**

Vous: _____

           I want to take the bus. Let's leave now!/**Partons maintenant!**

IV. Giving Directions. Proficiency in Speaking and Writing.

Situation: As you are getting off a bus in Paris, a gentleman asks you for directions to the Opera
House and the Café de la Paix.

You may vary and extend this guided conversation with your own words and ideas. Later, after you
have written what you said on the lines, exchange roles with a friend for more practice in speaking
and writing. Use the **vous** form of verbs because you do not know the gentleman.

You are going to use some common irregular verbs in the imperative (command) and in the present
indicative. They are on the preceding pages; for example, **aller, comprendre, dire, être, prendre,
savoir, vouloir.** Feel free to use some of the words that **Monsieur** uses when you make your statements.

Monsieur: **Pardonnez-moi, s'il vous plaît. Je suis touriste. Je veux aller à l'Opéra et au
            Café de la Paix. Quelle est la bonne direction?**/*Which is the right way?*

Vous: _____

            Take this street/**cette rue.** Go straight ahead/**tout droit.**

Monsieur:	Je vais répéter ce que/*what* vous dites. Je prends cette rue et je vais tout droit. Et puis?/*And then?*
Vous:	_____
	And then, at the end of this street, turn to the left/**tournez à gauche.**
Monsieur:	**Et puis, au bout de cette rue, je tourne à droite/***to the right.*
Vous:	_____
	No! At the end of this street, turn to the left!
Monsieur:	**Je tourne à gauche.**
Vous:	_____
	That's right/**C'est ça.** At the end of this street, turn left. And then, you are there!/**là.**
Monsieur:	**Je ne sais pas si je comprends.**
Vous:	_____
	You say you don't know if you understand?
Monsieur:	**C'est ça. Je dis que je ne sais pas si je comprends.**
Vous:	_____
	I'm going to repeat what I am saying. Take this street. Go straight ahead. Then, at the end of this street, turn to the left. And then, you are there. That's all!/**C'est tout!** Do you understand now?
Monsieur:	**Merci beaucoup. Je comprends maintenant. C'est clair/***It's clear.*
Vous:	_____
	Don't get lost!/**Ne vous perdez pas!**

Oh! Monsieur! Votre autographe, s'il vous plaît! Voici mon programme et voici mon stylo.
(Oh! Sir! Your autograph, please! Here is my program and my pen.)

Work Unit 12
The Passé Composé

Have you ever asked someone for an autograph? That's what Janine did while she was at the Paris Opera House during intermission.

L'autographe spécial

Hier soir la famille Paquet est allée à l'opéra. Ils ont vu la représentation de *Faust*. Ils ont quitté la maison à sept heures et demie et ils sont arrivés à l'opéra à huit heures. Ils sont entrés dans le théâtre et ils ont pris leurs places à huit heurs et quart. La représentation a commencé à huit heures et demie.

Pendant l'entracte, Madame Paquet est allée parler avec quelques dames. Monsieur Paquet est allé faire un appel sur son téléphone portable, Pierre est allé acheter du chocolat, et Janine est allée boire un jus d'orange.

Madame Paquet a parlé avec les dames, et, puis, elle est retournée à sa place. Monsieur Paquet a fait son appel et il est retourné à sa place aussi. Pierre a mangé son chocolat et il est retourné à sa place. Janine a bu son jus d'orange, mais avant de retourner à sa place, elle a vu un homme et elle a dit:

—Oh! Monsieur! vous êtes le grand acteur Philippe Jirard!

—Mais … mademoiselle … a répondu le monsieur.

—Oh! Monsieur! Votre autographe, s'il vous plaît! Voici mon programme et voici mon stylo. Vous pouvez écrire votre autographe sur mon programme, a dit Janine.

—Mais … Mais … a dit le monsieur.

—Vous êtres très modeste, a dit Janine.

—Mais … Ce n'est pas que je suis modeste, mademoiselle … Mais si vous insistez … Voilà mon autographe! a dit le monsieur.

—Merci, monsieur. Merci mille fois, monsieur! a dit Janine.

Janine est retournée à sa place.

L'opéra se termine et tout le monde quitte le théâtre.

Dehors, Janine a annoncé:

—Regardez mon programme! J'ai l'autographe de Philippe Jirard!

—Philippe Jirard?! Vraiment? Incroyable! a dit la mère.

Janine a donné son programme à sa mère et elle a lu: "Je ne suis pas Philippe Jirard. Je m'appelle Jean Leblanc."

—Ce n'est pas possible! Oh! J'ai fait une bêtise! a dit Janine.

—Ce n'est pas si bête. Tu as l'autographe de Jean Leblanc. Tout le monde n'a pas l'autographe de Jean Leblanc sur un programme! a répondu Pierre.

—Qui est Jean Leblanc? a demandé le père.

—C'est une personne ordinaire, comme toi et moi! a répondu la mère. Maintenant nous avons un autographe spécial!

Et ils ont ri.

VOCABULAIRE

l'acteur *m.*, l'actrice *f.*, *n.*, the actor, the actress

allé *past part. of* aller (to go); **la famille Paquet est allée** the Paquet family went

un appel a phone call

s'appeler *v.*, to be named, to call oneself; **Je m'appelle Jean Leblanc** My name is John Leblanc

arrivé *past part. of* arriver (to arrive); **ils sont arrivés** they arrived

bête *adj.*, foolish, dumb; **une bêtise** a foolish mistake

bu *past part. of* boire (to drink); **Janine a bu** Janine drank

commencé *past part. of* commencer (to begin); **la représentation a commencé** the performance began

la dame *n.*, the lady

dehors *adv.*, outside

demandé *past part. of* demander (to ask); **le père a demandé** the father asked

dit *past part. of* dire (to say, to tell); **a dit Janine** said Janine

donné *past part. of* donner (to give); **Janine a donné** Janine gave

l'entracte *n. m.*, intermission

entré *past part. of* entrer (to enter, to go in); **ils sont entrés** they entered

faire un appel to make a phone call

fait *past part. of* faire (to do, to make); **j'ai fait** I did

hier *adv.*, yesterday

incroyable *adj.*, unbelievable

insistez *v. form of* insister (to insist); **vous insistez** you insist

leurs *poss. adj. pl.*, their; **leurs places** their seats

lu *past part. of* lire (to read); **elle a lu** she read

mangé *past part. of* manger (to eat); **il a mangé** he ate

modeste *adj.*, modest

parlé *past part. of* parler (to talk, to speak); **elle a parlé** she talked

pouvez *v. form of* pouvoir (can, to be able); **vous pouvez écrire** you can write

pris *past part. of* prendre (to take); **ils ont pris** they took

le programme *n.*, the program

quitté *past part. of* quitter (to leave); **tout le monde a quitté le théâtre** everybody left the theater

répondu *past part. of* répondre (to reply); **a répondu Pierre** replied Pierre

retourné *past part. of* retourner (to return, go back); **elle est retournée** she returned

ri *past part. of* rire (to laugh); **ils ont ri** they laughed

si *conj.*, if; *as an adv.*, so

le stylo *n.*, the pen

terminé *past part. of* terminer (to end)

voici here is, here are; **voilà** there is, there are (used when pointing out)

vu *past part. of* voir (to see); **elle a vu un homme** she saw a man

EXERCISES

Review the story and vocabulary before starting these exercises.

I. **Answer the following questions in complete sentences. They are based on the story in this unit.**

1. A quelle heure est-ce qu'ils ont quitté la maison pour aller à l'opéra?

_____

2. A quelle heure sont-ils arrivés à l'opéra?

_____

3. A quelle heure est-ce qu'ils ont pris leurs places?

_____

4. A quelle heure la représentation a-t-elle commencé?

_____

II. Activities. Proficiency in Speaking.

A. Expressing personal feelings.
Situation: You are at a concert. During intermission, a friend of yours sees you and asks you how you like the concert. Tell him/her what you think of it. You may use your own words and the vocabulary at the beginning of this work unit.

B. Friendly persuasion.
Situation: You are going out for the evening with a friend. You want to see a French movie but your friend wants to go to a French opera. Persuade your friend to see a French film with you. You may use your own words and the vocabulary at the beginning of this work unit.

III. Fill in the blank lines with the past participle. Refer to the story if you have to. The answers are there!

1. Hier soir la famille Paquet est _____ à l'opéra.

2. Ils ont _____ la représentation de *Faust*.

3. Ils ont _____ la maison à sept heures et demie.

4. Ils sont _____ à l'opéra à huit heures.

5. Ils sont _____ dans le théâtre.

6. Ils ont _____ leurs places.

7. Madame Paquet est _____ parler avec quelques dames.

8. Monsieur Paquet est _____ faire un appel sur son téléphone portable.

9. Pierre est _____ acheter du chocolat.

10. Janine est _____ boire un jus d'orange.

IV. Word Search. Find the past participles *in French* in this puzzle and circle them.

1. allé   6. parlé
2. bu   7. pris
3. dit   8. quitté
4. fait   9. répondu
5. lu   10. ri

A	L	L	É	T	F	U	M	É	L
P	A	R	L	É	A	L	A	B	U
P	R	I	S	D	I	T	N	T	O
R	Q	U	I	T	T	É	U	R	I
U	R	É	P	O	N	D	U	F	T

184

STRUCTURES DE LA LANGUE

THE PASSÉ COMPOSÉ
(PAST INDEFINITE *OR* COMPOUND PAST)

A. Verbs conjugated with **avoir**

	1st Conjugation	2nd Conjugation	3rd Conjugation
	-ER	**-IR**	**-RE**
INFINITIVES ⟶	**danser** *to dance*	**finir** *to finish*	**vendre** *to sell*
	I danced, *or*	I finished, *or*	I sold, *or*
	I have danced, *or*	I have finished, *or*	I have sold, *or*
	I did dance;	I did finish;	I did sell;
	you danced, etc.	you finished; etc.	you sold, etc.
SINGULAR			
1. **j'** (I)	**ai dansé**	**ai fini**	**ai vendu**
2. **tu** (you—*familiar only*)	**as dansé**	**as fini**	**as vendu**
3. **il** (he *or* it) / **elle** (she *or* it)	**a dansé**	**a fini**	**a vendu**
PLURAL			
1. **nous** (we)	**avons dansé**	**avons fini**	**avons vendu**
2. **vous** (you)	**avez dansé**	**avez fini**	**avez vendu**
3. **ils** / **elles** (they)	**ont dansé**	**ont fini**	**ont vendu**

RULES AND OBSERVATIONS:

1. To form the passé composé of verbs conjugated with **avoir**, use the present indicative of **avoir** plus the past participle of the verb. Almost all verbs are conjugated with **avoir** except *all reflexive verbs and the 17 verbs listed in section C of this lesson.*

2. To form the past participle of a regular **-er** verb, drop the **-er** ending and add **é**.

3. To form the past participle of a regular **-ir** verb, drop the **-ir** ending and add **i**.

4. To form the past participle of a regular **-re** verb, drop the **-re** ending and add **u**.

5. The passé composé is used to express an action that was completed in the past. It is used in conversation and in informal writing.

6. The passé composé can be translated into English in three different ways, as noted in the table above.

7. To form the negative, place **n'** in front of the present indicative of **avoir**, which in the passé composé is called the auxiliary or helping verb. Then put **pas** after it:

1st Conjugation	2nd Conjugation	3rd Conjugation
je n'ai **pas** dansé	je n'ai **pas** fini	je n'ai **pas** vendu
tu n'as **pas** dansé	tu n'as **pas** fini	tu n'as **pas** vendu
il (*or*) elle **n'a pas** dansé	il (*or*) elle **n'a pas** fini	il (*or*) elle **n'a pas** vendu
nous **n'avons pas** dansé	nous **n'avons pas** fini	nous **n'avons pas** vendu
vous **n'avez pas** dansé	vous **n'avez pas** fini	vous **n'avez pas** vendu
ils (*or*) elles **n'ont pas** dansé	ils (*or*) elles **n'ont pas** fini	ils (*or*) elles **n'ont pas** vendu

8. To form the interrogative, use either (a) the **est-ce que** form in front of the subject, or (b) the inverted form, both of which you learned when you formed the present indicative tense:

(a) Est-ce que j'ai dansé?	(b) ai-je dansé?
Est-ce que tu as dansé?	as-tu dansé?
Est-ce qu'il a dansé?	a-t-il dansé?
Est-ce qu'elle a dansé?	a-t-elle dansé?
Est-ce que nous avons dansé?	avons-nous dansé?
Est-ce que vous avez dansé?	avez-vous dansé?
Est-ce qu'ils ont dansé?	ont-ils dansé?
Est-ce qu'elles ont dansé?	ont-elles dansé?

Note: In box (b) above, if you use the inverted form, you need to add **-t-** in the third person singular between the auxiliary verb and the subject pronoun. You already learned to do this when you used the inverted form in the present indicative tense.

9. To form the negative interrogative, use either (a) the **est-ce que** form in front of the subject in the negative form or (b) the inverted form in the negative.

(a) Est-ce que je n'ai pas dansé?	(b) n'ai-je pas dansé?
Est-ce que tu n'as pas dansé?	n'as-tu pas dansé?
Est-ce qu'il n'a pas dansé?	n'a-t-il pas dansé?
Est-ce qu'elle n'a pas dansé?	n'a-t-elle pas dansé?
Est-ce que nous n'avons pas dansé?	n'avons-nous pas dansé?
Est-ce que vous n'avez pas dansé?	n'avez-vous pas dansé?
Est-ce qu'ils n'ont pas dansé?	n'ont-ils pas dansé?
Est-ce qu'elles n'ont pas dansé?	n'ont-elles pas dansé?

Note: In boxes (a) and (b) above, it is very easy to form the negative interrogative of a verb in the passé composé. If you just drop, for a minute, the past participle *dansé*, what you have left is actually what you already learned: the negative interrogative of the present indicative tense of the verb **avoir**. See the summary at the end of Work Unit 11.

EXERCISES

Review the preceding material before starting these exercises.

I. **Write the answers to the following in complete sentences.**

A. Passé composé with **avoir** in the affirmative—answer in the affirmative.

    Model: **Avez-vous vendu la maison?**   You answer: **Oui, j'ai vendu la maison.**
             (Did you sell the house?)   (Yes, I sold the house.)

1. Avez-vous vendu la voiture?

_____

2. Avez-vous acheté la propriété?

_____

3. Avez-vous fini les leçons?

_____

4. Avez-vous réussi la vente de la propriété?

_____

5. Avez-vous fermé les portes et les fenêtres?

_____

B. Passé composé with **avoir** in the negative—answer in the negative.

    Model: **Janine a-t-elle dansé**   You answer: **Non, elle n'a pas**
                hier soir?   **dansé hier soir.**
                (Did Janine dance last   (No, she did not dance last
                evening?)   evening.)

> Use a pronoun subject in your answer where
> a noun subject is given in the question.

1. Janine a-t-elle chanté hier soir?

_____

2. Robert a-t-il choisi une jolie cravate?

_____

3. As-tu mangé l'éclair?

_____

4. Janine et Pierre ont-ils étudié les leçons?

_____

5. Avons-nous fini le travail?

_____

C. Passé composé with **avoir** in the interrogative—change to the interrogative in the inverted form.

> Model: **Janine a parlé à Madame Richy.**
> (Janine talked to Mrs. Richy.)
>
> You ask: **Janine a-t-elle parlé à Madame Richy?**
> (Did Janine talk to Mrs. Richy?)

1. Pierre a vu Madame Richy.

_____

2. Hélène a choisi une jolie robe.

_____

3. Coco a mangé le gâteau.

_____

Coco a mangé le gâteau.

4. Suzanne et Georges ont navigué sur Internet.

_____

5. Marie et Betty ont voyagé en France.

_____

D. Passé composé with **avoir** in the interrogative—change to the interrogative with **est-ce que**.

> Model: **Madame Banluc a chanté hier soir.**
> (Mrs. Banluc sang last evening.)
>
> You ask: **Est-ce que Madame Banluc a chanté hier soir?**
> (Did Mrs. Banluc sing last evening?)

1. Madame Paquet a acheté un beau chapeau.

_____

2. Pierre a perdu sa montre.

_____

3. Monsieur Paquet a fait un appel sur son téléphone portable.

_____

4. Paul a mangé du chocolat.

_____

5. Janine a bu un jus d'orange.

_____

E. Passé composé with **avoir** in the negative interrogative—change into the negative interrogative using the inverted form only.

Model: **Madame Paquet n'a pas**   You ask: **Madame Paquet n'a-t-elle**
             acheté un beau chapeau.   **pas acheté un beau chapeau?**
             (Mrs. Paquet did not buy a   (Didn't Mrs. Paquet buy a
             beautiful hat.)   beautiful hat?)

1. Madame Richy n'a pas acheté une automobile.

_____

2. Monsieur Richy n'a pas voyagé aux États-Unis.

_____

3. Madame et Monsieur Armstrong n'ont pas aimé le dessert.

_____

4. Mathilde n'a pas entendu la musique.

_____

5. Joseph n'a pas choisi une jolie cravate.

_____

F. Passé composé with **avoir** in the negative interrogative—change into the negative interrogative using the **est-ce que** form only.

Model: **Suzanne n'a pas fini le livre.**   You ask: **Est-ce que Suzanne n'a pas**
         (Suzanne did not finish the book.)   **fini le livre?**
                                              (Didn't Suzanne finish the book?)

1. Robert n'a pas dansé hier soir.

_____

2. Joséphine n'a pas chanté ce matin.

_____

3. Guy et Michel n'ont pas fini leurs leçons.

_____

4. Françoise et Simone n'ont pas entendu la musique.

_____

5. Charles n'a pas perdu son ami.

_____

II. **Match the following.**

1. She drank some milk.   _____ Il a vendu sa voiture.

2. They heard a big noise.   _____ Elles ont fini le travail.

3. She played in the park.   _____ Il a fermé la fenêtre.

4. She worked yesterday.   _____ Ils ont oublié de venir.

5. They lost their dog.   _____ Il a expliqué la leçon.

6. He explained the lesson.   _____ Elle a joué dans le parc.

7. He sold his car.   _____ Elles ont perdu leur chien.

8. He closed the window.   _____ Ils ont entendu un grand bruit.

9. They forgot to come.   _____ Elle a bu du lait.

10. They finished the work.   _____ Elle a travaillé hier.

III. **Change the infinitive in parentheses to the past participle.**

> **Model:** **(voir)** **Ils ont** _____ You write on the blank line: vu (saw)
> **la représentation de *Carmen*.**
> (They _____ the performance of *Carmen*.)

1. (aimer)   Ils ont _____ la représentation de *Carmen*.

2. (quitter)   Ils ont _____ la maison à sept heures et demie.

3. (prendre)   Ils ont _____ leurs places à huit heures et quart.

4. (commencer)   La représentation a _____ à huit heures et demie.

5. (parler)   Madame Paquet a _____ avec les dames.

6. (parler)   Monsieur Paquet a _____ au téléphone.

7. (manger)   Pierre a _____ son chocolat.

8. (boire)   Janine a _____ son jus d'orange.

9. (voir)   Elle a _____ un homme.

10. (dire)   Elle a _____ . —Oh! Monsieur! Votre autographe!

IV. **Give the three English translations for each of the following French verb forms in the passé composé. Refer to the chart in section A. Verbs conjugated with avoir.**

1. J'ai dansé.   _____   _____   _____

2. Vous avez fini.   _____   _____   _____

3. Nous avons vendu. _____   _____   _____

V. **For each of the following verbs in the passé composé, write the correct form of avoir (i.e., the present indicative tense of avoir).**

1. J'_____ joué.   7. Vous _____ perdu.

2. Tu _____ pleuré.   8. Ils _____ répondu.

3. Il _____ fini.   9. J' _____ étudié.

4. Elle _____ choisi.   10. Il _____ parlé.

5. Janine _____ chanté.   11. Robert _____ travaillé.

6. Nous _____ dansé.   12. Marie et Bob _____ dîné.

190

B. Verbs conjugated with **être**

MASCULINE SUBJECTS		FEMININE SUBJECTS	
Singular	Plural	Singular	Plural
je suis allé	nous sommes allés	je suis allée	nous sommes allées
tu es allé	vous êtes allé(s)	tu es allée	vous êtes allée(s)
il est allé	ils sont allés	elle est allée	elles sont allées
English equivalents: I went, *or* I have gone, *or* I did go; you went, *or* you have gone, *or* you did go; etc.			

RULES AND OBSERVATIONS:

1. To form the *passé composé* of verbs conjugated with **être**, use the present indicative of **être** plus the past participle of the verb. All reflexive verbs are conjugated with **être** as are the 17 verbs in the chart in section **C**.

2. The past participle of a verb conjugated with **être** agrees in gender (*i.e.*, whether masculine or feminine) and number (*i.e.*, whether singular or plural) with the subject, as shown in the box. The past participle of a verb conjugated with **être**, therefore, is like an adjective because it describes the subject in some way.

> Compare: **Elle est jolie.**   **Elle est partie.**
> (She is pretty.)   (She has left.)

3. To form the negative, interrogative, and negative interrogative, do the same as you did for verbs conjugated with **avoir** in the passé composé. The word order is the same. See the summary at the end of Work Unit 11.

C. The 17 most common verbs conjugated with **être***

1. **aller**   to go

2. **arriver**   to arrive

3. ***descendre**   to go down, come down

   Elle est descendue vite.
   She came down quickly.

   BUT: *Elle a descendu la valise.*
   She brought down the suitcase.

4. **devenir**   to become

5. **entrer**   to enter, go in, come in

6. ***monter**   to go up, come up

   Elle est montée lentement.
   She went up slowly.

   BUT: *Elle a monté l'escalier.*
   She went up the stairs.

7. **mourir**   to die

8. **naître**   to be born

9. **partir**   to leave

10. ***passer**   to go by, pass by

    Elle est passée chez moi.
    She came by my house.

    BUT: *Elle m'a passé le sel.*
    She passed me the salt.

    AND: *Elle a passé un examen.*
    She took an exam.

Some of these verbs, as noted above, are conjugated with **avoir if the verb is used in a transitive sense and has a direct object.*

11. *rentrer to go in again, to return (home)	14. revenir to come back
Elle est rentrée tôt.	15. *sortir to go out
She returned home early.	Elle est sortie hier soir.
BUT: Elle a rentré le chat dans la maison.	She went out last night.
She brought (took) the cat into the house.	BUT: Elle a sorti son mouchoir.
12. rester to remain, stay	She took out her handkerchief.
13. retourner to return, go back	16. tomber to fall
	17. venir to come

*Some of these verbs, as noted on page 191, are conjugated with avoir if the verb is used in a transitive sense and has a direct object.

D. Some irregular past participles

	INFINITIVE	PAST PARTICIPLE		INFINITIVE	PAST PARTICIPLE
1.	apprendre *to learn*	appris	16.	naître *to be born*	né
2.	avoir *to have*	eu	17.	ouvrir *to open*	ouvert
3.	boire *to drink*	bu	18.	paraître *to appear, seem*	paru
4.	comprendre *to understand*	compris	19.	permettre *to permit*	permis
5.	couvrir *to cover*	couvert	20.	pouvoir *to be able, can*	pu
6.	croire *to believe*	cru	21.	prendre *to take*	pris
7.	devenir *to become*	devenu	22.	promettre *to promise*	promis
8.	devoir *to owe, have to, should*	dû	23.	recevoir *to receive*	reçu
9.	dire *to say, tell*	dit	24.	revenir *to come back*	revenu
10.	écrire *to write*	écrit	25.	rire *to laugh*	ri
11.	être *to be*	été	26.	savoir *to know*	su
12.	faire *to do, make*	fait	27.	tenir *to hold*	tenu
13.	lire *to read*	lu	28.	venir *to come*	venu
14.	mettre *to put, place*	mis	29.	voir *to see*	vu
15.	mourir *to die*	mort	30.	vouloir *to want*	voulu

EXERCISES

Review the preceding material before starting these exercises.

I. Write the answers to the following in complete sentences.

A. Passé composé with **être** in the affirmative—answer the questions in the affirmative.

Drill on **aller**

REMEMBER TO WATCH FOR AN AGREEMENT OF THE
PAST PARTICIPLE WITH THE SUBJECT IN THE PASSÉ
COMPOSÉ WHEN THE VERB IS CONJUGATED WITH **être**!

Model: **Madame Paquet est-elle**   You answer: **Oui, Madame Paquet est**
       allée à l'opéra?   **allée à l'opéra.**
       (Did Mrs. Paquet go to the opera?)   (Yes, Mrs. Paquet went to the
                                                         opera.)

1. Janine est-elle allée au cinéma?

---

2. Monique est-elle allée à l'école?

---

3. Robert est-il allé au théâtre?

---

4. Pierre et Raymond sont-ils allés au parc?

---

5. Anne et Béatrice sont-elles allées au Canada?

---

6. Jacques et Jeanne sont-ils allés à l'aéroport?

---

7. Monsieur et Madame Beaupuy sont-ils allés aux États-Unis?

---

8. La mère est-elle allée dans le garage?

---

9. Le père est-il allé dans la cuisine?

---

10. La jeune fille est-elle allée à la pharmacie?

193

B. Passé composé with **être** in the negative—answer the questions in the negative.

Model:	**Janine est-elle arrivée à l'opéra à huit heures et demie?**	You answer:	**Non, elle n'est pas arrivée à l'opéra à huit heures et demie.**
	(Did Janine arrive at the opera at eight-thirty?)		(No, she did not arrive at the opera at eight-thirty.)

> Use a pronoun subject in your answer where a noun subject is given in the question.

1. Madame Paquet est-elle arrivée à l'opéra à huit heures et demie?

   _____

2. Est-ce qu'ils sont entrés dans le théâtre à huit heures?

   _____

3. Monsieur et Madame Paquet sont-ils partis de bonne heure?

   _____

4. Est-ce qu'il est resté à la maison?

   _____

5. Simone est-elle sortie ce soir?

   _____

C. Passé composé with **être** in the interrogative—change to the interrogative in the inverted form.

Model:	**Monique est tombée dans la rue.**	You ask:	**Monique est-elle tombée dans la rue?**
	(Monique fell in the street.)		(Did Monique fall in the street?)

1. Yolande est venue ce soir.

   _____

2. François est retourné à midi.

   _____

3. Les garçons sont restés dans l'école.

   _____

4. Les jeunes filles sont descendues vite.

   _____

5. Monsieur et Madame Paquet sont rentrés à minuit.

   _____

D. Passé composé with **être** in the interrogative—change to the interrogative with **est-ce-que**.

Model:	**Madame Banluc est née à la Martinique.**	You ask:	**Est-ce que Madame Banluc est née à la Martinique?**
	(Mrs. Banluc was born in Martinique.)		(Was Mrs. Banluc born in Martinique?)

1. John James Audubon est né aux Cayes à Haïti.

    _____

2. Napoléon Bonaparte est mort à Sainte-Hélène.

    _____

3. Marie-Antoinette est née à Vienne.

    _____

4. Jacques Chirac est devenu président de la République Française en 1995.

    _____

5. Joséphine est née à la Martinique.

    _____

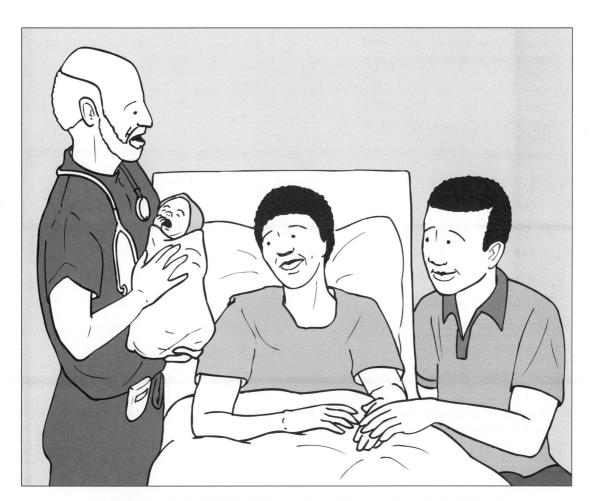

Joséphine est née à la Martinique. (Josephine was born in Martinique.)

6. Marie-Antoinette est morte à Paris.

    _____

7. Joséphine est devenue impératrice en 1804.

    _____

E. Passé composé with **être** in the negative interrogative—change the following negative sentences into the negative interrogative using the inverted form only.

Model: **Tu n'es pas sorti hier soir.**   You ask: **N'es-tu pas sorti hier soir?**
(You did not go out last evening.)   (Didn't you go out last evening?)

1. Tu n'es pas resté à la maison.

_____

2. Elle n'est pas tombée dans le jardin.

_____

3. Il n'est pas parti ce matin.

_____

4. Vous n'êtes pas arrivé à dix heures.

_____

5. Elles ne sont pas allées à l'école aujourd'hui.

_____

II.   Match the following.

1. She has left.   _____ Il a bu du vin.

2. They have read some books.   _____ Elle est partie.

3. They died.   _____ Ils ont lu des livres.

4. He drank some wine.   _____ Elles sont mortes.

5. We went into the living room.   _____ Vous avez appris la leçon.

6. You went to the restaurant.   _____ Nous sommes entrés dans le salon.

7. He has had an accident.   _____ Tu es allée au restaurant.

8. She has been sick.   _____ Vous êtes devenu médecin.

9. You became a doctor.   _____ Il a eu un accident.

10. You learned the lesson.   _____ Elle a été malade.

III.   Give the three English translations for each of the following French verb forms in the passé composé. Refer to the chart in section B.

1. Je suis allé au cinéma.   _____ _____ _____

2. Elle est partie.   _____ _____ _____

3. Nous sommes arrivés.   _____ _____ _____

IV. **For each of the following verbs in the passé composé write the correct form of either avoir or être, depending on which is required.**

1. Suzanne _____ parlé.

2. Il _____ monté.

3. Elle _____ sortie.

4. Elle _____ compris.

5. Nous _____ arrivés.

6. Vous _____ dit.

7. Elles _____ lu.

8. Tu _____ fait.

9. Robert _____ resté.

10. Ils _____ ri.

11. Je _____ allé.

12. Madame Paquet _____ bu.

V. **Identify the following past particles by writing the infinitive form. These past participles are all irregular.**

Model: dit   You write: dire

1. appris _____

2. devenu _____

3. eu _____

4. couvert _____

5. cru _____

6. compris _____

7. permis _____

8. reçu _____

9. promis _____

10. voulu _____

11. dû _____

12. vu _____

13. dit _____

14. venu _____

15. écrit _____

16. été _____

17. bu _____

18. fait _____

19. tenu _____

20. lu _____

21. ouvert _____

22. mis _____

23. su _____

24. mort _____

25. ri _____

26. né _____

27. revenu _____

28. paru _____

29. pu _____

30. pris _____

VI. **Write the past participle for each of the following verbs. Some are regular, some are irregular.**

Model: vendre   You write: vendu

1. avoir _____

2. être _____

3. faire _____

4. finir _____

5. savoir _____

6. lire _____

7. apprendre _____

8. défendre _____

9. choisir _____

10. aller _____

11. sortir _____

12. saisir _____

13. aider _____

14. bâtir _____

15. jouer _____

16. voir _____

17. danser _____

18. vendre _____

197

VII. Some verbs in French are conjugated with **avoir** to form the passé composé and some verbs are conjugated with **être**. For each of the following verbs write on the blank line either **avoir** or **être**, depending on which is required to form the passé composé.

Models: **aller**　　　　　　You write: **être**
　　　　　parler　　　　　You write: **avoir**

1. rester _____
2. danser _____
3. finir _____
4. vendre _____
5. arriver _____
6. entrer _____
7. aimer _____

8. chanter _____
9. mourir _____
10. donner _____
11. dire _____
12. naître _____
13. aller _____
14. étudier _____

15. partir _____
16. chercher _____
17. retourner _____
18. choisir _____
19. avoir _____
20. être _____
21. venir _____

VIII. Change from the passé composé to the present indicative tense.

Model: **Il a bu du lait.**　　　You write: **Il boit du lait.**
　　　　(He drank milk.)　　　　　　　　　(He is drinking milk.)

1. Il a lu un bon livre.

_____

2. J'ai vendu la voiture.

_____

3. Elle est allée à l'opéra.

_____

4. Nous avons écrit des lettres.

_____

5. Vous êtes arrivé de bonne heure.

_____

IX. Change from the present indicative tense to the passé composé.

Model: **Monsieur Paquet a une belle**　You write: **Monsieur Paquet a eu**
　　　　voiture grise.　　　　　　　　　　**une belle voiture grise.**
　　　　(Mr. Paquet has a beautiful gray car.)　　(Mr. Paquet had a beautiful gray car.)

1. Madame Paquet a un beau chapeau rouge.

_____

2. Janine boit un jus d'orange.

3. Pierre mange du chocolat.

_____

4. Monique va au cinéma.

_____

5. Jeanne et Joséphine entrent dans le théâtre.

_____

X. Fill in the ending of the past participle with the appropriate agreement, if needed. If none is needed, write a dash (—). Refer to the story at the beginning of this unit if you have to. The answers are there!

Model: **La famille Paquet est**   Fill in the ending of the past participle if an
allé_____ à l'opéra.   agreement is needed: **é** or **s**
(The Paquet family went to
the opera.)

1. La famille Paquet est allé_____ à l'opéra.

2. Monsieur Paquet est retourné_____ à sa place.

3. Madame Paquet est retourné_____ à sa place.

4. Janine est retourné_____ à sa place.

5. Ils sont arrivé_____ à l'opéra à huit heures.

6. Ils sont entré_____ dans le théâtre.

7. Pierre est retourné_____ à sa place.

XI. On the blank line, write the appropriate past participle of the verb in parentheses. Refer to the story at the beginning of this unit if you have to. The answers are there!

Model: **(aller) La famille Paquet est** _____   Write on the blank line: **allée**
à l'opéra.

1. (aller)   La famille Paquet est _____ à l'opéra.

2. (arriver)   Ils sont _____ à l'opéra à huit heures.

3. (entrer)   Ils sont _____ dans le théâtre.

4. (aller)   Madame Paquet est _____ parler avec quelques dames.

5. (aller)   Monsieur Paquet est _____ faire un appel sur son téléphone portable.

6. (aller)   Pierre est _____ acheter du chocolat.

7. (aller)   Janine est _____ boire un jus d'orange.

8. (retourner) Madame Paquet est _____ à sa place.

9. (retourner) Monsieur Paquet est _____ à sa place.

10. (retourner) Janine est _____ à sa place.

199

XII. French Opera. Proficiency in Speaking and Writing.

Situation: Last night you went to the Opera House in Paris. You saw the opera *Pelléas et Mélisande*, music composed by Claude Debussy.

Say aloud at least three statements in French using the **passé composé** tense. You may use your own ideas and words, those used in the story at the beginning of this lesson, and/or the following: **Hier soir, je suis allé(e) à l'Opéra**/*last night, I went to the Opera*. **J'ai vu l'opéra *Pelléas et Mélisande*/** *I saw the opera Pelléas et Mélisande*; **Pendant l'entracte, j'ai bu un jus d'orange et j'ai mangé du chocolat**/*During intermission, I drank an orange juice and I ate some chocolate.* Now, write what you said on the following lines:

_____

_____

_____

The Opera House, Paris.

XIII. Folklore Basque. Proficiency in Speaking and Writing.

Situation: Look at the picture on the following page of the young men dressed in costume doing the saber dance. Basque is located in southwest France.

In at least three sentences, tell us what the young men are doing, what they are wearing, and something about their berets. You may use your own ideas and words and/or the following: **Dans ce dessin les jeunes hommes sont habillés en costume**/*In this drawing the young men are dressed in costume.* **Ils portent des bérets noirs**/*They are wearing black berets.* **Ils dansent**/*They are dancing.* **C'est La Danse des Sabres**/*It's the Sabre Dance.* **Ils sont beaux et magnifiques!**/*They are handsome and magnificent!* **Ils sont extraordinaires**/*They are extraordinary.*

Now, write what you said on the following lines:

1. _____

2. _____

3. _____

Folklore Basque. La Danse des Sabres.

XIV. Word Game. Proficiency in Writing.

Situation: You are playing word games at a French Club party. Change one letter in each of the past participles given and get the past participle of another verb. Write the new words on the lines. Make up a few more. They are in this work unit.

1. **pu** (past part. of **pouvoir**)   _____ (past part. of **savoir**)

2. **eu** (past part. of **avoir**)   _____ (past part. of **lire**)

XV. Obtaining and Providing Information. Proficiency in Speaking and Writing.

Situation: You are on a school trip in Paris with your classmates and Mr. Durand, your French teacher. Last night Catherine, a classmate, returned very late to the hotel. Mr. Durand and the others were worried about her. Catherine has been asked to explain where she was and what she did.

Your role is **Catherine.** You may vary and extend this guided conversation with your own words and ideas. Later, after you have written what you said on the lines, you may exchange roles with Mr. Durand for more practice in speaking and writing. Here, you are going to practice using verbs in the **passé composé.** Feel free to use some of the words that Mr. Durand uses when you make your statements.

M. Durand: **Catherine, hier soir vous êtes rentrée à l'hôtel très tard. Où êtes-vous allée?**

Catherine: _____

Tell him you went to the theater.

M. Durand: **Vous êtes allée au théâtre? Avec qui?**

Catherine: _____

Tell him you went alone to the theater.

M. Durand: **Vous êtes allée seule au théâtre? À quel théâtre?**/*To which theater?* **Et vous avez vu quelle pièce?**/*what play?*

Catherine: _____

Yes, I went alone to the theater. To **La Comédie Française.** I saw the play *L'Avare*/*The Miser.* It's a comedy by Molière.

M. Durand: **Avez-vous aimé la comédie?**

Catherine: _____

Yes, I liked the comedy very much. Very funny/**très drôle.**

M. Durand: **Avez-vous vu quelques personnes au théâtre que vous connaissez?**/*Did you see any people at the theater that you know?*

Catherine: _____

Yes, I saw the Paquet family—the mother, father, Janine, and Pierre.

M. Durand: **Pendant l'entracte, qu'est-ce que vous avez bu et mangé?**

Catherine: _____

During intermission I ate chocolate with Pierre, I drank orange juice with Janine, and I talked with Madame Paquet and some ladies.

M. Durand: **Est-ce que vous êtes allée boire du café?**

Catherine: _____

Yes, I went to drink some coffee with Mr. Paquet.

M. Durand: **D'accord**/*Okay.* **Tout est bien qui finit bien!**/*All's well that ends well!*

XVI. Providing Information. Proficiency in Writing.

Situation: You are checking out of your hotel in Rennes and you have been asked to answer a questionnaire of services provided.

Answer the following questions in complete sentences.

1. **Avez-vous été satisfait des services dans notre hôtel pendant votre séjour? /**
   Have you been satisfied with the services in our hotel during your stay?

   _____

   _____

2. **Avez-vous aimé votre chambre? Est-ce qu'elle a été propre? Confortable? /**
   Did you like your room? Was it clean? Comfortable?

   _____

   _____

3. **Avez-vous été satisfait de notre service téléphonique? /**
   Were you satisfied with our telephone service?

   _____

   _____

4. **Est-ce que les employés ont montré de la politesse? /**
   Did the employees show politeness?

   _____

   _____

5. **Est-ce que les repas dans le restaurant ont été bons? Excellents? /**
   Were the meals in the restaurant good? Excellent?

   _____

   _____

6. **Est-ce que le service dans le restaurant a été rapide? /**
   Was the service in the restaurant fast?

   _____

   _____

7. **Est-ce que les prix ont été bons? Trop chers? /**
   Were the prices good? Too expensive?

   _____

   _____

XVII. A Letter to a Friend. Proficiency in Writing.

Situation: Before you left for Paris you promised your friend Yvette that you would write her a letter about your activities. Here's your chance to keep your promise!

Refer to Exercise XV above where you had a conversation with Monsieur Durand about how you spent the evening at La Comédie Française.

Now, using the statements you made in the conversation, write a letter to Yvette telling her how you spent yesterday evening. Write at least seven sentences.

Dimanche, le 14 janvier 2007

Chère amie Yvette,

_____

_____

_____

_____

_____

Grosses bises de/_Love and kisses from,_

_____

XVIII. Word Game. Proficiency in Writing.

Situation: You are playing more word games at a French Club party. Change one letter in each of the irregular past participles given below and get the irregular past participle of another verb. Write the new words on the lines. If you need any help, review them all in section **D** in this work unit.

1. **vu** (past part. of **voir**)   Change it to →   _____ (past part. of **pouvoir**)

2. **lu** (past part. of **lire**)   Change it to →   _____ (past part. of **savoir**)

3. **bu** (past part. of **boire**)   Change it to →   _____ (past part. of **avoir**)

4. **pu** (past part. of **pouvoir**)   Change it to →   _____ (past part. of **lire**)

5. **eu** (past part. of **avoir**)   Change it to →   _____ (past part. of **boire**)

Here's a recipe in French for a stew. Try making it yourself. It's fun!

RAGOÛT DE MOUTON
À L'IRLANDAISE (IRISH STEW)

Pour 6 personnes   cuisson: 2 heures, 35 min.

1500 grammes de mouton coupé en morceaux
3 grosses pommes de terre
300 grammes d'oignons
sel, poivre, blanc de céleri, et 3 gousses d'ail
3 cuillères à soupe de farine blanche

1. Disposez dans une cocotte:

   (a) une couche d'oignons hachés
   (b) une grosse pomme de terre coupée en lamelles
   (c) un tiers des morceaux de mouton
   (d) du sel, du poivre
   (e) une gousse d'ail haché (si vous désirez)

2. Répétez en disposant une deuxième couche d'oignons hachés, une grosse pomme de terre coupée en lamelles, un tiers des morceaux de mouton, du sel, du poivre, une gousse d'ail haché.

3. Répétez en disposant une troisième couche d'oignons hachés, une grosse pomme de terre coupée en lamelles, un tiers des morceaux de mouton, du sel, du poivre, une gousse d'ail haché.

4. Ajoutez une tasse et demie d'eau chaude.

5. Faites bouillir pendant 5 min.

6. Laissez cuire doucement, à couvert, pendant 1 heure 30 min.

7. Après une heure et demie, si le mélange est épais, ajoutez un peu d'eau chaude. Maintenant, mettez dans la cocotte le céleri coupé en petits morceaux.

8. Laissez cuire doucement pendant 1 heure.

9. Maintenant, ajoutez 3 cuillères à soupe de farine blanche, lentement, pendant que vous remuez le mélange.

10. Bonne chance! Ne le brûlez pas!

Work Unit 13
Direct Object Pronouns, Including *en*

*Let's see how the family stew
turns out!*

À chacun son goût

Ce soir Madame Paquet a préparé le dîner. Pierre a servi le dîner pour la famille et les voisins, Monsieur et Madame Richy. Il a servi un ragoût de mouton à l'irlandaise. La recette pour le ragoût est sur la page d'en face.

Pierre:	**Voici le ragoût! Je vais le servir maintenant. À table, s'il vous plaît!**
	(Tout le monde va s'asseoir à table: Monsieur et Madame Paquet, Janine, Pierre, Monsieur et Madame Richy.)
Janine:	**Oh! Il sent bon!**
Monsieur Paquet:	**Et comment! Il sent très bon. Moi, j'ai grand faim.**
Madame Paquet:	**Il est magnifique, n'est-ce pas? . . . Excusez-moi, je vais dans la cuisine. Vous pouvez commencer sans moi.**
	(Madame Paquet se lève. Elle quitte la table pour aller dans la cuisine.)
Madame Richy:	**Vraiment extraordinaire!**
Monsieur Richy:	**J'adore les ragoûts.**
Madame Richy:	**Moi aussi. Pierre, tu es un bon garçon!**
Pierre:	**Alors, qui va commencer?**
Monsieur Paquet:	**Après toi, Pierre. Tu peux commencer si tu veux.**
Janine:	**Vas-y, Pierre! Tu goûtes le premier.**
Pierre:	**Bon. Alors, je vais commencer . . . Maintenant, je goûte le ragoût . . .**
Janine:	**Je vais le goûter aussi . . . Oh! Oh! Il est brûlé! C'est dégoûtant. Je vais être malade. Il est brûlé! Goûtez-en!**
	(Janine se lève et quitte la table.)
Pierre:	**Oui. Il est brûlé. Janine a raison. Il est brûlé. Je ne l'aime pas. Je vais être malade aussi. Goûtez-en!**
	(Pierre se lève et quitte la table.)
Monsieur Paquet:	**Je vais le goûter aussi... Oui. Il est brûlé. Janine et Pierre ont raison. Je ne l'aime pas.**
	(Monsieur Paquet se lève et quitte la table.)
Monsieur Richy:	**Moi, je vais le goûter maintenant... Ce ragoût est délicieux! Il est bien cuit, comme le ragoût de ma mère. Bien cuit! Excellent... Chérie, pourqoi ne fais-tu pas un ragoût si bien cuit aussi?**
Madame Richy:	**Tu as raison, chéri. La prochaine fois je vais le faire trop cuire. Je vais le brûler pour toi et tu peux le manger seul. Tiens! Mange toute la cocotte!**
	(Madame Richy se lève. Monsieur Richy reste seul à la table avec la cocotte de ragoût brûlé devant lui.)
	(Madame Paquet rentre dans la salle à manger avec le dessert.)
Madame Paquet:	**Alors, est-ce que tout le monde aime mon ragoût? J'ai un dessert que j'ai fait aussi. Qui veut une crème brûlée? Goûtez-en!**

VOCABULAIRE

à couvert   covered

à table   to (at) the table, come to the table!

l'ail   *n. m.,* garlic; **une gousse d'ail** a clove of garlic

aime   *v. form of* aimer; **Je ne l'aime pas!** I don't like it!

ajouter   *v.,* to add

avoir faim   *v.,* to be hungry; **avoir raison** to be right; **J'ai grand faim** I'm very hungry; **Janine et Pierre ont raison!** Janine and Peter are right!

blanc   *m.,* **blanche** *f., adj.,* white

bouillir   *v.,* to boil

brûler   *v.,* to burn; **brûlé** burned; **ne le brûlez pas!** don't burn it!

le céleri   *n.,* celery; **le blanc de céleri** celery stalk

chacun   *pron.,* each one; **à chacun son goût** to each his/her own (taste)

la chance   *n.,* chance, luck; **bonne chance!** good luck!

chaud *m.,* **chaude** *f., adj.,* hot

la cocotte   *n.,* the stewing pot; **toute la cocotte** the whole pot

comment   *adv.,* how

connaît   *v. form of* **connaître** to know (someone), to be acquainted with (someone); **Est-ce que Pierre connaît Madeleine?** Does Peter know Madeleine? *(pres. indicative):* **je connais, tu connais, il (elle) connaît, nous connaissons, vous connaissez, ils (elles) connaissent**

la couche   *n.,* layer

couper   *v.,* to cut; **coupé** sliced

la crème brûlée   crème brûlée (a custard dessert with caramelized sugar on top)

la cuillère   *n.,* the spoon; **cuillère à soupe** soup spoon

cuire   *v.,* to cook; **cuit** cooked; **cuisson** cooking time; **bien cuit** well done (cooked); **trop cuit** overdone (overcooked)

dégoûtant   *adj.,* disgusting, revolting

devant   *prep.,* in front of; **devant lui** in front of him

disposer   *v.,* to dispose, to arrange; **en disposant** arranging

doucement   *adv.,* gently (low flame)

en   *partitive,* some; **goûtez-en!** taste some!

épais   *m.,* **épaisse** *f., adj.,* thick

la faim   *n.,* hunger; **avoir faim** to be hungry

faire bouillir   *v.,* to boil; **faire trop cuire** to overcook

la farine   *n.,* flour

goûter   *v.,* to taste; **le goût** the taste; **Qui veut en goûter?** Who wants to taste some? **Goûtez-en!** Taste some!

le gramme   *n.,* the gram (metric unit of measurement); 1 gram equals about .035 ounce; 500 grams equal about 1.1 lbs.; 300 grams equal about 10 oz.

gros *m.,* **grosse** *f., adj.,* big, fat, large

hacher   *v.,* to chop (up); **haché** chopped

irlandais *m.,* **irlandaise** *f., adj.,* Irish; **à l'irlandaise** Irish style

le kilogramme   *n.,* kilogram (1,000 grams; 1 kilo equals about 2.2 lbs.)

laisser   *v.,* to let, to allow

la lamelle   *n.* the thin slice

malade   *adj.,* sick

le mélange   *n.,* the mixture

mettez   *v. form of* **mettre** (to put, to place)

le morceau   *n.,* the piece, morsel

le mouton   *n.,* the mutton

l'oignon   *n. m.,* the onion

la page   *n.,* the page; **page d'en face** opposite page

pendant   *prep.,* during; **pendant que** *conj.,* while

peux   *v. form of* **pouvoir; tu peux commencer** you can begin

le poivre   *n.,* the pepper

la pomme de terre   *n.,* the potato

prochain *m.,* **prochaine** *f., adj.,* next; **la prochaine fois** the next time

le ragoût   *n.,* the stew

la raison   *n.,* the reason; **avoir raison** to be right

la recette   *n.,* the recipe

remuer   *v.,* to stir

le sel   *n.,* the salt

sent   *v. form of* **sentir** (to smell, to feel); **il sent très bon!** it smells very good!

servir   *v.,* to serve; **je vais le servir maintenant** I'm going to serve it now

seul   *m.,* **seule** *f., adj.,* alone

tiens!   *exclam.,* here!

un tiers   one-third

vas-y!   go to it!

veux   *v. form of* **vouloir** (to want); **si tu veux** if you want

le voisin, la voisine   *n.,* the neighbor

EXERCISES

Review the story and vocabulary before starting these exercises.

I.   **Answer the following questions in complete sentences. They are based on the story "À chacun son goût."**

1. Qui a servi le dîner ce soir?

_____

2. Pour qui a-t-il servi le dîner?

_____

3. Qui commence à goûter le ragoût?

_____

4. Qui aime le ragoût?

_____

5. Pourquoi aime-t-il le ragoût?

_____

6. Qui a fait le ragoût?

_____

_____

II. **Answer the following questions in complete sentences. They are personal questions and require answers of your own.**

1. Aimez-vous manger du ragoût?

_____

2. Savez-vous faire un ragoût?

_____

3. Aimez-vous le ragoût brûlé?

_____

III. **Comment dit-on en français . . . ?** Find these statements in the story and write them in French.

1. And how! It smells very good. I'm very hungry.

_____

2. Janine is right. It's burned. I don't like it. Taste some!

_____

3. I'm going to taste it.

_____

4. Mrs. Paquet comes back into the dining room with the dessert.

_____

5. Does everybody like my stew? I have a dessert that I made also. Who wants a crème brûlée? Taste some!

_____

_____

STRUCTURES DE LA LANGUE

A. Direct object pronouns

	Singular			Plural
me or **m'**	me		**nous**	us
te or **t'**	you *(familiar)*		**vous**	you *(sing. polite or plural)*
le or **l'**	him, it ⎫		**les**	them *(persons or things)*
la or **l'**	her, it ⎭ *person or thing*			

RULES AND OBSERVATIONS:

1. A direct object **pronoun** takes the place of a direct object **noun**.

2. A direct object noun ordinarily comes after the verb, but a direct object pronoun is ordinarily placed *in front of* the verb.

3. The vowel **e** in **me**, **te**, **le** and the vowel **a** in **la** drop and an apostrophe is added if the verb right after it starts with a vowel or a silent *h*; e.g., **je l'aime**. (I like it.)

4. You might say that the direct object "receives" the action of the verb.

5. Study the direct object pronouns in the above box and the model sentences in the boxes below.

B. Direct object pronoun referring to a thing in the present indicative

The noun as direct object of the verb.	The pronoun in place of the noun.
(a) **Janine lit le poème.**	(a) **Janine le lit.**
Janine is reading the poem.	*Janine is reading it.*
(b) **Pierre lit la lettre.**	(b) **Pierre la lit.**
Peter is reading the letter.	*Peter is reading it.*
(c) **Janine apprend le poème.**	(c) **Janine l'apprend.**
Janine is learning the poem.	*Janine is learning it.*
(d) **Pierre écrit la lettre.**	(d) **Pierre l'écrit.**
Peter is writing the letter.	*Peter is writing it.*
(e) **Janine lit les poèmes.**	(e) **Janine les lit.**
Janine is reading the poems.	*Janine is reading them.*

RULES AND OBSERVATIONS:

1. The direct object pronoun must agree in gender and number with the noun it is replacing. Gender means masculine or feminine. Number means singular or plural.

2. Actually, what you do is drop the noun direct object. The definite article that remains becomes the pronoun direct object. Put it *in front of* the verb. If the verb starts with a vowel or a mute *h*, drop the **e** in **le** and the **a** in **la** and add an apostrophe.

(a) From: **Janine lit le poème.** You get: **Janine le lit.**	Janine lit le poème.
(b) From: **Pierre lit la lettre.** You get: **Pierre la lit.**	Pierre lit la lettre.
(c) From: **Janine apprend le poème.** You get: **Janine l'apprend.**	Janine apprend le poème.
(d) From: **Pierre écrit la lettre.** You get: **Pierre l'écrit.**	Pierre écrit la lettre.
(e) From: **Janine lit les poèmes.** You get: **Janine les lit.**	Janine lit les poèmes.

C. Direct object pronoun referring to a person in the present indicative

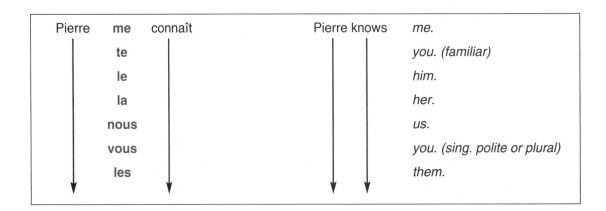

Pierre	**me**	connaît		Pierre knows	*me.*
	te				*you. (familiar)*
	le				*him.*
	la				*her.*
	nous				*us.*
	vous				*you. (sing. polite or plural)*
	les				*them.*

RULES AND OBSERVATIONS:

1. Direct object pronouns, whether they refer to persons or things, are ordinarily placed *in front of* the verb.

2. If the verb is negative, put **ne** *in front of the direct object pronoun* and **pas** *after* the verb, as in the examples in this box.

Pierre	ne **me**	connaît pas.		Peter	does	not	know	*me.*
	ne **te**	pas.						*you. (familiar)*
	ne **le**	pas.						*him.*
	ne **la**	pas.						*her.*
	ne **nous**	pas.						*us.*
	ne **vous**	pas.						*you. (sing. polite or plural)*
	ne **les**	pas.						*them.*

D. Direct object pronoun in the affirmative and negative command

Affirmative command		Negative command	
with noun direct object	with pronoun direct object	with noun direct object	with pronoun direct object
Apprenez le poème!	**Apprenez-le!**	N'apprenez pas le poème.	**Ne l'apprenez pas!**
Écrivez la lettre!	**Écrivez-la!**	N'écrivez pas la lettre.	**Ne l'écrivez pas!**
Étudiez les leçons!	**Étudiez-les!**	N'étudiez pas les leçons.	**Ne les étudiez pas!**

RULES AND OBSERVATIONS:

1. In the affirmative command, a direct object pronoun is placed *right after* the verb and joined with a hyphen.

2. In the negative command, a direct object pronoun is placed *in front of* the verb, where it ordinarily goes.

3. In the negative command, the **ne** is placed *in front of* the direct object pronoun and the **pas** *after* the verb.

E. Direct object pronoun as object of an infinitive

(a) **Monsieur Richy veut goûter le ragoût.** ⟶ **Monsieur Richy veut le goûter.**

(Mr. Richy wants to taste the stew.) *(Mr. Richy wants to taste it.)*

(b) **Janine veut apprendre le poème.** ⟶ **Janine veut l'apprendre.**

(Janine wants to learn the poem.) *(Janine wants to learn it.)*

(c) **Pierre ne veut pas écrire la lettre.** ⟶ **Pierre ne veut pas l'écrire.**

(Peter does not want to write the letter.) *(Peter does not want to write it.)*

RULES AND OBSERVATIONS:

1. A pronoun as object of an infinitive is placed *in front* of the infinitive.

2. In a negative statement with a pronoun as object of an infinitive, **ne** is placed in front of the verb and **pas** after it (as is usual) and the pronoun as object of the infinitive still remains in front of the infinitive.

3. The point is that the verb can be made negative and it has nothing to do with the logical position of the pronoun as object of an infinitive.

F. Direct object pronoun with a verb in the passé composé

The noun as direct object of the verb.	The pronoun in place of the noun.
(a) **Marie a préparé le dîner.**	(a) **Elle l'a préparé.**
(Mary prepared the dinner.)	*(She prepared it.)*
(b) **Robert a préparé la salade.**	(b) **Il l'a préparée.**
(Robert prepared the salad.)	*(He prepared it.)*
(c) **Jean a préparé les dîners.**	(c) **Il les a préparés.**
(John prepared the dinners.)	*(He prepared them.)*
(d) **Anne a préparé les salades.**	(d) **Elle les a préparées.**
(Anne prepared the salads.)	*(She prepared them.)*

RULES AND OBSERVATIONS:

1. The verb form **a préparé** is in the passé composé, third person, singular tense. Review how to form the passé composé in Work Unit 12.

2. You still put the direct object pronoun *in front of* the verb form (**a préparé**), just as you put it *in front of* the simple verb form in the present indicative. Review the position of the direct object pronoun in the present indicative in section **B**.

3. There is one new thing to be learned here: the past participle (**préparé**) of the verb in the passé composé must agree in gender (masculine or feminine) and number (singular or plural) with the *preceding* direct object pronoun, if there is one.

4. If the *preceding* direct object pronoun is **le** (masculine, singular), no agreement is required on the past participle.

5. If the *preceding* direct object pronoun is **la** (feminine, singular), you must add **e** to the past participle.

6. If the *preceding* direct object pronoun is **les** (masculine, plural), you must add **s** to the past participle.

7. If the *preceding* direct object pronoun is **les** (feminine, plural), you must add **es** to the past participle.

8. To sum it up: There must be an agreement in both gender and number in the past participle of a verb conjugated with **avoir** with the *preceding* direct object pronoun if there is one. No agreement if the direct object is a *noun* and it follows the verb. Compare the column on the right and the column on the left in the box on this page.

9. A reminder: When we conjugate a verb with **être**, there is an agreement between the past participle and the subject (e.g., **Janine est allée au théâtre**). Review sections **B** and **C** in Work Unit 12.

G. Meanings and positions of **en** as an object pronoun

(a)	Avez-vous **du café?**	Oui, j'**en** ai.
	(Have you *any coffee?*) (Have you *some coffee?*)	(Yes, I have *some* [*of it*].)
(b)	Buvez-vous **de l'eau?**	Oui, j'**en** bois.
	(Do you drink *any water?*)	(Yes, I drink *some*.)
(c)	Mangez-vous **de la glace?**	Oui, j'**en** mange.
	(Do you eat *any ice cream?*)	(Yes, I eat *some*.)
(d)	Mangez-vous **des pommes?**	Oui, j'**en** mange.
	(Do you eat *any apples?*)	(Yes, I eat *some*.)
(e)	Avez-vous **des soeurs?**	Oui, j'**en** ai deux.
	(Do you have *any sisters?*)	(Yes, I have two [*of them*].)
(f)	Vient-il **de Paris?**	Oui, il **en** vient.
	(Does he come *from Paris?*)	(Yes, he comes *from there*.)
(g)	Avez-vous peur **des serpents?**	Oui, j'**en** ai peur.
	(Are you afraid *of snakes?*)	(Yes, I'm afraid *of them*.)
(h)	Buvez **du café!**	Buvez-**en!**
	(Drink *some coffee!*)	(Drink *some!*)
(i)	Ne buvez pas **de café!**	N'**en** buvez pas!
	(Don't drink *any coffee!*)	(Don't drink *any* [*of it*]*!*)

RULES AND OBSERVATIONS:

1. The pronoun **en** has more than one translation in English, as you can see from the model sentences in the box.

2. **En** is used to replace a noun preceded by the preposition **de** or any combination of **de** (e.g., **du, de l', de la, des**).

3. **En** is used to refer to persons or things if the noun is used in a partitive sense.

4. **En** is used to refer to places and things but not to persons, if the noun is not used in a partitive sense. See (f) and (g) in section **G**.

5. In the affirmative imperative, **en** is placed *right after* the verb and joined with a hyphen. In the negative imperative, **en** is placed in front of the verb, where it is ordinarily placed, e.g., **Goûtez-en!** (Taste some!), **N'en goûtez pas!** (Don't taste any!)

EXERCISES

I. Change the following sentences by substituting a pronoun as object of the verb in place of the noun object. Rewrite the entire sentence.

Model: **Janine lit *le poème.***　　　You write: **Janine le lit.**
(Janine is reading the poem.)　　　　　　　(Janine is reading it.)

1. Pierre lit *la lettre.*

_____

2. Janine écrit *la leçon.*

_____

3. Michel apprend *l'espagnol.*

_____

4. Christophe fait *les devoirs.*

_____

5. Alexandre écoute *la musique.*

_____

6. Yolande prononce *le mot.*

_____

7. Théodore voit *l'hôtel.*

_____

8. Monique dit *la phrase.*

_____

9. Joséphine attend *l'autobus.*

_____

10. Anne mange *les gâteaux.*

_____

II. Answer the following questions in the affirmative, substituting a pronoun as object of the verb in place of the noun object. Also, substitute a pronoun in place of the noun subject. Rewrite the entire sentence.

   Model: **Janine écrit-elle *la leçon*?**   You write: **Oui, elle l'écrit.**
           (Is Janine writing the lesson?)   (Yes, she is writing it.)

1. Monique dit-elle *la phrase*?

   _____

2. Joséphine attend-elle *l'autobus*?

   _____

3. Pierre lit-il *la lettre*?

   _____

4. Michel mange-t-il *les gâteaux*?

   _____

5. Yolande écoute-t-elle *la musique*?

   _____

III. Answer the following questions in the negative, substituting a pronoun as object of the verb in place of the noun object. Also, substitute a pronoun in place of the noun subject. Rewrite the entire sentence.

   Model: **Est-ce que Janine boit le**   You write: **Non, elle ne le boit pas.**
           jus d'orange?
           (Is Janine drinking the   (No, she is not drinking it.)
           orange juice?)

1. Est-ce que Pierre mange la saucisse?

   _____

2. Est-ce que Joséphine prononce le mot?

   _____

3. Est-ce qu'Henri aime le saucisson?

   _____

4. Est-ce que Georges lit la lettre?

   _____

5. Est-ce que Georgette apporte les gâteaux?

   _____

IV. Answer the following questions in complete sentences in the affirmative, substituting a direct object pronoun for the noun object.

Model: **Apprenez-vous le français**   You write: **Oui, je l'apprends**
         maintenant?   **maintenant.**
         (Are you learning French now?)   (Yes, I am learning it now.)

1. Comprenez-vous la leçon aujourd'hui?

_____

2. Dites-vous toujours la vérité?

_____

3. Faites-vous les devoirs maintenant?

_____

4. Lisez-vous le journal tous les jours?

_____

5. Écrivez-vous la phrase en ce moment?

_____

V. Answer the following questions in the affirmative in complete sentences, substituting a direct object pronoun for the noun object. Also, substitute a pronoun for the noun subject.

Model: **Est-ce que Pierre connaît**   You write: **Oui, il la connaît.**
         Madeleine?
         (Does Peter know Madeleine?)   (Yes, he knows her.)

1. Est-ce que Janine connaît Monique?

_____

2. Est-ce que Monique connaît Robert?

_____

3. Est-ce que Robert connaît Pierre et Hélène?

_____

4. Est-ce que Marie connaît Monsieur et Madame Paquet?

_____

5. Est-ce qu'Henri connaît Anne et Françoise?

_____

VI. Answer the following questions in the affirmative.

Model: **Est-ce qu'elle vous voit?**   You write: **Oui, elle me voit.**
         (Does she see you?)   (Yes, she sees me.)

1. Est-ce qu'elle vous connaît?

_____

2. Est-ce qu'il te voit?

_____

3. Est-ce qu'elle nous aime?

_____

4. Est-ce qu'ils les attendent?

_____

5. Est-ce qu'il l'adore?

_____

VII. Answer the following questions in the affirmative.

    Model: **Est-ce que vous m'aimez bien?**   You write: **Oui, je vous aime bien.**
        (Do you like me?)   (Yes, I like you.)

1. Est-ce que tu m'aimes bien?

_____

2. Est-ce que vous l'aimez bien aussi?

_____

3. Est-ce que tu l'aimes bien aussi?

_____

4. Est-ce qu'il vous aime bien?

_____

5. Est-ce qu'elle vous aime bien aussi?

_____

VIII. Answer the following questions in the negative.

    Model: **Est-ce que vous m'aimez?** You write: **Non, je ne vous aime pas.**
        (Do you love me?)   (No, I do not love you.)

1. Est-ce que tu m'aimes?

_____

2. Est-ce qu'il vous aime?

_____

3. Est-ce que vous l'aimez aussi?

_____

4. Est-ce qu'il t'aime?

_____

5. Est-ce qu'elle vous aime?

_____

IX. **For each statement write a response in the affirmative imperative. Use a pronoun object in place of the noun object. Review the imperative in Work Units 10 and 11.**

Model: **Je veux apprendre le poème!**   You write: **Bon! Alors, apprenez-le!**
(I want to learn the poem!)   (Good! Then learn it!)

1. Je veux écrire la lettre!

_____

2. Je veux étudier les leçons!

_____

3. Je veux lire le livre!

_____

4. Je veux boire le lait!

_____

5. Je veux faire les devoirs!

_____

X. **For each statement write a response in the negative imperative. Use a pronoun object in place of the noun object. Review the imperative in Work Units 10 and 11.**

Model: **Je ne veux pas apprendre**   You write: **Bon! Alors, ne l'apprenez**
le poème!   **pas!**
(I don't want to learn the poem!)   (Good! Then don't learn it!)

1. Je ne veux pas écrire la lettre!

_____

2. Je ne veux pas étudier les leçons!

_____

3. Je ne veux pas lire le livre!

_____

4. Je ne veux pas boire le lait!

_____

5. Je ne veux pas faire les devoirs!

_____

XI. **Change the following sentences by substituting a pronoun as object of the infinitive in place of the noun object. Rewrite the entire sentence.**

Model: **Janine veut lire *la lettre*.**   You write: **Janine veut la lire.**
(Janine wants to read the letter.)   (Janine wants to read it.)

1. Pierre veut lire *le livre.*

_____

2. Madeleine veut apprendre *le poème.*

_____

3. Paul ne veut pas écrire *la lettre.*

_____

4. Philippe ne veut pas manger *la saucisse.*

_____

5. Gertrude ne veut pas apporter *les gâteaux.*

_____

XII. **Answer the following questions in the affirmative, substituting en as a pronoun object of the verb in place of the words indicated.**

     Model: **Avez-vous du café?**   You write: **Oui, j'en ai.**
             (Do you have any coffee?)   (Yes, I have some.)

1. Avez-vous *du lait?*

_____

2. Buvez-vous *de l'eau?*

_____

3. Mangez-vous *de la glace?*

_____

4. Mangez-vous *des pommes?*

_____

5. Avez-vous *des soeurs?*

_____

XIII. **Answer the following questions in the negative, substituting en as a pronoun object of the verb in place of the words indicated.**

     Model: **Avez-vous du vin?**   You write: **Non, je n'en ai pas.**
             (Do you have any wine?)   (No, I don't have any.)

1. Avez-vous *du café?*

_____

2. Avez-vous *de l'eau?*

_____

3. Avez-vous *de la glace?*

_____

4. Avez-vous *des gâteaux?*

_____

5. Avez-vous *des frères?*

_____

XIV. For each statement write a response in the affirmative imperative, substituting **en** in place of the words indicated. Review the imperative in Work Units 10 and 11.

Model: **Je veux boire *du café*!**   You write: **Bon! Alors, buvez-en!**
(I want to drink some coffee!)   (Good! Then drink some!)

1. Je veux boire *du lait!*

_____

2. Je veux manger *du gâteau!*

_____

3. Je veux écrire *des lettres!*

_____

4. Je veux boire *de l'eau!*

_____

5. Je veux manger *de la salade!*

_____

XV. For each statement write a response in the negative imperative, substituting **en** in place of the words indicated. Review the imperative in Work Units 10 and 11.

Model: **Je ne veux pas boire *de café*!**   You write: **Bon! Alors, n'en buvez pas!**
(I don't want to drink any coffee!)   (Good! Then don't drink any!)

1. Je ne veux pas boire *de vin!*

_____

2. Je ne veux pas manger *de gâteau!*

_____

3. Je ne veux pas écrire *de lettres!*

_____

XVI. Change the following sentences in the passé composé by substituting a pronoun as object of the verb in place of the noun object. Rewrite the entire sentence. Watch for agreement of the past participle with a preceding direct object pronoun.

Model: **Pierre a préparé *la leçon*.**   You write: **Pierre l'a préparée.**
(Peter prepared the lesson.)   (Peter prepared it.)

1. Madame Paquet a préparé *le dîner.*

_____

2. Monsieur Richy a mangé *le ragoût.*

_____

3. Pierre a servi *le dîner.*

_____

4. Janine a préparé *les devoirs.*

_____

5. Monsieur Paquet a préparé *les salades.*

_____

XVII. Answer the following questions in the affirmative, substituting a pronoun as object of the verb in place of the noun object. Also, substitute a pronoun in place of the noun subject. Rewrite the entire sentence. Watch for agreement on the past participle!

> Model: **Est-ce que Pierre a**   You write: **Oui, il l'a préparée.**
> **préparé *la salade?***
> (Did Peter prepare the salad?)   (Yes, he prepared it.)

1. Est-ce que Pierre a servi *le dîner?*

_____

2. Est-ce que Madame Paquet a préparé *le dîner?*

_____

3. Est-ce que Monsieur Richy a mangé *le ragoût?*

_____

4. Est-ce que Janine a écrit *la lettre?*

_____

5. Est-ce que Christophe a fait *les devoirs?*

_____

XVIII. Answer the following questions in the negative, substituting a pronoun as object of the verb in place of the noun object. Also, substitute a pronoun in place of the noun subject. Rewrite the entire sentence. Watch for agreement of the past participle!

> Model: **Est-ce que Pierre a préparé**   You write: **Non, il ne l'a pas**
> **le dîner?**   **préparé.**
> (Did Peter prepare the dinner?)   (No, he did not prepare it.)

1. Est-ce que Guy a préparé *la salade?*

_____

2. Est-ce que Pierre a fait *le dîner?*

_____

3. Est-ce que Janine a lu *le poème?*

_____

4. Est-ce que Madame Richy a mangé *le ragoût?*

_____

5. Est-ce que Robert a fait *les devoirs?*

_____

XIX. Appreciating French Sculpture. Proficiency in Speaking and Writing.

Situation: You are at the Musée Rodin in Paris admiring a work of art by the French sculptor Auguste Rodin. The Rodin Museum in Philadelphia also has many sculptures by Rodin.

Look at the photograph below. Make three statements about it. Then write what you said. You may use your own ideas and words and/or the following: **Cette oeuvre de Rodin est superbe/**_This work by Rodin is superb._ **Les hommes sont tristes parce qu'ils souffrent beaucoup/**_The men are sad because they are suffering a great deal._ **Ils n'ont pas de liberté/**_They don't have any freedom._

Les Bourgeois de Calais *(The Burghers of Calais)* by Auguste Rodin, French sculptor.
Reprinted with permission of Michael Nicholson / The Corbis Collection.

XX. Talking to an Animal or Pet. Proficiency in Speaking and Writing.

Situation: The little girl in the picture on the next page seems to be talking to the cow. She is holding a pail in her hand/**Elle tient un seau à la main.**

What do you suppose she is saying to the cow? You may use your own ideas and words and/or the following: **Salut, mon amie!/**_Hello, my friend!_ **J'aime le lait/**_I like milk._ **As-tu du lait pour moi aujourd'hui?/**_Do you have any milk for me today?_

Make at least three statements in French that the little girl might say to the cow. Then write what you said on the lines below. Note that when we talk to an animal or pet in French, we use the familiar **tu** form. **La vache** is the word for cow.

1. _____

2. _____

3. _____

As-tu du lait pour moi? *(Have you any milk for me?)*

XXI. Dinner Talk. Proficiency in Speaking, Reading, and Writing.

Situation: Monsieur and Madame Dufy are dinner guests at your home.

In this guided conversation, you are providing the needed French words on the blank lines. This gives you practice to say what someone else would say. You may use your own ideas and words or follow the suggested words under the blank lines. Later, write what you said on the lines.

Mme Dufy:	**La salade est délicieuse. Qui l'a préparée?**
Janine:	_____
	My brother Peter prepared it.
M. Dufy:	**Les pommes de terre sont vraiment excellentes. Qui les a préparées?**
Pierre:	_____
	Me/**Moi.** I prepared them.
M. Paquet:	**Janine, veux-tu un peu de salade?**
Janine:	_____
	No, thank you, Dad. I don't want any [of it].
Mme Paquet:	**Tu n'en veux pas, Janine? Pourquoi?**
Janine:	_____
	I already ate some [of it]./**J'en ai déjà mangé.**
Mme Dufy:	_____
	_____
	I would like a cup of tea with the dessert, please. I don't drink any coffee./**J'aimerais une tasse de thé avec le dessert, s'il vous plaît.**
Mme Paquet:	**Avec citron ou crème?**/With lemon or cream?
Mme Dufy:	_____
	Lemon, please, if there is any/**s'il y en a.**

223

Mme Paquet: _____

Peter, go into the kitchen, please/**s'il te plaît.** The lemon is on the table.

Pierre: _____

Yes, Mom. Right away/**Tout de suite.**

Après quelques minutes/After a few minutes

Pierre: _____

Mom, there isn't any lemon on the table in the kitchen/**Maman, il n'y a pas de citron ...**

Mme Dufy: **Ce n'est pas important. Merci tout de même, Pierre**/Thank you anyway, Peter.

XXII. Snack Time. Proficiency in Speaking, Reading, and Writing.

Situation: You and some friends are having afternoon snacks at your kitchen table.

In this guided conversation, you are providing the needed French words on the blank lines. This gives you practice to say what someone else would say. The familiar form **tu** is used in this conversation because the participants are all friends. You may use your own ideas and words or follow the suggested words under the blank lines. Then, switch roles with your friends.

Pierre: **Raymond, passe-moi la pizza, s'il te plaît.**

Raymond: _____

Okay. Here it is/**La voici.**

Pierre: **Robert, tu n'en manges pas. Tu ne l'aimes pas?**

Robert: _____

No, I don't like it.

Pierre: _____

Why not?/**Pourquoi pas?**

Robert: **C'est brûlé. Et le fromage est trop élastique**/And the cheese is too elastic. **C'est gommeux**/It's gummy.

Janine: _____

_____

That makes me laugh!/**Ça me fait rire!** He thinks the cheese is too elastic and gummy! He doesn't like to eat rubber bands!/**(les élastiques).**

Robert: _____

Tell me, Peter, did you do the biology assignments **(les devoirs de biologie)** for tomorrow?

Janine: _____

No. He didn't do them.

Monique: **Pierre, passe-moi les hamburgers, s'il te plaît.**

Pierre: **Les voici. Robert, tu n'aimes pas les hamburgers?**

Robert: _____

No. I don't like them. I don't eat them. I don't like fast food/ **la cuisine rapide.**

Monique: Qui a apporté les pâtisseries?

Pierre: _____

Robert brought them.

Robert: _____

I like pastries. I'm going to eat them all/**tous.**

Metropolitain (entrance to subway).

XXIII.   Appreciating French Art. Proficiency in Speaking and Writing.

Situation: You are at the Metropolitan Museum of Art in New York City admiring the painting **(le tableau)** *La Mort de Socrate (The Death of Socrates)* by the great French artist Louis David. He was the head of the neoclassical school of painting **(le chef de l'école néo-classique).**

The scene shows Socrates, a famous philosopher of Ancient Greece, on a bed. He is being handed a cup of hemlock to drink. His philosophical and political ideas were contrary to those of the government. After his trial, he was condemned to die by drinking a goblet of hemlock **(une coupe de ciguë).**

Look at the picture below and tell us what is happening. Use your own words and ideas or the following in at least two short sentences. First, say them aloud; then write them on the lines. For example: **Socrate, grand philosophe grec, est condamné à mort à cause de ses idées philosophiques et politiques**/ Socrates, a great Greek philosopher, is condemned to die because of his philosophical and political ideas. **Il est sur un lit**/He is on a bed. **Un homme lui donne une coupe de ciguë à boire**/A man is giving him a goblet of hemlock to drink. **Le tableau est superbe.**

1. _____

2. _____

La Mort de Socrate (The Death of Socrates) by Louis David (1748–1825).
Reprinted with permission of Francis G. Mayer / The Corbis Collection.

Qui a mon téléphone portable? (Who has my cell phone?)

Work Unit 14
Indirect Object Pronouns, Including *y*

Janine lent her cell phone to a friend. Now she doesn't know where it is. Let's see how Janine finds her phone.

Prête à prêter

Ce matin, Janine a prêté son téléphone portable à son amie Suzanne. Suzanne avait besoin du portable pour téléphoner à son petit ami. Maintenant, Janine veut son téléphone portable pour téléphoner à sa mère. Elle va voir son amie Suzanne et elle lui dit:

Janine:	**Suzanne, je t'ai prêté mon téléphone portable à neuf heures du matin. Il est maintenant trois heures de l'après-midi et il faut que je téléphone à ma mère. Veux-tu me rendre mon portable, s'il te plaît?**
Suzanne:	**Je ne l'ai pas, Janine. Je l'ai donné à Monique. Va la voir. Je lui ai donné le portable.**
Janine:	**Monique, j'ai prêté mon portable à Suzanne et elle m'a dit que tu l'as maintenant. Je lui ai donné mon portable ce matin.**
Monique:	**Je ne l'ai pas, Janine. Je l'ai prêté à Mimi. Va la voir. Je lui ai donné le portable.**
	(Janine va voir Mimi.)
Janine:	**Mimi, as-tu mon téléphone portable? Tu l'as, je sais. Je l'ai prêté à Suzanne, elle l'a donné à Monique, et Monique m'a dit que tu l'as maintenant.**
Mimi:	**Oh! Le portable! Quel portable? Le portable avec appareil photo numérique?**
Janine:	**Oui. C'est ça.**
Mimi:	**Non. Je ne l'ai pas. Je l'ai donné à Raymond. Va le voir. Je lui ai donné le portable.**
	(Janine cherche Raymond. Elle ne le trouve pas. Janine va voir Paul, qui a un téléphone portable.)
Janine:	**Paul, pourrais-tu me prêter ton portable?**
Paul:	**Pas de problème, Janine. Vas-y!**
	(Janine prend le téléphone portable et elle compose son propre numéro de téléphone. C'est Raymond qui répond.)
Raymond:	**Allô. Ici Raymond.**
Janine:	**Raymond, c'est Janine. Rends-moi mon téléphone portable!**

VOCABULAIRE

l'ami *m.*, l'amie *f., n.*, the friend

l'appareil *m. n.* photo numérique digital camera

l'après-midi *m. n.*, afternoon; **de l'après-midi** in the afternoon (time)

le besoin *n.* need; **avoir besoin de (quelque chose)** to need (something)

écouter *v.*, to listen (to)

faut *v. form of* **falloir** to be necessary; **il faut que** it is necessary (that). This expression takes the subjunctive mood.

l' (**la** or **le** before vowel), *direct obj. pron.*, it

le *direct obj. pron.*, it

les *direct obj. pron.*, them

lui *indirect obj. pron.*, to her, to him

le matin *n.*, morning; **du matin** in the morning (time)

me *indirect obj. pron.*, to me

mes *poss. adj. pl.*, my

le portable *n.* the cell phone (short for **le téléphone portable**); can also mean laptop computer

prêt, prête *adj. m. f.*, ready

prêté *past part. of* **prêter** *v.* to lend

propre *adj.*, own; **son propre numéro (de téléphone)** her own (phone) number

rendre *v.*, to return (something), to give back; **rends-moi…** Give me back…

reprendre *v.*, to take back, get back

ses *poss. adj. pl.*, his, her

s'il te plaît please *(fam. use)*; **s'il vous plaît** *(polite use)*

te *indirect obj. pron.*, to you *(fam.)*

le téléphone portable cell phone

va la (le) voir go see her (him)

Vas-y! *v. form of* **aller** Go ahead!

EXERCISES

Review the story and vocabulary before starting these exercises.

I. **Answer the following questions in complete sentences. They are all based on the dialogue in this unit, "Prête à prêter."**

1. Qui a prêté son téléphone portable à Suzanne?

_____

2. Pourquoi Janine veut-elle reprendre son téléphone portable?

_____

3. Qui prête son téléphone portable à Janine?

_____

II. **Comment dit-on en français…?** Refer to the dialogue in this unit if you have to.

1. She said to me that you have it now.

_____

2. I don't have it. I gave it to Monique. Go see her.

_____

3. I gave the cell phone to Mimi. Mimi gave it to Raymond.

_____

4. I gave the cell phone to him. Go see him.

_____

III. Unscramble the French words listed below and write them in the appropriate squares.

1. BLATEROP

2. ENDERR

3. RÊTEP

4. RÈST

5. ETROCUE

6. REPROP

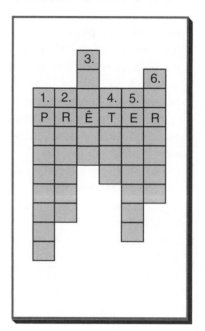

STRUCTURES DE LA LANGUE

A. Indirect object pronouns

	Singular		Plural
me or **m'**	to me	**nous**	to us
te or **t'**	to you (familiar)	**vous**	to you (sing. polite or plural)
lui	to him, to her, to it	**leur**	to them

RULES AND OBSERVATIONS:

1. An indirect object pronoun takes the place of an indirect object noun.

2. You might say that an indirect object "receives" the direct object because it is usually a matter of something "going" to someone (e.g., *to me, to you, to him, to her, to it, to us, to them*). Sometimes the *to* is not mentioned in English: *I am giving him the book*; what we really mean to say is, *I am giving the book to him.* Then, too, some verbs in French take an indirect object pronoun because the verb takes the preposition **à** (*to*); for example, **Je lui réponds** can be translated into English as *I am answering her (or) him*, or, *I am responding to her (or) to him.*

3. An indirect object pronoun is ordinarily placed *in front of* the verb.

4. Study the indirect object pronouns in the preceding box and the model sentences in the box below.

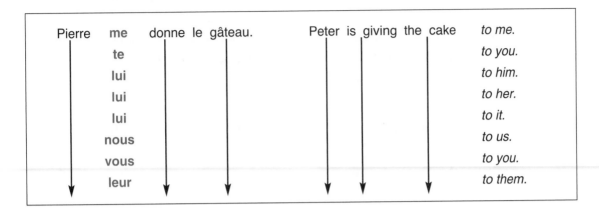

Pierre	me	donne le gâteau.	Peter is giving the cake	*to me.*
	te			*to you.*
	lui			*to him.*
	lui			*to her.*
	lui			*to it.*
	nous			*to us.*
	vous			*to you.*
	leur			*to them.*

5. To make the verb negative, put **ne** *in front of the indirect object pronoun* and **pas** after the verb, as you did for the direct object pronouns:

> **Pierre ne me donne pas le gâteau.**
>
> *(Peter is not giving the cake to me.)*

6. In the affirmative imperative, do the same as you did for the direct object pronouns. The indirect object pronoun is put *right after* the verb and joined with a hyphen:

> **Donnez-lui le gâteau!**   *(Give the cake to him/her.)*

7. In the affirmative imperative, **me** changes to **moi** when it is tacked on to the verb and joined with a hyphen:

> **Donnez-moi le gâteau!**   *(Give me the cake!)*

8. In the negative imperative, do the same as you did for the direct object pronouns. Put the indirect object pronoun *in front of* the verb, where it ordinarily goes:

> **Ne me donnez pas le gâteau!**   *(Don't give me the cake!)*
>
> **Ne lui donnez pas le gâteau!**   *(Don't give her/him the cake!)*

9. If the indirect object pronoun is the object of an infinitive, do the same as you did for the direct object pronouns. Put the indirect object pronoun *in front of* the infinitive:

> **Janine veut leur parler.**   *(Janine wants to talk to them.)*

10. Remember that there is *no agreement* between the past participle of a verb conjugated with **avoir** in the passé composé if there is an indirect object. However, *an agreement* (both in gender and in number) is *required if there is a preceding direct object*. Compare:

Je lui ai donné les disques.	**Je les ai donnés à Mimi.**
(I *gave* the records *to her.*)	(I *gave them* to Mimi.)

B. **Y** is an indirect object form that is used to refer to places or to things. It ordinarily replaces a noun preceded by the preposition **à**, **dans**, or **sur**:

(a) Allez-vous **à la bibliothèque**?   Oui, j'**y** vais.
(Are you going *to the library?*)   (Yes, I'm going *there.*)

(b) Les gants sont-ils **dans le tiroir**?   Oui, ils **y** sont.
(Are the gloves *in the drawer?*)   (Yes, they are *there.*)

(c) Est-ce que le chapeau est **sur la commode**?   Oui, il **y** est.
(Is the hat *on the dresser?*)   (Yes, it is *there.*)

(d) Aimez-vous aller **au cinéma**?   Oui, j'aime **y** aller.
(Do you like going *to the movies?*)   (Yes, I like going *there.*)

EXERCISES

Review the preceding material before starting these exercises.

I. Change the following sentences by substituting an indirect object pronoun in place of the nouns. Put the indirect object pronoun in its proper position. Rewrite the entire sentence.

Model: **Pierre donne le gâteau à Janine.**   You write: **Pierre lui donne le gâteau.**
(Peter is giving the cake to Janine.)   (Peter is giving the cake to her.)

1. Janine donne le journal *à Pierre.*

_____

2. Madeleine donne le livre *à Mathilde.*

_____

3. Gloria donne la fleur *à Hélène.*

_____

4. Robert donne la balle *aux garçons.*

_____

5. Monique donne les stylos *à Marie et à Henri.*

_____

II. **Answer the following questions in complete sentences, using an appropriate indirect object pronoun in place of the words in parentheses.**

A. Model: **A qui parlez-vous? (à la jeune fille)**   You write: **Je lui parle.**
To whom are you talking? (to the girl)   (I am talking to her.)

1. A qui parlez-vous? (à la femme)

_____

2. A qui parlez-vous? (au garçon)

_____

3. A qui parlez-vous? (à Madeleine)

_____

4. A qui parlez-vous? (à l'ami)

_____

5. A qui parlez-vous? (à Robert)

_____

B. Model: **A qui donnez-vous les fleurs?**   You write: **Je leur donne les fleurs.**
(aux femmes)
To whom are you giving the flowers?   (I am giving the flowers to them.)
(to the women)

1. A qui donnez-vous les gâteaux? (aux garçons)

_____

2. A qui donnez-vous les livres? (à Marie et à Robert)

_____

3. A qui donnez-vous le ragoût brûlé? (aux chiens)

_____

4. A qui donnez-vous les lettres? (à la mère et au père)

_____

5. A qui donnez-vous le jus? (à Janine et à Pierre)

_____

233

À qui donnez-vous le ragoût brûlé? (To whom are you giving the burned stew?)

III. **Answer the following questions in the affirmative using an indirect object pronoun in each answer.**

Model: **Est-ce que vous me parlez?** You write: **Oui, je vous parle.**

1. Est-ce que vous me parlez?

_____

2. Est-ce que vous lui parlez?

_____

3. Est-ce que vous nous parlez?

_____

IV. **For each statement write a response in the affirmative imperative. Use an indirect object pronoun in place of the words indicated.**

Model: **Je veux donner le ragoût à Pierre.**
(I want to give the stew to Peter.)

You write: **Bon! Alors, donnez-lui le ragoût!**
(Good! Then give him the stew!)

1. Je veux donner le gâteau *à Marie.*

_____

2. Je veux donner le parapluie *à la femme.*

_____

3. Je veux donner le bonbon *à l'enfant.*

_____

4. Je veux donner le jus de fruit *à Robert.*

_____

5. Je veux donner le ragoût brûlé *à Monsieur Richy.*

_____

V. **For each statement write a response in the negative imperative. Use an indirect object pronoun in place of the words indicated.**

Model: **Je ne veux pas donner les bonbons *aux enfants.***
(I don't want to give the candies to the children.)

You write: **Bon! Alors, ne leur donnez pas les bonbons!**
(Good! Then don't give them the candies!)

1. Je ne veux pas donner le chocolat *aux garçons.*

_____

2. Je ne veux pas donner les devoirs *à la maîtresse.*

_____

3. Je ne veux pas donner le billet *à Françoise.*

_____

VI. **For each statement write a response in the affirmative imperative. Use an indirect object pronoun in your response.**

Model: **Je veux vous parler.**
(I want to talk to you.)

You write: **Bon! Alors, parlez-moi!**
(Good! Then talk to me!)

1. Je veux vous parler.

_____

2. Je veux lui parler.

_____

3. Je veux leur parler.

_____

VII. For each statement write a response in the negative imperative. Use an indirect object pronoun in your response.

> Model: **Je ne veux pas vous parler.**   You write: **Bon! Alors, ne me parlez pas!**
> (I don't want to talk to you.)   (Good! Then don't talk to me!)

1. Je ne veux pas vous parler!

_____

2. Je ne veux pas lui parler!

_____

3. Je ne veux pas leur parler!

_____

VIII. Match the following.

1. He is giving the assignments to them.   _____ Elle me donne le gâteau.

2. She is giving him the hat.   _____ Il te donne le livre.

3. She is giving you the juice.   _____ Elle lui donne le chapeau.

4. She is giving me the cake.   _____ Il nous donne le chocolat.

5. He is giving you the book.   _____ Elle vous donne le jus.

6. He is giving us the chocolate.   _____ Il leur donne les devoirs.

IX. Answer the following questions in the affirmative using y in your answer to take the place of the words indicated.

> Model: **Allez-vous à la bibliothèque?**   You write: **Oui, j'y vais.**
> (Are you going to the library?)   (Yes, I am or I'm going there.)

1. Allez-vous *à la maison?*

_____

2. Allez-vous *au cinéma?*

_____

3. Allez-vous *à l'aéroport?*

_____

X. The words in the following boxes are scrambled. Unscramble them to find a meaningful sentence. Write the sentence on the line.

Model:

donne	me	ragoût
Pierre	**le**	

You write: **Pierre me donne le ragoût.**

1.

lui	parlez	Bon!	Alors,

2.

leur	parler
veut	Janine

1. _____

2. _____

XI. Providing and Obtaining Information. Proficiency in Speaking and Writing.

Situation: You are talking to your friend Anne on the telephone. You are trying to obtain information about the whereabouts of the CDs (**les disques compacts**, *m. n.*) you let her borrow in September. She is providing you with some information.

You may use your own ideas and words or follow the suggested words under the blank lines. Say your words aloud; then write them on the lines.

Vous: _____
_____
Anne, I lent you my CDs in the month of September and today is December first.

Anne: Oui, je sais. Je ne les ai pas.

Vous: _____
You don't have them? Where are they?

Anne: Je ne sais pas. Je les ai donnés à Suzanne. Va la voir.

Vous: _____
I can't go to see her. She is on vacation in Canada./Elle est en vacances au Canada.

Anne: Oh! Je sais maintenant! Suzanne les a donnés à Jacqueline. Elle les a.

Vous: _____
No. She does not have them. I talked to her yesterday.

Anne: Qu'est-ce qu'elle t'a dit?/What did she say to you?

Vous: _____
She told me that (que) you have them.

Anne: Elle t'a dit que je les ai? Impossible! Je ne les ai pas, je te dis.

Vous: _____
And I am telling you that I don't have them! Apparently my CDs are lost!/**Apparemment mes disques compacts sont perdus!** Good-bye! And have a nice day!/**Et passe une bonne journée!**

XII. Picture Interpretation. Proficiency in Speaking and Writing.

Respond orally in French to **A** and **B**. (Later, you may write your responses for intensive practice.)

A. Look at this picture of two people talking. Read the captions that describe what they are saying to each other. Do you find the pronoun **y** that you learned in this work unit? Do you notice that it is placed in front of the infinitive? What does the **y** refer to?

B. In at least ten words, describe to a friend what you see in the picture below.

XIII. Picture Interpretation. Proficiency in Speaking.

Situations A, B, C:

A. Look at the picture at the beginning of this work unit. Describe it in at least ten words.

B. Look at the following advertisement. In at least eleven words, state in French the name of the shop, what is sold there, something about their prices, when the shop is open, the address, telephone number, and any ideas of your own.

═══ **OMEGA** ═══

un magasin moderne

disques	vidéo-cassettes
cassettes	jeux vidéo

Ouvert tous les jours de midi à minuit
prix bas

29, rue des Amants, Paris   Tél. 42-34-84-56

C. Look at the picture on page 234. Describe it in at least twelve words. Make sure you use direct and indirect object nouns and pronouns. They are in this lesson and in previous work units.

XIV. Obtaining Information. Proficiency in Speaking and Writing.

First, say aloud the French words you plan to use; then write three sentences on the lines below.

Situation: In school, while walking to your next class, a friend stops you in the hall and says: **Où sont mes CDs?** (Where are my CDs?) **Je te les ai donnés la semaine passée** (I gave them to you last week). Respond to your friend by stating at least three things that happened to the CDs. You may use any or all of the following: **avoir, prêter, donner, aller, voir, les, lui, demander, penser.**

_____

_____

_____

_____

Place de la Concorde, Paris, France.

Qui suis-je?
Who am I?

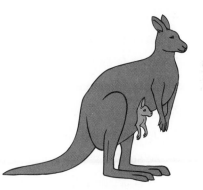

Qui suis-je?
Who am I?

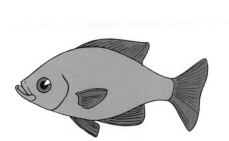

Qui suis-je?
Who am I?

Que suis-je?
What am I?

Qu'est-ce que je suis?
What am I?

241

Work Unit 15
Interrogative Pronouns

Have you ever guessed any riddles in English? In French? Here are fifteen riddles in French; some are easy, some are not so easy. The answers are upside down at the bottom of the riddles.

Quinze devinettes

1. Je porte toujours un chapeau mais je n'ai pas de tête. Que suis-je?

2. Je vole comme un oiseau. Qu'est-ce que je suis?

3. J'ai un cou très, très long et je peux voir les autres animaux de très haut. Qui suis-je?

4. Je suis toujours au milieu de Paris. Que suis-je?

5. J'habite dans l'eau. J'ai des yeux mais je n'ai pas de paupières. Qui suis-je?

6. J'ai des jambes et j'ai des bras mais je n'ai pas de mains. Qu'est-ce que je suis?

7. Je vais, je viens, je sors, je retourne, sans quitter ma maison. Qui suis-je?

8. Je n'ai pas de pieds et de jambes. J'ai seulement deux aiguilles. Que suis-je?

9. Je suis un animal qui porte mes petits enfants dans ma poche. Qui suis-je?

10. Je suis jaune dedans et blanc dessus. Qu'est-ce que je suis?

11. Quand je quitte la maison, je ne sors jamais par la porte et jamais par la fenêtre. Je sors par la cheminée. Que suis-je?

12. J'entre le premier dans la maison. Qu'est-ce que je suis?

13. Je peux traverser une vitre sans la casser. Que suis-je?

14. Je suis le plus sale de la maison. Qu'est-ce que je suis?

15. Je suis utile pour surfer, mais ne me mets pas dans l'eau! Que suis-je?

1. un champignon	6. un fauteuil	11. la fumée
2. un avion	7. une tortue	12. une clef
3. une girafe	8. une horloge	13. la lumière
4. la lettre "r"	9. un kangourou	14. un balai
5. un poisson	10. un oeuf	15. un ordinateur

VOCABULAIRE

l'aiguille   *n. f.*, the needle, hand of a clock

l'animal   *n. m.*, **les animaux** *pl.*, the animal, the animals

l'avion   *n. m.*, the airplane

le balai   *n.*, the broom

le bras   *n.*, the arm

casser   *v.*, to break; **sans la casser** without breaking it

le champignon   *n.*, the mushroom

la cheminée   *n.*, the chimney

la clef   *n.*, the key

le cou   *n.*, the neck

dedans   *adv.*, inside

dessus   *adv.*, on top, above

deviner   *v.*, to guess; **une devinette** a riddle

le fauteuil   *n.*, the armchair

la fenêtre   *n.*, the window

la fumée *n.,* the smoke
la girafe *n.,* the giraffe
habite *v. form of* **habiter** (to live, reside, inhabit)
haut *adv.,* high
l'horloge *n. f.,* the clock
jamais *adv.,* ever; **ne … jamais** never
la jambe *n.,* the leg
le kangourou *n.,* the kangaroo
le lait *n.,* the milk
la lumière *n.,* the light
la main *n.,* the hand
le milieu *n.,* the middle; **au milieu de** in the middle of
l'oeuf *n. m.,* the egg

la paupière *n.,* the eyelid
peux *v. form of* **pouvoir** (to be able, may, can); **je peux** I can
le pied *n.,* the foot
la poche *n.,* the pocket
le poisson *n.,* the fish
porte *v. form of* **porter** (to wear, carry)
que *interrog. pron.,* what
que suis-je? what am I?
qu'est-ce que je suis? what am I?
qui suis-je? who am I?
quitter *v.,* to leave; **sans quitter** without leaving

sale *adj.,* dirty, soiled; **le plus sale de la maison** the dirtiest in the house
sors *v. form of* **sortir** (to go out); **je sors** I go out; **je ne sors jamais** I never go out
suis *v. form of* **être** (to be); **je suis** I am
la tortue *n.,* the turtle
tourner *v.,* to turn, to turn sour
traverser *v.,* to cross, to go through
viens *v. form of* **venir** (to come); **je viens** I come
la vitre *n.,* the windowpane (glass)

EXERCISES

Review the preceding material before starting these exercises.

I.   **Fill in the blank lines after each picture by writing the French word for it. Use the indefinite article. They are based on the riddles in this unit.**

Model:

U N E   M A I S O N

1.___ ___ _____

4.   _____ _____

2.___ _____

5.   ___ _____

3._____ _____

243

II. **Complete the following statements by writing the appropriate words in French. They are based on the fifteen riddles in this unit.**

1. Je suis un kangourou. Je _____ mes petits enfants dans ma poche.

2. Je suis un poisson. J'ai des _____ , mais je _____ de paupières.

3. Je suis un balai et je _____ le plus sale de la maison.

4. Je suis un fauteuil. J'ai deux bras mais je _____ de mains.

5. Je suis une girafe. J'ai un cou très, très _____ et je _____ voir les autres animaux de très haut.

III. **Fill in the squares by writing the French words across for the English words in the list.**

1. ten

2. I am

3. he sells

4. giraffe

5. kangaroo

6. window

7. armchair

8. very

9. I can

10. fish

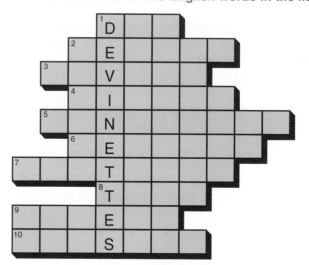

STRUCTURES DE LA LANGUE

A. Interrogative pronouns

1. Qui

1. **Qui** parle?	1. *Who* is talking?
2. **Qui** aimez-vous?	2. *Whom* do you love?
3. **À qui** parlez-vous?	3. *To whom* are you talking?
4. **De qui** parlez-vous?	4. *About whom* are you talking?

RULES AND OBSERVATIONS:

1. **Qui** is used as a subject. See example 1 in the above box.

2. **Qui** is used as a direct object and translated into English as *whom*. See example 2 in the above box.

3. **Qui** is used as an object of a preposition. See example 3 in the box above (**qui** is the object of the preposition *à*).

4. In example 4 in the box above, **qui** is used as the object of the preposition *de*.

5. The *i* in **qui** never drops. Note that **qui** can mean *who* or *whom*.

244

2. **Que** and **Qu'est-ce que**

1. **Que** mangez-vous?	1. *What* are you eating?
2. **Qu'est-ce que** vous mangez?	2. *What* are you eating?

RULES AND OBSERVATIONS:

1. **Que** is used as a direct object of a verb for things.

2. **Qu'est-ce que** can be used instead of **que** as direct object of a verb, but when you use it, keep the normal word order of what follows (i.e., subject plus verb). See example 2 in the above box.

3. The **e** in **que** drops if the word that follows begins with a vowel or silent *h* and an apostrophe replaces it.

EXERCISES

Review the preceding material before starting these exercises.

I.   Match the following.

1. De qui parlez-vous?	_____ Who is talking?
2. Que dites-vous?	_____ Whom do you love?
3. Qui aimez-vous?	_____ Whom are you talking to?
4. Qu'est-ce que vous mangez?	_____ About whom are you talking?
5. À qui parlez-vous?	_____ What are you eating?
6. Qui parle?	_____ What are you saying?

II. Fill in the missing words with either qui, que, or qu'est-ce que, as required.

1. _____ parle?	6. _____ vous mangez?
2. _____ est à la porte?	7. _____ dites-vous?
3. À _____ parlez-vous?	8. _____ vous dites?
4. De _____ parlez-vous?	9. _____ arrive?
5. _____ mangez-vous?	10. _____ faites-vous?

III. Riddles. Proficiency in Speaking.

Situations A and B:

A. Look at the five drawings in the picture at the beginning of this work unit. Answer the five questions.

B. Make up a riddle of your own in French and ask a friend to solve it. If your friend can't solve it, give a couple more hints. Or, select a riddle at the beginning of this work unit.

IV. Vocabulary Building. Proficiency in Writing.

Write the names of four animals that you could describe in a riddle.

1. _____   2. _____   3. _____   4. _____

V. Giving Something to Someone. Proficiency in Speaking and Writing.

Situation: You bought six cookies (**un biscuit**) in a pastry shop (**une pâtisserie**) and you plan to give them to six persons in your French class.

In the following guided conversation, first say aloud the words you have in mind. Then write your statements on the lines for practice, following the English words under them. You may change and extend this dialogue with your own ideas and words. Review the direct object pronouns in Work Unit 13 and the indirect object pronouns in Work Unit 14. Use the **tu** form with your friends and **vous** with your teacher.

Vous: _____

_____

I am giving a cookie to you, Claire, because you are a good person. Do you like cookies?

Claire: Oh, tu me donnes un biscuit! J'aime les biscuits. Je les adore. Merci!

Vous: _____

_____

Now I'm giving a cookie to Pierre. I am giving a cookie to him because he is my friend (**mon ami**).

Pierre: Pour moi? Merci beaucoup. J'aime les biscuits. Je les aime beaucoup.

Vous: _____

And now I'm offering (**j'offre**) a cookie to Catherine. I'm offering a cookie to her because she is pretty.

Catherine: Merci! Tu es aimable.

Vous: _____

Now I'm offering two cookies to them, to Gigi and Mimi, because they are very beautiful.

Gigi et Mimi: Pour nous? Tu es vraiment aimable. Nous les acceptons avec plaisir. Merci mille fois.

Vous: _____

I am giving a cookie to you (*polite, sing.* ***vous***), Madame Marin, because you are kind.

Mme Marin: Je te remercie beaucoup. Tu es bien généreux/généreuse. Qu'est-ce que je peux te donner?

Vous: _____

You can give me a good grade (**une bonne note**) because I'm talking in French!

Mme Marin: D'accord! Je te donne une bonne note!

VI. Dining Out. Proficiency in Speaking and Writing.

Situation: You are in a French restaurant having dinner. The waiter brought you a cup of tea instead of coffee. What would you say to him?

You may use your own words and ideas and/or the following: You brought me (**Vous m'avez apporté**) a cup of tea (**une tasse de thé**) instead of (**au lieu de**) coffee. Bring me a cup of coffee, please.

First, say your statements aloud; then write them on these lines:

_____

_____

VII. Look Who's Talking to Whom! Proficiency in Speaking and Writing.

Situation: You have been on the phone for about an hour. Your brother wants to call someone and he is pestering you by asking you one question after the next. You interrupt your telephone conversation every few seconds to answer his questions.

After you have finished answering his questions, you may practice writing what you said on the lines. You may add your own words and ideas to expand this conversation. Ask a classmate to play the role of your brother or, if you prefer, your sister. Use the **tu** form with your brother or sister.

Le frère: **Je veux téléphoner à un ami.**

Vous: _____

Don't you see that I'm talking to someone?

Le frère: **Oui, je vois que tu parles à quelqu'un. À qui parles-tu? Tu parles à Micheline?**

Vous: _____

No. I'm not talking to her.

Le frère: **Tu ne lui parles pas?**

Vous: _____

_____

I'm not talking to her this minute/**en ce moment.** I talked to her yesterday.

Le frère: **Tu parles à Marie et à Monique?**

Vous: _____

I'm not talking to them now. I talked to them this morning/**ce matin.**

Le frère: **À qui parles-tu?**

Vous: _____

I'm talking to you, to you!/**Je te parle, à toi!** Go away!/**Va-t'en!***

*Va-t'en is the 2nd pers., sing., familiar form, imperative of **s'en aller**/to go away.

Test 3

This test is based on Work Units 11 to 15. Review them before starting this test.

PART ONE   SPEAKING PROFICIENCY

Directions: Read the twelve situations given below. Take a few minutes to organize your thoughts about the words you are going to speak. Select ten of them.

1. **Situation:** You are playing guessing games at a party. Describe an object and then ask what it is.

2. **Situation:** A new student was transferred to your French class today. Her name is Debbie. Greet her and introduce yourself. Then tell her about the French guessing games you are playing in class.

3. **Situation:** Select an advertisement in a French newspaper or magazine in your French class. In a few words tell us what it is about.

4. **Situation:** You are looking at a picture of two children playing together. In a few words tell us something about them and what they are doing.

5. **Situation:** You are home from college for the Christmas holidays. Your friend Anne, who lives next door, is visiting you. You are talking about how to spend the day together. Make at least three statements in French.

6. **Situation:** As you are getting off a bus in Paris, a gentleman asks you for directions to get to the Opera House and the Café de la Paix. What would you say to him? Make at least three statements.

7. **Situation:** You are at a concert. During intermission, a friend of yours sees you, comes to you, and asks you how you like the concert. In two or more sentences, tell your friend what you think of it.

8. **Situation:** You are going out for the evening with a friend. You want to see a French movie but your friend wants to go to the theater. In two or more sentences, persuade your friend to see a French film with you.

9. **Situation:** Last night you went to the Opera House in Paris. In two or more sentences, tell us about it.

10. **Situation:** You are on a school trip in Paris with your classmates and Mr. Durand, your French teacher. Last night you returned very late to the hotel. Mr. Durand and the others were worried about you. In two or three sentences, explain where you went and what you did.

11. **Situation:** You are checking out of your hotel and you have been asked to answer a questionnaire of services provided. In two or more sentences, tell us about the hotel's services.

12. **Situation:** In three statements tell us how you spent yesterday evening.

PART TWO   LISTENING PROFICIENCY

Directions: Your teacher will read aloud four short paragraphs. Each one will contain only a few sentences. You will hear each paragraph twice. Then you will hear one question based on each. You will hear the question only once. It is printed below. Choose the best suggested answer and check the letter of your choice.

Selection Number 1

1. Qu'est-ce que c'est?

    A. une banane
    B. du lait
    C. de la glace
    D. un jus de fruit

Selection Number 2

2. À quelle heure sont-ils arrivés au théâtre?

    A. à sept heures et demie
    B. à huit heures
    C. à huit heures et quart
    D. à huit heures et demie

Selection Number 3

3. Qui a servi le dîner?

    A. Madame Paquet
    B. Pierre
    C. Monsieur Richy
    D. Monsieur Paquet

Selection Number 4

4. Pourquoi Janine veut-elle reprendre ses CDs?

    A. au mois de septembre
    B. le premier décembre
    C. pour les écouter pendant les fêtes de Noël
    D. pour aller voir son amie Suzanne

PART THREE   READING PROFICIENCY

Directions: In the following passage there are five blank spaces numbered 1 through 5. Each blank space represents a missing word. For each blank space, four possible completions are provided. Only one of them makes sense in the context of the passage.

First, read the passage in its entirety to determine its general meaning. Then read it a second time. For each blank space choose the completion that makes the best sense and is grammatically correct. Write its letter in the space provided.

Suzanne, je _____ ai prêté _____ CDs au mois de septembre et

1. A. te
   B. t'
   C. le
   D. les

2. A. mon
   B. ma
   C. mes
   D. ses

aujourd'hui c'est le premier décembre. Je veux _____ jouer pendant les fêtes

3. A. les
   B. leur
   C. lui
   D. la

de Noël. Veux-tu _____ rendre mes CDs, s'il te plaît?

4. A. le
   B. lui
   C. leur
   D. me

Je ne les ai pas, Janine. Je les ai _____ à Monique. Va la voir.

5. A. donné
   B. donnée
   C. donnés
   D. données

PART FOUR   WRITING PROFICIENCY

Directions: Of the twelve situations in Part One (Speaking Proficiency) in this test, select ten and write what you said on the lines below.

Situation No. __ _____

_____

_____

Situation No. __ _____

_____

_____

Situation No. __ _____

_____

_____

Situation No. __ _____

_____

_____

Situation No. __ _____

_____

_____

Situation No. __ _____

_____

_____

Situation No. __ _____

_____

_____

Situation No. __ _____

_____

_____

Situation No. __ _____

_____

_____

Situation No. __ _____

_____

_____

Il est trois heures. La leçon est terminée! (It is three o'clock. The lesson is over!)

Work Unit 16
Demonstrative Pronouns—*ceci, cela, ça*

Do you like answering true-false questions? Let's see how Mrs. Ravel's students make out.

Vrai ou faux?

Madame Ravel est professeur de géographie. Elle pose des questions à la classe.

Madame Ravel: Paris est la capitale de la France. Marie, ceci est vrai ou faux?
Marie: Cela est vrai, madame.
Madame Ravel: Bravo, Marie! Maintenant, Suzanne. Marseille est un port sur la Méditerranée. Suzanne, ceci est vrai ou faux?
Suzanne: Cela est faux, madame.
Madame Ravel: Non! Non! Non! Ceci est vrai: Marseille est un port sur la Méditerranée . . . Maintenant, Georges. La Seine est un fleuve. Georges, ceci est vrai ou faux?
Georges: Cela est vrai, madame. La Seine est un fleuve.
Madame Ravel: Bravo, Georges! C'est ça!
(La directrice de l'école entre dans la salle de classe.)
La Directrice: Madame Ravel, on vous demande au téléphone dans mon bureau.
Madame Ravel: Oh! Merci, madame. Je viens tout de suite.
(La directrice quitte la salle de classe.)
Madame Ravel: Marie, tu es chargée de continuer la leçon. Viens ici devant la classe.
(Madame Ravel quitte la salle et Marie va devant la classe.)
Tous les élèves: Paris est la capitale de la France. Ceci est vrai ou faux, Madame Marie? Oh, cela est vrai! Oh, bravo, Madame Marie! Tu as du génie! Quelle intelligence!
(Tous les élèves rient.)
(Robert lance un avion en papier contre l'horloge.)
Robert: J'ai lancé un avion en papier contre l'horloge. Ceci est vrai ou faux, Madame Marie? Oh, cela est vrai! Oh, bravo, Madame Marie! Quel génie! Quelle intelligence!
Marie: Silence! Silence! Robert, tu es insolent!
Robert: Cela est vrai? Je suis insolent? Oh! pardonnez-moi, Madame Marie!
(Madame Ravel rentre dans la salle de classe.)
Madame Ravel: Bon! Merci, Marie. Tu peux t'asseoir. Nous allons continuer la leçon . . . Hélène, pose une question à Raymond.
Hélène: Raymond, où se trouve la Grande Bretagne?
Raymond: Près de la petite Bretagne!
(Tous les élèves rient.)
Madame Ravel: Raymond, ta réponse est ridicule! . . . Suzanne, pose une question à Georges.
Suzanne: Georges, qui habite le pôle nord?
Georges: Un bonhomme de neige!

(Tous les élèves rient.)

Madame Ravel: **Georges, ta réponse est absurde!**

Georges: **Peut-être le Père Noël? Ho! Ho! Ho!**

(Tous les élèves rient.)

Madame Ravel: **Ça suffit! . . . Soyons sérieux! Paulette, où est Nancy?**

Paulette: **Elle est absente!**

Madame Ravel: **Je ne parle pas de Nancy. Je parle de Nancy. Je parle de Nancy, la ville en France. Oh! Quelle classe!**

Hélène: **Madame Ravel, j'ai une question à poser à Robert. Robert, où est Cadillac?**

Robert: **Dans le garage de mon père!**

(Tous les élèves rient.)

Madame Ravel: **Oh! Quelle classe! Je deviens folle!**

Robert: **Madame, il est trois heures. La leçon est terminée! C'est vrai ou faux, madame?**

Madame Ravel: **C'est superbe!**

VOCABULAIRE

le bonhomme de neige *n.,* the snowman

le bureau *n.,* the office

ça *dem. pron.,* that (ça is short for **cela**)

ceci *dem. pron.,* this

cela *dem. pron.,* that

c'est ça! that's right!

contre *prep.,* against

demander *v.,* to ask (for); **on vous demande au téléphone** you're wanted on the phone

deviens *v. form of* **devenir** (to become); **je deviens folle!** I'm going crazy!

le directeur, la directrice *n.,* the director, the principal

faux *m.,* **fausse** *f., adj.,* false

le fleuve *n.,* the river

le génie *n.,* genius

la Grande Bretagne *n.,* Great Britain

l'horloge *n.,* the clock

lancer *v.,* to throw, fling

la Méditerranée *n.,* the Mediterranean (Sea)

la neige *n.,* the snow; **un bonhomme de neige** a snowman

le nord *n.,* the north; **le pôle nord** the North Pole

le papier *n.,* paper

pardonner *v.,* to pardon, to forgive; **pardonnez-moi** forgive me

le Père Noël *n.,* Santa Claus

peut-être *adv.,* maybe, perhaps

poser une question to ask a question

près (de) *adv.,* near

quel génie! what genius! **quelle classe!** what a class!

rentrer *v.,* to return

la réponse *n.,* the answer; **ta réponse est ridicule!** your answer is ridiculous!

rient *v. form of* **rire** (to laugh); **tous les élèves rient** all the students laugh

sérieux *m.,* **sérieuse** *f., adj.,* serious; **soyons sérieux!** let's be serious!

suffit *v. form of* **suffire** (to suffice, to be enough); **ça suffit** that's enough

trouver *v.,* to find: **se trouver** to be located

viens *v. form of* **venir** (to come); **je viens tout de suite** I'm coming right away; **viens ici!** come here!

vrai *m.,* **vraie** *f., adj.,* true

EXERCISES

Review the story and vocabulary before starting these exercises.

I. **Vrai ou faux?** On the blank line write **vrai** if the statement is true or **faux** if the statement is false.

1. Paris est la capitale de la France.   _____

2. Marseille est un port sur la Méditerranée.   _____

3. La Seine est un flueve.   _____

4. Madame Ravel est professeur de mathématiques.   _____

5. La directrice de l'école n'entre pas dans la classe.   _____

6. Suzanne est chargée de continuer la leçon.   _____

7. Robert a lancé un avion en papier contre la fenêtre.   _____

8. Il est trois heures, la leçon est terminée, et Madame Ravel est   _____
    heureuse.

II. Complete the following statements by writing the appropriate words.

1. Madame Ravel est _____ de _____ .

2. La capitale de la France est _____ .

3. Marseille est un _____ sur la Méditerranée.

4. La Seine est un _____ .

5. La directrice de l'école entre _____ la salle de _____ .

6. Madame Ravel, on vous demande _____ téléphone dans mon _____ .

7. Marie, tu es chargée de _____ la _____ .

8. J'ai une question à _____ à Robert.

III. Answer the following questions in complete sentences.

1. Qui est Madame Ravel?

_____

2. Qui entre dans la salle de classe?

_____

3. Quand Madame Ravel quitte la salle, où va-t-elle?

_____

4. Qui a lancé un avion en papier contre l'horloge?

_____

5. À quelle heure est-ce que la leçon finit?

_____

STRUCTURES DE LA LANGUE

A. Demonstrative pronouns: **ceci, cela, ça**

1.	**Ceci** est vrai.	1.	*This* is true.
2.	**Cela** est faux.	2.	*That* is false.
3.	C'est **ça**!	3.	*That's* right!
4.	Je fais **cela**.	4.	I do *that*.
5.	Je fais **ceci**.	5.	I do *this*.

RULES AND OBSERVATIONS:

1. **Ça** is a contraction of **cela**.

2. **Ceci** and **cela** are demonstrative pronouns in a neuter sense. They usually refer to a general or indefinite concept, to an idea or to a statement. As pronouns, they do not refer to any particular masculine or feminine noun.

3. **Ceci** or **cela** can be used as the subject of a sentence. See examples 1 and 2 in the preceding box. They can also be used as the direct object of a verb. See examples 4 and 5 in the above box. They can also be used as the object of a preposition. **Elle parle toujours de cela**. (She always talks about that.)

Cela est vrai ou faux? (Is that true or false?)

256

EXERCISES

Review the preceding material before doing these exercises.

I. Match the following.

1. Je fais ceci.   _____ This is true.

2. C'est ça.   _____ That is true.

3. Je fais cela.   _____ That's right.

4. Cela est vrai.   _____ I do this.

5. Ceci est vrai.   _____ I do that.

II. Answer the following questions in French, using Oui in your answer and a complete statement.

> Model: **Cela est vrai?**   You write: **Oui, cela est vrai.**
> (Is that true?)   (Yes, that is true.)

1. Cela est faux?

_____

2. Ceci est vrai?

_____

3. C'est ça?

_____

III. Find the following demonstrative pronouns in the puzzle and circle them.

1. ceci

2. cela

3. ça

E	C	E	L
C	E	I	C
E	C	A	E
I	I	Ç	L
L	C	A	A

IV. Sports. Proficiency in Reading.

Situation: Look at the picture below and read the statements. After each statement, write on the line **C'est vrai** if the statement is true or **C'est faux** if the statement is false.

1. Les deux garçons jouent au football.

_____

2. Le ballon est près des pieds des deux joueurs.

_____

3. Derrière les deux garçons il y a des arbres.

_____

4. Les deux joueurs sont en shorts.

_____

5. Les deux garçons jouent sous la pluie.

_____

V. Appreciating French Art. Proficiency in Speaking and Writing.

Situation: You are at the Metropolitan Museum of Art in New York City. You are admiring the painting _Répétition d'un ballet sur la scène_/_Rehearsal of a ballet on the stage,_ by Edgar Degas, a great French artist/**grand artiste français.** He studied painting in Paris at the **École des Beaux-Arts**/School of Fine Arts.

Look at the picture on the following page and say aloud French words that come to mind. Then write them on the lines or use them in two or three sentences. You may use your own ideas and words and/or the following suggestions.

J'admire le tableau de Degas/_I am admiring the painting by Degas;_ **C'est une répétition d'un ballet sur la scène**/_It's a rehearsal of a ballet on stage;_ **Les danseuses sont jolies**/_The dancers are pretty;_ **Leurs tutus sont beaux**/_Their ballet skirts are beautiful;_ **Je vois le chorégraphe habillé en noir au milieu de la scène**/_I see the choreographer dressed in black in the middle of the stage;_ **Ce tableau exprime l'art des formes et du mouvement**/_This painting expresses the art of forms and movement;_ **C'est un tableau magnifique**/_It's a magnificent painting;_ **Je l'aime beaucoup**/_I like it a lot;_ **La peinture est signée en haut, à gauche**/_The painting is signed at the top, on the left;_ **Quel beau tableau!**/_What a beautiful picture!_

_____

_____

_____

Répétition d'un ballet sur la scène (The Rehearsal of a Ballet) by Edgar Degas.
Reprinted with permission Edimédia / The Corbis Collection.

VI. Introducing Yourself. Proficiency in Speaking.

Situation: Your French teacher is absent today because of illness and you have a substitute in class. Greet the substitute teacher, introduce yourself, and tell her or him that you would like to play a game of **Vrai ou Faux** similar to the story at the beginning of this work unit. Say **J'aimerais jouer un jeu de ...** for *I would like to play a game of...*

VII. True or False? Proficiency in Speaking.

Situation: You are in French class. Each student has to make one statement in French followed by **Cela est vrai? Cela est faux?** It's your turn. Make at least three statements and then ask if that's true or false. You may use your own ideas and words and/or the following: **Paris, être, la capitale de la France, la Seine, un fleuve, Marseille, un port, la Méditerranée, une mer.** Use the map of France in Work Unit 9.

VIII. Obtaining and Providing Information. Proficiency in Speaking and Writing.

Situation: Your friend Richard did not go to school today because he is not feeling well. He has called you at home to find out what you did in French class.

You may vary and extend this telephone conversation with your own words and ideas. Use the **tu** form with him because he is your friend. In this exercise you are again practicing the **passé composé.** Later, switch roles for more practice.

Richard: **Qu'est-ce que tu as fait dans la classe de français aujourd'hui?**

Vous: _____

I talked a lot in French.

Richard: **Et les autres étudiants, aussi?**

Vous: _____

Some students talked in French. Some students said nothing/**Quelques étudiants n'ont rien dit.**

Richard: **Est-ce que tu as écrit en français au tableau?**

Vous: _____

Yes, I wrote in French on the chalkboard.

Richard: **Qui a gagné le grand prix aujourd'hui dans la classe?**

Vous: _____

Me!/**Moi!** I won the first prize today!

Richard: **Félicitations!/Congratulations!**

—**Nous sommes très heureux de vous voir.** (We're very happy to see you.)

Work Unit 17
Disjunctive Pronouns

*Monsieur and Madame Paquet
received an invitation for dinner at
the home of some neighbors. Are
they in for a big surprise!*

R. S. V. P.

Monsieur et Madame Paquet ont reçu une invitation à dîner chez leurs voisins, Monsieur et Madame Berger. Voici l'invitation:

> Madame Berger
> vous invite à dîner
> vendredi, 15 avril, à 20 h.
> R.S.V.P.   21, rue des Jardins Paris

Madame Paquet: **Eh bien, François, est-ce que nous y allons ou est-ce que nous n'y allons pas? Il faut répondre à l'invitation.**

Monsieur Paquet: **Claire, tu sais que je ne veux pas aller chez eux parce que je ne les aime pas. Lui et elle sont des snobs.**

Madame Paquet: **Tu as raison. Quand je l'ai vue au supermarché hier, elle m'a parlé, mais elle m'a regardée d'un air supérieur.**

Monsieur Paquet: **D'ailleurs, ils sont ennuyeux.**

Madame Paquet: **Oui. Ils m'ennuient aussi. Mais tu sais que si nous refusons l'invitation, tout est fini entre eux et nous.**

Monsieur Paquet: **Il faut accepter pour rester amis avec eux.**

Claire accepte l'invitation. Quand ils arrivent pour dîner chez les Berger, ils entrent dans le salon. Ils voient d'autres voisins chez eux. Tout le monde crie: Surprise! Surprise!

—Nous sommes très heureux de vous voir. Ce dîner est en votre honneur, leur dit Madame Berger.

—Pour nous?! En notre honneur?! s'exclament Claire et François.

—Oui, répond Monsieur Berger.

—Mais pourquoi? Qu'est-ce que nous avons fait? leur demande Claire.

—Parce que vous êtes bons! Et vous êtes aimables et gentils! répond Madame Berger.

—Merci, merci, disent les Paquet.

Tout le monde a mangé, bu, chanté, et dansé jusqu'à minuit. Claire et François Paquet sont rentrés contents chez eux.

Quand ils arrivent chez eux, Monsieur Paquet dit à sa femme:

—Tu sais, Claire, j'ai toujours dit que les Berger étaient aimables et gentils. Je les aime beaucoup.

—Moi aussi, j'ai toujours dit cela, François.

VOCABULAIRE

d'ailleurs *adv.,* besides
aimable *adj.,* likable
chez *prep.,* at (to) the home (place) of; **chez eux** at their house; **chez moi** at my house; **chez leurs voisins** at the home of their neighbors; **chez les Berger** at the Bergers
ennuient *v. form of* **ennuyer** (to bore, annoy); **ils m'ennuient** they bore me; **ennuyeux** *adj. m. pl.,* boring

entre *prep.,* between; **entre eux et nous** between them and us
eux *disj. pron.,* them; **avec eux** with them
faut *v. form of* **falloir**; **il faut** it is necessary
gentil *m.,* **gentille** *f., adj.,* nice, kind
h. *abbrev. for* **heures**; **20 h.** is 8 o'clock in the evening
l'honneur *n. m.,* honor

leur dit Madame Berger Mrs. Berger says to them
pour *prep.,* for, in order (to)
R.S.V.P. please reply (Répondez, **s**'il vous plaît)
reçu *past part. of* **recevoir** (to receive); **ils ont reçu** they received
refusons *v. form of* **refuser** (to refuse); **si nous refusons** if we refuse
rester *v.,* to remain, to stay

Note: **étaient** verb form of **être**, were.

Review the story and vocabulary before starting these exercises.

I. **Complete the dialogue in French between Mr. and Mrs. Paquet. They are deciding whether or not to accept a dinner invitation. Refer to the story if you have to.**

Madame Paquet: **Eh bien, François, est-ce que nous acceptons l'invitation à dîner chez les Berger?**

Monsieur Paquet: _____

Madame Paquet: **Pourquoi?**

Monsieur Paquet: _____

Madame Paquet: **Oui. Tu as raison. Ils m'ennuient aussi.**

Monsieur Paquet: _____

II. **Complete the following statements by writing the appropriate words from among these:**

(a) à l'invitation   (b) chez eux   (c) je ne les aime pas   (d) entre eux et nous   (e) vous voir

1. Si nous refusons l'invitation, tout est fini

_____

2. Nous sommes très heureux de

_____

3. Ils voient d'autres voisins

_____

4. Je ne veux pas y aller parce que

_____

5. Il faut répondre

_____

III. Choose the correct answer based on the story in this unit.

1. M. et Mme Paquet ont reçu

   (a) un balai.   (b) une voiture.   (c) un ami.   (d) une invitation.   _____

2. M. Paquet ne veut pas aller chez les Berger parce qu'

   (a) il est malade. (b) il est heureux. (c) il est aimable. (d) il ne les aime pas.   _____

3. M. et Mme Berger sont très heureux

   (a) de recevoir les Paquet.   (b) d'aller dîner.   (c) d'accepter l'invitation.
   (d) d'aller au supermarché.   _____

STRUCTURES DE LA LANGUE

A. Disjunctive pronouns (also known as stressed pronouns or tonic pronouns)

Singular		Plural	
moi	me *or* I	**nous**	us *or* we
toi	you *(familiar)*	**vous**	you *(formal singular or plural)*
soi	oneself	**eux**	them, they *(masculine)*
lui	him *or* he	**elles**	them, they *(feminine)*
elle	her *or* she		

RULES AND OBSERVATIONS:

1. The disjunctive pronoun is used when it is the object of a preposition:

   Elle parle avec moi. (She is talking with me.)

   Nous allons chez eux. (We are going to their house.)

2. The disjunctive pronoun is used in a compound subject:

   Lui et elle sont intelligents. (He and she are intelligent.)

3. The disjunctive pronoun is used in a compound object:

   Je vous connais—toi et lui. (I know you—you and him.)

4. You may use **à** with a disjunctive pronoun to express possession only if the verb is **être** and if the subject is a noun, personal pronoun, or a demonstrative pronoun:

   Ce livre est à moi. (This book is mine.)

   Ces livres sont à elles. (These books are theirs.)

   Ces livres sont à eux. (These books are theirs.)

5. The disjunctive pronoun **moi** is used instead of **me** in the affirmative imperative when it is tacked on to the verb and joined with a hyphen; example:

   Excusez-moi. (Excuse me.)

6. A disjunctive pronoun is also known as a *stressed* or a *tonic* pronoun.

EXERCISES

Review the preceding material before starting these exercises.

I. **On the blank line write the disjunctive pronoun that expresses possession as needed, according to what is given in English in parentheses.**

Model: **Les livres sont à** _____ (mine).   You write: **moi**
(The books are _____.)   (me)

1. Le parapluie est à _____ (mine).

2. Les balles sont à _____ (his).

3. L'orange est à _____ (hers).

4. La maison est à _____ (ours).

5. La voiture est à _____ (yours, *pl.*).

6. Les gâteaux sont à _____ (theirs, *m.*).

II. **On the blank line write in French the proper disjunctive pronoun for the English given in parentheses.**

Model: (me) **Elle parle avec** _____ .   You write: **Elle parle avec moi.**
(She is talking with _____ .)   (She is talking with me.)

1. (him)   Je suis allée au cinéma avec _____ .

2. (me)   Il va partir sans _____ .

3. (he)   Madeleine et _____ sont intelligents.

4. (she)   Marie et _____ écrivent les leçons.

5. (us)   Le ragoût est pour _____ .

6. (you, *formal singular*)   Elle va partir avec _____ .

7. (you, *familiar singular*)   Nous allons sortir avec _____ .

8. (them, *masculine*)   Ce courriel est pour _____ .

9. (them, *feminine*)   Ces petits fours sont pour _____ .

10. (he and I)   _____ nous allons au cinéma.

III. **Fill in the missing pronouns. They are not all disjunctive!**

Monsieur Paquet annonce: J'ai les billets pour le théâtre. Ces quatre billets sont pour

_____ . Ce billet est pour _____ , ce billet est pour _____ , Claire;
(us)   (me)   (you)

et ces deux billets sont pour _____ deux, Janine et Pierre. Prenez- _____ .
(you)   (them)

Madame Paquet dit: François, ne _____ donne pas les billets. Je préfère
(to them)

_____ mettre dans ma poche.
(them)

Monsieur Paquet répond: Non, Claire, ne _____ mets pas dans ta poche. Je veux

(them)

_____ garder sur _____ .

(them)   (me)

Janine demande: Papa, est-ce que nous allons au théâtre ce soir?

Monsieur Paquet répond: Oui, nous _____ allons ce soir.

(there)

IV. Expressing Personal Feelings. Proficiency in Speaking and Writing.

Situation: You are at a dinner party at the home of some friends. Express your personal feelings by telling the hostess you like very much the dinner that she prepared, thank her for the invitation, and tell her that she is very nice and likable. You may use these suggestions or your own ideas and words. Make at least three statements. After you say them aloud, write them on the lines for practice.

1. _____

2. _____

3. _____

V. An Invitation. Proficiency in Speaking and Writing.

Situation: A girl has called a friend to invite him to go to a dance this Saturday night. Complete the conversation in French according to the English words under the lines. You may vary and extend the conversation with your own ideas and words. First, say aloud the French words you plan to use. Then write them on the lines.

1. **Elle:**   **Allô! Robert? C'est toi? C'est moi—Janine.**

2. **Lui:**   _____

               (Respond with a greeting and ask how she is.)

3. **Elle:**   **Très bien, merci. Écoute. Je te téléphone pour te demander si tu veux aller à un bal ce samedi soir. Veux-tu y aller avec moi?**

4. **Lui:**   _____

               (Say you can't because your father is sick and you have to stay home with him.)

5. **Elle:**   **C'est dommage. Ta mère ne peut pas rester chez toi avec lui?**

6. **Lui:**   _____

               (Tell her your mother went to visit her sister in France.)

7. **Elle:**   **Est-ce que je peux venir chez toi pour regarder la télé avec toi?**

8. **Lui:**   _____

               (Tell her yes, she can come to your place.)

9. **Elle:**   **D'accord. Je vais venir chez toi à huit heures.**

10. **Lui:**   _____

               (Tell her to bring a big chocolate cake with her.)

11. **Elle:** **Un grand gâteau au chocolat?! Avec moi? Okay. D'accord.**

12. **Lui:** _____

(Tell her to bring the music and words of the song _Sur le Pont d'Avignon._)*

13. **Elle:** **D'accord. Et nous allons chanter pour ton père qui est malade!**

*The words are below.

Sur le pont d'Avignon
Sur le pont d'Avignon
On y danse, on y danse
Sur le pont d'Avignon
On y danse tout en rond

267

Non! Non! Es-tu fou? (No! No! Are you crazy?)

Work Unit 18
Adjectives

Janine and her brother Pierre have nothing to do. They get into mischief when Pierre persuades her to look under the hood of their father's car. In this scene Pierre does something foolish despite his sister's objections.

Tour d'écrou

Quelle voiture! La famille Paquet a une belle voiture grise qui ne leur donne jamais de problèmes. Même les grosses voitures neuves ne sont pas meilleures que la voiture de la famille Paquet.

Aujourd'hui Pierre fait quelque chose de bête. Il regarde dans le moteur de la voiture de leur père.

Pierre:	**Janine, donne-moi le tournevis.**
Janine:	**Pourquoi? Que vas-tu faire, Pierre?**
Pierre:	**Je vais régler le moteur. Je te dis, donne-moi le tournevis.**
Janine:	**Quel tournevis? Il y en a beaucoup.**
Pierre:	**Le plus petit.**
Janine:	**Mais, que vas-tu faire, Pierre?**
Pierre:	**Je vais engager le tournevis dans cette vis et je vais tourner.**
Janine:	**Non! Non! Non!**
Pierre:	**Maintenant je tourne le tournevis . . . là . . . là . . . là . . . J'enlève la vis et l'écrou. Ils ne sont pas utiles. Maintenant je les mets dans la poubelle.**
Janine:	**Non! Es-tu fou?**
Pierre:	**C'est fait.**

Quand Monsieur Paquet veut aller faire des courses dans sa voiture, il va au garage, il monte dans sa voiture, et il tourne la clef pour mettre le moteur en marche. Il entend du bruit et le moteur ne marche pas.

Il appelle la station-service et le garagiste arrive; il emporte la voiture de Monsieur Paquet au garage de service.

Le lendemain, le garagiste téléphone à Monsieur Paquet et lui dit: Le montant à payer est de 200 euros, monsieur. Voilà le problème: Il manque une vis dans le moteur.

VOCABULAIRE

appeler *v.,* to call

beau *m.,* **belle** *f., adj.,* beautiful

bête *adj. m. f.,* foolish, dumb

le bruit *n.,* the noise

c'est fait it's done

la couleur *n.,* the color: **de quelle couleur est . . .** what color is . . .

l'écrou *n. m.,* nut that fits on a screw or bolt

emporter *v.,* to take (carry) away

engager *v.,* to engage, to put (machinery) in gear

enlever *v.,* to remove, to take off

entendre *v.,* to hear

faire des courses to do (go) shopping

fou *m.,* **folle** *f., adj.,* crazy

le garagiste *n.,* the garage mechanic

gris *m.,* **grise** *f., adj.,* gray

il y a there is, there are; **il y en a beaucoup** there are many (of them)

269

là *adv.,* there
le lendemain *n.,* the following day
manquer *v.,* to miss, to be missing, to be lacking something; **il manque une vis dans le moteur** a screw is missing in the motor
marcher *v.,* to walk, to run (a motor or apparatus); **mettre en marche** to put into operation
meilleur *m.,* **meilleure** *f.,* *adj.,* better
même *adv.,* even
le montant *n.,* total amount (of an account)

monter *v.,* to climb, to mount, to get into
le moteur *n.,* the motor, the engine
neuf *m.,* **neuve** *f., adj.,* new
petit *m.,* **petite** *f., adj.,* small; **plus petit, plus petite** smaller; **le plus petit, la plus petite** the smallest
la poubelle *n.,* the garbage can
que *conj.,* than, that; *pron.,* what

quel *m.,* **quelle** *f., interrog. adj.,* what, which; **quel tournevis?** which screwdriver? **quelle voiture!** what a car!
qui *pron.,* which, who
régler *v.,* to adjust, to tune (engine)
le tour *n.,* the turn; **tour d'écrou** turn of the nut
le tournevis *n.,* the screwdriver
utile *adj.,* useful
la vis *n.,* the screw
la voiture *n.,* the car, automobile

EXERCISES

Review the story and vocabulary before starting these exercises.

I. **Answer the following questions in complete sentences. They are based on the story "Tour d'écrou."**

1. Qui a une belle voiture grise?

_____

2. Est-ce que les grosses voitures neuves sont meilleures que la voiture de Monsieur Paquet?

_____

3. Pourquoi Pierre veut-il le tournevis?

_____

4. Où est-ce que Pierre met la vis et l'écrou?

_____

II. **Answer the following questions in complete sentences. They are personal questions and require answers of your own.**

1. Est-ce que votre famille a une voiture?

_____

2. Allez-vous faire des courses dans la voiture de votre famille?

_____

3. De quelle couleur est la voiture de votre famille?

_____

III. Vocabulary building. Proficiency in Writing

A. A car salesperson is showing you a brand new car. Write five adjectives to describe it.

1. _____ 2. _____ 3. _____ 4. _____ 5. _____

B. Your next door neighbors have just renovated their garage. Write five adjectives to describe it.

1. _____ 2. _____ 3. _____ 4. _____ 5. _____

STRUCTURES DE LA LANGUE

A. Agreement and position of descriptive adjectives

Masculine	Feminine
un chapeau **gris**	une voiture **grise** (gray)
des chapeaux **gris**	des voitures **grises**
un passage **étroit**	une rue **étroite** (narrow)
des passages **étroits**	des rues **étroites**
un homme **libre**	une femme **libre** (free)
des hommes **libres**	des femmes **libres**

RULES AND OBSERVATIONS:

1. Most descriptive adjectives follow the noun in French.

2. Here are some common adjectives that normally precede the noun: **autre, beau, bon, chaque, gros, jeune, joli, long, mauvais, petit, plusieurs, vieux,** and **grand** (exception: **un homme grand,** a tall man; **un grand homme,** a great man).

3. Adjectives must agree in gender and number with the nouns they modify.

B. Formation of masculine descriptive adjectives in the plural

1. To form the plural of a masculine singular adjective, ordinarly add **s**.

2. If a masculine singular adjective ends in **s**, it remains the same in the plural: **gris**.

3. If a masculine singular adjective ends in **x**, it remains the same in the plural: **dangereux**.

4. If a masculine singular adjective ends in **al**, it ordinarily changes to **aux** in the plural: **loyal, loyaux**.

C. Formation of regular feminine descriptive adjectives

1. To form the feminine singular of an adjective, ordinarily add **e** to the masculine singular, e.g., **gris, grise**.

2. If the masculine singular adjective ends in **e**, the feminine singular is the same, e.g., **libre**.

271

D. Formation of irregular feminine descriptive adjectives

Masculine		Feminine	
Singular	*Plural*	*Singular*	*Plural*
neuf	neufs	neuve	neuves
furieux	furieux	furieuse	furieuses
dernier	derniers	dernière	dernières
ancien	anciens	ancienne	anciennes
bon	bons	bonne	bonnes
cruel	cruels	cruelle	cruelles
muet	muets	muette	muettes

RULES AND OBSERVATIONS:

1. A masculine singular adjective that ends in -f changes to -ve to form the feminine singular: neuf, neuve.

2. A masculine singular adjective that ends in -eux changes to -euse to form the feminine singular: furieux, furieuse.

3. A masculine singular adjective that ends in -ier changes to ière to form the feminine singular: dernier, dernière.

4. Some adjectives double the final consonant in the masculine singular to form the feminine singular; then an e is added: ancien, ancienne.

E. Other irregular feminine forms of descriptive adjectives

Masculine		Feminine	
Singular	*Plural*	*Singular*	*Plural*
beau	beaux	belle	belles
frais	frais	fraîche	fraîches
sec	secs	sèche	sèches
gros	gros	grosse	grosses
long	longs	longue	longues
blanc	blancs	blanche	blanches
favori	favoris	favorite	favorites
public	publics	publique	publiques
doux	doux	douce	douces

EXERCISES

I. Answer the following questions in French, substituting the appropriate form of the descriptive adjective in parentheses for the one indicated. Use **non** in your answer, but write your sentence in the affirmative.

Model: **Avez-vous une voiture**   You write: **Non, j'ai une voiture**
        grise? (blanc)   **blanche.**
        Do you have a gray car? (white)   (No, I have a white car.)

1. Avez-vous une maison blanche?   (gris)

_____

2. Avez-vous un bon ordinateur?   (mauvais)

_____

3. Avez-vous une grosse pomme?   (beau)

_____

4. Avez-vous une pêche fraîche?   (doux)

_____

5. Avez-vous un joli chapeau?   (vieux)

_____

II. Answer the following questions in the affirmative in complete French sentences. In answer (a) use **oui**. In answer (b) use **aussi**. Write the appropriate form of the descriptive adjective in your answers. Use subject pronouns in your answers. Study the models.

Model: (a) **Est-ce que Monsieur**   You answer: (a) **Oui, il est bon.**
            Paquet est bon?   (Yes, he is good.)
            (Is Mr. Paquet good?)
        (b) **Et Madame Paquet?**   You answer: (b) **Elle est bonne**
            (And Mrs. Paquet?)   **aussi.**
                                                            (She is good, too.)

1. (a) Est-ce que Janine est petite?

_____

   (b) Et Pierre?

_____

2. (a) Est-ce que Monsieur Paquet est furieux?

_____

   (b) Et Madame Paquet?

_____

3. (a) Est-ce que Monique est gentille?

_____

(b) Et Pierre?

_____

4. (a) Est-ce que Janine et Monique sont belles?

_____

(b) Et Pierre et Robert?

_____

5. (a) Est-ce que la maison est neuve?

_____

(b) Et les voitures?

_____

III. Answer the following questions in the negative in complete French sentences. In answer (a) use **non**. In answer (b) use **non plus**. Write the appropriate form of the descriptive adjective in your answers. Use subject pronouns in your answers. Study the models.

Model: (a) **Est-ce que Madame Paquet est cruelle?** (Is Mrs. Paquet cruel?)

You answer: (a) **Non, elle n'est pas cruelle.** (No, she is not cruel.)

(b) **Et Monsieur Paquet?** (And Mr. Paquet?)

You answer: (b) **Il n'est pas cruel non plus.** (He is not cruel either.)

1. (a) Est-ce que Madame Paquet est petite?

_____

(b) Et Monsieur Paquet?

_____

2. (a) Est-ce que le professeur de français est mauvais?

_____

(b) Et le professeur d'espagnol?

_____

3. (a) Est-ce que le maître d'italien est gros?

_____

(b) Et la maîtresse d'allemand?

_____

4. (a) Est-ce que le petit garçon est muet?

_____

(b) Et la petite fille?

_____

IV. Choose the form of the adjective that does not belong in the group.

Model: (a) **beau**   (b) **sec**   (c) **gros**   (d) **longue**   _____d_____

1. (a) neuf   (b) ancien   (c) bon   (d) cruelle   _____

2. (a) muets   (b) cruels   (c) dernière   (d) beaux   _____

3. (a) neuve   (b) furieuse   (c) étroits   (d) bonne   _____

4. (a) belles   (b) grise   (c) fraîches   (d) blanches   _____

5. (a) beau   (b) longs   (c) sec   (d) blanc   _____

F. Possessive adjectives

Masculine			
Singular		*Plural*	
mon livre	my book	**mes livres**	my books
ton stylo	your pen	**tes stylos**	your pens
son ballon	his (her, its) balloon	**ses ballons**	his (her, its) balloons
notre parapluie	our umbrella	**nos parapluies**	our umbrellas
votre sandwich	your sandwich	**vos sandwichs**	your sandwiches
leur gâteau	their cake	**leurs gâteaux**	their cakes

Feminine			
Singular		*Plural*	
ma robe	my dress	**mes robes**	my dresses
ta jaquette	your jacket	**tes jaquettes**	your jackets
sa balle	his (her, its) ball	**ses balles**	his (her, its) balls
notre maison	our house	**nos maisons**	our houses
votre voiture	your car	**vos voitures**	your cars
leur soeur	their sister	**leurs soeurs**	their sisters

RULES AND OBSERVATIONS:

1. A possessive adjective agrees in gender and number *with the noun* it modifies, *not with the possessor.*

2. Some possessive adjectives do not agree with the gender of the noun *in the singular.* They are all the same, whether in front of a masculine or feminine singular noun: **notre**, **votre**, **leur**.

3. Some possessive adjectives do not agree with the gender of the noun *in the plural.* They are all the same, whether in front of a masculine or feminine plural noun: **mes**, **tes**, **ses**, **nos**, **vos**, **leurs**.

4. Be aware of the following possessive adjectives: **mon** or **ma**, **ton** or **ta**, **son** or **sa**.

5. In front of a *feminine singular noun* beginning with a vowel or silent *h*, use the masculine singular forms: **mon**, **ton**, **son**—instead of **ma**, **ta**, **sa**.

mon adresse	my address	**son** amie	his (or her) friend
ton opinion	your opinion	**mon** habitude	my habit (custom)

6. Since **son, sa,** and **ses** can mean *his* or *her*, you may add **à lui** or **à elle** to make the meaning clear.

sa maison à lui	his house	**son livre à elle**	her book
sa maison à elle	her house	**ses livres à lui**	his books
son livre à lui	his book	**ses livres à elle**	her books

7. If there is more than one noun, a possessive adjective must be used in front of each noun: **ma mère et mon père** (my mother and father).

8. Use the definite article instead of the possessive adjective when referring to parts of the body if it is clear who the possessor is.

J'ai de l'argent **dans la main.**	(I have some money *in my hand.*)

EXERCISES

Review the preceding material before starting these exercises.

I.   Answer the following questions in the affirmative, using the appropriate form of the possessive adjective. Use oui in your answer.

Model:	**Aimes-tu ta robe grise?**	You answer:	**Oui, j'aime ma robe grise.**
	(Do you like your gray dress?)		(Yes, I like my gray dress.)

1. Aimes-tu ta petite voiture neuve?

_____

2. Aimez-vous mon parapluie rouge?

_____

3. Aimez-vous notre maison blanche?

_____

4. Aimes-tu mon amie Monique?

_____

5. Aimes-tu ton petit frère?

_____

II. Answer the following questions in the affirmative, using the appropriate form of the possessive adjective. Use **oui** in your answer.

> Model: **Est-ce votre maison?**　　　You answer: **Oui, c'est ma maison.**
> (Is it your house?)　　　　　　　　　　　　　　　(Yes, it is my house.)

1. Est-ce votre voiture?

_____

2. Est-ce ton chapeau?

_____

3. Est-ce son livre à lui?

_____

4. Est-ce votre maîtresse de français?

_____

5. Est-ce leur maison?

_____

III. Answer the following questions in the affirmative, using the appropriate form of the possessive adjective. Use **oui** in your answer.

> Model: **Ce sont vos livres?**　　　You answer: **Oui, ce sont mes livres.**
> (Are they your books?)　　　　　　　　　　　　　(Yes, they are my books.)

1. Ce sont vos stylos?

_____

2. Ce sont leurs crayons?

_____

3. Ce sont tes gâteaux?

_____

4. Ce sont mes pommes?

_____

5. Ce sont nos pêches?

_____

IV. Fill in the missing words, using the appropriate form of a possessive adjective so that the rest of the sentence and dialogue will make sense.

Madame Paquet:　Bonjour, Madame Richy! Oh! Vous avez un joli chapeau! J'aime beaucoup
_____ chapeau.

Madame Richy:　Merci! J'ai aussi une nouvelle robe. Aimez-vous _____ nouvelle
robe rouge?

Madame Paquet:　Oui, j'aime beaucoup _____ nouveau chapeau et
_____ nouvelle robe rouge. J'adore _____ vêtements!

Madame Richy:　Mon mari a une nouvelle jaquette. J'aime beaucoup _____ nouvelle jaquette.

Madame Paquet: Et mon mari a un nouveau complet. J'aime beaucoup _____

nouveau complet.

Madame Richy: Alors, _____ maris ont de nouveaux vêtements. Nous aimons

beaucoup _____ nouveaux vêtements.

V. Answer in a complete sentence, using the appropriate form of a possessive adjective. In your answer, use the noun given in parentheses.

Model: **Que mangez-vous? (pomme)** You answer: **Je mange ma pomme.**
(What are you eating? [apple]) (I am eating my apple.)

1. Que mangez-vous? (pêche)

_____

2. Que mange-t-il? (sandwich)

_____

3. Que mangent-ils? (chocolat)

_____

4. Que mangent-elles? (soupe)

_____

5. Que mangez-vous? (petits fours)

_____

VI. Activities. Proficiency in Speaking.

A. Look at the picture at the beginning of this work unit. Using at least ten words in French, describe the scene to a friend. Make sure you use adjectives to describe the garage, the car, the girl, and the boy.

B. Describe the house you live in. You may want to use adjectives like the following: new or old, big or small, beautiful, pretty, the color. If you live in an apartment, describe it.

C. Talk about the people you live with. Describe them by using as many adjectives as you can that are found in this lesson.

VII. Obtaining and Providing Information. Proficiency in Speaking.

Situation: Your father's brand new car is parked in the driveway. You decided to lift the hood to inspect the motor and the parts. With a screwdriver, you try to remove a screw or bolt. Your father comes rushing out of the house and says to you: **Que fais-tu?** (What are you doing?) He is furious. Respond by telling him what you are doing and why. You may use any or all of the following words: **la vis, l'écrou, j'enlève, dans la poubelle.** Use some adjectives, for example: **petit, gros, utile, furieux, bon, neuf,** or any others you prefer.

VIII. Picture Interpretation. Proficiency in Speaking.

Situation: Describe what you see in the picture shown below. Use at least ten words in French. You may want to use some or all of the following: **un jeune homme, marcher, un bâtiment, vieux, ancien, des briques,** or any others you prefer.

IX. Sports. Proficiency in Speaking and Writing.

Situation: Two boys and a coach are practicing soccer **(le football).**

Look at the picture below. First, organize your thoughts and practice aloud the words you plan to say. Then write two sentences on the lines. You may use your own ideas and words and/or the following suggestions: **Les trois personnes jouent au football/***The three people are playing soccer;* **Le jeune homme est l'entraîneur/***The young man is the coach;* **C'est le gardien de but/***He is the goalie;* **garder le but/***to guard the goal;* **le filet/***the net;* **envoyer le ballon au fond des filets/***to send the ball into the back of the net;* **Les deux garçons jouent/***The two boys are playing;* **Un garçon a envoyé le ballon au fond des filets/***One boy sent the ball into the back of the net;* **L'autre garçon est surpris!/***The other boy is surprised!* **Ils se sont bien amusés/***They had a lot of fun.*

1. _____

2. _____

X. Appreciating French Art. Proficiency in Speaking and Writing.

Situation: You and your friend Janine are at a museum admiring the painting *Rue de Tahiti*/*Street in Tahiti,* by Paul Gauguin.

Look at the picture below and complete the conversation. You may use your own ideas and words and/or the suggestions under the lines.

Janine: Quel beau tableau de Gauguin! L'aimes-tu?

Vous: _____

Yes, I like it very much.

Janine: Cette femme à droite, que fait-elle? Est-ce qu'elle dort?

Vous: _____

I think she is waiting for a friend.

Janine: Évidemment, cette rue de Tahiti est tranquille! Les montagnes au fond/*in the background* sont belles, n'est-ce pas?

Vous: _____

Yes, they are beautiful. I would like to go/**J'aimerais aller** to Tahiti.

Rue de Tahiti by Paul Gauguin (1848–1903)
The Granger Collection, New York.

Les Signes du Zodiaque. (Signs of the Zodiac.)

Work Unit 19
Adjectives (Continued)

Let's see what Pierre's horoscope reveals for today. What does yours say?

Zodiaque

Pierre lit le journal dans la cuisine. Il a la page de l'horoscope devant lui.

 I **Le Bélier** (Aries)

(21 mars–20 avril)

Vous êtes le meilleur juge de vos actions.

 II **Le Taureau** (Taurus)

(21 avril–21 mai)

Votre plus grande qualité, c'est votre patience. Attendez des nouvelles!

 III **Les Gémeaux** (Gemini)

(22 mai–21 juin)

La personne qui vous aime le plus attend un courriel de vous. Écrivez-lui.

 IV **Le Cancer** (Cancer)

(22 juin–23 juillet)

Méfiez-vous des obstacles dangereux.

 V **Le Lion** (Leo)

(24 juillet–23 août)

Demain va être un jour parfait pour finir vos projets.

 VI **La Vierge** (Virgo)

(24 août–23 septembre)

Méfiez-vous des petites automobiles vertes.

 VII **La Balance** (Libra)

(24 septembre–23 octobre)

Quelle chance! Vous allez voir un grand changement.

VIII **Le Scorpion** (Scorpio)

(24 octobre–22 novembre)

Vous avez un esprit inventif. Soyez prudent!

IX **Le Sagittaire** (Sagittarius)

(23 novembre–21 décembre)

Votre plus grande qualité, c'est votre imagination.

X **Le Capricorne** (Capricorn)

(22 décembre–20 janvier)

Ne sortez pas aujourd'hui. Restez dans votre maison. Il y a du danger dans les rues.

XI **Le Verseau** (Aquarius)

(21 janvier–19 février)

Il faut profiter du moment. Quelle semaine! Bonnes nouvelles!

XII **Les Poissons** (Pisces)

(20 février–20 mars)

N'allez pas à la plage aujourd'hui. Il y a un requin affamé dans l'eau.

Le téléphone sonne. Voici la conversation entre Pierre et Monique:

Monique: **C'est toi, Pierre? Ici Monique.**
Pierre: **Oui, c'est moi. Comment vas-tu?**
Monique: **Ça va. Écoute, Pierre. Il y a une grande soirée chez moi ce soir. Nous allons danser et chanter. Ma mère a préparé un gâteau délicieux. Nous allons beaucoup nous amuser. Henri va venir, ainsi que Paul, Robert, Raymond, Suzanne, Hélène, ta soeur Janine, et d'autres amis. Veux-tu venir?**
Pierre: **Attends, Monique. Je vais regarder dans le journal. Je n'ai pas lu mon horoscope pour aujourd'hui.**

Pierre regarde l'horoscope dans le journal. Il lit sous son signe du Zodiaque, Le Capricorne. Il retourne au téléphone.

Pierre: **Monique, mon horoscope dit qu'il faut rester à la maison aujourd'hui parce qu'il y a du danger dans les rues.**
Monique: **Es-tu superstitieux? Tu es fou!**
Pierre: **Écoute. Je vais venir tout de même.**

Plus tard, Pierre quitte la maison pour aller à la soirée chez Monique. Quand il traverse la rue, il voit un grand camion venant à toute vitesse. Pierre _____

_____

_____

(Note to the student: Write your own ending to this story in one or two sentences—in French, of course!)

VOCABULAIRE

affamé *adj.,* starved, famished

ainsi que *conj.,* as well as

amuser *v.,* to amuse; **s'amuser** *refl. v.,* to have a good time, to amuse oneself; **nous allons beaucoup nous amuser** we are going to have a very good time; **amusez-vous bien!** have a good time!

ça va *interj.,* I'm fine, it's fine, it's okay

le changement *n.,* the change, alteration

comment vas-tu? how are you?

un courriel *n.,* e-mail

écrivez *v. form of* **écrire**; **écrivez-lui** write to him/to her

fort *m.,* **forte** *f., adj.,* strong: **votre qualité la plus forte** your strongest quality

ici *adv.,* here; **ici Monique** this is Monique here

intelligent *m.,* **intelligente** *f., adj.;* **l'élève le plus intelligent de la classe** the most intelligent student in the class

inventif *m.,* **inventive** *f., adj.,* inventive; **un esprit inventif** an inventive spirit

lit *v. form of* **lire**; **il lit** he is reading (he reads); **lu** *past part.*; **je n'ai pas lu** I haven't read

lui *disj. pron.,* him; **devant lui** in front of him; *as an indir. obj. pron.,* to him/to her

méfiez-vous *v. form (imperative) of* **se méfier** (to beware); **méfiez-vous des obstacles dangereux** beware of dangerous obstacles

meilleur *m.,* **meilleure** *f., adj.,* better; **le meilleur, la meilleure** the best

même *adj.,* same; **tout de même** all the same, just the same

la nouvelle *n.,* (piece of) news; **bonnes nouvelles** good news

la plage *n.,* the beach

plus *adv.,* more; **le plus** the most

profiter *v.,* to profit, to take advantage (of); **il faut profiter du moment** you must take advantage of the moment

la qualité *n.,* the quality; **la qualité la plus forte** the strongest quality

le requin *n.,* the shark

le signe *n.,* the sign; **les signes du Zodiaque** the signs of the Zodiac

le soir *n.,* the evening; **ce soir** this evening, tonight; **une soirée** an evening party

sortez *v. form (imperative) of* **sortir**; **ne sortez pas** don't go out

soyez *v. form (imperative) of* **être**; **soyez prudent!** be prudent!

EXERCISES

Review the story and vocabulary before starting these exercises.

I. Complete the following statements by writing the appropriate words. They are all in the story. Refer to it if you have to.

1. Pierre _____ le journal dans la cuisine. Il a la page _____ devant
   _____ .

2. Vous êtes _____ juge de vos actions.

3. Votre qualité la _____ est la patience.

4. La personne qui vous aime _____ attend un courriel de vous.

5. Il faut profiter _____ . Quelle _____ ! Bonnes _____ !

II. **Letters or Notes. Proficiency in Writing.**

Situation: Your best friend has invited you to a **soirée** at her house. Write a note to her expressing your thanks, but say that you cannot come and explain why. Write at least twelve words in French, using your own ideas and words. You may refer to the story at the beginning of this work unit.

III. **Unscramble the words to find a meaningful sentence. Write it on the blank line. Refer to the story in this unit if you have to.**

1. Pierre / horoscope / son / lit.

_____

2. Demain / parfait / jour / être / va / un.

_____

3. Une / personne / aime / vous / beaucoup.

_____

4. Il / a / y / requin / un / l'eau / dans.

_____

5. Téléphone / sonne / le.

_____

STRUCTURES DE LA LANGUE

A. Forms of the interrogative adjective **Quel**

Masculine		Feminine	
Singular	*Plural*	*Singular*	*Plural*
quel *(what, which)*	quels	quelle *(what, which)*	quelles

RULES AND OBSERVATIONS:

1. The interrogative adjective quel agrees in gender and number with the noun it modifies.

2. Here are four examples to illustrate each form:

    1. **Quel livre** lisez-vous?   *Which (what) book are you reading?*

    2. **Quels fruits** aimez-vous?   *Which (what) fruits do you like?*

    3. **Quelle leçon** étudiez-vous?   *Which (what) lesson are you studying?*

    4. **Quelles phrases** écrivez-vous?   *Which (what) sentences are you writing?*

3. In exclamations, **quel** and **quelle** mean *what a . . . !*

Quel homme! (What a man!)

Quel homme!	*What a* man!
Quelle femme!	*What a* woman!
Quelle semaine!	*What a* week!

4. When the verb **être** is used, the form of **quel** is not ordinarily in front of the noun it modifies:

Quel est votre nom?	*What* is your name?
Quelle est votre adresse?	*What* is your address?

EXERCISES

Review the preceding material before starting these exercises.

I.   Write in French the questions that must have been asked.

Model: **Il est dix heures et quart.**   You write the question: **Quelle heure est-il?**
(It is 10:15.)   (What time is it?)

1. Mon nom est Pierre Paquet.

_____

2. Mon adresse est 17, rue de Rivoli.

_____

3. J'ai vingt ans.

_____

II. **Answer the following questions in complete sentences. They are personal questions and require answers of your own.**

1. Quel est votre nom?

_____

2. Quelle est votre adresse?

_____

3. Quel âge avez-vous?

_____

III. **Write the appropriate form of quel on the blank line.**

1. Vous lisez un livre! _____ livre lisez-vous?

2. Vous écrivez des phrases! _____ phrases écrivez-vous?

3. Vous aimez les fruits! _____ fruits aimez-vous?

4. Vous étudiez une leçon! _____ leçon étudiez-vous?

IV. **Match the following.**

1. Quel homme!   _____ What a car!

2. Quelle femme!   _____ What a stew!

3. Quel ragoût!   _____ What a man!

4. Quel livre!   _____ What a book!

5. Quelle voiture!   _____ What a woman!

V. **Vocabulary Building. Proficiency in Writing.**

A. Write five adjectives in French that the three girls have in mind to describe the young man (see page 286).

1. _____ 2. _____ 3. _____ 4. _____ 5. _____

B. Write five adjectives in French that the young man has in mind to describe the three girls.

1. _____ 2. _____ 3. _____ 4. _____ 5. _____

B. Demonstrative adjectives

1. **ce** garçon	1. this (that) boy
2. **cet** arbre	2. this (that) tree
3. **cet** homme	3. this (that) man
4. **cette** femme	4. this (that) woman
5. **cette** église	5. this (that) church
6. **ces** femmes	6. these (those) women
7. **ces** hommes	7. these (those) men

RULES AND OBSERVATIONS:

1. **Ce** is used before a masculine singular noun that begins with a consonant. See example 1 in the box on the preceeding page.

2. **Cet** is used before a masculine singular noun that begins with a vowel or silent *h.* See examples 2 and 3 in the box on the preceeding page.

3. **Cette** is used before *all* feminine singular nouns.

4. **Ces** is used in front of *all* nouns in the plural.

5. These demonstrative adjectives can mean *this* or *that* in the singular, depending on the meaning intended. **Ces** can mean *these* or *those.*

6. If there is any doubt as to the meaning (*this, that, these, those*), just add **-ci** to the noun to give it the meaning of *this* or *these.* Actually, **-ci** is a shortening of *ici,* which means *here.* Add **-là** (which means *there*) to the noun to give it the meaning of *that* or *those.* Examples:

ce livre-ci	*this book*	**cette page-ci**	*this page*
ce livre-là	*that book*	**cette page-là**	*that page*
ces livres-ci	*these books*	**ces pages-ci**	*these pages*
ces livres-là	*those books*	**ces pages-là**	*those pages*

7. If there is more than one noun, a demonstrative adjective must be used in front of each noun; **cette dame et ce monsieur** *(this lady and gentleman).*

EXERCISES

Review the preceding material before starting these exercises.

I.   **Substitute the noun in parentheses for the noun in italics. Rewrite the sentence, using the appropriate form of the demonstrative adjective given.**

Model: **Je mange ce *fruit.* (pomme)**   You write: **Je mange cette pomme.**
(I am eating this fruit. [apple])   (I am eating this apple.)

A. Je mange cette *soupe.*

1. (pêche)

_____

2. (gâteau)

_____

3. (petits fours)

_____

4. (ananas)

_____

5. (tomate)

_____

B. Etudiez-vous ce *vocabulaire*?

1. (leçon)

_____

2. (livre)

_____

3. (pages)

_____

4. (phrases)

_____

5. (poème)

_____

C. Nous allons au cinéma avec ces *garçons.*

1. (jeunes filles)

_____

2. (ami)

_____

3. (amie)

_____

4. (jeune homme)

_____

5. (étudiants)

_____

II. For each imperative that is given, write a response indicating that you are doing what you are told to do.

Model: **Donnez-moi ce livre!**   You write: **Bien! Je vous donne ce livre!**
(Give me this book!)   (Good! I am giving you this book!)

1. Donnez-moi ce journal!

_____

2. Donnez-lui cette pomme!

_____

3. Donnez-leur ces pommes frites!

_____

III. Change the demonstrative adjective and the noun, which are in italics, to the singular or plural, depending on what is given. Rewrite the sentence.

Model: **Je vais lire _ces livres_ et _cette lettre._**
(I am going to read these books and this letter.)

You write: **Je vais lire ce livre et ces lettres.**
(I am going to read this book and these letters.)

1. Je vais manger _ces ananas_ et _cette tomate._

_____

2. Je vais écrire _ces leçons_ et _cette phrase._

_____

3. Je vais boire _ce vin_ et _cette bière._

_____

4. Je vais envoyer _ces lettres._

_____

5. Je vais acheter _ces livres._

_____

C. Regular comparative and superlative adjectives

Adjective (masc. and fem.)	Comparative	Superlative
grand tall	**plus grand (que)** taller (than)	**le plus grand (de)** (the) tallest (in)
grande tall	**plus grande (que)** taller (than)	**la plus grande (de)** (the) tallest (in)
grand tall	**moins grand (que)** less tall (than)	**le moins grand (de)** (the) least tall (in)
grande tall	**moins grande (que)** less tall (than)	**la moins grande (de)** (the) least tall (in)
grand tall	**aussi grand (que)** as tall (as)	
grande tall	**aussi grande (que)** as tall (as)	
intelligent intelligent	**plus intelligent (que)** more intelligent (than)	**le plus intelligent (de)** (the) most intelligent (in)
intelligente intelligent	**plus intelligente (que)** more intelligent (than)	**la plus intelligente (de)** (the) most intelligent (in)
intelligent intelligent	**moins intelligent (que)** less intelligent (than)	**le moins intelligent (de)** (the) least intelligent (in)
intelligente intelligent	**moins intelligente (que)** less intelligent (than)	**la moins intelligente (de)** (the) least intelligent (in)
intelligent intelligent	**aussi intelligent (que)** as intelligent (as)	
intelligente intelligent	**aussi intelligente (que)** as intelligent (as)	

RULES AND OBSERVATIONS:

1. In making a comparison in English, we ordinarily add **-er** to the adjective (*tall, taller*) or we place *more* or *less* in front of the adjective (*more intelligent, less intelligent*). In French, we use **plus** or **moins** in front of the adjective. See the examples in the preceding box.

2. In order to express *as . . . as* in French, we use **aussi . . . que**.

3. The adjective must agree in gender and number with the noun it modifies. Example: Marie est plus **intelligente** que son frère. (Mary is more intelligent than her brother.)

4. In making a comparison, we use **que** in French to express *than*; we also use **que** in French to express *as*.

5. If the adjective is one that ordinarily is placed in front of the noun, then it remains in front of the noun when making a comparison. If the adjective is one that ordinarily is placed after the noun, then it remains after the noun when making a comparison. Examples:

   une jolie robe, une plus jolie robe, la plus jolie robe
   a pretty dress, a prettier dress, the prettiest dress

   une personne intelligente, une personne plus intelligente, la personne la plus intelligente
   an intelligent person, a more intelligent person, the most intelligent person

D. Irregular comparative and superlative adjectives

Adjective (*masc.*)	Comparative	Superlative
bon, *good*	**meilleur**, *better*	**le meilleur**, *(the) best*
mauvais, *bad*	**plus mauvais**, *worse*	**le plus mauvais**, *(the) worst*
	pire, *worse*	**le pire**, *(the) worst*
petit, *small*	**plus petit**, *smaller (in size)*	**le plus petit**, *(the) smallest*
	moindre, *less (in importance)*	**le moindre**, *(the) least*

RULES AND OBSERVATIONS:

1. Actually, there are no rules that apply to these irregular adjectives of comparison. Just study them and make observations of your own.

2. Observe that **mauvais** and **petit** have regular and irregular comparisons.

3. Note that **de** is used (and not **dans**) to express *in* when using the superlative.

EXERCISES

Review the preceding material before starting these exercises.

I. Answer the following questions in French, substituting the appropriate forms of the words in parentheses for the ones indicated. Use **non** in your answer, but write your sentence in the affirmative. Also, use a pronoun subject in place of the noun subject.

Model: **Est-ce que Paul est *plus* intelligent que son frère? (moins)** (Is Paul more intelligent than his brother? [less]) You write: **Non, il est moins intelligent que son frère.** (No, he is less intelligent than his brother.)

1. Est-ce que Pierre est *plus* grand que sa mère?   (moins)

_____

2. Est-ce que Janine est *plus* grande que son père?   (moins)

_____

3. Est-ce que Monique est *plus* intelligente que Janine?   (moins)

_____

II. Answer the following questions in complete sentences. Use the noun in parentheses in your answer. Make all required changes in the forms of the adjectives.

Model: **Qui est plus grand que Robert? (Janine)** (Who is taller than Robert?) You write: **Janine est plus grande que Robert.** (Janine is taller than Robert.)

1. Qui est plus grand que Janine?   (Madame Paquet)

_____

2. Qui est moins grand que Pierre?   (Janine)

_____

3. Qui est plus petit que Monique?   (Mathilde)

_____

4. Qui est moins petit que Joseph?   (Suzanne)

_____

5. Qui est aussi grand que Monsieur Paquet?   (Monsieur Richy)

_____

6. Qui est aussi petit que Madame Banluc?   (Madame Paquet)

_____

III. For each statement, write in French a response contradicting the statement. Begin your response with **Non, ce n'est pas vrai**. Then use the name in parentheses in your answer in place of the noun subject in the statement, which is in italics. Make all required changes in agreement.

Model: ***Monique* est la plus intelligente du cours d'anglais. (Joseph)**
(Monique is the most intelligent in the English course.) (Joseph)

You write: **Non, ce n'est pas vrai. Joseph est le plus intelligent du cours d'anglais.** (No, it's not true. Joseph is the most intelligent in the English course.)

1. *Raymond* est le plus intelligent du cours de mathématiques. (Janine)

_____

2. *Bob* est le plus grand du cours de français. (Suzanne)

_____

Michelle est la moins grande de la famille. (Michelle is the least tall in the family.)

3. *Michelle* est la moins grande de la famille. (Simon)

_____

4. *Béatrice* est la plus belle du groupe. (Charles)

_____

5. *Henri* est le plus petit. (Hélène)

_____

IV. Answer the following questions in the affirmative in complete French sentences. In answer (a) use **oui** and write a complete sentence. In answer (b) write a complete answer and add **aussi**. Make the required changes in the adjectives.

Models: **(a) Ce livre est-il plus long que les autres?** (Is this book longer than the others?)

You write: **(a) Oui, ce livre est plus long que les autres.** (Yes, this book is longer than the others.)

(b) Et cette lettre? (And this letter?)

You write: **(b) Cette lettre est plus longue que les autres aussi.** (This letter is longer than the others also.)

1. (a) Cette phrase est-elle moins facile que les autres?

   _____

   (b) Et ces questions?

   _____

2. (a) Ce poème est-il plus difficile que les autres?

   _____

   (b) Et cette leçon?

   _____

3. (a) Cette voiture est-elle plus belle que les autres?

   _____

   (b) Et ces maisons?

   _____

4. (a) Ce garçon est-il plus beau que les autres?

   _____

   (b) Et ces jeunes filles?

   _____

5. (a) Cette banane est-elle plus délicieuse que les autres?

   _____

   (b) Et ces gâteaux?

   _____

V. On the blank line write the French equivalent for the English words in parentheses.

1. (more)   Simone est _____ intelligente que sa soeur.

2. (tall)   Alain est aussi _____ que sa mère.

3. (as)   Monique est _____ petite que son père.

4. (prettier)   Anne est _____ que Suzanne.

5. (the least)   Michel est _____ grand.

VI. **Le Mot Mystère.** (Mystery Word). In order to find the mystery word, you must first find and circle in the puzzle the French words given under it. The letters that remain in the puzzle are scrambled. Unscramble them to find **le mot mystère.**

E	M	A	R	C	H	E	E	T	R
N	V	Q	U	I	O	T	T	O	F
A	M	I	E	I	L	U	A	U	A
G	E	B	R	U	I	T	Y	R	I
R	M	Ê	M	E	I	P	N	N	R
I	D	A	N	S	À	L	O	E	E
S	P	A	Y	E	R	U	N	V	T
E	U	Q	U	E	L	S	E	I	S
P	O	U	B	E	L	L	E	S	O
	B	E	A	U	C	O	U	P	N

à	grise	poubelle
amie	il	quel
au	marche	qui
beaucoup	me	se
bruit	même	son
dans	non	tournevis
en	payer	tu
et	plus	y
faire		

VII. **Earning a Living. Proficiency in Speaking and Writing.**

Situation: You are a salesclerk (**le vendeur, la vendeuse**) in a UNISEX shop. A customer (**le client, la cliente**) comes in to buy a few articles of clothing.

Greet the customer by saying: **Bonjour! Vous désirez?** The customer wants to buy a T-shirt, a big black hat, a long coat, and other items. After your opening statement, show the customer a few things and ask questions. You may use your own ideas and words and/or all of the following: **ce, cet, cette, ces, quel, quelle, quels, quelles; regarder, joli, meilleur, aimer, préférer, plus joli(e) que, plus beau (belle) que, plus grand(e) que.** Use as many comparative and superlative adjectives as you can. They are in this work unit.

Ask a friend to act out the role of the customer in this conversation. Later, switch roles for more practice. When you are satisfied with what you both said, write the conversation for practice. For starters, consider the following:

Vous: Bonjour! Vous désirez?

Le client: Je désire acheter un grand chapeau noir.

Vous: Ce grand chapeau noir est beau. Ce chapeau-là est plus grand et plus beau. L'aimez-vous?

Now, continue the conversation.

295

VIII. Helping Others. Speaking and Writing Proficiency

Situation: You are the best student in your French class. Robert, a classmate is having problems with adjectives and needs your help. You are together at your kitchen table with your French books and some paper on which to practice.

You may use your own ideas and words and/or the suggestions under the lines. First, respond in spoken French; then write your words on the lines. Later, you may switch roles. Use the **tu** form with each other because you are friends.

Robert: **Je ne comprends pas les adjectifs, les comparatifs, les superlatifs, et leur position. J'ai besoin de pratique/**I need practice.

Vous: _____

*There's no problem/*Il n'y a pas de problème. *Tell me, is Anne prettier than Monique?/*Dis-moi, est-ce qu'Anne est plus jolie que Monique?

Robert: **Non. Anne n'est pas plus jolie que Monique. Monique est la plus jolie de la classe.**

Vous: _____

*Tell me, is my father taller than your father?/*Dis-moi, mon père est-il plus grand que ton père?

Robert: **Non. Ton père n'est pas plus grand que mon père. Mais ta mère est plus grande que ma mère.**

Vous: _____

Tell me, who is the best student in our French class?

Robert: **C'est toi! Tu es le meilleur (la meilleure) étudiant(e) de notre classe de français.**

Vous: _____

*Me?!/*Moi?! *You think that I am the best student in our French class?!/*Tu penses que je suis le meilleur (la meilleure) étudiant(e) de notre classe de français?!

Robert: **Oui, oui. Je t'assure!**

Vous: _____

*Thank you! Now, let's eat some chocolate mousse/*Merci! Maintenant, mangeons de la mousse au chocolat. *It's the best in the world!!/*C'est la meilleure du monde.

IX. Expressing Love on Mother's Day. Proficiency in Speaking and Writing.

Situation: Next Sunday is Mother's Day. In the space provided, write your own card and give it to your mother or to some friend or relative who has been like a mother to you. Before you start, take a few minutes to gather your thoughts, jot down a few words in French that you will use, then say them aloud.

You may also use the following: **à la plus sympa de toutes les mamans**/*to the nicest of all Moms*; **de tout coeur**/*with all my heart*; **Je te souhaite une joyeuse Fête des Mères**/*I wish you a Happy Mother's Day*; **Je t'aime**/*I love you*; **Chez nous, j'ai appris la valeur de l'amour depuis mon enfance**/*In our home, I learned the value of love since childhood*.

Donne-moi la boîte de chocolats! (Give me the box of chocolates!)

Work Unit 20
Adverbs and Tag Questions—*n'est-ce pas?*

Janine receives a phone call from a neighbor, Madame Bédier. She wants her to babysit with Renée, her five-year-old daughter, while she and her husband are at the movies. What do you suppose happens to the box of chocolates while they are out?

La boîte de chocolats

C'est samedi. Janine n'a rien à faire. Elle est à la fenêtre dans sa chambre. Elle regarde les oiseaux sur les branches du pommier dans le jardin.

Le téléphone sonne.

—Janine! C'est pour toi, dit sa mère.

Janine quitte sa chambre et descend l'escalier.

—C'est Madame Bédier, dit sa mère. Elle va au cinéma ce soir avec son mari et elle a besoin de toi.

—Allô! J'écoute. Ici Janine . . . . Comment allez-vous, madame? . . . . Très bien, merci . . . . Je ne fais rien ce soir . . . . Vous allez au cinéma . . . Ah! Bon! . . . . D'accord . . . . Oui, je peux venir chez vous ce soir et rester avec Renée . . . . Oui, je sais . . . . Oh, elle a déjà cinq ans! . . . . Oui, elle est grande pour son âge . . . . Oui, je sais qu'elle est capricieuse . . . . Oui, je sais qu'elle parle plus vite que les autres enfants . . . . Oui, je sais qu'elle marche moins vite que les autres enfants . . . . Bon! . . . . D'accord! À six heures et demie . . . . À ce soir, madame.

À six heures vingt, Janine quitte la maison pour aller chez les Bédier qui habitent à côté de la maison des Paquet.

—Ah! Janine! s'exclame Madame Bédier. Philippe! C'est Janine! La meilleure gardienne d'enfants du voisinage! N'est-ce pas, Philippe!

Monsieur et Madame Bédier ont mis leurs chapeaux, manteaux, et gants. Avant de sortir, Madame Bédier dit:

—Renée, sois sage! À huit heures et demie tu vas te coucher, n'est-ce pas? Janine, tu sais où est la chambre de Renée, n'est-ce pas? La boîte de chocolats est là-bas sur la petite table ronde. Seulement un morceau pour Renée. Elle en a mangé trois aujourd'hui. Janine, tu peux en avoir deux morceaux si tu veux parce que tu es plus grande que Renée. Il y a une comédie à la télévision ce soir. Nous allons voir le film *La Lettre* au Bijou. À tout à l'heure!

Ils partent.

—Janine, je veux mon morceau de chocolat maintenant, dit Renée. J'aime mieux la cerise à la crème. Quel morceau est la cerise à la crème, Janine? demande Renée.

—Je ne sais pas! J'aime beaucoup les chocolats et mon favori est le nougat. Quel morceau est le nougat, Renée? demande Janine.

—Je ne sais pas! . . . . Ah! . . . . je sais comment savoir!

—Comment? demande Janine.

—Je vais écraser chaque morceau avec le doigt, répond Renée.

—Non! Renée! Non! Tu vas les abîmer! s'exclame Janine.

—Ça ne fait rien. Laisse-moi! crie Renée.

Renée arrache vigoureusement la boîte de chocolats des mains de Janine et elle commence à piquer chaque morceau avec son doigt.

—Voilà, Janine! Voilà la cerise à la crème pour moi et le nougat pour toi!

—Oh! Tous les morceaux de chocolat sont écrasés! Tout est abîmé! Qu'est-ce que je vais dire à tes parents? s'exclame Janine.

Renée quitte le salon avec la boîte de chocolats. Après quelques minutes, elle revient dans le salon et elle dit:

—Janine, ne t'inquiète pas. J'ai jeté la boîte de chocolats dans la poubelle avec les ordures! Maintenant, tu n'as pas besoin d'expliquer à mes parents.

—Ta mère a raison, lui dit Janine. Tu es vraiment capricieuse. Méchante! Va te coucher! Vite!

Trois heures plus tard, Monsieur et Madame Bédier rentrent à la maison. Madame entre dans le salon et dit:

—Janine, tu peux avoir toute la boîte de chocolats. Emporte la boîte avec toi. Bonsoir, et merci!

VOCABULAIRE

à tout à l'heure! see you in a little while!

abîmer *v.*, to spoil, to ruin

l'accord *n. m.*, the agreement; **d'accord** okay, agreed

allô *interj.*, hello (used when answering the telephone)

arracher *v.*, to pull away, to pull out

avant *prep.*, before; **avant de sortir** before going out

le besoin *n.*, the need; **avoir besoin de** to have need of, to need

la boîte *n.*, the box

bonsoir *salutation*, good evening

ça ne fait rien! that doesn't matter!

capricieux *m.*, **capricieuse** *f.*, *adj.*, capricious, whimsical

la cerise *n.*, the cherry

chaque *adj.*, each

le côté *n.*, the side, **à côté de** next to

déjà *adv.*, already; **elle a déjà cinq ans!** she is already five years old!

descendre *v.*, to descend, to come (go) down

écraser *v.*, to crush

en *pron.*, *partitive*, of them; **elle en a mangé trois!** she ate three (of them)

l'escalier *n. m.*, the staircase

le gant *n.*, the glove

le gardien, la gardienne *n.*, the guardian; **gardien (gardienne) d'enfants** babysitter

s'inquiéter *refl. v.*, to worry, to be upset; **ne t'inquiète pas!** don't worry!

jeter *v.*, to throw

laisse-moi! let me!

le manteau *n.*, the coat

méchant *m.*, **méchante** *f.*, *adj.*, mean, nasty, naughty

mieux *adv.*, better; **j'aime mieux** I prefer, I like better

mignon *m.*, **mignonne** *f.*, *adj.*, darling, cute

le morceau *n.*, piece; **les morceaux** *n. pl.*, pieces; **un morceau de chocolat** a piece of chocolate

l'oiseau *n. m.*, the bird

l'ordure *n. f.*, garbage, rubbish

piquer *v.*, to poke, to puncture

le pommier *n.*, the apple tree

sois *v. form of* être; **sois sage!** be good!

va te coucher! go to bed! (*v. form of* aller se coucher)

le voisinage *n.*, the neighborhood

EXERCISES

Review the story and vocabulary before starting these exercises.

I. Resolving a Quarrel. Proficiency in Speaking and Writing.

Situation: You are babysitting in your neighbor's house next door. They have two children—Robert, who is five years old, and Debbie, who is seven. They are quarreling with each other about what to watch on TV. You do your best to settle the argument. In five sentences resolve the quarrel and restore order. You may use your own ideas or ideas suggested by the following: **avoir, être, sois (soyez) sage(s), avoir besoin de, capricieux, capricieuse, abîmer, laisse-moi! jeter, méchant(e), va te coucher! vite** (quickly).

First, say aloud the French words you plan to use. Then write five short sentences using them.

_____

_____

_____

_____

_____

II. Choose the correct answer.

1. Janine est à la fenêtre dans

(a) le salon.   (b) la cuisine.   (c) la salle de bains.   (d) sa chambre.   _____

2. Madame et Monsieur Bédier vont

(a) au cinéma.   (b) à l'église.   (c) au théâtre.   (d) à l'opéra.   _____

3. Renée a jeté la boîte de chocolats

(a) par la fenêtre.   (b) dans la rue.   (c) dans la poubelle.   (d) contre le mur.   _____

4. La boîte de chocolats est

(a) dans le tiroir. (b) sur la petite table ronde. (c) dans la cuisine. (d) sous le lit.   _____

5. Renée est

(a) très mignonne.   (b) très gentille.   (c) capricieuse.   (d) fatiguée.   _____

III. Vocabulary Building. Proficiency in Writing.

A. Describe how your neighbor talks, using three adverbs that end in **-ment.**

1. _____   2. _____   3. _____

B. Describe how a friend of yours eats, using four adverbs that do not end in **-ment.**

1. _____   2. _____   3. _____   4. _____

STRUCTURES DE LA LANGUE

A. Position of an adverb

1. Janine aime **beaucoup** les chocolats.	(Janine likes chocolates *very much.*)
2. Madame Bédier a parlé **distinctement.**	(Mrs. Bédier spoke *distinctly.*)
3. Madame Bédier a **bien** parlé.	(Mrs. Bédier spoke *well.*)

RULES AND OBSERVATIONS:

1. An adverb is a word that describes a verb, an adjective, or another adverb.

2. In French, an adverb ordinarily *follows* the simple verb it modifies, as in the first model sentence in the above box.

3. If a verb is compound, as in the passé composé (model sentence 2), the adverb generally *follows* the past participle only if it is a long adverb. The adverb **distinctement** is long.

4. If a verb is compound, as in the passé composé (model sentence 3), *short common adverbs* (like **beaucoup**, **bien**, **déjà**, **encore**, **mal**, **mieux**, **souvent**, **toujours**) *must precede* the past participle.

B. Formation of some adverbs

1. Many adverbs are formed in French by adding the ending **-ment** to the *feminine singular* form of an adjective. This is similar to adding *-ly* to an adjective in English to form an adverb: *quick/quickly.*

seule/seulement	**furieuse/furieusement**
(alone/only)	(furious/furiously)

2. Ordinarily, adjectives that end in **-ant** are transformed into adverbs by dropping **-ant** and adding **-amment**.

constant/constamment	(constant/constantly)

3. Ordinarily, adjectives that end in **-ent** are transformed into adverbs by dropping **-ent** and adding **-emment**.

patient/patiemment	(patient/patiently)

C. Regular comparison of adverbs

Adverb	Comparative	Superlative
vite *(quickly)*	**plus vite (que)** *more quickly (than)* *faster (than)*	**le plus vite** *(the) most quickly* *(the) fastest*
	moins vite (que) *less quickly (than)*	**le moins vite** *(the) least quickly*
	aussi vite (que) *as quickly (as)* *as fast (as)*	

D. Tag question: **n'est-ce pas?**

The phrase *n'est-ce pas?* is tagged to a statement when the speaker expects the listener to agree. It can be translated into English in any number of ways: *isn't that right? isn't that so?* etc. The appropriate translation into English depends on the meaning of the statement in French.

| Renée a cinq ans, **n'est-ce pas?** | (Renée is five years old, *isn't she*?) |

EXERCISES

Review the preceding material before starting these exercises.

I.   **Change the following adjectives to adverbs.**

Model: **furieuse**   **furieusement**
         (furious)   (furiously)

1. distincte _____

2. seule _____

3. courageuse _____

4. constant _____

5. patient _____

6. fière _____

II.   **Rewrite each sentence, adding the adverb in parentheses in its proper position.**

Model: **Madame Coty aime le**   You write: **Madame Coty aime**
         café. (beaucoup)   **beaucoup le café.**
         (Mrs. Coty likes coffee.   (Mrs. Coty likes coffee
         [very much])   very much.)

1. Monsieur Richy aime le ragoût brûlé. (beaucoup)

_____

2. Le professeur a parlé. (bien)

_____

3. Janine a parlé. (constamment)

_____

4. Elle est partie. (déjà)

_____

5. Pierre a mangé. (beaucoup)

_____

303

III. **Write the French adverb for the English in italics.**

> **Model:** Pierre marche aussi *quickly* que son père.   **You write:**   vite
> (Pierre walks as *quickly* as his father.)   (quickly)

1. Janine parle aussi *well* que sa mère.   _____

2. Joseph mange *more* vite que son frère.   _____

3. Bob marche *as* lentement *as* son cousin.   _____   _____

4. Raymond étudie *more* souvent *than* Michel.   _____   _____

5. Mathilde parle *less* vite que sa soeur.   _____

IV. **Le Mot Mystère** (Mystery Word). In order to find the *mystery word*, you must first find and circle in this puzzle the French words given under it. The letters that remain in the puzzle are scrambled. Unscramble them to find *le mot mystère.*

```
A  E  M  V  P  Y  G  R  I  S
U  N  O  O  L  A  L  L  E  R
T  F  I  I  U  A  L  A  C  A
O  J  N  T  S  A  U  S  S  I
M  O  S  U  G  A  R  Ç  O  N
O  L  P  R  R  F  E  M  M  E
B  I  E  E  A  N  E  P  A  S
I  R  T  B  N  N  L  U  I  E
L  I  I  O  D  L  U  N  D  I
E  L  T  N  O  P  É  R  A  S
```

à	garçon	moins petit
aller	gris	ne
aussi	il	opéras
automobile	joli	pas
bon	la	plus grand
en	lui	voiture
femme	lundi	y

V. **Human Behavior. Proficiency in Speaking and Writing.**

Situation: Your parents would like to know something about the behavior of two children in your neighborhood, a girl and a boy, before they give you permission to babysit. Tell your parents something about the way the children talk, eat, play. You may want to use your own ideas and adverbs or those suggested here: **bien, mal, beaucoup, constamment, furieusement, distinctement, souvent, toujours, vite.** You may also want to compare their behavior; for example, one of the two talks more or less distinctly than the other, plays better than the other, and so on. Of course, mention the names of the children.

First, say aloud the French words you plan to use. Then write at least three sentences using them.

_____

_____

_____

Test 4

This test is based on Work Units 16 to 20. Review them before starting this test.

PART ONE SPEAKING PROFICIENCY

Directions: Read the twelve situations given below. Take a few minutes to organize your thoughts about the words you are going to speak. Select ten of them.

1. **Situation:** You saw a soccer game. Tell us about it in at least three sentences.

2. **Situation:** You are at the Metropolitan Museum of Art in New York City admiring the painting *Répétition d'un ballet sur la scène* by Edgar Degas, a great French artist. Tell us about it in at least three sentences.

3. **Situation:** Your French teacher is absent today because of illness and you have a substitute in class. Greet the substitute teacher, introduce yourself, and tell her or him that you would like to play a game of true or false in class today because you like to practice speaking French.

4. **Situation:** The substitute teacher has agreed to playing true or false games in French. You have the pleasure of starting. Make at least three statements. After each statement, ask if it's true or false.

5. **Situation:** Your friend Richard did not go to school today because he is not feeling well. He has called you at home to find out what you did in French class. Make at least three statements in French using the **passé composé.**

6. **Situation:** A friend has telephoned inviting you to go to a dance this Saturday night. Make at least three statements that you would say in this conversation.

7. **Situation:** You are at a dinner party at the home of some friends. Express your personal feelings by telling the hostess you like very much the dinner that she prepared, thank her for the invitation, and tell her that she is very nice and likable.

8. **Situation:** A car salesperson is showing you a brand new car. Use five adjectives to describe it.

9. **Situation:** In at least three short sentences, describe the house or apartment you live in.

10. **Situation:** You and a friend are at a museum admiring the painting *Rue de Tahiti* by the great French artist, Paul Gauguin. Make three statements about what you see in the painting.

11. **Situation:** Your best friend has invited you to an evening party (**une soirée**) at her house. Thank her for the invitation but say you cannot come and explain why.

12. **Situation:** Next Sunday is Mother's Day. Make three statements that you plan to write on a card.

PART TWO   LISTENING PROFICIENCY

Directions: Your teacher will read aloud four short paragraphs. Each one will contain only a few sentences. You will hear each paragraph twice. Then you will hear one question based on each. You will hear the question only once. It is printed below. Choose the best suggested answer and check the letter of your choice.

Selection Number 1

1. Qui est entré dans la salle de classe?

    A. Madame Ravel
    B. La directrice
    C. Les deux dames
    D. Les étudiants

Selection Number 2

2. Qui a crié "Surprise! Surprise!"?

    A. Claire
    B. François
    C. Monsieur Berger
    D. Toutes les personnes dans la maison

Selection Number 3

3. Pourquoi Monsieur Paquet appelle-t-il la station-service?

    A. parce qu'il monte dans sa voiture
    B. parce qu'il veut aller faire des courses
    C. parce que le garagiste n'est pas arrivé
    D. parce que la voiture ne marche pas

Selection Number 4

4. Pourquoi Monique a-t-elle téléphoné à Pierre?

    A. pour danser et chanter chez lui
    B. parce que sa mère a préparé un gâteau délicieux
    C. parce que ses amis vont s'amuser
    D. pour l'inviter à une soirée chez elle

PART THREE   READING PROFICIENCY

Directions: In the following passage there are five blank spaces numbered 1 through 5. Each blank space represents a missing word. For each blank space, four possible completions are provided. Only one of them makes sense in the context of the passage.

First, read the passage in its entirety to determine its general meaning. Then read it a second time. For each blank space choose the completion that makes the best sense and is grammatically correct. Write its letter in the space provided.

Monsieur et Madame Durand ont _____ une invitation à dîner chez leurs

    1. A. recevoir
        B. reçu
        C. reçoivent
        D. reçoit

voisins, Monsieur et Madame Dufy. Monsieur et Madame Durand ont _____

    2. A. accepte
        B. acceptent
        C. accepté
        D. accepter

l'invitation. Quand ils _____ arrivés chez leurs amis, ils sont _____

    3. A. ont   4. A. entré
        B. sont   B. entrée
        C. a   C. entrées
        D. est   D. entrés

dans le foyer. Ils ont _____ d'autres voisins chez eux.

    5. A. voir
        B. voient
        C. voit
        D. vu

PART FOUR   WRITING PROFICIENCY

Directions: Of the twelve situations in Part One (Speaking Proficiency) in this test, select ten and write what you said on the lines below.

Situation No. __ _____

_____

_____

Situation No. __ _____

_____

_____

Situation No. __ _____

_____

_____

Situation No. __ _____

_____

_____

Situation No. __ _____

_____

_____

Situation No. __ _____

_____

_____

Situation No. __ _____

_____

_____

Situation No. __ _____

_____

_____

Situation No. __ _____

_____

_____

Situation No. __ _____

_____

_____

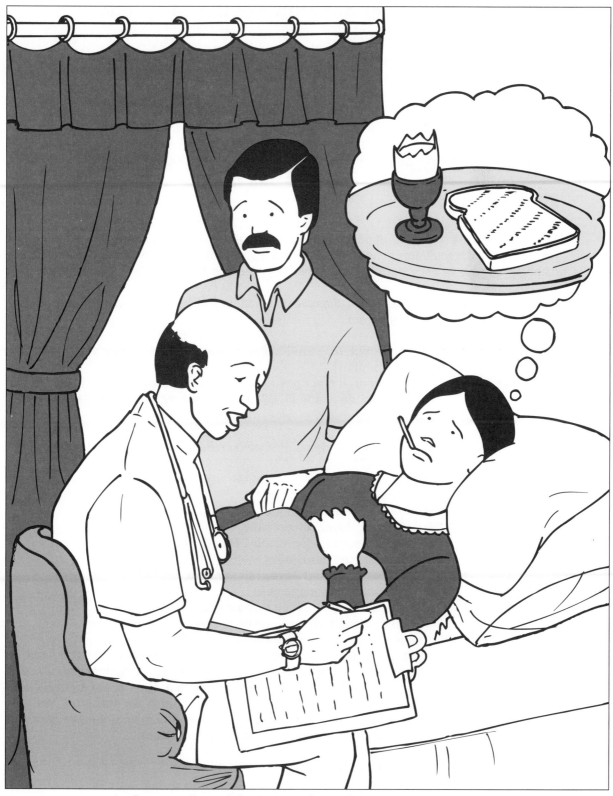

Le Docteur: Il est ridicule de croire qu'il faut manger pour vivre.
(The Doctor: It is ridiculous to believe that one must eat in order to live.)

Work Unit 21
Negations and Other Structures of the Language

*Mrs. Paquet has been sick since
yesterday. She has indigestion.
What do you think of the doctor's
advice? Would you do what he says
or what she does?*

Manger pour vivre ou vivre pour manger?

Madame Paquet est malade depuis hier. Elle a mangé quelque chose qui lui a donné mal à l'estomac. Elle est souffrante dans son lit. Son mari a appelé le docteur pour lui donner un médicament. Le docteur va venir dans quelques minutes. Madame Paquet l'attend patiemment depuis vingt minutes.

Le docteur est arrivé. Il est dans la chambre de Madame Paquet depuis quinze minutes. Il l'examine. Monsieur Paquet est avec eux.

Monsieur Paquet:	Dites-moi, docteur, faut-il appeler une ambulance pour transporter ma femme à l'hôpital?
Le Docteur:	Non, monsieur. Il n'est pas nécessaire de la transporter à l'hôpital. Elle peut rester ici dans son lit. Elle n'est pas gravement malade. Les ambulances rendent grand service, mais dans ce cas votre femme peut rester où elle est. J'insiste, chère madame. Prenez ce médicament et ne mangez rien.
Madame Paquet:	Rien manger?!
Le Docteur:	Absolument rien!
Madame Paquet:	Pas même un oeuf à la coque?
Le Docteur:	Pas même un oeuf à la coque!
Monsieur Paquet:	Mais, docteur, soyez raisonnable.
Madame Paquet:	Oui, docteur, soyez raisonnable? Rien à manger?
Le Docteur:	Pendant au moins deux jours.
Madame Paquet:	Je vais mourir de faim! Soyez raisonnable, docteur.
Le Docteur:	Je suis raisonnable, madame.
Madame Paquet:	Pas même un petit morceau de pain grillé?
Le Docteur:	Pas même un petit morceau de pain grillé!
Madame Paquet:	. . . sans beurre . . . sans confiture . . . ?
Le Docteur:	Pas de pain grillé, pas de beurre, pas de confiture. Rien. Il est ridicule de croire qu'il faut manger pour vivre. Rappelez-vous, madame, qu'une personne ne se nourrit pas seulement par le pain. Manger est mauvais pour la santé. Tout le monde mange mal. La chimie du corps ne peut pas tolérer les aliments modernes . . . Excusez-moi maintenant. Je dois partir parce que je vais dîner au Coq d'or: du poisson . . .
Madame Paquet:	Du poisson! Ah!
Le Docteur:	Un beau filet mignon . . .
Madame Paquet:	Ah!
Le Docteur:	Une belle salade . . .
Madame Paquet:	Ah!
Le Docteur:	Rappelez-vous, aussi, que quand j'ai pris le serment d'Hippocrate, j'ai promis de remplir mes devoirs.

Le docteur va à la porte.

Madame Paquet: **Hippocrate ou hypocrite?! Docteur, n'oubliez pas le proverbe: "Dis-moi ce que tu manges et je te dirai ce que tu es!"**

Le docteur sort.

Madame Paquet: **François, y a-t-il quelque chose à manger dans le réfrigérateur? Et donne-moi mon médicament.**

VOCABULAIRE

absolument *adv.,* absolutely

l'aliment *n. m.,* the food

la chimie *n.,* chemistry

Le Coq d'or Golden Rooster (name of a restaurant)

la coque *n.,* the shell (of an egg); **un oeuf à la coque** soft-boiled egg

depuis *adv., prep.,* since: **depuis quand** since when; **depuis combien de temps** since how long (a time); **Madame Paquet est malade depuis hier** Mrs. Paquet has been sick since yesterday

dîner *v.,* to dine, to have dinner

dis-moi ce que tu manges et je te dirai ce que tu es! tell me what you eat and I'll tell you what you are!

dois *v. form of* **devoir** (ought to, have to, must); **je dois** I have (to)

l'estomac *n. m.,* the stomach

griller *v.,* to grill, to toast; **grillé** toasted

Hippocrate *n. m.,* Hippocrates (ancient Greek physician)

le mal *n.,* pain, ache; **mal à l'estomac** stomachache

malade *adj.,* sick, ill

manger *v.,* to eat

le médicament *n.,* medicine

moins *adv.,* less; **au moins** at least

le morceau *n.,* morsel, piece

mourir *v.,* to die

nourrir *v.,* to nourish; **se nourrir** *refl. v.,* to nourish oneself

l'oeuf *n. m.,* the egg

le pain *n.,* the bread; **pain grillé** toast

pas de pain no bread; **pas de beurre** no butter; **pas même** not even

patiemment *adv.,* patiently

pour *prep.,* for, in order (to)

prenez *v. form (imperative) of* **prendre**; **prenez** take

pris *past part. of* **prendre** (to take)

promis *past part. of* **promettre** (to promise)

quelque *adj.,* some; **quelques** a few; **quelque chose** something

rappelez-vous *v. form (imperative) of* **se rappeler** (to remember)

rendre service to perform a service

le serment *n.,* oath; **le serment d'Hippocrate** Hippocratic Oath (a code of medical ethics imposed by Hippocrates upon his students of medicine)

souffrir *v.,* to suffer; **souffrant** *m.,* **souffrante** *f., adj.,* sick

soyez *v. form (imperative) of* **être**; **soyez raisonnable!** be reasonable!

vivre *v.,* to live

EXERCISES

Review the story and vocabulary before starting these exercises.

I. **Answer the following questions in complete sentences. They are based on the story in this unit.**

1. Qui est malade?

_____

2. Pourquoi est-elle malade?

_____

3. Depuis quand est-elle malade?

_____

4. Qui lui donne un médicament?

_____

5. Pourquoi le docteur doit-il partir?

_____

II. **Comment dit-on en français . . . ?** Write the French equivalent for the English given. Refer to the story in this unit if you have to.

1. Mrs. Paquet has been sick since yesterday.

_____

2. Absolutely nothing!

_____

3. Not even a soft-boiled egg!

_____

4. Tell me what you eat and I'll tell you what you are!

_____

5. Take this medicine and don't eat anything!

_____

III. The words in the following boxes are scrambled. Unscramble them to find a **meaningful** sentence. Write the sentence in French on the line provided.

Model:

le	est
arrivé	docteur

You write: Le docteur est arrivé. (The doctor arrived.)

1.

le	est	n'
arrivé	docteur	pas

_____

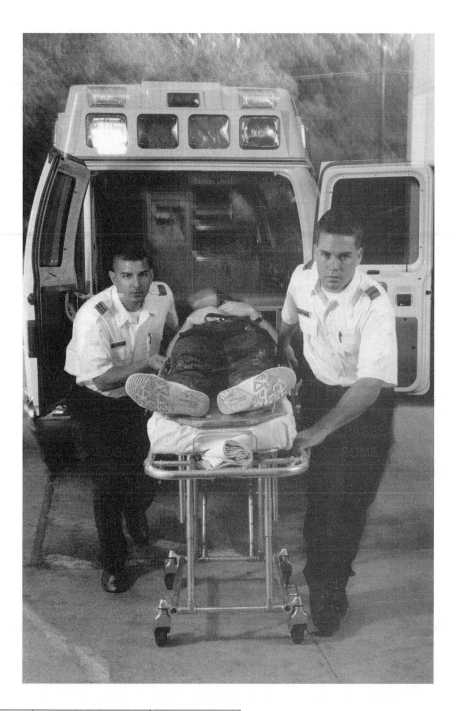

2.

est	Madame Paquet	hier
depuis	malade	n'est-ce pas?

_____

3.

est	la	dans	quinze
chambre	il	depuis	minutes

_____

313

IV. **Mots-croisés.** (Crossword Puzzle). Give the French words for the English.

Verticalement

1. third person sing., pres. indicative of **devoir**

2. to call

5. butter

6. year

7. since

8. bed

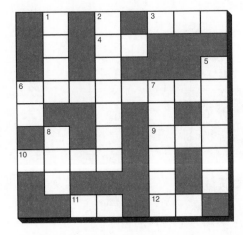

Horizontalement

3. _____ à l'estomac

4. past part. of **pouvoir**

6. to wait

9. by

10. yesterday

11. past part. of **lire**

12. reflexive pronoun

STRUCTURES DE LA LANGUE

A. Negations: **ne . . . pas / ne . . . jamais / ne . . . rien**

Present Indicative	Passé Composé
1. Je **ne** fume **pas**. (I do not smoke.)	4. Je **n'ai pas** fumé. (I did not smoke.)
2. Je **ne** fume **jamais**. (I never smoke.)	5. Je **n'ai jamais** fumé. (I have never smoked.)
3. Elle **ne** mange **rien**. (She's eating nothing. or: She's not eating anything.)	6. Elle **n'a rien** mangé. (She has eaten nothing. or: She hasn't eaten anything.)

RULES AND OBSERVATIONS:

1. To make a sentence negative in the present indicative (as you already know from experience in previous work units), merely put **ne** in front of the verb and **pas** after it.

2. If you want to negate the verb by saying **never** in the present indicative, merely put **ne** in front of the verb and **jamais** after it.

3. If you want to negate a verb by saying **nothing** in the present indicative, merely put **ne** in front of the verb and **rien** after it.

4. In the passé composé, put **ne** in front of the auxiliary (or helping) verb and put **pas** or **jamais** or **rien** after it.

5. If the first letter of the verb is a vowel, drop the **e** in **ne** and add an apostrophe: **Je n'ai . . .**

B. Subordination with **quand, parce que,** and **que**

---

1. **Quand** j'ai faim, je mange.

   (*When* I'm hungry, I eat.)

2. Madame Paquet est dans son lit **parce qu'**elle est malade.

   (Mrs. Paquet is in her bed *because* she is sick.)

3. Je sais **que** vous **êtes** intelligent.

   (I know *that* you are intelligent.)

RULES AND OBSERVATIONS:

1. Each sentence in the preceding box contains two clauses: a main clause and a subordinate clause. In model sentence 1, the main clause is **je mange** and the subordinate clause is **quand j'ai faim**. As a main clause, **je mange** can stand alone. However, **quand j'ai faim** cannot stand alone; it is incomplete and subordinate to the main clause.

2. In model sentence 2, the main clause is **Madame Paquet est dans son lit** and the subordinate clause is **parce qu'elle est malade**. As a main clause, **Madame Paquet est dans son lit** can stand alone and make sense. However, **parce qu'elle est malade** cannot stand alone; it is incomplete and subordinate to the main clause. Of course, subordinate clauses are used frequently as fragmentary replies to questions or statements in conversation and informal writing. Nevertheless, a subordinate clause is not a complete sentence.

3. In model sentence 3, the main clause is **Je sais** and the subordinate clause is **que vous êtes intelligent**.

C. **Dans** and a duration of time

Le docteur va venir **dans quelques minutes**.

(The doctor is going to come *in a few minutes*.)

RULES AND OBSERVATIONS:

1. **Dans** and a duration of time indicates a definite time in the future when something will happen.

2. In the model sentence above, **dans quelques minutes** means *at the end of a few minutes*.

3. **Dans** and a duration of time can be at the beginning or the end of a sentence, but future time must be implied.

D. **En** and a duration of time

En une heure, le docteur est venu.

(*In one hour*, the doctor came.)

RULES AND OBSERVATIONS:

1. **En** and a duration of time indicates the completion of an action at any time *within* that period of time.

2. In the model sentence above, **en une heure** means *in* or *within* one hour; in other words, any time before the one hour is up. If that is what you mean, use **en** for *in*.

3. **En** and a duration of time must be at the beginning of a sentence if the action has already been completed (as a general rule).

E. **Depuis** and a duration of time

---

1. **Depuis quand** Madame Paquet **est**-elle malade?

   (*Since when has* Mrs. Paquet been sick?)

2. Madame Paquet est malade **depuis hier**.

   (Mrs. Paquet has been sick *since yesterday*.)

3. **Depuis combien de temps** Mme Paquet **attend**-elle le docteur?

   (*How long has* Mrs. Paquet *been waiting* for the doctor?)

4. Madame Paquet **attend** le docteur **depuis vingt minutes**.

   (Mrs. Paquet *has been waiting* for the doctor *for twenty minutes*.)

RULES AND OBSERVATIONS:

1. In model sentence 1 in the above box, **depuis quand** is used in the question to express *since when*; in other words, at what point in the past. When you use this structure, you must use the present indicative tense of the verb.

2. In model sentence 2, which is the answer to 1, **depuis hier** is used to express *since yesterday* and the verb is still in the present indicative tense. (Note the verb tense in English in the question and in the answer in both model sentences: *has been*.) In French, however, we use the simple present tense because the thought expressed in the verb still holds right *now* in the present.

3. In model sentences 3 and 4, **depuis combien de temps** has a slightly different meaning. It asks: for how long. The answer to the question asked in this type of sentence structure usually requires a certain length of time to be stated (e.g., twenty minutes, three hours, a month, etc.). Note here, too, that in French we use the verb in the present tense because the action of the verb (in this case, *waiting*) is carried on right up to the present.

Non, je ne fume pas. (No, I do not smoke.)

EXERCISES

I. Answer the following questions in French in the negative using **ne . . . pas**.

Model: **Fumez-vous?**   You answer: **Non, je ne fume pas.**
(Do you smoke?)   (No, I do not smoke.)

1. Dansez-vous bien?

_____

2. Votre père chante-t-il souvent?

_____

3. Votre mère lit-elle beaucoup?

_____

4. Vos amis écrivent-ils bien?

_____

5. Fumes-tu?

_____

II. Answer the following questions in the negative using **ne . . . jamais.**

Model: **Mangez-vous beaucoup?**   You answer: **Non, je ne mange jamais**
(Do you eat a lot?)   **beaucoup.**
                                            (No, I never eat a lot.)

1. Parlez-vous beaucoup?

_____

2. Votre père boit-il beaucoup de lait?

_____

3. Votre soeur travaille-t-elle beaucoup?

_____

4. Ton ami étudie-t-il beaucoup?

_____

5. Buvez-vous beaucoup d'eau?

_____

III. Answer the following questions in the negative using **ne . . . rien.**

Model: **Est-ce que Madame Paquet** You answer: **Non, Madame Paquet ne**
mange quelque chose?   **mange rien.**
(Is Mrs. Paquet eating something?)   (No, Mrs. Paquet isn't eating
                                       anything.)

1. Lucille mange-t-elle quelque chose?

_____

2. Guy écrit-il quelque chose?

_____

3. Lis-tu quelque chose?

_____

4. Madame Paquet fait-elle quelque chose?

_____

5. Étudiez-vous quelque chose?

_____

IV. Answer the following questions in the negative, using the negation requested.

(A) Use ne . . . rien in your answers.

Model: **Avez-vous mangé quelque chose?** You answer: **Non, je n'ai rien**
(Have you eaten something?)   **mangé.** (No, I haven't
                                          eaten anything.)

1. Avez-vous dit quelque chose?

_____

2. Janine a-t-elle bu quelque chose?

_____

3. Vos amis ont-ils étudié quelque chose?

_____

4. Avez-vous lu quelque chose?

_____

5. Avez-vous écrit quelque chose?

_____

6. As-tu bu quelque chose?

_____

7. Julie et Lucille ont-elles mangé quelque chose?

_____

(B) Use **ne . . . jamais** in your answers.

| Model: | **Avez-vous jamais voyagé en France?** (Have you ever traveled to France?) | You answer: | **Non, je n'ai jamais voyagé en France.** (No, I have never traveled to France.) |

> NOTE THAT SOME OF THESE VERBS IN THE PASSÉ COMPOSÉ ARE CONJUGATED WITH **AVOIR**, SOME WITH **ÊTRE**. BE CAREFUL!

1. Avez-vous jamais voyagé en Angleterre?

_____

2. Êtes-vous jamais allé au Canada?

_____

3. Avez-vous jamais vu un film français?

_____

4. Juliette est-elle jamais allée à l'opéra?

_____

5. Robert a-t-il jamais lu un journal français?

_____

6. Monsieur et Madame Paquet sont-ils jamais allés en Espagne?

_____

7. Lucille et Marie-Louise ont-elles jamais mangé un éclair?

_____

V. The words in the following boxes are scrambled. Unscramble them to find a meaningful sentence. Write the sentence in French on the line provided.

Model:

sais	vous	que
êtes	intelligent	je

You write: **Je sais que vous êtes intelligent.** (I know you are intelligent.)

1.

êtes	malade	je
sais	vous	que

_____

2.

dans	est	lit	elle	est
son	Madame Paquet	parce qu'	malade	n'est-ce pas?

_____

3.

j'ai	je	faim
mange	quand	

_____

4.

venir	va	quelques
le docteur	minutes	dans

_____

5.

heure	le docteur	est
une	venu	en

_____

VI. Identify the following verb forms by giving the infinitive for each. They are all in the story in this unit.

Model: **dis**   You write: **dire**

1. est _____   4. attend _____

2. a _____   5. dites _____

3. va _____   6. prenez _____

VII. Answer the following questions in complete sentences. Use the French words in parentheses in your answers. Use a pronoun in place of the noun as subject.

Model: **Depuis quand Madame Paquet**   You answer: **Elle est malade**
est-elle malade? (hier) (Since   **depuis hier.** (She has
when has Mrs. Paquet been sick?)   been sick since yesterday.)

1. Depuis quand Pierre est-il absent? (lundi)

_____

2. Depuis combien de temps Madame Paquet attend-elle le docteur? (vingt minutes)

_____

3. Depuis combien de temps attendez-vous l'autobus? (dix minutes)

_____

4. Depuis quand travaillez-vous ici? (le premier avril)

_____

5. Depuis combien de temps lisez-vous ce livre? (une heure)

_____

6. Depuis quand lisez-vous ce livre? (ce matin)

_____

VIII. Answer the following questions in the affirmative in complete sentences.

Model: **Faut-il manger pour vivre?**   You answer: **Oui, il faut manger pour**
(Is it necessary to eat in order   **vivre.** (Yes, it is necessary
to live?)   to eat in order to live.)

1. Faut-il boire pour vivre?

_____

2. Faut-il étudier pour apprendre?

_____

3. Faut-il parler français dans la classe de français?

_____

4. Faut-il parler espagnol dans la classe d'espagnol?

_____

5. Faut-il faire les devoirs pour apprendre?

_____

321

IX. Educational Tour. Proficiency in Speaking and Writing.

Situation: You have just arrived in Paris on an educational tour with a group of students. Your guide is Madame Simard, an assistant at the Université de Paris. You have been asking her questions about Paris. Now she has a few questions to ask you because she is impressed with your ability to speak some French.

You may vary and extend this conversation with your own ideas and words.

Mme Simard: **Vous parlez français extraordinairement bien.**

Vous: _____

Thank her.

Mme Simard: **Depuis combien de temps étudiez-vous le français?**

Vous: _____

Tell her you have been studying French for one year.

Mme Simard: **Vous étudiez le français depuis un an? C'est tout? C'est extraordinaire! Où avez-vous appris à parler si bien le français?**

Vous: _____

Tell her you learned to speak French in school.

Mme Simard: **Où habitez-vous? Avec qui? Dans quel pays?**

Vous: _____

Tell her you live with your parents in the United States/**aux États-Unis.**

Mme Simard: **Quelles matières étudiez-vous?**

Vous: _____

Tell her what subjects you are studying. (Include computer science/l'**informatique,** _n.f.;_ computers/**les ordinateurs,** _n.m._)

Mme Simard: **Aimez-vous mon pays?**

Vous: _____

Tell her you like her country, the French people, the culture, music, and art/**les Français, la culture, la musique, et l'art.**

Mme Simard: **Merci bien. Maintenant, nous allons au marché aux puces.**

Vous: _____

_____

Say, "Oh, the flea market!" Tell her you want to buy a pillow/**un oreiller** because you don't like the pillow on the bed in your room at the hotel.

Mme Simard: **Attention aux puces!***

*Watch out for the fleas!

X. Expressing Personal Feelings. Proficiency in Speaking, Reading, and Writing.

Situation: You are in a florist shop **(chez un fleuriste)** because you want to buy a plant for a friend. You are talking with the florist. Use your own ideas and words. To know what to say and write on the lines, you must read what the florist says before and after your lines.

Le fleuriste: Bonjour! Vous désirez?

Vous: _____

Le fleuriste: Une plante? C'est pour vous? Ou c'est pour offrir comme cadeau?

Vous: _____

Le fleuriste: Ah, bon! C'est pour offrir! C'est pour une occasion spéciale?

Vous: _____

Le fleuriste: Aimez-vous cette plante rouge? Elle est très jolie.

Vous: _____

Le fleuriste: C'est trente euros. La prenez-vous?

Vous: _____

XI. Storytelling. Proficiency in Speaking and Writing.

Situation: Alice, one of your classmates, was absent when this lesson was done in class. She wants you to tell her what is going on in the picture at the beginning of this work unit where Madame Paquet is sick in bed. It was summarized in class.

You may use your own words and key words following the story. When you tell her, make at least five statements. Then practice writing them on the lines below.

1. _____

2. _____

3. _____

4. _____

5. _____

XII. Expressing Love on Father's Day. Proficiency in Speaking and Writing.

Situation: Next Sunday is Father's Day. Below, write your own card and give it to your father or to some friend or relative who has been like a father to you. Before you start, take a few minutes to gather your thoughts, jot down a few words in French that you will use, then say them aloud.

You may also use the following: **au plus sympa de tous les papas**/to the nicest of all Dads; **de tout coeur**/with all my heart; **Je te souhaite une joyeuse Fête des Pères**/I wish you a Happy Father's Day; **Je t'aime**/I love you; **Chez nous, j'ai appris la valeur de l'amour depuis mon enfance**/In our home, I learned the value of love since childhood.

XIII. Entertainment. Proficiency in Speaking and Reading.

Situation: The members of your French Club are planning a party to entertain some students who are thinking of joining the club. As president of the French Club, you have proposed to help the members practice to sing a song. You have asked a member to play the piano.

Say aloud the words to the song *Frère Jacques*. The words and music are below.

Courtesy of French Cultural Services, New York.

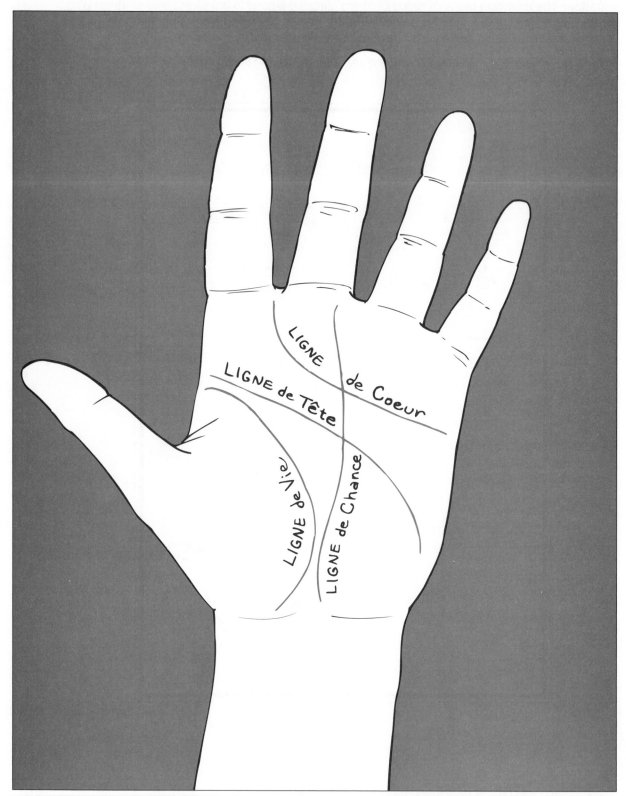

Les secrets de votre main. (The secrets of your hand.)

Work Unit 22
Orthographically Changing Verbs in the Present Indicative and Other Structures of the Language

Some people like to have their palms read. It can be fun—believe it or not.

Les secrets de votre main

Claire et François Paquet sont allés à la foire samedi. Là, ils se sont bien amusés. Ils ont vu des expositions, ils ont acheté des souvenirs, et ils sont entrés chez une chiromancienne pour se faire lire les lignes de la main.

—Tiens! François! Une chiromancienne! s'exclame Claire.

—Où? lui a demandé François.

—Là, devant nous. Ne vois-tu pas?

> Madame Sétou,
> chiromancienne,
>
> révèle les secrets de votre main.

—François, je vais me faire lire les lignes de la main. Toi aussi? lui a demandé Claire.

—Oui, je veux bien. Mais, tu sais que je n'y crois pas, dit François.

Ils entrent chez la chiromancienne.

—Est-ce que nous vous dérangeons, madame?

—Mais non, pas du tout! Entrez! Entrez! répond Madame Sétou.

—Je veux me faire lire les lignes de la main. Et mon mari aussi, dit Claire.

—Bon! répond la chiromancienne. Asseyez-vous et donnez-moi votre main.

Madame Sétou regarde fixement la main de Claire et elle commence à lire les lignes:

—Ah! Je vois dans votre ligne de chance que vous allez faire un voyage aux États-Unis avec un homme, s'exclame Madame Sétou.

—C'est curieux! dit Claire. Mon mari et moi, nous commençons à faire des préparations pour un autre voyage aux États-Unis.

—Maintenant, dit Madame Sétou, je regarde votre ligne de coeur. Je vois que vous êtes amoureuse d'un homme.

—C'est curieux! dit Claire. Vous avez raison. Je suis amoureuse de mon mari!

—Maintenant, monsieur, asseyez-vous et donnez-moi votre main, dit Madame Sétou.

François Paquet lui donne sa main.

—Ah! Je vois dans votre ligne de chance que vous allez faire un voyage aux États-Unis avec une femme, s'exclame Madame Sétou.

—C'est curieux! dit François. Ma femme et moi, nous commençons à faire des préparations pour un autre voyage aux États-Unis.

—Maintenant, dit Madame Sétou, je regarde votre ligne de coeur. Je vois que vous êtes amoureux d'une femme.

—C'est curieux! dit François. Vous avez raison. Je suis amoureux de ma femme! La main révèle tout, n'est-ce pas?

—Oui, monsieur, la main révèle les secrets de votre vie. Ça fait dix euros pour les révélations.

François lui paye les dix euros.

Dehors, Claire dit à François:

—Madame Sétou sait tout, n'est-ce pas?

—Oui, Madame Sétou sait tout, mais je n'ai rien appris de nouveau. Et toi?

—Moi non plus. Nous savons déjà que nous voyageons aux États-Unis et que nous sommes amoureux!

VOCABULAIRE

l'amour   *n. m.,* love; amoureux *m.,* amoureuse *f. adj.,* in love; **nous sommes amoureux** we are in love

s'amuser   *refl. v.,* to have a good time; **ils se sont bien amusés** they had a good time

appris   *past part. of* **apprendre**; **je n'ai rien appris de nouveau** I didn't learn anything new

asseyez-vous   *imperative of* **s'asseoir** (to sit down)

la chance   *n.,* luck, fortune, chance

le chiromancien, la chiromancienne   *n.,* the palm reader

le coeur   *n.,* the heart

crois   *v. form of* **croire** (to believe); **je n'y crois pas** I don't believe in it

curieux   *m.,* curieuse *f., adj.,* curious, odd

déranger   *v.,* to disturb

donnez-moi la main   give me your hand

fixement   *adv.,* intently, fixedly

la foire   *n.,* the fair

la ligne   *n.,* the line; **se faire lire les lignes de la main** to have one's palm read (to have the lines of one's hand read)

pas du tout   not at all

plus   *adv.,* more; **non plus** neither; **moi non plus** me neither

révéler   *v.,* to reveal

sais   *v. form of* **savoir**; **tu sais** you know

veux   *v. form of* **vouloir**; **veux-tu?** do you want to?; **je veux bien** I'd like to; **je veux me faire lire les lignes de la main** I want to have my palm read

vois   *v. form of* **voir**; **ne vois-tu pas?** don't you see?

voyager   *v.,* to travel

y   *advl. pron.,* **je n'y crois pas** I don't believe *in it*

EXERCISES

Review the story and vocabulary before starting these exercises.

I.   **Vocabulary Building. Proficiency in Writing.**

Situation: You are planning to go to a county fair with some friends. Write six things you would like to do there; for example, **regarder les animaux**.

1. _____   2. _____   3. _____

4. _____   5. _____   6. _____

II. Write appropriate responses on the blank lines. The following is a conversation between Claire and François Paquet, who are about to have their palms read.

Claire: Tiens! François! Une chiromancienne!

François: _____

Claire: Là, devant nous. Je vais me faire lire les lignes de la main. Veux-tu?

François: _____

Claire: Madame Sétou sait tout, n'est-ce pas?

François: _____

Claire: Je n'ai rien appris de nouveau. Et toi?

François: _____

III. Write complete sentences using the cue words given below. Change the infinitives where necessary to either the present tense or the **passé composé**, whichever you prefer. Supply other words as needed.

Model: Claire et François Paquet/ aller/ la foire.
(Claire and François Paquet/ to go/ to the fair.)

You write: Claire et François Paquet sont allés à la foire.
(Claire and François Paquet went to the fair.)

or:

Claire et François Paquet vont à la foire.
(Claire and François Paquet are going to the fair.)

1. Joseph et Joséphine / aller / cinéma / samedi.

_____

2. Ils / entrer / chez / chiromancienne.

_____

3. Ils / ne / apprendre / rien / chez / chiromancienne.

_____

4. François Paquet / lui / payer / euros / pour / révélations.

_____

STRUCTURES DE LA LANGUE

A. Orthographically changing verbs in the present indicative

appeler (to call)	
Singular	*Plural*
j'appelle	nous appelons
tu appelles	vous appelez
il, elle, on appelle	ils, elles appellent

RULES AND OBSERVATIONS:

1. An orthographically changing verb is a verb that changes in spelling.

2. In the preceding box, **appeler** doubles the l in the three persons of the singular and in the third person plural. This is done because the stress falls on the syllable that contains the l when pronounced. The letter l does not double in the first and second persons of the plural because the stress is on the final syllable (**-ons** and **-ez**).

3. There are other verbs that double the consonant in the same persons as just described. For example: **jeter** (to throw) and **rappeler** (to recall, to call (someone) back).

employer (to use, employ)	
Singular	*Plural*
j'emploie	nous employons
tu emploies	vous employez
il, elle, on emploie	ils, elles emploient

4. For verbs ending in **-oyer** or **-uyer**, you must change the y to i before a silent e, as noted in the preceding box.

5. Other verbs that end in **-oyer** or **-uyer** are **nettoyer** (to clean), **envoyer** (to send), **ennuyer** (to bore, to bother), **essuyer** (to wipe).

6. Verbs ending in **-ayer** may change the y to i or may keep the y before silent e. Two examples are **essayer** (to try, to try on) and **payer** (to pay, to pay for).

manger (to eat)	
Singular	*Plural*
je mange	nous mangeons
tu manges	vous mangez
il, elle, on mange	ils, elles mangent

7. For verbs ending in **-ger**, add a silent **e** after **g** if the vowels **a** or **o** follow **g**. This is done in order to preserve the soft sound of **g** as it is pronounced in the infinitive. If a silent **e** were not inserted between **g** and **a** or **g** and **o**, the **g** would then have to be pronounced hard, as in the English word *go*.

8. Here are other verbs ending in **-ger** that are treated in the same way:

   arranger (to arrange); **changer** (to change); **corriger** (to correct); **déranger** (to disturb); **nager** (to swim); **obliger** (to oblige); **songer** (to think, to dream); **voyager** (to travel).

prononcer (to pronounce)	
Singular	*Plural*
je prononce	nous prononçons
tu prononces	vous prononcez
il, elle, on prononce	ils, elles prononcent

9. For verbs ending in **-cer**, change **c** to **ç** before the vowels **a**, **o**, **u**. This is done in order to preserve the soft sound of **c** (like *s*) as it is pronounced in the infinitive. The little mark under the **c** (**ç**) is called *une cédille*. Actually, it is the lower half of the consonant *s* and indicates that **ç** should be pronounced as *s*.

10. Here are other verbs ending in **-cer** that are treated in the same way:

    annoncer (to announce); **avancer** (to advance); **commencer** (to begin); **effacer** (to efface, to erase); **lancer** (to hurl, to lance, to launch); **menacer** (to threaten, to menace); **placer** (to place, to put, to set); **remplacer** (to replace).

acheter (to buy)	
Singular	*Plural*
j'achète	nous achetons
tu achètes	vous achetez
il, elle, on achète	ils, elles achètent

11. If there is a silent **e** in the syllable just before the infinitive ending (as in acheter), it changes to **è** in a verb form—provided that the syllable right after it contains another silent **e**. Study the changes in spelling in the preceding box.

12. Other verbs that change in the same way are **lever** (to lift, to raise), **se lever** (to get up), and **enlever** (to remove, to take off).

EXERCISES

Review the preceding material before starting these exercises.

I. Answer the following questions in complete sentences (in French) in the affirmative. Substitute **nous** as the subject pronoun in place of **"Et vous et votre soeur?"** Also, substitute an object pronoun for the noun direct object, as shown in these two models:

Model: **Bob arrange les fleurs. Et vous et votre soeur?**
(Bob arranges the flowers. And you and your sister?)

You answer: **Nous les arrangeons aussi.**
(We are arranging them too.)

Model: **Simone efface le tableau. Et vous et votre soeur?**
(Simone is erasing the board. And you and your sister?)

You answer: **Nous l'effaçons aussi.**
(We are erasing it too.)

1. Hélène change la phrase. Et vous et votre soeur?

_____

2. Yves corrige le devoir. Et vous et votre soeur?

_____

3. Monique appelle les garçons. Et vous et votre soeur?

_____

4. Guy emploie le dictionnaire. Et vous et votre soeur?

_____

5. Lucille achète les roses. Et vous et votre soeur?

_____

Store front, Paris, France.

II. **Change to the passé composé.**

    Model: **Claire et François Paquet vont à la foire.** (Claire and François Paquet are going to the fair.)   **You write:**   **Claire et François Paquet sont allés à la foire.** (Claire and François Paquet went to the fair.)

1. Janine et Monique vont au cinéma.

    _____

2. Nous voyageons aux États-Unis.

    _____

3. Madame Sétou regarde fixement la main de Madame Paquet.

    _____

4. Madame Sétou révèle les secrets de votre main.

    _____

5. Claire et François Paquet achètent des souvenirs.

    _____

333

III. **Change to the present indicative.**

Model: **Nous avons mangé les pommes.**   You write: **Nous mangeons les**
(We ate the apples.)   **pommes.**
                                                                                          (We are eating the apples.)

1. Nous avons arrangé les fleurs.

_____

2. Il a acheté une cravate.

_____

3. Ils ont appelé la police.

_____

4. Tu as employé le dictionnaire.

_____

5. Nous avons prononcé le mot.

_____

B. **Aller** in the present indicative with an infinitive

Je vais faire mes devoirs.	**Il va voir** ses amis.
(*I am going to do* my homework.)	(*He's going to see* his friends.)

RULE:

It is customary to use **aller** in the present indicative with an infinitive form of a verb, as we do in English.

C. **Vouloir** in the present indicative with an infinitive

Elle **veut acheter** une nouvelle robe.	Monsieur Paquet **veut vendre** son auto.
(She *wants to buy* a new dress.)	(Mr. Paquet *wants to sell* his car.)

RULE:

It is customary to use **vouloir** in the present indicative with an infinitive form of a verb, as we do in English.

D. The use of **il y a, y a-t-il . . .?**, **voici**, and **voilà**

(a) **Il y a** un bon restaurant près d'ici.	(*There is* a good restaurant near here.)
(b) **Il y a** dix étudiants dans cette classe.	(*There are* ten students in this class.)
(c) J'ai vu Janine **il y a deux heures**.	(I saw Janine *two hours ago*.)
(d) **Y a-t-il** un arrêt d'autobus près d'ici?	(*Is there* a bus stop near here?)
(e) **Est-ce qu'il y a** des fruits sur la table?	(*Are there* fruits on the table?)
(f) **N'y a-t-il pas** de sel dans la soupe?	(*Isn't there* any salt in the soup?)
(g) Non, **il n'y a pas** de sel dans la soupe.	(No, *there isn't* any salt in the soup.)
(h) Je l'ai vue **il y a un an**.	(I saw her *a year ago*.)
(i) **Voici** ma mère et **voilà** mon père!	(*Here's* my mother and *there's* my father!)
(j) **Voici** un taxi et **voilà** un taxi!	(*Here is* a taxi and *there is* a taxi!)

(k) **Me voici!**	**Le voici!**	**Vous voilà!**	**Les voilà!**	**La voici!**
(*Here I am!*)	(*Here he is!* *Here it is!*)	(*There you are!*)	(*There they are!*)	(*Here she is!* *Here it is!*)

RULES AND OBSERVATIONS:

1. **Il y a** is used simply to mention the existence of something that may or may not be known to the listener. It may be about people, things, or facts. Its equivalent in English is *there is* or *there are*.

2. **Il y a** also means *ago* when a length of time is stated right after it. See models (c) and (h) in the preceding box.

3. The interrogative form of **il y a** is given in models (d) and (e).

4. The negative form of **il y a** is given in model sentence (g).

5. The negative-interrogative form of **il y a** is given in model sentence (f). **Est-ce qu'il n'y a pas** is also a correct form.

6. **Voici** and **voilà** have a demonstrative characteristic. They are used to point out, to call attention to someone or something. They are based on **vois + ici (+ là)**. If you analyze the word, it actually means: *See (look) here! See (look) there!* See models (i) and (j).

7. If you regard **voici** or **voilà** as a "verb form" you will understand why the object pronoun is placed in front of it, as in the model sentences in (k).

EXERCISES

Review the preceding material before starting these exercises.

I. Answer the following questions in the affirmative in complete sentences.

Model: **Allez-vous faire vos devoirs?**
(Are you going to do your homework?)

You answer: **Oui, je vais faire mes devoirs.**
(Yes, I am going to do my homework.)

1. Allez-vous faire un voyage au Canada?

_____

2. Va-t-elle écrire une lettre?

_____

3. Est-ce qu'il va jouer dans le parc?

_____

4. Vont-ils voyager en Angleterre?

_____

5. Allons-nous répondre à la question?

_____

II. Answer the following questions in the negative in complete sentences.

Model: **Voulez-vous acheter un nouveau chapeau?**
(Do you want to buy a new hat?)

You answer: **Non, je ne veux pas acheter un nouveau chapeau.**
(No, I do not want to buy a new hat.)

1. Voulez-vous acheter une nouvelle voiture?

_____

2. Le professeur de français veut-il corriger les devoirs?

_____

3. L'étudiant veut-il prononcer le mot?

_____

4. Janine veut-elle employer le dictionnaire?

_____

5. Monsieur Paquet veut-il fumer une cigarette?

_____

III. Match the following.

1. There you are!   _____ Me voici!

2. Here she is!   _____ Vous voilà!

3. Here they are!   _____ Les voici!

4. Here I am!   _____ Le voilà!

5. There it is!   _____ La voici!

IV. Change to the negative.

> Model: **Il y a un bon restaurant près d'ici.**   You write: **Il n'y a pas un bon restaurant près d'ici.**
> (There is a good restaurant near here.)   (There is not a good restaurant near here.)

1. Il y a un grand parc dans cette ville.

_____

2. Y a-t-il un arrêt d'autobus ici?

_____

3. Est-ce qu'il y a dix garçons dans la classe?

_____

V. Answer the following questions in the affirmative in complete sentences, using French for the English in parentheses.

> Model: **Avez-vous vu Janine? (two hours ago)**   You answer: **Oui, j'ai vu Janine il y a deux heures.**
> (Have you seen Janine?)   (Yes, I saw Janine two hours ago.)

1. Avez-vous lu *Le livre de mon ami* d'Anatole France? (three months ago)

_____

2. A-t-il vu Pierre? (ten minutes ago)

_____

3. Êtes-vous allé en Californie? (a year ago)

_____

4. Sont-elles arrivées? (a half hour ago)

_____

5. Est-elle partie? (an hour ago)

_____

337

VI. Physical Activities. Proficiency in Speaking and Writing.

Situation: In your French Club students are looking at pictures in an album that one of the students brought to stimulate speaking in French.

Look at the picture below. Say aloud the French words you plan to write. Then answer the questions in complete sentences. Verbs you may want to use: **jouer**/*to play*; **s'amuser**/*to have fun*; **être debout**/*to be standing*; **être prêt à sauter**/ *to be ready to jump*; **grimper sur un arbre abattu**/ *to climb onto a felled (cut down, knocked down) tree.*

1. Combien d'enfants y a-t-il dans cette photo?

_____

2. Où sont-ils? Dans un parc?

_____

3. Qu'est-ce qu'ils font?

_____

4. Que fait le petit garçon à gauche?

_____

5. Que fait le garçon au milieu/*in the middle?*

_____

6. Que fait le troisième garçon à droite?

_____

VII. Leisure. Proficiency in Speaking and Writing.

Situation: A boy and a girl are riding their bicycles by the beach. They stop for a moment to rest. What do they say to each other?

Write two statements on the following lines.

Le garçon: _____

La jeune fille: _____

Papa! Papa! Attends! Attends! (Papa! Papa! Wait! Wait!)

Work Unit 23
Prepositions and Infinitives and Other Structures of the Language

*In this story, the Paquet family is
celebrating the wedding
anniversary of Mr. and Mrs. Paquet.
After a festive lunch, they attempt to
play some music on their brand-
new stereo that Mr. Paquet had
bought as a present for his wife.*

Le beau cadeau

C'est aujourd'hui samedi.

Monsieur Paquet est allé acheter une chaîne stéréo. C'est un cadeau pour sa femme à l'occasion de leur vingtième anniversaire de mariage. Madame Paquet est allée chez le coiffeur pour une
nouvelle coiffure. Janine a préparé un grand déjeuner toute la matinée dans la cuisine, et Pierre est
allé aux grands magasins acheter un petit cadeau pour sa mère de la part de lui et da sa soeur. Il
est allé, aussi, chez un confiseur pour acheter une boîte de chocolats et chez un fleuriste pour
acheter des fleurs.

Après un déjeuner délicieux, Monsieur Paquet dit:

—Et maintenant nous allons écouter un peu de musique. Elle est belle, cette chaîne stéréo,
n'est-ce pas?

Monsieur Paquet essaye d'allumer la chaîne stéréo, mais il n'y a pas de musique! Il n'y a pas
de son! Il n'y a rien!

—Zut, alors! J'ai horreur de réparer les chaînes stéréo! dit-il.

—D'abord, le téléviseur il y a un an! Et maintenant, une nouvelle chaîne stéréo qui ne marche
pas! Incroyable! Ces appareils gouvernent notre vie! s'exclame Madame Paquet. Monsieur Paquet
va téléphoner au magasin où il a acheté la chaîne stéréo.

—Il faut appeler le magasin, dit-il.

A ce moment-là, Pierre s'exclame:

—Papa! Papa! Attends! Attends! Tu n'as pas branché la chaîne stéréo sur la prise de courant!

VOCABULAIRE

agréable   *adj.*, pleasant
l'anniversaire   *n. m.*,
   anniversary, birthday
brancher   *v.*, to plug in, to
   connect (an electrical
   apparatus)
le cadeau   *n.*, the gift,
   present
la chaîne   *n.* **stéréo** stereo
   system

le coiffeur, la coiffeuse   *n.*,
   the hairdresser; **une
   coiffure** *n.*, a hair style
le confiseur, la confiseuse
   n., the confectioner, candy
   maker; **une confiserie** a
   candy store
d'abord   *advl. phrase*, at
   first, first
essayer   *v.*, to try
la fleur   *n.*, the flower

le fleuriste, la fleuriste   *n.*,
   the florist
gouverner   *v.*, to govern, to
   rule, to direct
l'horreur   *n. f.*, horror; **J'ai
   horreur de** + *inf.* I hate +
   pres. part.
le magasin   *n.*, the store; **le
   grand magasin** the
   department store
le mariage   *n.*, the marriage

le matin *n.,* the morning; **la matinée** the morning (long); **toute la matinée** all morning long

l'occasion *n. f.,* the occasion
la part *n.,* part, behalf; **de la part de lui** on his behalf
peu *adv.,* little

la prise *n.,* hold, grip; **une prise de courant** electric outlet (in the wall)
le son *n.,* the sound

EXERCISES

Review the story and vocabulary before starting these exercises.

I. Answer the following questions in complete sentences. They are all based on the story in this unit.

1. Où Monsieur Paquet est-il allé?

_____

2. Qui a préparé un grand déjeuner?

_____

3. Qui est allé chez le coiffeur?

_____

4. Qui a acheté une boîte de chocolats?

_____

5. Pourquoi la chaîne stéréo ne marche-t-elle pas d'abord?

_____

II. Picture Interpretation. Proficiency in Speaking.

Situations:

A. Take a good look at the picture at the beginning of this work unit. Describe the scene to a friend, telling what's going on, in at least ten words.

B. Notice that Coco, **le petit chien,** is on the floor. Give the French for at least five other animals. Refer to previous lessons in this book. Then say which is your favorite pet, for example, **Mon animal favori est le chat.**

III. Write short sentences using the cue words in each group. They are all based on the story in this work unit. Use the present indicative or the passé composé, whichever you prefer. Supply other words as needed.

1. Monsieur Paquet / acheter / chaîne stéréo.

_____

2. Janine / préparer / déjeuner.

_____

3. Pierre / aller / confiseur / chocolats.

_____

4. Madame Paquet / aller / coiffeuse / nouvelle coiffure.

_____

5. Pierre / aller / fleuriste / fleurs.

_____

STRUCTURE DE LA LANGUE

A. The use of **de** with an infinitive after certain idiomatic expressions

1. **avoir besoin de + inf.**	4. **avoir peur de + inf.**
(to need + inf.)	(to be afraid + inf.)
2. **avoir envie de + inf.**	5. **avoir raison de + inf.**
(to feel like + pres. part.)	(to be right + inf.)
3. **avoir horreur de + inf.**	6. **avoir tort de + inf.**
(to hate, to detest + pres. part. or inf.)	(to be wrong + inf.)

Models:

1. **J'ai besoin d'aller** chez le dentiste.   (*I need to go* to the dentist.)
2. **Tu as envie de dormir.**   (*You feel like sleeping.*)
3. **Il a horreur de réparer** les chaînes stéréo.   (*He hates repairing (to repair)* stereo systems.)
4. **Nouns avons peur de traverser** la mer.   (*We are afraid to cross* the sea.)
5. **Vous avez raison d'avoir** peur.   (*You are right to be* afraid.)
6. **Vous avez tort d'avoir** peur.   (*You are wrong to be* afraid.)

RULE:

These idiomatic expressions take **de + infinitive form**. Note that in English we sometimes use a present participle (or gerund) instead of an infinitive, as in model sentences 2 and 3 in the box.

B. The use of **il est** + adjective + **de** + infinitive

1. **Il est agréable d'aller** à un bal.   (*It is pleasant to go (going)* to a dance.)
2. **Il est amusant d'aller** à un cirque.   (*It is fun to go (going)* to a circus.)
3. **Il est désagréable d'aller** chez le dentiste.   (*It is unpleasant to go (going)* to the dentist.)
4. **Il est impossible de lire** ce gros livre en une heure.   (*It is impossible to read* this thick book within an hour.)
5. **Il est intéressant d'aller** à un musée.   (*It is interesting to go (going)* to a museum.)

RULE:

Use **Il est** (not **C'est**) + adjective + **de** + infinitive.

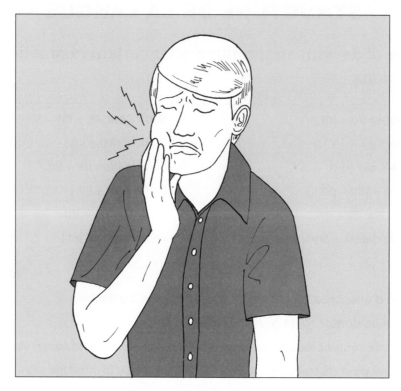

J'ai besoin d'aller chez le dentiste. (I have to go to the dentist.)

C. The use of **à** after certain verbs + infinitive

1. **J'apprends à lire** en français.   (*I am learning to read* in French.)
2. **Je commence à écrire** en français.   (*I am beginning to write* in French.)
3. **J'hésite à sortir** parce qu'il pleut.   (*I hesitate going (to go) out* because it's raining.)

RULE:

In French, some verbs take **à** between the verb form and the infinitive. Study the above models.

D. The use of **pour, sans, avant de, au lieu de**, and **afin de** + infinitive

1. Il est parti **pour aller** voir ses amis.   (He left *to go* see his friends.)
2. Elle est sortie **sans dire** un mot.   (She went out *without saying* a word.)
3. Nous mangeons et buvons **pour vivre**.   (We eat and drink *(in order) to live*.)
4. Ils sont allés au cinéma **avant de finir** leurs devoirs.   (They went to the movies *before finishing* their homework.)
5. Elles sont sorties **au lieu de rester** à la maison.   (They went out *instead of staying* home.)
6. Il est revenu **afin de voir** ses amis.   (He came back *in order to* see his friends.)

RULE:

The infinitive form of the verb is used *after* prepositions and prepositional phrases, except after **en**.

E. The use of no preposition after certain verbs + infinitive

1. **J'aime aller** au cinéma.   (*I like to go (going)* to the movies.)
2. **Tu aimes mieux aller** au théâtre.   (*You prefer to go (going)* to the theater.)
3. **Il déteste aller** chez le dentiste.   (*He hates to go (going)* to the dentist.)
4. **Elle veut aller** au Canada.   (*She wants to go* to Canada.)
5. **Nous pensons aller** en Angleterre.   (*We intend to go (going)* to England.)
6. **Vous pouvez aller** à l'opéra ce soir.   (*You can go* to the opera tonight.)
7. **Ils veulent aller** en Australie.   (*They want to go* to Australia.)
8. **Elles doivent aller** à la bibliothèque.   (*They have to go* to the library.)

ALSO MAKE A NOTE OF THE IMPERSONAL EXPRESSION **Il faut**, as in:

Il faut étudier pour apprendre. (*It is necessary to study* in order to learn.)

RULE:

No preposition is needed between the verb form and the infinitive when you use the verbs that are listed above.

F. The use of **de** after certain verbs + infinitive

1. **J'ai oublié de fermer** la fenêtre.   (*I forgot to close* the window.)
2. **Je promets de venir** chez vous.   (*I promise to come* to your house.)
3. **Elle a refusé de sortir** hier soir.   (*She refused to go out* last night.)
4. **Je tâche de faire** mes devoirs.   (*I try to do* my homework.)

RULE:

The preceding verbs require **de** + infinitive.

EXERCISES

Review the preceding material before starting these exercises.

I. Write the appropriate preposition in French, either **à** or **de,** on the blank line. If no preposition is needed, write a dash (—).

Model: **Elle a oublié __de__ fermer la porte.**

1. Tu as envie _____ jouer, n'est-ce pas?

2. Elle apprend _____ lire en espagnol.

3. J'aime _____ aller au cinéma.

4. Il a besoin _____ travailler.

5. Nous commençons _____ écrire en français.

6. Veux-tu _____ aller au Canada?

7. J'aime mieux _____ prendre du thé.

8. Elle hésite _____ fumer.

9. Vous avez raison _____ partir.

10. Nous avons tort _____ rester.

II. Answer the following questions in the affirmative in complete French sentences. In answer (a) use **oui.** In answer (b) use **aussi.** Study the models.

Models: (a) **Avez-vous envie de sortir?**   You answer: (a) **Oui, j'ai envie de**
(Do you feel like going out?)   **sortir.** (Yes, I feel
like going out.)

(b) **Et Robert?**   (b) **Il a envie de sortir**
(And Robert?)   **aussi.** (He feels like
going out too.)

| USE SUBJECT PRONOUNS IN YOUR ANSWERS. |

1. (a) As-tu envie d'aller au cinéma?

   _____

   (b) Et tes amis?

   _____

2. (a) Madame Paquet a-t-elle besoin d'aller au supermarché?

   _____

   (b) Et Louise et Antoinette?

   _____

3. (a) Êtes-vous sorti sans dire un mot?

   _____

   (b) Et Joséphine?

   _____

4. (a) Apprenez-vous à lire en français?

   _____

   (b) Et Robert?

   _____

5. (a) Avez-vous horreur de manger dans un restaurant sale?

_____

(b) Et Michel et Marie?

_____

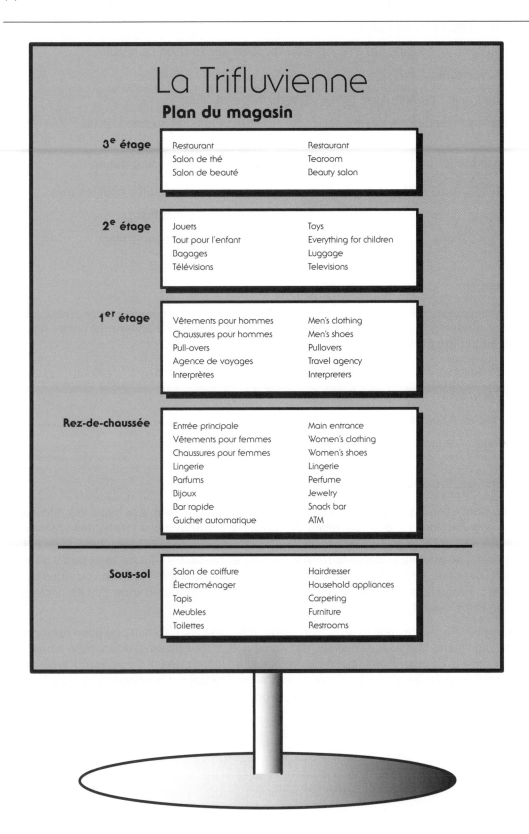

347

III. Choose the correct answer after studying the picture on the preceding page.

1. Un jouet est généralement pour

    (a) une dame.   (b) un monsieur.   (c) un enfant.   (d) un agent de police.   _____

2. Si vous avez faim, vous allez

    (a) au salon de coiffure. (b) à l'agence de voyages. (c) au salon de beauté.

    (d) au restaurant.   _____

3. Si vous voulez prendre de la pâtisserie et du thé, vous allez

    (a) au salon de beauté. (b) aux tapis. (c) aux interprètes. (d) au salon de thé.   _____

IV. Match the following after studying the picture on the preceding page.

1. everything for children   _____ chaussures pour femmes

2. carpeting   _____ bar rapide

3. women's shoes   _____ tout pour l'enfant

4. toys   _____ tapis

5. snack bar   _____ jouets

V. After studying the picture on the preceding page, choose the word that does not belong in the group.

1. (a) pull-overs   (b) chaussures   (c) vêtements   (d) parfums   _____

2. (a) interprètes   (b) agence de voyages   (c) lingerie

    (d) guichet automatique   _____

3. (a) tapis   (b) jouets   (c) bar rapide   (d) meubles   _____

VI. Activities. Proficiency in Speaking.

A. Situation: Your friend John has a toothache. Talk to him about it. Ask him a few questions. Use your own ideas and words and/or the following: **As-tu mal aux dents, Jean?**/Do you have a toothache, John? **As-tu besoin d'aller chez le dentiste?**/Do you have to go to the dentist? **Vas-tu chez le dentiste?**/Are you going to the dentist? **Tu ne veux pas y aller?**/You don't want to go there? **Pourquoi? As-tu peur des dentistes?**/Why? Are you afraid of dentists? **Je sais qu'il est désagréable d'aller chez le dentiste**/I know that it's unpleasant going to the dentist.

B. Situation: Persuade John to go to the dentist. If he refuses, give him one good reason why he has to go there. Use your own ideas and words and/or the following: **Jean, mon ami, il faut aller chez le dentiste**/John, my friend, you must go to the dentist; **Tu as tort d'avoir peur**/You are wrong to be afraid; **Le dentiste va t'aider**/The dentist is going to help you; **La douleur va disparaître**/The pain is going to disappear.

VII. Vocabulary Building. Proficiency in Writing.

A. You need to buy a wedding present and you are wondering what the bride would like. Write three things that you are considering.

1. _____ 2. _____ 3. _____

B. You need to furnish your new apartment. Write three things you plan to buy.

1. _____ 2. _____ 3. _____

VIII. Appreciating French Art. Proficiency in Speaking and Writing.

Situation: You and your friend Anne are at the National Gallery of Art in Washington, D.C., admiring the painting *La Liseuse*/*A Young Girl Reading* by Jean-Honoré Fragonard. Look at the picture on the next page.

Anne: Ce tableau de Fragonard est très beau, n'est-ce pas?

Vous: _____

Yes, it's superb. The young girl is reading a book. She's a reader. What book is she reading?

Anne: Oui, elle tient un livre à la main droite. Je ne sais pas quel livre elle lit. C'est peut-être la Bible ou un livre de poèmes.

Vous: _____

She's beautiful, isn't she? My French teacher has the same hairdo/la même coiffure. I suppose/je suppose que she has seen this painting.

Anne: J'aime beaucoup le noeud de ruban dans sa coiffure. Et toi?

Vous: _____

Yes, I like the bow of ribbon in her hairdo. It's simple and pretty.

Anne: J'ai envie d'aller chez un coiffeur pour une nouvelle coiffure.

Vous: _____

Don't forget to bring a little book with you and a bow of ribbon!

La Liseuse/*A Young Girl Reading* by Jean-Honoré Fragonard (1732–1806).
The Corbis Collection.

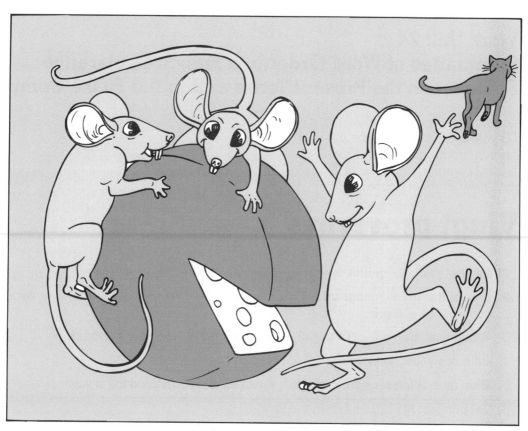

Le chat parti, les souris dansent. (When the cat is away, the mice will play [dance]).

L'appétit vient en mangeant. (The more you have, the more you want. [Appetite comes while eating.])

Work Unit 24
Summaries of Word Order in a French Declarative Sentence in the Present Tense and in the Passé Composé

Do you know any proverbs in French? In English? Here are twenty common proverbs in French with their English equivalents.

Vingt proverbes

1. **Le chat parti, les souris dansent.**   (When the cat is away, the mice will play.)

2. **L'appétit vient en mangeant.**   (The more you have, the more you want.) (*i.e.,* Appetite comes while eating.)

3. **À bon chat, bon rat.**   (Tit for tat). (*i.e.,* A good cat is entitled to a good rat.)

4. **Loin des yeux, loin du coeur.**   (Out of sight, out of mind.)

5. **Bien faire et laisser dire.**   (Do your work well and never mind the critics.)

6. **Tel père, tel fils.**   (Like father, like son.)

7. **Telle mère, telle fille.**   (Like mother, like daughter.)

8. **Il n'y a pas de fumée sans feu.**   (Where there's smoke, there's fire.)

9. **Mains froides, coeur chaud.**   (Cold hands, warm heart.)

10. **Mieux vaut tard que jamais.**   (Better late than never.)

11. **Les murs ont des oreilles.**   (Walls have ears.)

12. **À chacun son goût.**   (To each his own.) (*i.e.,* Each person has his/her own tastes.)

13. **Tout est bien qui finit bien.**   (All's well that ends well.)

14. **Qui se ressemble s'assemble.**   (Birds of a feather flock together.)

15. **Qui ne risque rien n'a rien.**   (Nothing ventured, nothing gained.)

16. **Vouloir, c'est pouvoir.**   (Where there's a will, there's a way.)

17. **Beaucoup de bruit pour rien.**   (Much ado about nothing.)

18. **Qui vivra verra.**   (Time will tell.)

19. **L'habit ne fait pas le moine.**   (Clothes don't make the person.)

20. **Rira bien qui rira le dernier.**   (She/He who laughs last laughs best.)

VOCABULAIRE

l'appétit   *n.,* the appetite
assembler   *v.,* to assemble;
   s'assembler *refl. v.,* to
   gather, to meet
le bruit   *n.,* the noise
le feu   *n.,* the fire
la fumée   *n.,* the smoke
l'habit   *n. m.,* attire,
   costume, dress
loin   *adv.,* far
mangeant   *pres. part. of*
   manger; en mangeant
   while eating

le moine   *n.,* the monk
le mur   *n.,* the wall
l'oeil   *n. m.,* the eye; **les
   yeux** the eyes
l'oreille   *n. f.,* the ear
pouvoir   *v.,* to be able
qui *pron.,* who (sometimes:
   he/she who)
se ressembler   *refl. v.,* to
   resemble each other

rira   *v. form of* **rire** (to laugh)
risquer   *v.,* to risk
la souris   *n.,* the mouse
tel *m.,* **telle** *f.,*   *adj.,* such
vaut   *v. form of* **valoir** (to be
   worth)
verra   *v. form of* **voir** (to see)
vivra   *v. form of* **vivre** (to
   live)
vouloir   *v.,* to want

EXERCISES

Review the proverbs and vocabulary before starting these exercises.

I.   Write the French proverb for the English one.

1. When the cat is away, the mice will play.

_____

2. Tit for tat.

_____

3. Better late than never.

_____

4. Where there's a will, there's a way.

_____

5. To each his own.

_____

II.   Fill in the missing words in French. Refer to the proverbs in this unit.

1. Le _____ parti, les souris _____.

2. Loin des _____, loin _____ coeur.

3. Tel _____, tel _____.

4. Telle _____, telle _____.

III.   Match the following.

1. Better late than never.   _____ À bon chat, bon rat.

2. To each his own.   _____ Mieux vaut tard que jamais.

3. Where there's a will, there's a way.   _____ Tout est bien qui finit bien.

4. All's well that ends well.   _____ À chacun son goût.

5. Tit for tat.   _____ Vouloir, c'est pouvoir.

IV. Picture Interpretation. Proficiency in Speaking.

Situation: Look at the two pictures at the beginning of this work unit. Choose either the three mice and the cat or the man eating an enormous amount of food. Describe the picture to a friend in at least ten words. If you choose the mice, tell how many mice there are in the picture, what they are doing and why, and something about the cat. If you choose the man, tell something about his appearance, what he is doing, and why.

V. Vocabulary Building. Proficiency in Writing.

A. Look again at the picture of the mice and cat. Write two verbs you would use if you described this picture.

1. _____ 2. _____

B. Look again at the picture of the man who is eating. Write the names of four foods on the table.

1. _____ 2. _____ 3. _____ 4. _____

STRUCTURES DE LA LANGUE

A. Summary of word order of elements in a French declarative sentence in the present tense

SUBJECT	ne	me	le	lui	y	en	VERB	pas
	n'	m'	la	leur				
		te	l'					
		t'	les					
		se						
		s'						
		nous						
		vous						

Models:

Affirmative

1. Janine lit le poème.
   Janine le lit.

2. Pierre écrit la lettre.
   Pierre l'écrit.

3. M. Richy me donne le ragoût.

Negative

1. Janine ne lit pas le poème.
   Janine ne le lit pas.

2. Pierre n'écrit pas la lettre.
   Pierre ne l'écrit pas.

3. M. Richy ne me donne pas le ragoût.

B. Summary of word order of elements in a French declarative sentence in the passé composé

SUBJECT	ne	me	le	lui	y	en	VERB	pas	past participle
	n'	m'	la	leur			(Auxiliary		
		te	l'				verb		
		t'	les				**avoir** or		
		se					**être** in		
		s'					the		
		nous					present		
		vous					tense)		

Models:

Affirmative	Negative
1. Louis a préparé le dîner. Louis l'a préparé.	1. Louis n'a pas préparé le dîner. Louis ne l'a pas préparé.
2. Pierre a préparé la salade. Pierre l'a préparée.	2. Pierre n'a pas préparé la salade. Pierre ne l'a pas préparée.
3. Louise a préparé les dîners. Louise les a préparés.	3. Louise n'a pas préparé les dîners. Louise ne les a pas préparés.
4. Rita a préparé les salades. Rita les a préparées.	4. Rita n'a pas préparé les salades. Rita ne les a pas préparées.

EXERCISES

Review the preceding material before starting these exercises.

I. The following sentences are scrambled. Each sentence is in the present tense and contains a subject, a verb, a direct object pronoun, a direct object noun, or an indirect object pronoun. Some contain y and some contain en; some contain both. Some are in the negative, some are in the affirmative. Rewrite them in correct word order. (Refer to Summary A above if you have to.)

1. Janine / la lettre / écrit.

_____

2. Janine / écrit / l'.

_____

3. Monique / la lettre / n' / pas / écrit.

_____

4. Madame Richy / donne / me / un cadeau.

_____

5. Le professeur / ne / donne / lui / pas / le stylo.

_____

6. Il / pas / n' / y / a / bon / un / restaurant / près d'ici.

_____

7. Il / a / une mouche / y / la soupe / dans.

_____

8. Il / en / a / y / beaucoup / la soupe / dans.

_____

9. Je / donne / leur / de l'argent.

_____

10. Je / vous / ne / pas / donne / l'éclair.

_____

II. **Do the same in this exercise as you did in the above one. (Refer to Summary B above if you have to.)**

1. Louis / le dîner / préparé / a.

_____

2. Marie / préparé / a / l'.

_____

3. Il / pas / n' / préparé / a / le dîner.

_____

4. Janine / la salade / préparé / a / pas / n'.

_____

5. Robert / préparé / a / les salades.

_____

6. Jacques / a / préparées / les / ne / pas.

_____

7. Monique / lui / ne / pas / a / donné / les chocolats.

_____

8. Raymond / donné / a / vous / les disques.

_____

9. Madame Paquet / leur / ne / pas / donné / a / l'argent.

_____

10. Je / leur / ne / ai / donné / en / pas.

_____

III. Eating, Drinking, and Socializing. Proficiency in Speaking.

Situation: Below is a photo of a sidewalk café in Paris. It is located on the **avenue des Champs-Élysées** near the **Arc de Triomphe.** Describe the scene to a friend; for example, there are many people eating, drinking, and talking. You may also want to select one particular person and describe his or her appearance. You may use your own ideas and words or any of the following: **boire, manger, parler, lui, leur, il y a, étudiants.**

A sidewalk café in Paris.

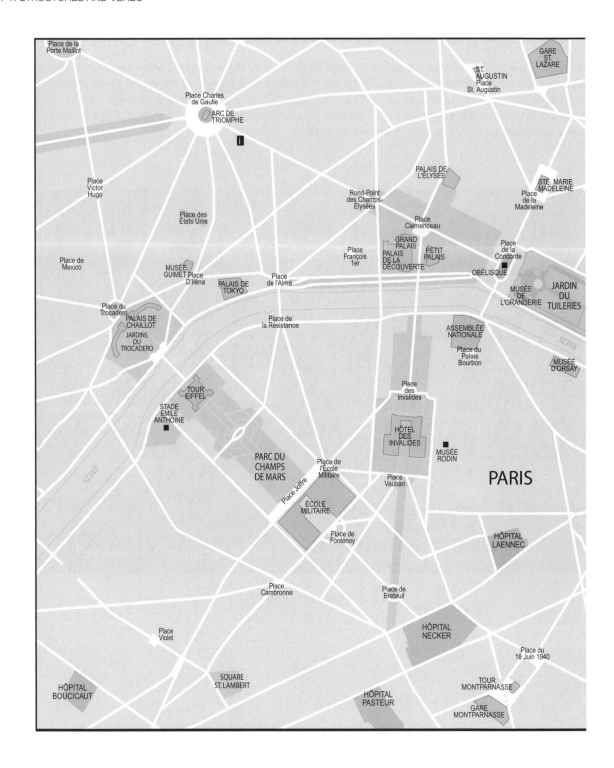

Map showing the quays in the **Île de la Cité** area.
From the Michelin Green Guide to Paris, 2nd Edition, of Pneu Michelin, Services de Tourisme.

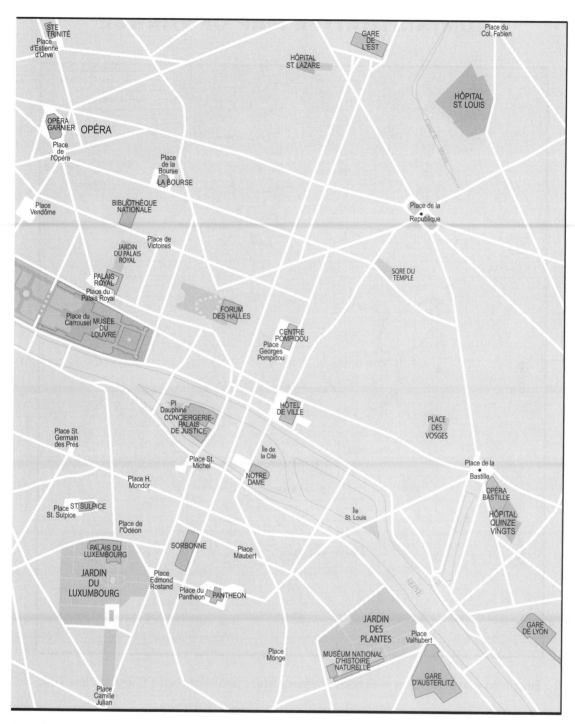

Autrefois (formerly), Paris s'appelait (used to be called) Lutèce. Lutèce était (was) le village des Parisii, le nom d'une tribu gauloise (Gallic tribe). La ville de Paris a reçu son nom des Parisii.

L'Île de la Cité, le berceau (the cradle) de Paris, est une île de la Seine, le fleuve qui passe par Paris. Dans la Cité vous pouvez voir, par exemple (for example), la cathédrale Notre-Dame de Paris, la Sainte-Chapelle, le Palais de Justice, et la Préfecture de Police. Pour une belle vue (view) de cette île, tournez à la page 432 dans ce livre.

ADMINISTRATIVE MAP OF FRANCE

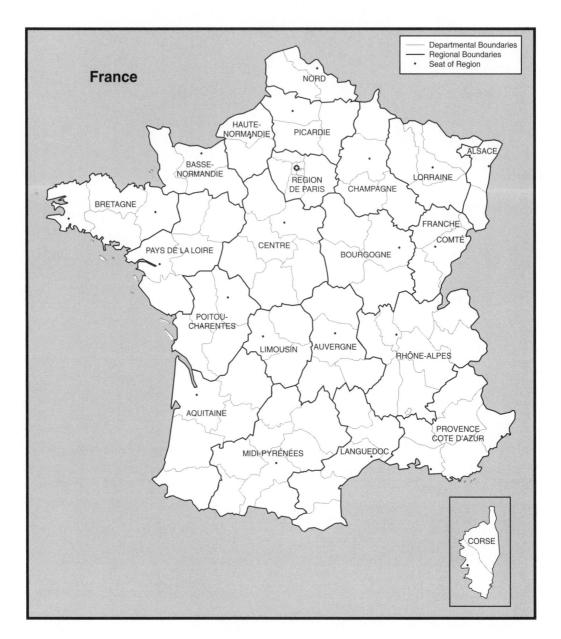

Reprinted with permission of French Embassy Press and Information Division, New York.

IV. Culture. French Proverbs. Proficiency in Speaking and Writing.

Situation: The fun activity today in Madame Marin's class is to see who can finish a French proverb that a student begins. The one who finishes the most proverbs wins a prize **(gagner un prix).** In this exercise, provide the French for all the players. First, say the words aloud. After the game is completed, write the French words on the lines. Later, switch roles with the other players.

Mme Marin:	**Bon. Alors, qui veut commencer un proverbe français? Qui veut le finir?**
Robert:	_____
	Me! Me! I want to begin a French proverb. Tonya can finish it.
Mme Marin:	**D'accord. Vous pouvez commencer, Robert.**
Robert:	_____
	Better late …
Mme Marin:	**Excellent! Mieux vaut tard … Tonya, finissez le proverbe.**
Tonya:	**Je ne sais pas.**
Yvette:	_____
	I know! It's … than never. Better late than never!
Mme Marin:	**C'est ça. Bravo, Yvette! Mieux vaut tard que jamais!**
André:	_____
	Me! Me! I want to begin a French proverb.
Mme Marin:	**D'accord. Allez-y!/Okay. Go ahead!**
André:	_____
	All's well …
Mme Marin:	**Éric, finissez ce proverbe, s'il vous plaît.**
Éric:	_____
	… that ends well.
Mme Marin:	**C'est épatant!/That's wonderful! Tout est bien qui finit bien!**
Robert:	_____
	Who has won the prize, Madame Marin?
Mme Marin:	**Qui a gagné le prix? Personne/Nobody. Nous allons continuer demain avec les autres étudiants. C'est tout pour aujourd'hui.**

V. Culture. French Proverbs. Proficiency in Speaking and Writing.

Say a proverb in French that would make a point in the following situations. Then write it on the line. Review the proverbs at the beginning of this work unit.

A. Situation: You just arrived twenty minutes late to French class for a test. What might the teacher say to you?

_____

B. Situation: Your French teacher has to leave the room for about ten minutes to make an urgent phone call in the main office. What might one of the students say when the teacher is out of the room?

_____

C. Situation: Annie tells her mother that she doesn't feel like having dinner because she doesn't have an appetite. What might her mother say to her?

_____

D. Situation: Yvette is gossiping with Mimi about Julie. Mimi whispers to her that somebody might be listening. What proverb might she use?

_____

E. Situation: Robert is telling his friend Louis that he would like to have a summer job in the fast-food restaurant near his house but he doesn't know how to get the job he wants. What might Louis say to him?

_____

VI. Culture. French Proverbs. Proficiency in Writing.

Situation: Write two situations in English and the French proverbs that would apply to them.

1. Situation: _____

_____

2. Situation: _____

_____

VII. Appreciating French Art. Proficiency in Speaking and Writing.

Situation: You are on a field trip at a museum with your French teacher, Monsieur Martin, and other students. You are in awe as you admire the masterpiece of French art, *Terrasse à Sainte-Adresse*/*Garden at Sainte-Adresse* by Claude Monet, **grand artiste français.** Sainte-Adresse is located near Le Havre, a port in northern France on the English Channel/**La Manche.**

In this exercise, for maximum practice, provide the French for all the students. First, say the words aloud, then write them on the lines. You may vary and expand the conversation with your own ideas and words. Refer to the vocabulary under the picture on the next page.

M. Martin: **Alors, aimez-vous ce tableau de Claude Monet?**

Simone: _____

I think it's beautiful! What a painting! I want to be an artist.

Éric: _____

I think it's great! What an artist! I want to be an artist, too.

M. Martin: **Regardez la structure géométrique marquée par les deux mâts.**

Robert: _____

It's marvelous! Look at the railing that separates the terrace garden from the sea.

Anne: _____

If only I could paint like that!

Monique: _____

Where there's a will, there's a way!

Nathalie: _____

Look at all the boats on the horizon! And look at the sailboat near the woman with the white parasol.

Jacques: _____

The garden is beautiful. I have never seen a garden so beautiful!

M. Martin: **Je vois trois plans dans ce tableau—la terrasse, la mer, et le ciel. Au premier plan, les fleurs, les feuilles, et les ombres sont impressionnistes.**

Georges: _____

The pennant on the left is splendid. The French flag on the right is impressive.

M. Martin: **Bon. Alors, maintenant que vous avez apprécié un tableau impressionniste, allons sur la terrasse pour un rafraîchissement!**

Terrasse à Sainte-Adresse/Garden at Sainte-Adresse by Claude Monet (1840–1926).

all the boats   **tous les bateaux**

alors   *adv.* well, then, so

au premier plan   on the first level

French flag   **le drapeau français**

I have never seen a garden so beautiful!   **Je n'ai jamais vu un jardin si beau!**

I think it's great!   **Je pense que c'est épatant!**

I want to be an artist   **Je veux être artiste.**

If only I could paint like that!   **Si je pouvais peindre comme ça!**

impressionniste   *adj.* impressionist

impressive   *adj.* **impressionnant**

Je vois trois plans   I see three levels.

Look at …   **Regardez …**

marquée   *adj.* marked

marvelous   *adj.* **merveilleux**

mât   *n. m.* mast

mer   *n. f.* sea

near   *adv.* **près de**

ombre   *n. f.* shadow

on the horizon   **à l'horizon**

par   *prep.* by

pennant   *n.* **le fanion**

rafraîchissement   *n. m.* refreshment

railing   *n.* **la balustrade**

sailboat   *n.* **le bateau à voiles; le voilier**

separate   *v.* **séparer**

terrasse   *n. f.* terrace

that separates   **qui sépare**

too, also   *adv.* **aussi**

What a painting!   **Quel tableau!**

What an artist!   **Quel artiste!**

with the white parasol   **au parasol blanc**

La fourmi répond à la cigale: "Ah! Vous avez chanté! Dansez maintenant!"
(The ant answers the cicada, "Ah, you have sung! Dance now!")

Work Unit 25
Summaries of Word Order of Elements in a French Imperative Sentence in the Affirmative and Negative

Do you plan ahead like the cicada or the ant?

Une fable

La cigale et la fourmi

—adapté de la fable de Jean de La Fontaine

La cigale a chanté tout l'été.
Elle n'a pas travaillé.

L'hiver arrive et
Elle n'a rien à manger.

Elle n'a pas un seul petit morceau
De mouche ou de vermisseau.

Elle va chez la fourmi, sa voisine,
Et elle lui dit:

> —Ma chère amie, je n'ai rien à manger et j'ai
> faim. Pouvez-vous me prêter un grain de
> quelque chose jusqu'au printemps?

Mais la fourmi ne donne jamais
Rien à ses voisins.

Elle a travaillé pendant l'été
Pour avoir quelque chose à manger
Pendant l'hiver.

La fourmi demande à la cigale:

> —Qu'est-ce que vous avez fait pendant l'été?
> Avez-vous travaillé?

La cigale répond à la fourmi:

> —Je n'ai pas travaillé.
> J'ai chanté.

Et la fourmi lui dit:

> —Ah! Vous avez chanté! Dansez maintenant!

VOCABULAIRE

la cigale   *n.,* the cicada (an insect; the male cicada makes a prolonged shrill, droning sound on hot days in the summer)

l'été   *n. m.,* the summer
la fourmi   *n.,* the ant
l'hiver   *n. m.,* the winter
jusque   *prep.,* as far as, up to; **jusqu'au printemps**

until spring
le printemps   *n.,* the spring
travailler   *v.,* to work
le vermisseau   *n.,* the small worm

EXERCISES

Review the fable and vocabulary before starting these exercises.

I.   Vrai ou Faux?

1. La cigale a chanté tout l'été. _____

2. La cigale n'a pas travaillé pendant l'été. _____

3. La fourmi n'a pas travaillé. _____

4. La cigale n'a rien à manger. _____

5. La fourmi a beaucoup à manger. _____

6. Quand l'hiver arrive, la cigale a besoin de nourriture. _____

7. La fourmi refuse de donner à manger à la cigale. _____

8. La fourmi a chanté tout l'été. _____

9. La cigale a faim. _____

10. La fourmi dit à la cigale de danser. _____

367

II. Fill in the squares by writing the French words across for the English words in the list.

1. to her or to him

2. dance!

3. hunger

4. fly (insect)

5. or

6. grain

7. to eat

8. the cicada

III. Fill in the missing words. (Refer to the fable if you have to.)

1. La cigale _____ _____ tout l'été.

2. Elle n'a _____ à manger.

3. Elle n'a _____ travaillé.

4. Elle n'a pas un seul petit morceau de _____ ou de vermisseau.

5. Elle _____ chez la fourmi, sa voisine.

6. La fourmi _____ donne _____ rien à ses voisins.

7. Qu'est-ce que vous _____ fait pendant l'été?

8. J'_____ chanté.

9. La fourmi demande _____ la cigale.

10. Ah! Vous _____ chanté! _____ maintenant!

IV. Answer the following questions in complete simple sentences.

1. Qui a chanté tout l'été?

_____

2. Est-ce que la cigale a travaillé?

_____

3. Quand l'hiver arrive, est-ce que la cigale a quelque chose à manger?

_____

4. Qui a travaillé tout l'été?

_____

5. Est-ce que la fourmi donne quelque chose à manger à la cigale?

_____

STRUCTURES DE LA LANGUE

A. Summary of word order of elements in a French affirmative imperative sentence

VERB	le	moi	lui	y	en
	la	m'	leur		
	l'	toi			
		t'			
	les	nous			
		vous			

Models: (Compare these affirmative imperatives with those in the negative below.)

1. **Répondez à la lettre!**
   Répondez-y!
2. **Écrivez la lettre!**
   Écrivez-la!
3. **Achetez les chocolats!**
   Achetez-les!
4. **Donnez-moi le livre!**
5. **Donnez-nous l'argent!**
6. **Donnez-le à Marie!**
   Donnez-lui le gâteau!
7. **Lève-toi!**
8. **Écrivez-lui!**
9. **Parlez-leur!**
10. **Allez à la plage!**
    Allez-y!
11. **Mangez du gâteau!**
    Mangez-en!
12. **Donnez-m'en!**

1. Answer the letter!
   Answer it!
2. Write the letter!
   Write it!
3. Buy the chocolates!
   Buy them!
4. Give me the book!
5. Give us the money!
6. Give it to Marie!
   Give (to) her the cake!
7. Get up!
8. Write to him (to her)!
9. Speak to them!
10. Go to the beach!
    Go there (to it)!
11. Eat some cake!
    Eat some!
12. Give me some!

B. Summary of word order of elements in a French negative imperative sentence

Ne	me, m'	le	lui	y	en	VERB	pas
N'		la	leur				
	te, t'	l'					
		les					
	nous						
	vous						

Models: (Compare these negative imperatives with those in the affirmative above.)

1. **Ne répondez pas à la lettre!**
   N'y répondez pas!
2. **N'écrivez pas la lettre!**
   Ne l'écrivez pas!
3. **N'achetez pas les chocolats!**
   Ne les achetez pas!
4. **Ne me donnez pas le livre!**
5. **Ne nous donnez pas l'argent!**
6. **Ne le donnez pas à Marie!**
   Ne lui donnez pas le gâteau!
7. **Ne te lève pas!**
8. **Ne lui écrivez pas!**
9. **Ne leur parlez pas!**
10. **N'allez pas à la plage!**
    N'y allez pas!
11. **Ne mangez pas de gâteau!**
    N'en mangez pas!
12. **Ne m'en donnez pas!**

1. Don't answer the letter!
   Don't answer it!
2. Don't write the letter!
   Don't write it!
3. Don't buy the chocolates!
   Don't buy them!
4. Don't give me the book!
5. Don't give us the money!
6. Don't give it to Marie!
   Don't give (to) her the cake!
7. Don't get up!
8. Don't write to him (to her)!
9. Don't speak to them!
10. Don't go to the beach!
    Don't go there (to it)!
11. Don't eat any cake!
    Don't eat any of it!
12. Don't give me any (of it)!

EXERCISES

Review the preceding material before starting these exercises.

I. The following sentences are scrambled. Rewrite them in correct word order. (Refer to Summary A if you have to.)

1. Moi / donnez / le livre / !

_____

2. Lui / écrivez / la lettre / !

_____

3. Le gâteau / lui / donnez / !

_____

4. Y / répondez / !

_____

5. Vous / asseyez / et / donnez / la main / moi / !

_____

II. The following sentences are scrambled. Rewrite them in correct word order. (Refer to Summary B if you have to.)

1. Apprenez / l' / ne / pas / !

_____

2. Ne / pas / les / étudiez / !

_____

3. Donnez / m' / ne / en / pas / !

_____

4. N' / en / pas / mangez / !

_____

5. Leur / ne / pas / parlez / !

_____

III. Giving Commands. Proficiency in Speaking.

Situation: You and a girlfriend are at a party. You see a young man who is coming toward both of you. You know that he recently broke off with your friend, and you think he has a lot of nerve to come over to talk. Tell your friend not to get up, not to talk to him, not to answer him. When he approaches, tell him to go away. You may use your own ideas and words or any in this work unit.

Test 5

This test is based on Work Units 21 to 25. Review them before starting this test.

PART ONE   SPEAKING PROFICIENCY

Directions: Read the seventeen situations below. Take a few minutes to organize your thoughts about the words you are going to speak. Select fifteen of them.

1. **Situation:** You have just arrived in Paris on an educational tour with a group of students. Your guide is Madame Simard, an assistant at the Université de Paris. You have been asking her questions about Paris. Now she has a few questions to ask you because she is impressed with your ability to speak some French. Make three statements that you would say to her.

2. **Situation:** You are in a florist shop because you want to buy a plant for a friend. You are talking with the florist. Make three statements.

3. **Situation:** Alice, one of your classmates, was absent when Work Unit 21 was done in class. She wants you to tell her what is going on in the picture at the beginning of that work unit where Madame Paquet is sick in bed. Make three statements.

4. **Situation:** You are preparing to make your own Father's Day card to give to your father or to some friend or relative who has been like a father to you. Make three statements.

5. **Situation:** The members of your French Club are planning a party to entertain some students who are thinking of joining the club. As president of the French Club, you have proposed to help the members practice to sing a song. You have asked a member to play the piano. Say aloud the words to the song *Frère Jacques*. The words and music are in Work Unit 21.

6. **Situation:** You are planning to go to a county fair with some friends. Tell us six things you would like to do there; for example, **regarder les animaux.**

7. **Situation:** Three children are in a park playing on a tree that has been felled. Look at the picture in Work Unit 22 and, in three statements, tell us what they are doing.

8. **Situation:** You are riding on a bicycle on a country road in France. In front of you there is another cyclist with a young boy sitting behind him. The boy has turned his head and is looking at you. What is he saying to you? What are you saying to him?

9. **Situation:** Take another good look at the picture at the beginning of Work Unit 23. Describe the scene to a friend, telling what's going on, in three statements.

10. **Situation:** Your friend John has a toothache but he does not want to go to the dentist. Ask him three questions or make three statements.

11. **Situation:** You and your friend Anne are at the National Gallery of Art in Washington, D.C., admiring the painting *La Liseuse*/*A Young Girl Reading* by Jean-Honoré Fragonard. Look at the picture again in Work Unit 23. Make three statements about it.

12. **Situation:** You are looking at the two pictures at the beginning of Work Unit 24. Choose either the three mice and the cat or the man eating. Describe the scene to a friend in at least three statements.

13. **Situation:** If you are looking at the picture of the three mice and the cat in Work Unit 24, state two verbs you would use to describe what is going on. If you are looking at the picture of the man eating, say aloud the names of four foods on the table.

14. **Situation:** Look again at the picture of the **Café de Flore** in Work Unit 24. In three statements, tell us what the people are doing.

15. **Situation:** State three French proverbs.

16. **Situation:** You are on a field trip at a museum with your French teacher, Monsieur Martin, and other students. You are in awe as you admire the masterpiece **(le chef-d'oeuvre)** of French art, *Terrasse à Sainte-Adresse/Garden at Sainte-Adresse* by Claude Monet, a French impressionist painter. Make three statements about the painting. It is in Work Unit 24.

17. **Situation:** Imagine a situation. State it in English; then make three statements about it in French.

PART TWO   LISTENING PROFICIENCY

Directions: Your teacher will read aloud four short paragraphs. Each one will contain only a few sentences. You will hear each paragraph twice. Then you will hear one question based on each. You will hear the question only once. It is printed below. Choose the best suggested answer and check the letter of your choice.

Selection Number 1

1. Depuis quand Madame Paquet est-elle malade?
   - A. depuis ce matin
   - B. depuis la semaine passée
   - C. depuis quelques heures
   - D. depuis hier

Selection Number 2

2. Où sont-ils allés samedi?
   - A. au théâtre
   - B. au cinéma
   - C. à la foire
   - D. à l'hôpital

Selection Number 3

3. Où Pierre est-il allé?
   - A. aux grands magasins
   - B. chez un confiseur
   - C. chez le coiffeur
   - D. aux grands magasins et chez un confiseur

Selection Number 4

4. Pourquoi la cigale est-elle allée chez la fourmi?
   - A. pour chanter au plaisir de la fourmi
   - B. pour donner quelque chose à la fourmi
   - C. pour lui donner à manger
   - D. pour lui demander de la nourriture

PART THREE   READING PROFICIENCY

Directions: In the following passage there are five blank spaces numbered 1 through 5. Each blank space represents a missing word. For each blank space, four possible completions are provided. Only one of them makes sense in the context of the passage.

First, read the passage in its entirety to determine its general meaning. Then read it a second time. For each blank space choose the completion that makes the best sense and is grammatically correct. Write its letter in the space provided.

Madame Paquet est malade _____ hier. Elle _____ mangé quelque chose

1. A. de	2. A. est
B. d'	B. a
C. pour	C. va
D. depuis	D. ont

qui _____ a donné mal à l'estomac. Elle est _____ dans son lit. Son

3. A. la	4. A. souffrant
B. le	B. souffrante
C. lui	C. souffrants
D. leur	D. souffrantes

mari a _____ le docteur pour lui donner un médicament.

5. A. appeler
   B. appelé
   C. appelée
   D. appelés

PART FOUR   WRITING PROFICIENCY

Directions: Of the eighteen situations in Part One (Speaking Proficiency) in this test, select fifteen and write what you said on the lines below. If you need more space for writing, use a sheet of paper.

Situation No. __ _____

_____

Situation No. __ _____

_____

Situation No. __ _____

_____

Situation No. __ _____

_____

Situation No. __ _____

_____

Situation No. __ _____

_____

Situation No. __ _____

_____

Situation No. __ _____

_____

Situation No. __ _____

_____

Situation No. __ _____

_____

Situation No. __ _____

_____

Situation No. __ _____

_____

Situation No. __ _____

_____

Situation No. __ _____

_____

Situation No. __ _____

_____

Part 2: Vocabulary

© Corbis 2007

Unit 1
L'école

le **banc** *n.*, the seat, the bench
la **bibliothèque** *n.*, the library
le **bureau** *n.*, the desk, the office
le **cahier** *n.*, the notebook
la **calculatrice** *n.*, the calculator
le **calendrier** *n.*, the calendar
le **carnet** *n.*, the small notebook
la **carte** *n.*, the map
la **classe** *n.*, the class; **la classe de français** French class
le **congé** *n.*, leave, permission; **jour de congé** day off (from school or work)
la **cour** *n.*, the playground, the courtyard
la **craie** *n.*, the chalk
le **crayon** *n.*, the pencil; **le crayon-feutre** felt-tip pen
les **devoirs** *n. m.*, homework assignments
la **dictée** *n.*, the dictation
le **drapeau** *n.*, the flag

l'**école** *n. f.*, the school
écrire *v.*, to write
l'**élève** *n. m. f.*, the pupil
l'**encre** *n. f.*, the ink
étudier *v.*, to study; **les études** *n. f. pl.*, the studies
l'**étudiant** *m.*, l'**étudiante** *f.*, *n.*, the student
l'**examen** *n. m.*, the examination
l'**exercice** *n. m.*, the exercise
expliquer *v.*, to explain
la **faute** *n.*, the mistake
la **leçon** *n.*, the lesson; **leçon de français** French lesson
le **livre** *n.*, the book
le **livret d'exercices** *n.*, the workbook
le **lycée** *n.*, the high school
le **maître** *m.*, la **maîtresse** *f.*, *n.*, the teacher
l'**ordinateur** *n. m.*, the computer
le **papier** *n.*, the paper; **une feuille de papier** a sheet of paper

passer *v.*, to pass; **passer un examen** to take an exam
poser *v.*, to pose; **poser une question** to ask a question
le **professeur** *m.*, la **professeur-dame, une femme professeur** *f.*, *n.*, the professor
le **pupitre** *n.*, the desk (student's)
la **règle** *n.*, the rule, the ruler
répondre *v.*, to respond, to answer, to reply
la **réponse** *n.*, the answer
réussir *v.*, to succeed; **réussir à un examen** to pass an exam
la **salle** *n.*, the room; **la salle de classe** the classroom
le **stylo** *n.*, the pen
le **tableau noir** *n.*, the blackboard, the chalkboard
l'**université** *n. f.*, the university
le **vocabulaire** *n.*, the vocabulary

EXERCISES

Review the above material before doing these exercises.

I.   Choose the word that does not belong in the group.

1. (a) élève   (b) étudiant   (c) maître   (d) stylo   _____

2. (a) écrire   (b) répondre   (c) université   (d) expliquer   _____

3. (a) crayon   (b) drapeau   (c) stylo   (d) craie   _____

4. (a) vocabulaire   (b) école   (c) lycée   (d) université   _____

5. (a) cahier   (b) cour   (c) carnet   (d) livre   _____

II. All the words in each group are either masculine or feminine, except one. Choose the word whose gender is not like the others.

1. (a) examen   (b) drapeau   (c) bureau   (d) dictée   _____

2. (a) règle   (b) stylo   (c) crayon   (d) cahier   _____

3. (a) exercice   (b) école   (c) cour   (d) faute   _____

4. (a) classe   (b) leçon   (c) bibliothèque   (d) bureau   _____

5. (a) ordinateur   (b) pupitre   (c) carte   (d) stylo   _____

III. Choose the word that can be substituted for the italicized word and still give meaning to the sentence.

1. Janine veut lire *le livre.*

    (a) la leçon   (b) le tableau noir   (c) l'encre   (d) la cour   _____

2. Tu peux écrire dans *le cahier.*

    (a) la faute   (b) le stylo   (c) le carnet   (d) l'encre   _____

3. L'étudiant doit faire ses *études.*

    (a) pupitres   (b) devoirs   (c) craies   (d) lycées   _____

4. La maîtresse commence *la dictée.*

    (a) les bureaux   (b) le crayon   (c) la craie   (d) la leçon   _____

5. L'élève ne veut pas *répondre.*

    (a) poser une question   (b) réponse   (c) bibliothèque   (d) cahier   _____

IV. Match the following.

1. le stylo   _____ map

2. le cahier   _____ rule, ruler

3. la carte   _____ notebook

4. la cour   _____ pen

5. la règle   _____ playground

V. Under each drawing, write the French word for the object shown. Include the definite article; e.g., le bureau, le cahier, etc.

_____   _____   _____

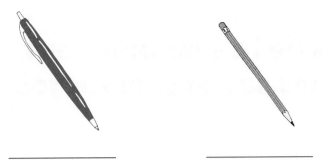

_____   _____

VI. Vocabulary Building. Proficiency in Writing.

A. Write five things that are usually found in a classroom.

1. _____ 2. _____ 3. _____ 4. _____ 5. _____

B. Write four things you can use to write.

1. _____ 2. _____ 3. _____ 4. _____

Unit 2

Les jours de la semaine, les mois de l'année, les saisons, et les jours de fête

Les jours de la semaine:

le **dimanche,** Sunday
le **lundi,** Monday
le **mardi,** Tuesday
le **mercredi,** Wednesday
le **jeudi,** Thursday
le **vendredi,** Friday
le **samedi,** Saturday

Les saisons:

le **printemps,** spring
l'**été** *(m.),* summer
l'**automne** *(m.),* autumn, fall
l'**hiver** *(m.),* winter

don't pronounce "n"

Les mois de l'année:

janvier, January
février, February
mars, March
avril, April
mai, May
juin, June
juillet, July
août, August
septembre, September
octobre, October
novembre, November
décembre, December

Les jours de fête:

fêter *v.,* to celebrate a holiday; **bonne fête!** happy holiday!
l'**anniversaire** *m.,* anniversary, birthday; **bon anniversaire!** happy anniversary! *or* happy birthday!
le **Jour de l'An,** New Year's Day
Bonne année! Happy New Year!
les **Pâques,** Easter; **Joyeuses Pâques,** Happy Easter
la **Pâque,** Passover
le **quatorze juillet** (Bastille Day), July 14, French "Independence Day"
les **grandes vacances,** summer vacation
la **Toussaint,** All Saints' Day (le premier novembre)
le **Noël,** Christmas; **Joyeux Noël!** Merry Christmas!
à vous de même! the same to you!
le **ramadan,** Ramadan
la **Hanoukka,** Hanukkah

EXERCISES

Review the above material before doing these exercises.

I.   **Choose the answer that is the best rejoinder.**

1. C'est Noël!

   (a) Bonne année!   (b) Joyeux Noël!   (c) À vous de même!
   (d) Pâques!

382

2. C'est le Jour de l'An!

    (a) À vous de même!   (b) Bonne année!   (c) Joyeuses Pâques!
    (d) Fête!   _____

3. Janine a seize ans aujourd'hui!

    (a) Bon anniversaire, Janine!   (b) Venez demain, Janine!
    (c) Ce n'est pas aujourd'hui, Janine!   (d) Au revoir, Janine!   _____

II.   **Choose the word or group of words that does not belong in the group.**

1. (a) samedi   (b) vendredi   (c) jeudi   (d) août   _____

2. (a) mai   (b) mardi   (c) juin   (d) février   _____

3. (a) printemps   (b) Noël   (c) été   (d) hiver   _____

4. (a) le Jour de l'An   (b) le Jour de la Bastille   (c) la Toussaint
    (d) anniversaire   _____

5. (a) le premier novembre   (b) le 14 juillet   (c) le premier janvier
    (d) les grandes vacances   _____

III.   **Choose the word that can be substituted for the italicized word and still give meaning to the sentence.**

1. *Le printemps* est une saison.

    (a) L'anniversaire   (b) La fête   (c) L'hiver   (d) Le jour   _____

2. *Mardi* est un jour de la semaine.

    (a) Noël   (b) Pâques   (c) Mai   (d) Samedi   _____

3. *Décembre* est un mois de l'année.

    (a) Janvier   (b) Noël   (c) L'été   (d) Dimanche   _____

4. *Noël* est un jour de fête.

    (a) Décembre   (b) Le Jour de l'An   (c) Janvier   (d) L'automne   _____

5. Il y a des fleurs dans le jardin en *juin*.

    (a) juillet   (b) décembre   (c) janvier   (d) hiver   _____

IV.   **Write in French the season of the year that is suggested by the picture.**

_____   _____

_____   _____

V. Activities. Proficiency in Speaking and Writing.

A. Choose one of the holidays under the heading **Les jours de fête** in this unit, and say what you do to celebrate it. Use at least ten words in French.

B. Choose one of the months under the heading **Les mois de l'année** in this unit, and give two reasons why it is your favorite month of the year.

C. Choose one of the days of the week under the heading **Les jours de la semaine** in this unit, and state two things you do on that special day of the week.

Les légumes, les poissons, les viandes, les produits laitiers, les desserts, les fromages, et les boissons

Les légumes:

l'aubergine   *f.,* the eggplant
la carotte,   the carrot
le champignon,   the mushroom
les épinards   *m.,* the spinach
les haricots verts   *m.,* the string beans
le maïs,   the corn
l'oignon   *m.,* the onion
les petits pois   *m.,* the peas
la pomme de terre,   the potato

Les viandes:

l'agneau   *m.,* the lamb; **la côte d'agneau,** the lamb chop
le biftek,   the steak
le jambon,   the ham
le porc,   the pork
le poulet,   the chicken
le rosbif,   the roast beef
le veau,   the veal; **la côte de veau,** the veal chop

Les poissons:

le maquereau,   the mackerel
la morue,   the cod
le saumon,   the salmon
la sole,   the sole
la truite,   the trout

Les produits laitiers:

le beurre,   the butter
la crème,   the cream
le fromage,   the cheese
le lait,   the milk
l'oeuf   *m.,* the egg

Les desserts:

le biscuit,   the cookie
le fruit,   the fruit
le gâteau,   the cake; **le gâteau sec,** the cookie
la glace,   the ice cream
la pâtisserie,   the pastry

Les fromages:

le brie
le camembert
le gruyère
le petit suisse
le port-salut
le roquefort

Les boissons:

la bière,   the beer
le cacao,   the cocoa
le café,   the coffee
le chocolat chaud,   the hot chocolate
le cidre,   the cider
l'eau minérale   *f.,* the mineral water
le jus,   the juice; **le jus de tomate,**   the tomato juice
le thé,   the tea
le vin,   the wine

EXERCISES

Review the above material before doing these exercises.

I.   **Choose the word that belongs in the same class as the italicized word.**

1. Donnez-moi un *jus,* s'il vous plaît.

   (a) oignon   (b) oeuf   (c) gâteau   (d) café   _____

2. J'aime beaucoup la *truite.*

   (a) morue   (b) crème   (c) glace   (d) pâtisserie   _____

3. Je n'aime pas le *roquefort.*

   (a) beurre   (b) lait   (c) porc   (d) camembert   _____

4. Le *jambon* est délicieux!

    (a) vin   (b) thé   (c) port-salut   (d) rosbif   _____

5. Je préfère des *pommes de terre.*

    (a) petits pois   (b) fruits   (c) fromages   (d) oeufs   _____

II. Choose the word that does not belong in the group.

1. (a) veau   (b) pâtisserie   (c) rosbif   (d) jambon   _____

2. (a) bière   (b) thé   (c) roquefort   (d) vin   _____

3. (a) morue   (b) sole   (c) beurre   (d) saumon   _____

4. (a) haricot vert   (b) carotte   (c) aubergine   (d) crème   _____

5. (a) brie   (b) camembert   (c) porc   (d) gruyère   _____

III. In this puzzle, find the French words for the English words listed. Circle them.

1. eggs
2. milk
3. wine
4. eggplant
5. ham

V	O	C	A	F	E	L	V	S
I	E	V	E	A	U	A	I	O
A	U	B	E	R	G	I	N	E
L	F	J	A	M	H	T	U	I
I	S	J	A	M	B	O	N	L

IV. Choose the best answer that completes the sentence.

1. Monsieur Paquet aime boire

    (a) des fruits.   (b) du vin.   (c) de la glace.   (d) du veau.   _____

2. Madame Paquet aime manger

    (a) du jambon.   (b) du café.   (c) de la bière.   (d) du lait.   _____

3. Le poisson que j'aime mieux est

    (a) le porc.   (b) la pomme de terre.   (c) le port-salut.   (d) le saumon.   _____

4. Pour le petit déjeuner je prends du lait dans

    (a) mon café.   (b) mes oeufs.   (c) mes petits pois.   (d) ma glace.   _____

5. La pomme de terre est

    (a) un produit laitier.   (b) un légume.   (c) un fruit.   (d) une viande.   _____

V. Vocabulary Building. Proficiency in Writing.

A. It is your turn to bring three different desserts to the next meeting of the French Club. Write your three choices.

    1. _____   2. _____   3. _____

B. You are in a restaurant. Write four things you would like to eat.

    1. _____   2. _____   3. _____   4. _____

VI. On the line write in French the name of the food shown in the drawing. Use the definite article; e.g., **le beurre, les petits pois,** etc.

_____   _____   _____

_____   _____   _____

_____   _____   _____

_____

Unit 4

Les animaux, les fleurs, les couleurs, les arbres, et les fruits

Les animaux:

l'âne   *m.,* the donkey
le chat   *m.,* la chatte *f.,* the cat
le cheval,   the horse
le chien   *m.,* la chienne *f.,* the dog
le cochon,   the pig
le coq,   the rooster
l'éléphant   *m.,* the elephant
le lapin,   the rabbit
le lion,   the lion
l'oiseau   *m.,* the bird
la poule,   the hen
le poulet,   the chicken
le renard,   the fox
la souris,   the mouse
le tigre,   the tiger
la vache,   the cow

Les fleurs:

l'iris   *m.,* the iris
le lilas,   the lilac
le lis,   the lily
la marguerite,   the daisy
l'oeillet   *m.,* the carnation
la rose,   the rose
la tulipe,   the tulip
la violette,   the violet

Les couleurs:

blanc,   white
bleu,   blue
brun,   brown
gris,   gray
jaune,   yellow
noir,   black
rouge,   red
vert,   green

Les arbres:

le bananier,   the banana tree
le cerisier,   the cherry tree
le citronnier,   the lemon tree
l'oranger   *m.,* the orange tree
le palmier,   the palm tree
le pêcher,   the peach tree
le poirier,   the pear tree
le pommier,   the apple tree

Les fruits:

la banane,   the banana
la cerise,   the cherry
le citron,   the lemon; **citron vert,** lime
la fraise,   the strawberry
la framboise,   the raspberry
l'orange   *f.,* the orange
le pamplemousse,   the grapefruit
la pêche,   the peach
la poire,   the pear
la pomme,   the apple
le raisin,   the grape
la tomate,   the tomato

EXERCISES

Review the above material before doing these exercises.

I.   Choose the word that does not belong in the group.

1. (a) vache   (b) éléphant   (c) poire   (d) cochon   _____

2. (a) fraise   (b) banane   (c) poire   (d) gris   _____

3. (a) poirier   (b) pêcher   (c) cerisier   (d) pomme   _____

4. (a) tulipe   (b) oiseau   (c) marguerite   (d) rose   _____

5. (a) jaune   (b) bleu   (c) rouge   (d) oeillet   _____

II. **Un acrostiche.** Complete the French words in the squares across in this puzzle.

1. green
2. carnation
3. horse
4. eggplant
5. banana
6. university
7. lilac
8. year
9. iris
10. grape
11. ink

| V |
| O |
| C |
| A |
| B |
| U |
| L |
| A |
| I |
| R |
| E |

III. **Choose the word that is defined or described in the sentence.**

1. C'est un animal domestique.

   (a) tigre   (b) lion   (c) chat   (d) renard   _____

2. Cet animal donne du lait.

   (a) cochon   (b) vache   (c) oiseau   (d) chien   _____

3. Cet animal est plus grand que les autres.

   (a) âne   (b) éléphant   (c) chat   (d) cheval   _____

IV. **Choose the word that belongs in the same class as the italicized word.**

1. *Un poirier* est un arbre.

   (a) haricot vert   (b) banc   (c) renard   (d) cerisier   _____

2. Janine aime la jupe *verte* de Monique.

   (a) rouge   (b) poire   (c) morue   (d) oignon   _____

3. Pierre a donné un bouquet de *marguerites* à sa mère.

   (a) citrons   (b) fraises   (c) cerisiers   (d) roses   _____

4. *Une pomme* est un fruit.

   (a) un citron   (b) un oiseau   (c) un pêcher   (d) une tulipe   _____

5. *Un chat* est un animal.

   (a) un lilas   (b) un poirier   (c) une vache   (d) une fraise   _____

V. **Write the French words for what is shown in the drawings. Use the indefinite article;
e.g. un âne, une poule, etc.**

Unit 5

Le corps humain, les vêtements, la toilette

Le corps humain:

la bouche,   mouth
le bras,   arm
les cheveux   *m.,* hair
le cou,   neck
les dents   *f.,* teeth
le doigt,   finger; **doigt de pied, l'orteil**   *m.,* toe
l'épaule   *f.,* shoulder
l'estomac   *m.,* stomach
le genou,   knee
la jambe,   leg
la langue,   tongue
les lèvres   *f.,* lips
la main,   hand
le menton,   chin
le nez,   nose
l'oeil   *m.,* eye; **les yeux,** eyes
l'oreille   *f.,* ear
la peau,   skin
le pied,   foot
la poitrine,   chest
la tête,   head
le visage,   face

La toilette:

se baigner   *v.,* to bathe oneself
la baignoire   *n.,* the bathtub
le bain   *n.,* the bath
la brosse   *n.,* the brush; **brosse à dents,** toothbrush

brosser   *v.,* to brush; **se brosser les dents,** to brush one's teeth
la cuvette   *n.,* the toilet bowl
le dentifrice   *n.,* the toothpaste
le déodorant   *n.,* deodorant
déshabiller   *v.,* to undress; **se déshabiller,** to undress oneself
la douche   *n.,* the shower; **prendre une douche,** to take a shower
enlever   *v.,* to remove, to take off
le gant de toilette   *n.,* the washcloth
la glace   *n.,* the hand mirror
s'habiller   *v.,* to dress oneself
le lavabo   *n.,* the washroom, washstand
laver   *v.,* to wash; **se laver,** to wash oneself
mettre   *v.,* to put on
le miroir   *n.,* the mirror
ôter   *v.,* to take off, to remove
le peigne   *n.,* the comb; **se peigner les cheveux,** to comb one's hair
porter   *v.,* to wear
la salle de bains   *n.,* the bathroom
le savon   *n.,* the soap
la serviette   *n.,* the towel
le shampooing   *n.,* the shampoo

Les vêtements:

le bas,   stocking
le béret,   beret
la blouse,   blouse, smock
le blouson,   jacket (often with zipper)
le chandail,   sweater
le chapeau,   hat
la chaussette,   sock
la chaussure,   shoe
la chemise,   shirt
le collant,   pantyhose
le complet,   suit
le costume,   suit
la cravate,   necktie
l'écharpe   *f.,* scarf
le gant,   glove
le jean,   jeans
la jupe,   skirt
le maillot de bain,   swimsuit
le manteau,   coat
le pantalon,   trousers, pants
la pantoufle,   slipper
le pardessus,   overcoat
la poche,   pocket
le pull-over,   pullover or long-sleeved sweater
la robe,   dress
le slip,   underpants
le soulier,   shoe
le soutien-gorge,   bra
le veston,   (suit) coat

EXERCISES

Review the above material before doing these exercises.

I.   **Choose the word that belongs in the same class as the italicized word.**

1. Lucille a *les cheveux* noirs.

(a) les poches   (b) les yeux   (c) les gants   (d) les bains   _____

2. *Les oreilles* sont une partie de la tête.

   (a) les pantoufles   (b) les souliers   (c) les lèvres   (d) les bas   _____

3. Yolande a des *souliers* rouges.

   (a) jupes   (b) brosses   (c) savons   (d) serviettes   _____

4. Marthe aime les chemises *jaunes.*

   (a) gants   (b) blanches   (c) pantoufles   (d) robes   _____

5. *Le menton* se trouve sur le visage.

   (a) la poche   (b) le manteau   (c) l'écharpe   (d) le nez   _____

II.   Choose the word whose meaning completes the sentence.

1. Je veux me brosser les dents mais il n'y a pas de

   (a) savon.   (b) déodorant.   (c) dentifrice.   (d) shampooing.   _____

2. Il y a un lavabo dans

   (a) le salon.   (b) la voiture.   (c) la salle de bains.   (d) la rue.   _____

3. Pour me laver les cheveux j'ai besoin d'un

   (a) peigne.   (b) nez.   (c) shampooing.   (d) oeil.   _____

4. Après une douche, j'emploie une

   (a) cuvette.   (b) glace.   (c) chaussette.   (d) serviette.   _____

5. Une personne porte des pantoufles

   (a) aux pieds.   (b) sur la tête.   (c) aux cheveux.   (d) aux mains.   _____

III. Choose the word that does not belong in the group.

1. (a) bouche   (b) jambe   (c) oeil   (d) complet   _____

2. (a) doigt   (b) bas   (c) bras   (d) menton   _____

3. (a) se peigner   (b) se baigner   (c) se laver   (d) mettre   _____

4. (a) dent   (b) dentifrice   (c) lèvres   (d) jambe   _____

5. (a) chaussette   (b) chaussure   (c) soulier   (d) chapeau   _____

IV. Complete the following sentences by choosing the best answer.

1. Nous entendons avec les

   (a) pieds.   (b) visages.   (c) mains.   (d) oreilles.   _____

2. Nous courons avec les

   (a) bras.   (b) jambes.   (c) doigts.   (d) lèvres.   _____

3. La main contient cinq

   (a) doigts.   (b) visages.   (c) yeux.   (d) langues.   _____

4. Je porte un pardessus

   (a) en été.   (b) au printemps.   (c) en hiver.   (d) en juillet.   _____

5. La langue est une partie de

   (a) l'estomac.   (b) la bouche.   (c) la jambe.   (d) l'oeil.   _____

6. Pour me peigner, je regarde dans

    (a) un savon.   (b) un peigne.   (c) un miroir.   (d) une serviette.   _____

7. Quand je nage, je porte

    (a) un gant.   (b) une écharpe.   (c) une cravate.   (d) un maillot.   _____

8. Nous portons des souliers aux

    (a) cheveux.   (b) pieds.   (c) jambes.   (d) nez.   _____

9. Je mets de l'argent dans

    (a) les dents.   (b) la poche.   (c) le pull-over.   (d) la douche.   _____

10. J'emploie du savon pour

    (a) me brosser les dents.   (b) me laver.   (c) m'habiller.   (d) me peigner.   _____

V. Match the following.

1. bas   _____ tête

2. gant   _____ pied

3. soulier   _____ jambe

4. chapeau   _____ main

VI. Write in French the parts of the body where the arrows are pointing. Include the definite article, e.g., la tête, le pied, etc.

VII. Under each drawing, write in French the word for the article of clothing. Include the indefinite article; e.g., **un chapeau**, **une robe**, etc.

Unit 6
La famille, la maison, les meubles

La famille:

le **cousin**, la **cousine**, cousin

l'**enfant** *m. f.*, child

l'**époux** *m.*, l'**épouse** *f.*, spouse (husband/wife)

la **femme**, wife

la **fille**, daughter

le **fils**, son

le **frère**, brother; le **beau-frère**, brother-in-law

la **grand-mère**, grandmother

le **grand-père**, grandfather

les **grands-parents**, grandparents

le **mari**, husband

la **mère**, la **maman**, mother; la **belle-mère**, mother-in-law

le **neveu**, nephew

la **nièce**, niece

l'**oncle** *m.*, uncle

le **père**, le **papa**, father; le **beau-père**, father-in-law

le **petit-fils**, grandson

la **petite-fille**, granddaughter

les **petits-enfants**, grandchildren

la **soeur**, sister; la **belle-soeur**, sister-in-law

la **tante**, aunt

La maison:

la **cave**, the cellar

la **chambre**, the room; **chambre à coucher**, bedroom

la **cheminée**, the fireplace, chimney

la **cuisine**, the kitchen

l'**escalier** *m.*, the stairs, staircase

la **fenêtre**, the window

le **mur**, the wall

la **pièce**, the room

le **plafond**, the ceiling

le **plancher**, the floor

la **porte**, the door

la **salle**, the room; la **salle à manger**, the dining room; la **salle de bains**, bathroom

le **salon**, the living room

le **toit**, the roof

Les meubles:

l'**armoire** *f.,* the wardrobe closet (movable)

le **bureau**, the desk

le **canapé**, the sofa, couch

la **chaîne stéréo**, the stereo system

la **chaise**, the chair

la **commode**, the dresser, chest of drawers

la **couchette**, the bunk

l'**évier** *m.,* the kitchen sink

le **fauteuil**, the armchair

le **four**, the oven

la **fournaise**, the furnace

le **fourneau**, the kitchen stove, range

la **lampe**, the lamp

le **lit**, the bed

le **piano**, the piano

la **table**, the table

le **tapis**, the carpet

le **téléphone**, the telephone

le **téléviseur**, the television (set)

EXERCISES

Review the preceding material before doing these exercises.

I. **Choose the word whose meaning completes the statement.**

1. La soeur de mon père est ma

   (a) cousine.   (b) tante.   (c) mère.   (d) fille.   _____

2. On s'assied sur une

   (a) pièce.   (b) fenêtre.   (c) cave.   (d) chaise.   _____

3. Le fils de mon oncle est mon

   (a) neveu.   (b) frère.   (c) cousin.   (d) père.   _____

4. On met les petits fours dans

    (a) un four.   (b) un tapis.   (c) une couchette.   (d) une armoire.   _____

5. La fille de ma tante est ma

    (a) mère   (b) grand-mère.   (c) soeur.   (d) cousine.   _____

6. Le frère de ma cousine est

    (a) mon cousin.   (b) mon frère.   (c) ma soeur.   (d) mon père.   _____

7. Je fais ma toilette dans

    (a) le salon.   (b) la cuisine.   (c) la cave.   (d) la salle de bains.   _____

8. On prépare les repas dans

    (a) la salle à manger.   (b) le salon.   (c) la cuisine.   (d) la cave.   _____

9. On prend les repas dans

    (a) l'évier.   (b) la fournaise.   (c) la salle à manger   (d) l'armoire.   _____

10. J'allume la lampe pour

    (a) courir.   (b) dormir.   (c) lire.   (d) entendre.   _____

II. **Choose the word that does not belong in the group.**

1. (a) lit   (b) tapis   (c) fauteuil   (d) salade   _____

2. (a) grand-père   (b) père   (c) fils   (d) fille   _____

3. (a) mère   (b) soeur   (c) tante   (d) neveu   _____

4. (a) table   (b) oeil   (c) buffet   (d) radio   _____

5. (a) canapé   (b) téléphone   (c) couchette   (d) lit   _____

6. (a) phonographe   (b) table   (c) piano   (d) radio   _____

7. (a) salon   (b) cuisine   (c) toit   (d) chambre   _____

8. (a) épouse   (b) époux   (c) mari   (d) escalier   _____

9. (a) mur   (b) vin   (c) plafond   (d) plancher   _____

10. (a) mari   (b) soeur   (c) tante   (d) nièce   _____

III. **Choose the word that belongs in the same class as the italicized word.**

1. Il y a quatre *chaises* dans cette pièce.

    (a) tapis   (b) lampes   (c) fauteuils   (d) lits   _____

2. Madame Paquet a un bon *mari*.

    (a) chapeau   (b) soulier   (c) époux   (d) bureau   _____

3. Monsieur Paquet a une bonne *femme*.

    (a) épouse   (b) chambre   (c) radio   (d) cravate   _____

4. Il y a une *porte* dans cette chambre.

    (a) cuisine   (b) fenêtre   (c) salle   (d) cave   _____

5. Il y a une *douche* dans la salle de bains.

    (a) baignoire   (b) pièce   (c) cheminée   (d) couchette   _____

IV. Match the following.

1. le lit   _____ la salle de bains

2. le fourneau   _____ la salle à manger

3. le canapé   _____ la cuisine

4. la table   _____ le salon

5. la cuvette   _____ la chambre à coucher

V. Write the French word for what is shown in the drawings. Use the definite article; e.g., la grand-mère, etc.

_____   _____   _____

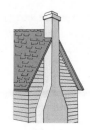

_____   _____   _____

_____   _____

399

Unit 7

La ville, les bâtiments, les magasins, les divers modes de transport

La ville:

l'avenue   *f.,* the avenue
la boîte aux lettres,   the mailbox
la bouche de métro,   the subway entrance
le boulevard,   the boulevard
le bruit,   the noise
la chaussée,   the road
défense d'afficher,   post no bills
les feux   *m.,* the traffic lights
le parc,   the park
la pollution,   the pollution
la rue,   the street
le trottoir,   the sidewalk
la voiture de police,   the police car

Les bâtiments:

la banque,   the bank
la bibliothèque,   the library
le bureau de poste,   the post office
la cathédrale,   the cathedral
la chapelle,   the chapel
le château,   the castle
le cinéma,   the movie theatre
l'école   *f.,* the school
l'église   *f.,* the church
la gare,   the railroad station
la grange,   the barn

le gratte-ciel,   the skyscraper
l'hôpital   *m.,* the hospital
l'hôtel   *m.,* the hotel
l'hôtel de ville,   the city hall
la hutte   *f.,* the hut, cabin
l'immeuble d'habitation,   the apartment building
la mosquée   the mosque
le musée,   the museum
le palais,   the palace
la synagogue,   the synagogue
le temple,   the temple
le théâtre,   the theater
l'usine   *f.,* the factory

Les divers modes de transport:

l'autobus   *m.,* the city bus
l'autocar   *m.,* the interurban bus
l'automobile   *f.,* the car
l'avion   *m.,* the plane
le bateau,   the boat
la bicyclette,   the bicycle
le camion,   the truck
le chemin de fer,   the railroad
le métro,   the subway
la moto,   the motorcycle
le train,   the train
le train à grande vitesse (le TGV),   the high-speed train
le transatlantique,   the ocean liner
le vélo,   the bike
la voiture,   the car

Les magasins:

la bijouterie,   the jewelry shop
la blanchisserie,   the laundry
la boucherie,   the butcher shop
la boulangerie,   the bakery (mostly for bread)
la boutique,   the (small) shop
le bureau de tabac,   the tobacco shop
le café,   the café
la charcuterie,   the pork store, delicatessen
la crémerie,   the dairy store
l'épicerie   *f.,* the grocery store
le grand magasin,   the department store
la librairie,   the bookstore
le magasin,   the store
la pâtisserie,   the pastry shop
la pharmacie,   the drugstore
le supermarché,   the supermarket

EXERCISES

Review the above material before doing these exercises.

I.   Choose the word that does not belong in the group.

1.   (a) train   (b) vélo   (c) camion   (d) musée   _____

2.   (a) trottoir   (b) bateau   (c) rue   (d) chaussée   _____   **401**

3. (a) palais   (b) épicerie   (c) charcuterie   (d) boulangerie   _____
4. (a) église   (b) temple   (c) synagogue   (d) gratte-ciel   _____
5. (a) boucherie   (b) charcuterie   (c) bijouterie   (d) pâtisserie   _____
6. (a) avion   (b) bateau   (c) boutique   (d) autobus   _____
7. (a) voiture   (b) bicyclette   (c) moto   (d) vélo   _____
8. (a) avenue   (b) rue   (c) boulevard   (d) grange   _____
9. (a) cathédrale   (b) bureau de tabac   (c) chapelle   (d) église   _____
10. (a) immeuble d'habitation   (b) autobus   (c) autocar   (d) automobile   _____

II.   Complete the following sentences by writing the appropriate word from the list below.

boulangerie   bruit   gratte-ciel   librairie   boucherie

musée   voitures   charcuterie   banque   transatlantique

1. On vend du pain dans une _____

2. Pour voir des objets d'art, je vais au _____

3. On achète du porc dans une _____

4. En général, on entend beaucoup de _____ dans une grande ville.

5. Pour acheter des livres j'entre dans une _____

6. Le trottoir est pour les personnes et la chaussée est pour les _____

7. Il y a de l'argent dans une _____

8. Pour acheter de la viande j'entre dans une _____

9. On peut aller de New York à Cherbourg dans un _____

10. On appelle un bâtiment à très grand nombre d'étages un _____

III.   Choose the word that belongs in the same class as the italicized word.

1. J'entre dans *l'église* pour prier.

   (a) le théâtre   (b) la synagogue   (c) le cinéma   (d) l'hôtel   _____

2. Janine attend l'autobus pour aller *à la bibliothèque.*

   (a) au parc   (b) voir ses amies   (c) faire du shopping   (d) à l'école   _____

3. Je préfère voyager de Cherbourg à New York dans un *bateau.*

   (a) avion   (b) transatlantique   (c) train   (d) métro   _____

4. Pour voir une représentation, je vais *à l'opéra.*

   (a) à une banque   (b) à un bureau de poste   (c) au théâtre   (d) à la gare   _____

5. Pour acheter quelque chose à manger, j'entre dans une *boulangerie.*

   (a) librairie   (b) épicerie   (c) bijouterie   (d) blanchisserie   _____

IV.   Choose the word that is defined or described in the sentence.

1. On trouve ce mode de transport dans une ville.

   (a) une grange   (b) un autobus   (c) les feux   (d) le bruit   _____

2. Dans ce magasin on vend des éclairs.

    (a) une charcuterie   (b) une bijouterie   (c) une blanchisserie   (d) une pâtisserie _____

3. Dans ce magasin on vend des médicaments.

    (a) un café   (b) une pharmacie   (c) une boucherie   (d) une crémerie   _____

4. C'est un bâtiment à très grand nombre d'étages.

    (a) un temple   (b) une église   (c) un gratte-ciel   (d) une hutte   _____

5. C'est un mode de transport de marchandises.

    (a) une boîte   (b) un camion   (c) un magasin   (d) une usine   _____

V. **Write the French word for what is shown in the drawing. Use the indefinite article; e.g., un train, un parc, etc.**

_____   _____   _____

_____   _____   _____

_____   _____

VI. On the line write the French word for what is suggested. Choose from the following:

une gare   une boucherie   une voiture   un avion   un hôtel
un théâtre   un cinéma   une boulangerie   une pharmacie

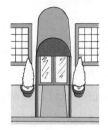

_____   _____   _____

_____   _____   _____

_____   _____   _____

Unit 8
Les métiers et les professions, les langues, les pays et la technologie

Les métiers et les professions:

l'acteur   *m.,* l'actrice *f.,*
actor, actress

l'agent de police   *m.,* police officer

l'auteur,   author (of a book) *or* composer (of a song) *or* painter (of a picture)

l'avocat   *m.,* la femme-avocat *f.,* lawyer

le bijoutier, la bijoutière, jeweler

le blanchisseur, la blanchisseuse,   launderer

le boucher, la bouchère, butcher

le boulanger, la boulangère, baker

le charcutier, la charcutière, pork butcher

le chauffeur,   driver, chauffeur

le coiffeur, la coiffeuse, hairdresser, barber

le, la dentiste,   dentist

l'épicier, l'épicière,   grocer

le facteur,   letter carrier

le fermier, la fermière, farmer

le, la libraire,   bookseller

le maître, la maîtresse, teacher

le marchand, la marchande, merchant

le médecin, la femme-médecin,   doctor

le pâtissier, la pâtissière, pastry chef

le pharmacien, la pharmacienne, pharmacist

le professeur, la femme-professeur,   professor

le sénateur,   senator

le serveur, la serveuse, waiter, waitress

le tailleur, la tailleuse, tailor

le vendeur, la vendeuse, salesperson

Les langues (all are masculine):

allemand,   German
anglais,   English
chinois,   Chinese
danois,   Danish
espagnol,   Spanish; castillan, Castilian (Spanish)
français,   French
grec ancien,   ancient Greek
grec moderne,   modern Greek
hébreu,   Hebrew
italien,   Italian
japonais,   Japanese
latin,   Latin
norvégien,   Norwegian
portugais,   Portuguese
russe,   Russian
suédois,   Swedish

Les pays:

l'Allemagne   *f.,* Germany
l'Angleterre   *f.,* England
l'Australie   *f.,* Australia
la Belgique,   Belgium
le Canada,   Canada
la Chine,   China
le Danemark,   Denmark
l'Espagne   *f.,* Spain
les États-Unis   *m.,* United States
l'Europe   *f.,* Europe
la France,   France
la Grande-Bretagne,   Great Britain
la Grèce,   Greece
la Hollande,   Holland

l'Irlande   *f.,* Ireland
l'Israël   *m.,* Israel
l'Italie   *f.,* Italy
le Japon,   Japan
le Luxembourg, Luxembourg
le Mexique,   Mexico
la Norvège,   Norway
la Pologne,   Poland
le Portugal,   Portugal
la Russie,   Russia
la Suède,   Sweden
la Suisse,   Switzerland

La technologie (Technology):

la banque de données, database

le billet électronique, electronic ticket, e-ticket

la boîte vocale,   voice mail

le bouton de démarrage, power button

le bouton du pavé tactile, touch pad button

la calculatrice,   calculator

la carte bancaire/la carte de crédit,   credit card

la carte d'embarquement, boarding pass

le CD,   CD

le cédérom, le CD-ROM, CD-ROM

le clavardage,   chat (Internet)

clavarder,   to chat (Internet)

le clavier,   keyboard

le clavier d'identification personnelle,   PIN pad

le commerce électronique, e-commerce

le contrôle de sécurité, security check (for transportation in airports, public buildings)

le **courriel**, e-mail
le **courrier électronique**, e-mail
le **cybercafé**, cybercafé
le **disque compact**, compact CD
le **disque dur**, hard drive
le **disque DVD**, DVD
l'**écran** *m.,* display screen (computer)
l'**écran** *m.* plasma, plasma screen, plasma display
l'**écran** *m.* tactile, touch screen
le **fichier MP3**, MP3
le **guichet automatique (bancaire)**, ATM (automated teller machine)
l'**Internet** *m.,* Internet
l'**iPod** *m.,* iPod
le **lecteur de CD**, CD player
le **lecteur de DVD**, DVD player
le **lecteur multimédia**, multimedia player

la **machine à rayons X**, X-ray machine (in airports)
la **messagerie**, voice mail
naviguer (sur Internet), to navigate, to surf the Internet
le **NIP (le numéro d'identification personnelle)**, PIN
l'**ordinateur** *m.,* computer
l'**ordinateur** *m.* de bureau *m.,* desktop computer
l'**ordinateur** *m.* de poche, PDA (personal digital assistant), handheld computer
l'**ordinateur** *m.* portable, laptop computer (A laptop computer may just be called "**un portable.**" The same word is sometimes used for a cell phone.)
la **pagette**, pager
le **pavé tactile**, touch pad

le **portable**, cell phone (le **téléphone portable**), laptop computer (l'**ordinateur** *m.,* **portable**)
le **répondeur**, answering machine
le **sac de vol**, carry-on bag
le **salon de clavardage**, chat room
la **souris**, mouse
surfer, to surf (the Internet)
la **télécopie**, fax
télécopier, to fax
le **télécopieur**, fax machine
le **téléphone portable**, cell phone (A cell phone may just be called "**un portable.**" The same word is sometimes used for a laptop computer.)
le **téléviseur à écran plasma**, plasma screen television set
la **touche d'appel**, talk key
la **touche de sélection**, selection key

1. Organisation des Nations Unies (ONU), Nations Unies—United Nations (UN)

2. Organisation des Nations Unies pour l'Éducation, la Science et la Culture (ONUESCO)—United Nations Educational, Scientific, and Cultural Organization (UNESCO)

3. Organisation Mondiale de la Santé (OMS)—World Health Organization (WHO)

EXERCISES

Review the above material before doing these exercises.

I.   Choose the word that does not belong in the group.

1. (a) boucher   (b) charcutier   (c) boulanger   (d) dentiste   _____

2. (a) pharmacien   (b) dentiste   (c) médecin   (d) chauffeur   _____

3. (a) français   (b) Italie   (c) espagnol   (d) hébreu   _____

4. (a) Allemagne   (b) Angleterre   (c) portugais   (d) Belgique   _____

5. (a) bijoutier   (b) danois   (c) serveur   (d) serveuse   _____

II. Write in French the name of the language spoken in each of these countries.

    Model: **États-Unis**   Answer: **l'anglais**

1. l'Allemagne _____   5. l'Italie _____

2. l'Angleterre _____   6. le Porto Rico _____

3. la France _____   7. le Japon _____

4. l'Espagne _____   8. la Chine _____

III. Answer the following questions in French in complete sentences in the affirmative.

    Model: **Est-ce qu'on parle hébreu** Answer: **Oui, on parle hébreu**
            en Israël?   **en Israël.**
            (Do they speak   (Yes, they speak
            Hebrew in Israel?)   Hebrew in Israel.)

1. Est-ce qu'on parle italien en Italie? _____

2. Est-ce qu'on parle anglais aux États-Unis?_____

3. Est-ce qu'on parle français et anglais au Canada?_____

4. Est-ce qu'on parle français en Belgique? _____

5. Est-ce qu'on parle français en France?_____

6. Est-ce qu'on parle espagnol en Espagne? _____

7. Est-ce qu'on parle français en Suisse? _____

8. Est-ce qu'on parle portugais au Portugal? _____

9. Est-ce qu'on parle espagnol au Mexique? _____

10. Est-ce qu'on parle grec en Grèce? _____

IV. Write the feminine form in French for each of the following occupations.

    Model: **un boulanger** (a baker, *m.*)   Answer: **une boulangère** (a baker, *fem.*)

1. un boulanger _____   6. un pharmacien _____

2. un bijoutier _____   7. un maître _____

3. un serveur _____   8. un épicier _____

4. un fermier _____   9. un coiffeur _____

5. un acteur _____   10. un blanchisseur _____

V. Write in French the name of the store where the following persons work. Review the vocabulary on page 401.

    Model: **un pâtissier** (a pastry chef)   Answer: **une pâtisserie** (a pastry shop)

1. un pâtissier _____   4. un charcutier _____

2. une pharmacienne _____   5. un bijoutier _____

3. une libraire _____   6. une blanchisseuse _____

407

VI. Write in French the name of the store where you can buy the item given. Review the vocabulary on page 401.

     Model: **un livre** (a book)   **Answer:** **une librairie** (a bookstore)

1. un livre _____

2. du médicament _____

3. de la crème _____

4. une tasse de café _____

5. un gâteau _____

6. du pain _____

VII. On the line write the French word for what is illustrated. Choose from the following:

  un dentiste   **un tailleur**   **une boulangère**   **une vendeuse**   **un facteur**
      une fermière   **une maîtresse**   **un fermier**   **un coiffeur**

_____   _____   _____

_____   _____   _____

_____   _____   _____

Unit 9

Poids, mesures, valeurs (Weights, Measures, Values*)

un gramme = 0.035274 ounce (1 gram)

28.3 grammes = 1 ounce

100 grammes = 3.52 ounces

453.6 grammes = 1 pound

500 grammes = 17.63 ounces (about 1.1 pounds)

1,000 grammes = 1 kilogram

un kilogramme = 2.2 pounds (1 kilogram)

une livre = 17.63 ounces (about 1.1 pounds)

un litre = 1.0567 quarts (0.26417 gallon)

---

un euro = $1.20

5 euros = $6.00

20 euros = $24.00

50 euros = $60.00

---

un kilomètre = 0.62137 mile (about ⅝ mile or 1000 meters)

1.61 kilomètres = 1 mile

10 kilomètres = 6.21 miles

---

un centimètre = 0.39 inch (1 centimeter)

2.54 centimètres = 1 inch

30.5 centimètres = 1 foot

91.4 centimètres = 1 yard

un mètre = 39.37 inches (100 centimeters)

0.9144 mètre = 1 yard

---

1. To convert Fahrenheit degrees into Celsius (Centigrade): subtract 32, multiply by 5, and divide by 9.
2. To convert Celsius (Centigrade) into Fahrenheit: multiply by 9, divide by 5, and add 32.
3. A Fahrenheit degree is smaller than a Celsius degree. One F degree is ⅝ of a C degree.
4. France uses the Celsius scale.

*All the equivalents given are approximate. For the current rate of exchange (euros for U.S. dollars), inquire at the international exchange office of a commercial bank or check online.

EXERCISE

Review the preceding material before doing this exercise.

I. **Match the following. The equivalent figures are all approximate.**

1. $1.20   _____ un gramme

2. 39.37 inches   _____ un kilogramme

3. 1.1 pounds   _____ une livre

4. 1 yard   _____ un litre

5. 2.2 pounds   _____ 28.3 grammes

6. 1.0567 quarts   _____ un euro

7. 1 ounce   _____ un mètre

8. 0.62137 mile   _____ 0.9144 mètre

9. 20 euros   _____ un kilomètre

10. 0.035274 ounce   _____ $24.00

Unit 10
Antonymes et synonymes

absent, absente *adj.,* absent	**présent, présente** *adj.,* present
acheter *v.,* to buy	**vendre** *v.,* to sell
agréable *adj.,* pleasant, agreeable	**désagréable** *adj.,* unpleasant, disagreeable
aimable *adj.,* kind	**méchant, méchante** *adj.,* mean, nasty
ami, amie *n.,* friend	**ennemi, ennemie** *n.,* enemy
beau, belle *adj.,* beautiful, handsome	**laid, laide** *adj.,* ugly
beaucoup (de) *adv.,* much, many	**peu (de)** *adv.,* little, some
beauté *n. f.,* beauty	**laideur** *n. f.,* ugliness
bête *adj.,* stupid	**intelligent, intelligente** *adj.,* intelligent
blanc, blanche *adj.,* white	**noir, noire** *adj.,* black
bon, bonne *adj.,* good	**mauvais, mauvaise** *adj.,* bad
bonheur *n. m.,* happiness	**malheur** *n. m.,* unhappiness
chaud, chaude *adj.,* hot, warm	**froid, froide** *adj.,* cold
content, contente *adj.,* glad, pleased	**mécontent, mécontente** *adj.,* displeased
court, courte *adj.,* short	**long, longue** *adj.,* long
dedans *adv.,* inside	**dehors** *adv.,* outside
dernier, dernière *adj.,* last	**premier, première** *adj.,* first
derrière *adv., prep.,* behind	**devant** *adv., prep.,* in front of
dessous *adv., prep.,* below, underneath	**dessus** *adv., prep.,* above, over
différent, différente *adj.,* different	**même** *adj.,* same
difficile *adj.,* difficult	**facile** *adj.,* easy
domestique *adj.,* domestic	**sauvage** *adj.,* wild
donner *v.,* to give	**recevoir** *v.,* to receive
étroit, étroite *adj.,* narrow	**large** *adj.,* wide
faible *adj.,* weak	**fort, forte** *adj.,* strong
fin *n. f.,* end	**commencement** *n. m.,* beginning
finir *v.,* to finish	**commencer** *v.,* to begin
gai, gaie *adj.,* gay, happy	**triste** *adj.,* sad
grand, grande *adj.,* large, tall, big	**petit, petite** *adj.,* small, little
gros, grosse *adj.,* fat	**maigre** *adj.,* thin
heureux, heureuse *adj.,* happy	**malheureux, malheureuse** *adj.,* unhappy
homme *n. m.,* man	**femme** *n. f.,* woman
inutile *adj.,* useless	**utile** *adj.,* useful
jamais *adv.,* never	**toujours** *adv.,* always
jeune *adj.,* young	**vieux, vieille** *adj.,* old
jeune fille *n. f.,* girl	**garçon** *n. m.,* boy
joli, jolie *adj.,* pretty	**laid, laide** *adj.,* ugly
jour *n. m.,* day	**nuit** *n. f.,* night
lentement *adv.,* slowly	**vite** *adv.,* quickly
mal *adv.,* badly	**bien** *adv.,* well
moins *adv.,* less	**plus** *adv.,* more
oui *adv.,* yes	**non** *adv.,* no
paix *n. f.,* peace	**guerre** *n. f.,* war
partir *v.,* to leave	**arriver** *v.,* to arrive
pauvre *adj.,* poor	**riche** *adj.,* rich
plein, pleine *adj.,* full	**vide** *adj.,* empty
question *n. f.,* question	**réponse** *n. f.,* answer, reply, response
refuser *v.,* to refuse	**accepter** *v.,* to accept
rire *v.,* to laugh	**pleurer** *v.,* to cry, to weep
sans *prep.,* without	**avec** *prep.,* with

silence   *n. m.,* silence   bruit   *n. m.,* noise
sûr, sûre   *adj.,* sure, certain   incertain, incertaine   *adj.,* unsure
tôt   *adv.,* early   tard   *adv.,* late
travailler   *v.,* to work   jouer   *v.,* to play

Synonymes

aimer mieux *v.,* **préférer**	to prefer
auteur *n. m.,* **écrivain**	author, writer
bâtiment *n. m.,* **édifice**	building, edifice
certain, certaine *adj.,* **sûr, sûre**	certain, sure
content, contente *adj.,* **heureux, heureuse**	content, happy
docteur *n. m.,* **médecin**	doctor, physician
erreur *n. f.,* **faute**	error, mistake
façon *n. f.,* **manière**	manner, way
fameux, fameuse *adj.,* **célèbre**	famous
favori, favorite *adj.,* **préféré, préférée**	favorite, preferred
femme *n. f.,* **épouse**	wife, spouse
finir *v.,* **terminer**	to finish, end, terminate
glace *n. f.,* **le miroir**	mirror
habiter *v.,* **demeurer**	to live (in), dwell, inhabit
image *n. f.,* **le tableau**	picture
lieu *n. m.,* **endroit**	place
maîtresse *n. f.,* **institutrice**	teacher (woman)
mari *n. m.,* **époux**	husband, spouse
pays *n. m.,* **la nation**	country, nation
rester *v.,* **demeurer**	to stay, to remain
sérieux, sérieuse *adj.,* **grave**	serious, grave
tout de suite *adv.,* **immédiatement**	right away, immediately
triste *adj.,* **malheureux, malheureuse**	sad, unhappy
vêtements *n. m.,* **habits**	clothes, clothing
vite *adv.,* **rapidement**	quickly, fast, rapidly

EXERCISES

Review the preceding material before doing these exercises.

I.   Choose the word that completes the sentence.

1. La leçon pour aujourd'hui est

    (a) dedans   (b) étroite   (c) facile   (d) contente   _____

2. Cet arbre est

    (a) petit   (b) difficile   (c) bête   (d) triste   _____

3. Ce problème est bien

    (a) difficile   (b) dehors   (c) même   (d) présent   _____

4. Cette rue est longue et

    (a) certaine   (b) large   (c) dessous   (d) dessus   _____

5. J'aime ce manteau parce qu'il est

    (a) sauvage   (b) mécontent   (c) heureux   (d) joli   _____

II. Choose the word that can replace the italicized word and still give meaning to the sentence.

1. Pierre a *plus* d'argent que moi.

   (a) moins   (b) jamais   (c) toujours   (d) aussi   _____

2. Monsieur Paquet marche *vite.*

   (a) fort   (b) faible   (c) lentement   (d) inutile   _____

3. Je pense que *oui.*

   (a) tard   (b) mal   (c) devant   (d) non   _____

4. Michel va arriver *tôt.*

   (a) longtemps   (b) tard   (c) seulement   (d) étroit   _____

5. La voiture marche *mal.*

   (a) jamais   (b) faible   (c) fort   (d) bien   _____

III. Choose the word that is defined or described in the sentence.

1. Une chose qui plaît.

   (a) bête   (b) agréable   (c) désagréable   (d) malheureux   _____

2. Le contraire de froid.

   (a) chaud   (b) beau   (c) court   (d) grand   _____

3. Ce qui n'est pas difficile.

   (a) faible   (b) fort   (c) facile   (d) dessus   _____

4. Donner une réponse.

   (a) finir   (b) commencer   (c) répondre   (d) recevoir   _____

5. Le contraire de jamais.

   (a) toujours   (b) joli   (c) beau   (d) laid   _____

IV. Choose the response that is the best rejoinder.

    Model: **Paul a perdu son petit chien.**
            (a) Il est heureux.
            (b) Il est malheureux.
            (c) Il est riche.
            (d) Il est pauvre.   _b_

1. Lucille a perdu son argent.

   (a) Elle pleure.
   (b) Elle refuse.
   (c) Elle accepte.
   (d) Elle arrive.   _____

2. Veux-tu aller au parc avec moi?

   (a) Je n'ai pas le temps maintenant.
   (b) Il est utile.
   (c) Je veux monter.
   (d) Je n'aime pas la guerre.   _____

3. La femme ouvre le tiroir.

   (a) Il est vide.
   (b) Elle est jolie.
   (c) Elle travaille mal.
   (d) Elle veut descendre.   _____

4. Vous ne mangez pas beaucoup.

   (a) Vous aimez la paix.
   (b) Vous aimez les pommes de terre.
   (c) Vous êtes maigre.
   (d) C'est rare.   _____

5. Pourquoi veux-tu travailler?

   (a) Pour jouer.
   (b) Pour recevoir de l'argent.
   (c) Pour faire du bruit.
   (d) Pour être sûr.   _____

V. **Fill in the blank lines by writing the French word for each picture given below. Use the indefinite article with the word.**

   Model: **U N E C A R O T T E**

   1   2   3   4   5

   6   7   8   9

   10   11   12   13

1. _ _ _   _ _ _ _ _ _   8. _ _   _ _ _ _ _ _ _

2. _ _ _   _ _ _ _ _ _ _   9. _ _ _   _ _ _ _ _ _ _ _ _ _ _

3. _ _ _   _ _ _ _ _   10. _ _   _ _ _ _ _ _ _ _ _ _

4. _ _ _   _ _ _ _ _ _ _ _   11. _ _ _   _ _ _ _ _ _ _

5. _ _   _ _ _ _ _ _   12. _ _   _ _ _ _ _ _ _ _ _ _

6. _ _   _ _ _ _ _ _   13. _ _   _ _ _

7. _ _   _ _ _ _ _ _ _

Toulouse-Lautrec's Poster for the Moulin Rouge
Courtesy of The Granger Collection.

Part 3: Idioms, Verbal Expressions, and Dialogues

Unit 1
With à, with au

with à	
à bientôt so long, see you soon	**à la page …** on page …
à cause de on account of, because of	**à l'heure** on time
à cette heure at the present moment	**à mon avis** in my opinion
à côté de beside, next to	**à propos** by the way
à demain see you tomorrow	**à temps** in time
à droite at (on, to) the right	**à voix basse** in a low voice, softly
à gauche at (on, to) the left	**aller à pied** to walk (go on foot)
à haute voix aloud, in a loud voice	**c'est-à-dire** that is, that is to say
à la campagne at (in, to) the country(side)	**jouer à** to play (a game)
à la maison at home	**peu à peu** little by little

with au	
au bout de at the end of, at the tip of	**au lieu de** instead of
au contraire on the contrary	**au milieu de** in the middle of
au début in the beginning	**au moins** at least
au-dessous de below, underneath	**au printemps** in the spring
au-dessus de above, over	**au revoir** good-bye

DIALOGUE

Madame Banluc:	À propos, Claire, dis-moi, où est Madame Richy? Elle n'est pas à la maison.
Madame Paquet:	Tu parles à voix basse, Joséphine. Je n'entends rien. Parle à haute voix!
Madame Banluc:	J'ai dit: où est Madame Richy? Elle n'est pas à la maison.
Madame Paquet:	Lucille Richy? Elle est à la campagne.
Madame Banluc:	À mon avis, elle peut nous dire quand elle va à la campagne, au moins!
Madame Paquet:	Au contraire, Joséphine, elle n'est pas obligée de nous dire où elle va.
Madame Banluc:	Mais elle va toujours à la campagne au printemps. Pourquoi est-elle allée à la campagne maintenant?
Madame Paquet:	À cause de la pluie. Il pleut beaucoup ici, mais il ne pleut pas à la campagne.
Madame Banluc:	Où est-elle exactement?
Madame Paquet:	Elle est à Denfert-Rochereau. C'est un village à côté du village de Val.
Madame Banluc:	Est-ce que c'est à droite ou à gauche de Val en arrivant à Denfert-Rochereau?
Madame Paquet:	Je pense que c'est à gauche. Pourquoi?
Madame Banluc:	Parce que je voudrais aller la voir.
Madame Paquet:	Ah, bon! Et moi, aussi, je veux aller la voir. Veux-tu y aller avec moi demain?
Madame Banluc:	Oui. Nous pouvons aller la voir demain.
Madame Paquet:	Au revoir, Joséphine.
Madame Banluc:	Au revoir, Claire. À demain.

EXERCISES

Review the preceding material before starting these exercises.

I.   Comment dit-on en français?   Find these idioms and verbal expressions in the dialogue and write them in French.

1. by the way

_____

2. at home

_____

3. in a low voice

_____

4. in my opinion

_____

5. at least

_____

6. good-bye

_____

II.   Fill in the blank line with either à or au, depending on which is required.

1. _____ contraire	6. _____ gauche	11. _____ bout de
2. _____ la campagne	7. _____ revoir	12. _____ lieu de
3. _____ cause de	8. _____ demain	13. _____ l'heure
4. _____ côté de	9. _____ bientôt	14. aller _____ pied
5. _____ droite	10. _____ haute voix	15. peu _____ peu

III. Complete the following dialogue by writing an appropriate response on the blank line. Use as many idioms and verbal expressions in this unit as you can. Refer to the dialogue in this unit if you have to.

Madame Banluc: À propos, où est Lucille?

Madame Paquet: _____

Madame Banluc: Pourquoi est-elle à la campagne?

Madame Paquet: _____

Madame Banluc: Où est-elle exactement?

Madame Paquet: _____

Madame Banluc: Je veux aller la voir.

Madame Paquet: _____

Madame Banluc: Oui. À demain. Au revoir.

Madame Paquet: _____

IV. Match the following.

1. at the present moment	_____ au lieu de
2. instead of	_____ à mon avis
3. below, underneath	_____ au-dessous de
4. to walk	_____ à cette heure
5. in my opinion	_____ aller à pied
6. little by little	_____ jouer à
7. in the spring	_____ peu à peu
8. good-bye	_____ au printemps
9. on the left	_____ au revoir
10. to play (a game)	_____ à gauche

Unit 2
With **comment**, with **en**

with comment	
Comment allez-vous? How are you?	**Comment ça va?** How goes it?
Comment vas-tu? How are you? *(familiar)*	**Comment vous appelez-vous?** What's your name?
Comment vous portez-vous? How do you feel?	**Comment t'appelles-tu?** What's your name? *(familiar)*
Comment te portes-tu? How do you feel? *(familiar)*	**Comment dit-on … ?** How do you say … ?

with en	
en français, en anglais, *etc.* in French, in English	**en même temps** at the same time
en automne, en hiver, en été in the fall, in winter, in summer	**en retard** late (*i.e.,* not on time)
en bas downstairs, below, at the bottom	**en ville** downtown
en face de opposite	**Je vous en prie!** I beg you! You're welcome!

DIALOGUE

Pierre meets a new friend in school. He is talking to him at lunch.

Pierre:	**Comment t'appelles-tu?**
Jacques:	**Je m'appelle Jacques. Comment t'appelles-tu?**
Pierre:	**Je m'appelle Pierre. Où demeures-tu, Jacques?**
Jacques:	**15, rue de Clichy. C'est en face du bureau de poste.**
Pierre:	**C'est bien en ville, n'est-ce pas? C'est loin de l'école!**
Jacques:	**Oui, je demeure loin de l'école. Aujourd'hui je suis arrivé en retard et le maître m'a envoyé en bas, au bureau du directeur.**
Pierre:	**J'étais là, aussi. Nous sommes arrivés en même temps!**
Jacques:	**Ah, oui, je t'ai vu là!**
Pierre:	**Il faut aller en classe maintenant. À bientôt, Jacques!**
Jacques:	**À bientôt, Pierre!**

EXERCISES

Review the above material before doing these exercises.

I. **Vocabulary Building. Proficiency in Writing.**

A. Write three idiomatic expressions that begin with **Comment ... ?**

1. _____   2. _____   3 _____

B. Write three idiomatic expressions that begin with **en.**

1. _____   2. _____   3 _____

II. **Comment dit-on en français?**   Find the following expressions either in the dialogue or preceding list and write them in French.

1. In French, in English, in Spanish

_____

2. In the fall, in winter, in summer

_____

3. It's far from school!

_____

4. You're welcome!

_____

5. What's your name? My name is Jacques.

_____

Unit 3
With **avoir**, with **être**

with avoir	

avoir … an(s)   to be … year(s) old
  Quel âge a-t-il?   How old is he?
  Il a un an.   He is a year old.
  Il a dix-neuf ans.   He is 19 years old.
 	
avoir besoin de
  to need, have need (of)
 	
avoir chaud
  to feel (be) warm
 	
avoir faim
  to feel (be) hungry
 	
avoir froid
  to feel (be) cold
 	
avoir l'habitude de
  to be in the habit of
 	
avoir l'intention de
  to intend (to)
	avoir lieu
	  to take place
	
	avoir mal
	  to feel sick
	
	avoir mal à …
	  to have a pain (ache) in …
	
	avoir peur (de)
	  to be afraid (of)
	
	avoir raison, avoir tort
	  to be right, to be wrong
	
	avoir soif
	  to be thirsty
	
	avoir sommeil
	  to be sleepy

with être	

être à l'heure
  to be on time
 	
être en retard
  to be late
 	
Cela est égal.
  It's all the same.
  It doesn't matter.
  It makes no difference.
 	
Cela m'est égal.
  It doesn't matter to me.
  It's all the same to me.
 	
C'est dommage.
  It's a pity.
  It's too bad.
	C'est entendu.
	  It's understood.
	  It's agreed.
	
	Quel jour est-ce aujourd'hui?
	  What day is it today?
	
	C'est aujourd'hui lundi.
	  Today is Monday.
	
	Quelle heure est-il?
	  What time is it?
	
	Il est trois heures et quart.
	  It is 3:15.
	
	Qu'est-ce que c'est?
	  What is it?

DIALOGUE

Janine forgot to study for a test in school. She wants to stay home in bed all day so she plays sick.

Janine:	**J'ai mal, maman. J'ai chaud, puis j'ai froid. J'ai mal au cou, je suis faible, et j'ai sommeil.**
Madame Paquet:	**Tout cela? C'est dommage. Mais si tu veux être à l'heure, il faut te lever. Lève-toi, Janine!**
Janine:	**Tu sais, maman, je n'ai pas l'habitude de dire des histoires. Je ne peux pas sortir aujourd'hui.**
Madame Paquet:	**Alors, c'est entendu. Tu vas rester au lit toute la journée … À propos, tu ne peux pas aller chez Monique pour déjeuner avec elle aujourd'hui. Il faut lui téléphoner pour dire que tu es malade.**
Janine:	**Quoi?! Quel jour est-ce aujourd'hui?**
Madame Paquet:	**C'est aujourd'hui samedi.**
Janine:	**Samedi?! Ce n'est pas vendredi?! Je vais me lever.**
Madame Paquet:	**Ah non! Non, non, non! Tu as raison. Aujourd'hui tu es malade et tu restes au lit.**
Janine:	**Oh, je suis bête!**

EXERCISES

Review the above material before doing these exercises.

I.   Answer the following questions in French in complete sentences.

1. Quel jour est-ce aujourd'hui?

_____

2. Quelle heure est-il?

_____

3. Avez-vous peur des serpents?

_____

4. Comment vous appelez-vous?

_____

5. Où demeurez-vous?

_____

II. Answer the following questions in the affirmative in complete French sentences. In answer (a) use **Oui**. In answer (b) use **aussi**. Study the models. Use subject pronouns in your answers.

Models:	(a) **Avez-vous l'intention d'aller au cinéma?** (Do you intend to go to the movies?)	Answer:	(a) **Oui, j'ai l'intention d'aller au cinéma.** (Yes, I intend to go to the movies?)
	(b) **Et Pierre?** (And Pierre?)		(b) **Il a l'intention d'aller au cinéma aussi.** (He intends to go to the movies also.)

1. (a) Avez-vous l'intention d'aller au cinéma?

   _____

   (b) Et Pierre?

   _____

2. (a) Avez-vous l'habitude d'étudier dans la bibliothèque?

   _____

   (b) Et vos amis?

   _____

3. (a) Avez-vous chaud dans cette classe?

   _____

   (b) Et les autres étudiants?

   _____

4. (a) Avez-vous faim en ce moment?

   _____

   (b) Et votre amie Monique?

   _____

5. (a) Avez-vous soif en ce moment?

   _____

   (b) Et Pierre et Jacques?

   _____

III. **Complete the following dialogue by writing an appropriate response on the blank line. Use as many idioms and verbal expressions in this unit as you can. Refer to the dialogue in this unit if you have to.**

Pierre doesn't want to go to school today, so he plays sick.

Pierre:	_____
Sa mère:	**C'est dommage. Tu es vraiment malade?**
Pierre:	_____
Sa mère:	**Il est difficile de trouver un docteur parce que c'est dimanche.**
Pierre:	_____
Sa mère:	**Oui, oui. C'est bien dimanche aujourd'hui!**
Pierre:	_____
Sa mère:	**Es-tu malade ou non?!**
Pierre:	_____

Unit 4
With **de, du, d'**

with de	
de bon appétit with good appetite	**jouer de** to play (a musical instrument) **Ma soeur joue du piano.** My sister plays the piano.
de bonne heure early	**près de** near
de cette façon in this way	**de quelle couleur ...** what color ... **De quelle couleur est ta nouvelle chemise?** What color is your new shirt?
de façon à + inf. so as to	
de jour en jour from day to day	
de l'autre côté (de) on the other side (of)	**quelque chose de + adj.** something + adj. **J'ai mangé quelque chose de bon!** I ate something good!
de nouveau again	
de plus en plus more and more	**quoi de neuf?** what's new?
de rien you're welcome	**rien de neuf!** nothing new!
de temps en temps from time to time	**venir de + inf.** to have just + past part. **Elle vient de partir.** She has just left.
pas de mal! no harm!	**Il n'y a pas de quoi!** You're welcome!

with du	
du matin au soir from morning until night	**pas du tout!** not at all!

with d'	
d'abord first, at first	**d'aujourd'hui en huit** a week from today
d'accord agreed, O.K.	**d'habitude** *or* **d'ordinaire** ordinarily, usually

DIALOGUE

In this conversation, Pierre is telling Paul about his new shirt. Then Janine arrives on the scene to tell Pierre what their father has just done.

Pierre:	**Quoi de neuf?**
Paul:	**Rien de neuf! Et toi?**
Pierre:	**J'ai une nouvelle chemise.**
Paul:	**De quelle couleur est ta nouvelle chemise?**
Pierre:	**D'habitude, j'aime les chemises blanches, mais cette chemise blanche a un peu de vert et un peu de bleu.**
Paul:	**Et tu aimes ça?**
Pierre:	**Oui. Je vais la porter du matin au soir!**

(Janine arrive.)

Janine:	**Pierre! Papa a fait quelque chose de terrible! Il vient de peindre les murs de la cuisine en jaune et il a employé ta chemise pour nettoyer le pinceau!**
Pierre:	**Encore? Il a fait la même chose hier quand il a peint les murs de la salle de bains en bleu et en vert!**

(Pierre rit.)

Janine:	**Tu n'es pas fâché?**
Pierre:	**Non, pas du tout. Maintenant ma nouvelle chemise blanche a les couleurs d'un arc-en-ciel!**

EXERCISES

Review the preceding material before doing these exercises.

I. **Answer the following questions in complete sentences. They are based on the dialogue in this unit.**

1. Qui a une nouvelle chemise?

_____

2. Qui vient de peindre les murs de la cuisine?

_____

3. Pourquoi y a-t-il un peu de vert, de bleu, et de jaune sur la nouvelle chemise blanche de Pierre?

_____

II. **Write three simple sentences in French using each of the following expressions. If you need to, review the idioms, verbal expressions, and dialogue in this unit.**

1. venir de + inf.

_____

2. de bonne heure

_____

3. de quelle couleur

_____

III. Find the following idiomatic expressions in French in this puzzle and circle them.

1. not at all
2. at first
3. ordinarily
4. O.K.
5. no harm
6. again
7. from time to time

P	D	D	P	A	S	P	D	E	N	E	M	A	L
A	U	A	U	D	H	A	B	I	T	U	D	E	U
D	E	T	E	M	P	S	E	N	T	E	M	P	S
A	M	A	P	A	S	D	U	T	O	U	T	D	E
B	D	U	D	O	D	E	N	O	U	V	E	A	U
O	T	E	M	P	S	M	T	U	T	E	M	P	S
R	C	C	O	R	D	A	C	C	O	R	D	D	U
D	E	N	O	U	V	L	P	A	S	M	L	A	E

Unit 5
With **par**, with **tout**, with **tous**, and miscellaneous

with par	
par bonheur fortunately	**par ici** this way
par ci par là here and there	**par jour** per day, daily
par conséquent consequently	**par là** that way
par exemple for example	**apprendre par coeur** to memorize, learn by heart

with tout	
tout à coup suddenly	**tout d'abord** first of all
tout d'un coup all of a sudden	**tout de suite** immediately, at once, right away
tout à fait completely, entirely	**tout le monde** everybody
tout à l'heure in a little while, a little while ago	**tout le temps** all the time

with tous	
tous les deux both	**tous les matins** every morning
tous les jours every day	**tous les soirs** every evening

Miscellaneous	
s'il vous plaît please *(polite form)* **s'il te plaît** please *(familiar form)*	**vouloir bien** to be willing **Je veux bien sortir avec vous.** I'm willing to go out with you. **vouloir dire** to mean **Que veut dire ce mot?** What does this word mean?

DIALOGUE

Janine and Pierre are in a museum because they want to see the dinosaurs.

Pierre:	**Pour aller voir les dinosaures, c'est par ici, Janine.**
Janine:	**Non, Pierre. Ils sont par là.**
Pierre:	**Je te dis que c'est par ici. Je sais, moi!**
Janine:	**Non, Pierre. Ils ont tout changé dans ce musée. Maintenant les dinosaures sont par là.**
Pierre:	**Es-tu folle?! Ils ne changent jamais les expositions dans ce musée.**
Janine:	**Je te dis que tous les jours ils changent tout.**
Pierre:	**Je vais demander au gardien.**
	(Pierre s'approche du gardien.)
Pierre:	**Excusez-moi, monsieur, mais où sont les dinosaures aujourd'hui?**
Gardien:	**Il n'y a pas de dinosaures ici. Ils sont dans le petit musée de l'autre côté de la rue. Il est ouvert maintenant. Vous pouvez y aller tout de suite parce qu'il ferme à cinq heures.**
	(Pierre et Janine se regardent l'un à l'autre.)
Pierre et Janine:	**Tu vois! Tu vois!**

EXERCISES

Review the above material before doing these exercises.

I. **Answer the following questions in complete sentences. They are based on the dialogue in this unit.**

1. Où sont Janine et Pierre?

_____

2. Pourquoi sont-ils dans le musée?

_____

3. Est-ce qu'il y a des dinosaures dans ce musée?

_____

4. Est-ce que Pierre a raison?

_____

5. Est-ce que Janine a tort?

_____

6. Est-ce que tous les deux ont tort?

_____

II. **Find these idiomatic expressions in the dialogue and write them in French.**

1. this way _____   3. every day _____

2. that way _____   4. across the street _____

429

III. Match the following.

1. vouloir bien   __ please
2. par exemple   __ everybody
3. vouloir dire   __ for example
4. tout le monde   __ daily
5. par jour   __ to mean
6. s'il vous plaît   __ to be willing

Unit 6
With **faire**

with **faire**	

faire attention
    to pay attention
	faire un voyage
	    to take a trip

faire de l'autostop
    to hitchhike
	faire une malle
	    to pack a trunk

faire de son mieux
    to do one's best
	faire une promenade
	    to take a walk

faire des emplettes **faire des courses** } to do (go) shopping **faire du shopping**	**faire une promenade en voiture** to go for a drive

faire des progrès
    to make progress
	Quel temps fait-il?
	    What's the weather like?

faire du vélo
    to bike,
    to ride a bike
	Il fait beau.
	    The weather is nice.

faire jour
    to be daylight
	Il fait mauvais.
	    The weather is bad.

faire le ménage
    to do housework
	Il fait chaud.
	    It's warm (hot).

faire les valises
    to pack the suitcases
	Il fait froid.
	    It's cold.

faire nuit
    to be night(time)
	Il fait frais.
	    It's cool.

faire peur
    to frighten
	Il fait du soleil.
	    It's sunny.

faire ses bagages
    to pack one's baggage
	Il fait du vent.
	    It's windy.

	Cela ne fait rien.
	    It doesn't matter.
	    It makes no difference.

DIALOGUE

Dad is home because he has the day off from work. Mom wants him to take her out.

Maman: **Il fait beau aujourd'hui, n'est-ce pas?**
Papa: **Oui.**
Maman: **Il fait du soleil aujourd'hui, n'est-ce pas?**
Papa: **Oui.**
Maman: **Je veux faire une promenade.**
Papa: **Oui.**
Maman: **Je veux faire une promenade en voiture. Et toi? Et TOI??!**
Papa: **Que dis-tu?**
Maman: **Tu ne fais pas attention! Moi, je te parle, et tu ne fais pas attention.**
Papa: **Tu as tort, ma chérie. Je t'écoute. Que dis-tu?**
Maman: **Je dis que je veux faire une promenade en voiture. Enfin, je veux sortir!**
Papa: **Bon! Alors, tu vas faire les bagages. Moi, je vais faire la malle, et nous allons faire un voyage! D'accord?**

Maman:	Tu te moques de moi!
Papa:	Où veux-tu aller?
Maman:	Moi, je sais où je veux aller; et toi, tu sais où tu veux aller!
Papa:	Terrible, terrible. Tu t'es fâchée. Tu me fais peur. Je travaille tous les jours, je fais de mon mieux, le samedi je fais des courses avec toi. Et aujourd'hui … et aujourd'hui, j'ai un jour de congé et je ne peux pas rester tranquillement à la maison.
Maman:	Et moi? Et MOI?? Je travaille aussi; je fais le ménage dans cette maison tous les jours, je fais de mon mieux aussi. Je dors quand il fait nuit, je travaille quand il fait jour. Aujourd'hui tu as un jour de congé et tu ne veux pas sortir avec moi!
Papa:	Veux-tu aller au cinéma?
Maman:	Oui, si c'est un bon film, pourquoi pas?
Papa:	Bon! Allons au cinéma. Allons voir le film *Un Homme et une femme.*

EXERCISES

Review the preceding material before doing these exercises.

I.   **Find these idiomatic expressions in the dialogue and write them in French.**

1. The weather is nice today, isn't it?

_____

2. It's sunny today, isn't it?

_____

3. I want to take a walk.

_____

4. I want to go for a drive.

_____

5. You are going to pack the bags, I am going to pack the trunk, and we are going to take a trip.

_____

An aerial view of l'Île de la Cité, Paris

II. Complete the following dialogue in French. The conversation is between a man and a woman. They can't decide on what to do or where to go.

Lui: Veux-tu sortir ce soir?

Elle: _____

Lui: Si tu ne veux pas sortir, que veux-tu faire?

Elle: _____

Lui: Pourquoi veux-tu rester à la maison?

Elle: _____

Lui: Veux-tu une aspirine?

Elle: _____

Lui: M'aimes-tu?

Elle: _____

III. **Le Mot Mystère**   (Mystery Word).   In order to find the mystery word, you must first find and circle in this puzzle the French words given next to it. The letters that remain in the puzzle are scrambled. Unscramble them to find **le mot mystère.**

à	me
attention	mieux
autostop	non
beau	nuit
chaud	oui
emplettes	peur
faire	se
jour	soleil
la	tu
mauvais	y

A	M	N	O	N	À	N	U	I	T
T	I	F	A	I	R	E	M	E	O
T	E	M	A	U	V	A	I	S	U
E	U	C	H	A	U	D	Y	P	I
N	X	S	O	L	E	I	L	E	J
T	S	M	A	U	O	R	A	U	O
I	E	B	E	A	U	T	U	R	U
O	A	U	T	O	S	T	O	P	R
N	E	M	P	L	E	T	T	E	S

433

Part 4: Skill in Listening Comprehension

I. **Auditory-pictorial stimuli.** Listen to the questions that will be read to you based on the pictures shown. Then choose the correct answer and write the letter on the blank line. Each statement or question will be read twice only.

1. (a) deux   (b) trois   (c) quatre   (d) cinq _____

2. (a) dans une salle   (b) dans un train   (c) dans un autobus   (d) dans un autocar _____

3. (a) un agent de police   (b) un facteur   (c) un contrôleur   (d) un prêtre _____

4. (a) deux   (b) trois   (c) quatre   (d) cinq   _____

5. (a) Ils courent   (b) Ils marchent   (c) Ils sautent   (d) Il fait beau   _____

6. (a) de chez eux   (b) du cinéma   (c) du théâtre   (d) de l'école   _____

7. (a) sur les arbres   (b) dans l'école   (c) sur le toit   (d) sur le trottoir   _____

There are four pictures on this page. Under each picture there is a letter identifying it. Your teacher will read a series of four statements, numbered 8 to 11. Match each statement that you hear with the appropriate picture by writing the letter of the picture on the blank line.

A

B

C

D

8. _____   9. _____   10. _____   11. _____

L'Arc de Triomphe à Paris.

Instructions: Do the same here as on the previous pages. This is practice in listening comprehension. Study carefully the picture above.

12. (a) à la Place Charles de Gaulle   (b) à la Place de la Concorde
    (c) à l'Opéra   (d) aux Invalides   _____

13. (a) Napoléon Ier   (b) Louis XIV   (c) Louis XVI   (d) les Romains   _____

14. (a) Avenue des Champs-Élysées   (b) Boulevard St.-Michel   (c) Rue du Bac
    (d) Avenue Foch   _____

15. (a) dix   (b) onze   (c) douze   (d) treize   _____

16. (a) de Jeanne d'Arc   (b) de Napoléon   (c) du Soldat Inconnu   (d) de Louis XIV   _____

Instructions: Do the same here as on the previous pages. This is practice in listening comprehension. Study carefully the picture above.

17. (a) un grand livre   (b) un petit livre   (c) des lunettes   (d) un verre   _____

18. (a) une croix   (b) des lunettes   (c) un livre   (d) une bague   _____

19. (a) un tout petit livre   (b) un gros livre   (c) une chaise   (d) des fleurs   _____

There are four pictures on this page. Under each picture there is a letter identifying it. Your teacher will read a series of four statements, numbered 20 to 23. Match each statement that you hear with the appropriate picture by writing the letter of the picture on the blank line.

A

B

C

D

20. _____   21. _____   22. _____   23. _____

II. **Differentiating sounds.** Choose the word that is pronounced and write the letter on the blank line. Each will be read three times only.

1. (a) coeur
   (b) cour
   (c) car
   (d) cure   _____

2. (a) pour
   (b) pur
   (c) par
   (d) peur   _____

3. (a) de
   (b) du
   (c) des
   (d) doux   _____

4. (a) vent
   (b) vigne
   (c) vin
   (d) viens   _____

5. (a) deux
   (b) Dieu
   (c) de
   (d) dur   _____

6. (a) ceci
   (b) ceux-ci
   (c) souci
   (d) sucer   _____

7. (a) heure
   (b) heureux
   (c) heureuse
   (d) eurent   _____

8. (a) grand
   (b) grain
   (c) grande
   (d) gris   _____

9. (a) du
   (b) doux
   (c) deux
   (d) des   _____

10. (a) était
    (b) été
    (c) thé
    (d) tu   _____

III. **Choosing the correct answer to a question.** Listen carefully to each question. Then choose the correct answer and write the letter on the blank line. Each will be read three times only.

1. (a) sept
   (b) huit
   (c) neuf
   (d) dix   _____

2. (a) onze
   (b) douze
   (c) treize
   (d) quatorze   _____

3. (a) Fontainebleau
   (b) Arc de Triomphe
   (c) Paris
   (d) Versailles   _____

4. (a) dix-sept
   (b) sept
   (c) treize
   (d) quarante   _____

5. (a) Comment allez-vous?
   (b) Bonjour
   (c) Au revoir
   (d) De rien   _____

6. (a) une fourchette
   (b) un couteau
   (c) un plat
   (d) une cuillère   _____

7. (a) Paris
   (b) Bordeaux
   (c) Marseille
   (d) Domrémy   _____

8. (a) On boit
   (b) On dort
   (c) On court
   (d) On mange   _____

9. (a) septembre
   (b) mai
   (c) janvier
   (d) décembre   _____

10. (a) une valise
    (b) un parapluie
    (c) une canne
    (d) une leçon   _____

IV. **Pattern responses.** Listen carefully to each statement or question that is read to you. Then choose the correct response and write the letter on the blank line. Each will be read three times only.

1. (a) Je vais à la porte aussi.
   (b) Je vois la porte aussi.
   (c) Je ferme la porte aussi.
   (d) J'ouvre la porte aussi. _____

2. (a) Elles les lèvent aussi.
   (b) Elles les lavent aussi.
   (c) Elles les aiment aussi.
   (d) Elles ont lavé les chemises aussi. _____

3. (a) Je le fais tous les matins aussi.
   (b) J'ai pris le petit déjeuner aussi.
   (c) Je le prends tous les matins aussi.
   (d) Je le prépare tous les matins aussi. _____

4. (a) Il a eu peur des lions.
   (b) Il adore les lions.
   (c) Il a peur des lions.
   (d) Il déteste les lions. _____

5. (a) Je vais l'étudier aussi.
   (b) J'ai étudié la leçon aussi.
   (c) Je veux bien l'étudier aussi.
   (d) J'aime étudier mes leçons aussi. _____

6. (a) Je ne peux pas lire.
   (b) Je ne sais pas lire.
   (c) Je sais écrire.
   (d) Elle a lu un livre aussi. _____

7. (a) Il n'a pas de devoir.
   (b) Il n'étudie jamais.
   (c) Il va étudier sa leçon dans le train.
   (d) Il étudie. _____

8. (a) On met une voiture dans un garage.
   (b) Le garage est blanc aussi.
   (c) Si on n'a pas de voiture, on n'a pas de garage.
   (d) Le garage est vert aussi. _____

V. **Choosing rejoinders to statements or questions.** Listen carefully to each statement or question. Then choose the correct response and write the letter on the blank line. Each will be read three times only.

1. (a) Oui, il pleut aujourd'hui.
   (b) Non, je ne crois pas.
   (c) Très bien, merci, et vous?
   (d) Je vais faire des emplettes. _____

2. (a) Alors, dépêchez-vous.
   (b) Alors, couchez-vous.
   (c) Alors, téléphonez-moi.
   (d) Alors, allez-y. _____

3. (a) Je vais mettre mon pardessus.
   (b) Il faut ouvrir les fenêtres.
   (c) J'aime beaucoup l'été.
   (d) J'adore le printemps quand il fait frais. _____

4. (a) Elles sont belles.
   (b) Elles coûtent cher.
   (c) Elles sont rouges.
   (d) Elles sont grandes. _____

5. (a) Très bien, merci.
   (b) Au revoir, monsieur.
   (c) Bonjour, monsieur.
   (d) Oui, il fait beau jour. _____

6. (a) Suzanne dit "bonjour."
   (b) Je dis "bonjour."
   (c) Au revoir, Suzanne.
   (d) Bonjour, Suzanne. _____

7. (a) Il est midi.
   (b) Il est tôt.
   (c) Il fait du bruit.
   (d) Il fait beau. _____

8. (a) Demandez-moi quel temps il fait.
   (b) Je ne sais pas quel temps il fait.
   (c) Quel temps fait-il?
   (d) Il fait mauvais. _____

443

VI. Choosing the word or words whose meaning completes each statement. Listen carefully to each incomplete statement. Then choose the correct answer and write the letter on the blank line. Each will be read three times only.

1. (a) joue bien au tennis
   (b) obéit à ses parents
   (c) se couche tard
   (d) désobéit à ses parents _____

2. (a) heureux
   (b) confus
   (c) bête
   (d) malade _____

3. (a) j'ai mangé
   (b) j'ai bu
   (c) je vais me lever
   (d) je vais me coucher _____

4. (a) la raison
   (b) la clef
   (c) la balle
   (d) l'adresse _____

5. (a) couches-vous
   (b) peignez-vous
   (c) dépêchez-vous
   (d) lavez-vous _____

6. (a) une chaise
   (b) une table
   (c) un lit
   (d) un trottoir _____

7. (a) laver
   (b) lever
   (c) coucher
   (d) amuser _____

8. (a) s'amuser
   (b) défendre son pays
   (c) prendre le train
   (d) apprendre le français _____

VII. Choosing the word that belongs in the same class as the word that is read to you. Listen carefully to the word that your teacher pronounces. Then choose the word that belongs in the same class and write the letter on the blank line. Each word will be read three times only.

1. (a) chat
   (b) chien
   (c) lion
   (d) oiseau _____

2. (a) tablier
   (b) fleurs
   (c) pain
   (d) couteau _____

3. (a) panorama
   (b) vélo
   (c) crayon
   (d) marquis _____

4. (a) soleil
   (b) vent
   (c) lis
   (d) ferme _____

5. (a) pluie
   (b) pommes
   (c) orages
   (d) art _____

6. (a) complet
   (b) genou
   (c) conte
   (d) ruban _____

7. (a) main
   (b) tête
   (c) chapeau
   (d) pied _____

8. (a) panier
   (b) congé
   (c) salon
   (d) épingle _____

VIII. **Choosing the word that is defined.** Listen carefully to the definition that your teacher reads to you. Then choose the word which is defined and write the letter on the blank line. Each definition will be read three times only.

1. (a) la cuisine
   (b) la salle à manger
   (c) la chambre
   (d) la salle de bains   _____

2. (a) un chanteur
   (b) un camionneur
   (c) un conducteur
   (d) un pâtissier   _____

3. (a) mon neveu
   (b) mon cousin
   (c) ma tante
   (d) mon oncle   _____

4. (a) un professeur
   (b) un agent de police
   (c) un avocat
   (d) un étudiant   _____

5. (a) un stylo
   (b) une craie
   (c) un petit bâton
   (d) une lettre   _____

6. (a) le lapin
   (b) le cheval
   (c) la vache
   (d) le chat   _____

7. (a) une boulangerie
   (b) une épicerie
   (c) un musée
   (d) une pâtisserie   _____

8. (a) de la soupe
   (b) de la glace
   (c) des petits pois
   (d) des pommes de terre   _____

IX. **Choosing the synonym of the word that is pronounced.** Listen carefully to the word that your teacher pronounces. Then choose the synonym of it and write the letter on the blank line. Each word will be read three times only.

1. (a) la femme
   (b) le prêtre
   (c) l'instituteur
   (d) l'agent de police   _____

2. (a) demeurer
   (b) me reposer
   (c) détester
   (d) travailler   _____

3. (a) mot
   (b) réponse
   (c) phrase
   (d) erreur   _____

4. (a) commencer
   (b) rompre
   (c) préparer
   (d) terminer   _____

5. (a) guérir
   (b) demeurer
   (c) dîner
   (d) descendre   _____

6. (a) nuire
   (b) interroger
   (c) désirer
   (d) voler   _____

7. (a) fâché
   (b) heureux
   (c) fatigué
   (d) malheureux   _____

8. (a) les pieds
   (b) les mains
   (c) le chapeau
   (d) la figure   _____

La Marseillaise—paroles en français

Allons enfants de la Patrie
Le jour de gloire est arrivé!
Contre nous de la tyrannie
L'étendard sanglant est levé
Entendez-vous dans nos campagnes
Mugir ces féroces soldats?
Ils viennent jusque dans vos bras.
Égorger vos fils, vos compagnes!

    Aux armes citoyens
    Formez vos bataillons
    Marchons, marchons
    Qu'un sang impur
    Abreuve nos sillons

Que veut cette horde d'esclaves
De traîtres, de rois conjurés?
Pour qui ces ignobles entraves
Ces fers dès longtemps préparés?
Français, pour nous, ah! quel outrage
Quels transports il doit exciter?
C'est nous qu'on ose méditer
De rendre à l'antique esclavage!

Quoi ces cohortes étrangères!
Feraient la loi dans nos foyers!
Quoi! ces phalanges mercenaires
Terrasseraient nos fils guerriers!
Grand Dieu! par des mains enchaînées
Nos fronts sous le joug se ploieraient
De vils despotes deviendraient
Les maîtres des destinées.

Tremblez, tyrans et vous perfides
L'opprobre de tous les partis
Tremblez! vos projets parricides
Vont enfin recevoir leurs prix!
Tout est soldat pour vous combattre
S'ils tombent, nos jeunes héros
La France en produit de nouveaux,
Contre vous tout prêts à se battre.

Français, en guerriers magnanimes
Portez ou retenez vos coups!
Épargnez ces tristes victimes
À regret s'armant contre nous
Mais ces despotes sanguinaires
Mais ces complices de Bouillé
Tous ces tigres qui, sans pitié
Déchirent le sein de leur mère!

Nous entrerons dans la carrière
Quand nos aînés n'y seront plus
Nous y trouverons leur poussière
Et la trace de leurs vertus
Bien moins jaloux de leur survivre
Que de partager leur cercueil
Nous aurons le sublime orgueil
De les venger ou de les suivre!

Amour sacré de la Patrie
Conduis, soutiens nos bras vengeurs
Liberté, Liberté chérie
Combats avec tes défenseurs!
Sous nos drapeaux, que la victoire
Accoure à tes mâles accents
Que tes ennemis expirants
Voient ton triomphe et notre gloire!

Château des Fines Roches, Provence, France
Reprinted with permission of the French Embassy Press and Information Division,
French Cultural Services, New York.

X. Choosing the idiom or expression whose meaning completes each statement. Listen carefully to each incomplete statement. Then choose the answer that completes the thought and write the letter on the blank line. Your teacher will read each incomplete statement three times only.

1. (a) j'ai raison
   (b) j'ai tort
   (c) j'ai sommeil
   (d) je veux faire des emplettes _____

2. (a) a raison
   (b) a froid
   (c) est arrivé à l'heure
   (d) a tort _____

3. (a) fait froid ici
   (b) fait chaud ici
   (c) vient ici
   (d) fait du vent ici _____

4. (a) à voix basse
   (b) à haute voix
   (c) au moins
   (d) à mon avis _____

5. (a) corriger
   (b) envoyer
   (c) lire
   (d) écrire _____

6. (a) faire des emplettes
   (b) aller à pied
   (c) faire attention
   (d) aller en ville _____

7. (a) le soleil brille
   (b) je n'ai pas fait la leçon
   (c) je travaille trop
   (d) c'est un jour de congé _____

8. (a) j'ai chaud
   (b) j'ai faim
   (c) j'ai sommeil
   (d) j'ai peur _____

XI. Choosing the antonym of the word that is pronounced. Listen carefully to the word that your teacher pronounces. Then choose the antonym of it and write the letter on the blank line. Each word will be read three times only.

1. (a) vent
   (b) pluie
   (c) neige
   (d) chaud _____

2. (a) le bonheur
   (b) la laideur
   (c) la vente
   (d) la richesse _____

3. (a) vieux
   (b) difficile
   (c) faible
   (d) courte _____

4. (a) avant
   (b) debout
   (c) nouveau
   (d) avec _____

5. (a) la tristesse
   (b) le bonheur
   (c) la guerre
   (d) le bonbon _____

6. (a) vendre
   (b) emprunter
   (c) acheter
   (d) écrire _____

7. (a) mieux
   (b) meilleur
   (c) fort
   (d) cher _____

8. (a) le bonheur
   (b) la pluie
   (c) le silence
   (d) le vent _____

XII. Choosing the word or words that are suggested by the situation described in a sentence. Listen carefully to the statement that your teacher reads to you. Then choose the word or words that are suggested by the situation described and write the letter on the blank line. Each statement will be read three times only.

1. (a) la salle à manger
   (b) la rue
   (c) le toit
   (d) la cave _____

2. (a) un livre
   (b) une addition
   (c) un repas
   (d) un voyage _____

3. (a) rire
   (b) sourire
   (c) manger
   (d) étudier _____

4. (a) la danse
   (b) le bal
   (c) le parc
   (d) la maison _____

5. (a) la boucherie
   (b) la boulangerie
   (c) la pâtisserie
   (d) la bijouterie _____

6. (a) chez le coiffeur
   (b) chez le dentiste
   (c) chez l'avocat
   (d) chez le médecin _____

7. (a) la France et l'Angleterre
   (b) heureux
   (c) malheureux
   (d) triste _____

8. (a) le trottoir
   (b) le toit
   (c) la cave
   (d) le mur _____

XIII. True-False statements. Listen carefully to the statement that your teacher reads to you. Then on the blank line write **vrai** if the statement is true or **faux** if the statement is false. The teacher will read each statement only three times.

1. _____   3. _____   5. _____   7. _____   9. _____

2. _____   4. _____   6. _____   8. _____   10. _____

XIV. Responding to statements on content. Your teacher will read a statement to you. Listen carefully. Then choose the best response based on the content of the statement and write the letter on the blank line. Each statement will be read three times only.

1. L'enfant
   (a) veut quelque chose
   (b) refuse quelque chose
   (c) écrit quelque chose
   (d) mange quelque chose _____

2. L'enfant va le donner à
   (a) un animal
   (b) son frère
   (c) sa soeur
   (d) une personne _____

3. L'enfant
   (a) a maintenant de l'argent
   (b) ne fait rien
   (c) ne veut rien
   (d) ne demande rien _____

4. L'enfant
   (a) dit *merci*
   (b) ne dit rien
   (c) regarde l'heure
   (d) est fâché _____

5. L'enfant
   (a) dort
   (b) sort
   (c) parle
   (d) écoute _____

6. L'enfant est
   (a) courageux
   (b) généreux
   (c) diligent
   (d) scrupuleux _____

449

XV. **Determining who the two speakers are in a short dialogue.** Your teacher will read a short dialogue to you. It will be read three times. Listen carefully. Then choose the answer that indicates who the two speakers are and write the letter on the blank line.

1. (a) un docteur et une personne malade
   (b) un vendeur et un client
   (c) un maître et un élève
   (d) un père et son fils _____

2. (a) un dentiste et une femme
   (b) un chef et un client
   (c) un garçon et une fille
   (d) une mère et son enfant _____

3. (a) deux jeunes filles
   (b) une concierge et un professeur
   (c) un agent de police et une femme
   (d) un astronome et son élève _____

4. (a) un facteur et un homme
   (b) un médecin et un malade
   (c) un client et une vendeuse
   (d) deux acteurs _____

Part 5: Skill in Reading Comprehension

Part Five:
Skill in Reading Comprehension

I. **True-False statements.** Read the following statements and on the blank lines write **vrai** if the statement is true or **faux** if the statement is false.

1. Il y a sept jours dans une semaine. _____

2. Il y a treize mois dans une année. _____

3. Trois et quatre font sept. _____

4. Quand on dit *merci,* on répond *de rien.* _____

5. Quand on dit *bonjour,* on répond *c'est ça.* _____

6. Quand on dit *au revoir,* on répond *bonjour.* _____

7. Le jour de la semaine qui précède jeudi est vendredi. _____

8. Quand on a froid, on porte un maillot de bain. _____

9. La Loire est un fleuve. _____

10. Le jour de la semaine qui suit vendredi est samedi. _____

11. Quand on a faim on mange. _____

12. Janvier est le premier mois de l'année. _____

13. Le boulanger vend du lait. _____

14. Quand il pleut, on prend un parapluie. _____

15. Une vache donne du lait. _____

16. Les Pyrénées se trouvent entre la France et l'Italie. _____

17. On emploie un crayon pour écrire au tableau noir. _____

18. La cerise est un fruit. _____

19. Quand on a soif on boit. _____

20. Pour prendre le train on va à la gare. _____

21. Le printemps est une saison. _____

22. Il neige généralement en été. _____

23. Le chat est un animal domestique. _____

24. Le boucher vend de la viande. _____

25. Il y a soixante minutes dans une heure. _____

II. **Pictorial stimuli.** Choose the correct statement and write the letter on the blank line.

1. (a) Il est une heure.
   (b) Il est midi.
   (c) Il est douze heures.
   (d) Il est une heure cinq.   _____

2. (a) Il est six heures.
   (b) Il est midi cinq.
   (c) Il est une heure et demie.
   (d) Il est midi.   _____

3. (a) Il est neuf heures et demie.
   (b) Il est cinq heures.
   (c) Il est neuf heures vingt-cinq.
   (d) Il est cinq heures moins
       quinze.   _____

Degas—Danseuse au repos

4. Dans ce tableau la danseuse
   (a) se repose.
   (b) mange.
   (c) danse.
   (d) regarde le plafond. _____

5. Dans ce tableau la danseuse
   (a) est debout.
   (b) est assise.
   (c) est couchée par terre.
   (d) chante. _____

6. Cette danseuse a la main droite sur
   (a) le pied gauche.
   (b) le pied droit.
   (c) le genou.
   (d) la tête. _____

Edwin Aldrin, astronaute américain, photographié par Neil Armstrong sur le sol lunaire, 1969.
(Edwin Aldrin, American astronaut, photographed by Neil Armstrong on the lunar surface, 1969.)
Official NASA Photograph.

7. Dans cette photo l'astronaute
    (a) marche.
    (b) danse.
    (c) monte.
    (d) court. _____

8. L'astronaute se trouve sur
    (a) la terre.
    (b) la plage.
    (c) la lune.
    (d) un tapis. _____

Manet—*Le Balcon*

9. Dans ce tableau la femme à droite tient
   (a) une brosse.
   (b) un parapluie.
   (c) une chaussure.
   (d) une clef. _____

10. Dans ce tableau le monsieur porte
    (a) un maillot de bain.
    (b) un chapeau haut-de-forme.
    (c) une cravate.
    (d) des gants. _____

11. Dans ce tableau on est
    (a) au restaurant.
    (b) sur le balcon.
    (c) dans la cuisine.
    (d) au cinéma. _____

12. Ce tableau est une oeuvre de
    (a) Degas.
    (b) Renoir.
    (c) Manet.
    (d) Dufy. _____

A l'heure des petites filles en fleurs
Des petites robes d'été pratiques
comme des tee-shirts, faciles à porter, et très romantiques.

ROBE coton.
haut style "Tee-shirt".
jupe et manches
toile écrue imprimée
"fleurs".
Coloris écru/rose
ou écru/bleu.
Du 18 mois au 8 ans.
Le 4 ans.

AUX TROIS QUARTIERS

boulevard de la Madeleine
ouvert tous les jours de 9 h 45 à 18 h 30
4 parkings gratuits
Madeleine, Concorde
Garages de Paris, Malesherbes

Reprinted with permission of AUX TROIS QUARTIERS, Paris.

III. Match the following. Study the French words in the picture on this page.

1. petites filles	6. manche	_____ to wear	_____ skirt
2. fleurs	7. jupe	_____ easy	_____ sleeve
3. porter	8. robe	_____ dress	_____ little girls
4. facile	9. chapeaux	_____ to smile	_____ summer
5. sourire	10. été	_____ flowers	_____ hats

457

IV. **Oui ou Non?** Study the picture on page 457, then answer.

1. Ces deux petites filles portent des robes d'été. _____

2. Leurs robes sont longues. _____

3. Ces jolies petites filles portent des chapeaux. _____

4. La plus petite regarde la main de son amie. _____

5. Les deux petites filles tiennent des fleurs à la main. _____

V. **Choose the best answer.** Study the picture on this page; then answer the questions.

1. L'homme dans cette image porte sur la tête
   (a) un journal.
   (b) deux yeux.
   (c) une main.
   (d) un chapeau. _____

2. Il tient
   (a) un chapeau
   (b) une main.
   (c) un détective.
   (d) un journal. _____

3. Il est probablement dans
   (a) sa maison.
   (b) une église.
   (c) un train.
   (d) une grange. _____

4. L'homme est probablement
   (a) fermier.
   (b) facteur.
   (c) avocat.
   (d) dentiste. _____

5. Sans doute, il va
   (a) à la plage.
   (b) au bureau.
   (c) au supermarché.
   (d) au cinéma. _____

VI. **There are two pictures on this page. Under each picture there is a letter identifying it. Match each statement that you read with the appropriate picture by writing the letter of the picture on the blank line opposite each statement.**

A

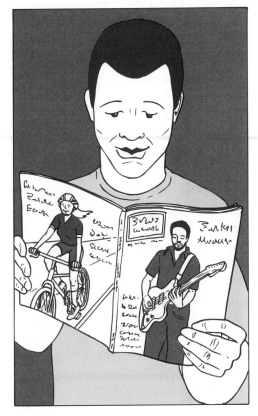

B

1. Dans cette photo il y a des personnes qui dansent. _____

2. Un homme lit un magazine. _____

3. Une personne au milieu d'un groupe. _____

4. Un homme qui sourit. _____

5. Une femme qui fait du vélo. _____

6. Un homme qui joue de la guitare. _____

VIII. Pattern responses. Choose the correct response and write the letter on the blank line.

1. Albertine va à la porte. Et vous?
   - (a) Je vais à la porte aussi.
   - (b) Je vois la porte aussi.
   - (c) Je ferme la porte aussi.
   - (d) J'ouvre la porte aussi. _____

2. Cette femme lave les chemises. Et les autres femmes?
   - (a) Elles les lèvent aussi.
   - (b) Elles les lavent aussi.
   - (c) Elles les aiment aussi.
   - (d) Elles ont lavé les chemises aussi. _____

3. Je prends le petit déjeuner tous les matins. Et vous?
   - (a) Je le fais tous les soirs aussi.
   - (b) J'ai pris le petit déjeuner aussi.
   - (c) Je le prends tous les matins aussi.
   - (d) Je le prépare tous les matins aussi. _____

4. Paul a peur des lions. Et toi?
   - (a) J'ai eu peur des lions aussi.
   - (b) J'adore les lions aussi.
   - (c) J'ai peur des lions aussi.
   - (d) Il a peur des lions aussi. _____

5. J'ai étudié la leçon. Et toi?
   - (a) Je vais l'étudier aussi.
   - (b) J'ai étudié le livre aussi.
   - (c) Je veux bien étudier aussi.
   - (d) J'ai étudié la leçon aussi. _____

6. J'ai un livre. Et Antoine?
   - (a) Nous avons un livre aussi.
   - (b) Il a un livre aussi.
   - (c) Je n'ai pas de livre.
   - (d) Elle a un livre aussi. _____

7. Hélène est bien fatiguée. Et vous?
   - (a) Je vais me reposer aussi.
   - (b) Je suis fatigueé aussi.
   - (c) Je suis bien content aussi.
   - (d) Je vais travailler aussi. _____

8. Louis sait jouer du piano. Et les autres garçons?
   - (a) Ils aiment jouer du piano aussi.
   - (b) Ils savent jouer du piano aussi.
   - (c) Ils entendent la musique aussi.
   - (d) Ils ont un piano aussi. _____

9. Cette maison est blanche. Et le garage?
   - (a) Il y a une voiture dans le garage.
   - (b) Il est blanc aussi.
   - (c) Si on n'a pas de voiture, on n'a pas de garage.
   - (d) Le garage est vert aussi. _____

10. Ils vont faire un voyage. Et vous?
    - (a) Nous allons rester chez nous aussi.
    - (b) Nous allons faire un voyage aussi.
    - (c) Quand on voyage, on apprend.
    - (d) Je vais faire la malle aussi. _____

IX. Choosing rejoinders to statements or questions. Choose the best rejoinder that is logically related to the statement or question.

1. Bonjour, Janine. Comment allez-vous?
   - (a) Oui, il pleut aujourd'hui.
   - (b) Je vais à l'école.
   - (c) Très bien, merci, et vous?
   - (d) Je vais faire des emplettes. _____

2. Je suis bien fatigué.
   - (a) Alors, dépêchez-vous.
   - (b) Alors, couchez-vous.
   - (c) Alors, téléphonez-moi.
   - (d) Alors, allez-y. _____

3. Je dois sortir et il fait froid.
   - (a) Je vais mettre mon pardessus.
   - (b) Il faut ouvrir les fenêtres.
   - (c) Il faut fermer les fenêtres.
   - (d) Il fait beau en été. _____

4. La femme refuse d'acheter les pommes. Elle dit:
   - (a) Elles sont belles.
   - (b) Elles coûtent cher.
   - (c) Elles sont rouges.
   - (d) Elles sont grandes. _____

5. Le maître dit: Pierre, dis-moi "bonjour."—Pierre répond:
   - (a) Très bien, merci.
   - (b) Au revoir, monsieur.
   - (c) Bonjour, monsieur.
   - (d) Oui, il fait beau jour. _____

6. La maîtresse dit: André, dis "bonjour" à Suzanne. —André dit:
   - (a) Suzanne dit "bonjour."
   - (b) Je dis "bonjour."
   - (c) Au revoir, Suzanne.
   - (d) Bonjour, Suzanne. _____

7. Quel temps fait-il aujourd'hui?
   - (a) Il est midi.
   - (b) Il est tôt.
   - (c) Il fait du bruit.
   - (d) Il fait beau. _____

8. La maîtresse dit: Charles, demande-moi quel temps il fait.—Charles dit:
   - (a) Demandez-moi quel temps il fait.
   - (b) Je ne sais pas.
   - (c) Quel temps fait-il?
   - (d) Il fait mauvais. _____

9. Le maître dit: Denise, combien font dix et trois?—Denise répond correctement:
   - (a) Ils font onze.
   - (b) Dix et trois font douze.
   - (c) Dix et trois font treize.
   - (d) Dix et trois font quatorze. _____

10. Le professeur dit: Joseph, combien font dix moins un? —Joseph répond correctement:
    - (a) Dix moins un font onze.
    - (b) Dix moins un font sept.
    - (c) Dix moins un font huit.
    - (d) Dix moins un font neuf. _____

11. Madame Jodelle est dans la cuisine.
    - (a) Elle fait le lit.
    - (b) Elle vend des pommes.
    - (c) Elle prépare le dîner.
    - (d) Elle efface le tableau. _____

12. Un homme enseigne le français à un groupe d'élèves.
    - (a) C'est un médecin.
    - (b) C'est un avocat.
    - (c) C'est un pâtissier.
    - (d) C'est un professeur. _____

13. Dominique dit: Je sais qu'il va faire beau le jour du match. Vous dites:
    - (a) Je sais qu'il va faire beau aussi.
    - (b) Moi, aussi, je vais aller au match.
    - (c) Oui, il fait beau aujourd'hui.
    - (d) Il pleut. _____

14. Simone dit: Paul, qu'est-ce que tu fais avec ces valises? —Il répond:
    - (a) Il vaut mieux être en retard.
    - (b) Je suis rentré hier soir.
    - (c) Je vais faire un voyage.
    - (d) Vous avez des valises. _____

461

IX. **Choosing the word or words whose meaning completes a sentence.**

1. En été il fait généralement
   (a) froid.
   (b) chaud.
   (c) mauvais.
   (d) un temps terrible. _____

2. Hier soir je suis allé à un bal et j'ai
   (a) rappelé.
   (b) dansé.
   (c) coupé.
   (d) couché. _____

3. Le petit déjeuner est un repas qu'on prend
   (a) le soir.
   (b) le matin.
   (c) l'après-midi.
   (d) le midi. _____

4. Un bon enfant
   (a) joue bien au tennis.
   (b) se couche tard.
   (c) obéit à ses parents.
   (d) désobéit à ses parents. _____

5. Tu as les mains sales. Va te
   (a) laver.
   (b) lever.
   (c) coucher.
   (d) coiffer. _____

6. Généralement on se couche sur
   (a) une chaise.
   (b) une table.
   (c) un lit.
   (d) un trottoir. _____

7. Le train va partir et si vous voulez l'attraper,
   (a) couchez-vous.
   (b) coiffez-vous.
   (c) dépêchez-vous.
   (d) lavez-vous. _____

8. Pauline ne peut pas ouvrir la porte parce qu'elle a perdu
   (a) la raison.
   (b) la clef.
   (c) la balle.
   (d) l'adresse. _____

9. Le réveil a sonné et
   (a) j'ai mangé.
   (b) j'ai bu.
   (c) je vais me lever.
   (d) je vais me coucher. _____

10. Monsieur Bernard ne peut pas marcher parce qu'il est très
    (a) malade.
    (b) heureux.
    (c) confus.
    (d) bête. _____

X. **Choosing the word that belongs in the same class as the italicized word.**

1. La maîtresse écrit avec *un crayon.*
   (a) une cravate
   (b) une jupe
   (c) un stylo
   (d) une leçon _____

2. *Le tigre* est un animal sauvage.
   (a) le chat
   (b) le chien
   (c) l'oiseau
   (d) le lion _____

3. La mère met *une fourchette* sur la table.
   (a) un tablier
   (b) des fleurs
   (c) du pain
   (d) un couteau _____

4. Il a lu *un conte.*
   (a) un panorama
   (b) un vélo
   (c) un crayon
   (d) une histoire _____

5. Madame Boileau a de belles
   roses dans son jardin.
   (a) soleil
   (b) vent
   (c) tulipes
   (d) ferme _____

6. Madame Duval adore *les cerises.*
   (a) la pluie
   (b) les pommes
   (c) les orages
   (d) l'art _____

7. Monsieur Paquet a acheté
   un nouveau *costume.*
   (a) complet
   (b) genou
   (c) conte
   (d) chapeau _____

8. Le pauvre garçon a mal à
   l'épaule.
   (a) l'école
   (b) la tête
   (c) la veste
   (d) l'église _____

9. Cette maison a une grande
   cuisine.
   (a) salle de bains
   (b) porte
   (c) fenêtre
   (d) table _____

10. J'ai lu plusieurs livres de cet
    auteur.
    (a) éclair
    (b) écrivain
    (c) arbre
    (d) hôtel _____

XI. Choosing the word that is defined or described.

1. La pièce où on prend une douche.
   (a) la cuisine
   (b) la salle à manger
   (c) la chambre
   (d) la salle de bains _____

2. L'homme qui prépare des gâteaux.
   (a) chanteur
   (b) boucher
   (c) conducteur
   (d) pâtissier _____

3. Le frère de mon père.
   (a) mon neveu
   (b) mon cousin
   (c) ma tante
   (d) mon oncle _____

4. Une personne qui enseigne.
   (a) professeur
   (b) agent de police
   (c) détective
   (d) étudiant _____

5. On les met aux mains.
   (a) souliers
   (b) gants
   (c) chaussettes
   (d) manteau _____

6. On emploie cette chose pour
   écrire au tableau noir.
   (a) stylo
   (b) craie
   (c) bâton
   (d) lettre _____

7. On l'emploie pour parler.
   (a) jambes
   (b) yeux
   (c) langue
   (d) pieds _____

8. Animal qui donne du lait.
   (a) lapin
   (b) cheval
   (c) vache
   (d) chat _____

9. C'est un dessert.
   (a) soupe
   (b) glace
   (c) petits pois
   (d) pommes de terre _____

10. Où on voit des objets d'art.
    (a) boulangerie
    (b) épicerie
    (c) musée
    (d) boucherie _____

463

XII. Choosing the synonym of the italicized word.

1. Je vois *le maître.*
   (a) la femme
   (b) le monsieur
   (c) la maîtresse
   (d) le boulanger _____

2. Je préfère *rester* chez moi aujourd'hui.
   (a) demeurer
   (b) me reposer
   (c) détester
   (d) travailler _____

3. Rose-Marie a fait *une faute* dans ses devoirs.
   (a) une réponse
   (b) un mot
   (c) une phrase
   (d) une erreur _____

4. Jules va *finir* sa leçon ce soir.
   (a) commencer
   (b) terminer
   (c) lire
   (d) écrire _____

5. Monsieur et Madame Girard *demeurent* près d'ici.
   (a) jouent
   (b) habitent
   (c) dînent
   (d) descendent _____

6. Qu'est-ce que vous *voulez* faire?
   (a) refusez de
   (b) pouvez
   (c) désirez
   (d) oubliez de _____

7. La pauvre petite fille est *triste.*
   (a) fâchée
   (b) heureuse
   (c) fatiguée
   (d) malheureuse _____

8. Paul a *le visage* sale.
   (a) les mains
   (b) le chapeau
   (c) la figure
   (d) les pieds _____

9. Elle se lève, *puis* elle se lave.
   (a) ensuite
   (b) avant
   (c) avec
   (d) naturellement _____

10. Monsieur Roche marche *rapidement.*
    (a) lentement
    (b) facilement
    (c) vraiment
    (d) vite _____

XIII. Choosing the idiom or expression whose meaning completes the sentence.

1. Je n'ai pas pris mon déjeuner ce matin et maintenant
   (a) j'ai chaud.
   (b) j'ai faim.
   (c) j'ai sommeil.
   (d) j'ai peur. _____

2. Je vais me coucher parce que
   (a) j'ai raison.
   (b) j'ai sommeil.
   (c) j'ai tort.
   (d) j'ai du travail. _____

3. J'ai rendez-vous chez le dentiste parce que
   (a) je veux m'amuser.
   (b) j'ai besoin d'argent.
   (c) je veux être à l'heure.
   (d) j'ai mal aux dents. _____

4. Richard fait ses excuses parce qu'il
   (a) a raison.
   (b) a froid.
   (c) a tort.
   (d) est arrivé à l'heure. _____

5. Je vais ouvrir la fenêtre
   parce qu'il
   (a) fait froid ici.
   (b) fait chaud ici.
   (c) vient ici.
   (d) fait du vent ici. _____

6. Je n'ai pas une voiture,
   alors je vais
   (a) faire des emplettes.
   (b) aller à pied.
   (c) faire attention.
   (d) aller en ville. _____

7. André a fait beaucoup de
   fautes dans ses devoirs et il
   va les
   (a) corriger.
   (b) lire.
   (c) écrire.
   (d) envoyer. _____

8. Il n'y a pas de classes
   aujourd'hui parce que
   (a) le soleil brille.
   (b) je n'ai pas fait la leçon.
   (c) je travaille beaucoup.
   (d) c'est un jour de congé. _____

9. Edmond ne comprend pas
   et il demande au professeur:
   (a) Comment vous
       appelez-vous, monsieur?
   (b) Comment allez-vous,
       monsieur?
   (c) Qu'est-ce que cela
       veut dire, monsieur?
   (d) Que faites-vous, monsieur? _____

10. Madame Paquet ne peut
    pas bien entendre parce
    qu'on lui parle
    (a) à voix basse.
    (b) à haute voix.
    (c) à mon avis.
    (d) au moins. _____

XIV. Choosing the antonym of the italicized word.

1. Janine a *ouvert* le livre à la page dix.
   (a) déchiré
   (b) commencé
   (c) fini
   (d) fermé _____

2. Monsieur et Madame Picot vont
   sortir *après* le dîner.
   (a) avant
   (b) en même temps
   (c) à droite
   (d) à gauche _____

3. Il y a du *bruit* dans la rue.
   (a) silence
   (b) vent
   (c) froid
   (d) large _____

4. Cet animal est *sauvage.*
   (a) beau
   (b) mauvais
   (c) bon
   (d) domestique _____

5. Cet étudiant est *mécontent.*
   (a) content
   (b) intelligent
   (c) bête
   (d) grand _____

6. Cette rue est *large.*
   (a) longue
   (b) étroite
   (c) petite
   (d) courte _____

7. C'est un *bon* garçon.
   (a) mauvais
   (b) grand
   (c) petit
   (d) beau _____

8. Hugo a *acheté* un vélo.
   (a) envoyé
   (b) vendu
   (c) nettoyé
   (d) reçu _____

XVI. Choosing the missing word or words in each sentence that contains a particular structure or idiom.

1. Janine vient _____ partir.
   (a) pour
   (b) dans
   (c) de
   (d) à   _____

2. Le sénateur parle _____ haute voix.
   (a) de
   (b) pour
   (c) à
   (d) avec   _____

3. Gigi a peur _____ chien.
   (a) du
   (b) au
   (c) à
   (d) de   _____

4. Monsieur le Président _____ toujours raison.
   (a) affirme
   (b) fait
   (c) est
   (d) a   _____

5. Alfred a répondu: "Il n'y a pas de _____, monsieur."
   (a) qui
   (b) que
   (c) quel
   (d) quoi   _____

6. L'élève a appris le poème _____ coeur.
   (a) de
   (b) par
   (c) pour
   (d) du   _____

7. Ce livre est _____ moi.
   (a) le
   (b) au
   (c) aux
   (d) à   _____

8. Je pense _____ un voyage.
   (a) prendre
   (b) venir
   (c) aller
   (d) faire   _____

9. Hugo aime jouer _____ la balle.
   (a) de
   (b) du
   (c) à
   (d) des   _____

10. Louise aime jouer _____ piano.
    (a) du
    (b) de la
    (c) à
    (d) au   _____

XVII. Summarizing. Read the following paragraphs. Then choose the statement that best summarizes the main point of each and write the letter on the blank line.

1. Mon père a un ami très intéressant. Il est vieux maintenant, mais quand il était *(was)* jeune, il voyageait *(used to travel)* dans tous les coins du monde. Quand il nous rend visite, je passe beaucoup de temps avec lui.
   (a) Les meilleurs amis de mon père sont vieux.
   (b) Mon père a fait beaucoup de voyages avec son ami intéressant.
   (c) J'aime les visites de l'ami de mon père parce qu'il est très intéressant.
   (d) L'ami de mon père ne peut plus voyager parce qu'il est vieux maintenant.   _____

2. En hiver je me lève tard le samedi matin. Je descends à la cuisine où je prends le petit déjeuner avec mon frère et ma soeur. Je lis le journal, surtout la page comique. Puis je vais en ville acheter des choses pour ma mère. J'achète des légumes, des fruits, de la viande, du fromage, et du pain.

   (a) Je prends toujours mon petit déjeuner dans la cuisine.

   (b) Ma mère achète des légumes et des fruits et je les mange.

   (c) Mon frère et ma soeur n'aiment pas aller en ville.

   (d) Après le petit déjeuner je lis un peu et puis je vais acheter des choses pour ma mère. _____

XVII. **Answering questions on content.** Read each of the following passages. Then choose the best answer to each question and write the letter on the blank line.

I

Jean est un garçon de quinze ans. Il a une amie, appelée Marie, avec qui il passe beaucoup de temps. Dans quelques jours, Marie va célébrer son anniversaire. Jean veut lui donner un très beau cadeau mais il n'a pas d'argent. Il en demande à son père, mais il lui répond:
—Il faut travailler pour recevoir de l'argent.
Maintenant Jean cherche des idées. Comment trouver du travail pour avoir de l'argent? À ce moment-là il regarde par la fenêtre. Que voit-il? Il neige. Il neige beaucoup. Maintenant il a du travail.

1. Pourquoi Jean veut-il donner un cadeau à la jeune fille?

   (a) C'est son anniversaire.

   (b) C'est une très jolie fille.

   (c) Elle a fait beaucoup pour Jean.

   (d) Il l'aime. _____

2. Pourquoi est-ce que Jean n'a pas encore acheté un cadeau pour elle?

   (a) Il neige.

   (b) Il n'a pas d'argent.

   (c) Il ne l'aime pas.

   (d) Son père ne l'aime pas. _____

3. Qu'est-ce que son père lui dit?

   (a) Maintenant Jean cherche des idées.

   (b) Jean, cherche des idées.

   (c) Il faut faire du travail.

   (d) Il neige beaucoup. _____

II

Un diplomate de Chine représente son pays aux États-Unis. Ce monsieur est un homme très intelligent et il prend beaucoup de plaisir à parler américain comme un Américain. Un jour une dame lui écrit une lettre pour l'inviter à dîner chez elle. Sa lettre est très élégante.

Plusieurs jours après, la dame a une réponse dans un courriel. Imaginez sa surprise! Au lieu d'écrire une longue lettre, le diplomate a répondu simplement "O.K."

1. De quel pays est le diplomate?

   (a) de Chine.

   (b) des États-Unis.

   (c) de l'Amérique du Sud.

   (d) Il est Américain. _____

467

2. Qu'est-ce qu'il aime faire?
   (a) Il aime représenter son pays.
   (b) Il aime beaucoup les invitations.
   (c) Il aime écrire des courriels.
   (d) Il aime parler américain comme un Américain. _____

3. Pourquoi est-ce que la dame lui écrit?
   (a) Pour avoir le plaisir de parler avec lui.
   (b) Pour l'inviter aux États-Unis.
   (c) Pour l'inviter à dîner chez elle.
   (d) Pour représenter son pays. _____

4. Qu'est-ce qu'elle a reçu quelques jours après?
   (a) Une lettre.
   (b) Un courriel.
   (c) Un cadeau.
   (d) Un dîner. _____

III

Une jeune dame entre dans un petit magasin. Elle passe beaucoup de temps devant un miroir où elle essaye un chapeau après l'autre, mais elle n'achète pas de chapeau. La vendeuse n'est pas contente d'attendre si longtemps. Elle devient impatiente et enfin elle demande:
—Avez-vous choisi un chapeau, madame?
La jeune femme répond:
—Je ne suis pas venue pour acheter. Je suis venue pour m'amuser.

1. Où entre la jeune dame?
   (a) Dans une église.
   (b) Dans une maison.
   (c) Dans une boutique.
   (d) Dans une chapelle. _____

2. Que fait-elle dans le magasin?
   (a) Elle passe longtemps devant le magasin.
   (b) Elle devient impatiente.
   (c) Elle est venue pour acheter.
   (d) Elle essaye beaucoup de chapeaux. _____

3. Pourquoi la vendeuse est-elle impatiente?
   (a) La jeune dame passe beaucoup de temps devant le miroir.
   (b) Elle aime bien attendre.
   (c) La jeune dame ne veut pas payer.
   (d) La jeune dame achète trois chapeaux. _____

4. Pourquoi la dame est-elle entrée dans ce magasin?
   (a) Pour acheter un chapeau.
   (b) Pour s'amuser.
   (c) Pour devenir impatiente.
   (d) Pour manger quelque chose. _____

Le Sacré-Coeur, Paris.

Part 6: Skill in Writing

Part Six:
Skill in Writing

I. **Copying sentences.** First, read each sentence in French silently or aloud. Do not translate. After you have understood it, copy it accurately on the blank line. Then, compare your sentence with the one you copied. Make any necessary corrections yourself.

1. La cerise est un fruit.

_____

2. Quand on a soif on boit.

_____

3. Le boulanger vend du pain.

_____

4. Janine est une belle jeune fille.

_____

5. Hugo est un beau jeune homme.

_____

6. Pierre est un bon garçon.

_____

7. Le printemps est une saison.

_____

8. Il y a sept jours dans une semaine.

_____

9. Il neige généralement en hiver.

_____

10. Trois et quatre font sept.

_____

II. **Dictées.** Your teacher will read a few sentences to you in French. Each will be read three times only. During the first reading, just listen. Write during the second reading. Check what you have written during the third reading. Do not answer or translate. Just write what you hear.

1. Monsieur Paquet cherche ~~son~~ son chappeau

2. Madame Paquet cherche le chappeau dans l'armoire, Janine cherche dans la commode, Et Pierre cherche sous le lit

3. La chien est sous la commode

2. Venez   tout la monde venez Nous Pouvons
de jéjeuner sur l'herbe maintanant. Nous allons
commeneer   avec les viandes

3. _____
_____
_____

4. _____
_____
_____

5. _____
_____
_____

III. **Writing the word that your teacher reads to you; choosing the word that is the antonym of the word you write.** Your teacher will pronounce a word and will repeat it twice. Write it on the blank line. Then choose the antonym of that word from among the words given and write the letter on the short blank line.

Model: **(Your teacher says the word *long*)**

You hear and write:

long	(a) large (b) étroit (c) court (d) haut	**c**
1. _____	(a) mauvais (b) bon (c) frais (d) chaud	_____
2. _____	(a) presque (b) jamais (c) tout (d) rien	_____
3. _____	(a) tôt (b) en retard (c) toujours (d) encore	_____
4. _____	(a) heureux (b) joyeux (c) malheur (d) de bonne heure	_____
5. _____	(a) jeune (b) vieille (c) content (d) mauvais	_____
6. _____	(a) paysage (b) vérité (c) visage (d) figure	_____
7. _____	(a) pleurer (b) gagner (c) jouer (d) travailler	_____
8. _____	(a) offrir (b) venir (c) partir (d) naître	_____
9. _____	(a) travailler (b) commencer (c) faire (d) oublier	_____
10. _____	(a) sortie (b) entrée (c) neige (d) bruit	_____

IV. **Combining short sentences into one sentence.** Rewrite the two sentences as a single sentence by adding one or two words. Make any required changes.

Model: **Je danse. Je chante.**   Answer: **Je danse et je chante.**

1. J'ai soif. J'ai faim.

_____

2. Je suis dans la maison. Je suis malade.

_____

3. La mère est dans la cuisine. L'enfant est dans la cuisine.

_____

4. Monsieur Christian est beau. Monsieur Christian est grand.

_____

5. Madame Bernard veut faire un voyage. Madame Bernard n'a pas d'argent.

_____

V. **Forming a sentence from word cues.** Write a sentence using the following words.

Model: **acheter … pain … ma mère**

Je vais acheter du pain pour ma mère.

_____

1. acheter … pain … ma mère

_____

2. avoir … quinze ans

_____

3. père … vendre … maison

_____

4. poire … fruit

_____

5. boulanger … vendre … pain

_____

6. vache … donner … lait

_____

7. trois … quatre … sept

_____

8. printemps … saison

_____

9. neiger … généralement … hiver

_____

10. aller … plage … se baigner

_____

VI. **Writing the word that your teacher reads to you; choosing the word that is the synonym of the word you write.** Your teacher will pronounce a word and will repeat it twice. Write it on the blank line. Then choose the synonym of that word from among the words given and write the letter on the short blank line.

Model: **(Your teacher says the word *bâtiment*)**

You hear and write:

bâtiment	(a) boulevard (b) avenue (c) édifice (d) clef	**c**
1. _____	(a) désirer (b) oublier (c) voler (d) avoir	_____
2. _____	(a) incertain (b) sûr (c) plusieurs (d) beaucoup	_____
3. _____	(a) mécontent (b) content (c) malheureux (d) retard	_____
4. _____	(a) soulier (b) chapeau (c) chaussette (d) pied	_____
5. _____	(a) oublier (b) finir (c) commencer (d) entendre	_____
6. _____	(a) pharmacien (b) boulanger (c) pâtissier (d) docteur	_____
7. _____	(a) image (b) fourchette (c) plat (d) lit	_____
8. _____	(a) complet (b) repas (c) chemise (d) jupe	_____
9. _____	(a) cour (b) centre (c) sous (d) sur	_____
10. _____	(a) habiter (b) aimer mieux (c) demeurer (d) sortir	_____

VII. **Converting sentences.** Change the following sentences to the singular or plural, as indicated.

Model: Change to the singular: Answer: **La leçon est difficile.**
        Les leçons sont difficiles.

(a) Change to the singular.

1. Ces livres sont faciles.

_____

2. Elles sont descendues vite.

_____

3. Les garçons ont bien mangé.

_____

4. Ils ont écrit à leurs amis.

_____

5. Elles ont acheté deux chapeaux.

_____

(b) Change to the plural.

1. Cette femme est heureuse.

_____

2. Cet homme est beau.

_____

3. Cette jeune fille est jolie.

_____

4. Le garçon a joué avant d'étudier.

_____

5. La maîtresse a corrigé le devoir.

_____

VIII. Parallel writing. Write a simple sentence in French of your own imitating the model sentence. If you are not ready to do this, then copy the model sentence.

    Model: **Je m'appelle Robert.**   **Answer:**   **Je m'appelle** (and add your name).

1. Je m'appelle Bob.

_____

2. J'ai quinze ans.

_____

3. Je me lève à sept heures.

_____

4. Je vais à l'école avec Marilyn.

_____

5. Je m'assieds dans l'autobus avec elle.

_____

6. Nous arrivons à l'école à huit heures et quart.

_____

7. Ma première classe commence à neuf heures moins le quart.

_____

8. J'aime beaucoup ma classe de français.

_____

9. Je suis un bon élève.

_____

10. J'étudie le soir avant le dîner.

_____

IX. **Writing a substitute for a certain portion of a sentence.** Copy each sentence on the blank line, except for the words in italics. In place of them, write your own words.

Model: **J'ouvre *la porte*.**   Answer: **J'ouvre le livre.**

1. J'ouvre *la porte*.

   _____

2. Je ferme *la fenêtre*.

   _____

3. Je vais *à la gare ce soir*.

   _____

4. Mon ami raconte *des histoires intéressantes*.

   _____

5. Il y a *du café* dans la tasse.

   _____

6. Je commence *mes devoirs* à six heures.

   _____

7. Ils écoutent *des disques*.

   _____

8. Mon père m'a donné *deux cents euros*.

   _____

9. Madame Molet vient *nous* voir *souvent*.

   _____

10. Guy lève *les bras*.

   _____

X. **Building a sentence.** Expand the first sentence which is given to you in (a) by adding one or two words in each step (b), (c), and (d).

Model: (a) Monsieur Bernard parle.
         (b) Monsieur Bernard parle lentement.
         (c) Monsieur Bernard parle lentement aux élèves.
         (d) Monsieur Bernard parle lentement aux élèves dans la classe.

1. (a) Monsieur Marin parle.

   (b) _____

   (c) _____

   (d) _____

2. (a) Madame Duval chante.

    (b) _____

    (c) _____

    (d) _____

3. (a) Monique arrive.

    (b) _____

    (c) _____

    (d) _____

4. (a) Jacques joue.

    (b) _____

    (c) _____

    (d) _____

5. (a) Nicolette étudie.

    (b) _____

    (c) _____

    (d) _____

XI. Writing an appropriate response to one line of dialogue. On the blank line write an appropriate response to the line of dialogue that is given.

    Model: Dialogue: **Bonjour, Pierre. Comment vas-tu?**   Answer: **Très bien, merci, et toi?**

1. Bonjour, Anne. Comment vas-tu?

_____

2. Oh! J'ai perdu mes devoirs!

_____

3. Veux-tu aller au cinéma avec moi?

_____

4. Quel âge avez-vous?

_____

5. Où est le musée, s'il vous plaît?

_____

XII. **Writing a response that would logically fit in with two lines of dialogue.**

Model: Dialogue: **Bonjour, Mimi.**
 Bonjour, Anne. Où vas-tu?   Answer: **Je vais chez moi.**

1. Jean: Bonjour, Georges.
 Georges: Bonjour, Jean. Où vas-tu?

 Jean: _____

2. Marie: Que fais-tu, Anne?
 Anne: Mes devoirs. Et toi?

 Marie: _____

3. Jeanne: Aimez-vous votre classe de français?
 Paul: Oui, beaucoup. Et vous?

 Jeanne: _____

4. Pierre: Est-ce qu'il fait froid dehors?
 Albert: Non. Pourquoi veux-tu le savoir?

 Pierre: _____

5. Le Voyageur: À quelle heure arrive le train pour Paris?
 Le Porteur: À deux heures, monsieur.

 Le Voyageur: _____

XIII. **Writing pattern responses.** Write an automatic response in the affirmative for each of the following questions.

Model: Question: **Marguerite va à la porte. Et vous?**   Answer: **Je vais à la porte aussi.**

1. Marguerite va à la porte. Et vous?

   _____

2. Alfred s'assied près de la fenêtre. Et vous?

   _____

3. Robert prend le petit déjeuner tous les matins. Et vous?

   _____

4. Paul a peur des lions. Et vous?

   _____

5. Marie a étudié la leçon. Et vous?

   _____

6. Philippe lit un livre. Et vous?

   _____

7. Suzanne est bien fatiguée. Et vous?

   _____

8. Louis sait jouer du piano. Et vous?

_____

9. Marc a lu un livre. Et vous?

_____

10. Mimi a faim. Et vous?

_____

XIV. **Writing answers to written questions.** Answer each question in a complete sentence in French.

1. Quel est votre nom?

_____

2. Quel âge avez-vous?

_____

3. Où demeurez-vous?

_____

4. Avec qui allez-vous à l'école?

_____

5. À quelle heure arrivez-vous à l'école?

_____

XV. **Writing answers to oral questions.** Your teacher will ask you a question in French and will then repeat it. Write your answer in French after you hear the question for the second time. When the question is repeated the third time, check your answer.

1. _____

2. _____

3. _____

4. _____

5. _____

XVI. **Answering questions on content.** Read the following selections. Then, on the lines provided, answer in French the questions based on them.

I

Après les cours, Jean-Luc, Paul, Denise, et Maryse vont au café qui se trouve en face du campus. Ils prennent un café, un thé, ou un chocolat chaud. Les quatre amis parlent de leurs cours, de la politique, et de la musique. Quand il fait beau, ils se promènent dans le parc. Quand il fait mauvais, ils vont au cinéma. Tout le monde s'amuse bien après les cours.

1. Où vont Jean-Luc, Paul, Denise, et Maryse après les cours?

_____

2. Qu'est-ce qu'ils prennent au café?

_____

3. De quoi les amis parlent-ils?

_____

4. Qu'est-ce qu'ils font quand il fait beau?

_____

5. Qu'est-ce qu'ils font quand il fait mauvais?

_____

II

Tous les jours, pour aller en classe, Paul passe dans la même rue. C'est une petite rue charmante et il l'aime beaucoup. C'est une rue tranquille quand il est en classe, mais quand il sort de l'école, il y a beaucoup de bruit. Quelquefois il y a des autos qui passent. Il aime bien les voir, et souvent il va au grand garage près de sa maison pour les regarder. C'est pourquoi il arrive à l'école en retard!

1. Pourquoi Paul aime-t-il la petite rue?

_____

2. Comment est la rue quand Paul est en classe?

_____

3. Comment est la rue quand il sort de l'école?

_____

4. Qu'est-ce qu'il aime bien voir?

_____

5. Pourquoi arrive-t-il à l'école en retard?

_____

479

III

Le Ciel est, par-dessus le toit ...

Le ciel est, par-dessus le toit,
    Si bleu, si calme!
Un arbre, par-dessus le toit,
    Berce sa palme.

La cloche, dans le ciel qu'on voit,
    Doucement tinte.
Un oiseau sur l'arbre qu'on voit
    Chante sa plainte.

Mon Dieu, mon Dieu, la vie est là,
    Simple et tranquille.
Cette paisible rumeur-là
    Vient de la ville.

—Qu'as-tu fait, ô toi que voilà
    Pleurant sans cesse,
Dis, qu'as-tu fait, toi que voilà
    De ta jeunesse?

(Paul Verlaine, *Sagesse*)

1. De quelle couleur est le ciel?

_____

2. Que fait l'arbre?

_____

3. Que fait la cloche?

_____

4. Que fait l'oiseau?

_____

5. D'où vient la paisible rumeur?

_____

6. Le poète est-il heureux?

_____

XVII. **Writing three simple sentences as directed.** Write three sentences about yourself in French. State your name, your age, and your nationality.

Model: **Je m'appelle Bob Jones. J'ai quinze ans. Je suis américain.**

1. Write three sentences about yourself. State your name, your age, and your nationality.

_____

_____

_____

2. Write three sentences about what you do in the mornings. State at what time you get up, that you wash your face and hands, and that you get dressed.

_____

_____

_____

3. Write three sentences about what you do in the evenings. State at what time you have dinner, that you do your homework, and that you go to bed early.

_____

_____

_____

_____

XVIII. **Writing a question, then answering it; both in French, of course.**

Model: **Quel temps fait-il aujourd'hui? Il fait beau.**

1. _____

2. _____

3. _____

XIX. Writing two sentences based on an opening sentence. Read the opening sentence. Then write two sentences of your own continuing the thought expressed in the first sentence.

Model: **Georges sait nager. Il nage bien. Il aime la natation.**

1. Georges a étudié.

_____

2. Je vais en ville.

_____

3. J'aime beaucoup le français.

_____

4. Madame Bernard est malade.

_____

5. Nous allons faire un voyage.

_____

XX. Graphic stimuli. Answer the following questions in French on the lines provided.

Models:

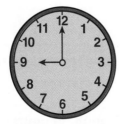

Quelle heure est-il? <u>Il est neuf heures.</u>   1. Quelle heure est-il? _____

_____

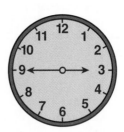

2. Quelle heure est-il? _____   3. Quelle heure est-il? _____

_____   _____

XXI. **Pictorial stimuli.**

1. Write at least three sentences in French describing the above scene.

_____

_____

_____

_____

Edwin Aldrin, astronaute américain photographié par Neil Armstrong sur le sol lunarie, 1969.
(Edwin Aldrin, American astronaut, photographed by Neil Armstrong on the lunar surface, 1969.)
Official NASA photograph.

2. Write at least three sentences in French describing the above scene.

_____

_____

_____

_____

_____

Appendix

Definitions of Basic Grammatical Terms with Examples

Active voice

When we speak or write in the active voice, the subject of the verb performs the action. The action falls on the direct object.

Example:

Everyone loves Janine. / **Tout le monde aime Janine.**

The subject is *everyone*/**tout le monde.** The verb is *loves*/**aime.** The direct object is *Janine.*

Review **aimer** in the verb tables. See also *passive voice* in this list. Compare the preceding sentence with the example in the passive voice.

Adjective

An adjective is a word that modifies a noun or a pronoun. In grammar, to modify a word means to describe, limit, expand, or make the meaning particular. In French an adjective agrees in gender (masculine or feminine) and in number (singular or plural) with the noun or pronoun it modifies.

Examples:

This garden is beautiful. / **Ce jardin est beau.**

She is beautiful. / **Elle est belle.**

The adjective *beautiful*/**beau** modifies the noun *garden*/**jardin.** It is masculine singular because **le jardin** is masculine singular. The adjective *beautiful*/**belle** modifies the pronoun *She*/**Elle.** It is feminine singular because *she* is feminine singular.

Review **être** in the verb tables. Review adjectives in Work Units 18 and 19. In French there are different kinds of adjectives. *See also* comparative adjective, demonstrative adjective, descriptive adjective, interrogative adjective, limiting adjective, possessive adjective, superlative adjective.

Adverb

An adverb is a word that modifies a verb, an adjective, or another adverb. An adverb says something about how, when, where, to what extent, or in what way.

Examples:

Jane runs swiftly. / **Jeanne court rapidement.** The adverb *swiftly*/**rapidement** modifies the verb *runs*/**court.** The adverb shows *how* she runs.

Jack is a very good friend. / **Jacques est un très bon ami.** The adverb *very*/**très** modifies the adjective *good*/**bon.** The adverb shows *how good* a friend he is.

485

The boy is eating too fast now. / **Le garçon mange trop vite maintenant.** The adverb *too*/**trop** modifies the adverb *fast*/**vite.** The adverb shows *to what extent* he is eating *fast.* The adverb *now*/**maintenant** tells us *when.*

The post office is there. / **Le bureau de poste est là.** The adverb *there*/**là** modifies the verb *is*/**est.** It tells us *where* the post office is.

Mary writes carefully. / **Marie écrit soigneusement.** The adverb *carefully*/**soigneusement** modifies the verb *writes*/**écrit.** It tells us *in what way* she writes.

Review adverbs in Work Unit 20. Review **courir, écrire, être, manger** in the verb tables.

Affirmative statement, negative statement

A statement in the affirmative is the opposite of a statement in the negative. To negate an affirmative statement is to make it negative.

Examples:

In the affirmative: I like chocolate ice cream. / **J'aime la glace au chocolat.**

In the negative: I do not like chocolate ice cream. / **Je n'aime pas la glace au chocolat.**

Review **aimer** in the verb tables.

Agreement of adjective with noun

Agreement is made on the adjective with the noun it modifies in gender (masculine or feminine) and number (singular or plural).

Examples:

a white house / **une maison blanche.** The adjective **blanche** is feminine singular because the noun **une maison** is feminine singular.

two white houses / **deux maisons blanches.** The adjective **blanches** is feminine plural because the noun **maisons** is feminine plural.

Review Work Unit 18.

Agreement of past participle of a reflexive verb with its reflexive pronoun

Agreement is made on the past participle of a reflexive verb with its reflexive pronoun in gender (masculine or feminine) and number (singular or plural) if that pronoun is the *direct object* of the verb. The agreement is determined by looking at the subject to see its gender and number, which is the same as its reflexive pronoun. If the reflexive pronoun is the *indirect object*, an agreement is *not* made.

Examples:

to wash oneself / **se laver**

She washed herself. / **Elle s'est lavée.** There is a feminine agreement on the past participle **lavée** (added **e**) with the reflexive pronoun **se** (here, **s'**) because it serves as a direct object pronoun. What or whom did she wash? Herself, which is expressed in **se (s').**

But:

She washed her hair. / **Elle s'est lavé les cheveux.** There is no feminine agreement on the past participle **lavé** here because the reflexive pronoun (**se**, here, **s'**) serves as an *indirect object*. The direct object is **les cheveux** and it is stated *after* the verb. What did she wash? She washed her hair *on herself (s').*

Review reflexive verbs in Work Unit 7. Review **se laver** and other reflexive verbs, in the verb tables. *See also* reflexive pronoun and reflexive verb.

Agreement of past participle with its preceding direct object

Agreement is made on the past participle with its direct object in gender (masculine or feminine) and number (singular or plural) when the verb is conjugated with **avoir** in the compound tenses. Agreement is made when the direct object, if there is one, *precedes* the verb.

Examples:

Where are the little cakes? Paul ate them. / **Où sont les petits gâteaux? Paul les a mangés.** The verb **a mangés** is in the *passé composé*; **manger** is conjugated with **avoir**. There is a plural agreement on the past participle **mangés** (added **s**) because the *preceding* direct object *them/les* is masculine plural, referring to *les petits gâteaux,* which is masculine plural.

Who wrote the letters? Robert wrote them. / **Qui a écrit les lettres? Robert les a écrites.** The verb **a écrites** is in the *passé composé*; **écrire** is conjugated with **avoir**. There is a feminine plural agreement on the past participle **écrites** (added **e** and **s**) because the *preceding* direct object *them/les* is feminine plural, referring to *les lettres*, which is feminine plural. A past participle functions as an adjective. An agreement in gender and number is *not* made with *an indirect object. See* indirect object noun, indirect object pronoun.

Review the **passé composé** in Work Units 12 and 13. Review **écrire, être, manger** in the verb tables. *See also* direct object noun, direct object pronoun.

Agreement of past participle with the subject

Agreement is made on the past participle with the subject in gender (masculine or feminine) and number (singular or plural) when the verb is conjugated with **être** in the compound tenses.

Examples:

She went to Paris. / **Elle est allée à Paris.** The verb **est allée** is in the *passé composé*; **aller** is conjugated with **être**. There is a feminine agreement on the past participle **allée** (added **e**) because the subject **elle** is feminine singular.

The boys have arrived. / **Les garçons sont arrivés.** The verb **sont arrivés** is in the *passé composé*; **arriver** is conjugated with **être**. There is a plural agreement on the past participle **arrivés** (added **s**) because the subject **les garçons** is masculine plural. Review Work Unit 12 to find out about verbs conjugated with either **avoir** or **être** to form the **passé composé** tense. Review **aller** and **arriver** in the verb tables. *See also* past participle and subject.

Agreement of verb with its subject

A verb agrees in person (1st, 2nd, or 3rd) and in number (singular or plural) with its subject.

Examples:

Does he always tell the truth? / **Dit-il toujours la vérité?** The verb **dit** (of **dire**) is third person singular because the subject **il**/*he* is third person singular.

Where are they going? / **Où vont-ils?** The verb **vont** (of **aller**) is third person plural because the subject **ils**/*they* is third person plural. Review **aller** and **dire** in the verb tables. For subject pronouns in the singular and plural, review Work Unit 4.

Antecedent

An antecedent is a word to which a relative pronoun refers. It comes *before* the pronoun.

Examples:

The girl who is laughing over there is my sister. / **La jeune fille qui rit là-bas est ma soeur.** The antecedent is *girl*/**la jeune fille.** The relative pronoun *who*/**qui** refers to the girl.

The car that I bought is expensive. / **La voiture que j'ai achetée est chère.** The antecedent is *car*/**la voiture.** The relative pronoun *that*/**que** refers to the car. Note also that the past participle **achetée** is feminine singular because it refers to *la voiture* (fem. sing.), which precedes the verb. Review **acheter** and **rire** in the verb tables. *See also* relative pronoun.

Auxiliary verb

An auxiliary verb is a helping verb. In English grammar it is *to have.* In French grammar it is **avoir** (to have) or **être** (to be). An auxiliary verb is used to help form the **passé composé** tense.

Examples:

I have eaten. / **J'*ai* mangé.**   She has left. / **Elle *est* partie.**

Review Work Unit 12 to find out about verbs conjugated with either **avoir** or **être** as helping verbs to form the **passé composé.** Also, review **manger** and **partir** in the verb tables.

Cardinal number

A cardinal number is a number that expresses an amount, such as *one, two, three,* and so on. Review Work Unit 8. *See also* ordinal number.

Causative *faire*

In English grammar, a causative verb causes something to be done. In French grammar the idea is the same. The subject of the verb causes the action expressed in the verb to be carried out by someone else.

Examples:

Mrs. Roth makes her students work in French class. / **Madame Roth fait travailler ses élèves dans la classe de français.**

Mr. Reis is having a house built. / **Monsieur Reis fait construire une maison.**

Review **construire, faire,** and **travailler** in the verb tables.

Clause

A clause is a group of words that contains a subject and a predicate. A predicate may contain more than one word. A conjugated verb form is revealed in the predicate.

Example:

Mrs. Coty lives in a small apartment. / **Madame Coty demeure dans un petit appartement.**

The subject is *Mrs. Coty/**Madame Coty***. The predicate is *lives in a small apartment/**demeure dans un petit appartement***. The verb is *lives/**demeure***.

See also dependent clause, independent clause, predicate.

Comparative adjective

When making a comparison between two persons or things, an adjective is used to express the degree of comparison in the following ways.

Examples:

Of the same degree of comparison:

Raymond is *as tall as* his father. / **Raymond est *aussi grand que* son père.**

Of a lesser degree of comparison:

Monique is *less intelligent than* her sister. / **Monique est *moins intelligente que* sa soeur.**

Of a higher degree of comparison:

This apple is *more delicious than* that apple. / **Cette pomme-ci est *plus délicieuse que* cette pomme-là.**

Review comparative and superlative adjectives in Work Unit 19. *See also* superlative adjective.

Comparative adverb

An adverb is compared in the same way as an adjective is compared. *See* comparative adjective.

Examples:

Of the same degree of comparison:

Mr. Bernard speaks *as fast as* Mr. Claude. / **Monsieur Bernard parle *aussi vite que* Monsieur Claude.**

Of a lesser degree of comparison:

Alice studies *less seriously than* her sister. / **Alice étudie *moins sérieusement que* sa soeur.**

Of a higher degree of comparison:

Albert works *more slowly than* his brother. / **Albert travaille *plus lentement que* son frère.**

Review comparative and superlative adverbs in Work Unit 20. Review **étudier, parler, travailler** in the verb tables. *See also* superlative adverb.

Complex sentence

A complex sentence contains one independent clause and one or more dependent clauses.

Examples:

One independent clause and one dependent clause:

Jack is handsome but his brother isn't. / **Jacques est beau mais son frère ne l'est pas.** The independent clause is *Jack is handsome.* It makes sense when it stands alone because it expresses a complete thought. The dependent clause is *but his brother isn't.* The dependent clause, which is introduced by the conjunction *but*, does not make complete sense when it stands alone because it *depends* on the thought expressed in the independent clause.

One independent clause and two dependent clauses:

Mary gets good grades in school because she studies but her sister never studies. / **Marie reçoit de bonnes notes à l'école parce qu'elle étudie mais sa soeur n'étudie jamais.** The independent clause is *Mary gets good grades in school.* It makes sense when it stands alone because it expresses a complete thought. The first dependent clause is *because she studies.* This dependent clause, which is introduced by the conjunction *because*, does not make complete sense when it stands alone because it *depends* on the thought expressed in the independent clause. The second dependent clause is *but her sister never studies.* That dependent clause, which is introduced by the conjunction *but*, does not make complete sense either when it stands alone because it *depends* on the thought expressed in the independent clause. Review **étudier** and **recevoir** in the verb tables. *See also* dependent clause, independent clause.

Compound sentence

A compound sentence contains two or more independent clauses.

Example:

Mrs. Dubois went to the supermarket, she bought some groceries, and then she returned home. / **Madame Dubois est allée au supermarché, elle a acheté des provisions, et puis elle est rentrée chez elle.** This compound sentence contains three independent clauses. They are independent because they make sense when they stand alone. Review the **passé composé** in Work Unit 12. Review **acheter, aller, rentrer** in the verb tables. *See also* clause, independent clause.

Conjugation

The conjugation of a verb is the fixed order of all its forms showing their inflections (changes) in the three persons of the singular and the three persons of the plural in a particular tense.

In French there are three major types of regular verb conjugations:

> 1st conjugation type: regular verbs that end in **er**, for example, **donner**.
>
> 2nd conjugation type: regular verbs that end in **ir**, for example, **finir**.
>
> 3rd conjugation type: regular verbs that end in **re**, for example, **vendre**.

Review Work Units 4, 5, 6. Review also the verb tables for the conjugation of verbs used in this book.

Conjunction

A conjunction is a word that connects words or groups of words.

Examples:

and/**et**, or/**ou**, but/**mais**

You *and* I are going downtown. / **Toi *et* moi, nous allons en ville.**

You can stay home *or* you can come with us. / **Tu peux rester à la maison *ou* tu peux venir avec nous.**

Review **aller, pouvoir, rester, venir** in the verb tables.

Declarative sentence

A declarative sentence makes a statement.

Example:

I have finished the work. / **J'ai fini le travail.**

Review the **passé composé** in Work Unit 12. Review **finir** in the verb tables.

Definite article

The definite article in French has four forms and they all mean *the.*

They are: **le, la, l', les,** as in:

le livre/the book, **la maison**/the house, **l'école**/the school, **les enfants**/the children

Review Work Units 1, 2, 3. The definite articles are also used as direct object pronouns. *See* direct object pronoun.

Demonstrative adjective

A demonstrative adjective is an adjective that points out. It is placed in front of a noun.

Examples:

this book/**ce livre;** this hotel/**cet hôtel;** this child/**cet enfant;** this house/**cette maison;** these flowers/**ces fleurs**

Review Work Unit 19.

Demonstrative pronoun

A demonstrative pronoun is a pronoun that points out. It takes the place of a noun. It agrees in gender and number with the noun it replaces.

Examples:

I have two apples; do you prefer *this one* or *that one?* / **J'ai deux pommes; préférez-vous *celle-ci* ou *celle-là*?**

Sorry, but I prefer *those.* / **Je regrette, mais je préfère *celles-là*.**

Do you like the ones that are on the table? / **Aimez-vous celles qui sont sur la table?**

Review **aimer, avoir, être, préférer, regretter** in the verb tables. For demonstrative pronouns that are neuter, *see* neuter.

Dependent clause

A dependent clause is a group of words that contains a subject and a predicate. It does not express a complete thought when it stands alone. It is called *dependent* because it depends on the independent clause for a complete meaning. Subordinate clause is another term for dependent clause.

Example:

Mary is absent today because she is sick. / **Marie est absente aujourd'hui parce qu'elle est malade.** The independent clause is *Mary is absent today.* The dependent clause is *because she is sick.* Review **être** in the verb tables. *See also* clause, independent clause.

Descriptive adjective

A descriptive adjective is an adjective that describes a person, place, or thing.

Examples:

a pretty girl/**une jolie jeune fille;** a handsome boy/**un beau garçon;** a small house/**une petite maison;** a big city/**une grande ville;** an expensive car/**une voiture chère.**

Review Work Unit 18. *See also* adjective.

Direct object noun

A direct object noun receives the action of the verb *directly*. That is why it is called a *direct* object, as opposed to an indirect object. A direct object noun is normally placed *after* the verb.

Examples:

I am writing a letter. / **J'écris une lettre.** The subject is *I/J' (Je).* The verb is *am writing/écris.* The direct object is the noun *letter/une lettre.*

I wrote a letter. / **J'ai écrit une lettre.** The subject is *I/J' (Je).* The verb is *wrote/ai écrit.* The direct object is the noun *letter/une lettre.*

Review Work Unit 13. Also, review **écrire** in the verb tables. *See also* direct object pronoun.

Direct object pronoun

A direct object pronoun receives the action of the verb *directly.* It takes the place of a direct object noun. In French a pronoun that is a direct object of a verb is ordinarily placed *in front of* the verb.

Example:

I am reading it [the letter]. / **Je *la* lis.**

A direct object pronoun is placed *after* the verb and joined with a hyphen *in the affirmative imperative.*

Example:

Write it [the letter] now. / **Écrivez-*la* maintenant.**

Review Work Unit 13. Also, review **écrire** and **lire** in the verb tables. The direct object pronouns are summed up here:

Person	Singular		Plural	
1st	**me (m')**	me	**nous**	us
2nd	**te (t')**	you *(fam.)*	**vous**	you (sing. polite or pl.)
3rd	**le (l')**	him, it (person or thing)	**les**	them (persons or things)
	la (l')	her, it (person or thing)		

See also imperative. Review the imperative (command) in Work Units 10 and 11. Also, review word order in a sentence in Work Unit 14.

Disjunctive pronoun

In French grammar a disjunctive pronoun is a pronoun that is stressed; in other words, emphasis is placed on it.

Examples:

I speak well; *he* does not speak well. / *Moi,* **je parle bien;** *lui,* **il ne parle pas bien.**

Talk to me. / **Parlez-***moi.*

A disjunctive pronoun is also object of a preposition.

Examples:

She is talking with me. / **Elle parle** *avec moi.*

I always think of you. / **Je pense toujours** *à toi.*

The disjunctive pronouns are summed up here:

Person	Singular		Plural	
1st	**moi**	me	**nous**	us
2nd	**toi**	you *(fam.)*	**vous**	you (sing. polite or pl.)
3rd	**soi** **lui** **elle**	oneself him, he her, she	**eux** **elles**	them, they *(m.)* them, they *(f.)*

Review **parler** and **penser** in the verb tables. Review Work Unit 17. Also review word order in a sentence in Work Unit 14.

Ending of a verb

In French grammar the ending of a verb form changes according to the person and number of the subject and the tense of the verb.

Example:

To form the present indicative tense of a regular **-er** type verb like **parler,** drop the **er** ending of the infinitive and add the following endings: **-e, -es, -e** for the first, second, and third persons of the singular; **-ons, -ez, -ent** for the first, second, and third persons of the plural.

You then get: **je parle, tu parles, il (elle, on) parle;**
        nous parlons, vous parlez, ils (elles) parlent

Review Work Units 4, 5, 6. Review **parler** in the verb tables. *See also* stem of a verb.

Feminine

In French grammar the gender of a noun, pronoun, or adjective is feminine or masculine, not female or male.

Examples:

Masculine			Feminine		
noun	**pronoun**	**adjective**	**noun**	**pronoun**	**adjective**
le garçon	**il**	**grand**	**la femme**	**elle**	**grande**
the boy	*he*	*tall*	*the woman*	*she*	*tall*
le livre	**il**	**petit**	**la voiture**	**elle**	**petite**
the book	*it*	*small*	*the car*	*it*	*small*

See also gender.

Gender

In French and English grammar, gender means masculine or feminine.

Examples:

Masculine: the boy/**le garçon;** he, it/**il;** the rooster/**le coq;** the book/**le livre**

Feminine: the girl/**la jeune fille;** she, it/**elle;** the hen/**la poule;** the house/**la maison**

Gerund

In English grammar, a gerund is a word formed from a verb. It ends in *ing.* Actually, it is the present participle of a verb. But it is not used as a verb. It is used as a noun.

Example:

Seeing is believing. / **Voir c'est croire.**

However, in French grammar, the infinitive form of the verb is used, as in the preceding example, when the verb is used as a noun. In French, *seeing is believing* is expressed as *to see is to believe.*

The French gerund is also a word formed from a verb. It ends in ***ant.*** It is also the present participle of a verb. As a gerund, it is normally preceded by the preposition **en.**

Example:

En partant, il a fait ses excuses. / While leaving, he made his excuses.

Review **faire** and **partir** in the verb tables. *See also* present participle.

Imperative

The imperative is a mood, not a tense. It is used to express a command. In French it is used in the second person of the singular **(tu),** the second person of the plural **(vous),** and in the first person of the plural **(nous).** Review the imperative (command) with examples in Work Units 10 and 11. *See also* person (1st, 2nd, 3rd).

Indefinite article

In English the indefinite articles are *a, an*, as in *a book, an apple.* They are indefinite because they do not refer to any definite or particular noun.

In French there are two indefinite articles in the singular: one in the masculine form **(un)** and one in the feminine form **(une).**

Examples:

Masculine singular: **un livre**/*a book*

Feminine singular: **une pomme**/*an apple*

In French they both change to **des** in the plural.

Examples:

I have a brother. / **J'ai un frère;** I have brothers. / **J'ai des frères.**

I have a sister. / **J'ai une soeur;** I have sisters. / **J'ai des soeurs.**

I have an apple. / **J'ai une pomme;** I have apples. / **J'ai des pommes.**

Review Work Units 1, 2, 3. Review **avoir** in the verb tables. *See also* definite article.

Indefinite pronoun

An indefinite pronoun is a pronoun that does not refer to any definite or particular noun.

Examples:

something/**quelque chose;** someone, somebody/**quelqu'un, quelqu'une;** one, "they"/**on** (3rd pers., sing.), as in **On ne sait jamais**/One never knows; **On dit qu'il va neiger**/They say it's going to snow; each one/**chacun, chacune;** anything/**n'importe quoi.**

Independent clause

An independent clause is a group of words that contains a subject and a predicate. It expresses a complete thought when it stands alone.

Example:

The cat is sleeping under the bed. / **Le chat dort sous le lit.**

Review **dormir** in the verb tables. *See also* clause, dependent clause, predicate.

Indicative mood

The indicative mood is used in sentences that make a statement or ask a question. The indicative mood is used most of the time when we speak or write in English or French.

Examples:

I am going home now. / **Je vais chez moi maintenant.**

Where are you going? / **Où allez-vous?**

Review **aller** in the verb tables.

Indirect object noun

An indirect object noun receives the action of the verb *indirectly*.

Example:

I am writing a letter to Mary *or* I am writing Mary a letter. / **J'écris une lettre à Marie.**

The subject is *I/**Je**. The verb is *am writing/**écris**. The direct object noun is *a letter/**une lettre**. The indirect object noun is *to Mary/**à Marie**. An agreement is not made with an indirect object noun. Review Work Unit 14. *See also* indirect object pronoun, direct object noun, direct object pronoun.

Indirect object pronoun

An indirect object pronoun takes the place of an indirect object noun. It receives the action of the verb *indirectly*. In French a pronoun that is the indirect object of a verb is ordinarily placed *in front of* the verb.

Example:

I am writing a letter to her *or* I am writing her a letter. / **Je lui écris une lettre.** The indirect object pronoun is *(to) her/**lui**.

An agreement is not made with an indirect object pronoun. An indirect object pronoun is placed *after* the verb and joined with a hyphen *in the affirmative imperative.*

Example:

Write to her now. / **Écris-lui maintenant.**

The indirect object pronouns are summed up below:

Person	Singular		Plural	
1st	**me (m')**	to me	**nous**	to us
2nd	**te (t')**	to you *(fam.)*	**vous**	to you (sing. polite or pl.)
3rd	**lui**	to him, to her	**leur**	to them

Review Work Unit 14. Also review the imperative (command) in Work Units 10 and 11. *See also* indirect object noun.

Infinitive

An infinitive is a verb form. In English, it is normally stated with the preposition *to*, as in *to talk, to finish, to sell*. In French, the infinitive form of a verb consists of three major types: those of the first conjugation that end in **-er,** those of the second conjugation that end in **-ir,** and those of the third conjugation that end in **-re.**

Examples:

parler/*to talk, to speak*; **finir**/*to finish*; **vendre**/*to sell*

Review these verbs in the verb tables.

Interjection

An interjection is a word that expresses emotion, a feeling of joy, of sadness, an exclamation of surprise, and other exclamations consisting of one or two words.

Examples:

Ah!/**Ah!**   Oh!/**Oh!**   Darn it!/**Zut!**   Whew!/**Ouf!**   My God!/**Mon Dieu!**

Interrogative adjective

An interrogative adjective is an adjective used in a question. It agrees in gender and number with the noun it modifies.

Examples:

What book do you want? / ***Quel* livre désirez-vous?**

What time is it? / ***Quelle* heure est-il?**

Review Work Unit 19. Also, review **désirer** and **être** in the verb tables.

Interrogative adverb

An interrogative adverb is an adverb that introduces a question. As an adverb, it modifies the verb.

Examples:

How are you? / ***Comment* allez-vous?**

How much does this book cost? / ***Combien* coûte ce livre?**

When are you leaving? / ***Quand* partez-vous?**

Review **aller, coûter, partir** in the verb tables.

Interrogative pronoun

An interrogative pronoun is a pronoun that asks a question. There are interrogative pronouns that refer to persons and those that refer to things.

Examples:

Who is on the phone? / *Qui* **est à l'appareil?**

What are you saying? / *Que* **dites-vous?** or *Qu'est-ce* **que vous dites?**

Review Work Unit 15. Also, review **dire, être** in the verb tables.

Interrogative sentence

An interrogative sentence asks a question.

Example:

What are you doing? / **Que faites-vous?** or **Qu'est-ce que vous faites?**

Review Work Unit 15. Also, review **faire** in the verb tables.

Intransitive verb

An intransitive verb is a verb that does not take a direct object.

Example:

The professor is talking too fast. / **Le professeur parle trop rapidement.**

An intransitive verb takes an indirect object.

Example:

The professor is talking to us. / **Le professeur nous parle.**

Review **parler** in the verb tables. *See also* indirect object pronoun, transitive verb.

Irregular verb

An irregular verb is a verb that does not follow a fixed pattern in its conjugation in the various verb tenses.

Examples of basic irregular verbs in French:

aller/to go   **avoir**/to have   **être**/to be   **faire**/to do, to make

Review irregular verbs in the present indicative tense and the imperative (command) in Work Unit 11. Review the verb tables. *See also* conjugation, regular verb.

Limiting adjective

A limiting adjective is an adjective that limits a quantity.

Example:

three tickets/**trois billets**

Review numbers in Work Unit 8.

Main clause

Main clause is another term for independent clause. *See* independent clause.

Masculine

In French grammar the gender of a noun, pronoun, or adjective is masculine or feminine, not male or female. For examples, *see* gender.

Mood of verbs

Some grammarians use the term *the mode* instead of *the mood* of a verb. Either term means *the manner or way* a verb is expressed. In English and in French grammar, a verb expresses an action or state of being in the following three moods (modes, *ways*): the indicative mood, the imperative mood, and the subjunctive mood. In French grammar, there is also the infinitive mood when the whole infinitive is used, *e.g.*, **voir, croire,** as in **Voir c'est croire** / *Seeing is believing (to see is to believe).* Most of the time in English and French, we speak and write in the indicative mood.

Negative statement, affirmative statement

See affirmative statement, negative statement.

Neuter

A word that is neuter is neither masculine nor feminine. Common neuter demonstrative pronouns are **ce (c')**/*it*, **ceci**/*this*, **cela**/*that*, **ça**/*that*. They are invariable, which means they do not change in gender and number.

Examples:

It's not true/**Ce n'est pas vrai;** it is true/**c'est vrai;** this is true/**ceci est vrai;** that is true/**cela est vrai;** what is that?/**qu'est-ce que c'est que ça?**

For demonstrative pronouns that are not neuter, *see* demonstrative pronoun.

There is also the neuter pronoun **le**, as in **Je le crois** / I believe it; **Je le pense** / I think so.

Review Work Unit 16.

Noun

A noun is a word that names a person, animal, place, thing, condition or state, or quality.

Examples:

the man/**l'homme,** the woman/**la femme,** the horse/**le cheval,** the house/**la maison,**

the book/**le livre,** happiness/**le bonheur,** excellence/**l'excellence** *(fem.)*

In French the noun **le nom** is the word for name and noun. Review Work Units 1, 2, 3.

Number

In English and French grammar, number means singular or plural.

Examples:

Masc. sing.:	the boy/**le garçon**; the arm/**le bras**; the eye/**l'oeil**
Masc. pl.:	the boys/**les garçons**; the arms/**les bras**; the eyes/**les yeux**
Fem. sing.:	the girl/**la jeune fille**; the house/**la maison**; the hen/**la poule**
Fem. pl.:	the girls/**les jeunes filles**; the houses/**les maisons**; the hens/**les poules**

Ordinal number

An ordinal number expresses position in a series, such as *first, second, third*, and so on. In English and French grammar we talk about first person, second person, third person singular or plural regarding subjects and verbs. Review the ordinal numbers in Work Unit 8. *See also* cardinal number, and person (1st, 2nd, 3rd).

Orthographical changes in verb forms

An orthographical change in a verb form is a change in spelling.

Examples:

The second letter **c** in the verb **commencer**/*to begin* changes to **ç** if the letter after it is **a, o,** or **u,** as in *nous commençons/we begin.* The reason for this spelling change is to preserve the sound of *s* as it is pronounced in the infinitive form **commencer.**

Ordinarily, when **a, o,** or **u** follow the letter **c,** the **c** is pronounced as in the sound of **k.** The mark under the letter **ç** is called **une cédille**/*cedilla.* Some linguists say it is the lower part of the letter **s** and it tells you to pronounce **ç** as an **s** sound. Other linguists say that the letter **ç** was borrowed from the Greek alphabet, which represents the sound of **s.**

The verb **s'appeler**/*to call oneself, to be named* contains a single **l.** When a verb form is stressed on the syllable containing one **l,** it doubles, as in **je m'appelle.../***I call myself..., my name is...*

Review orthographically changing verbs in Work Unit 22.

Partitive

In French grammar the partitive denotes a *part* of a whole. In English we express the partitive by saying *some* or *any* in front of the noun. In French we use the following partitive forms in front of the noun:

Masculine singular: **du** or **de l'**   *Feminine singular:* **de la** or **de l'**

Masculine or feminine plural: **des**

Examples:

I have some coffee. / **J'ai du café.**

Bring me some water, please. / **Apportez-moi de l'eau, s'il vous plaît.**

Is there any meat? / **Y a-t-il de la viande?**

Do you have any candies? / **Avez-vous des bonbons?**

In the negative, these partitive forms change to **de** or **d'**:

I don't have any coffee. / **Je n'ai pas de café.**

I don't want any water. / **Je ne veux pas d'eau.**

There isn't any meat. / **Il n'y a pas de viande.**

No, I don't have any candies. / **Non, je n'ai pas de bonbons.**

Review the partitive in Work Unit 3.

Passé composé

The name of a commonly used past tense is the **passé composé.** It is defined with examples in French and English in Work Units 12, 13, 14.

Passive voice

When we speak or write in the active voice and change to the passive voice, the direct object becomes the subject, the subject becomes the object of a preposition, and the verb becomes *to be* plus the past participle of the active verb. The past participle functions as an adjective.

Example:

Janine is loved by everyone. / **Janine est aimée de tout le monde.** The subject is *Janine.* The verb is *is*/**est.** The object of the preposition *by*/**de** is *everyone*/**tout le monde.** *See also* active voice. Compare the preceding sentence with the example in the active voice.

Past indefinite tense

In French this tense is the **passé composé.** Review it in Work Units 12, 13, 14.

Past participle

A past participle is derived from a verb. It is used to form the compound tenses, for example, the **passé composé.** Its auxiliary verb in English is *to have.* In French, the auxiliary verb is **avoir**/*to have* or **être**/*to be.* It is part of the verb tense.

Examples:

with **avoir** as the auxiliary verb:

Elle a mangé. / She has eaten. The subject is *elle*/*she.* The verb is *a mangé*/*has eaten.* The tense of the verb is the **passé composé.** The auxiliary verb is *a*/*has.* The past participle is *mangé*/*eaten.*

with **être** as the auxiliary verb:

Elle est arrivée. / She has arrived. The verb is *est arrivée*/*has arrived.* The tense of the verb is the **passé composé.** The auxiliary verb is *est*/*has.* The past participle is *arrivée*/*arrived.*

Review Work Unit 12 for the regular formation of a past participle and a list of commonly used irregular past participles. In Work Unit 12 you can also find out about which verbs are conjugated with either **avoir** or **être** to form the **passé composé.**

Person (1st, 2nd, 3rd)

Verb forms in a particular tense are learned systematically according to person (1st, 2nd, 3rd) and number (singular, plural).

Example, showing the present indicative tense of the verb **aller**/to go:

Singular		Plural	
1st person:	**je vais**	1st person:	**nous allons**
2nd person:	**tu vas**	2nd person:	**vous allez**
3rd person:	**il, elle va**	3rd person:	**ils, elles vont**

Personal pronoun

A personal pronoun refers to a person. Review the personal subject pronouns in Work Unit 4. For examples of other types of pronouns, *see also* demonstrative pronoun, direct object pronoun, disjunctive pronoun, indefinite pronoun, indirect object pronoun, interrogative pronoun, reflexive pronoun, relative pronoun.

Plural

Plural means more than one. *See also* person (1st, 2nd, 3rd), and singular.

Possessive adjective

A possessive adjective is an adjective that is placed in front of a noun to show possession. In French their forms change in gender (masculine or feminine) and number (singular or plural) to agree with the noun they modify.

Examples:

my book/**mon livre**   my books/**mes livres**

my dress/**ma robe**   my dresses/**mes robes**

Review them all in Work Unit 18.

Predicate

The predicate is that part of the sentence that tells us something about the subject. The main word of the predicate is the verb.

Example:

The tourists are waiting for the tour bus. / **Les touristes attendent l'autocar.**

The subject is *the tourists/**les touristes**.* The predicate is *are waiting for the tour bus/**attendent l'autocar**.* The verb is *are waiting/**attendent**.* The direct object is *the tour bus/l'autocar.* Review **attendre** in the verb tables.

Preposition

A preposition is a word that establishes a rapport between words.

Examples: with, in, on, at, between

with me/*avec* moi   *in* the drawer/*dans* le tiroir   *on* the table/*sur* la table

at six o'clock/*à* six heures   *between* him and her/*entre* lui et elle

Review prepositions in Work Unit 23.

Present indicative tense

This is a commonly used tense. It is defined with examples in French and English in Work Units 4, 5, 6.

Present participle

A present participle is derived from a verb form. In French it is regularly formed like this: Take the **nous** form of the present indicative tense of the verb you have in mind, then drop the ending **ons** and add **ant.** In English a present participle ends in *ing.*

Examples:

Infinitive	Present Indicative **nous** form	Present participle
chanter to sing	**nous chantons** we sing	**chantant** singing
finir to finish	**nous finissons** we finish	**finissant** finishing
vendre to sell	**nous vendons** we sell	**vendant** selling

Review these three verbs in the verb tables. Regular and irregular present participles are given in the verb tables also.

Pronoun

A pronoun is a word that takes the place of a noun.

Examples:

l'homme/*il* the man/*he*	**la femme/***elle* the woman/*she*	**l'arbre/***il* the tree/*it*	**la voiture/***elle* the car/*it*

For examples of other kinds of pronouns, *see also* demonstrative pronoun, direct object pronoun, disjunctive pronoun, indefinite pronoun, indirect object pronoun, interrogative pronoun, reflexive pronoun, relative pronoun.

Reflexive pronoun and reflexive verb

In English a reflexive pronoun is a personal pronoun that contains *self* or *selves*. In French and English a reflexive pronoun is used with a verb that is called reflexive because the action of the verb falls on the reflexive pronoun.

In French, as in English, there is a required set of reflexive pronouns for a reflexive verb.

Examples:

se laver/to wash oneself   **Je me lave.** / I wash myself.

se blesser/to hurt oneself   **Elle s'est blessée.** / She hurt herself.

In French a reflexive verb is conjugated with **être** to form a compound tense. The French term for a reflexive verb is **un verbe pronominal** because a pronoun goes with the verb.

Review the reflexive verbs **s'appeler, se blesser, se laver,** and **se lever** in the verb tables. Review reflexive verbs in Work Units 7 and 10. *See also* agreement of past participle of a reflexive verb with its reflexive pronoun.

Regular verb

A regular verb is a verb that is conjugated in the various tenses according to a fixed pattern. For examples, review regular **er, ir,** and **re** verbs in the present indicative tense in Work Units 4, 5, 6. *See also* conjugation, irregular verb.

Relative pronoun

A relative pronoun is a pronoun that refers to its antecedent.

Example:

The girl who is laughing over there is my sister. / **La jeune fille qui rit là-bas est ma soeur.** The antecedent is *girl*/*la jeune fille*. The relative pronoun *who*/*qui* refers to the girl.

Review **rire** in the verb tables. *See also* antecedent.

Sentence

A sentence is a group of words that contains a subject and a predicate. The verb is contained in the predicate. A sentence expresses a complete thought.

Example:

The train leaves from the North Station at two o'clock in the afternoon. / **Le train part de la Gare du Nord à deux heures de l'après-midi.** The subject is *train*/*le train*. The predicate is *leaves from the North Station at two o'clock in the afternoon*/*part de la Gare du Nord à deux heures de l'après-midi*. The verb is *leaves*/*part*.

Review **partir** in the verb tables. *See also* complex sentence, compound sentence, simple sentence.

Simple sentence

A simple sentence is a sentence that contains one subject and one predicate. The verb is the core of the predicate. The verb is the most important word in a sentence because it tells us what the subject is doing.

Example:

Mary is eating an apple from her garden. / **Marie mange une pomme de son jardin.** The subject is *Mary*/*Marie*. The predicate is *is eating an apple from her garden*/*mange une pomme de son jardin*. The verb is *is eating*/*mange*. The direct object is *an apple*/*une pomme*. From her *garden*/*de son jardin* is an adverbial phrase. It tells you where the apple came from.

Review **manger** in the verb tables. *See also* complex sentence, compound sentence.

Singular

Singular means one. *See also* person (1st, 2nd, 3rd), and plural.

Stem of a verb

The stem of a verb is what is left after we drop the ending of its infinitive form. It is added to the required endings of a regular verb in a particular verb tense.

Examples:

Infinitive	Ending of infinitive	Stem
donner/to give	**er**	**donn**
choisir/to choose	**ir**	**chois**
vendre/to sell	**re**	**vend**

Review Work Units 4, 5, 6. Review **choisir, donner, vendre** in the verb tables. *See also* ending of a verb.

Subject

A subject is that part of a sentence that is related to its verb. The verb says something about the subject.

Examples:

Mary and Catherine are beautiful. / **Marie et Catherine sont belles.**

Peter and Paul are handsome. / **Pierre et Paul sont beaux.**

Subjunctive mood

The subjunctive mood of a verb is used in specific cases, *e.g.*, after certain verbs expressing a wish, doubt, emotion, fear, joy, uncertainty, an indefinite expression, an indefinite antecedent, certain conjunctions, and others, for example, in the imperative mood of **avoir** and **être.** Review the present subjunctive in the imperative mood of **avoir** and **être** in Work Unit 11. *See also* mood of verbs.

Subordinate clause

Subordinate clause is another term for dependent clause. *See* dependent clause.

Superlative adjective

A superlative adjective is an adjective that expresses the highest degree when making a comparison of more than two persons or things.

Examples:

	Adjective	Comparative	Superlative
(masc.)	**bon**/good	**meilleur**/better	**le meilleur**/(the) best
(fem.)	**bonne**/good	**meilleure**/better	**la meilleure**/(the) best
(masc.)	**mauvais**/bad	**plus mauvais**/worse	**le plus mauvais**/(the) worst
(fem.)	**mauvaise**/bad	**plus mauvaise**/worse	**la plus mauvaise**/(the) worst

Review Work Unit 19. *See also* comparative adjective.

Superlative adverb

A superlative adverb is an adverb that expresses the highest degree when making a comparison of more than two persons or things.

Example:

Adverb	Comparative	Superlative
vite/quickly	**plus vite**/more quickly	**le plus vite**/most quickly
	moins vite/less quickly	**le moins vite**/least quickly

Review Work Unit 20. *See also* comparative adverb.

Tense of verb

In English and French grammar, tense means time. The tense of the verb indicates the time of the action or state of being. The three major segments of time are past, present, and future. Review the verb tables.

Transitive verb

A transitive verb is a verb that takes a direct object.

Example:

I am closing the window. / **Je ferme la fenêtre.** The subject is *I*/*Je.* The verb is *am closing*/*ferme.* The direct object is *the window*/*la fenêtre.* Review **fermer** in the verb tables. *See also* intransitive verb.

Verb

A verb is a word that expresses action or a state of being.

Examples:

> *Action:* **Nous sommes allés au cinéma hier soir** / We went to the movies last night.
> The verb is *sommes allés* / *went*.

> *State of being:* **La jeune fille est heureuse** / The girl is happy.
> The verb is *est* / *is*.

Review **aller** and **être** in the verb tables.

French Verb Conjugation Tables

Regular and irregular verbs in these tables are presented alphabetically in Part A. Reflexive verbs are in Part B. They are arranged separately by the reflexive pronoun **se** or **s'** plus the verb so you can see them all in one place, in alphabetical order. In this way, you can make your own observations about their repeated patterns. All verbs given here are used in this book.

For the various translations into English of the **présent de l'indicatif,** review Work Unit 4.

For the translation into English of the **impératif** (imperative, command), of reflexive and nonreflexive verbs in the affirmative and negative, review Work Units 10 and 11.

For the various translations into English of the **passé composé,** review Work Unit 12.

In the **passé composé,** the vowel **e** in parentheses denotes a feminine agreement if required; **s** in parentheses denotes a plural agreement if required.

For orthographical (spelling) changes in verb forms, review Work Unit 22.

The abbreviation *pr. part.* denotes *present participle*; *past part.* denotes *past participle.* See these two terms in the section on Definitions of Basic Grammatical Terms with Examples.

In the Imperative (Command), the first verb form is 2nd pers., sing. **(tu)**; the second verb form is 1st pers., pl. **(nous)**/let's...; the third verb form is 2nd pers., pl. or sing. **(vous).**

Examples:

In the Affirmative Imperative

danser/to dance	**finir**/to finish	**vendre**/to sell
danse/dance!	**finis**/finish!	**vends**/sell!
dansons/let's dance!	**finissons**/let's finish!	**vendons**/let's sell!
dansez/dance!	**finissez**/finish!	**vendez**/sell!

In the Negative Imperative

ne danse pas!	**ne finis pas!**	**ne vends pas!**
ne dansons pas!	**ne finissons pas!**	**ne vendons pas!**
ne dansez pas!	**ne finissez pas!**	**ne vendez pas!**

Part A

acheter/to buy, to purchase   *pr. part.* **achetant**   *past part.* **acheté**

    Singular   Plural

PRESENT INDICATIVE   IMPERATIVE (AFFIRMATIVE)

j'achète	nous achetons	achète
tu achètes	vous achetez	achetons
il/elle achète	ils/elles achètent	achetez

PASSÉ COMPOSÉ   IMPERATIVE (NEGATIVE)

j'ai acheté	nous avons acheté	n'achète pas
tu as acheté	vous avez acheté	n'achetons pas
il/elle a acheté	ils/elles ont acheté	n'achetez pas

---

aimer/to like, to love   *pr. part.* **aimant**   *past part.* **aimé**

    Singular   Plural

PRESENT INDICATIVE   IMPERATIVE (AFFIRMATIVE)

j'aime	nous aimons	aime
tu aimes	vous aimez	aimons
il/elle aime	ils/elles aiment	aimez

PASSÉ COMPOSÉ   IMPERATIVE (NEGATIVE)

j'ai aimé	nous avons aimé	n'aime pas
tu as aimé	vous avez aimé	n'aimons pas
il/elle a aimé	ils/elles ont aimé	n'aimez pas

In this book the conditional of **aimer** is used at times to express courtesy when asking for something: j'aimerais.../I would like...

---

aller/to go   *pr. part.* **allant**   *past part.* **allé**

    Singular   Plural

PRESENT INDICATIVE   IMPERATIVE (AFFIRMATIVE)

je vais	nous allons	va
tu vas	vous allez	allons
il/elle va	ils/elles vont	allez

PASSÉ COMPOSÉ   IMPERATIVE (NEGATIVE)

je suis allé(e)	nous sommes allé(e)s	ne va pas
tu es allé(e)	vous êtes allé(e)(s)	n'allons pas
il est allé	ils sont allés	n'allez pas
elle est allée	elles sont allées	

annoncer/to announce   *pr. part.* **annonçant**   *past part.* **annoncé**

Singular   Plural

PRESENT INDICATIVE   IMPERATIVE (AFFIRMATIVE)

j'annonce   nous annonçons   annonce
tu annonces   vous annoncez   annonçons
il/elle annonce   ils/elles annoncent   annoncez

PASSÉ COMPOSÉ   IMPERATIVE (NEGATIVE)

j'ai annoncé   nous avons annoncé   n'annonce pas
tu as annoncé   vous avez annoncé   n'annonçons pas
il/elle a annoncé   ils/elles ont annoncé   n'annoncez pas

---

appeler/to call   *pr. part.* **appelant**   *past part.* **appelé**

Singular   Plural

PRESENT INDICATIVE   IMPERATIVE (AFFIRMATIVE)

j'appelle   nous appelons   appelle
tu appelles   vous appelez   appelons
il/elle appelle   ils/elles appellent   appelez

PASSÉ COMPOSÉ   IMPERATIVE (NEGATIVE)

j'ai appelé   nous avons appelé   n'appelle pas
tu as appelé   vous avez appelé   n'appelons pas
il/elle a appelé   ils/elles ont appelé   n'appelez pas

---

apporter/to bring   *pr. part.* **apportant**   *past part.* **apporté**

Singular   Plural

PRESENT INDICATIVE   IMPERATIVE (AFFIRMATIVE)

j'apporte   nous apportons   apporte
tu apportes   vous apportez   apportons
il/elle apporte   ils/elles apportent   apportez

PASSÉ COMPOSÉ   IMPERATIVE (NEGATIVE)

j'ai apporté   nous avons apporté   n'apporte pas
tu as apporté   vous avez apporté   n'apportons pas
il/elle a apporté   ils/elles ont apporté   n'apportez pas

---

apprendre/to learn   *pr. part.* **apprenant**   *past part.* **appris**

Singular   Plural

PRESENT INDICATIVE   IMPERATIVE (AFFIRMATIVE)

j'apprends	nous apprenons	apprends
tu apprends	vous apprenez	apprenons
il/elle apprend	ils/elles apprennent	apprenez

PASSÉ COMPOSÉ   IMPERATIVE (NEGATIVE)

j'ai appris	nous avons appris	n'apprends pas
tu as appris	vous avez appris	n'apprenons pas
il/elle a appris	ils/elles ont appris	n'apprenez pas

---

arriver/to arrive   *pr. part.* **arrivant**   *past part.* **arrivé**

Singular   Plural

PRESENT INDICATIVE   IMPERATIVE (AFFIRMATIVE)

j'arrive	nous arrivons	arrive
tu arrives	vous arrivez	arrivons
il/elle arrive	ils/elles arrivent	arrivez

PASSÉ COMPOSÉ   IMPERATIVE (NEGATIVE)

je suis arrivé(e)	nous sommes arrivé(e)s	n'arrive pas
tu es arrivé(e)	vous êtes arrivé(e)(s)	n'arrivons pas
il est arrivé	ils sont arrivés	n'arrivez pas
elle est arrivée	elles sont arrivées	

---

attendre/to wait (for)   *pr. part.* **attendant**   *past part.* **attendu**

Singular   Plural

PRESENT INDICATIVE   IMPERATIVE (AFFIRMATIVE)

j'attends	nous attendons	attends
tu attends	vous attendez	attendons
il/elle attend	ils/elles attendent	attendez

PASSÉ COMPOSÉ   IMPERATIVE (NEGATIVE)

j'ai attendu	nous avons attendu	n'attends pas
tu as attendu	vous avez attendu	n'attendons pas
il/elle a attendu	ils/elles ont attendu	n'attendez pas

513

avoir/to have   *pr. part.* **ayant**   *past part.* **eu**

Singular   Plural

PRESENT INDICATIVE   IMPERATIVE (AFFIRMATIVE)

j'ai	nous avons	aie
tu as	vous avez	ayons
il/elle a	ils/elles ont	ayez

PASSÉ COMPOSÉ   IMPERATIVE (NEGATIVE)

j'ai eu	nous avons eu	n'aie pas
tu as eu	vous avez eu	n'ayons pas
il/elle a eu	ils/elles ont eu	n'ayez pas

---

boire/to drink   *pr. part.* **buvant**   *past part.* **bu**

Singular   Plural

PRESENT INDICATIVE   IMPERATIVE (AFFIRMATIVE)

je bois	nous buvons	bois
tu bois	vous buvez	buvons
il/elle boit	ils/elles boivent	buvez

PASSÉ COMPOSÉ   IMPERATIVE (NEGATIVE)

j'ai bu	nous avons bu	ne bois pas
tu as bu	vous avez bu	ne buvons pas
il/elle a bu	ils/elles ont bu	ne buvez pas

---

chanter/to sing   *pr. part.* **chantant**   *past part.* **chanté**

Singular   Plural

PRESENT INDICATIVE   IMPERATIVE (AFFIRMATIVE)

je chante	nous chantons	chante
tu chantes	vous chantez	chantons
il/elle chante	ils/elles chantent	chantez

PASSÉ COMPOSÉ   IMPERATIVE (NEGATIVE)

j'ai chanté	nous avons chanté	ne chante pas
tu as chanté	vous avez chanté	ne chantons pas
il/elle a chanté	ils/elles ont chanté	ne chantez pas

---

chercher/to look for, search   *pr. part.* **cherchant**   *past part.* **cherché**

Singular   Plural

PRESENT INDICATIVE

		IMPERATIVE (AFFIRMATIVE)
je cherche	nous cherchons	cherche
tu cherches	vous cherchez	cherchons
il/elle cherche	ils/elles cherchent	cherchez

PASSÉ COMPOSÉ

		IMPERATIVE (NEGATIVE)
j'ai cherché	nous avons cherché	ne cherche pas
tu as cherché	vous avez cherché	ne cherchons pas
il/elle a cherché	ils/elles ont cherché	ne cherchez pas

---

choisir/to choose   *pr. part.* **choisissant**   *past part.* **choisi**

Singular   Plural

PRESENT INDICATIVE

		IMPERATIVE (AFFIRMATIVE)
je choisis	nous choisissons	choisis
tu choisis	vous choisissez	choisissons
il/elle choisit	ils/elles choisissent	choisissez

PASSÉ COMPOSÉ

		IMPERATIVE (NEGATIVE)
j'ai choisi	nous avons choisi	ne choisis pas
tu as choisi	vous avez choisi	ne choisissons pas
il/elle a choisi	ils/elles ont choisi	ne choisissez pas

---

commencer/to begin, commence   *pr. part.* **commençant**   *past part.* **commencé**

Singular   Plural

PRESENT INDICATIVE

		IMPERATIVE (AFFIRMATIVE)
je commence	nous commençons	commence
tu commences	vous commencez	commençons
il/elle commence	ils/elles commencent	commencez

PASSÉ COMPOSÉ

		IMPERATIVE (NEGATIVE)
j'ai commencé	nous avons commencé	ne commence pas
tu as commencé	vous avez commencé	ne commençons pas
il/elle a commencé	ils/elles ont commencé	ne commencez pas

---

comprendre/to understand   *pr. part.* **comprenant**   *past part.* **compris**

Singular   Plural

PRESENT INDICATIVE

		IMPERATIVE (AFFIRMATIVE)
je comprends	nous comprenons	comprends
tu comprends	vous comprenez	comprenons
il/elle comprend	ils/elles comprennent	comprenez

PASSÉ COMPOSÉ

		IMPERATIVE (NEGATIVE)
j'ai compris	nous avons compris	ne comprends pas
tu as compris	vous avez compris	ne comprenons pas
il/elle a compris	ils/elles ont compris	ne comprenez pas

---

connaître/to know, be acquainted with   *pr. part.* **connaissant**   *past part.* **connu**

Singular   Plural

PRESENT INDICATIVE

		IMPERATIVE (AFFIRMATIVE)
je connais	nous connaissons	connais
tu connais	vous connaissez	connaissons
il/elle connaît	ils/elles connaissent	connaissez

PASSÉ COMPOSÉ

		IMPERATIVE (NEGATIVE)
j'ai connu	nous avons connu	ne connais pas
tu as connu	vous avez connu	ne connaissons pas
il/elle a connu	ils/elles ont connu	ne connaissez pas

---

construire/to construct, build   *pr. part.* **construisant**   *past part.* **construit**

Singular   Plural

PRESENT INDICATIVE

		IMPERATIVE (AFFIRMATIVE)
je construis	nous construisons	construis
tu construis	vous construisez	construisons
il/elle construit	ils/elles construisent	construisez

PASSÉ COMPOSÉ

		IMPERATIVE (NEGATIVE)
j'ai construit	nous avons construit	ne construis pas
tu as construit	vous avez construit	ne construisons pas
il/elle a construit	ils/elles ont construit	ne construisez pas

---

corriger/to correct	*pr. part.* corrigeant	*past part.* corrigé

Singular	Plural	

PRESENT INDICATIVE		IMPERATIVE (AFFIRMATIVE)
je corrige	nous corrigeons	corrige
tu corriges	vous corrigez	corrigeons
il/elle corrige	ils/elles corrigent	corrigez

PASSÉ COMPOSÉ		IMPERATIVE (NEGATIVE)
j'ai corrigé	nous avons corrigé	ne corrige pas
tu as corrigé	vous avez corrigé	ne corrigeons pas
il/elle a corrigé	ils/elles ont corrigé	ne corrigez pas

courir/to run	*pr. part.* courant	*past part.* couru

Singular	Plural	

PRESENT INDICATIVE		IMPERATIVE (AFFIRMATIVE)
je cours	nous courons	cours
tu cours	vous courez	courons
il/elle court	ils/elles courent	courez

PASSÉ COMPOSÉ		IMPERATIVE (NEGATIVE)
j'ai couru	nous avons couru	ne cours pas
tu as couru	vous avez couru	ne courons pas
il/elle a couru	ils/elles ont couru	ne courez pas

coûter/to cost	*pr. part.* coûtant	*past part.* coûté

Singular	Plural	

PRESENT INDICATIVE		IMPERATIVE (AFFIRMATIVE)
il/elle coûte	ils/elles coûtent	[not used]

PASSÉ COMPOSÉ		IMPERATIVE (NEGATIVE)
il/elle a coûté	ils/elles ont coûté	[not used]

Note that this verb is generally regarded as impersonal. That is why it is not conjugated in all six persons here. It is used primarily in the third person singular (it) and plural (they).

couvrir/to cover   *pr. part.* **couvrant**   *past part.* **couvert**

Singular   Plural

PRESENT INDICATIVE

je couvre   **nous couvrons**
tu couvres   **vous couvrez**
il/elle couvre   **ils/elles couvrent**

IMPERATIVE (AFFIRMATIVE)

couvre
couvrons
couvrez

PASSÉ COMPOSÉ

j'ai couvert   **nous avons couvert**
tu as couvert   **vous avez couvert**
il/elle a couvert   **ils/elles ont couvert**

IMPERATIVE (NEGATIVE)

ne couvre pas
ne couvrons pas
ne couvrez pas

---

croire/to believe   *pr. part.* **croyant**   *past part.* **cru**

Singular   Plural

PRESENT INDICATIVE

je crois   **nous croyons**
tu crois   **vous croyez**
il/elle croit   **ils/elles croient**

IMPERATIVE (AFFIRMATIVE)

crois
croyons
croyez

PASSÉ COMPOSÉ

j'ai cru   **nous avons cru**
tu as cru   **vous avez cru**
il/elle a cru   **ils/elles ont cru**

IMPERATIVE (NEGATIVE)

ne crois pas
ne croyons pas
ne croyez pas

---

cuire/to cook   *pr. part.* **cuisant**   *past part.* **cuit**

Singular   Plural

PRESENT INDICATIVE

je cuis   **nous cuisons**
tu cuis   **vous cuisez**
il/elle cuit   **ils/elles cuisent**

IMPERATIVE (AFFIRMATIVE)

cuis
cuisons
cuisez

PASSÉ COMPOSÉ

j'ai cuit   **nous avons cuit**
tu as cuit   **vous avez cuit**
il/elle a cuit   **ils/elles ont cuit**

IMPERATIVE (NEGATIVE)

ne cuis pas
ne cuisons pas
ne cuisez pas

---

danser/to dance   *pr. part.* dansant   *past part.* dansé

Singular   Plural

PRESENT INDICATIVE

		IMPERATIVE (AFFIRMATIVE)
je danse	nous dansons	danse
tu danses	vous dansez	dansons
il/elle danse	ils/elles dansent	dansez

PASSÉ COMPOSÉ

		IMPERATIVE (NEGATIVE)
j'ai dansé	nous avons dansé	ne danse pas
tu as dansé	vous avez dansé	ne dansons pas
il/elle a dansé	ils/elles ont dansé	ne dansez pas

---

déjeuner/to lunch, have lunch, breakfast   *pr. part.* déjeunant   *past part.* déjeuné

Singular   Plural

PRESENT INDICATIVE

		IMPERATIVE (AFFIRMATIVE)
je déjeune	nous déjeunons	déjeune
tu déjeunes	vous déjeunez	déjeunons
il/elle déjeune	ils/elles déjeunent	déjeunez

PASSÉ COMPOSÉ

		IMPERATIVE (NEGATIVE)
j'ai déjeuné	nous avons déjeuné	ne déjeune pas
tu as déjeuné	vous avez déjeuné	ne déjeunons pas
il/elle a déjeuné	ils/elles ont déjeuné	ne déjeunez pas

---

demander/to ask (for), request   *pr. part.* demandant   *past part.* demandé

Singular   Plural

PRESENT INDICATIVE

		IMPERATIVE (AFFIRMATIVE)
je demande	nous demandons	demande
tu demandes	vous demandez	demandons
il/elle demande	ils/elles demandent	demandez

PASSÉ COMPOSÉ

		IMPERATIVE (NEGATIVE)
j'ai demandé	nous avons demandé	ne demande pas
tu as demandé	vous avez demandé	ne demandons pas
il/elle a demandé	ils/elles ont demandé	ne demandez pas

519

demeurer/to live (somewhere), reside   *pr. part.* **demeurant**   *past part.* **demeuré**

Singular   Plural

PRESENT INDICATIVE

		IMPERATIVE (AFFIRMATIVE)
je demeure	nous demeurons	demeure
tu demeures	vous demeurez	demeurons
il/elle demeure	ils/elles demeurent	demeurez

PASSÉ COMPOSÉ

		IMPERATIVE (NEGATIVE)
j'ai demeuré	nous avons demeuré	ne demeure pas
tu as demeuré	vous avez demeuré	ne demeurons pas
il/elle a demeuré	ils/elles ont demeuré	ne demeurez pas

---

descendre/to descend, go (bring) down   *pr. part.* **descendant**   *past part.* **descendu**

Singular   Plural

PRESENT INDICATIVE

		IMPERATIVE (AFFIRMATIVE)
je descends	nous descendons	descends
tu descends	vous descendez	descendons
il/elle descend	ils/elles descendent	descendez

PASSÉ COMPOSÉ

		IMPERATIVE (NEGATIVE)
je suis descendu(e)	nous sommes descendu(e)s	ne descends pas
tu es descendu(e)	vous êtes descendu(e)(s)	ne descendons pas
il est descendu	ils sont descendus	ne descendez pas
elle est descendue	elles sont descendues	

This verb is conjugated with **avoir** in the **passé composé** when it has a direct object.
Examples: **J'ai descendu l'escalier**/*I went down the stairs;* **J'ai descendu les valises**/*I brought down the suitcases.* But: **Elle est descendue vite**/*She came down quickly.*

---

désirer/to desire   *pr. part.* **désirant**   *past part.* **désiré**

Singular   Plural

PRESENT INDICATIVE

		IMPERATIVE (AFFIRMATIVE)
je désire	nous désirons	désire
tu désires	vous désirez	désirons
il/elle désire	ils/elles désirent	désirez

PASSÉ COMPOSÉ

		IMPERATIVE (NEGATIVE)
j'ai désiré	nous avons désiré	ne désire pas
tu as désiré	vous avez désiré	ne désirons pas
il/elle a désiré	ils/elles ont désiré	ne désirez pas

devenir/to become　　　　　*pr. part.* devenant　　　　*past part.* devenu

　　Singular　　　　　　　　　Plural

PRESENT INDICATIVE

		IMPERATIVE (AFFIRMATIVE)

je deviens　　　　　　　nous devenons　　　　　　deviens
tu deviens　　　　　　　vous devenez　　　　　　　devenons
il/elle devient　　　　　ils/elles deviennent　　　　devenez

PASSÉ COMPOSÉ　　　　　　　　　　　　　　IMPERATIVE (NEGATIVE)

je suis devenu(e)　　　　nous sommes devenu(e)s　　ne deviens pas
tu es devenu(e)　　　　　vous êtes devenu(e)(s)　　　ne devenons pas
il est devenu　　　　　　ils sont devenus　　　　　　ne devenez pas
elle est devenue　　　　　elles sont devenues

---

devoir/to have to, must, ought, owe, should　　　*pr. part.* devant　　　*past part.* dû

　　Singular　　　　　　　　　Plural

PRESENT INDICATIVE　　　　　　　　　　　　IMPERATIVE (AFFIRMATIVE)

je dois　　　　　　　　　nous devons　　　　　　　dois
tu dois　　　　　　　　　vous devez　　　　　　　　devons
il/elle doit　　　　　　　ils/elles doivent　　　　　devez

PASSÉ COMPOSÉ　　　　　　　　　　　　　　IMPERATIVE (NEGATIVE)

j'ai dû　　　　　　　　　nous avons dû　　　　　　ne dois pas
tu as dû　　　　　　　　vous avez dû　　　　　　　ne devons pas
il/elle a dû　　　　　　　ils/elles ont dû　　　　　　ne devez pas

---

dîner/to dine, have dinner　　　　　*pr. part.* dînant　　　*past part.* dîné

　　Singular　　　　　　　　　Plural

PRESENT INDICATIVE　　　　　　　　　　　　IMPERATIVE (AFFIRMATIVE)

je dîne　　　　　　　　　nous dînons　　　　　　　dîne
tu dînes　　　　　　　　vous dînez　　　　　　　　dînons
il/elle dîne　　　　　　　ils/elles dînent　　　　　dînez

PASSÉ COMPOSÉ　　　　　　　　　　　　　　IMPERATIVE (NEGATIVE)

j'ai dîné　　　　　　　　nous avons dîné　　　　　ne dîne pas
tu as dîné　　　　　　　vous avez dîné　　　　　　ne dînons pas
il/elle a dîné　　　　　　ils/elles ont dîné　　　　　ne dînez pas

---

dire/to say, tell   *pr. part.* **disant**   *past part.* **dit**

Singular   Plural

PRESENT INDICATIVE

		IMPERATIVE (AFFIRMATIVE)

je dis   nous disons   dis
tu dis   vous dites   disons
il/elle dit   ils/elles disent   dites

PASSÉ COMPOSÉ

IMPERATIVE (NEGATIVE)

j'ai dit   nous avons dit   ne dis pas
tu as dit   vous avez dit   ne disons pas
il/elle a dit   ils/elles ont dit   ne dites pas

---

donner/to give   *pr. part.* **donnant**   *past part.* **donné**

Singular   Plural

PRESENT INDICATIVE

IMPERATIVE (AFFIRMATIVE)

je donne   nous donnons   donne
tu donnes   vous donnez   donnons
il/elle donne   ils/elles donnent   donnez

PASSÉ COMPOSÉ

IMPERATIVE (NEGATIVE)

j'ai donné   nous avons donné   ne donne pas
tu as donné   vous avez donné   ne donnons pas
il/elle a donné   ils/elles ont donné   ne donnez pas

---

dormir/to sleep   *pr. part.* **dormant**   *past part.* **dormi**

Singular   Plural

PRESENT INDICATIVE

IMPERATIVE (AFFIRMATIVE)

je dors   nous dormons   dors
tu dors   vous dormez   dormons
il/elle dort   ils/elles dorment   dormez

PASSÉ COMPOSÉ

IMPERATIVE (NEGATIVE)

j'ai dormi   nous avons dormi   ne dors pas
tu as dormi   vous avez dormi   ne dormons pas
il/elle a dormi   ils/elles ont dormi   ne dormez pas

écouter/to listen (to) *pr. part.* écoutant *past part.* écouté

Singular Plural

PRESENT INDICATIVE

Singular	Plural	IMPERATIVE (AFFIRMATIVE)
j'écoute	nous écoutons	écoute
tu écoutes	vous écoutez	écoutons
il/elle écoute	ils/elles écoutent	écoutez

PASSÉ COMPOSÉ / IMPERATIVE (NEGATIVE)

j'ai écouté	nous avons écouté	n'écoute pas
tu as écouté	vous avez écouté	n'écoutons pas
il/elle a écouté	ils/elles ont écouté	n'écoutez pas

écrire/to write *pr. part.* écrivant *past part.* écrit

Singular Plural

PRESENT INDICATIVE / IMPERATIVE (AFFIRMATIVE)

j'écris	nous écrivons	écris
tu écris	vous écrivez	écrivons
il/elle écrit	ils/elles écrivent	écrivez

PASSÉ COMPOSÉ / IMPERATIVE (NEGATIVE)

j'ai écrit	nous avons écrit	n'écris pas
tu as écrit	vous avez écrit	n'écrivons pas
il/elle a écrit	ils/elles ont écrit	n'écrivez pas

---

effacer/to erase *pr. part.* effaçant *past part.* effacé

Singular Plural

PRESENT INDICATIVE / IMPERATIVE (AFFIRMATIVE)

j'efface	nous effaçons	efface
tu effaces	vous effacez	effaçons
il/elle efface	ils/elles effacent	effacez

PASSÉ COMPOSÉ / IMPERATIVE (NEGATIVE)

j'ai effacé	nous avons effacé	n'efface pas
tu as effacé	vous avez effacé	n'effaçons pas
il/elle a effacé	ils/elles ont effacé	n'effacez pas

---

employer/to use, employ   *pr. part.* **employant**   *past part.* **employé**

Singular   Plural

PRESENT INDICATIVE   IMPERATIVE (AFFIRMATIVE)

j'emploie   nous employons   emploie
tu emploies   vous employez   employons
il/elle emploie   ils/elles emploient   employez

PASSÉ COMPOSÉ   IMPERATIVE (NEGATIVE)

j'ai employé   nous avons employé   n'emploie pas
tu as employé   vous avez employé   n'employons pas
il/elle a employé   ils/elles ont employé   n'employez pas

Verbs ending in *-oyer* must change *y* to *i* before mute *e.*

---

ennuyer/to annoy, bore, weary   *pr. part.* **ennuyant**   *past part.* **ennuyé**

Singular   Plural

PRESENT INDICATIVE   IMPERATIVE (AFFIRMATIVE)

j'ennuie   nous ennuyons   ennuie
tu ennuies   vous ennuyez   ennuyons
il/elle ennuie   ils/elles ennuient   ennuyez

PASSÉ COMPOSÉ   IMPERATIVE (NEGATIVE)

j'ai ennuyé   nous avons ennuyé   n'ennuie pas
tu as ennuyé   vous avez ennuyé   n'ennuyons pas
il/elle a ennuyé   ils/elles ont ennuyé   n'ennuyez pas

Verbs ending in *-uyer* must change *y* to *i* before mute *e.*

---

entendre/to hear   *pr. part.* **entendant**   *past part.* **entendu**

Singular   Plural

PRESENT INDICATIVE   IMPERATIVE (AFFIRMATIVE)

j'entends   nous entendons   entends
tu entends   vous entendez   entendons
il/elle entend   ils/elles entendent   entendez

PASSÉ COMPOSÉ   IMPERATIVE (NEGATIVE)

j'ai entendu   nous avons entendu   n'entends pas
tu as entendu   vous avez entendu   n'entendons pas
il/elle a entendu   ils/elles ont entendu   n'entendez pas

entrer/to enter, come in, go in   *pr. part.* entrant   *past part.* entré

Singular   Plural

PRESENT INDICATIVE

		IMPERATIVE (AFFIRMATIVE)
j'entre	nous entrons	entre
tu entres	vous entrez	entrons
il/elle entre	ils/elles entrent	entrez

PASSÉ COMPOSÉ

		IMPERATIVE (NEGATIVE)
je suis entré(e)	nous sommes entré(e)s	n'entre pas
tu es entré(e)	vous êtes entré(e)(s)	n'entrons pas
il est entré	ils sont entrés	n'entrez pas
elle est entrée	elles sont entrées	

---

envoyer/to send   *pr. part.* envoyant   *past part.* envoyé

Singular   Plural

PRESENT INDICATIVE

		IMPERATIVE (AFFIRMATIVE)
j'envoie	nous envoyons	envoie
tu envoies	vous envoyez	envoyons
il/elle envoie	ils/elles envoient	envoyez

PASSÉ COMPOSÉ

		IMPERATIVE (NEGATIVE)
j'ai envoyé	nous avons envoyé	n'envoie pas
tu as envoyé	vous avez envoyé	n'envoyons pas
il/elle a envoyé	ils/elles ont envoyé	n'envoyez pas

Verbs ending in *-oyer* must change *y* to *i* before mute *e*.

---

espérer/to hope   *pr. part.* espérant   *past part.* espéré

Singular   Plural

PRESENT INDICATIVE

		IMPERATIVE (AFFIRMATIVE)
j'espère	nous espérons	espère
tu espères	vous espérez	espérons
il/elle espère	ils/elles espèrent	espérez

PASSÉ COMPOSÉ

		IMPERATIVE (NEGATIVE)
j'ai espéré	nous avons espéré	n'espère pas
tu as espéré	vous avez espéré	n'espérons pas
il/elle a espéré	ils/elles ont espéré	n'espérez pas

525

essayer/to try, try on   *pr. part.* **essayant**   *past part.* **essayé**

Singular   Plural

PRESENT INDICATIVE   IMPERATIVE (AFFIRMATIVE)

j'essaye	nous essayons	essaye
tu essayes	vous essayez	essayons
il/elle essaye	ils/elles essayent	essayez

PASSÉ COMPOSÉ   IMPERATIVE (NEGATIVE)

j'ai essayé	nous avons essayé	n'essaye pas
tu as essayé	vous avez essayé	n'essayons pas
il/elle a essayé	ils/elles ont essayé	n'essayez pas

Verbs ending in *-ayer* may change *y* to *i* before mute *e* or may keep *y*.

---

essuyer/to wipe   *pr. part.* **essuyant**   *past part.* **essuyé**

Singular   Plural

PRESENT INDICATIVE   IMPERATIVE (AFFIRMATIVE)

j'essuie	nous essuyons	essuie
tu essuies	vous essuyez	essuyons
il/elle essuie	ils/elles essuient	essuyez

PASSÉ COMPOSÉ   IMPERATIVE (NEGATIVE)

j'ai essuyé	nous avons essuyé	n'essuie pas
tu as essuyé	vous avez essuyé	n'essuyons pas
il/elle a essuyé	ils/elles ont essuyé	n'essuyez pas

Verbs ending in *-uyer* must change *y* to *i* before mute *e.*

être/to be   *pr. part.* **étant**   *past part.* **été**

Singular   Plural

PRESENT INDICATIVE   IMPERATIVE (AFFIRMATIVE)

je suis	nous sommes	sois
tu es	vous êtes	soyons
il/elle est	ils/elles sont	soyez

PASSÉ COMPOSÉ   IMPERATIVE (NEGATIVE)

j'ai été	nous avons été	ne sois pas
tu as été	vous avez été	ne soyons pas
il/elle a été	ils/elles ont été	ne soyez pas

étudier/to study   *pr. part.* étudiant   *past part.* étudié

Singular   Plural

PRESENT INDICATIVE   IMPERATIVE (AFFIRMATIVE)

j'étudie	nous étudions	étudie
tu étudies	vous étudiez	étudions
il/elle étudie	ils/elles étudient	étudiez

PASSÉ COMPOSÉ   IMPERATIVE (NEGATIVE)

j'ai étudié	nous avons étudié	n'étudie pas
tu as étudié	vous avez étudié	n'étudions pas
il/elle a étudié	ils/elles ont étudié	n'étudiez pas

---

faire/to do, make   *pr. part.* faisant   *past part.* fait

Singular   Plural

PRESENT INDICATIVE   IMPERATIVE (AFFIRMATIVE)

je fais	nous faisons	fais
tu fais	vous faites	faisons
il/elle fait	ils/elles font	faites

PASSÉ COMPOSÉ   IMPERATIVE (NEGATIVE)

j'ai fait	nous avons fait	ne fais pas
tu as fait	vous avez fait	ne faisons pas
il/elle a fait	ils/elles ont fait	ne faites pas

---

falloir/to be necessary, need to, must   *pr. part.* [not in use]   *past part.* fallu

Singular

PRESENT INDICATIVE   IMPERATIVE (AFFIRMATIVE)

il faut   [not in use]

PASSÉ COMPOSÉ   IMPERATIVE (NEGATIVE)

il a fallu   [not in use]

This is an impersonal verb that is used in the third person singular. *Examples:* Il faut manger et boire pour vivre/*It is necessary to eat and drink in order to live;* Il a fallu partir/*It was necessary to leave.*

527

fermer/to close   *pr. part.* fermant   *past part.* fermé

Singular   Plural

PRESENT INDICATIVE   IMPERATIVE (AFFIRMATIVE)

je ferme	nous fermons	ferme
tu fermes	vous fermez	fermons
il/elle ferme	ils/elles ferment	fermez

PASSÉ COMPOSÉ   IMPERATIVE (NEGATIVE)

j'ai fermé	nous avons fermé	ne ferme pas
tu as fermé	vous avez fermé	ne fermons pas
il/elle a fermé	ils/elles ont fermé	ne fermez pas

---

finir/to finish   *pr. part.* finissant   *past part.* fini

Singular   Plural

PRESENT INDICATIVE   IMPERATIVE (AFFIRMATIVE)

je finis	nous finissons	finis
tu finis	vous finissez	finissons
il/elle finit	ils/elles finissent	finissez

PASSÉ COMPOSÉ   IMPERATIVE (NEGATIVE)

j'ai fini	nous avons fini	ne finis pas
tu as fini	vous avez fini	ne finissons pas
il/elle a fini	ils/elles ont fini	ne finissez pas

---

habiter/to live (somewhere), inhabit   *pr. part.* habitant   *past part.* habité

Singular   Plural

PRESENT INDICATIVE   IMPERATIVE (AFFIRMATIVE)

j'habite	nous habitons	habite
tu habites	vous habitez	habitons
il/elle habite	ils/elles habitent	habitez

PASSÉ COMPOSÉ   IMPERATIVE (NEGATIVE)

j'ai habité	nous avons habité	n'habite pas
tu as habité	vous avez habité	n'habitons pas
il/elle a habité	ils/elles ont habité	n'habitez pas

---

jeter/to throw   *pr. part.* jetant   *past part.* jeté

Singular	Plural

PRESENT INDICATIVE		IMPERATIVE (AFFIRMATIVE)
je jette	nous jetons	jette
tu jettes	vous jetez	jetons
il/elle jette	ils/elles jettent	jetez

PASSÉ COMPOSÉ		IMPERATIVE (NEGATIVE)
j'ai jeté	nous avons jeté	ne jette pas
tu as jeté	vous avez jeté	ne jetons pas
il/elle a jeté	ils/elles ont jeté	ne jetez pas

jouer/to play   *pr. part.* jouant   *past part.* joué

Singular	Plural

PRESENT INDICATIVE		IMPERATIVE (AFFIRMATIVE)
je joue	nous jouons	joue
tu joues	vous jouez	jouons
il/elle joue	ils/elles jouent	jouez

PASSÉ COMPOSÉ		IMPERATIVE (NEGATIVE)
j'ai joué	nous avons joué	ne joue pas
tu as joué	vous avez joué	ne jouons pas
il/elle a joué	ils/elles ont joué	ne jouez pas

lire/to read   *pr. part.* lisant   *past part.* lu

Singular	Plural

PRESENT INDICATIVE		IMPERATIVE (AFFIRMATIVE)
je lis	nous lisons	lis
tu lis	vous lisez	lisons
il/elle lit	ils/elles lisent	lisez

PASSÉ COMPOSÉ		IMPERATIVE (NEGATIVE)
j'ai lu	nous avons lu	ne lis pas
tu as lu	vous avez lu	ne lisons pas
il/elle a lu	ils/elles ont lu	ne lisez pas

manger/to eat   *pr. part.* **mangeant**   *past part.* **mangé**

Singular   Plural

PRESENT INDICATIVE   IMPERATIVE (AFFIRMATIVE)

je mange   nous mangeons   mange
tu manges   vous mangez   mangeons
il/elle mange   ils/elles mangent   mangez

PASSÉ COMPOSÉ   IMPERATIVE (NEGATIVE)

j'ai mangé   nous avons mangé   ne mange pas
tu as mangé   vous avez mangé   ne mangeons pas
il/elle a mangé   ils/elles ont mangé   ne mangez pas

---

mettre/to put, place   *pr. part.* **mettant**   *past part.* **mis**

Singular   Plural

PRESENT INDICATIVE   IMPERATIVE (AFFIRMATIVE)

je mets   nous mettons   mets
tu mets   vous mettez   mettons
il/elle met   ils/elles mettent   mettez

PASSÉ COMPOSÉ   IMPERATIVE (NEGATIVE)

j'ai mis   nous avons mis   ne mets pas
tu as mis   vous avez mis   ne mettons pas
il/elle a mis   ils/elles ont mis   ne mettez pas

---

monter/to go up, bring up   *pr. part.* **montant**   *past part.* **monté**

Singular   Plural

PRESENT INDICATIVE   IMPERATIVE (AFFIRMATIVE)

je monte   nous montons   monte
tu montes   vous montez   montons
il/elle monte   ils/elles montent   montez

PASSÉ COMPOSÉ   IMPERATIVE (NEGATIVE)

je suis monté(e)   nous sommes monté(e)s   ne monte pas
tu es monté(e)   vous êtes monté(e)(s)   ne montons pas
il est monté   ils sont montés   ne montez pas
elle est montée   elles sont montées

This verb is conjugated with **avoir** in the **passé composé** when it has a direct object. *Examples:* **J'ai monté l'escalier**/*I went up the stairs;* **J'ai monté les valises**/*I brought up the suitcases.* But: **Elle est montée vite**/*She went up quickly.*

mourir/to die   *pr. part.* mourant   *past part.* mort

Singular   Plural

PRESENT INDICATIVE

je meurs	nous mourons	
tu meurs	vous mourez	
il/elle meurt	ils/elles meurent	

IMPERATIVE (AFFIRMATIVE)

meurs
mourons
mourez

PASSÉ COMPOSÉ

je suis mort(e)	nous sommes morte(e)s
tu es mort(e)	vous êtes mort(e)(s)
il est mort	ils sont morts
elle est morte	elles sont mortes

IMPERATIVE (NEGATIVE)

ne meurs pas
ne mourons pas
ne mourez pas

---

nager/to swim   *pr. part.* nageant   *past part.* nagé

Singular   Plural

PRESENT INDICATIVE

je nage	nous nageons
tu nages	vous nagez
il/elle nage	ils/elles nagent

IMPERATIVE (AFFIRMATIVE)

nage
nageons
nagez

PASSÉ COMPOSÉ

j'ai nagé	nous avons nagé
tu as nagé	vous avez nagé
il/elle a nagé	ils/elles ont nagé

IMPERATIVE (NEGATIVE)

ne nage pas
ne nageons pas
ne nagez pas

---

naître/to be born   *pr. part.* naissant   *past part.* né

Singular   Plural

PRESENT INDICATIVE

je nais	nous naissons
tu nais	vous naissez
il/elle naît	ils/elles naissent

IMPERATIVE (AFFIRMATIVE)

nais
naissons
naissez

PASSÉ COMPOSÉ

je suis né(e)	nous sommes né(e)s
tu es né(e)	vous êtes né(e)(s)
il est né	ils sont nés
elle est née	elles sont nées

IMPERATIVE (NEGATIVE)

ne nais pas
ne naissons pas
ne naissez pas

531

neiger/to snow *pr. part.* **neigeant** *past part.* **neigé**

Singular

PRESENT INDICATIVE	IMPERATIVE (AFFIRMATIVE)
il neige	[not in use]

PASSÉ COMPOSÉ	IMPERATIVE (NEGATIVE)
il a neigé	[not in use]

This is an impersonal verb that is used in the third person singular with the subject pronoun il/it.

---

nettoyer/to clean *pr. part.* **nettoyant** *past part.* **nettoyé**

Singular   Plural

PRESENT INDICATIVE		IMPERATIVE (AFFIRMATIVE)
je nettoie	**nous nettoyons**	**nettoie**
tu nettoies	**vous nettoyez**	**nettoyons**
il/elle nettoie	**ils/elles nettoient**	**nettoyez**

PASSÉ COMPOSÉ		IMPERATIVE (NEGATIVE)
j'ai nettoyé	**nous avons nettoyé**	**ne nettoie pas**
tu as nettoyé	**vous avez nettoyé**	**ne nettoyons pas**
il/elle a nettoyé	**ils/elles ont nettoyé**	**ne nettoyez pas**

Verbs ending in *-oyer* must change *y* to *i* before mute *e.*

---

offrir/to offer *pr. part.* **offrant** *past part.* **offert**

Singular   Plural

PRESENT INDICATIVE		IMPERATIVE (AFFIRMATIVE)
j'offre	**nous offrons**	**offre**
tu offres	**vous offrez**	**offrons**
il/elle offre	**ils/elles offrent**	**offrez**

PASSÉ COMPOSÉ		IMPERATIVE (NEGATIVE)
j'ai offert	**nous avons offert**	**n'offre pas**
tu as offert	**vous avez offert**	**n'offrons pas**
il/elle a offert	**ils/elles ont offert**	**n'offrez pas**

---

oublier/to forget   *pr. part.* oubliant   *past part.* oublié

Singular   Plural

PRESENT INDICATIVE

Singular	Plural	IMPERATIVE (AFFIRMATIVE)
j'oublie	nous oublions	oublie
tu oublies	vous oubliez	oublions
il/elle oublie	ils/elles oublient	oubliez

PASSÉ COMPOSÉ / IMPERATIVE (NEGATIVE)

Singular	Plural	IMPERATIVE (NEGATIVE)
j'ai oublié	nous avons oublié	n'oublie pas
tu as oublié	vous avez oublié	n'oublions pas
il/elle a oublié	ils/elles ont oublié	n'oubliez pas

---

ouvrir/to open   *pr. part.* ouvrant   *past part.* ouvert

Singular   Plural

PRESENT INDICATIVE

Singular	Plural	IMPERATIVE (AFFIRMATIVE)
j'ouvre	nous ouvrons	ouvre
tu ouvres	vous ouvrez	ouvrons
il/elle ouvre	ils/elles ouvrent	ouvrez

PASSÉ COMPOSÉ / IMPERATIVE (NEGATIVE)

Singular	Plural	IMPERATIVE (NEGATIVE)
j'ai ouvert	nous avons ouvert	n'ouvre pas
tu as ouvert	vous avez ouvert	n'ouvrons pas
il/elle a ouvert	ils/elles ont ouvert	n'ouvrez pas

---

parler/to talk, speak   *pr. part.* parlant   *past part.* parlé

Singular   Plural

PRESENT INDICATIVE

Singular	Plural	IMPERATIVE (AFFIRMATIVE)
je parle	nous parlons	parle
tu parles	vous parlez	parlons
il/elle parle	ils/elles parlent	parlez

PASSÉ COMPOSÉ / IMPERATIVE (NEGATIVE)

Singular	Plural	IMPERATIVE (NEGATIVE)
j'ai parlé	nous avons parlé	ne parle pas
tu as parlé	vous avez parlé	ne parlons pas
il/elle a parlé	ils/elles ont parlé	ne parlez pas

533

partir/to leave, depart   *pr. part.* **partant**   *past part.* **parti**

Singular   Plural

PRESENT INDICATIVE   IMPERATIVE (AFFIRMATIVE)

je pars   nous partons   pars
tu pars   vous partez   partons
il/elle part   ils/elles partent   partez

PASSÉ COMPOSÉ   IMPERATIVE (NEGATIVE)

je suis parti(e)   nous sommes parti(e)s   ne pars pas
tu es parti(e)   vous êtes parti(e)(s)   ne partons pas
il est parti   ils sont partis   ne partez pas
elle est partie   elles sont parties

---

passer/to pass, spend (time)   *pr. part.* **passant**   *past part.* **passé**

Singular   Plural

PRESENT INDICATIVE   IMPERATIVE (AFFIRMATIVE)

je passe   nous passons   passe
tu passes   vous passez   passons
il/elle passe   ils/elles passent   passez

PASSÉ COMPOSÉ   IMPERATIVE (NEGATIVE)

j'ai passé   nous avons passé   ne passe pas
tu as passé   vous avez passé   ne passons pas
il/elle a passé   ils/elles ont passé   ne passez pas

This verb is conjugated with **être** in the **passé composé** when it means *to pass by, go by:* **Elle est passée chez moi**/*She came by my house.* It is conjugated with **avoir** when it has a direct object: **Elle a passé un examen**/*She took an exam;* **Elle m'a passé le sel**/*She passed me the salt.*

---

payer/to pay (for)   *pr. part.* **payant**   *past part.* **payé**

Singular   Plural

PRESENT INDICATIVE   IMPERATIVE (AFFIRMATIVE)

je paye   nous payons   paye
tu payes   vous payez   payons
il/elle paye   ils/elles payent   payez

PASSÉ COMPOSÉ   IMPERATIVE (NEGATIVE)

j'ai payé   nous avons payé   ne paye pas
tu as payé   vous avez payé   ne payons pas
il/elle a payé   ils/elles ont payé   ne payez pas

Verbs ending in *-ayer* may change *y* to *i* before mute *e* or may keep *y*.

penser/to think   *pr. part.* **pensant**   *past part.* **pensé**

Singular   Plural

PRESENT INDICATIVE

		IMPERATIVE (AFFIRMATIVE)
je pense	nous pensons	pense
tu penses	vous pensez	pensons
il/elle pense	ils/elles pensent	pensez

PASSÉ COMPOSÉ

		IMPERATIVE (NEGATIVE)
j'ai pensé	nous avons pensé	ne pense pas
tu as pensé	vous avez pensé	ne pensons pas
il/elle a pensé	ils/elles ont pensé	ne pensez pas

---

perdre/to lose   *pr. part.* **perdant**   *past part.* **perdu**

Singular   Plural

PRESENT INDICATIVE

		IMPERATIVE (AFFIRMATIVE)
je perds	nous perdons	perds
tu perds	vous perdez	perdons
il/elle perd	ils/elles perdent	perdez

PASSÉ COMPOSÉ

		IMPERATIVE (NEGATIVE)
j'ai perdu	nous avons perdu	ne perds pas
tu as perdu	vous avez perdu	ne perdons pas
il/elle a perdu	ils/elles ont perdu	ne perdez pas

---

pleuvoir/to rain   *pr. part.* **pleuvant**   *past part.* **plu**

Singular

PRESENT INDICATIVE

	IMPERATIVE (AFFIRMATIVE)
il pleut	[not in use]

PASSÉ COMPOSÉ

	IMPERATIVE (NEGATIVE)
il a plu	[not in use]

This is an impersonal verb that is used in the third person singular with the subject pronoun il/it.

---

pouvoir/to be able, can   *pr. part.* **pouvant**   *past part.* **pu**

Singular	Plural

PRESENT INDICATIVE

		IMPERATIVE (AFFIRMATIVE)
je peux *or* je puis	nous pouvons	[not in use]
tu peux	vous pouvez	
il/elle peut	ils/elles peuvent	

PASSÉ COMPOSÉ

		IMPERATIVE (NEGATIVE)
j'ai pu	nous avons pu	[not in use]
tu as pu	vous avez pu	
il/elle a pu	ils/elles ont pu	

---

préférer/to prefer   *pr. part.* **préférant**   *past part.* **préféré**

Singular	Plural

PRESENT INDICATIVE

		IMPERATIVE (AFFIRMATIVE)
je préfère	nous préférons	préfère
tu préfères	vous préférez	préférons
il/elle préfère	ils/elles préfèrent	préférez

PASSÉ COMPOSÉ

		IMPERATIVE (NEGATIVE)
j'ai préféré	nous avons préféré	ne préfère pas
tu as préféré	vous avez préféré	ne préférons pas
il/elle a préféré	ils/elles ont préféré	ne préférez pas

---

prendre/to take   *pr. part.* **prenant**   *past part.* **pris**

Singular	Plural

PRESENT INDICATIVE

		IMPERATIVE (AFFIRMATIVE)
je prends	nous prenons	prends
tu prends	vous prenez	prenons
il/elle prend	ils/elles prennent	prenez

PASSÉ COMPOSÉ

		IMPERATIVE (NEGATIVE)
j'ai pris	nous avons pris	ne prends pas
tu as pris	vous avez pris	ne prenons pas
il/elle a pris	ils/elles ont pris	ne prenez pas

---

recevoir/to receive   *pr. part.* **recevant**   *past part.* **reçu**

Singular   Plural

PRESENT INDICATIVE

Singular	Plural
je reçois	nous recevons
tu reçois	vous recevez
il/elle reçoit	ils/elles reçoivent

IMPERATIVE (AFFIRMATIVE)

reçois
recevons
recevez

PASSÉ COMPOSÉ

Singular	Plural
j'ai reçu	nous avons reçu
tu as reçu	vous avez reçu
il/elle a reçu	ils/elles ont reçu

IMPERATIVE (NEGATIVE)

ne reçois pas
ne recevons pas
ne recevez pas

---

regarder/to look (at), watch   *pr. part.* **regardant**   *past part.* **regardé**

Singular   Plural

PRESENT INDICATIVE

Singular	Plural
je regarde	nous regardons
tu regardes	vous regardez
il/elle regarde	ils/elles regardent

IMPERATIVE (AFFIRMATIVE)

regarde
regardons
regardez

PASSÉ COMPOSÉ

Singular	Plural
j'ai regardé	nous avons regardé
tu as regardé	vous avez regardé
il/elle a regardé	ils/elles ont regardé

IMPERATIVE (NEGATIVE)

ne regarde pas
ne regardons pas
ne regardez pas

---

rendre/to give back, to return (something)   *pr. part.* **rendant**   *past part.* **rendu**

Singular   Plural

PRESENT INDICATIVE

Singular	Plural
je rends	nous rendons
tu rends	vous rendez
il/elle rend	ils/elles rendent

IMPERATIVE (AFFIRMATIVE)

rends
rendons
rendez

PASSÉ COMPOSÉ

Singular	Plural
j'ai rendu	nous avons rendu
tu as rendu	vous avez rendu
il/elle a rendu	ils/elles ont rendu

IMPERATIVE (NEGATIVE)

ne rends pas
ne rendons pas
ne rendez pas

537

rentrer/to go in again, return (home)   *pr. part.* **rentrant**   *past part.* **rentré**

Singular   Plural

PRESENT INDICATIVE   IMPERATIVE (AFFIRMATIVE)

je rentre	nous rentrons	rentre
tu rentres	vous rentrez	rentrons
il/elle rentre	ils/elles rentrent	rentrez

PASSÉ COMPOSÉ   IMPERATIVE (NEGATIVE)

je suis rentré(e)	nous sommes rentré(e)s	ne rentre pas
tu es rentré(e)	vous êtes rentré(e)(s)	ne rentrons pas
il est rentré	ils sont rentrés	ne rentrez pas
elle est rentrée	elles sont rentrées	

This verb is conjugated with **avoir** when it has a direct object. *Example:* **Elle a rentré le chat dans la maison**/*She brought (took) the cat back into the house.* But: **Elle est rentrée tôt**/*She returned (has returned) home early.*

---

répondre/to answer, respond, reply   *pr. part.* **répondant**   *past part.* **répondu**

Singular   Plural

PRESENT INDICATIVE   IMPERATIVE (AFFIRMATIVE)

je réponds	nous répondons	réponds
tu réponds	vous répondez	répondons
il/elle répond	ils/elles répondent	répondez

PASSÉ COMPOSÉ   IMPERATIVE (NEGATIVE)

j'ai répondu	nous avons répondu	ne réponds pas
tu as répondu	vous avez répondu	ne répondons pas
il/elle a répondu	ils/elles ont répondu	ne répondez pas

---

rester/to remain, stay   *pr. part.* **restant**   *past part.* **resté**

Singular   Plural

PRESENT INDICATIVE   IMPERATIVE (AFFIRMATIVE)

je reste	nous restons	reste
tu restes	vous restez	restons
il/elle reste	ils/elles restent	restez

PASSÉ COMPOSÉ   IMPERATIVE (NEGATIVE)

je suis resté(e)	nous sommes resté(e)s	ne reste pas
tu es resté(e)	vous êtes resté(e)(s)	ne restons pas
il est resté	ils sont restés	ne restez pas
elle est restée	elles sont restées	

Do not confuse this verb with **se reposer**/to rest.

retourner/to go back, return   *pr. part.* **retournant**   *past part.* **retourné**

Singular   Plural

PRESENT INDICATIVE

IMPERATIVE (AFFIRMATIVE)

je retourne	nous retournons	retourne
tu retournes	vous retournez	retournons
il/elle retourne	ils/elles retournent	retournez

PASSÉ COMPOSÉ

IMPERATIVE (NEGATIVE)

je suis retourné(e)	nous sommes retourné(e)s	ne retourne pas
tu es retourné(e)	vous êtes retourné(e)(s)	ne retournons pas
il est retourné	ils sont retournés	ne retournez pas
elle est retournée	elles sont retournées	

---

revenir/to come back, return   *pr. part.* **revenant**   *past part.* **revenu**

Singular   Plural

PRESENT INDICATIVE

IMPERATIVE (AFFIRMATIVE)

je reviens	nous revenons	reviens
tu reviens	vous revenez	revenons
il/elle revient	ils/elles reviennent	revenez

PASSÉ COMPOSÉ

IMPERATIVE (NEGATIVE)

je suis revenu(e)	nous sommes revenu(e)s	ne reviens pas
tu es revenu(e)	vous êtes revenu(e)(s)	ne revenons pas
il est revenu	ils sont revenus	ne revenez pas
elle est revenue	elles sont revenues	

---

rire/to laugh   *pr. part.* **riant**   *past part.* **ri**

Singular   Plural

PRESENT INDICATIVE

IMPERATIVE (AFFIRMATIVE)

je ris	nous rions	ris
tu ris	vous riez	rions
il/elle rit	ils/elles rient	riez

PASSÉ COMPOSÉ

IMPERATIVE (NEGATIVE)

j'ai ri	nous avons ri	ne ris pas
tu as ri	vous avez ri	ne rions pas
il/elle a ri	ils/elles ont ri	ne riez pas

539

savoir/to know (how), to know (a fact)   *pr. part.* **sachant**   *past part.* **su**

Singular   Plural

PRESENT INDICATIVE

		IMPERATIVE (AFFIRMATIVE)

je sais   nous savons   sache
tu sais   vous savez   sachons
il/elle sait   ils/elles savent   sachez

PASSÉ COMPOSÉ

IMPERATIVE (NEGATIVE)

j'ai su   nous avons su   ne sache pas
tu as su   vous avez su   ne sachons pas
il/elle a su   ils/elles ont su   ne sachez pas

---

sentir/to smell, feel   *pr. part.* **sentant**   *past part.* **senti**

Singular   Plural

PRESENT INDICATIVE

IMPERATIVE (AFFIRMATIVE)

je sens   nous sentons   sens
tu sens   vous sentez   sentons
il/elle sent   ils/elles sentent   sentez

PASSÉ COMPOSÉ

IMPERATIVE (NEGATIVE)

j'ai senti   nous avons senti   ne sens pas
tu as senti   vous avez senti   ne sentons pas
il/elle a senti   ils/elles ont senti   ne sentez pas

---

servir/to serve   *pr. part.* **servant**   *past part.* **servi**

Singular   Plural

PRESENT INDICATIVE

IMPERATIVE (AFFIRMATIVE)

je sers   nous servons   sers
tu sers   vous servez   servons
il/elle sert   ils/elles servent   servez

PASSÉ COMPOSÉ

IMPERATIVE (NEGATIVE)

j'ai servi   nous avons servi   ne sers pas
tu as servi   vous avez servi   ne servons pas
il/elle a servi   ils/elles ont servi   ne servez pas

---

sortir/to go out, leave   *pr. part.* **sortant**   *past part.* **sorti**

Singular   Plural

PRESENT INDICATIVE	**IMPERATIVE (AFFIRMATIVE)**

Singular	Plural	
je sors	nous sortons	**sors**
tu sors	vous sortez	**sortons**
il/elle sort	ils/elles sortent	**sortez**

PASSÉ COMPOSÉ	**IMPERATIVE (NEGATIVE)**

Singular	Plural	
je suis sorti(e)	nous sommes sorti(e)s	**ne sors pas**
tu es sorti(e)	vous êtes sorti(e)(s)	**ne sortons pas**
il est sorti	ils sont sortis	**ne sortez pas**
elle est sortie	elles sont sorties	

This verb is conjugated with **avoir** in the **passé composé** when it has a direct object. *Example:* **Elle a sorti son mouchoir**/*She took out her handkerchief.* But: **Elle est sortie**/*She went out (She has gone out).*

---

souffrir/to suffer, endure   *pr. part.* **souffrant**   *past part.* **souffert**

Singular   Plural

PRESENT INDICATIVE	**IMPERATIVE (AFFIRMATIVE)**

Singular	Plural	
je souffre	nous souffrons	**souffre**
tu souffres	vous souffrez	**souffrons**
il/elle souffre	ils/elles souffrent	**souffrez**

PASSÉ COMPOSÉ	**IMPERATIVE (NEGATIVE)**

Singular	Plural	
j'ai souffert	nous avons souffert	**ne souffre pas**
tu as souffert	vous avez souffert	**ne souffrons pas**
il/elle a souffert	ils/elles ont souffert	**ne souffrez pas**

---

suffire/to suffice, be enough   *pr. part.* **suffisant**   *past part.* **suffi**

Singular

PRESENT INDICATIVE	**IMPERATIVE (AFFIRMATIVE)**
il suffit	[not in use]

PASSÉ COMPOSÉ	**IMPERATIVE (NEGATIVE)**
il a suffi	[not in use]

This verb is generally impersonal and is used frequently in the third person singular with the subject pronoun **il**/it. The subject **cela** may be used, as in **Cela suffit**/*That is enough.*

541

téléphoner/to telephone *pr. part.* **téléphonant** *past part.* **téléphoné**

Singular Plural

PRESENT INDICATIVE

IMPERATIVE (AFFIRMATIVE)

je téléphone nous téléphonons téléphone
tu téléphones vous téléphonez téléphonons
il/elle téléphone ils/elles téléphonent téléphonez

PASSÉ COMPOSÉ

IMPERATIVE (NEGATIVE)

j'ai téléphoné nous avons téléphoné ne téléphone pas
tu as téléphoné vous avez téléphoné ne téléphonons pas
il/elle a téléphoné ils/elles ont téléphoné ne téléphonez pas

---

tenir/to hold *pr. part.* **tenant** *past part.* **tenu**

Singular Plural

PRESENT INDICATIVE

IMPERATIVE (AFFIRMATIVE)

je tiens nous tenons tiens
tu tiens vous tenez tenons
il/elle tient ils/elles tiennent tenez

PASSÉ COMPOSÉ

IMPERATIVE (NEGATIVE)

j'ai tenu nous avons tenu ne tiens pas
tu as tenu vous avez tenu ne tenons pas
il/elle a tenu ils/elles ont tenu ne tenez pas

---

tomber/to fall *pr. part.* **tombant** *past part.* **tombé**

Singular Plural

PRESENT INDICATIVE

IMPERATIVE (AFFIRMATIVE)

je tombe nous tombons tombe
tu tombes vous tombez tombons
il/elle tombe ils/elles tombent tombez

PASSÉ COMPOSÉ

IMPERATIVE (NEGATIVE)

je suis tombé(e) nous sommes tombé(e)s ne tombe pas
tu es tombé(e) vous êtes tombé(e)(s) ne tombons pas
il est tombé ils sont tombés ne tombez pas
elle est tombée elles sont tombées

---

travailler/to work   *pr. part.* **travaillant**   *past part.* **travaillé**

Singular   Plural

PRESENT INDICATIVE

je travaille   nous travaillons
tu travailles   vous travaillez
il/elle travaille   ils/elles travaillent

PASSÉ COMPOSÉ

j'ai travaillé   nous avons travaillé
tu as travaillé   vous avez travaillé
il/elle a travaillé   ils/elles ont travaillé

IMPERATIVE (AFFIRMATIVE)

travaille
travaillons
travaillez

IMPERATIVE (NEGATIVE)

ne travaille pas
ne travaillons pas
ne travaillez pas

---

trouver/to find   *pr. part.* **trouvant**   *past part.* **trouvé**

Singular   Plural

PRESENT INDICATIVE

je trouve   nous trouvons
tu trouves   vous trouvez
il/elle trouve   ils/elles trouvent

PASSÉ COMPOSÉ

j'ai trouvé   nous avons trouvé
tu as trouvé   vous avez trouvé
il/elle a trouvé   ils/elles ont trouvé

IMPERATIVE (AFFIRMATIVE)

trouve
trouvons
trouvez

IMPERATIVE (NEGATIVE)

ne trouve pas
ne trouvons pas
ne trouvez pas

---

vendre/to sell   *pr. part.* **vendant**   *past part.* **vendu**

Singular   Plural

PRESENT INDICATIVE

je vends   nous vendons
tu vends   vous vendez
il/elle vend   ils/elles vendent

PASSÉ COMPOSÉ

j'ai vendu   nous avons vendu
tu as vendu   vous avez vendu
il/elle a vendu   ils/elles ont vendu

IMPERATIVE (AFFIRMATIVE)

vends
vendons
vendez

IMPERATIVE (NEGATIVE)

ne vends pas
ne vendons pas
ne vendez pas

venir/to come	*pr. part.* venant	*past part.* venu

Singular   Plural

PRESENT INDICATIVE   IMPERATIVE (AFFIRMATIVE)

je viens	nous venons	viens
tu viens	vous venez	venons
il/elle vient	ils/elles viennent	venez

PASSÉ COMPOSÉ   IMPERATIVE (NEGATIVE)

je suis venu(e)	nous sommes venu(e)s	ne viens pas
tu es venu(e)	vous êtes venu(e)(s)	ne venons pas
il est venu	ils sont venus	ne venez pas
elle est venue	elles sont venues	

---

vivre/to live	*pr. part.* vivant	*past part.* vécu

Singular   Plural

PRESENT INDICATIVE   IMPERATIVE (AFFIRMATIVE)

je vis	nous vivons	vis
tu vis	vous vivez	vivons
il/elle vit	ils/elles vivent	vivez

PASSÉ COMPOSÉ   IMPERATIVE (NEGATIVE)

j'ai vécu	nous avons vécu	ne vis pas
tu as vécu	vous avez vécu	ne vivons pas
il/elle a vécu	ils/elles ont vécu	ne vivez pas

---

voir/to see	*pr. part.* voyant	*past part.* vu

Singular   Plural

PRESENT INDICATIVE   IMPERATIVE (AFFIRMATIVE)

je vois	nous voyons	vois
tu vois	vous voyez	voyons
il/elle voit	ils/elles voient	voyez

PASSÉ COMPOSÉ   IMPERATIVE (NEGATIVE)

j'ai vu	nous avons vu	ne vois pas
tu as vu	vous avez vu	ne voyons pas
il/elle a vu	ils/elles ont vu	ne voyez pas

---

voler/to fly; to steal   *pr. part.* **volant**   *past part.* **volé**

Singular   Plural

PRESENT INDICATIVE

je vole	nous volons
tu voles	vous volez
il/elle vole	ils/elles volent

IMPERATIVE (AFFIRMATIVE)

vole
volons
volez

PASSÉ COMPOSÉ

j'ai volé	nous avons volé
tu as volé	vous avez volé
il/elle a volé	ils/elles ont volé

IMPERATIVE (NEGATIVE)

ne vole pas
ne volons pas
ne volez pas

---

vouloir/to want   *pr. part.* **voulant**   *past part.* **voulu**

Singular   Plural

PRESENT INDICATIVE

je veux	nous voulons
tu veux	vous voulez
il/elle veut	ils/elles veulent

IMPERATIVE (AFFIRMATIVE)

veuille
veuillons
veuillez

PASSÉ COMPOSÉ

j'ai voulu	nous avons voulu
tu as voulu	vous avez voulu
il/elle a voulu	ils/elles ont voulu

IMPERATIVE (NEGATIVE)

ne veuille pas
ne veuillons pas
ne veuillez pas

---

voyager/to travel   *pr. part.* **voyageant**   *past part.* **voyagé**

Singular   Plural

PRESENT INDICATIVE

je voyage	nous voyageons
tu voyages	vous voyagez
il/elle voyage	ils/elles voyagent

IMPERATIVE (AFFIRMATIVE)

voyage
voyageons
voyagez

PASSÉ COMPOSÉ

j'ai voyagé	nous avons voyagé
tu as voyagé	vous avez voyagé
il/elle a voyagé	ils/elles ont voyagé

IMPERATIVE (NEGATIVE)

ne voyage pas
ne voyageons pas
ne voyagez pas

545

Part B

This part contains only reflexive verbs. They are grouped here so you can make your own observations about the repeated patterns. All reflexive verbs are conjugated with **être** to form the **passé composé** tense.

---

s'amuser/to have a good time, have fun *pr. part.* **s'amusant** *past part.* **amusé**

Singular	Plural

PRESENT INDICATIVE

		IMPERATIVE (AFFIRMATIVE)
je m'amuse	nous nous amusons	amuse-toi
tu t'amuses	vous vous amusez	amusons-nous
il/elle s'amuse	ils/elles s'amusent	amusez-vous

PASSÉ COMPOSÉ

		IMPERATIVE (NEGATIVE)
je me suis amusé(e)	nous nous sommes amusé(e)s	ne t'amuse pas
tu t'es amusé(e)	vous vous êtes amusé(e)(s)	ne nous amusons pas
il s'est amusé	ils se sont amusés	ne vous amusez pas
elle s'est amusée	elles se sont amusées	

---

s'appeler/to be named, call oneself *pr. part.* **s'appelant** *past part.* **appelé**

Singular	Plural

PRESENT INDICATIVE

		IMPERATIVE (AFFIRMATIVE)
je m'appelle	nous nous appelons	appelle-toi
tu t'appelles	vous vous appelez	appelons-nous
il/elle s'appelle	ils/elles s'appellent	appelez-vous

PASSÉ COMPOSÉ

		IMPERATIVE (NEGATIVE)
je me suis appelé(e)	nous nous sommes appelé(e)s	ne t'appelle pas
tu t'es appelé(e)	vous vous êtes appelé(e)(s)	ne nous appelons pas
il s'est appelé	ils se sont appelés	ne vous appelez pas
elle s'est appelée	elles se sont appelées	

---

s'asseoir/to sit down *pr. part.* **s'asseyant** *past part.* **assis**

Singular	Plural

PRESENT INDICATIVE

		IMPERATIVE (AFFIRMATIVE)
je m'assieds	nous nous asseyons	assieds-toi
tu t'assieds	vous vous asseyez	asseyons-nous
il/elle s'assied	ils/elles s'asseyent	asseyez-vous

PASSÉ COMPOSÉ

		IMPERATIVE (NEGATIVE)
je me suis assis(e)	nous nous sommes assis(es)	ne t'assieds pas
tu t'es assis(e)	vous vous êtes assis(e)(es)	ne nous asseyons pas
il s'est assis	ils se sont assis	ne vous asseyez pas
elle s'est assise	elles se sont assises	

---

s'en aller/to go away   *pr. part.* s'en allant   *past part.* en allé

Singular   Plural

PRESENT INDICATIVE

		IMPERATIVE (AFFIRMATIVE)

je m'en vais   nous nous en allons   **va-t'en**
tu t'en vas   vous vous en allez   **allons-nous-en**
il/elle s'en va   ils/elles s'en vont   **allez-vous-en**

PASSÉ COMPOSÉ   IMPERATIVE (NEGATIVE)

je m'en suis allé(e)   nous nous en sommes allé(e)s   **ne t'en va pas**
tu t'en es allé(e)   vous vous en êtes allé(e)(s)   **ne nous en allons pas**
il s'en est allé   ils s'en sont allés   **ne vous en allez pas**
elle s'en est allée   elles s'en sont allées

---

s'habiller/to dress (oneself)   *pr. part.* s'habillant   *past part.* habillé

Singular   Plural

PRESENT INDICATIVE   IMPERATIVE (AFFIRMATIVE)

je m'habille   nous nous habillons   **habille-toi**
tu t'habilles   vous vous habillez   **habillons-nous**
il/elle s'habille   ils/elles s'habillent   **habillez-vous**

PASSÉ COMPOSÉ   IMPERATIVE (NEGATIVE)

je me suis habillé(e)   nous nous sommes habillé(e)s   **ne t'habille pas**
tu t'es habillé(e)   vous vous êtes habillé(e)(s)   **ne nous habillons pas**
il s'est habillé   ils se sont habillés   **ne vous habillez pas**
elle s'est habillée   elles se sont habillées

---

se blesser/to hurt (injure) oneself   *pr. part.* se blessant   *past part.* blessé

Singular   Plural

PRESENT INDICATIVE   IMPERATIVE (AFFIRMATIVE)

je me blesse   nous nous blessons   **blesse-toi**
tu te blesses   vous vous blessez   **blessons-nous**
il/elle se blesse   ils/elles se blessent   **blessez-vous**

PASSÉ COMPOSÉ   IMPERATIVE (NEGATIVE)

je me suis blessé(e)   nous nous sommes blessé(e)s   **ne te blesse pas**
tu t'es blessé(e)   vous vous êtes blessé(e)(s)   **ne nous blessons pas**
il s'est blessé   ils se sont blessés   **ne vous blessez pas**
elle s'est blessée   elles se sont blessées

547

se coucher/to go to bed, to lie down   *pr. part.* se couchant   *past part.* couché

Singular   Plural

PRESENT INDICATIVE   IMPERATIVE (AFFIRMATIVE)

je me couche   nous nous couchons   couche-toi
tu te couches   vous vous couchez   couchons-nous
il/elle se couche   ils/elles se couchent   couchez-vous

PASSÉ COMPOSÉ   IMPERATIVE (NEGATIVE)

je me suis couché(e)   nous nous sommes couché(e)s   ne te couche pas
tu t'es couché(e)   vous vous êtes couché(e)(s)   ne nous couchons pas
il s'est couché   ils se sont couchés   ne vous couchez pas
elle s'est couchée   elles se sont couchées

---

se dépêcher/to hurry   *pr. part.* se dépêchant   *past part.* dépêché

Singular   Plural

PRESENT INDICATIVE   IMPERATIVE (AFFIRMATIVE)

je me dépêche   nous nous dépêchons   dépêche-toi
tu te dépêches   vous vous dépêchez   dépêchons-nous
il/elle se dépêche   ils/elles se dépêchent   dépêchez-vous

PASSÉ COMPOSÉ   IMPERATIVE (NEGATIVE)

je me suis dépêché(e)   nous nous sommes dépêché(e)s   ne te dépêche pas
tu t'es dépêché(e)   vous vous êtes dépêché(e)(s)   ne nous dépêchons pas
il s'est dépêché   ils se sont dépêchés   ne vous dépêchez pas
elle s'est dépêchée   elles se sont dépêchées

---

se laver/to wash oneself   *pr. part.* se lavant   *past part.* lavé

Singular   Plural

PRESENT INDICATIVE   IMPERATIVE (AFFIRMATIVE)

je me lave   nous nous lavons   lave-toi
tu te laves   vous vous lavez   lavons-nous
il/elle se lave   ils/elles se lavent   lavez-vous

PASSÉ COMPOSÉ   IMPERATIVE (NEGATIVE)

je me suis lavé(e)   nous nous sommes lavé(e)s   ne te lave pas
tu t'es lavé(e)   vous vous êtes lavé(e)(s)   ne nous lavons pas
il s'est lavé   ils se sont lavés   ne vous lavez pas
elle s'est lavée   elles se sont lavées

---

se lever/to get up   *pr. part.* se levant   *past part.* levé

Singular   Plural

PRESENT INDICATIVE

		IMPERATIVE (AFFIRMATIVE)
je me lève	nous nous levons	lève-toi
tu te lèves	vous vous levez	levons-nous
il/elle se lève	ils/elles se lèvent	levez-vous

PASSÉ COMPOSÉ

		IMPERATIVE (NEGATIVE)
je me suis levé(e)	nous nous sommes levé(e)s	ne te lève pas
tu t'es levé(e)	vous vous êtes levé(e)(s)	ne nous levons pas
il s'est levé	ils se sont levés	ne vous levez pas
elle s'est levée	elles se sont levées	

---

se reposer/to rest   *pr. part.* se reposant   *past part.* reposé

Singular   Plural

PRESENT INDICATIVE

		IMPERATIVE (AFFIRMATIVE)
je me repose	nous nous reposons	repose-toi
tu te reposes	vous vous reposez	reposons-nous
il/elle se repose	ils/elles se reposent	reposez-vous

PASSÉ COMPOSÉ

		IMPERATIVE (NEGATIVE)
je me suis reposé(e)	nous nous sommes reposé(e)s	ne te repose pas
tu t'es reposé(e)	vous vous êtes reposé(e)(s)	ne nous reposons pas
il s'est reposé	ils se sont reposés	ne vous reposez pas
elle s'est reposée	elles se sont reposées	

---

se souvenir/to remember   *pr. part.* se souvenant   *past part.* souvenu

Singular   Plural

PRESENT INDICATIVE

		IMPERATIVE (AFFIRMATIVE)
je me souviens	nous nous souvenons	souviens-toi
tu te souviens	vous vous souvenez	souvenons-nous
il/elle se souvient	ils/elles se souviennent	souvenez-vous

PASSÉ COMPOSÉ

		IMPERATIVE (NEGATIVE)
je me suis souvenu(e)	nous nous sommes souvenu(e)s	ne te souviens pas
tu t'es souvenu(e)	vous vous êtes souvenu(e)(s)	ne nous souvenons pas
il s'est souvenu	ils se sont souvenus	ne vous souvenez pas
elle s'est souvenue	elles se sont souvenues	

549

French-English Glossary

A

à   *prep.* at, to; **à bientôt** see you soon; **à ce moment-là** at that moment; **à couvert** covered; **à tout à l'heure** see you in a little while *see also idioms with* à, Part III, Unit 1

a   *v. form of* **avoir**; **il, elle a**/he, she, it has; **a eu** *v. form, passé composé of* **avoir**

abîmer   *v.* to spoil, to damage

accepté   *past part. of* **accepter** (to accept)

achat   *n. m.* purchase; **achète** *v. form of* **acheter** (to buy); **acheté** *past part.*

addition   *n. f.* bill, check (tab)

adieu   *n. m.* farewell, good-bye

Afrique   *n. f.* Africa

agent de police   *n. m.* police officer

agréable   *adj.* pleasant

ai   *v. form of* **avoir**; **j'ai**/I have; **je n'ai pas**/I don't have

aidé   *past part. of* **aider** (to help)

ail   *n. m.* garlic

aile   *n. f.* wing

aime   *v. form of* **aimer** (to love, to like); **aimé** *past part.*; **aimer bien** to like; **aimer mieux** to prefer, to like better

ainsi que   *conj.* as well as, (just) as

ajoute, ajoutez   *v. forms of* **ajouter** (to add)

aliment   *n. m.* **alimentation** *n. f.* food, nourishmnent

allé *past part. of* **aller** (to go); **allez, allons** *v. forms of* **aller**; **allez-y!** go there! go to it! **allez! go! n'allez pas!** don't go! **allons!** let's go!

allemand   *n. m.* German (language); **Allemagne** *n. f.* Germany

allô   *interj.* hello (used when answering a telephone)

allumer   *v.* to turn on, switch on (an apparatus), to light

alors   *adv.* so, then, well

américain   *n. m.* American (language); **l'Amérique** *n. f.* America

ami   *n. m.* **amie** *n. f.* friend; **amitié** *n. f.* friendship

amour   *n. m.* love; **amoureux, amoureuse** *adj. m. f.* in love; **amoureuse de** in love with; **nous sommes amoureux** we are in love

amusant, amusante   *adj.* amusing, enjoyable; **amuser** *v.* to amuse; **s'amuser** *refl. v.* to have a good time, amuse oneself, enjoy oneself; **nous allons beaucoup nous amuser** we are going to have a very good time; **amusez-vous bien!** have a good time! **ils se sont bien amusés** they had a very good time

an   *n. m.* **année** *n. f.* year

ananas   *n. m.* pineapple

ancien   *adj. m. s.* **ancienne** *adj. f. s.* ancient, old, former

anglais   *n. m.* English (language)

Angleterre   *n. f.* England

animaux   *n. m. pl.* animals

anniversaire   *n. m.* birthday, anniversary

annoncé   *past part. of* **annoncer** (to announce)

août   *n. m.* August

appareil *n. m.* apparatus (telephone)

appelé   *past part. of* **appeler** (to call); **s'appeler** to be called, be named; **Comment vous appelez-vous?**/What is your name? **Je m'appelle Janine.**/My name is Janine.

apporte   *v. form of* **apporter** (to bring); **apporté** *past part.*; **apporte!**/bring!

apprendre   *v.* to learn; **appris** *past part.*; **Je n'ai rien appris de nouveau**/I didn't learn anything new

s'approcher (de)   *refl. v.* to approach, come (go) near

après   *prep.* after; **après-midi** *n. m.* afternoon; **l'après-midi** in the afternoon

arbre   *n. m.* tree

arc-en-ciel   *n. m.* rainbow

argent   *n. m.* money

armoire   *n. f.* closet, wardrobe

arracher   *v.* to pull (away)

arrêt *n. m.* stop; **arrêt d'autobus** bus stop; **arrêté** *past part. of* **arrêter** (to arrest), **s'arrêter** (to stop)

arrivent   *v. form of* **arriver** (to arrive); **arrivé** *past part.*

as   *v. form of* **avoir** (to have); **tu as**/you have; **as-tu?**/do you have

s'assembler   *refl. v.* to gather together

s'assied   *v. form of* **s'asseoir** (to sit down); **assis** *past part.*; **assis(e)** *adj.* seated, sitting; **assieds-toi!**/sit down! **asseyez-vous!**/sit down!

assiette   *n. f.* plate, dish

assister à   *v.* to attend, be present at

assourdissant(e)   *adj. m. (f.) s.* deafening (very loud)

attendre   *v.* to wait (for), expect

attention   *n. f.* **à** watch out for

attraper   *v.* to catch

au (*combining of* à + **le**) at the, to the, in the, with; *see also idioms with* **au**, Part III, Unit 1; **au caissier**/at the cashier's; **au courant**/in the know; **au four**/in the oven; **au guichet**/at the ticket window; **au lit**/in bed; **au mois de**/in the month of; **au régime**/on a diet; **au revoir**/good-bye, until we meet again

aujourd'hui *adv.* today

aussi *adv.* also, too, as

auteur *n. m.* author, writer

autobus *n. m.* city bus; **autocar** *n. m.* interurban bus

automne *n. m.* autumn, fall

autour *adv.* around

autre(s) *adj., pron.* other(s), another; **l'autre** the other one; **un (une) autre** another one

aux (*combining of* à + **les**) to the, in the, at the, with; **aux États-Unis** to (in) the United States

avancer *v.* to advance

avant *prep.* before; **avant de sortir** before going out

avec *prep.* with; **avec eux** with them

avez *v. form of* **avoir** (to have); **vous avez** you have, you do have

avion *n. m.* airplane

avis *n. m.* opinion; **avisé** *adj.* shrewd, smart

avocat *n. m.* lawyer

avoir *v.* to have

avoué *n. m.* attorney, lawyer

B

bague *n. f.* ring

se baigner *v. refl.* to bathe oneself

bal *n. m.* dance

balai *n. m.* broom

balançoir *n. f.* swing, seesaw

balle *n. f.* ball, bullet

ballon *n. m.* ball, balloon, football

banc *n. m.* bench (seat)

banque *n. f.* **de données** database

bar *n. m.* **rapide** snack bar

barrière *n. f.* fence

bas *n. m.* stocking; *adj.* low; *adv.* low down; **les plus bas** the lowest

basse *adj. f.* low

bat *v. form of* **battre** (to beat)

bâti *past part. of* **bâtir** (to build); **bâtiment** *n. m.* building

bâton *n. m.* wand, stick, baton

beau *adj. m. s.* beautiful, handsome; **beaux** *pl.*

beaucoup (de) *adv.* much, a lot, many

beauté *n. f.* beauty

bébé *n. m.* baby

belge *adj.* Belgian; **Belgique** *n. f.* Belgium; **Il est belge, Elle est belge**/He (She) is Belgian

belle *adj. f. s.* beautiful

bercer *v.* to rock, lull

besoin *n. m.* need; *see also idioms with* **avoir** in Part III, Unit 3

bête *adj.* foolish, dumb; **bêtise** *n. f.* foolish thing, dumb thing

beurre *n. m.* butter

bibliothèque *n. f.* library

bien *adv.* well; **bien sûr** of course; **bientôt** *adv.* soon

bière *n. f.* beer

billet *n. m.* ticket

billet *n. m.* **électronique** electronic ticket, e-ticket

blanc *adj. m. s.* **blanche** *adj. f. s.* white

blé *n. m.* wheat

blesser *v.* to hurt, injure

bleu *n. m., adj. m. sing.* **bleus** *adj. m. pl.* blue

boire *v.* to drink

bois *n. m.* woods

boisson *n. f.* drink, beverage

boit *v. form of* **boire**

boîte *n. f.* tin can, box

boîte *n. f.* **vocale** voice mail

bon *adj. m. s.,* **bons** *pl.*; **bonne** *adj. f. s.,* **bonnes** *pl.* good

bon voyage! have a good trip! **bon retour!** have a good return trip!

bonbon *n. m.* candy

bonheur *n. m.* happiness

bonhomme *n. m.* **de neige** snowman

bonjour *n. m.* hello, good day, good morning, good afternoon

bonne *adj. f. s.* good; **bonne chance!** good luck! **de bonne heure** early; **bonnes nouvelles!** good news!

bonsoir *n. m.* good night, good evening

bouche *n. f.* mouth

boucher *n. m.* butcher; **boucherie** *n. f.* butcher shop

bouillir *v.* to boil

boulanger *n. m.* baker; **boulangerie** *n. f.* bakery

bouteille *n. f.* bottle

boutique *n. f.* boutique, small shop

bouton *n. m.* **de démarrage** power button

bouton *n. m.* **du pavé tactile** touch pad button

bras *n. m.* arm

brave *adj. m.* good, fine, honest (when **brave** follows a noun, it means *brave*: **c'est un homme brave** he's a brave man; **c'est une femme brave** she's a brave woman)

briller *v.* to shine

brosse *n. f.* brush

bruit *n. m.* noise

brûler *v.* to burn; **brûlé** burned

bu *past part. of* **boire**

buffet *n. m.* china closet, hutch, sideboard

bureau *n. m.* desk, office

but *n. m.* goal

C

ça *dem. pron.* that (**ça** is short for **cela**); **Ça ne fait rien!** That doesn't matter! **Ça va!** (I'm) fine!

caché *adj. m. s.* hidden

cadeau *n. m.* present, gift

café *n. m.* coffee, café (coffeehouse)

cahier *n. m.* notebook

caisse *n. f.* cash box (register); **caissier** *n. m.* **caissière** *n. f.* cashier

calculatrice *n. f.* calculator

camarade *n. m. f.* comrade, buddy, pal, mate

camembert *n. m.* camembert (name of a cheese)

camion *n. m.* truck; **camionneur** *n. m.* truck driver

campagne *n. f.* countryside

Canada *n. m.* Canada; **Il est canadien**/He is Canadian; **Elle est canadienne**/She is Canadian

canne *n. f.* cane

carte *n. f.* map, menu

carte *n. f.* **bancaire/la carte de crédit** credit card

carte *n. f.* **d'embarquement** boarding pass

cas *n. m.* case

casser *v.* to break; **sans la casser** without breaking it

cave *n. f.* cellar

CD *n. m.* CD

ce *dem. adj. m. s.* this, that; **ce n'est pas...** it isn't...; **ce que** *pron.* that which, what; **ce qui** *pron.* that which; **ce soir** tonight; **ce sont...** they are... or it's...

ceci *dem. pron.* this; **cela** *dem. pron.* that; **Cela n'a pas d'importance** That has no importance; That's not important.

cédérom *n. m., le CD-ROM* CD-ROM

céleri *n. m.* celery; **blanc de céleri** celery stalk

cent *adj.* one hundred

cerise *n. f.* cherry

ces *dem. adj. m. f. pl.* these, those

cesse *n. f.* ceasing, stopping

c'est... he's... she's... it's... **c'est aujourd'hui le premier décembre** today is December 1st; **c'est ça!** that's right! **c'est bien ça!** that's quite right! **c'est fait!** it is done! **c'est fini!** it's finished

cet *dem. adj. m. s.* **cette** *f. s.* this

chacun *pron.* each one; **chacune** *fem.*

chaise *n. f.* chair

chambre *n. f.* room; **chambre à coucher** bedroom

champ *n. m.* field

champignon *n. m.* mushroom

chance *n. f.* luck, chance, fortune

changement *n. m.* change

chanté *past part. of* **chanter** (to sing); **chanteur** *n. m.,* **chanteuse** *n. f.* singer

chapeau *n. m.* hat

chapelle *n. f.* chapel

chaque *adj.* each

charmante *adj. f.* charming

chasser *v.* to chase away, hunt

chat *n. m.,* **chatte** *n. f.* cat

château *n. m.* castle

chaud, chaude *adj. m. f.* hot; *see also idioms with* **avoir** *in Part III, Unit 3*

chaussettes *n. f.* socks; **chaussure** *n. f.* shoe

cheminée *n. f.* chimney

chemise *n. f.* shirt

cher, chère *adj. m. s., f. s.* dear; **cher** *adj., adv.* expensive; **chéri, chérie** *n. m. f.* darling, honey

cherché *past part. of* **chercher** to look (for), search (for), get

cheval *n. m.* horse

cheveux *n. m. pl.* hair

chez *prep.* at (to) the home (place) of; **chez moi** at my house; **chez le dentiste** to (at) the dentist's; **chez le coiffeur** to (at) the hairdresser's, barber's; **chez le médecin** to (at) the doctor's; **chez vous** to (at) your house (place)

chien *n. m.* dog

choisi *part part. of* **choisir** (to choose, select)

choisit, choisissez *v. forms of* **choisir; il choisit** he chooses; **choisissez!** choose!

chose *n. f.* thing

chuchoter *v.* to whisper

ciel *n. m.* sky

cigale *n. f.* cicada

cinéma *n. m.* movies

cinq *adj.* five; **cinquième** fifth; **cinquante** fifty

clair *adj. m. s.* clear

clavardage *n. m.* chat (Internet)

clavarder *v.* to chat (Internet)

clavier *n. m.* keyboard

clavier *n. m.* **d'identification personnelle** PIN pad

clef *n. f.* key

client *n. m.* customer

cloche *n. f.* bell

coeur *n. m.* heart

coiffeur *n. m.* hairdresser, barber; **coiffe** *n. f.* headdress; **coiffure** *n. f.* hairstyle; **se coiffer** *v. refl.* to comb one's hair, style one's hair

coin *n. m.* corner

combien *adv.* how many, how much

comme *adv.* like, as; **comme il faut** as it should be, proper and correct

commencé *past part. of* **commencer** (to begin, commence)

comment *adv.* how; *see also idioms with* **comment** *in Part III, Unit 2*

commerce *n. m.* **électronique** e-commerce

commode *n. f.* dresser

comprendre *v.* to understand; **compris** *past part.* understood

confiture *n. f.* jam, perserves

congé *see* **jour de congé**

connaissez-vous...? *v. form of* **connaître** (to know someone, be acquainted with); do you know...? **Est-**

ce que Pierre connaît Robert? Does Pierre know Robert? (*pres. indicative;* je connais, tu connais, il (elle) connaît, nous connaissons, vous connaissez, ils (elles) connaissent)

conte *n. m.* story, tale

contraire *n. m., adj.* contrary, opposite

contre *prep.* against

contrôle *n. m.* de sécurité security check (travel)

contrôleur *n. m.* ticket taker, train conductor

cordiaux *adj. m. pl.* cordial

corps *n. m.* body

corriger *v.* to correct

côté *n. m.* side; à côté de next to

cou *n. m.* neck

couché *adj.* lying down; se coucher *v.* to go to bed

couleur *n. f.* color; de quelle couleur est...? what color is...?

couloir *n. m.* hallway, corridor

se couper *v. refl.* to cut oneself

courent, court *v. forms of* courir (to run)

courriel *n. m.* e-mail

courrier *n. m.* électronique e-mail

cours *n. m.* course; cours de français French course

court, courte *adj. m. s., f. s.* short

couteau *n. m.* knife

coûter *v.* to cost

couvert *past part. of* couvrir (to cover)

craie *n. f.* chalk

cravate *n. f.* necktie

crayon *n. m.* pencil

crémeux *adj. m.* creamy

crie, crient *v. forms of* crier (to shout, to cry out)

crois *v. form of* croire (to believe); Je n'y crois pas. I don't believe in it.

croix *n. f.* cross

cru *past part. of* croire

cuiller, cuillère *n. f.* spoon; cuillère à soupe soup spoon

cuire *v.* to cook; cuit *past part.*

cuisine *n. f.* kitchen, cooking (food); cuisine rapide *n. f.* fast food

cuisson *n. f.* cooking (time)

cybercafé *n. m.* cybercafé

D

d' *prep.* (*contraction of* de); *see idioms with* d' *in* Part III, Unit 4

d'abord *advl. expr.* at first, first

d'accord agreed, okay

d'ailleurs *adv.* besides

dame *n. f.* lady

dangereux *adj. m.* dangereuse *adj. f.* dangerous

dans *prep.* in

dansé *past part. of* danser (to dance); danseur *n. m.,* danseuse *n. f.* dancer

davantage *adj.* more

de *prep.* of, from, with; de bonne heure *adv.* early *see also idioms with* de *in* Part III, Unit 4

de quelle couleur est... what color is...

de rien you're welcome

debout *adv.* standing

décembre *n. m.* December

déchirer *v.* to tear

décision *n. f.* decision

décréter *v.* to decree, to enact, to give an executive order

dedans *adv.* inside

défendre *v.* to defend, forbid; défendu, *past part.*

dégoûtant *adj. m. s.* disgusting, revolting

dehors *adv.* outside

déjà *adv.* already

déjeuner *v.* to have lunch, to eat lunch, to lunch; *n. m.* lunch; le petit déjeuner breakfast

délicieux *adj. m. s. pl.,* délicieuse *adj. f. s.* delicious

demain *adv.* tomorrow

demander *v.* to ask (for); demandé *past part.*

demeurer *v.* to live, reside, inhabit, stay, remain

demi *m.,* demie *f., adj.* half

d'en face opposite

dent *n. f.* tooth

se dépêcher *refl. v.* to hurry

depuis *adv., prep.* since

déranger *v.* to disturb

dernier *m.,* dernière *f., adj.* last; la dernière mise the last bid

derrière *adv., prep.* behind

descendre *v.* to go down, come down; descendu *past part.*

désir *n. m.* desire; désirer *v.* to desire

désobéir *v.* to disobey

dessert *n. m.* dessert

dessus *adv.* on top, above

détail *n. m.* detail

détective *n. m.* detective

détester *v.* to detest, to hate

deux *n. m., adj.* two; tous les deux both

deuxième *n. m. f., adj.* second

devant *prep.* before, in front of

devenir *v.* to become; devenu *past part.*

deviens, devient *v. forms of* devenir; je deviens folle! je deviens fou! I'm going crazy!

devinette *n. f.* riddle

devoir *v.* to owe, ought to, must, have to

devoirs *n. m. pl.* homework, assignments, duties

dictionnaire *n. m.* dictionary

Dieu *n. m.* God

difficile *adj. m. f.* difficult

diligent *adj. m.* diligent, industrious

dîné *past part. of* dîner

dîner *v.* to dine, to have dinner; *n. m.* dinner

dire *v.* to say, to tell; dire des histoires to tell stories, make up stories, fibs

553

directeur *n. m.,* **directrice** *n. f.* director, principal

dis, disent *v. forms of* **dire**; **je dis** I say; **tu dis** you say; **ils, elles disent** they say; **dis-moi** tell me

disposer *v.* to dispose, arrange, prepare

disque *n. m.* record, disc, recording

disque *n. m.* **compact** CD

disque *n. m.* **dur** hard drive

disque *n. m.* **DVD** DVD

distinctement *adv.* distinctly

dit *v. form of* **dire**; **il/elle dit** he/she says, tells; *also past part. of* **dire**

dites-moi tell me; **dites-nous** tell us

divers *adj.* diverse, different

dix *n. m., adj.* ten

docteur *n. m.* doctor

dodo *n. m.* sleep; **fais dodo** go to sleep (child's language)

doigt *n. m.* finger

dois, doit, doivent *v. forms of* **devoir**; **je dois** I have to; **il/elle doit** he/she has to; **ils/elles doivent** they have to

domestique *adj.* domestic; **domestiqué** *adj.* domesticated

donne *v. form of* **donner**; **donne!** give! **donne-moi/donnez-moi** give me; **donné** *past part. of* **donner**

donner *v.* to give

dormir *v.* to sleep; **dors** *v. form of* **dormir**

dos *n. m.* back

dossier *n. m.* brief, file of papers

douane *n. f.* customs (duty or tax on imported goods)

douce *adj. f.* sweet, soft

doucement *adv.* softly, sweetly, gently (low flame)

douche *n. f.* shower

doute *n. m.* doubt; **sans doute** undoubtedly, without a doubt

doux *adj. m.* sweet, soft

drapeau *n. m.* flag

droite *n. f.* right (as opposed to left); **à droite, à la droite** to (on) the right

drôle *adj. m. f.* funny, droll

dû *past part. of* **devoir**

de (*contraction of* **de** + **le**); *see idioms with* **du** *in* Part III, Unit 4

E

eau *n. f.* water

échapper *v.* to escape, to get away; **le chapeau échappé** the hat that got away

éclair *n. m.* eclair

éclairant *pres. part. of* **éclairer** illuminating

éclairer *v.* to illuminate, to light up

école *n. f.* school

écouter *v.* to listen (to)

écran *n. m.* display screen (computer)

écran *n. m.* **plasma** plasma screen, plasma display

écran *n. m.* **tactile** touch screen

écraser *v.* to crush

écrire *v.* to write

écrit, écrivent, écrivez *v. forms of* **écrire**

écrivain *n. m.* writer, author

effacer *v.* to erase

église *n. f.* church

eh bien! *exclam.* well now!

élève *n. m. f.* pupil, student

elle *per. pron. f.* she, her, it; **elles** *per. pron. f. pl.* they, them; **avec elles** with them

embarras *n. m.* embarrassment, hindrance, fuss, distress

émission *n. f.* TV program, show

emplette *n. f.* purchase; *see also idioms with* **faire** *in* Part III, Unit 6

employer *v.* to use, to employ

emporter *v.* to take along, to take (carry) away

en *prep.* in, into, on, while; *see also idioms with* **en** *in* Part III, Unit 2; *as pron.,* some (of it, of them), of them; *see* Work Unit 13

en arrivant on (upon) arriving; **en courant** running; **en disposant** arranging; **en forme** in good shape; **en tenue d'exercice** in a gym suit; **en ville** downtown, into town

enchère *n. f.* bid, bidding

encore *adv.* again; **encore une fois** once more, yet, still

endroit *n. m.* place

enfant *n. m. f.* child

enfin *adv.* finally, at last, in short

engager *v.* to apply to, to put into gear

enlever *v.* to remove, to take off

ennuyer *v. to annoy, to bore;* **ennuyeux** annoying, boring

enseignement *n. m.* teaching, instruction

enseigner *v.* to teach

ensemble *adv.* together

ensuite *adv.* then, after, next

entendre *v.* to hear; **entendu** *past part.*

entracte *n. m.* intermission

entraîneur *n. m.* coach, sports instructor

entre *prep.* between; **entre eux et nous** between them and us

entrer (dans) *v.* to enter, to go (into), to come in; **entré** *past part.;* **entrée** *n. f.* entrance

envoyer *v.* to send

épais *adj.* thick

épaule *n. f.* shoulder

épicerie *n. f.* grocery store; **épicier** *m.* **épicière** *f.* grocer

épingle *n. f.* pin

épouse *n. f.* wife; **époux** *n. m.* husband

équipe *n. f.* team

érection *n. f.* construction, erection

erreur *n. f.* error, mistake

es *v. form of* **être**; **tu es** you are (*familiar use*); **es-tu...?** are you...?

espagnol *n. m.* Spanish

espérer *v.* to hope

esprit *n. m.* spirit

essayer *v.* to try

essence *n. f.* gasoline

est *v. form of* être; **il/elle est** he/she/it is

est-ce…? is it…?

estomac *n. m.* stomach

et *conj.* and

étage *n. m.* floor (of a building designated by number)

étais *v. form of* être (imperfect indicative); **j'étais** I was

États-Unis *n. m. pl.* United States; **aux États-Unis** in (to) the United States

été *n. m.* summer; *also past part. of* être (been); **j'ai été** I was, I have been

éteindre *v.* to extinguish, to snuff out

êtes *v. form of* être; **vous êtes** you are

être *v.* to be; *see also idioms with* être, Part III, Unit 3

êtroit *adj. m. s.* narrow

étudiant *n. m.* **étudiante** *n. f.,* student

étudié *past part. of* **étudier**

étudier *v.* to study

eu *past part. of* avoir; **j'ai eu** I had, I have had

euro *n. m.* euro

eux *disj. pron. m. pl.* them

éviter *v.* to avoid

exactement *adv.* exactly

examiner *v.* to examine

exclamer, s'exclamer *v., refl. v.* to exclaim

excuser *v.* to excuse

expliquer *v.* to explain

exposition *n. f.* exhibit

extraordinaire *adj. m. f. s.* extraordinary, unusual

extrêmement *adv.* extremely

F

fable *n. f.* fable

fâché *adj.* angry; **se fâcher** *refl. v.* to get angry

facile *adj.* easy; **facilement** *adv.* easily

façon *n. f.* way; **de façon à** so as to

facteur *n. m.* mail carrier

faible *adj.* weak

faim *n. f.* hunger; **avoir faim** to be hungry; **j'ai faim** I'm hungry; *see also other idioms with* avoir *in* Part III, Unit 3

faire *v.* to do, to make; **faire bouillir** to boil; **faire connaissance** to meet, to become acquainted with; **faire de la gymnastique** to do gymnastics, to do exercises; **faire la toilette** to wash and dress oneself; **se faire lire les lignes de la main** to have one's palm read, to have the lines of one's hand read; **se faire mal** to hurt oneself; **faire réparer** to have repaired; **faire trop cuire** to overcook; **faire visite** to visit, to pay a visit; *see also idioms with* faire, Part III, Unit 6

fais, fait, faites *v. forms of* **faire; fais dodo** go to sleep (child's language); **il/elle fait** he/she/it does (makes); **c'est fait** it's done, it's finished; **fait** *past part. of* **faire; elle a fait la leçon** she did (has done) the lesson; **faites le travail!** do the work! **faites bouillir l'eau, s'il vous plaît!** boil the water, please!

famille *n. f.* family

farine *n. f.* flour

fatigué *m.* **fatiguée** *f., adj.* tired

faut *v. form of* falloir (to be necessary, must); **il faut** it is necessary, you must, you have to, one must, we must, we have to, etc. (This is an impersonal verb and the subject is always il); **faut-il?** is it necessary?

faute *n. f.* mistake, error

fauteuil *n. m.* armchair

faux *adj.* false

favori *m.* favorite *f., adj.* favorite

femme *n. f.* woman, wife

fenêtre *n. f.* window

ferme *n. f.* farm

fermé *past part. of* **fermer** (to close)

fête *n. f.* holiday, feast, birthday

feu *n. m.* fire, traffic light

feuille *n. f.* leaf; **feuille de papier** sheet of paper

fichier *n. m.* **MP3** MP3

figure *n. f.* face

filer *v.* to go (away) quickly (*used familiarly*); **filez!** go away! beat it!

filet *n. m.* net

fille *n. f.* daughter; **une jeune fille** a girl

film *n. m.* film, movie

fils *n. m.* son

fin *n. f.* end

fini *m.,* **finie** *f. adj.* finished; **fini** *past part. of* **finir** (to finish)

finis, finissent, finissons, finit *v. forms of* **finir; finissons!** let's finish!

fixement *adv.* intently, fixedly

fleur *n. f.* flower; **fleuriste** *n. m. f.* florist

fleuve *n. m.* river

foire *n. f.* fair (as at a county or state fair)

fois *n. f.* time; **une fois** one time, once; **deux fois** two times, twice, etc.; **mille fois** a thousand times; **la prochaine fois** the next time

folle *adj. f. s.* crazy; **fou** *adj. m. s.*

font *v. form of* **faire**

football *n. m.* soccer (in the United States)

forme *n. f.* form, shape

formidable *adj.* terrific

fort *m.* **forte** *f., adj.* strong; **votre qualité la plus forte** your strongest quality; **le (la) plus fort (forte)** the strongest

fou *adj. m. s.* crazy

four *n. m.* oven

fourchette *n. f.* fork

555

fourmi   *n. f.* ant
foyer   *n. m.* hearth, home
frais   *m. s. pl.*, **fraîche** *f. s.*
   adj. fresh; **il fait frais** it's
   cool
fraise   *n. f.* strawberry
franc   *n. m.* franc (former
   French unit of money)
français   *n. m.* French
   (language); **Il est
   français**/He is French; **Elle
   est française**/She is
   French; **Je parle français**/I
   speak French
France   *n. f.* France
fréquence   *n. f.* frequency
frère   *n. m.* brother
froid   *n. m., adj.*, **froide** *f.*,
   adj. cold; *see idioms with*
   faire, Part III, Unit 6
fromage   *n. m.* cheese
fumé   *past part. of* **fumer** (to
   smoke); **la fumée** the
   smoke
furieux   *m. s. pl.*, **furieuse**
   adj. f. s. furious

G

gagner   *v.* to win
galant   *m.*, **galante** *f., adj.*
   gallant
gant   *n. m.* glove
garagiste   *n. m.* auto
   mechanic
garçon *n. m.* boy; **garçon (de
   restaurant);** (Nowadays, a
   customer addresses a waiter
   as *Monsieur*, not *garçon*;
   address a waitress as
   Mademoiselle or *Madame*)
garder   *v.* to guard, keep
gardien   *n. m.* guard; **un
   gardien (une gardienne)
   d'enfants** babysitter; **un
   gardien (une gardienne)
   de but** goalie
gare   *n. f.* station (bus, train,
   etc.)
gâteau   *n. m.* cake
gauche   *n. f.* left (as
   opposed to *right*); **à gauche**
   on (to) the left
généralement   *adv.*
   generally

généreux   *adj., m. s. pl.*
   generous
génie   *n. m.* genius
genou   *n. m.* knee
gentil   *adj., m. s.*, **gentille**
   adj., f. s. nice, kind
géographie   *n. f.* geography
gilet   *n. m.* vest
girafe   *n. f.* giraffe
glace   *n. f.* ice, ice cream,
   mirror; **glacé** *adj., m. s.*,
   glacée *adj., f. s.* glazed,
   frosted
gousse   *n. f.* clove; **une
   gousse d'ail** clove of garlic
goût   *n. m.* taste, flavor;
   goûter *v.* to taste; **goûtez-
   en!** taste some!
gouverner   *v.* to govern
grain   *n. m.* grain
gramme   *n. m.* gram; 1 gram
   = about .035 ounce; 500
   grams = about 1.1 lbs.; *see
   also* Part II, Unit 9
grand   *adj., m. s.*, **grande**
   adj., f. s. great, big, large,
   tall; **grand faim** (**J'ai grand
   faim** I'm very hungry);
   grand magasin *n. m.*
   department store; **grand
   prix** *n. m.* grand prize
Grand Bretagne   *n. f.* Great
   Britain
grande salle   *n. f.* auditorium
grange   *n. f.* barn
grave   *adj., m. f.* grave,
   serious; **gravement** *adv.*
   seriously, gravely
grillé   *adj., m. s.*, **grillée** *adj.,
   f. s.* toasted, grilled
gris   *adj., m. s. pl.*, **grise**
   adj., f. s. gray
gros   *adj., m. s. pl.*, **grosse**
   adj., f. s. big huge, large, fat
groupe   *n. m.* group
guérir   *v.* to cure
gueule   *n. f.* mouth (of an
   animal)
guichet   *n. m.* ticket window
guichet   *n. m.* **automatique
   (bancaire)** ATM (automated
   teller machine)
gymnase   *n. m.* gymnasium,
   gym; **gymnastique** *n. f.*
   gymnastics

H

habillement *n. m.* clothing;
   s'habiller *refl. v.* to get
   dressed, to dress
habit   *n. m.* clothing, attire
   (habit, *i.e.,* robe and hood of
   a monk)
habitant   *n. m.* inhabitant
habite   *v. form of* **habiter** (to
   live, to reside, to inhabit)
halte!   *interj.* halt! stop!
haut   *adv.* high, tall, **à haute
   voix** in a loud voice; **un
   chapeau haut de forme**
   top hat
herbe   *n. f.* grass
heure   *n. f.* hour; **heureux,
   heureuse** *adj., m. f.* happy
hideux   *adj. m. s. pl.* hideous
hier   *adv.* yesterday
histoire   *n. f.* story, history
hiver   *n. m.* winter; **en hiver**
   in winter
homme   *n. m.* man
honneur   *n. m.* honor
honte   *n. f.* shame, disgrace
hôpital   *n. m.* hospital
horizontalement   *adv.*
   horizontally
horloge   *n. f.* clock
horreur   *n. f.* horror
hôtel   *n. m.* hotel
huile   *n. f.* oil
huit   *adj.* eight
humain, humaine   *adj.*
   human
humble   *adj.* humble
hutte   *n. f.* hut

I

ici *adv.* here; **ici Monique** this
   is Monique here
idée   *n. f.* idea
identifier   *v.* to identify
il   *pron.* he *or* it; **il faut** it is
   necessary; **il y a** there is *or*
   there are; **il y en a
   beaucoup** there are many
   of them; **il n'y a pas (de)…**
   there isn't *or* aren't (any)…
   il y a un an a year ago
ils   *pron. m.* they
image   *n. f.* picture

immédiatement *adv.* immediately

immeuble *n. m.* building

incertain, incertaine *adj.* uncertain

incroyable *adj.* unbelievable

inquiet, inquiète *adj.* upset

s'inquiéter *refl. v.* to worry, to be upset; **ne t'inquiète pas!** don't worry!

insister *v.* to insist

insolent, insolente *adj., m. f.* insolent

intelligent, intelligente *adj., m. f.* intelligent; **l'élève le (la) plus intelligent (intelligente) de la classe** the most intelligent student in the class

intéressant, intéressante *adj., m. f.* interesting

Internet *n. m.* Internet

interroger *v.* to interrogate, to question

inventif, inventive *adj., m. f.* inventive

invitation *n. f.* invitation

inviter *v.* to invite

iPod *n. m.* iPod

irlandais, irlandaise *adj., m. f.* Irish

italien, italienne *adj., m. f.* Italian

J

j' (je) *per. pron.* I; **j'ai** I have; **j'ai grand faim** I'm very hungry; **j'ai seize ans** I'm sixteen years old

jamais *adv.* never, ever

jambe *n. f.* leg

jambon *n. m.* ham

jaquette *n. f.* jacket

jardin *n. m.* garden

jaune *n. m.* yellow

je *per. pron.* I; **je n'ai rien à faire** I have nothing to do; **je ne fais rien ce soir** I'm not doing anything tonight

jeter *v.* to throw

jeune *adj. m. f. s.* young; **jeune fille** *n. f.* girl

jeunesse *n. f.* youth

joli *adj. m. s.*, **jolie** *adj. f. s.* pretty

jouer *v.* to play; **joué** *past part.*

jouet *n. m.* toy

joueur *n. m.*, **joueuse** *n. f.* player

jour *n. m.* day; **jour de congé** day off (no school, no work); **Jour de la Bastille** Bastille Day (**le 14 juillet**)

journal *n. m.* newspaper

journée *n. f.* day; **toute la journée** all day long

joyeux, joyeuse *adj.* joyous, happy

juge *n. m.* judge

juillet *n. m.* July

jupe *n. f.* skirt

jus *n. m.* juice

jusque *prep.* until; **jusqu'à, jusqu'aux** until, up to; **jusqu'au printemps** until spring

juste *adj.* accurate, correct, exact

K

kangourou *n. m.* kangaroo

kilogramme *n. m.* kilogram; **1 kilogramme** = about 2.2 lbs.

kilomètre *n. m.* kilometer; **1 kilomètre** = about 0.621 mile

L

l' (le, la) *def. art. m. f.* the; *also, dir. obj. pron.* **Je la vois** (I see her *or* I see it.)

là *adv.* there; **là-bas** *adv.* over there

laideur *n. f.* ugliness

laisser *v.* to let, allow, leave (something behind); **laisse-moi!** let me!

lait *n. m.* milk

lamelle *n. f.* thin slice

lampe *n. f.* lamp

lancer *v.* to throw

langue *n. f.* language, tongue

lapin *n. m.* rabbit

large *n. m.* width, breadth; *adj.* wide

laver *v.* to wash; **se laver** *refl. v.* to wash oneself

le *def. art. m. s.* the; *also, dir. obj. pron.* **Je le vois** (I see him *or* I see it.)

leçon *n. f.* lesson

lecteur *n. m.* **de CD** CD player

lecteur *n. m.* **de DVD** DVD player

lecteur *n. m.* **multimédia** multimedia player

légume *n. m.* vegetable

lendemain *adv.* following day, next day

lentement *adv.* slowly

les *def. art. m. or f. pl.* the; *also, dir. obj. pron.* **Je les vois** (I see them.)

lettre *n. f.* letter

leur *indir. obj. pron.* (to) them; *also, poss. adj.* their; **Je leur parle** (I'm talking to them.); **J'aime leur voiture** (I like their car.); **J'aime leurs amis** (I like their friends.)

lever *v.* to raise, life; **se lever** *refl. v.* to get up; **elle lève la main** (she raises her hand); **levez-vous!** get up! **lève-toi!** get up!

libéré *adj. m.* **libérée** *adj. f.*, liberated

liberté *n. f.* liberty

lieu *n. m.* place; *see idioms with* **avoir** *in* Part III, Unit 3 *and with* **au** *in* Part III, Unit 1

ligne *n. f.* line

lire *v.* to read

lis, lit *v. forms of* **lire**

lit *n. m.* bed; **au lit** in bed

livre *n. m.* book; *n. f.,* pound

loi *n. f.* law

loin *adv.* far

long *adj. m. s.,* **longue** *adj. f. s.* long

Louisiane *n. f.* Louisiana

lu *past part. of* **lire**; **Je n'ai pas lu le livre.** (I haven't read the book/I didn't read the book.)

lui *indir. obj. pron.* (to) him, (to) her; *also, disj. pron.*

him; **avec lui** with him; **avec elle** with her

lumière   *n. f.* light

lunaire   *adj.* lunar

lune   *n. f.* moon

lunettes   *n. f. pl.* eyeglasses

lustre   *n. m.* chandelier

M

m' (me) *refl. pron., dir. and indir. obj. pron.* myself, me, to me

ma   *poss. adj. f. sing.* my (**ma maison**)

machine   *n. f.* **à rayons X** X-ray machine (in airports)

madame *n. f.* (*pl.* **mesdames**) Mrs., madam

mademoiselle   *n. f.* (pl. **mesdemoiselles**) Miss

magasin   *n. m.* store; **grand magasin** department store

magazine   *n. m.* magazine

magicien   *n. m.* **magicienne** *n. f.* magician

magnifique   *adj.* magnificent, wonderful

maillot   *n. m.* **de bain** swimsuit

main   *n. f.* hand

maintenant   *adv.* now

mais   *conj.* but; **mais non!** of course not! why, no! **mais oui!** of course!

maison   *n. f.* house

maître   *n. m.,* **maîtresse** *n. f.* teacher

mal *n. m.* pain, harm; *adv.* badly, poorly; **se faire mal** to hurt oneself; *see idioms with* **avoir** *in* Part III, Unit 3

malade   *adj.* sick, ill

malheur   *n. m.* unhappiness, misfortune

malheureux   *adj. m.,* **malheureuse** *adj. f.* unhappy

malle   *n. f.* trunk (luggage)

maman   *m. f.* mama, mom

manche   *n. f.* sleeve; **La Manche** English Channel

manger   *v.* to eat; **mangeant** *pres. part.* **en mangeant** while eating

manquer   *v.* to miss, be missing (lacking)

manteau   *n. m.* coat

marchand   *n. m.* **marchande** *n. f.* merchant

marchandise   *n. f.* merchandise, goods

marché   *n. m.* market; **le marché aux puces** flea market

marcher   *v.* to walk; to work, run (an apparatus or machine)

mari   *n. m.* husband; **le mariage** marriage

match   *n. m.* game, match (sport)

mathématiques   *n. f. pl.* mathematics

matin   *n. m.* morning; **le matin** in the morning

matinée   *n. f.* morning (all morning long); early afternoon theater performance

mauvais *adj. m.,* **mauvaise** *adj. f.* bad

me   *refl. pron., dir. and indir. obj. pron.* myself, me, to me

méchant   *adj. m.,* **méchante** *adj. f.* mean, nasty

mécontent   *adj. m.* **mécontente** *adj. f.* unhappy, discontent, malcontent

médecin   *n. m.* doctor

médicament   *n. m.* medicine

Méditerranée   *n. f.* Mediterranean (Sea)

se méfier   *refl. v.* to beware; **méfiez-vous de...** beware of...

meilleur, meilleure   *adj.* better; **le meilleur, la meilleure** the best

mélange   *n. m.* mixture

même   *adj.* same, self; **moi-même** myself; **la même chose** the same thing; **tout de même** all the same, just the same; **pas même** not even

ménagère   *n. f.* housewife

mensonge   *n. m.* lie, untruth, falsehood

merci   *n. m.* thanks, thank you

mère   *n. f.* mother

merveilleux, merveilleuse   *adj., m. f.* marvelous, wonderful

mes   *poss. adj. pl.* my (**mes livres**)

mesdames   *n. f. pl.* ladies

mesdemoiselles   *n. f. pl.* young ladies, Misses

messagerie   *n. f.* voice mail

messieurs   *n. m. pl.* gentlemen

mesure   *n. f.* measure

met   *v. form of* **mettre; elle met** she puts

métal   *n. m.* metal

métier   *n. m.* trade, occupation

métro, (métropolitain)   *n. m.* subway

mettez   *v. form of* **mettre** *v.* to put (on), place, wear; **mettre en marche** to put into operation, to start (a machine, apparatus)

meuble(s)   *n. m.* furniture

midi   *n. m.* noon; **le Midi** southern France

mieux   *adv.* better; **j'aime mieux** I prefer, I like better

mignon, mignonne   *adj., m. f.* darling, cute

milieu   *n. m.* middle; **au milieu de** in the middle of

mille   *adj.* thousand

minéral, minérale   *adj., m. f.* mineral

minuit   *n. m.* midnight

mis   *past part. of* **mettre** (to put on); **ils ont mis...** they put on...

misérable   *adj., m. or f.* miserable

mode   *n. m.* method, mode, kind

modeste   *adj.* modest

moi   *stressed per. pron.* me (**avec moi**)

moine   *n. m.* monk

moins   *adv.* less; **le moins, la moins...** the least; **au moins** at least; *see also idioms with* **au** *in* Part III, Unit 1

mois   *n. m.* month; **au mois de** in the month of

mon   *poss. adj. m. sing.* my (**mon livre**)

monde   *n. m.* world, **tout le monde** everybody

monsieur   *n. m.* sir, gentleman, Mr., mister

monstrueux, monstrueuse   *adj., m. f.* monstrous

montant   *n. m.* amount, sum

monté   *past part. of* **monter** (to get in, go up, come up)

montre   *n. f.* watch (wrist)

montrer   *v.* to show

se moquer de   *v. refl.* to make fun of

morceau   *n. m.* piece, morsel

mort   *past part. of* **mourir** (to die)

mot   *n. m.* word; **un petit mot** a note

moteur   *n. m.* motor

mouche   *n. f.* fly (insect)

mouchoir   *n. m.* handkerchief

mourir   *v.* to die

mouton   *n. m.* mutton

mouvement   *n. m.* action, movement

muet, muette   *adj.* mute

mur   *n. m.* wall

musée   *n. m.* museum

musique   *n. f.* music

N

nager *v.* to swim

naissance   *n. f.* birth; **l'anniversaire** (*n. m.*) **de naissance** birthday

naître   *v.* to be born

nappe   *n. f.* tablecloth

naturellement   *adv.* naturally

naviguer   **(sur Internet)** *v.* to navigate, to surf the Internet

né   *past part. of* **naître**

ne mangez rien   don't eat anything

ne   pas + *inf.* not to; **de ne pas révéler** not to reveal

nécessaire   *adj.* necessary

neige   *n. f.* snow; **neiger** *v.* to snow

n'est-ce pas?   isn't that so? isn't it? *see* Work Unit 20

nettoyer   *v.* to clean

neuf   *adj.* nine; **neuf, neuve** *adj., m. f.* new

neveu   *n. m.* nephew

nez   *n. m.* nose

NIP   *n. m.* (**le numéro d'identification personnelle**) PIN

Noël   *n. m.* Christmas

noir, noire   *adj.* black

nom   *n. m.* name

nombre   *n. m.* number; **nombreux, nombreuse** *adj., m. f.* numerous

non   *adv.* no; **non plus** neither; **moi non plus** me neither

notre   *poss. adj.* our; *pl.,* **nos** (**nos livres**)

nourriture   *n. f.* nourishment, food

nous   *per. pron.* we, us

nouveau, nouveaux   *adj.* new; **Je n'ai rien appris de nouveau/**I didn't learn anything new; **un nouveau livre** (a new book)

nouvel, nouvelle   *adj.* new; **un nouvel étudiant, une nouvelle étudiante/**a new student

Nouvelle-Orléans   *n. f.* New Orleans

nouvelles   *n. f. pl.* news; **bonnes nouvelles!** good news!

nuage   *n. m.* cloud;

nuageux, nuageuse   *adj.* cloudy

nuire   *v.* to harm, hurt

O

obéir *v.* to obey

objet   *n. m.* object, article

obscur, obscure   *adj.* dark, obscure

observer   *v.* to observe

occasion   *n. f.* occasion

oeil   *n. m.* eye; **yeux** *pl.*

oeuf   *n. m.* egg; **oeuf à la coque** soft-boiled egg

oeuvre   *n. f.* work; **une oeuvre d'art** a work of art

offre   *v. form of* **offrir** (to offer); *past part.* **offert**

oignon   *n. m.* onion

oiseau   *n. m.* bird; **oiseaux** *pl.*

on   *indef. per. pron.* one, people, you, someone, they; **On vous demande au téléphone/**You're wanted on the phone.

oncle   *n. m.* uncle

ont   *v. form of* **avoir** (to have); **ils (elles) ont** they have, they do have

opéra   *n. m.* opera

orage   *n. m.* storm

ordinateur   *n. m.* computer

ordinateur   *n. m.* **de bureau** *m.* desktop computer

ordinateur   *n. m.* **de poche** PDA (personal digital assistant), handheld computer

ordinateur   *n. m.* **portable** laptop computer (A laptop computer may just be called **"un portable."** The same word is sometimes used for a cell phone.)

ordures   *n. f. pl.* garbage

oreille   *n. f.* ear

ou   *conj.* or; **où** *adv.* where

oublié   *past part. of* **oublier** (to forget)

oui   *adv.* yes

ouvert, ouverte   *adj., m. f.* open; *also past part. of* **ouvrir** (to open)

ouvre   *v. form of* **ouvrir**; **elle ouvre** she opens

P

page *n. f.* page

pagette   *n. f.* pager

pain   *n. m.* bread; **pain grillé** toast

paisible   *adj.* peaceful

paix   *n. f.* peace

palme   *n. f.* palm branch

palmier   *n. m.* palm tree

pamplemousse   *n. m.* grapefruit

panier   *n. m.* basket

papa   *n. m.* papa, daddy, dad

papier *n. m.* paper; **une feuille de paper** a sheet of paper

par *prep.* by, through; **par terre** on the floor, on the ground; *see also idioms with par,* Part III, Unit 5

paraître *v.* to appear, seem

parapluie *n. m.* umbrella

parc *n. m.* park

parce que *conj.* because

par-dessous *adv.* underneath, below

par-dessus *adv.* over, above; **pardessus** *n. m.* coat, overcoat

parfait, parfaite *adj., m. f.* perfect

parle *v. form of* **parler** (to talk, to speak); **Qui parle?** Who is talking? **parlé** *past. part.*

part *n. f.* part, behalf; **de la part de lui**/on his behalf (from him)

part *v. form of* **partir** (to leave, to go away); **tout le monde part** everybody is leaving; **parti** *past part. of* **partir**

participe *n. m.* participle

partie *n. f.* part

partir *v.* to leave, to go away; **partons-nous?** are we leaving?

partout *adv.* everywhere

paru *past part. of* **paraître**

pas *adv.* not, none, no; **pas loin** not far; **pas du tout** not at all; **pas même** not even; *see also* **ne pas; Je n'ai pas de bananes**/I haven't any bananas, I don't have any bananas, I have no bananas

passage *n. m.* passage, passage way; **passage clouté** *n. m.* crosswalk

passé *n. m.* past; *also past part. of* **passer**

passe-moi le pain, passez-moi le beurre/pass me the bread, pass me the butter

passer *v.* to spend (time), to pass by, to go by

pâte *n. f.* dough, paste, "pasta" (macaroni, spaghetti, etc.)

patiemment *adv.* patiently

pâtisserie *n. f.* pastry, pastry shop

pâtissier, pâtissière *n. m. f.* pastry cook

patrie *n. f.* country (nation)

paupière *n. f.* eyelid

pauvre *adj.* poor

pavé *n. m.* **tactile** touch pad

payer *v.* to pay, to pay for; **payé** paid for

pays *n. m.* country (nation)

paysage *n. m.* countryside

peau *n. f.* skin

pêche *n. f.* peach

se peigner *v. refl.* to comb one's hair

peindre *v.* to paint; **peint** *past part.*

pendant *prep.* during; **pendant que** *conj.* while

perdre *v.* to lose; **perdu** *past part.*

père *n. m.* father; **Père Noël** *n. m.* Santa Claus

permettre *v.* to permit, to allow; **permis** *past part.*

personne *n. f.* person

petit, petite, petits, petites *adj.* small, little; **le plus petit, la plus petite, les plus petits, les plus petites** the smallest, the littlest; **le petit déjeuner** breakfast; **le petit four** little cake (usually square in shape with icing); **petits pois** *n. m. pl.* peas

peu *adv.* little, few, not much

peuple *n. m.* people (of a nation)

peur *n. f.* fear

peut *v. form of* **pouvoir**

peut-être *adv.* maybe, perhaps

peux *v. form of* **pouvoir**

pharmacie *n. f.* pharmacy, drugstore

pharmacien, pharmacienne *n.* pharmacist, druggist

photo *n. f.* photo

phrase *n. f.* sentence, phrase

pièce *n. f.* room, piece

pied *n. m.* foot; *see also idioms with à,* Part III, Unit 1

pinceau *n. m.* artist's brush

piquer *v.* to poke, puncture

piste *n. f.* track

pistolet *n. m.* pistol

placard *n. m.* closet

place *n. f.* place, seat, plaza

plafond *n. m.* ceiling

plage *n. f.* beach

plainte *n. f.* lamentation

plaire *v.* to please

plaisir *n. m.* pleasure

plaît *v. form of* **plaire; s'il vous plaît** please (if it is pleasing to you)

plat *n. m.* plate, dish

pleurer *v.* to cry, to weep

pleut *v. form of* **pleuvoir** (to rain); **il pleut** it's raining, it rains

pluie *n. f.* rain

plume *n. f.* feather

plus *adv.* more; **le plus, la plus, les plus** the most; **plus petit, plus petite** smaller; **plus tard** later; **ne...plus**/ no...longer, no...more

plusieurs *adv.* several

poche *n. f.* pocket

poème *n. m.* poem

poète, poétesse (femme poète) *n.* poet

poids *n. m.* weight

poire *n. f.* pear

pois *n. m.* pea; **les petits pois** peas

poisson *n. m.* fish

poivre *n. m.* pepper

pôle nord *n. m.* North Pole

pomme *n. f.* apple; **une pomme de terre** potato

pommes frites *n. f. pl.* French fries

pommier *n. m.* apple tree

porc *n. m.* pork

port *n. m.* port

portable *n. m.* cell phone (**le téléphone portable**), laptop computer (**l'ordinateur** *m.* **portable**)

porte *n. f.* door

porte *v. form of* **porter** (to wear, to carry)

poser *v.* to pose, to place; **poser une question** to ask a question

poubelle *n. f.* rubbish can

poulet *n. m.* chicken; **une poule** a hen

pour *prep.* for, in order (to)

pourquoi *adv.* why; **pourquoi pas?** why not?

pouvez, pouvons *v. forms of* **pouvoir** (can, to be able, may); **pu** *past part.*; **vous pouvez**/you can; **vous pouvez être**/you can be; **pouvez-vous?**/can you?

précéder *v.* to precede

préféré *past part. of* **préférer** (to prefer)

premier, première *adj., m. f.* first

prendre *v.* to take, to have (a meal); **Que prenez-vous pour le petit déjeuner?** What do you have for breakfast?

préparatoire *adj.* preparatory, preliminary

préparé *past part. of* **préparer** (to prepare); **se préparer** to prepare oneself

près (de) *adv.* near

présent *n. m.* present

presque *adv.* almost

prêt, prête *adj.* ready, prepared

prêté *past part. of* **prêter** (to lend)

prêtre, prêtresse *n.* priest, priestess

prier *v.* to beg, to request, to ask

printemps *n. m.* spring (season)

pris *past part. of* **prendre**

prise *n. f.* **de courant** electric outlet (wall)

prix *n. m.* price, prize; **le grand prix** the first prize

probablement *adv.* probably

prochain, prochaine *adj.* next; **la prochaine fois**/the next time

produits laitiers *n. m. pl.* dairy products

professeur, professeur-dame *n.* professor, teacher

profession *n. f.* profession

profiter *v.* to profit, to take advantage (of); **il faut profiter du moment**/you (one) must take advantage of the moment

programme *n. m.* program

projet *n. m.* project

se promener *v. refl.* to go for (to take) a walk, to stroll

promettre *v.* to promise; **promis** *past part.*

prononcer *v.* to pronounce

propriété *n. f.* property

proverbe *n. m.* proverb

pu *past part. of* **pouvoir**

public *n. m.* public; **public, publique** *adj.* public

puce *n. f.* flea; **le marché aux puces** flea market

puis *adv.* then

punit *v. form of* **punir** (to punish); **il punit**/he punishes

pupitre *n. m.* student's desk

Q

qualité *n. f.* quality; **la qualité la plus forte**/the strongest quality

quand *adv.* when

quatorze *adj.* fourteen

que *conj.* than, that; *interrog. pron.* what

quel *adj. m. s.* what, which; **quel sport?**/what (which) sport? **quel âge ont les enfants?**/how old are the children? what (a)...! what (an)...! **quel déjeuner!**/what a lunch! **quel embarras!**/what an embarrassment!

quelle *adj. f. s.* what, which; **quelle maison?**/what (which) house? what (a)...? what (an)...! **quelle classe!**/what a class! **quelle idée!**/what an idea! **Quelle heure est-il?**/What time is it? **Quelle est la date aujourd'hui?**/What's the date today? **De quelle couleur est...?** What color is...?

quelles *adj. f. pl.* what, which; **quelles maisons?**/what (which) houses? **quelles idées!**/what ideas!

quelque *adj.* some; **quelques** some, a few; **quelque chose**/something

quelquefois *adv.* sometimes

quels *adj. m. pl.* what, which; **quels livres?**/what (which) books?

qu'est-ce que c'est? what is it?

qu'est-ce que je suis? or **que suis-je?** what am I?

question *n. f.* question

qui *pron.,* who, whom, which, that; *in proverbs* he who/she who **Qui suis-je?**/Who am I? **Avec qui sortez-vous?**/With whom are you going out? **Le livre qui est sur la table est à moi**/The book which (that) is on the table is mine.

quinze *adj.* fifteen; **j'ai quinze ans**/I am fifteen years old.

quitte, quittent *v. forms of* **quitter** (to leave); **quitté** *past part.*; **Elle a quitté la maison à huit heures**/She left the house at 8 o'clock.

quoi *pron.* what; **Quoi?**/What?! **Quoi de neuf?** What's new?

R

R.S.V.P. **Répondez, s'il vous plaît**/Reply, please.

raconter *v.* to tell, to relate

ragoût *n. m.* stew

raisin *n. m.* grape

raison *n. f.* reason; **avoir raison**/to be right; **Vous avez raison**/You are right; **Tu as raison**/You (*fam. sing.*) are right.

raisonnable *adj.* reasonable

rang *n. m.* rank, row

rapide *adj.* rapid; **rapidement** *adv.* rapidly, fast, quickly

se rappeler *v.* to remember, to recall

rare *adj.* rare; **rarement** *adv.* rarely

rayonner *v.* to radiate symmetrically

recette *n. f.* recipe

recevoir *v.* receive; **reçu** *past. part.*

refuser *v.* to refuse

regarder *v.* to look, to look at, to watch; **Regarde!/**Look! **Regardez!/** Look! **se regarder** (l'un à l'autre) *v.* to look at each other

régime *n. m.* diet

règle *n. f.* rule, ruler

regretter *v.* to regret, to be sorry

religieuse *n. f.* nun (sister); *adj.* religious

religieux *n. m.* monk, friar; *adj.* religious

rembourser *v.* to reimburse

remercier *v.* to thank; **Je vous remercie/**I thank you.

remplir *v.* to fill, fulfill

remuer *v.* to stir

rendez-vous *n. m.* appointment

rendre *v.* return (something), give back; **Rendez-moi mes disques/** Give me back my (phono) records.

rendre visite à quelqu'un to visit someone

rentrer *v.* to go in again, to return (home)

réparer *v.* to repair

repas *n. m.* meal

répéter *v.* to repeat

répondeur *n. m.* answering machine

répondre *v.* to answer, to reply, to respond; **répondu,** *past part.*

réponse *n. f.* answer, response, reply

repos *n. f.* answer, response, reply

repos *n. m.* rest, repose (sleep); **au repos** at rest

se reposer *v. refl.* to rest

reprendre *v.* to take back, get back, to resume

représentation *n. f.* presentation, show, performance

requin *n. m.* shark

se ressembler *v. refl.* to resemble each other, to look alike

restaurant *n. m.* restaurant

reste *n. m.* rest, remainder

rester *v.* to remain, to stay; **resté** *past part.*; **restons-nous?** are we staying?

retard *n. m.* delay; **être en retard/**to be late

retentir *v.* to resound, to ring

retourner *v.* to return, to go back

réussir *v.* to succeed

réveille-matin *n. m.* alarm clock

révéler *v.* to reveal

revenir *v.* to return, to come back; **revenu,** *past part.*

rêver *v.* to dream

reviens, revient, reviennent *v. forms of* **revenir**

revoir *v.* to see again; **au revoir** good-bye

ri *past part. of* **rire**

riche *adj.* rich

ridicule *adj.* ridiculous

rien *indef. pron.* nothing; **ne...rien** nothing; **Je n'étudie rien/**I study nothing (I don't study anything); **de rien** you're welcome

rient, rira *v. forms of* **rire;** **Tous les élèves rient/**All the students laugh.

rire *v.* to laugh

risquer *v.* to risk

rit *v. form of* **rire;** **Il rit tout le temps/**He laughs all the time.

robe *n. f.* dress

rompre *v.* to break

rond, ronde *adj.* round; **ronde** *n. f.* round, roundelay

rosbif *n. m.* roast beef

rose *n. f.* rose

roue *n. f.* wheel

rouge *adj.* red

rougit *v. form of* **rougir** (to blush); **Pierre rougit/**Peter blushes.

route *n. f.* road

ruban *n. m.* ribbon

rue *n. f.* street

rumeur *n. f.* stir, stirring, muffled din, hum

S

s' *contraction of* **se,** *refl. pron.*

sa *poss. adj., f. sing.* his, her, its, one's; **sa voiture/**his (her, etc.) car

sac *n. m.* **de vol** carry-on bag

sagesse *n. f.* wisdom, discretion

sais *v. form of* **savoir; je sais/**I know, **tu sais/**you know, **vous savez/**you know; **je ne sais pas/**I don't know.

saisir *v.* to seize, to grasp

saison *n. f.* season

sait *v. form of* **savoir; elle (il, on), sait/**she (he, one) knows

sale *adj.* soiled, dirty; **le plus sale/**the dirtiest

salle *n. f.* (large) room; **une salle des ventes/**auction sales room; **une salle à manger/**dining room; **une salle de bains/**bathroom; **une salle de classe/** classroom; **une grande salle/**auditorium

salon *n. m.* living room

salon *n. m.* **de clavardage** chat room

samedi *n. m.* Saturday

sans *prep.* without; **sans doute/** without doubt, undoubtedly; **sans la casser/**without breaking it

santé *n. f.* health

satisfaire *v.* to satisfy

saucisse *n. f.* sausage; **saucisson** *n. m.* bologna

sauter *v.* to jump, to leap

sauvage *adj.* wild, savage

savent, savez, savons *v. forms of* **savoir**

savoir *v.* to know (how), to find out; **savez-vous lire?**/do you know how to read?

scrupuleux, scrupuleuse *adj.* scrupulous

se *refl. pron.* himself, herself, oneself, themselves; (reflexive verbs are not alphabetized in this vocabulary under the refl. pron. **se**; they are alphabetized under the first letter of the verb, *e.g.,* **se dépêcher** is listed under the D's)

sec *adj. m. s.* dry; **sèche** *f.*

Seine *n. f.* Seine River (flows through Paris)

séjour *n. m.* stay, visit

sel *n. m.* salt

semaine *n. f.* week

sénateur *n. m.* senator

sent *v. form of* sentir (to smell); **Il sent bon!** It smells good!

sentiment *n. m.* feeling

serpent *n. m.* snake

service *n. m.* service

servir *v.* to serve; **se servir (de)** to serve oneself, to use

ses *poss. adj. pl.* his, her, its, one's; (**ses livres, ses parents**)

seul *adj. m. s.* alone, single

seulement *adv.* only

si *adv.* so; **si** *conj.* if

s'il te plaît please *(fam. use)*; **s'il vous plaît** *(polite use)*

silence *n. m.* silence

snob *n. m.* snob

soeur *n. f.* sister

soif *n. f.* thirst

soigneusement *adv.* carefully

soir *n. m.* evening; **ce soir** tonight; **le soir** in the evening

soirée *n. f.* evening party

sois *v. form of* être; **Sois sage!** Be good!

soixante *adj.* sixty

sol *n. m.* ground, soil

soldat *n. m.* soldier

soleil *n. m.* sun

sommeil *n. m.* slumber, sleep; *see also idioms with* **avoir**, Part III, Unit 3

sommes *v. form of* être; **nous sommes** we are

son *n. m.* sound

son *poss. adj. m. s.* his, her, its, one's; (**son livre**)

sonne *v. form of* sonner (to ring); **la cloche sonne** the bell rings

sont *v. form of* être; **ils, elles sont** they are

sors, sort *v. forms of* sortir (to go out, to leave); **Je sors** I go out/I do go out/I am going out; **Je ne sors jamais** I never go out.

sortez *v. form (imperative) of* sortir; **Ne sortez pas!** Don't go out!

sorti *past part. of* sortir

sortie *n. f.* exit

sortir *v.* to go out, to leave

souffrante *adj. f. s.* sick

souffrir *v.* to suffer

soulier *n. m.* shoe

soupe *n. f.* soup

sourire *n. m.* smile; *as a v.* to smile

souris *n. f.* mouse

sourit *v. form of* sourire

sous *prep.* under

souvent *adv.* often

soyez, soyons *v. forms of* être *(imperative)*; **Soyez à l'heure!** Be on time! **Soyez prudent!** Be prudent! **Soyons sérieux!** Let's be serious!

spécial, spéciale *adj.* special

spectacle *n. m.* show (entertainment, *e.g.,* movie, theater)

spectateur, spectatrice *n.* spectator (person in an audience)

splendide *adj.* splendid

sport *n. m.* sport

stade *n. m.* stadium

stupéfié(e) *adj.* stupefied, dumbfounded

stylo *n. m.* pen

su *past part. of* **savoir**

suffit *v. form of* être; **je suis**/I am; **je ne suis pas**/I am not

suisse *adj.* Swiss; **la Suisse** Switzerland

suit *v. form of* suivre (to follow); **Il suit la route**/He is following the route.

supermarché *n. m.* supermarket

superstitieux, superstitieuse *adj.* superstitious

sur *prep.* on, upon

sûr, sûre *adj.* sure, certain

sûrement *adv.* surely

surfer *v.* to surf (the Internet)

surtout *adv.* especially, above all

T

t' *contraction of* te, *refl. pron.*; (**Est-ce que tu t'appelles Janine?** Is your name Janine?)

ta *poss. adj., f. sing.* your *(fam. use)*; **ta maison** your house

tableau *n. m.* chalkboard, picture, painting

tablier *n. m.* apron

tambour *n. m.* drum

tante *n. f.* aunt

tapis *n. m.* carpet, rug

tard *adv.* late; **plus tard** later

tarte *n. f.* tart

tasse *n. f.* cup; **une tasse de café** a cup of coffee; **une tasse à café** a coffee cup

te *refl. pron., dir. and indir. obj. pron. (fam.)* yourself, you, to you

tel, telle *adj.* such

télécopie *n. f.* fax

télécopier to fax

télécopieur *n. m.* fax machine

télégramme *n. m.* telegram

téléphone *n. m.* telephone; **au téléphone** to the telephone, on the telephone

téléphone *n. m.* **portable** cell phone (A cell phone may be called "**un portable**." The same word is sometimes used for a laptop computer.)

téléviseur *n. m.* television set (apparatus)

téléviseur *n. m.* **à écran plasma** plasma screen television set

télé *n. f.* TV; **la télévision** television; **à la télévision** on television

temps *n. m.* tense, time (duration), weather; **Quel temps fait-il?** What's the weather like? **Il a beaucoup de temps**/He has a lot of time.

tendrement *adv.* tenderly

tenir *v.* to hold

tenu *past part. of* **tenir**

tenue *n. f.* suit, attire; **en tenue d'exercice** in a gym suit

terminé *past part. of* **terminer** (to terminate, to end, to finish)

terrasse *n. f.* terrace; **une terasse de café** a sidewalk café

tes *poss. adj. pl (fam.)* your; (**tes livres**/your books)

tête *n. f.* head

théâtre *n. m.* theater

tiennent *v. form of* **tenir**

tiens! here! look!

tiens *v. form of* **tenir**

tiers one third (⅓)

tigre *n. m.* tiger

tinte *v. form of* **tinter** (to ring, to toll)

tiroir *n. m.* drawer

toi *pron. (fam.)* you; **avec toi** with you; **toi que voilà...** you there...

toilette *n. f.* washing and dressing; **faire sa toilette** to groom oneself (wash and dress)

toit *n. m.* roof

tolérer *v.* to tolerate

tomate *n. f.* tomato

tombé *past part. of* **tomber** (to fall)

tombeau *n. m.* tombe, grave

ton *poss. adj. m. sing.* your (*fam. use*); (**ton stylo**/your pen)

tort *n. m.* wrong; **vous avez tort** you are wrong; *see also idioms with* **avoir**, Part III, Unit 3

tortue *n. f.* turtle

tôt *adv.* early

touche *n. f.* **d'appel** talk key

touche *n. f.* **de sélection** selection key

toujours *adv.* always, still

tour *n. m.* turn, tour; **un tour de force** trick

tourner *v.* to turn, to turn sour

tournevis *n. m.* screwdriver

tous *adj. m. pl.* all; *see also idioms with* **tous**, Part III, Unit 5; **tous les deux** both; **toutes les deux** *(fem.)* both; **tous les élèves** all the pupils; **tous les élèves rient** all the pupils laugh; **tous les enfants** all the children; **tous les matins** every morning; **tous les soirs** every evening

tout *adj. pron., adv.* all, everything, every; *see also idioms with* **tous**, Part III, Unit 5; **tout de même** just the same, all the same; **tout de suite** immediately; **tout d'un coup** all of a sudden; **Tout est bien qui finit bien!** All's well that ends well! **tout le monde** everybody; **tout l'été** all summer

toute, toutes *adj. f.* all; **toute la classe** the whole clase; **toutes les jeunes filles** all the girls; **toute la bôite de chocolats** the whole box of chocolates; **toute la cocotte!** the whole pot! **toute la journée** the whole day, all day long; **toute la matinée** all morning long, the whole morning

tranquille *adj.* calm, quiet, tranquil

tranquillement *adv.* calmly, peacefully, quietly

transporter *v.* to transport

travail *n. m.* work

travaille *past part. of* **travailler** (to work)

traverser *v.* to cross, to go through, to traverse; **à travers** through, across

très *adv.* very (*Note: never use* **très** *with* **beaucoup**)

tricolore *n. m. adj.* tricolor (French flag, consisting of three vertical bands of blue, white, red)

triompher *v.* to triumph

triste *adj. m. f.* sad, unhappy

trois *adj.* three; **troisième** *adj.* third

trop *adv.* too, too much, too many; **trop facile**/too easy; **il travaille trop**/he works too much; **il a trop d'argent**/he has too much money; **il fait trop de fautes**/he makes too many mistakes; (*Note: never say* **trop beaucoup**)

trottoir *n. m.* sidewalk

trouve *v. form of* **trouver** (to find); **il trouve**/he finds; **se trouver** to be located; **la bibliothèque se trouve près du parc**/the library is located near the park

tu *per. pron. fam.* you

tulipe *n. f.* tulip

U

un, une *adj.* one; *also, indef. art.* a, an; **j'ai un père**/I have a (one) father; **j'ai une mère**/I have a (one) mother; **j'ai un livre**/I have a (one) book; **j'ai une pomme**/I have an (one) apple

usine *n. f.* factory

usuel, usuelle *adj.* usual

utile *adj.* useful

V

va *v. form of* **aller**; **il, elle va**/he, she, it goes, does go, is going; **va te coucher!** go to bed! *(fam. use)*

vache *n. f.* cow

vais *v. form of* **aller**; **je vais**/I'm going, I do go, I go; **je vais me faire lire les lignes de la main**/ I'm going to have my palm read

valeur *n. f.* value

valise *n. f.* suitcase, valise

valoir *v.* to be worth

vanille *n. f.* vanilla; **j'aime la glace à la vanille**/I like vanilla ice cream

vas *v. form of* **aller**; **tu vas**/you go, you do go, you are going *(fam. use)*; **comment vas-tu?**/how are you? *(fam. use)*

vase *n. m.* vase

vas-y! go to it!/go there!

vaut *v. form of* **valoir**; **il vaut mieux**/it is better

veau *n. m.* veal

vélo *n. m.* bike

venant *v. form of* **venir**

vend, vends, vendez, vendu *v. forms of* **vendre**

vendeur, vendeuse *n. m. f.* salesman, saleswoman

vendre *v.* to sell

vendu *past part. of* **vendre**

venez *v. form of* **venir** (to come); **venir de** *see idioms with* **de**, Part III, Unit 4

vent *n. m.* wind; *see also idioms with* **faire**, Part III, Unit 6

vente *n. f.* sale; **une vente aux enchères** auction

venu *past part. of* **venir**

vérité *n. f.* truth

vermisseau *n. m.* small worm

verra *v. form of* **voir**; **il, elle verra**/he, she will see

verre *n. m.* glass (drinking); **je bois un verre de lait**/I'm drinking a glass of milk

vers *prep.* toward

vert *n. m. adj.* green; **aimez-vous le vert?**/do you like green? **j'aime les petites automobiles vertes**/I like small green cars.

verticalement *adv.* vertically

veste *n. f.* vest (worn under a suit coat)

veston *n. m.* coat (of a suit)

vêtements *n. m. pl.* clothing

veut, veux *v. forms of* **vouloir** (to want); **je veux, tu veux, il** *ou* **elle** *ou* **on veut**/I want, you *(fam.)* want, he *or* she *or* it wants

viande *n. f.* meat

vie *n. f.* life

vieille *adj. f. s.* old; **une vieille dame**/an old lady; **vieux** *adj. m. s. pl.* old

viens, vient *v. forms of* **venir** (to come)

vigueur *n. f.* force

ville *n. f.* town, city; *see also idioms with* **en**, Part III, Unit 2

vin *n. m.* wine

vingt *adj.* twenty; **vingtième** twentieth

violence *n. f.* violence

vis *n. f.* screw

visage *n. m.* face

visite *n. f.* visit; **rendre visite à quelqu'un** to visit someone

visiter *v.* to visit

vite *adv.* quickly, fast

vitesse *n. f.* speed; **à toute vitesse** at full speed, quickly

vitre *n. f.* window (glass) pane

vive, vivent *v. forms of* **vivre** (to live); **Vive le quatorze juillet!**/ Hurrah for July 14th! **Vive la France!**/ Long live France! **Vive l'Amérique!**/Long live America!

vivra *v. form of* **vivre**; **il** *ou* **elle vivra**/ he *or* she will live

vivre *v.* to live

vocabulaire *n. m.* vocabulary

voici here is, here are; **voici les livres!**/here are the books! **voici Robert!**/Here's Robert!

voient *v. form of* **voir** (to see); **ils** *ou* **elles voient**/they see

voilà there is, there are; **voilà les livres!**/there are the books! **voilà Robert!**/There's Robert!

voir *v.* to see

voisin, voisine *n. m. f.* neighbor

voisinage *n. m.* neighborhood

voit *v. form of* **voir**; **il** *ou* **elle voit**/he *or* she sees, does see, is seeing

voiture *n. f.* car, automobile

voix *n. f.* voice; **à voix basse**/in a low voice, softly; **à haute voix**/in a loud voice

vol *n. m.* flight

voler *v.* to fly, to steal

vont *v. form of* **aller**; **ils** *ou* **elles vont**/they go, do go, are going

vos *poss. adj. pl.* your; **Voici vos livres!**/Here are your books!

votre *poss. adj. s.* your; **Voici votre livre!**/Here's your book!

voudrais *v. form (conditional) of* **vouloir** (to want); **je voudrais une tasse de café**/I would like a cup of coffee

voulez *v. form of* **vouloir**; **Voulez-vous aller au cinéma avec moi?**/ Do you want to go to the movies with me?

vouloir *v.* to want; **vouloir dire** to mean, to signify; **Que veut dire ce mot?**/ What does this word mean?

voulu *past part. of* **vouloir**

vous *per. pron.* you; **vous deux**/you two

voyage *n. m.* trip; **faire un voyage** to take a trip

565

voyageons *v. form of* **voyager; nous voyageons/** we are travelling

voyager *v.* to travel

voyez-vous? do you see?

vrai *adj. m.,* **vraie** *f.* true, real

vraiment *adv.* really, truly

vu *past part. of* **voir** (to see); **Avez-vous vu Janine?**/Have you seen Janine?

Y

y *advl. pron., adv. of place* there; **il y a** there is, there are; **il y a vingt élèves dans cette classe**/there are 20 students in this class; **y a-t-il vingt étudiants dans cette classe?**/are there 20 students in this class? **il y a quelqu'un à la porte**/there is someone at the door.

yeux *n. m. pl.* eyes; **l'oeil** *n. m. s.* the eye

Z

zèbre *n. m.* zebra

zodiaque *n. m.* zodiac

zut *interj.* darn it!

English-French Glossary

A

a   un, une; un homme/a man; une femme/a woman
above   au-dessus, en haut
absolutely   absolument
to accept   accepter
accident   un accident
acrostic   un acrostiche
actor, actress   un acteur, une actrice
to add   ajouter
address   une adresse
to adore   adorer
to advance   avancer
to affirm   affirmer
after   après; afternoon/un après-midi; in the afternoon/l'après-midi
again   encore, de nouveau
age   un âge
agreed   d'accord
airplane   un avion
airport   un aéroport; air terminal/une aérogare
alarm clock   un réveille-matin
all   tout, toute, toutes, tous; all of a sudden/tout d'un coup; All's well that ends well/ Tout est bien qui finit bien; all summer/tout l'été; all day long/toute la journée; all morning long/toute la matinée; all the girls/toutes les jeunes filles; all the boys/tous les garçons
to allow   permettre (past part., permis)
almost   presque
already   déjà
also   aussi
always   toujours
American (language)   l'américain n. m.; He is American. She is American/Il est américain, Elle est américaine

to amuse   amuser; to amuse oneself/s'amuser
amusing   amusant, amusante
an   un, une; un tablier/an apron; une pomme/an apple
ancient   ancien, ancienne
and   et
angry   fâché, fâchée; to get angry/se fâcher
animal   un animal; animals/animaux
to announce   annoncer
to annoy   ennuyer
annoying   ennuyeux, ennuyeuse
another   un autre, une autre
answer   une réponse; to answer/ répondre (past part., répondu)
answering machine   le répondeur
ant   une fourmi
apparatus   un appareil
appetite   un appétit
apple   une pomme
apple tree   un pommier
appointment   un rendez-vous
to appreciate   apprécier
to approach   s'approcher (de)
arm   un bras
armchair   un fauteuil
around   autour; he is traveling around the world/il voyage autour du monde; it is around two o'clock/il est vers deux heures
to arrange   arranger, disposer
arrested   arrêté
to arrive   arriver
art   l'art, m.
artist   l'artiste, m. f.
as   comme
as well as (just as)   ainsi que
to ask (for)   demander

to ask a question   poser une question
aspirin   une aspirine
to assert   affirmer
assignments   les devoirs, m.
astronomer   un astronome
at   à
at first   d'abord
at last   enfin
at that moment   à ce moment-là
ATM (automated teller machine)   le guichet automatique (bancaire)
to attend   assister à
auditorium   une grande salle
August   août, m.
aunt   une tante
author   un auteur, une femme auteur
auto mechanic   un garagiste, une garagiste
autograph   un autographe
automobile   une automobile, une voiture
autumn   l'automne, m.
to avoid   éviter

B

baby   un bébé
babysitter   une gardienne d'enfants, un gardien d'enfants
bad   mauvais, mauvaise
badly   mal
baker   un boulanger, une boulangère
bakery   une boulangerie
ball   une balle, un ballon
balloon   un ballon
banana   une banane
barber   un coiffeur, une coiffeuse
basket   un painer
Bastille Day   Le Jour de la Bastille

to bathe **baigner**; to bathe oneself **se baigner**

bathroom **une salle de bains**

baton **un bâton**

to be **être**: *see also idioms with* **être**, *Part III, Unit 3*

to be able **pouvoir** (*past part.,* **pu**)

to be born **naître** (*past part.,* **né**)

to be late **être en retard**

to be located **se trouver**

to be present at **assister à, être présent(e) à**

to be right **avoir raison**

to be sorry **regretter**

to beat **battre** (*past part.,* **battu**)

beautiful **beau, beaux, bel, belle, belles** (**un beau cadeau, de beaux cadeaux, un bel arbre, une belle femme, de belles femmes**)

beauty **la beauté**

because **parce que**

to become **devenir**

bedroom **une chambre à coucher**

before **avant**; before going out/**avant de sortir**

to beg **prier**

to begin **commencer** (**à + inf.**); **je commence à travailler**/I'm beginning to work.

behind **derrière** (*in back of*)

Belgian **belge**; He is Belgian, She is Belgian/**Il est belge, Elle est belge**

Belgium **la Belgique**

to believe **croire** (*past part.,* **cru**)

below **par-dessous, au-dessous**

bench (seat) **un banc**

besides **d'ailleurs**

better *as an adj.,* **meilleur, meilleure**; *as an adv.,* **mieux**; the best **le meilleur, la meilleure, les meilleurs, les meilleures**; **cette pomme est meilleure**/this apple is better; **cette pomme est la meilleure**/this apple is the best; **Paul travaille mieux que Robert/Paul works better than Robert.**

between **entre**; **entre eux et nous**/between them and us

beverage **une boisson**

to beware **se méfier de**; **méflez-vous des obstacles dangereux/** beware of dangerous obstacles

bid, bidding **une enchère**

bike **un vélo**; **une bicyclette**/a bicycle

bill **une addition**

bird **un oiseau**

birth **une naissance**; birthday/**un anniversaire de naissance**

black **noir, noire, noirs, noires**

blue **bleu, bleue, bleus, bleues**

boarding pass **la carte d'embarquement**

body **un corps**

to boil **bouillir, faire bouillir**

book **un livre**

to bore **ennuyer**

boring **ennuyeux, ennuyeuse**

to be born **naître**; *past part.,* **né**

both **tous les deux, toutes les deux**

bottle **une bouteille**

boutique **une boutique**

box **une boîte**

boy **un garçon**

to break **briser, casser, rompre**

breakfast **le petit déjeuner**

to bring **apporter**

broom **un balai**

brother **un frère**

to brush **brosser, se brosser**; **je brosse le manteau**/I'm brushing the coat; **je me brosse les dents**/I brush my teeth

brush **une brosse**

to build **bâtir**

building **un bâtiment, un immeuble**

to burn **brûler**

bus **un autobus** (city bus); **un autocar** (interurban, long-distance bus)

but **mais**

butcher **un boucher, une bouchère**

butcher shop **une boucherie**

butter **le beurre**

to buy **acheter**

by **par**

C

cake **un gâteau, des gâteaux**

calculator **la calculatrice**

to call **appeler**; to be called, to be named **s'appeler**; **j'appelle le médecin**/I'm calling the doctor; **je m'appelle Janine, je m'appelle Pierre**/My name is Janine, my name is Peter.

can (may) **pouvoir**; **vous pouvez entrer**/you can (may) come in

Canada **le Canada**

Canadian *adj.* **canadien, canadienne**; *n.* **Canadien, Canadienne**; **un livre canadien**/a Canadian book; **Madame Dupont est canadienne**/ Mrs. Dupont is Canadian.

candy **un bonbon**

capital **une capitale**

capricious **capricieux, capricieuse**

car **une voiture, une automobile**

carefully **soigneusement**

carpet **un tapis**

to carry **porter**

to carry away **emporter**

carry-on bag **le sac de vol**

cash box (register) **une caisse**

cashier **un caissier, une caissière**

castle **un château**

cat **un chat, une chatte**

to catch **attraper**

CD **le disque compact, le CD**

CD player **le lecteur de CD**

CD-ROM le cédérom, le **CD-ROM**

ceiling un plafond

to celebrate célébrer

cell phone le téléphone portable (A cell phone may be called "un portable." The same word is sometimes used for a laptop computer.)

cellar une cave

center un centre

certain certain, certaine, sûr, sûre

chair une chaise

chalk une craie

change un changement

chapel une chapelle

charming charmant, charmante

to chase, to chase away chasser

chat (Internet) le clavardage

to chat (Internet) clavarder

chat room le salon de clavardage

check (bill) une addition

cheese un fromage

cherry une cerise

chicken un poulet

child un enfant, une enfant

chimney une cheminée

chocolate un chocolat

to choose choisir

Christmas le Noël; Merry Christmas/Joyeux Noël

church une église

city une ville

class une classe; classroom/une salle de classe; a French class/une classe de français

to clean nettoyer

clear clair, claire

clock une horloge; alarm clock/un réveille-matin

to close fermer

closet une armoire, un placard

clothing un vêtement, des vêtements

cloud un nuage; cloudy/nuageux, nuageuse; a cloudy sky/un ciel nuageux

coat (overcoat) un manteau, un pardessus

coffee le café

cold froid, froide; the cold/le froid; j'ai froid/I'm cold, I feel cold; il fait froid ici/It's cold here.

color la couleur; what color is…/de quelle couleur est…

comb un peigne; to comb one's hair/se peigner les cheveux

to come venir; to come back/revenir

to come down descendre

to come in entrer (dans)

computer l'ordinateur m.

to confess confesser

contrary contraire

to cook cuire, faire la cuisine

to correct corriger

to cost coûter

country un pays, une nation

countryside un paysage

courageous courageux, courageuse

course un cours; a French course/un cours de français

cousin un cousin, une cousine

to cover couvrir; *past part.,* couvert

cow une vache

crazy fou, fol, folle

credit card la carte bancaire/la carte de crédit

cross une croix; to cross/traverser

cruel cruel, cruelle

to crush écraser

to cry pleurer; to cry out/crier

cup une tasse; a coffee cup/une tasse à café; a cup of coffee/une tasse de café

curious curieux, curieuse

customer un client, une cliente

to cut couper; to cut oneself/se couper; j'ai coupé le pain/I cut the bread; je me suis coupé le doigt/I cut my finger.

cut mignon, mignonne, *adj. m. f.*

cybercafé le cybercafé

D

dad, daddy un papa

dance un bal; to dance/danser

dancer un danseur, une danseuse

dangerous dangereux, dangereuse

dark obscur, obscure

darling chéri, chérie

darn it! zut alors!

database la banque de données

daughter une fille

day un jour, une journée; all day long/toute la journée

dear cher, chère

December le décembre

decision une décision

to defend défendre

delicious délicieux, délicieuse

department store un grand magasin

desire un désir; to desire/désirer

desk un bureau; desk (pupil's, student's)/un pupitre

desktop computer l'ordinateur *n.* de bureau *m.*

dessert un dessert

detail un détail

detective un détective

to detest détester

dictionary un dictionnaire

to die mourir; *past part.,* mort

diet un régime; on a diet/au régime

difficult difficile

to dine dîner

dining room une salle à manger

dinner le dîner

dirty sale

disk (record) un disque

disgusting **dégoûtant, dégoûtante**

dish **un plat, une assiette**

to disobey **désobéir (à)**

display screen (computer) **l'écran** *m.*

to dispose **disposer**

distinctly **distinctement**

to disturb **déranger**

to do **faire**; *see also idioms with* **faire**, *Part III, Unit 6*

to do gymnastics **faire de la gymnastique**

doctor **un docteur, un médecin, une femme docteur, une femme médecin**

dog **un chien, une chienne**

door **une porte**

doubt **un doute**; to doubt/**douter, se douter**

dream **un rêve**; to dream/**rêver**

dress **une robe**; to dress/**s'habiller**

drink **une boisson**; to drink/**boire**; *past part.,* **bu**

drugstore **une pharmacie**

druggist **un pharmacien, une pharmacienne**

drum **un tambour**

dry **sec, sèche**

dumb **bête**; a dumb (stupid, foolish) thing/**une bêtise**

during **pendant**

DVD **le disque DVD**

DVD player **le lecteur de DVD**

E

each **chaque**; each one **chacun, chacune**

ear **une oreille**

early **de bonne heure, tôt**

easily **facilement**

easy **facile**

to eat **manger**

e-commerce **le commerce électronique**

egg **un oeuf**; soft-boiled egg/**un oeuf à la coque**

eight **huit**

electronic ticket, e-ticket **le billet électronique**

e-mail **le courriel, le courrier électronique**

to employ **employer**

to end **finir, terminer**; the end/**la fin**

English (language) **l'anglais**, *n. m.* He is English, She is English/**Il est anglais, Elle est anglaise**

English Channel **La Manche**

to enjoy oneself **s'amuser**

enjoyable **amusant, amusante**

to enter (in, into) **entrer (dans)**

entrance **une entrée**

to erase **effacer**

error **une faute, une erreur**

to escape **échapper, s'échapper**

euro **l'euro** *m.*

evening **le soir**; in the evening/**le soir**; this evening, tonight/**ce soir**; every evening/**tous les soirs**

evening party **une soirée**

everybody **tout le monde**

everything **tout, toutes les choses**

everywhere **partout**

exactly **exactement**

to examine **examiner**

to exclaim **exlamer, s'exclamer**

to excuse **excuser, s'excuser**

exhibit **une exposition**

to expect **attendre**

to explain **expliquer**

extraordinary **extraordinaire**

extremely **extrêmement**

eye **un oeil**; eyes/**les yeux**

eyeglasses **les lunettes**, *f.*

eyelid **la paupière**

F

face **le visage, la figure**

to fall **tomber**

false **faux, fausse**

family **la famille**

far **loin**

farewell **adieu**

farm **la ferme**

fast **vite, rapidement**

father **le père**

favorite **favori, favorite**

to fax **télécopier**

fax **la télécopie**

fax machine **le télécopieur**

fear **la peur**; to have fear, to be afraid/**avoir peur**; *see also idioms with* **avoir**, *Part III, Unit 3*

feast **la fête**

feel hungry **avoir faim**

fifteen **quinze**

to fill **remplir**

film **le film**

finally **enfin**

to find **trouver**

finger **le doigt**

to finish **finir, terminer**

fire **le feu**

first **premier, première**; at first/**d'abord**

fish **le poisson**

flag **le drapeau**

flea **la puce**; flea market/**le marché aux puces**

floor **le plancher**; floor (of a building designated by a number)/**un étage**; ground floor/**le rez de chaussée**; the first floor/**le premier étage**

florist **le, la fleuriste**

flour **la farine**

flower **la fleur**

fly (insect) **la mouche**

to fly **voler**

to follow **suivre**

food **la nourriture, l'aliment**, *m.,* **l'alimentation**, *f.* fast food **la cuisine rapide**

foolish **bête**; a foolish thing/**une bêtise**

foot **le pied**; *see also idioms with* **à**, *Part III, Unit 1*

football **un ballon**; jouer au football/to play soccer

for **pour**

to forbid **défendre**

to forget **oublier**

fork **la fourchette**

fourteen **quatorze**

franc **un franc** (former French unit of money)

French (language) **le français**; He is French, She is French/**Il est français, Elle est française**
French fries **les pommes frites,** *f.*
fresh **frais, fraîche**
friend **un ami, une amie**
friendship **une amitié**
from **de**
to fulfill **remplir**
funny **drôle**
furious **furieux, furieuse**
furniture **le meuble**

G

game **le match**
garage **le garage**
garbage **les ordures,** *f.*
garden **le jardin**
garlic **l'ail,** *m.*
gasoline **l'essence,** *f.*
generally **généralement**
generous **généreux, généreuse**
genius **un génie**
gentleman **le monsieur; les messieurs,** *pl.*
geography **la géographie**
German (language) **l'allemand,** *m.*
to get angry **se fâcher**
to get away **échapper, s'échapper**
to get dressed **s'habiller**
girl **la jeune fille**
to give **donner**
to give back **rendre**
glass (drinking) **un verre**
glove **le gant**
to go **aller**
to go away **partir, s'en aller**
to go back **retourner**
to go by **passer**
to go down **descendre**
to go for a walk **se promener**
to go in (into) **entrer dans**
to go out **sortir**
to go through **traverser**
to go to bed **se coucher;** go to bed!/**va te coucher! allez vous coucher!**
goalie **le gardien de but, la gardienne de but**

God **le Dieu**
good **bon, bonne**
good afternoon, good day, good morning **bonjour**
good-bye **au revoir**
good evening, good night **bonsoir**
good luck **bonne chance**
grape **le raisin** (raisin/**le raisin sec**)
grapefruit **le pamplemousse**
Great Britain **la Grande Bretagne**
green **vert, verte**
grocer **un épicier, une épicière**
grocery store **une épicerie**
group **un groupe**
to guard **garder**
guard **un gardien, une gardienne**

H

hair **les cheveux,** *m.*
hairdresser **le coiffeur, la coiffeuse**
half **demi, demie**
ham **le jambon**
hand **la main**
handkerchief **le mouchoir**
handsome **bel, beau, beaux; un bel homme**/a handsome man
happiness **le bonheur**
happy **heureux, heureuse, joyeux, joyeuse**
hard drive **le disque dur**
to harm **nuire**
harm **le mal**
hat **le chapeau**
to hate **détester**
to have **avoir**
to have a good time **s'amuser;** have a good time!/**amusez-vous bien!**
have a good trip! **bon voyage!**
have a good return trip! **bon retour!**
to have a meal **prendre un repas**
to have dinner **dîner**
to have lunch **déjeuner**
to have to **devoir**

he **il**
head **la tête**
headdress **la coiffe**
health **la santé**
to hear **entendre**
heart **le coeur**
hello **bonjour; allô** (*used when answering the telephone*)
to help **aider**
her *as a poss. adj.,* **son, sa, ses** (**Alice a son livre**/Alice has her book; **Hélène lit sa leçon**/Helen is reading her lesson; **Marie a ses livres**/Mary has her books); *as a dir. obj. pron.,* **la** (**Voyez-vous Marie? Oui, je la vois**/Do you see Mary? Yes, I see her); *as obj. of a prep.,* **elle** (**avec elle**/with her); *as an indir. obj. pron.,* **lui**/to her (**Je lui donne le livre**/I'm giving [to] her the book)
here **ici**
here is, here are **voici** (**Voici Robert!**/Here's Robert!); (**Voici les livres!**/Here are the books!)
herself **se** (**Monique se lave**/Monique is washing herself)
to hide **cacher**
him *as a direct obj. pron.,* **le** (**Je le vois**/I see him); *as obj. of a prep.,* **lui** (**avec lui**/with him); *as an indir. obj. pron.,* **lui**/to him (**Je lui donne le livre**/I'm giving [to] him the book)
himself **se** (**Robert se lave**/Robert is washing himself
his **son, sa, ses** (**Robert a son livre**/Robert has his book; **Henri lit sa leçon**/Henry is reading his lesson; **Raymond a ses livres**/Raymond has his books)
to hold **tenir**
holiday **la fête**
homework **le devoir, les devoirs**
honor **l'honneur,** *m.*
to hope **espérer**

571

horse **le cheval**
hospital **l'hôpital**, *m.*
hot **chaud, chaude**
hotel **l'hôtel**, *m.*
hour **l'heure**, *f.*
house **la maison**
how **comment**; *see also idioms with* **comment**, Part III, Unit 2
how many, how much **combien (de)**
human **humain, humaine**
hunger **la faim**; to be hungry/**avoir faim**; *see also idioms with* **avoir**, Part III, Unit 3
to hunt **chasser**
to hurry **se dépêcher**
to hurt **blesser, nuire**; to hurt oneself/**sa faire mal, se blesser**
husband **le mari, l'époux**, *m.*

I

ice **la glace**
ice cream **la glace**; vanilla ice cream/ **la glace à la vanille**; chocolate ice cream/**la glace au chocolat**
idea **l'idée**, *f.*
if **si**
ill **malade**
to illuminate **éclairer**
immediately **tout de suite, immédiatement**
in **dans**
in front of **devant**
in love **amoureux, amoureuse**; in love with/**amoureux de, amoureuse de**
in order (to) **pour**
industrious **diligent, diligente, industrieux, industrieuse**
inhabit **demeurer, habiter**
to injure **blesser**
inside **dedans**
instruction **l'enseignement**, *m.*
intermission **l'entracte**, *m.*
Internet **l'Internet** *m.*
iPod **l'iPod** *m.*

Irish **irlandais, irlandaise**; Irish style/**à l'irlandaise**
isn't it? isn't that so? **n'est-ce pas?** *see also* Work Unit 20
it *per. pron. f., as subj.,* **elle** (**elle est ici**); *per. pron. m., as subj.,* **il** (**il est ici**); *as obj. of prep., m.,* **lui** (**avec lui**); *f.,* **elle** (**avec elle**); *dir. obj. pron. f.,* **la** (**Voyez-vous la maison? Oui, je la vois**); *dir. obj. pron. m.,* **le** (**Voyez-vous le garage? Oui, je le vois**)
it is necessary **il faut, il est nécessaire (de)**
it's (it is) **C'est...** (**C'est samedi**/It's Saturday)
its **son sa, ses**, *poss. adj.* (**Le petit chat a son jouet, sa nourriture, et ses rubans**/The little cat has its toy, its food, and its ribbons)
Italian (language) **l'italien**, *m.; as an adj.,* **italien, italienne**

J

jacket **la jaquette**
joyous **joyeux, joyeuse**
juice **le jus**
July **juillet**, *m.*
to jump **sauter**
just as **ainsi que**

K

kangaroo **le kangourou**
to keep **garder**
key **la clef**
keyboard **le clavier**
kilogram **le kilogramme** (1 kilogram equals about 2.2 lbs.)
kilometer **le kilomètre** (1 kilometer equals about 0.621 miles)
kind **gentil, gentille**
kitchen **la cuisine**
knee **le genou, les genoux**
knife **le couteau, les couteaux**

to know (how) **savoir**; **Savez-vous lire?**/Do you know how to read? **Savez-vous la leçon?**/Do you know the lesson?
to know (to be acquainted with) **connaître**; **Connaissez-vous Monique?**/Do you know Monique?/**Connaissez-vous Paris?**/Do you know Paris?

L

lady **la dame, les dames**; young lady/**la demoiselle**; in direct address, **mesdames, mesdemoiselles**
lamp **la lampe**
language **la langue**
laptop computer **l'ordinateur** *m.* **portable** (A laptop computer may just be called **"un portable."** The same word is sometimes used for a cell phone.)
last **dernier, dernière**
late **tard**; later/**plus tard**; to be late/**être en retard**
to laugh **rire**; *past part.,* **ri**
lawyer **un avocat, une (femme) avocate**
leaf **la feuille**
to leap **sauter**
to learn **apprendre**
to leave **partir, quitter, laisser**; **elle est partie**/she left; **j'ai quitté mes amis à six heures**/I left my friends at six o'clock; **j'ai laissé mon livre à l'école**/I left my book at school; **sortir** (to go out); **elle est sortie sans argent**/she went out without any money
left *(as opposed to right)* **gauche**; **à gauche**/on (to) the left
leg **la jambe**
to lend **prêter**
less **moins**; **au moins**/at least; *see also idioms with* **au**, Part III, Unit 1
lesson **la leçon**

let's go! **allons!**
letter **la lettre**
liberty **la liberté**
library **la bibliothèque**
life **la vie**
light **la lumière;** to light/**allumer, éclairer**
to like **aimer bien;** to like better/**aimer mieux, préférer**
line **la ligne**
to listen (to) **écouter;** to listen to music/**écouter la musique**
little (small) *adj.* **petit, petite, petits, petites**
little (not much) *adv.* **peu;** a little/**un peu;** a little sugar/**un peu de sucre**
to live **demeurer, vivre**
living room **le salon**
long *adj.* **long, longue, longs, longues**
to look (at) **regarder;** I'm looking at the sky/**Je regarde le ciel**
to look (for) **chercher;** I'm looking for the book/**Je cherche le livre**
to lose **perdre**
to love **aimer;** love/**l'amour** *n. m.*
low *adj.* **bas, basse, bas, basses**
luck **la chance;** you're lucky/**vous avez de la chance**
lunch, luncheon **le déjeuner;** to lunch, to have lunch/**déjeuner**

M

magazine **le magazine, la revue**
magnificent *adj.* **magnifique**
mail carrier **le facteur**
to make **faire;** *see idioms with* **faire,** Part III, Unit 6
to make fun of **se moquer de**
mama **la maman**
man **un homme**
many **beaucoup (de);** I have many friends/**J'ai beaucoup d'amis**

map **la carte**
marriage **le mariage**
mathematics **les mathématiques** *n. f.*
may (can) *v.* **pouvoir;** you may come in/**vous pouvez entrer**
maybe *adv.* **peut-être**
me *pron.* **me, moi** (when stressed); he knows me/**il me connaît;** she is talking to me/**elle me parle;** give me the book/**donnez-moi le livre**
meal **le repas**
to mean **vouloir dire;** What do you mean/**Que voulez-vous dire?**
meat **la viande**
medicine **le médicament**
to meet **rencontrer, faire connaissance, faire la connaissance de;** I met my friend at the movies/**J'ai recontré mon ami au cinéma;** Today I met a new student/**Aujourd'hui j'ai fait la connaissance d'une nouvelle étudiante**
menu **la carte**
merchant **le marchand, la marchande**
middle **le milieu;** in the middle of/**au milieu de**
midnight **le minuit**
milk **le lait**
mirror **une glace** (hand mirror); **un miroir** (wall mirror)
mistake **une erreur, une faute**
mister **monsieur**
mom **la maman**
money **l'argent** *n. m.*
month **le mois;** in the month of/**au mois de**
moon **la lune**
more **plus**
morning **le matin;** in the morning/**le matin;** I worked all morning/**J'ai travaillé toute la matinée;** every morning/**tous les matins**
mother **la mère**
motor **le moteur**
mouse **la souris**
mouth **la bouche**

movie (film) **le film;** movies (theater)/**le cinéma**
MP3 **le fichier MP3**
Mr. **Monsieur, M.**
Mrs. **Madame, Mme**
much **beaucoup (de)**
multimedia player **le lecteur multimédia**
museum **le musée**
mushroom **un champignon**
music **la musique**
must *v.* **devoir, falloir;** I must work now/**Je dois travailler maintenant;** One must be honest/**Il faut être honnête;** One must not lie/**Il ne faut pas mentir**
my *poss. adj.* **mon, ma, mes;** my book/**mon livre;** my room/**ma chambre;** my friends/**mes amis**
myself *pron.* **me, moi-même;** I wash myself/**Je me lave;** I did it myself/**Je l'ai fait moi-même**

N

name **le nom**
naturally *adv.* **naturellement**
to navigate (the Internet) **naviguer (sur Internet), surfer**
near *adv.* **près (de)**
necessary *adj.* **nécessaire;** it is necessary/**il est nécessaire**
neck **le cou**
necktie **la cravate**
need **le besoin;** to need/**avoir besoin (de);** I need a pen/**J'ai besoin d'un stylo**
neighbor **le voisin, la voisine**
neighborhood **le voisinage**
neither **ni…ni;** I have neither pen nor pencil/**Je n'ai ni stylo ni crayon**
nephew **le neveu**
net **le filet**
never *adj.* **jamais**
new *adj.* **nouveau, nouvel, nouvelle;** a new book/**un nouveau livre;** a new friend

573

(boy)/**un nouvel ami**; a new friend (girl)/**une nouvelle amie**; a (brand) new suit/**un complet neuf**; a (brand) new dress/**une robe neuve**

New Orleans **la Nouvelle-Orléans**

news **la nouvelle, les nouvelles**; good news!/**bonnes nouvelles!**

newspaper **le journal**

next *adj.* **prochain, prochaine**; next time/**la prochaine fois**

next to **à côté de**

nice *adj.* **gentil, gentille**

nine *adj.* **neuf**

no *adv.* **non**

noise **le bruit**

noon **le midi**

nose **le nez, les nez**

not at all **pas du tout**; not far/**pas loin**

notebook **le cahier**

nourishment **la nourriture, l'aliment,** *m.,* **l'alimentation,** *f.*

now *adv.* **maintenant**

O

to obey **obéir (à)**; I obey my mother and father/**J'obéis à ma mère et à mon père**

of *prep.* **de**; *see also idioms with* **de**, *Part III, Unit 4*

of course **bien sûr, mais oui**; of course not! **mais non!**

to offer **offrir**

office **le bureau**

often *adv.* **souvent**

okay **d'accord**

old *adj.* **ancien, ancienne, vieux, vieil, vieille**

on *prep.* **sur**

once **une fois**; once more/**encore une fois**

one *adj.* **un, une**; one book/**un livre**; one apple/**une pomme**

oneself *refl. pron.* **se**; One washes oneself here/**On se lave ici**

onion **un oignon**

only *adv.* **seulement, ne...que**; I have only two euros/**J'ai seulement deux euros; Je n'ai que deux euros**

to open **ouvrir**

opinion **un avis, une opinion**

opposite *adv.* **d'en face**

or *conj.* **ou**

orange **une orange**

other **autre**; the other/**l'autre**; another/**un autre, une autre**

ought to **devoir**

our *poss. adj.* **notre, nos**; our house/ **notre maison**; our book/**notre livre**; our books/**nos livres**

outside *adv.* **dehors**

oven **un four**

over *adv.* **par-dessus**; over there/**là-bas**

overcoat **le pardessus**

to overcook **faire trop cuire**

to owe **devoir**

P

pager **la pagette**

pain **un mal**

to paint **peindre**

paper **le papier**; sheet of paper/**une feuille de papier**; newspaper/**le journal**; paper airplane/**un avion en papier**

park **le parc**

to pass (by) **passer**

past **le passé**

pastry **la pâtisserie**; pastry shop/**une pâtisserie**; pastry cook/**un pâtissier, une pâtissière**

patiently *adv.* **patiemment**

to pay a visit **faire visite**

to pay attention **faire attention**

to pay (for) **payer**; I paid for the book/**J'ai payé le livre**

PDA (personal digital assistant) **l'ordinateur** *m.* **de poche**

pea **le pois**; peas/**les petits pois**

peace **la paix**

peach **la pêche**

pear **la poire**

pen **le stylo**

pencil **le crayon**

pepper **le poivre**

perfect *adj.* **parfait, parfaite**

perhaps *adv.* **peut-être**

to permit **permettre**

person **une personne**

pharmacist **le pharmacien, la pharmacienne**

pharmacy **la pharmacie**

phonorecord **le disque**

picture **le tableau, une image**

piece **le morceau**

pin **une épingle**

PIN **le NIP (le numéro d'identification personnelle)**

PIN pad **le clavier d'identification personnelle**

pineapple **un ananas**

place **un endroit, un lieu**

to place **mettre**

plasma screen, plasma display **l'écran** *m.* **plasma**

plasma screen television set **le téléviseur à écran plasma**

plate **un plat, une assiette**

to play **jouer**; to play (a musical instrument)/**jouer de**; to play the piano/**jouer du piano**; to play (a sport)/**jouer à**; to play tennis/**jouer au tennis**

player **un joueur, une joueuse**

pleasant *adj.* **agréable**

please **s'il vous plaît** (polite form); **s'il te plaît** (familiar form)

to please **plaire (à)**

pocket **la poche**

poem **le poème**

poet **un poète, une poétesse**

police officer **un agent de police**

poor *adj.* **pauvre**

postman **le facteur**

potato **une pomme de terre**

pound **une livre**

power button **le bouton de démarrage**

574

to prefer **préférer, aimer mieux**

to prepare **préparer**; to prepare oneself/**se préparer**

present (gift) **un cadeau**; the present (time)/**le présent**

pretty *adj.* **joli, jolie**

priest **un prêtre**; priestess/**une prêtresse**

principal (of a school) **un directeur, une directrice**

probably *adv.* **probablement**

to profit **profiter**; to take advantage of the moment/**profiter du moment**

program (television) **l'émission** *f.*

promise **une promesse**; to promise/**promettre**

to pull (away), to pull (out) **arracher**

to punish **punir**

pupil **un élève, une élève**

purchase **un achat, une emplette**; to purchase/**acheter**

to put **mettre**; to put on/**mettre**

Q

quality **la qualité**

quick *adj.* **rapide**

quickly *adv.* **vite, rapidement**

R

R.S.V.P. **Répondez, s'il vous plaît**/Reply, please (please reply)

rabbit **le lapin**

rain **la pluie**; to rain/**pleuvoir**; it's raining/**il pleut**

rainbow **un arc-en-ciel**

to read **lire**

real *adj.* **vrai, vraie**

really *adv.* **vraiment**

to receive **recevoir**

record, recording **le disque**

red *adj.* **rouge**

to regret **regretter**

to relate **raconter**; to tell, to relate a story/**raconter une histoire**

religious *adj.* **religieux, religieuse**

to remain **rester, demeurer**

to remember **se rappeler, se souvenir (de)**

to remove **enlever**

to repair **réparer**; to have something repaired/**faire réparer quelque chose**

to repeat **répéter**

reply **la réponse**; to reply/**répondre (à)**

to request **demander, prier**

to reside **demeurer**

to respond **répondre (à)**

to return **retourner, revenir**; to return (home)/**rentrer**; to return something/**rendre quelque chose**; I returned the book to the library/**J'ai rendu le livre à la bibliothèque**

to reveal **révéler**

ribbon **le ruban**

riddle **une devinette**

to be right **avoir raison**; Janine is right!/**Janine a raison!**

right (*as opposed to left*) **la droite**; on (to) the right/**à droite, à la droite**

to ring **sonner**

ring (*worn on finger*) **une bague**

river **un fleuve**

roast beef **le rosbif**

room **la chambre, la pièce**

to ruin **abîmer**

ruler **une règle**

to run **courir**

S

sad *adj.* **triste, malheureux, malheureuse**

salt **le sel**

same *adj.* **même**; all the same, just the same/**tout de même**

Santa Claus **le Père Noël**

to satisfy **satisfaire**

to say **dire**

school **une école**

season **la saison**

seat **la place**; seated/**assis, assise**

second **une seconde**; Wait a second, please/**Attendez une seconde, s'il vous plaît**; *adj.,* **deuxième, second(e)**; February is the second month of the year/**Février est le deuxième mois de l'année**; the Second Empire/**le Second Empire**

security check (travel) **le contrôle de sécurité**

to see **voir**; to see again/**revoir**; see you in a little while!/**à tout à l'heure!** see you soon/**à bientôt**; *see also* Part III, Unit 5

to seize **saisir**

selection key **la touche de sélection**

to send **envoyer**

sentence **la phrase**

serious *adj.* **sérieux, sérieuse, sérieux, sérieuses**; seriously/**sérieusement**

several *adj.* **plusieurs**

shame **la honte**

shark **un requin**

she *per. pron. f.* **elle**

to shine **briller**

shirt **la chemise**

shoe **la chaussure, le soulier**

shoo! shoo! **Ch! Ch!**

shop (small) **une boutique**

short *adj.* **court, courte**

shoulder **une épaule**

to shout **crier**

to show **montrer**

shower **une douche**; to take a shower/**prendre une douche**

sick *adj.* **malade, souffrant, souffrante**

sidewalk **le trottoir**

since **depuis**

to sing **chanter**

singer **un chanteur, une chanteuse**

sister **une soeur**

575

to sit down **s'asseoir**; sit down! **assieds-toi!** *or* **asseyez-vous!** (polite form)

sixty *adj.* **soixante**

skin **la peau**

skirt **la jupe**

sky **le ciel**

to sleep **dormir**

sleeve **une manche**

slow *adj.* **lent, lente**

slowly **lentement**

small *adj.* **petit, petite**

to smell **sentir**

smoke **la fumée**; to smoke/**fumer**

snack bar **un bar rapide**

snow **la neige**; to snow/**neiger**; it is snowing!/**il neige!**

snowman **un bonhomme de neige**

so *adv.* **alors**; so as to/**de façon à**

soccer (in the United States) **le football**

socks **les chaussettes**, *n. f.*

soft *adj.* **doux, douce, doux, douces**

soiled *adj.* **sale**

some *(partitive)* **de l', de la, du, des**; I drink some water/**Je bois de l'eau**; I eat some meat/**Je mange de la viande**; I drink some milk/**Je bois du lait**; I eat some potatoes/**Je mange des pommes de terre**; some (of it, of them) **en**; I am eating some/**J'en mange**; see also pp. 46–47

something *indef. pron.* **quelque chose**

sometimes *adv.* **quelquefois**

son **le fils** (pronouce as *feess*)

soon *adv.* **bientôt**

to be sorry **regretter**

soup **la soupe, le potage**

Spain **l'Espagne**, *n. f.*

Spanish (language) **l'espagnol** *n. m.*

to speak **parler**

speed **la vitesse**; at full speed, quickly/**à toute vitesse**

to spend (time) **passer**; I am spending one week in Paris/**Je passe une semaine à Paris**

spirit **l'esprit**, *n. m.*

to spoil **abîmer**

spoon **une cuiller, une cuillère**

spring (season of the year) **le printemps**

standing *adv.* **debout**

station (bus, train, *etc.*) **une gare**

to stay **demeurer, rester**

to steal **voler**

still *adv.* **toujours, encore**

stocking **le bas**

stomach **l'estomac**, *n. m.*

to stop **arrêter**; to stop (oneself) **s'arrêter**; I am stopping the bus/ **J'arrête l'autobus**; I'm stopping to take the bus/**Je m'arrête pour prendre l'autobus**

store **le magasin**; department store/**le grand magasin**

storm **un orage**

story **un conte, une histoire**

strawberry **la fraise**

street **la rue**

strong *adj.* **fort, forte**; the strongest/ **le plus fort, la plus forte**; your strongest quality/**votre qualité la plus forte**

student **un étudiant, une étudiante, un élève, une élève**

to study **étudier**

subway **le métro** (short for **métropolitain**)

to succeed **réussir (à)**

suit **le complet, le costume**

suitcase **la valise**

summer **l'été**, *n. m.*

sun **le soleil**

supermarket **le supermarché**

sure *adj.* **sûr, sûre, certain, certaine**

to surf (the Internet) **surfer, naviguer**

sweet *adj.* **doux, douce**

to swim **nager**

swimsuit **un maillot de bain**

to swing, to sway **se balancer**; a swing/**une balançoire**

Switzerland **la Suisse**

T

table **la table**

tablecloth **la nappe**

to take **prendre**; to take a walk/**faire une promenade, se promener**; to take advantage of/**profiter (de)**; to take along; to take away/**emporter**; to take off, to remove/**enlever**

to talk **parler**

talk key **la touche d'appel**

taste **le goût**; to taste/ **goûter**; taste some!/ **goûtez-en!**

to teach **enseigner**

teacher **un maître, une maîtresse, un professeur, une femme professeur**

team **une équipe**

to tear **déchirer**

television **la télévision, la télé, la TV, la T.V.**; on television/**à la télévision**; television set/**le téléviseur**

to tell **dire**

ten *adj.* **dix**

tense (verb) **le temps**; present indicative/**le présent de l'indicatif**

to terminate **terminer, finir**

terrific *adj.* **formidable**

than *conj.* **que**; She is taller than her sister/**Elle est plus grande que sa soeur**

to thank **remercier**; thank you/**Je vous remercie** *or* **merci**

that I know *that* you are right/**Je sais que vous avez raison**; The book *that* is on the table is mine/**Le livre qui est sur la table est à moi**; that book/**ce livre-là**; that tree/**cet arbre-là**; that lady/**cette dame-là**; *That* is not important/ *Cela* **n'est pas important**

that's right! **c'est ça!**

the *def. art.* **l', le, la, les;** the tree/**l'arbre;** the man/**l'homme;** the boy/**le garçon;** the girl/**la jeune fille;** the children/**les enfants**

theater **le théâtre**

their *poss. adj.* **leur, leurs;** their house/**leur maison;** their houses/**leurs maisons**

them *dir. obj. pron.* **les;** I like them/**Je les aime;** *as obj. of a prep.,* for them/**pour elles** (*fem.*), for them/**pour eux** (*masc.*)

themselves *refl. pron.* **se;** They wash themselves every morning/**Ils se lavent tous les matins**

then *adv.* **puis, alors**

there *adv. of place; advl. pron.* **y; Janine va à l'école/**Janine is going to school; She is going there/**Elle y va; Où est Janine?**/ Where is Janine? She's there/**Elle est là;** there is, there are/**il y a;** There is a fly in the soup/**Il y a une mouche dans la soupe;** There are many flowers in the garden/**Il y a beaucoup de fleurs dans le jardin;** there isn't, there aren't/**il n'y a pas;** There's Paul!/**Voilà Paul!**

these *dem. adj.* **ces;** these boys/**ces garçons;** these girls/**ces jeunes filles**

they *per. pron.* **ils, elles**

thick *adj.* **épais, épaisse**

thing **une chose**

third *adj.* **troisième**

thirst **la soif;** to be thirsty/**avoir soif;** I'm thirsty/**J'ai soif**

this *dem. adj.* **ce, cet, cette;** this boy/**ce garçon;** this tree/**cet arbre;** this girl/**cette jeune fille;** *dem. pron.* **ceci;** this is true/**ceci est vrai**

those *dem. adj.* **ces;** those boys/**ces garçons-là;** those girls/**ces jeunes filles-là**

three *adj.* **trois**

through *prep.* **par, à travers**

to throw **jeter, lancer**

ticket **le billet**

time (hour, time of day) **l'heure,** *n. f.;* What time is it?/**Quelle heure est-il?**

time (duration) **le temps;** Paul spent a lot of time in France/**Paul a passé beaucoup de temps en France**

time (different instances) **la fois;** one time, once/**une fois;** two times, twice/**deux fois;** many times/**beaucoup de fois;** next time/**la prochaine fois**

tired *adj.* **fatigué, fatiguée**

to *prep.* **à**

toast **le pain grillé**

today *adv.* **aujourd'hui**

together *adv.* **ensemble**

tomato **la tomate**

tomorrow *adv.* **demain**

tongue **la langue**

tonight **ce soir**

too **aussi, trop (de);** Robert is coming too/**Robert vient aussi;** Janine works too much/**Janine travaille trop;** There is too much noise here/**Il y a trop de bruit ici;** There are too many people here/**Il y a trop de personnes ici**

tooth **la dent**

touch pad **le pavé tactile**

touch pad button **le bouton du pavé tactile**

touch screen **l'écran** *m.* **tactile**

town **la ville;** *see also idioms with* **en,** *Part III, Unit 2*

toy **le jouet**

traffic light **le feu;** red traffic light/**le feu rouge;** green traffic light/**le feu vert**

tree **un arbre**

trip **un voyage;** to take a trip/**faire un voyage**

truck **le camion;** truck driver/**le camionneur**

true *adj.* **vrai, vraie**

truly *adv.* **vraiment**

to try **essayer (de)**

to turn on (light) **allumer**

twentieth *adj.* **vingtième**

twenty *adj.* **vingt**

two *adj.* **deux**

U

umbrella **le parapluie**

unbelievable *adj.* **incroyable**

uncle **un oncle**

under *prep.* **sous;** underneath/ **dessous, par-dessous, en dessous**

to understand **comprendre**

undoubtedly *adv.* **sans doute**

unhappy *adj.* **malheureux, malheureuse, triste**

United States **les États-Unis;** to the United States/**aux États-Unis**

until *prep.* **jusque;** until spring/**jusqu'au printemps**

unusual *adj.* **extraordinaire**

upset *adj.* **inquiet, inquiète**

us *per. pron.* **nous;** for us/**pour nous**

to use **employer**

useful *adj.* **utile**

useless *adj.* **inutile**

V

vase **un vase**

vegetable **un légume**

very *adv.* **très**

vest **un gilet**

to visit **faire visite, visiter;** to visit someone/**rendre visite à quelqu'un**

voice **une voix;** in a loud voice/**à haute voix;** in a low voice, softly/**à voix basse**

voice mail **la boîte vocale, la messagerie**

W

to wait (for) **attendre**

waiter **un garçon (de café, de restaurant);** (Nowadays, a customer addresses a waiter as *Monsieur,* not *garçon*)

577

to walk **marcher, aller à pied**

wall **un mur**

to want **vouloir**

to wash **laver**; I washed the car/**J'ai lavé la voiture**; to wash oneself/**se laver**; I washed myself/**Je me suis lavé(e)**

to wash and get dressed **faire la toilette**

to watch **regarder**; to watch television/**regarder la télévision**

water **l'eau**, *n. f.*

way **la façon**; I like your way of talking/**J'aime votre façon de parler**

we *per. pron.* **nous**; We like French/**Nous aimons le français**

weak *adj.* **faible**

to wear **porter**

weather **le temps**; What's the weather like today?/**Quel temps fait-il aujourd'hui?**

week **la semaine**

to weep **pleurer**

well *adv.* **bien**; She works well with her sister/**Elle travaille bien avec sa soeur**

what *What* are you saying?/*Que* **dites-vous?** *What* am I?/*Que* **suis-je?** or *Qu'est-ce qu* **je suis?** *What* you are saying is right/*Ce que* **vous dites est juste**; *What* is on the table is mine/*Ce qui* **est sur la table est à moi**; *what* book?/*quel* **livre?** *what* books?/*quels* **livres?** *what* house?/*quelle* **maison?** *what* houses?/*quelles* **maisons?** *What* time is it?/*Quelle* **heure est-il?** *What?!/***Quoi?!** *What* is it?/*Qu'est-ce que* **c'est?** What's new?/ **Quoi de neuf?** *What* is the date today?/*Quelle* **est la date aujourd'hui?** *What* day is it

today?/*Quel* **jour est-ce aujourd'hui?** *What* color is your house?/**De** *quelle* **couleur est votre maison?**

wheel **la roue**

when *adv.* **quand**

where *adv.* **où**

which *pron.* The book *which* is on the table is mine/**Le livre** *qui* **est sur la table est à moi**; *as an adj.,* **quel, quelle, quels, quelles**; which boy?/**quel garçon?** which books?/**quels livres?** which girl?/**quelle jeune fille?** which colors?/**quelles couleurs?**

while *conj.* **pendant que**

white *adj.* **blanc, blanche**

who *pron.* **qui**; Who are you?/**Qui êtes-vous?**

whom *pron.* **qui, que**; Whom do you see?/**Qui voyez-vous?** with whom/**avec qui** The boy whom you see over there is my brother/ **Le garçon que vous voyez là-bas est mon frère**

why **pourquoi**; why not?/**pourquoi pas?**

wife **une femme, une épouse**

to win **gagner**

wind **le vent**; It is windy/**Il fait du vent**

window **une fenêtre**

wine **le vin**

wing **une aile**

winter **l'hiver**, *n. m.;* in winter/**en hiver**

with *prep.* **avec**

without *prep.* **sans**

woman **la femme**

wonderful *adj.* **magnifique, merveilleux, merveilleuse**

woods **le bois, les bois**

word **le mot; la parole** (the spoken word)

work **le travail, l'oeuvre**, *n. f.;* a work of art/**une oeuvre d'art**

to work **travailler**

world **le monde**

to worry **s'inquiéter**; Don't worry!/**Ne vous inquiétez pas!** *or* **Ne t'inquiète pas!**

to write **écrire**

writer **un écrivain, une femme écrivain**

wrong **un tort**; to be wrong/**avoir tort**; You are wrong/**Vous avez tort**; *see also idioms with* **avoir**, *Part III, Unit 3*

X

X-ray machine (in airports) **la machine à rayons X**

Y

year **un an, une année**

yellow *adj.* **jaune**

yes *adv.* **oui**

yesterday *adv.* **hier**

you *pron.* Where are you going?/**Où vas-tu? Où allez-vous?** with you/**avec toi, avec vous**; I am giving this book to you/**Je te donne ce livre, Je vous donne ce livre**

young *adj.* **jeune**

your *poss. adj.* **ton, ta, tes, votre, vos**; your book/**ton livre, votre livre**; your mother/**ta mère, votre mère**; your books/**tes livres, vos livres**

you're welcome **de rien, il n'y a pas de quoi**

yourself *refl. pron.* **te, vous**; You wash yourself every morning, don't you?/**Tu te laves tous les matins, n'est-ce pas? Vous vous lavez tous les matins, n'est-ce pas?**

Z

zodiac **le zodiaque**

Index

FRENCH NOW! Level 1

Teacher's Manual with Answers

Fourth Edition

by

Christopher Kendris, Ph.D.

Theodore Kendris, Ph.D.

Suggestions and Guidelines for the Teacher

HOW THIS WORKTEXT MAY BE USED IN CLASS AS A BASIC COURSE OR AS A SUPPLEMENT TO A TEXTBOOK

1. **In presenting structures and verbs, the teacher can use the following features:**
   a. model sentences for listening, repetition, reading practice and brief analysis
   b. generalizations or rules to reinforce conclusions reached through studying the model sentences
   c. initial exercises as audio-lingual drills for the immediate classroom application of newly presented material
   d. additional graded exercises for oral and written practice with the class as a whole, with groups, and with students making individual progress
   See TABLE OF CONTENTS in the text for additional special sections to develop vocabulary, idiomatic control and skills in listening, reading, and writing.

2. **Promoting speaking skills and oral production**
   a. Social interaction can be promoted by role-reading, and by judicious memorizing of the many illustrative and model sentences and exercises which are written in question-answer and in stimulus-rejoinder form. Idiomatic Dialogues will provide material for dramatizations. The teacher may make original variations on this material according to the needs, interests, and abilities of the students.
   b. The stories are in play form as well as narrative, so that they, too, can be read taking roles, and can be re-enacted.
   c. The many humorous pictures, sketches, and illustrations can be used to stimulate both directed and free oral production, followed by written composition. The teacher may use the illustrations to stimulate students to formulate questions for other students to answer, and may base his or her own questions on the sketches to elicit details, a retelling of the story, or giving another ending to the story. On the basis of the illustrations, students may be stimulated to tell their own stories guided by questions, key words or sentences to be completed.

3. **Reinforcement and re-entry**
   Selected lessons in the worktext may be practiced for periodic reinforcement and review as the need arises. The teacher may refer students to the model sentences and to the explanations in order to clarify understandings, and to the exercises in order to develop mastery.

4. **Testing**
   a. Complete or portions of exercises may be reserved for periodic testing of oral and written skills, or both.
   b. The **dictée** exercises are ideal for testing and they are very effective.
   c. After every five work units there is a major test. There are five major tests in all.

5. **In the teacher's absence**
   The worktext can be used to reinforce topics taught earlier in the term, when the class is under the guidance of a substitute teacher whose area of competence may not be French.

USING THE WORKTEXT AT HOME

1. **Exercises and drills for homework**
   Oral and written homework assignments to reinforce class work may be made from the exercises and drills to strengthen oral ability, writing ability, and conceptualization.

2. Enrichment

Additional exercises from the worktext may be assigned in place of, or in conjunction with, the regular homework assignment from any basic textbook. This may apply to the class as a whole or to individual students who can benefit from additional work or a more interesting level of challenge.

3. Reviewing before an examination

An abundance of simple basic exercises with model or sample sentences and explanations clarify all Level One topics. This provides a source of supplementary practice and self-testing material (using the Answer Key) from which the teacher can make appropriate selections for a particular class.

4. Remedial work

After testing, when a particular weakness has been revealed, selected lessons and exercises may be assigned to the class or to an individual student to improve skills, to clarify understanding and to develop mastery.

USING THE WORKTEST FOR INDEPENDENT STUDY

Students who are motivated to perfect their work, who wish to advance, or who need to absent themselves from class for long periods, may use to good advantage the step-by-step models and explanations, and the graded exercises with the Answers.

Answer Key

LEÇONS PRÉLIMINAIRES

I. La famille Paquet: Présentation (The Paquet family: Presentation)

Exercises, pp. 4–5

I. 1. le père, une bonne épouse. 2. suis, mère, ai, bon. 3. suis, une soeur. 4. la fille, bon. 5. suis le. J'ai, famille. **II.** 3, 4, 1, 5, 2. **III.** 1. Claire Paquet est la mère. 2. François Paquet est le père. 3. Janine est la fille. 4. Pierre est le fils. 5. Coco est le chien. **IV.** A. 1. bon. 2. intelligent. B. 1. bonne. 2. intelligente. **V.** 1. Janine. 2. Claire Paquet. 3. François Paquet. 4. Coco. 5. Pierre. **VI.** 1. la fille. 2. le frère. 3. la mère. 4. le chien. 5. le père.

II. Choses (Things)

Exercises, p. 6

I. 1. grand. 2. rond. 3. bonne. 4. petite. **II.** 1. petite. 2. bonne. 3. rond. 4. grand. **III.** 4, 3, 1, 2.

Exercises, pp. 6–7

I. 1. joli. 2. belle. 3. long. 4. jolie. **II.** 3, 1, 4, 2. **III.** 1. joli. 2. belle. 3. long. 4. jolie.

Exercises, pp. 7–8

I. 1. grand. 2. délicieux. 3. beau. 4. intéressant. **II.** 1. grand. 2. délicieux. 3. beau. 4. intéressant. **III.** 1. c'est un garage. est. 2. n'est pas. un. 3. c'est. beau. 4. c'est. est.

Exercises, pp. 8–9

I. 1. confortable. 2. splendide. 3. charmante. 4. blanc. **II.** 4, 3, 1, 2.

Exercises, p. 9

I. 1. ouvert. 2. magnifique. 3. mignonne. 4. délicieux. **II.** 1. un parapluie, est. 2. n'est pas, est. 3. ce n'est pas, une. 4. un, délicieux.

Exercises, p. 10

I. 1. long. 2. noir. 3. beau. 4. grand. **II.** 4, 5, 1, 6, 2, 3.

III. Personnes (People)

Exercises, p. 11

I. 1. boit, lait. 2. danse. 3. un livre. 4. courent. **II.** 1. Le garçon boit du lait. 2. La jeune fille danse. 3. Le garçon lit un livre (possibly: Un garçon lit le livre). 4. La jeune fille et le garçon courent (possibly: Le garçon et la jeune fille courent).

Exercises, p. 12

I. 1. chante. 2. écrit. 3. arrête, autos. **II.** 1. (b). 2. (a). 3. (c).

IV. L'École: la salle de classe (The School: the classroom)

Exercises, pp. 13–14

I. Column B: 1. Madame Duval est derrière le bureau. 2. Il est une heure. 3. Il y a une carte de France sur le mur. 4. La jeune fille lit un livre. 5. La jeune fille écrit une composition. 6. Le garçon est debout. 7. Le garçon lève la main. **II.** 1. Non, madame (mademoiselle, monsieur), ce n'est pas le stylo. C'est le crayon. 2. Non, madame (mademoiselle, monsieur), ce n'est pas la feuille de papier. C'est le livre. 3. Non, madame (mademoiselle, monsieur), ce n'est pas l'ordinateur. C'est l'horloge. 4. Non, madame (mademoiselle, monsieur), ce n'est pas un élève. C'est une élève. 5.

Non, madame (mademoiselle, monsieur), ce n'est pas la chaise. C'est le banc. 6. Non, madame (mademoiselle, monsieur), ce n'est pas une élève. C'est un élève. 7. Non, madame (mademoiselle, monsieur), ce n'est pas le petit banc. C'est la petite chaise (Teacher, please see p. 5 for introduction of "petite chaise"). 8. Non, madame (mademoiselle, monsieur), ce n'est pas l'horloge. C'est l'ordinateur (Teacher, please see p. 13 in the book for the picture of "l'ordinateur" on teacher's desk). 9. Non, madame (mademoiselle, monsieur), ce n'est pas le tableau. C'est le pupitre (Teacher, please see p. 13 in the book for the picture of "le pupitre").

V. La Maison: la salle à manger (The House: the dining room)

Exercises, p. 17
I. 1. C'est une fleur. 2. C'est une assiette. 3. C'est une tasse. 4. C'est une cuiller (OR cuillère). 5. C'est un verre. 6. C'est un couteau. II. 1. UNE CHAISE. 2. UNE ASSIETTE. 3. UN TAPIS. 4. UNE FOURCHETTE. 5. UN COUTEAU. 6. UNE NAPPE. 7. UN VERRE. 8. UNE TASSE. 9. UNE CUILLER. 10. UNE FLEUR.

VI. La Ville: dans la rue (The City: in the street)

Exercises, p. 19
I. 1. C'est une dame. 2. C'est un homme. 3. C'est une petite fille. 4. C'est un garçon. 5. C'est un agent de police. 6. C'est une voiture. 7. C'est un immeuble. 8. C'est un autobus. II. 1. UNE VALISE. 2. UN PETIT CHIEN. 3. LE TROTTOIR. 4. LE MÉTRO.

PART 1: STRUCTURES AND VERBS

WORK UNIT 1

Exercises, pp. 24–25
I. 1. (c). 2. (d). 3. (d). 4. (b). 5. (d). II. 1. Janine cherche dans la commode. 2. Madame Paquet cherche dans l'armoire. 3. Monsieur Paquet cherche sous la chaise. III. 2. Non. Je cherche. 4. Je cherche sous la chaise (la table, l'armoire, etc.).

IV. Un acrostiche

Exercises, p. 27
I. 1. le. 2. la. 3. le. 4. la. 5. l'. 6. l'. 7. le. 8. le. 9. l'. 10. la. 11. le. 12. l'. 13. le. 14. la. 15. l'.

II. Word Hunt

Exercises, pp. 27–29

III. Je désire un sandwich. Oui, un sandwich au jambon. Et avec le sandwich au jambon, une tasse de café avec crème et sucre. Je désire une pomme et une banane. **IV.** Je désire acheter une chaise. Oui, elles sont belles. Je désire acheter, aussi, un lit, une armoire, une lampe, et une table. **V.** Je cherche sous le lit, papa. Maintenant je cherche sous la chaise, papa. Cherchons dans la cuisine, dans le salon, dans la salle de bains, dans la cave, sous la commode, dans le garage. Partout dans la maison! **VI.** 1. Le chapeau est dans la cuisine. 2. Le chapeau est dans l'armoire. 3. Le chapeau est dans la maison. 4. Le chapeau est dans la commode. 5. Le chapeau est dans le garage.

Exercises, pp. 30–32

I. 1. un. 2. une. 3. un. 4. un. 5. une. 6. un. 7. un. 8. un. 9. une. 10. un. 11. un. 12. une. 13. une. 14. une. 15. un.

II. Word Hunt

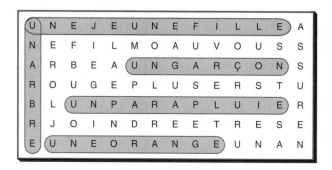

III. 2. C'est ma mère. 4. Elle cherche dans l'armoire. 6. Une nouvelle robe. 8. Elle va en ville avec une amie. **IV.** 1. Monsieur Paquet cherche son chapeau. 2. Le chien est sous le lit. 3. Nous cherchons partout. 4. Je vais en ville acheter un nouveau chapeau. 5. Coco mange le chapeau. **V.** 1. le. 2. la. 3. la. 4. l'. 5. la. 6. le. 7. le. 8. le. 9. un. 10. une. **VI. A.** 1. une banane. 2. un gâteau. 3. un jambon. 4. un oeuf. **B.** 1. une cuiller. 2. un couteau. 3. une fourchette. 4. une assiette. 5. un verre. 6. une tasse. **C.** 1. manger. 2. boire. 3. danser. 4. lire. 5. courir. 6. chanter. 7. écrire. 8. chercher.

WORK UNIT 2

Exercises, pp. 36–37

I. 1. (d). 2. (c). 3. (a). 4. (d). 5. (a). II. 1. Je désire apporter le poulet. 2. Je désire, aussi, apporter la saucisse et le rosbif. 3. Tu désires apporter le jambon, la glace, et le gâteau? III. 1. Pour moi, j'aime l'eau minérale. 2. C'est bon pour la santé. 3. Je n'aime pas le café. J'aime mieux l'eau minérale.

IV. Mots croisés

Exercises, pp. 39–40

I. 1. les garçons. 2. les fils. 3. les chapeaux. 4. les journaux. 5. les cieux. 6. les yeux. 7. les pères. 8. les voix. 9. les mères. 10. les chats. II. 1. la table. 2. le nez. 3. le genou. 4. la voix. 5. l'oeil. 6. le monsieur. 7. l'homme. 8. la jeune fille. 9. l'enfant. 10. l'arbre. III. 1. le père. 2. l'homme. 3. les eaux. 4. les fils. 5. les tables. 6. le journal. 7. les chevaux. 8. les oiseaux. 9. l'élève. 10. les pays.

Exercises, p. 42

I. 7, 8, 5, 3, 6, 2, 1, 4. II. 1. au. 2. à la. 3. aux. 4. à l'. III. 1. du. 2. de l'. 3. de la. 4. des.

Exercises, pp. 43–44

I. 4, 6, 7, 2, 10, 9, 8, 3, 5, 1. II. 1. des. 2. de la. 3. de. 4. du. 5. de l'. 6. de l'. 7. de. 8. du. 9. de l'. 10. de la. III. 1. C'est ma tante Sophie. Elle mange tout le temps. 2. C'est le parapluie de ma mère. 3. Ce sont les gants de mon père.

WORK UNIT 3

Exercises, p. 47

I. 1. (d). 2. (d). 3. (c). II. A. 1. une fourchette. 2. un couteau. 3. une cuiller. 4. une tasse. B. 1. un éclair. 2. une tarte. 3. un petit four glacé. 4. un gâteau.

III. Word Hunt

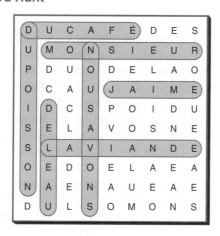

Exercises, pp. 49–51

I. 1. Oui, j'ai du pain. 2. Oui, j'ai de la viande. 3. Oui, j'ai de l'eau. 4. Oui, j'ai des bonbons. 5. Oui, j'ai du beurre. **II.** 1. Non, je n'ai pas de café. 2. Non, je n'ai pas de viande. 3. Non, je n'ai pas d'eau. 4. Non, je n'ai pas de bonbons. 5. Non, je n'ai pas de beurre. **III.** Mon ami Paul (Mon amie Paula): Je n'ai pas de bonbons. As-tu des bonbons pour moi? Merci. **IV.** 1. Non, je n'ai pas de bon café. 2. Non, je n'ai pas de jolis chapeaux. 3. Non, je n'ai pas de jolies jupes. 4. Non, je n'ai pas de bon vin. 5. Non, je n'ai pas de jolies cravates.

Exercises, p. 52

I. 1. Oui, j'ai les mains sales. 2. Oui, j'ai le visage sale. 3. Oui, j'ai le nez long. 4. Oui, j'ai les yeux bruns. 5. Oui, j'ai les cheveux noirs. **II.** 1. Non, je n'ai pas les pieds grands. 2. Non, je n'ai pas le visage sale. 3. Non, je n'ai pas les mains sales. 4. Non, je n'ai pas le chapeau sur la tête. 5. Non, je n'ai pas les cheveux noirs.

Exercises, pp. 53–54

I. 1. Oui, je vais à l'école les matins. 2. Oui, je vais à la bibliothèque les après-midi. (NOTE TO TEACHER: The French Academy writes *après-midi* with no *s* in the plural; but with *s* is acceptable.) 3. Oui, je vais au restaurant les soirs. 4. Oui, je vais au parc les après-midi. 5. Oui, je vais au café les soirs. **II.** 1. Non, je ne vais pas au cinéma les soirs. 2. Non, je ne vais pas à l'école les matins. 3. Non, je ne vais pas à la bibliothèque les soirs.

Exercises, pp. 55–59

I. 1. Il parle français. Il prononce bien le français. 2. Elle parle espagnol. Elle prononce bien l'espagnol. 3. Elle parle italien. Elle prononce bien l'italien. 4. Il parle anglais. Il prononce bien l'anglais. 5. Elle parle allemand. Elle prononce bien l'allemand. **II.** 1. Oui, j'ai cent dollars. 2. Oui, j'ai mille euros. 3. Oui, j'ai cent livres. 4. Oui, j'ai mille amis. **III.** 1. —. 2. l'. 3. —. 4. —. 5. la. 6. le. 7. les. 8. les. **IV.** 1. J'ai les sandwichs. 2. J'ai les éclairs. 3. J'ai la saucisse. 4. J'ai des dollars. 5. J'ai une jupe. 6. J'ai les chapeaux. 7. J'ai le dessert. 8. J'ai un gâteau.

V. Jeu de mots

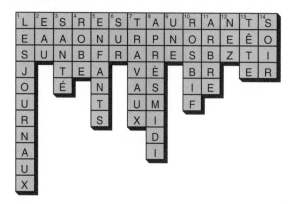

VI. J'ai les yeux bleus (bruns, gris, verts). J'ai les cheveux noirs (bruns, blonds, roux). J'ai les pieds grands (petits). J'ai le visage rond. J'ai les mains grandes (petites). **VII.** 1. Bonjour! Avez-vous du poisson aujourd'hui? 2. Avez-vous de la viande? 3. Avez-vous des saucisses? 4. Non, monsieur. Je regrette. Je ne veux pas (OR: Je ne désire pas) de viande. Je ne veux (désire) pas de saucisses. 5. Non, monsieur, je ne veux (désire) pas de poisson. Je regrette. 6. Non, monsieur, je ne veux (désire) pas de café. 7. Oui, oui. J'aime les éclairs et les tartes. **VIII.** 1. J'aimerais un grand gâteau au chocolat. 2. Avec ceci, j'aimerais deux éclairs et deux tartes aux pommes. 3. Oui, c'est tout, merci. **IX.** 1. Jacques est de France. Il parle français. Il prononce bien le français. 2. María est d'Espagne. Elle parle espagnol. Elle prononce bien l'espagnol. 3. Rosa est d'Italie. Elle parle italien. Elle prononce bien l'italien. 4. Ian est d'Angleterre. Il parle anglais. Il prononce bien l'anglais. 5. Marlena est d'Allemagne. Elle parle allemand. Elle prononce bien l'allemand. **X.** Bonjour, madame. J'aimerais savoir où se trouve le restaurant. Et où se trouve l'Agence de voyages, s'il vous plaît? À quelle heure est-ce que le magasin ferme? J'aimerais savoir aussi où se trouve le bar rapide. Et les toilettes? Merci, madame. Où se trouvent les interprètes?

WORK UNIT 4

Exercises, p. 63

I. 1. Janine et Pierre allument le téléviseur. 2. La mère et le père entrent dans le salon. 3. Pierre et Janine regardent dans les journaux. **II.** J'aime regarder la télévision (la télé) tous les samedis soirs. J'aime beaucoup "Jeopardy!," "Wheel of Fortune," et "Sports" parce que c'est très intéressant. J'aime mieux regarder la télé avec mes amis. **III.** 1. (b). 2. (c). 3. (b). **IV.** allument, marche, entrent, exclament, marche, regardez, demandent, mère, père.

Exercises, pp. 69–74

I. 1. Je travaille dans un restaurant cuisine rapide. 2. Je travaille tous les samedis. 3. Je regarde les films français à la télé tous les samedis soirs et je parle français tout le temps. **II.** 1. Elle. 2. Il. 3. Elles. 4. Ils. 5. Ils. **III.** 1. désirer. 2. demander. 3. montrer. 4. regarder. **IV.** 1. Bonjour, madame (monsieur). Désirez-vous parler français avec moi? 2. Parlez-vous français à la maison? 3. Est-ce que vous chantez en français avec les enfants? **V.** 1. Oui, je danse les matins; il danse aussi. 2. Oui, il cherche le chapeau; elle cherche le chapeau aussi. 3. Oui, elle étudie la leçon; j'étudie la leçon aussi. **VI.** 1. Non, je ne danse pas; il ne danse pas non plus. 2. Non, il n'étudie pas; elle n'é-tudie pas non plus. 3. Non, il ne cherche pas la balle; ils ne cherchent pas la balle non plus. 4. Non, elle n'écoute pas la musique; je n'écoute pas la musique non plus. 5. Non, je ne ferme pas la fenêtre; vous ne fermez pas la fenêtre non plus (possibly: nous ne fermons pas la fenêtre non plus). **VII.** 1. Je ferme. 2. Tu apportes. 3. Il étudie. 4. Elle parle. 5. Nous marchons. 6. Vous donnez. 7. Ils jouent. 8. Elles chantent. 9. Vous cherchez. 10. J'aime.

VIII. Word Search

IX. A. Nous préférons regarder "Le Tour de France" à la télé. C'est notre émission préférée. Nous aimons regarder les sports. Papa et maman aiment les sports aussi. **B.** Je n'aime pas aller au concert. J'aime mieux danser. J'aime la musique. Je préfère aller danser. **X.** Michel: Je désire danser. Michelle: Moi, j'aimerais voir un film français. **XI.** Je vais à la bibliothèque tous les jours. Je regarde la télé tous les soirs. J'étudie mes leçons de français tous les soirs aussi. **XII.** 1. Oui. Le menu est bon. Et les prix sont bons. Entrons! 2. Nous cherchons un bon restaurant français. 3. Apportez-nous la soupe du jour. 4. Quel restaurant! Quel serveur! Où est-il?! 5. Il y a des mouches dans la soupe! 6. Oui, Janine. Sortons d'ici tout de suite! Quel restaurant! **XIII.** 1. C'est Madame Georges Charpentier. Elle est belle. Elle est heureuse. 2. Il y a deux enfants dans ce tableau. 3. Le chien est grand. 4. Sur la table je vois un vase de fleurs, des fruits, et une carafe. 5. J'aime beaucoup ce tableau. C'est beau, c'est magnifique, c'est splendide!

WORK UNIT 5

Exercises, pp. 77–78
I. 1. (c). 2. (d). 3. (c). **II. A.** Je ne finis pas le devoir parce que l'exercice est très difficile. La leçon est difficile aussi. **B.** Madame Berty donne des devoirs difficiles. Pourquoi choisit-elle des exercices difficiles? Pour punir les élèves! Elle est méchante. **III.** 1. choisit. 2. rougit. 3. finit. 4. finissent. 5. retentit.

Exercises, pp. 79–85
I. J'aime la biologie mais je n'aime pas la maîtresse de biologie. Elle punit les élèves quand ils ne finissent pas les devoirs. Quand elle explique la leçon, je ne saisis rien. Elle choisit des questions très difficiles. **II.** Madame Durand est méchante. Elle punit les élèves quand ils ne finissent pas les leçons. Je n'aime pas Madame Durand. Elle n'est pas sympathique. Je déteste le cours et je déteste Madame Durand. **III.** 1. Ils finissent la leçon. 2. Tu finis la leçon. 3. Il finit la leçon. 4. Elle finit la leçon. 5. Vous finissez la leçon. 6. Elles finissent la leçon. **IV.** 1. Vous ne finissez pas le dîner. 2. Il ne finit pas le dîner. 3. Tu ne finis pas le dîner. 4. Elles ne finissent pas le dîner. 5. Ils ne finissent pas le dîner. 6. Nous ne finissons pas le dîner. **V.** 1. Oui, il finit le livre; je finis le livre aussi. 2. Oui, ils punissent les mauvais élèves; il punit les mauvais élèves aussi. 3. Oui, il choisit une nouvelle automobile; ils choisissent une nouvelle automobile aussi. 4. Oui, il obéit au garçon; ils obéissent au garçon aussi. 5. Oui, je finis la leçon aujourd'hui; elle finit la leçon aujourd'hui aussi. **VI.** 1. Non, il ne désobéit pas; je ne désobéis pas non plus (possibly: nous ne désobéissons pas non plus). 2. Non, je ne finis pas la leçon; il ne finit pas la leçon non plus. 3. Non, il ne choisit pas une auto; elle ne choisit pas une auto non plus. 4. Non, nous ne bâtissons pas une maison; ils ne bâtissent pas une maison non plus. 5. Non, je ne rougis pas (possibly: Non, nous ne rougissons pas); elles ne rougissent pas non plus. **VII.** 1. Je finis la leçon. 2. Tu saisis la balle. 3. Il accomplit les devoirs. 4. Elle bâtit une maison. 5. Nous choisissons un dessert. 6. Vous punissez le chien. 7. Ils rougissent facilement. 8. Elles désobéissent à leurs parents. 9. Je remplis le vase. 10. Vous finissez les devoirs.

VIII. Word Search

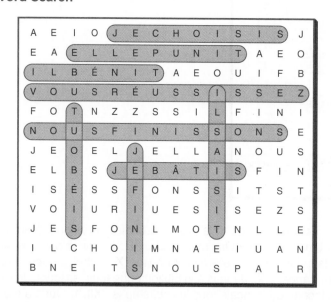

IX. 1. C'est une oeuvre d'art magnifique. 2. Je pense que cette statue est la plus belle de toutes les oeuvres de Rodin. 3. C'est une grande joie de regarder cette statue. **X.** 1. Le tableau de Tissot, artiste français, est superbe. 2. La jeune femme est belle. 3. Elle a de beaux yeux. 4. Elle porte une jolie robe. 5. Elle est assise. 6. Son grand chapeau noir est beau. 7. Elle a de belles mains. 8. Elle est chez elle.

TEST 1 (WORK UNITS 1–5)

Pages 87, 88, 89

PART ONE: Speaking Proficiency. (NOTE TO TEACHER: The ten situations given are a review of exercises in proficiency in speaking in Work Units 1 to 5. Your students will respond to you and you may grade them on this speaking test according to what they say in class or on a one-to-one basis at your desk.) **PART TWO: Listening Proficiency.** (NOTE TO TEACHER: Here are the four short paragraphs that you will read aloud to your students. The directions are given in the test.) **Selection Number 1.** Monsieur Paquet cherche son chapeau. Janine cherche dans la commode. Madame Paquet cherche dans l'armoire et Pierre cherche sous le lit. Tout le monde cherche dans la cuisine, dans le salon, dans la salle de bains, dans la cave, dans le garage, partout dans la maison. (Answer: **C**) **Selection Number 2.** Pour célébrer la Fête Nationale, la famille Paquet et la famille Banluc déjeunent sur l'herbe dans le Bois de Boulogne. Janine a apporté les gâteaux et les petits fours glacés. Pierre a apporté les éclairs. Monsieur Paquet a apporté la glace, et Monsieur Banluc a apporté une bouteille d'eau minérale. (Answer: **A**) **Selection Number 3.** Janine a les yeux bleus et les cheveux noirs. Pierre a les yeux verts et les cheveux roux. François a les pieds grands et Claire a les pieds petits. Raymond a les mains petites et Françoise a les mains grandes. (Answer: **A**) **Selection Number 4.** Janine et Pierre sont dans le salon. Ils allument le téléviseur mais il ne marche pas. Tous les deux sont inquiets parce que l'émission ce soir est "La violence triomphe!" Les deux enfants regardent trop de violence à la télé. La mère et le père entrent dans le salon et ils parlent. (Answer: **A**) **PART THREE: Reading Proficiency** 1. B 2. C 3. C 4. A 5. C **PART FOUR: Writing Proficiency.** (NOTE TO TEACHER: Your students will respond in writing in different ways, depending on which five situations they have chosen based on PART ONE. Speaking Proficiency in this test.)

WORK UNIT 6

Exercises, pp. 92–93
I. 1. oui. 2. non. 3. oui. 4. oui. 5. oui. II. 1. vendez. 2. vends, dix. 3. vraiment. 4. joli. III. 1. Je vends ce vase pour dix euros. 2. La marchande vend beaucoup de vases. 3. Après un moment, la femme ajoute: Attendez! Attendez!

Exercises, pp. 94–102
I. 1. Il défend sa patrie. 2. Elle vend des vases. 3. Ils entendent la musique. 4. Ils vendent leur maison. 5. Il rompt la petite barrière. II. A. 1. attendre. 2. descendre. 3. rendre. B. 1. entendre. 2. interrompre. 3. répondre. C. 1. danser. 2. rougir. 3. entendre.

III. 1. Bonjour, madame. Je désire acheter ce vase. 2. Pour combien vendez-vous ce vase? 3. Est-il rare? 4. Acceptez-vous les cartes de crédit? 5. Voici ma carte de crédit. 6. Voici mon passeport. IV. 1. Oui, il répond à la lettre; je réponds à la lettre aussi (possibly: nous répondons à la lettre aussi). 2. Oui, il vend la maison; il vend la maison aussi. 3. Oui, il défend la patrie; je défends la patrie aussi (possibly: nous défendons la patrie aussi). 4. Oui, il est joli; il est joli aussi. 5. Oui, elle est au marché aux puces; elle est au marché aux puces aussi. V. 1. Janine étudie-t-elle dans la bibliothèque? 2. Cherche-t-elle le chapeau? 3. Finit-il la leçon? 4. Choisit-elle une jolie robe? 5. Répondons-nous à la lettre? 6. Vendent-ils la maison? VI. Elles attendent. 2. Nous vendons. 3. Je danse. 4. Ils écoutent. 5. Vous finissez. 6. Il répond. VII. 1. Est-ce qu'elle finit le livre? 2. Est-ce que Monsieur Berty vend la voiture? 3. Est-ce qu'elle choisit un joli chapeau? 4. Est-ce qu'il défend la patrie? 5. Est-ce qu'Hélène ouvre la boîte?

VIII.

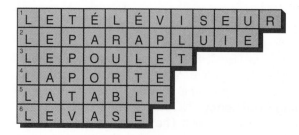

IX. 1. J'aime . . . 2. Vous chantez . . . 3. Janine étudie . . . 4. Je choisis . . . 5. Ils attendent . . . 6. Je vends . . . 7. Vous choisissez . . . 8. Nous finissons . . . **X.** 1. I dance, I do dance, I am dancing. 2. You finish, you do finish, you are finishing. 3. We sell, we do sell, we are selling.

XI. Word Search

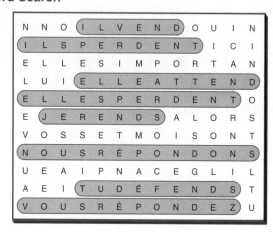

XII. 1. Claude Monet. l'artiste, est dans le bateau-atelier. 2. L'artiste se repose parce qu'il est fatigué. 3. L'eau est tranquille. 4. Les arbres sont beaux et le ciel est clair. **XIII.** 1. Merci, madame. 2. J'étudie le français depuis un an. 3. J'habite aux États-Unis dans la ville de New York. 4. J'aime beaucoup votre pays, la langue française, les Français, la culture, la musique, et l'art français. 5. Nous allons au marché aux puces. 6. Quel est le mot pour *flea* en français? **XIV.** 1. Oui, je désire acheter quelque chose. 2. J'ai assez d'argent et je désire acheter un oreiller. 3. L'oreiller sur mon lit à l'hôtel n'est pas bon. 4. Il y a beaucoup d'articles à bons prix ici. Où sont les oreillers? 5. Madame, pour combien vendez-vous les oreillers? 6. Je le prends. Voici un euro. 7. Merci, madame. Au revoir. Passez une bonne journée!

WORK UNIT 7

Exercises, pp. 106–107

I. 1. Le sport favori de Pierre est le football (possibly: Son sport favori est le football). 2. Il veut être toujours en forme parce qu'il est gardien de but dans son équipe à l'école. 3. Il mange seulement des aliments qui sont bons pour la santé. 4. Il se lève tôt (possibly: Il se lève avec le soleil). 5. Oui, Janine va jouer dans le match aussi. **II.** (NOTE TO TEACHER: These are personal questions asked of the students and they may answer in any number of ways.) **III. A.** 1. un sandwich. 2. une banane. 3. des pommes frites. 4. des bonbons. **B.** 1. jouer. 2. le joueur. 3. la joueuse. 4. le match.

IV. Un acrostiche

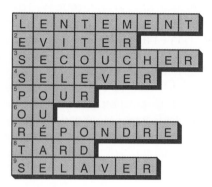

Exercises, pp. 111–119

I. 1. me. 2. me. 3. t'. 4. se. 5. s'. 6. nous. 7. vous. 8. s'. 9. se. 10. se. **II.** 8, 4, 9, 6, 2, 7, 1, 3, 5, 10.

III. Word Search

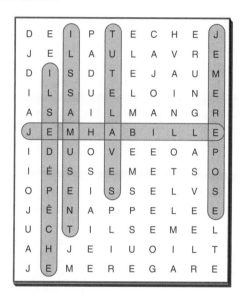

IV. 1. Je. 2. Tu. 3. Vous. 4. Ils, elles. 5. Il, elle. 6. Nous. 7. Vous. 8. Il, elle. 9. Ils, elles. 10. Je. **V.** 1. Oui, je m'amuse. 2. Oui, je me couche. 3. Oui, je me repose. 4. Oui, je m'habille. 5. Oui, je m'assieds. **VI.** 1. Non, je ne m'amuse pas ici. 2. Non, je ne me couche pas de bonne heure tous les soirs. 3. Non, je ne m'habille pas vite les matins. 4. Non, je ne m'appelle pas Jean-Jacques. 5. Non, je ne m'assieds pas ici. **VII.** 1. Se dépêche-t-il tous les soirs? 2. Je m'endors sur cette chaise. 3. Nous nous levons de bonne heure. 4. Il se lave vite. 5. Je m'amuse tous les jours. **VIII.** 1. Je m'habille dans ma chambre. 2. Ils s'amusent au théâtre tous les samedis (possibly: Tous les samedis, ils s'amusent au théâtre). 3. Tu te reposes après le dîner (possible: Après le dîner, tu te reposes). 4. Je me couche de bonne heure. 5. Nous nous dépêchons pour aller à l'école. 6. Je me lave tous les matins (possibly: Tous les matins, je me lave). **IX.** Je me couche tôt. Je m'endors facilement. Je me léve avec le soleil. Je me lave soigneusement. Je m'habille vite. Je m'amuse à Paris. **X.** 1. Se repose-t-elle après le dîner? 2. Vous levez-vous très tard le matin? 3. S'assied-elle devant la porte? 4. Nous dépêchons-nous? 5. Se couchent-ils tard? **XI.** 1. Pierre ne se couche-t-il pas de bonne heure? or: Est-ce que Pierre ne se couche pas de bonne heure? 2. Ne se lave-t-il pas soigneusement? or: Est-ce qu'il ne se lave pas soigneusement? 3. Ne s'habille-t-il pas vite? or: Est-ce qu'il ne s'habille pas vite? 4. Ne se dépêche-t-il pas? or: Est-ce qu'il ne se dépêche pas? 5. Ne se prépare-t-il pas à jouer au football? or: Est-ce qu'il ne se prépare pas à jouer au football? **XII.** 1. Je me lave. 2. Vous vous amusez. 3. Il s'endort. 4. Elle s'habille. 5. Nous nous couchons. 6. Tu t'amuses. 7. Ils se servent. 8. Elles s'endorment. 9. Je m'amuse. 10. Madame Paquet se dépêche. **XIII. A.** 1.

me lever. 2. m'habiller, 3. me coucher. 4. me reposer. **B.** 1. les glaces. 2. les pommes frites. 3. les pâtisseries. **XIV.** Est-ce que tu t'amuses tous les jours? Moi, je m'amuse beaucoup ici. Te couches-tu tard ou tôt? T'endors-tu facilement? Moi, je m'endors facilement. Te reposes-tu quand tu es fatiguée? Moi, je me repose quand je suis fatigué(e). **XV.** J'aime nager. Je nage tous les jours dans cette belle piscine. J'aime la natation. C'est mon sport favori. Voici une photo de la piscine. **XVI.** 1. Monsieur, désirez-vous déjeuner avec nous à l'école? 2. Monsieur, désirez-vous manger de la viande ou du poisson? 3. Monsieur, allez-vous parler en français aux étudiants du Cercle de Français à trois heures dans la salle 312? 4. À quelle heure allez-vous partir en taxi pour aller à l'aéroport? 5. Merci, monsieur. Bon voyage! **XVII.** 1. Le Moulin Rouge est un endroit de divertissement à Paris. 2. Les femmes portent de beaux manteaux longs, de belles robes longues, et de beaux chapeaux. 3. Les hommes et les femmes parlent pendant qu'ils dînent. Ils s'amusent. Dans quelques minutes la chanteuse Jane Avril va chanter dans un nouveau spectacle à minuit.

WORK UNIT 8

Exercises, pp. 122–123

I. 1. Madame Paquet aime beaucoup les ventes aux enchères. 2. Monsieur et Madame Paquet entrent dans la salle des ventes. 3. Elle lève la main pour chasser les mouches de son nez. 4. Madame paquet offre cent euros pour le fauteuil (sans le savoir, sans le vouloir, *or any acceptable answer*), quand elle lève la main pour chasser les mouches de son nez. 5. Tout le monde regarde Madame Paquet. **II.** (NOTE TO TEACHER: These are personal questions asked of the students and they may answer in any number of ways; they are "oui" or "non" questions to be answered in complete sentences in French.) **III.** 1. Monsieur Paquet parle à sa femme à voix basse. 2. Madame Paquet lève la main pour chasser les mouches de son nez. 3. J'ai cent euros. **IV.** 1. Ils entrent dans la salle des ventes. 2. Je n'aime pas ce fauteuil monstrueux. 3. Tout est si élégant dans cette salle. 4. Je veux une jolie petite table ronde.

Exercises, pp. 128–132

A. Cardinal numbers. I. 1. quatre. 2. sept. 3. douze. 4. dix. 5. dix-sept. 6. douze. **II.** 1. deux. 2. quatre. 3. six. 4. huit. 5. dix. 6. vingt. 7. vingt et un. 8. vingt-deux. 9. trente. 10. trente-sept. 11. soixante et un. 12. soixante-neuf. 13. soixante-dix. 14. quatre-vingts. 15. cent. **III. A.** Madame et Monsieur Paquet sont dans la salle des ventes avec beaucoup de personnes. Le commissaire-priseur parle. Madame Paquet veut acheter une petite table ronde pour le foyer dans la maison. (NOTE TO TEACHER: It is perfectly okay for the students to use words and sentences on p. 121 to describe the picture.) **B.** Je vais à un magasin de meubles d'occcasion pour acheter une table, quatre chaises, et un petit bureau pour ma chambre. **C.** Il y a cinq élèves (étudiants) dans le premier rang. Il y a six élèves dans le deuxième rang. Il y a quatre élèves dans le troisième rang. Il y a sept élèves dans le quatrième rang, etc. **IV.** 1. (c). 2. (a). 3. (c). 4. (d). 5. (c). **B. Ordinal numbers. I.** (First column) 3, 4, 1, 5, 2; (Second column) 7, 10, 6, 8, 9. **II.** Debbie, nous allons compter (to count) en français. Répète après moi: un (place one jelly bean on the table), deux (place another jelly bean on the table), trois (and another jelly bean), quatre, etc. Maintenant, où est le gâteau au chocolat?! **III.** 3, 5, 4, 2, 1. **C. Cardinals, fractions, approximate amounts, ordinals, simple arithmetical expressions, weights and measures. I.** 1. deux. 2. soixante. 3. vingt-cinq. 4. deux cents. 5. huit cents.

II. Word Search

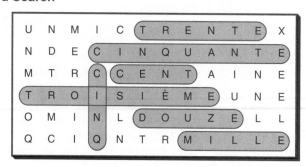

III. 7, 6, 8, 1, 10, 3, 5, 4, 9, 2. **IV.** 1. trois fois neuf font vingt-sept. 2. huit moins six font deux. 3. vingt divisés par cinq font quatre. 4. sept fois cent font sept cents. 5. quatre-vingts et dix font quatre-vingt-dix. **V.** C'est une classe de mathématiques. La maîtresse est au tableau. L'expression arithmétique est facile pour elle. Pour l'élève c'est très difficile. **VI.** 1. $3 \times 5 = 15$. 2. $12 - 10 = 2$. 3. $10 \div 2 = 5$. 4. $2 + 2 = 4$. 5. $9 \times 10 = 90$. **VII.** 1. J'aime la petite table ronde mais je n'aime pas les mouches dans cette salle des ventes. 2. Qui est la dame au premier rang qui offre soixante euros pour le fauteuil monstrueux? 3. Sûrement, elle doit être folle! 4. Oui, elle est parfaite pour ma chambre. 5. Oui, j'ai assez d'argent. Je vais offrir deux cents euros. 6. Oh, ces mouches! Filez! Filez! 7. N'importe. La petite table ronde est parfaite pour ma chambre.

WORK UNIT 9

Exercises, p. 136
I. 1. (c). 2. (d). 3. (c). 4. (d). 5. (d). **II.** 1. confortable. 2. facile. 3. économique. 4. agréable. **III.** 1. J'ai quinze ans. 2. Quelle heure est-il? 3. Quelle est la date aujourd'hui? **IV.** (NOTE TO TEACHER: These are personal questions asked of the students and they may answer in any number of ways.)

Exercises, pp. 140–144
I. 3, 4, 2, 1, 5, 6. **II.** 1. Il est trois heures et demie. 2. Il est dix heures moins huit. 3. Il est trois heures moins le quart. 4. Il est une heure et quart. **III.** 1. C'est aujourd'hui le premier octobre. 2. C'est aujourd'hui le dix novembre. **IV.** 1. Je me lève à six heures et demie du matin. 2. Je vais à l'école à huit heures du matin. 3. Je regarde la télévision à quatre heures de l'après-midi. 4. Je dîne à six heures du soir. 5. Je me couche à dix heures et demie du soir. **V.** 1. Nous désirons regarder l'art français à la télé. 2. Nous aimons l'art français. 3. Si nous avons la permission de regarder notre émission, nous promettons de laver la voiture et nettoyer la salle de bains. **VI.** 1. Non, ce n'est pas lundi; c'est aujourd'hui dimanche. 2. Non, ce n'est pas mardi; c'est aujourd'hui lundi. 3. Non, ce n'est pas mercredi; c'est aujourd'hui mardi. 4. Non, ce n'est pas vendredi; c'est aujourd'hui jeudi. 5. Non, ce n'est pas jeudi; c'est aujourd'hui mercredi. **VII.** 1. Quel âge a-t-il? 2. Quelle heure est-il? 3. Quel âge a-t-elle? 4. Quelle est la date aujourd'hui? 5. Quelle heure est-il? **VIII.** 1. Salut, Luc! Comment vas-tu? 2. Très bien, merci. Je vais faire un voyage en France avec ma famille. 3. Nous allons partir allons partir jeudi, le quatre avril. 4. En avion. 5. Nous allons partir à onze heures du soir. 6. Nous allons visiter Paris, Dijon, Lyon, Avignon, et Carcassonne. (NOTE TO TEACHER: Your students can locate these cities on the map of France in this work unit.) 7. À Paris, nous allons visiter le Musée du Louvre, la Tour Eiffel, et l'Arc de Triomphe.

Exercise, p. 145
IX. Je suis à l'aéroport Charles de Gaulle. Le terminal est énorme. Je pense que le plafond est impressionnant! (NOTE TO TEACHER: Answers may vary.)

Exercise, p. 146
X. J'aime la Corse. Je m'amuse bien ici. Il fait du soleil. Le port est très pittoresque. Les bateaux sont jolis. (NOTE TO TEACHER: Answers may vary.)

WORK UNIT 10

Exercises, pp. 150–151

I. 1. C'est aujourd'hui vendredi. 2. Dans le concours de talents, Pierre va jouer le magicien. 3. Janine est l'assistante de Pierre. 4. Non, ils n'ont pas le chapeau haut de forme, le bâton, la cape, et le lapin. 5. Coco arrive dans la grande salle. 6. Coco gagne le grand prix de talent. **II.** (NOTE TO TEACHER: These are personal questions asked of students and they may answer in any number of ways.) **III.** C'est aujourd'hui vendredi. 2. C'est le grand jour du concours de talents. 3. Apporte-moi mon bâton; apporte-moi le lapin. **IV.** Aujourd'hui c'est le grand jour du concours de talents dans la grande salle de l'école. Janine et Pierre sont dans le concours de talents. Pierre est le magicien et Janine l'assitante. Ils donnent leur représentation avec Coco, leur petit chien, un chapeau haut de forme, un bâton, une cape, et un lapin! Les spectateurs dans la grande salle crient:—Dansez! Chantez! Faites quelque chose! Tout d'un coup, Coco arrive en courant dans la grande salle. Sur la tête il a le chapeau haut de forme, dans la gueule le bâton et la cape, et sur le dos le lapin! C'est magnifique. Coco gagne le grand prix! … Oui, leur représentation est extraordinaire.

Exercises, pp. 152–153

I. **A. -ER verbs.** 1. donne, donnez, donnons. 2. apporte, apportez, apportons. 3. cherche, cherchez, cherchons. 4. aide, aidez, aidons. 5. chante, chantez, chantons. **B. -IR verbs.** 1. finis, finissez, finissons. 2. choisis, choisissez, choisissons. 3. bâtis, bâtissez, bâtissons. 4. punis, punissez, punissons. 5. obéis, obéissez, obéissons. **C. -RE verbs.** 1. vends, vendez, vendons. 2. attends, attendez, attendons. 3. descends, descendez, descendons. 4. réponds, répondez, répondons. 5. rends, rendez, rendons. **II.** 1. Ne chante pas, Janine! 2. Ne finissons pas le travail maintenant! 3. Ne vendez pas la maison, Monsieur Paquet! 4. N'écoute pas la musique, Pierre! 5. N'attendez pas l'autobus! **III.** Colette, mange tes épinards! … Non, je refuse … Colette, finis tes devoirs! … Non, je ne veux pas … Colette, chante! … Non, je ne veux pas chanter … Colette, danse! … Non, je refuse … Colette, va au cinéma! … Non, oh, oui, oui, j'aimerais aller au cinéma!

Exercises, pp. 155–159

I. 1. Lavez-vous. 2. Assieds-toi. 3. Levez-vous. 4. Asseyez-vous. 5. Lavons-nous. 6. Lève-toi. 7. Ne te lave pas. 8. Ne nous levons pas. 9. Ne vous asseyez pas. 10. Lave-toi. **II.** 1. Ne nous lavons pas! 2. Ne vous asseyez pas! 3. Ne te lave pas! 4. Ne t'assieds pas! 5. Ne vous lavez pas! 6. Ne te lève pas! **III. A.** 1. Donnez-moi …, s'il vous plaît! 2. Apportez-moi …, s'il vous plaît! 3. Finissez, s'il vous plaît! **B.** 1. Donne-moi …! 2. Apporte-moi …! 3. Viens! **IV.** 1. Z. 2. EZ. 3. EZ. 4. ISS. 5. EZ. 6. ONS. 7. DEZ. 8. PO, DE. 9. EN, EZ. 10. SS, EZ. 11. EZ. 12. A, Z. **V.** (NOTE TO TEACHER: These are only sample sentences. Your students may respond in different ways.) 1. Janine et Pierre sont dans le concours de talents sur la scène (on the stage) dans la grande salle de l'école. 2. Pierre est le magicien et Janine est l'assistante. 3. Ils ne font rien parce qu'ils n'ont rien pour commercer leur représentation. 4. Tout d'un coup, Coco arrive en courant sur la scène. 5. Sur la tête il a le chapeau haut de forme, dans la gueule il a le bâton et la cape, et sur le dos le lapin! **VI.** 1. Asseyez-vous, s'il vous plaît. 2. Ouvrez la bouche, s'il vous plaît. 3. Fermez les yeux, s'il vous plaît. 4. Fermez la bouche, s'il vous plaît. 5. Ouvrez les yeux, s'il vous plaît. 6. Levez-vous, s'il vous plaît. **VII.** 1. Mais tu danses très bien. 2. Oui, c'est vrai. 3. Vas-tu au grand bal en ville avec Roger ce soir? 4. Avec mon ami Pierre. 5. C'est un film passionnant!

VIII. (NOTE TO TEACHER: These are only sample sentences. Your students will respond in different ways.) 1. Ce tableau de Renoir est splendide. 2. Il est très impressionnant. 3. Je regarde les gens qui se promènent sur le grand boulevard. 4. Je vois deux enfants avec une femme, probablement leur mère. 5. Lex beaux arbres sont magnifiques. 6. Quel jour heureux!

TEST 2 (WORK UNITS 6–10)

Pages 160, 161, 162

PART ONE: Speaking Proficiency. (NOTE TO TEACHER: The eleven situations given are a review of exercises in proficiency in speaking in Work Units 6 to 10. Your students will respond to you and you may grade them on this speaking test according to what they say in class or on a one to one basis at your desk.) **PART TWO: Listening Proficiency.** (NOTE TO TEACHER: Here are four short paragraphs that you will read aloud to your students. The directions are given in the test.) **Selection Number 1.** Pierre aime les sports. Son sport favori est le football. Il veut être toujours en bonne forme parce qu'il est gardien de but dans son équipe à l'école. Il veut être toujours prêt à bien jouer. (Answer: **B**) **Selection Number 2.** Après la dernière classe. Pierre va au gymnase. Il se prépare pour le grand match. Il met sa tenue d'exercice. Il fait de la gymnastique avant de commencer le match. (Answer: **C**) **Selection Number 3.** Madame et Monsieur Paquet quittent la maison pour aller à une vente aux enchères. Elle aime beaucoup les ventes aux enchères. Elle veut acheter une petite table ronde pour le foyer dans sa maison. (Answer: **D**) **Selection Number 4.** La famille Paquet fait des préparations pour un voyage en avion aux États-Unis. Madame Paquet a une soeur qui habite à La Nouvelle-Orléans avec son mari et ses trois enfants. Maintenant, ils font les valises et dans quelques minutes ils vont quitter la maison pour aller à l'aéroport Charles de Gaulle. (Answer: **C**) **PART THREE: Reading Proficiency** 1. **B** 2. **C** 3. **C** 4. **D** 5. **A** **PART FOUR: Writing Proficiency.** (NOTE TO TEACHER: Your students will respond in writing in different ways, depending on which seven situations they have chosen based on PART ONE: Speaking Proficiency in this test.)

WORK UNIT 11

Exercises, pp. 165–166
I. 1. (b). 2. (b). 3. (d). **II.** (NOTE TO TEACHER: These are personal questions asked of students and they may answer in different ways.)

III. Un acrostiche

IV. 1. C'est un objet d'habillement. C'est pour une femme. Qu'est-ce que c'est? (C'est une robe.) 2. C'est une partie du corps humain. Elle a cinq doigts. Qu'est-ce que c'est? (C'est une main.) 3. C'est un meuble. Vous dormez sur ce meuble. Qu'est-ce que c'est? (C'est un lit.) 4. C'est un fruit. Il a la couleur jaune. Qu'est-ce que c'est? (C'est une banane.) **V. A.** 1. Qu'est-ce que c'est? C'est une chaise. 2. C'est une pomme. 3. C'est un cornet de glace (ice cream cone). 4. C'est un réveille-matin. 5. C'est un téléphone. **B.** 1. Qu'est-ce que c'est? C'est un livre. 2. C'est un stylo. 3. C'est un crayon.

Exercises, pp. 168–171
I. 1. Oui, je lis beaucoup; elle lit beaucoup aussi. 2. Oui, j'apprends le français; elle apprend le français aussi. 3. Oui, j'ai de la glace; il a de la glace aussi. 4. Oui, je bois du jus d'orange; il boit du jus d'orange aussi. 5. Oui, je comprends la leçon; elle comprend la leçon aussi. **II.** 1. Non, il ne lit pas beaucoup; je ne lis pas beaucoup; je ne lis pas beaucoup non plus (possibly: Nous ne lisons pas beaucoup non plus). 2. Non, elle ne met pas le vase sur la table; il ne met pas le vase sur la table non plus. 3. Non, je n'ouvre pas la porte; il n'ouvre pas la porte non plus. 4. Non, elle ne part pas à huit heures; il ne part pas à huit heures non plus. 5. Non, je ne peux (or: puis) pas aller au

cinéma ce soir; ils ne peuvent pas aller au cinéma ce soir non plus. **III.** 1. Ouvre-t-il la porte? 2. Est-ce qu'elle lit la lettre? 3. Prenez-vous du café? 4. Il ne fait pas la leçon. 5. Ecrivez-vous la date? **IV.** Bonjour (Salut), Debbie! Je m'appelle … (Je suis …). Comment vas-tu? Ça va? Ecoute, Debbie. Dans la classe de français nous jouons un jeu intéressant. Je vais donner la description d'une chose et tu dois deviner ce que c'est. Après la description, je demande, "Qu'est-ce que c'est?" et tu vas deviner (guess) la réponse; par exemple, je dis, "C'est un fruit. Il a la couleur rouge ou jaune ou verte. Qu'est-ce que c'est?" Tu dis, "C'est une pomme." Okay? D'accord? Maintenant, je commence. **V.** 1. Nous voyons. 2. Je sais. 3. Ils font. 4. Ils partent. 5. Tu bois. **VI.** 1. Ils comprennent bien aussi. 2. Elles écrivent bien aussi. 3. Ils vont bien aussi. 4. Elles lisent bien aussi. 5. Ils voient bien aussi.

Exercices, pp. 173–176

I. 1. Buvez! 2. Viens! 3. Dites! 4. Ecrivez! 5. Lisez! 6. Ouvre! 7. Sortons! 8. Soyons! 9. Buvons! 10. Revenez! **II.** 1. Dites la phrase. 2. Bois le lait. 3. Partez tout de suite. 4. Ferme la fenêtre. 5. Prends la valise là-bas. 6. Ecrivons la lettre. 7. Lisez le poème. 8. Sortons maintenant. 9. Revenez à l'heure. 10. Faisons la leçon. **III.** 7, 4, 6, 8, 3, 9, 1, 10, 5, 2. **IV. A.** 1. Bon! Alors, partez maintenant. 2. Bon! Alors, ouvrez la fenêtre. 3. Bon! Alors, faites la leçon. 4. Bon! Alors, écrivez une lettre. 5. Bon! Alors, lisez le journal. **B.** 1. Bon! Alors, sortez maintenant. 2. Bon! Alors, soyez ici à dix heures. 3. Bon! Alors, faites le travail ce soir. 4. Bon! Alors, apprenez l'anglais. 5. Bon! Alors, parlez français.

Exercices, pp. 177–180

I. 1. Il y a deux pièces dans l'appartement. 2. L'appartement est petit. 3. Le numéro de téléphone est 45-04-55-14. **II.** 1. Il y a deux enfants dans cette photo. 2. Ils jouent ensemble. 3. Ils sont dans une chambre chez eux. 4. Le garçon à gauche a probablement cinq ans. 5. Le garçon à droite a probablement trois ans. **III.** 1. Je veux acheter quelques cadeaux. C'est Noël, tu sais! Est-ce que tu dois acheter quelques cadeaux aussi? 2. Nous pouvons aller aux grands magasins ensemble. 3. J'ai beaucoup d'argent! Je peux acheter des cadeaux pour tous mes amis. 4. Je vois dans les journaux que le Père Noël est aux Galeries Lafayette aujourd'hui! 5. Je dis que le Père Noël est aux Galeries Lafayette aujourd'hui. 6. D'accord. Allons en ville tout de suite. 7. Je veux prendre le bus. Partons maintenant! **IV.** 1. Prenez cette rue. Allez tout droit. 2. Et puis, au bout de cette rue, tournez à gauche. 3. Non! Au bout de cette rue, tournez à gauche! 4. C'est ça. Au bout de cette rue, tournez à gauche. Et puis, vous êtes là. 5. Vous dites que vous ne savez pas si vous comprenez? 6. Je vais répéter ce que je dis. Prenez cette rue. Allez tout droit. Puis, au bout de cette rue, tournez à gauche. Et puis, vous êtes là. C'est tout! Comprenez-vous maintenant? 7. Ne vous perdez pas!

WORK UNIT 12

Exercices, pp. 183–184

I. 1. Ils ont quitté la maison à sept heures et demie pour aller à l'opéra. 2. Ils sont arrivés à l'opéra à huit heures. 3. Ils ont pris leurs places à huit heures et quart. 4. La repésentation a commencé à huit heures et demie. **II. A.** J'aime beaucoup le concert. La musique est excellente. **B.** Tu préfères aller à l'opéra? Moi, je préfère voir un film français. Pourquoi? Parce que c'est plus intéressant. Le film est "Les Aventures de la Famille Paquet" avec musique. Si tu viens voir le film avec moi, je vais acheter les billets. Après le film, nous allons manger quelque chose dans un café-restaurant et je vais payer. **III.** 1. allée. 2. vu. 3. quitté. 4. arrivés. 5. entrés. 6. pris. 7. allée. 8. allé. 9. allé. 10. allée.

IV. Word Search

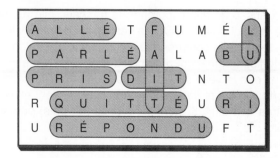

Exercises, pp. 187–190

I. A. 1. Oui, j'ai vendu la voiture. 2. Oui, j'ai acheté la propriété. 3. Oui, j'ai fini les leçons. 4. Oui, j'ai réussi la vente de la propriété. 5. Oui, j'ai fermé les portes et les fenêtres. **B.** 1. Non, elle n'a pas chanté hier soir. 2. Non, il n'a pas choisi une jolie cravate. 3. Non, je n'ai pas mangé l'éclair. 4. Non, ils n'ont pas étudié les leçons. 5. Non, nous n'avons pas fini le travail (possibly: Non, vous n'avez pas fini le travail). **C.** 1. Pierre a-t-il vu Madame Richy? 2. Hélène a-t-elle choisi une jolie robe? 3. Coco a-t-il mangé le gâteau? 4. Suzanne et Georges ont-ils navigué sur Internet? 5. Marie et Betty ont-elles voyagé en France? **D.** 1. Est-ce que Madame Paquet a acheté un beau chapeau? 2. Est-ce que Pierre a perdu sa montre? 3. Est-ce que Monsieur Paquet a fait un appel sur son téléphone portable? 4. Est-ce que Paul a mangé du chocolat? 5. Est-ce que Janine a bu un jus d'orange? **E.** 1. Madame Richy n'a-t-elle pas acheté une automobile? 2. Monsieur Richy n'a-t-il pas voyagé aux Etats-Unis? 3. Madame et Monsieur Armstrong n'ont-ils pas aimé le dessert? 4. Mathilde n'a-t-elle pas entendu la musique? 5. Joseph n'a-t-il pas choisi une jolie cravate? **F.** 1. Est-ce que Robert n'a pas dansé hier soir? 2. Est-ce que Joséphine n'a pas chanté ce matin? 3. Est-ce que Guy et Michel n'ont pas fini leurs leçons? 4. Est-ce que Françoise et Simone n'ont pas entendu la musique? 5. Est-ce que Charles n'a pas perdu son ami? **II.** 7, 10, 8, 9, 6, 3, 5, 2, 1, 4. **III.** 1. aimé. 2. quitté. 3. pris. 4. commencé. 5. parlé. 6. parlé. 7. mangé. 8. bu. 9. vu. 10. dit. **IV.** 1. I danced, I have danced. I did dance. 2. You finished, you have finished, you did finish. 3. We sold, we have sold, we did sell. **V.** 1. J'ai joué. 2. Tu as pleuré. 3. Il a fini. 4. Elle a choisi. 5. Janine a chanté. 6. Nous avons dansé. 7. Vous avez perdu. 8. Ils ont répondu. 9. J'ai étudié. 10. Il a parlé. 11. Robert a travaillé. 12. Marie et Bob ont dîné.

Exercises, pp. 193–204

I. A. 1. Oui, Janine est allée au cinéma. 2. Oui, Monique est allée à l'école. 3. Oui, Robert est allé au théâtre. 4. Oui, Pierre et Raymond sont allés au parc. 5. Oui, Anne et Béatrice sont allées au Canada. 6. Oui, Jacques et Jeanne sont allés à l'aéroport. 7. Oui, Monsieur et Madame Beaupuy sont allés aux Etats-Unis. 8. Oui, la mère est allée dans le garage. 9. Oui, le père est allé dans la cuisine. 10. Oui, la jeune fille est allée à la pharmacie. **B.** 1. Non, elle n'est pas arrivée à l'opéra à huit heures et demie. 2. Non, ils ne sont pas entrés dans le théâtre à huit heures. 3. Non, ils ne sont pas partis de bonne heure. 4. Non, il n'est pas resté à la maison. 5. Non, elle n'est pas sortie ce soir. **C.** 1. Yolande est-elle venue ce soir? 2. François est-il retourné à midi? 3. Les garçons sont-ils restés dans l'école? 4. Les jeunes filles sont-elles descendues vite? 5. Monsieur et Madame Paquet sont-ils rentrés à minuit? **D.** 1. Est-ce que John James Audubon est né aux Cayes à Haïti? 2. Est-ce que Napoléon Bonaparte est mort à Sainte-Hélène? 3. Est-ce que Marie-Antoinette est née à Vienne? 4. Est-ce que Jacques Chirac est devenu président de la République française en 1995? 5. Est-ce que Joséphine est née à la Martinique? 6. Est-ce que Marie-Antoinette est morte à Paris? 7. Est-ce que Joséphine est devenue impératrice en 1804? **E.** 1. N'es-tu pas resté à la maison? 2. N'est-elle pas tombée dans le jardin? 3. N'est-il pas parti ce matin? 4. N'êtes-vous pas arrivé à dix heures? 5. Ne sont-elles pas allées à l'école aujourd'hui? **II.** 4, 1, 2, 3, 10, 5, 6, 9, 7, 8. **III.** 1. I went . . . , I have gone . . . , I did go . . . . 2. She left, she has left, she did leave. 3. We arrived, we have arrived, we did arrive. **IV.** 1. Suzanne a parlé. 2. Il est monté. 3. Elle est sortie. 4. Elle a compris. 5. Nous sommes arrivés. 6. Vous avez dit. 7. Elles ont lu. 8. Tu as fait. 9. Robert est resté. 10. Ils ont ri. 11. Je suis allé. 12. Madame Paquet a bu. **V.** 1. apprendre. 2. devenir. 3. avoir. 4. couvrir. 5. croire. 6. comprendre. 7. permettre. 8. recevoir. 9. promettre. 10. vouloir. 11. devoir. 12. voir. 13. dire. 14. venir. 15. écrire. 16. être. 17. boire. 18. faire. 19. tenir. 20. lire. 21. ouvrir. 22. mettre 23. savoir. 24. mourir. 25. rire. 26. naître. 27. revenir. 28. paraître. 29. pouvoir. 30. prendre. **VI.** 1. eu. 2. été. 3. fait. 4. fini. 5. su. 6. lu. 7. appris. 8. défendu. 9. choisi. 10. allé. 11. sorti. 12. saisi. 13. aidé. 14. bâti. 15. joué. 16. vu. 17. dansé. 18. vendu. **VII.** 1. être. 2. avoir. 3. avoir. 4. avoir. 5. être. 6. être. 7. avoir. 8. avoir. 9. être. 10. avoir. 11. avoir. 12. être. 13. être. 14. avoir. 15. être. 16. avoir. 17. être. 18. avoir. 19. avoir. 20. avoir. 21. être. **VIII.** 1. Il lit un bon livre. 2. Je vends la voiture. 3. Elle va à l'opéra. 4. Nous écrivons des lettres. 5. Vous arrivez tôt. **IX.** 1. Madame Paquet a eu un beau chapeau rouge. 2. Janine a bu un jus d'orange. 3. Pierre a mangé du chocolat. 4. Monique est allée au cinéma. 5. Jeanne et Joséphine sont entrées dans le théâtre. **X.** 1. e. 2. —. 3. e. 4. e. 5. s. 6. s. 7. —. **XI.** 1. allée. 2. arrivés. 3. entrés. 4. allée. 5. allé. 6. allé. 7. allée. 8. retournée. 9. retourné. 10. retournée. **XII.** 1. Hier soir, je suis allé(e) à l'opéra. J'ai vu l'opéra *Pelléas et Mélisande*. Claude Debussy a composé la musique. Pendant l'entracte, j'ai bu un jus d'orange et j'ai mangé du chocolat. **XIII.** Dans ce dessin les jeunes hommes sont habillés en blanc. Ils portent des bérets noirs. Ils dansent. C'est La Danse des Sabres. Ils sont beaux et magnifiques! **XIV.** 1. su. 2. lu. **XV.** 1. Je suis allée au théâtre. 2. Je suis allée seule au théâtre. 3. Oui, je suis allée seule au théâtre. À La Comédie Française. J'ai vu la pièce *L'Avare*. C'est une comédie de Molière. 4. Oui, j'ai beaucoup aimé la comédie. Très drôle. 5. Oui, j'ai vu la famille Paquet—la mère, le père, Janine, et Pierre. 6. Pendant l'entracte, j'ai mangé du chocolat avec Pierre, j'ai bu un jus d'orange avec Janine, et j'ai parlé avec Madame Paquet et quelques dames. 7. Oui, je suis allée boire du café avec Monsieur Paquet. **XVI.** 1. Oui, j'ai été sat-isfait(e) des services dans votre hôtel pendant mon séjour. 2. Oui, j'ai beaucoup aimé ma chambre. Elle a été propre et confortable. 3. Oui, j'ai été satisfait(e) de votre service téléphonique. 4. Oui, les employés ont montré de la politesse. 5. Les repas dans le restaurant ont été excellents. 6. Oui, le service dans le restaurant a été rapide. 7. Non, les prix n'ont pas été bons. Les prix ont été très chers. **XVII.** Hier soir je suis allé(e) suel(e) au théâtre. J'ai vu la pièce *L'Avare* de Molière à La Comédie Française. Je l'ai beaucoup aimée. J'ai beaucoup ri. Au théâtre j'ai vu la famille Paquet—la mère, le père, Janine, et Pierre. Pendant l'entracte, j'ai mangé du chocolat avec Pierre, j'ai bu un jus d'orange avec Janine, et j'ai parlé avec Madame Paquet et quelques dames. J'ai bu, aussi, un café avec Monsieur Paquet. C'est tout pour maintenant. Je vais t'écrire un autre petit mot la semaine prochaine. Écris-moi! **XVIII.** 1. pu. 2. su. 3. eu. 4. lu. 5. bu.

WORK UNIT 13

Exercises, p. 208
I. 1. Pierre a servi le dîner ce soir. 2. Il a servi le dîner pour la famille et les voisins. 3. Pierre com-mence à goûter le ragoût. 4. Monsieur Richy aime le ragoût. 5. Le ragoût est bien cuit (possibly: Il aime le ragoût bien cuit; or, il aime le ragoût parce qu'il est bien cuit). 6. Madame Paquet a fait le ragoût. **II.** (NOTE TO TEACHER: These are personal questions asked of the students and they may answer in different ways.) **III.** 1. Et comment! Il sent très bon. (Moi), j'ai grand faim (j'ai très faim). 2. Janine a raison. Il est brûlé. Je ne l'aime pas. Goûtez-en! 3. Je vais le goûter. 4. Madame Paquet rentre dans la salle à manger avec le dessert. 5. Est-ce que tout le monde aime mon ragoût? J'ai un dessert que j'ai fait aussi. Qui veut une crème brûlée? Goûtez-en!

Exercises, pp. 214–226
I. 1. Pierre la lit. 2. Janine l'écrit. 3. Michel l'apprend. 4. Christophe les fait. 5. Alexandre l'écoute. 6. Yolande le prononce. 7. Théodore le voit. 8. Monique la dit. 9. Joséphine l'attend. 10. Anne les mange. **II.** 1. Oui, elle la dit. 2. Oui, elle l'attend. 3. Oui, il la lit. 4. Oui, il les mange. 5. Oui, elle l'é-coute. **III.** 1. Non, il ne mange pas. 2. Non, elle ne le prononce pas. 3. Non, il ne l'aime pas. 4. Non, il ne la lit pas. 5. Non, elle ne les apporte pas. **IV.** 1. Oui, je la comprends aujourd'hui. 2. Oui, je la dis toujours. 3. Oui, je les fais maintenant. 4. Oui, je le lis tous les jours. 5. Oui, je l'écris en ce moment. **V.** 1. Oui, elle la connaît. 2. Oui, elle le connaît. 3. Oui, il les connaît. 4. Oui, elle les connaît. 5. Oui, il les connaît. **VI.** 1. Oui, elle me connaît. 2. Oui, il me voit. 3. Oui, elle nous aime. 4. Oui, ils les atten-dent. 5. Oui, il l'adore. **VII.** 1. Oui, je t'aime bien. 2. Oui, je l'aime bien aussi. 3. Oui, je l'aime bien aussi. 4. Oui, il m'aime bien. 5. Oui, elle m'aime bien aussi. **VIII.** 1. Non, je ne t'aime pas. 2. Non, il ne nous aime pas./Non, il ne m'aime pas. 3. Non, nous ne l'aimons pas./Non, je ne l'aime pas. 4. Non, il ne m'aime pas. 5. Non, elle ne nous aime pas./Non, elle ne m'aime pas. **IX.** 1. Bon! Alors, écrivez-la! 2. Bon! Alors, étudiez-les! 3. Bon! Alors, lisez-le! 4. Bon! Alors, buvez-le! 5. Bon! Alors, faites-les! **X.** 1. Bon! Alors, ne l'écrivez-pas! 2. Bon! Alors, ne les étudiez pas! 3. Bon! Alors, ne le lisez pas! 4. Bon! Alors, ne le buvez pas! 5. Bon! Alors, ne les faites pas! **XI.** 1. Pierre veut le lire. 2. Madeleine veut l'apprendre. 3. Paul ne veut pas l'écrire. 4. Philippe ne veut pas la manger. 5. Gertrude ne veut pas les apporter. **XII.** 1. Oui, j'en ai. 2. Oui, j'en bois. 3. Oui, j'en mange. 4. Oui, j'en mange. 5. Oui, j'en ai. **XIII.** 1. Non, je n'en ai pas. 2. Non, je n'en ai pas. 3. Non, je n'en ai pas. 4. Non, je n'en ai pas. 5. Non, je n'en ai pas. **XIV.** 1. Bon! Alors, buvez-en! 2. Bon! Alors, mangez-en! 3. Bon! Alors, écrivez-en! 4. Bon! Alors, buvez-en! 5. Bon! Alors, mangez-en! **XV.** 1. Bon! Alors, n'en buvez pas! 2. Bon! Alors, n'en mangez pas! 3. Bon! Alors, n'en écrivez pas! **XVI.** 1. Madame Paquet l'a préparé. 2. Monsieur Richy l'a mangé. 3. Pierre l'a servi. 4. Janine les a préparés. 5. Monsieur Paquet les a préparées. **XVII.** 1. Oui, il l'a servi. 2. Oui, elle l'a préparé. 3. Oui, il l'a mangé. 4. Oui, elle l'a écrite. 5. Oui, il les a faits. **XVIII.** 1. Non, il ne l'a pas préparée. 2. Non, il ne l'a pas fait. 3. Non, elle ne l'a pas lu. 4. Non, elle ne l'a pas mangé. 5. Non, il ne les a pas faits. **XIX.** 1. Cette oeuvre de Rodin est superbe. 2. Je pense que les hommes sont tristes parce qu'ils souffrent beaucoup. 3. Ils n'ont pas de liberté. **XX.** 1. Salut, mon amie! 2. J'aime le lait. 3. J'ai soif. 4. As-tu du lait pour moi

aujourd'hui? **XXI.** 1. Mon frère Pierre l'a préparée. 2. Moi. Je les ai préparées. 3. Non, merci, papa. Je n'en veux pas. 4. J'en ai déjà mangé. 5. J'aimerais une tasse de thé avec le dessert, s'il vous plaît. Je ne bois pas de café. 6. Citron, s'il vous plaît, s'il y en a. 7. Pierre, va dans la cuisine, s'il te plaît. Le citron est sur la table. 8. Oui, maman. Tout de suite. 9. Maman, il n'y a pas de citron sur la table dans la cuisine. **XXII.** 1. D'accord. La voici. 2. Non, je ne l'aime pas. 3. Pourquoi pas? 4. Ça me fait rire! Il pense que le fromage est trop élastique et gommeux. Il n'aime pas manger les élastiques! 5. Dis-moi, Pierre, as-tu fait les devoirs de biologie pour demain? 6. Il ne les a pas faits. 7. Non. Je ne les aime pas. Je ne les mange pas. 8. Robert les a apportées. 9. J'aime les pâtisseries. Je vais les manger toutes. **XXIII.** 1. Socrate, grand philosophe grec, est condamné à mort à cause de ses idées philosophiques et politiques. 2. Il est sur un lit. 3. Un homme lui donne une coupe de ciguë à boire. 4. Je pense que le tableau de Louis David est superbe.

WORK UNIT 14

Exercises, pp. 229–230

I. 1. Janine a prêté son téléphone portable à Suzanne. 2. Elle veut téléphoner à sa mère. 3. Paul prête son téléphone portable à Janine. **II.** 1. Elle m'a dit que tu l'as maintenant. 2. Je ne l'ai pas. Je l'ai donné à Monique. Va la voir. 3. J'ai donné le (téléphone) portable à Mimi. Mimi l'a donné à Raymond. 4. Je lui ai donné le (téléphone) portable. Va le voir.

III.

```
          3.
          P              6.
1.   2.   R    4.   5.   P
 P    R   Ê    T    E    R
 O    E   T    R    C    O
 R    N   E    È    O    P
 T    D        S    U    R
 A    R             T    E
 B    E             E
 L                  R
 E
```

Exercises, pp. 232–240

I. 1. Janine lui donne le journal. 2. Madeleine lui donne le livre. 3. Gloria lui donne la fleur. 4. Robert leur donne la balle. 5. Monique leur donne les stylos. **II. A.** 1. Je lui parle. 2. Je lui parle. 3. Je lui parle. 4. Je lui parle. 5. Je lui parle. **B.** 1. Je leur donne les gâteaux. 2. Je leur donne les livres. 3. Je leur donne le ragoût brûlé. 4. Je leur donne les lettres. 5. Je leur donne le jus. **III.** 1. Oui, je vous parle. 2. Oui, je lui parle. 3. Oui, je vous parle. **IV.** 1. Bon! Alors, donnez-lui le gâteau! 2. Bon! Alors, donnez-lui le parapluie. 3. Bon! Alors, donnez-lui le bonbon. 4. Bon! Alors, donnez-lui le jus de fruit. 5. Bon! Alors, donnez-lui le ragoût brûlé. **V.** 1. Bon! Alors, ne leur donnez pas le chocolat! 2. Bon! Alors, ne lui donnez pas les devoirs! 3. Bon! Alors, ne lui donnez pas le billet! **VI.** 1. Bon! Alors, parlez-moi! 2. Bon! Alors, parlez-lui! 3. Bon! Alors, parlez-leur! **VII.** 1. Bon! Alors, ne me parlez pas! 2. Bon! Alors ne lui parlez pas! 3. Bon alors, ne leur parlez pas! **VIII.** 4, 5, 2, 6, 3, 1. **IX.** 1. Oui, j'y vais. 2. Oui, j'y vais. 3. Oui, j'y vais. **X.** 1. Bon! Alors, parlez-lui! 2. Janine veut leur parler. **XI.** 1. Anne, je t'ai prêté mes disques compacts au mois de septembre et aujourd'hui c'est le premier décembre. 2. Tu ne les as pas? Où sont-ils? 3. Je ne peux pas aller la voir. Elle est en vacances au Canada. 4. Non. Elle ne les a pas. Je lui ai parlé hier. 5. Elle m'a dit que tu les as. 6. Et, moi, je te dis que je ne les ai pas! Apparemment mes disques compacts sont perdus! Au revoir! **XII. A.** The "y" is translated as "there" and it refers to "à la soirée," meaning "to the evening party." **B.** Je vois un étudiant qui invite une étudiante à la soirée chez Michel. Elle est heureuse. (NOTE TO TEACHER: Answers will vary.) **XIII. A.** Je vois des étudiants. Janine est avec les étudiants. Elle est fâchée. Elle crie, "Où est mon téléphone portable?" **B.** Le nom du magasin est OMEGA. C'est un magasin moderne. On y vend des disques et des cassettes. Si vous aimez avoir des vidéo-cassettes et des jeux vidéo, vous pouvez les acheter dans ce magasin. Les prix sont bas. Le magasin est ouvert tous les jours de midi à minuit. L'adresse est vingt-neuf, rue des Amants, Paris. Le numéro de téléphone est quarante-deux, trente-quatre, quatre-vingt-quatre, cinquante-six. **C.** Je vois une femme et deux petits chiens. Elle leur donne le ragoût brûlé. Mais ils ne désirent pas le manger. Ils ne le regardent pas. Elle leur dit: "Mon ragoût est délicieux." Les petits chiens lui disent: "Nous ne le voulons pas! Vous pouvez le manger!" **XIV.** Tes CDs? Ah, oui! Je les ai donnés à Robert. Va le voir. Va lui demander. Je lui ai prêté tes CDs. Je pense qu'il les a prêtés à Suzanne. Va lui demander. Je pense qu'elle les a prêtés à Monique. Je ne les ai pas. Je le regrette.

WORK UNIT 15

Exercises, pp. 243–244
I. 1. UN CHAMPIGNON. 2. UN FAUTEUIL. 3. UNE HORLOGE. 4. UNE GIRAFE. 5. UN KAN-GOUROU. **II.** 1. porte. 2. yeux, n'ai pas. 3. suis. 4. n'ai pas. 5. long, peux.

III.

Exercises, pp. 245–247
I. 6, 3, 5, 1, 4, 2. **II.** 1. Qui. 2. Qui. 3. qui. 4. qui. 5. Que. 6. Qu'est-ce que. 7. Que. 8. Qu'est-ce que. 9. Qui. 10. Que. **III. A.** 1. Tu es (Vous êtes) un éléphant. 2. Tu es (Vous êtes) un kangourou. 3. Tu es (Vous êtes) un poisson. 4. Tu es (Vous êtes) un balai. 5. Tu es (Vous êtes) un ordinateur. **B.** J'ai des ailes et je vole comme un avion. Qui suis-je? (Tu es un oiseau.) **IV.** 1. une girafe. 2. un kangourou. 3. un poisson 4. une tortue. **V.** 1. Je te donne un sablé, Claire, parce que tu es une bonne personne. Aimes-tu les biscuits? 2. Maintenant, je donne un biscuit à Pierre. Je lui donne un biscuit parce qu'il est mon ami. 3. Et maintenant j'offre un biscuit à Catherine. Je lui offre un biscuit parce qu'elle est jolie. 4. Maintenant, je leur offre deux biscuits, à Gigi et à Mimi, parce qu'elles sont très belles. 5. Je vous donne un biscuit, Madame Marin, parce que vous êtes aimable. 6. Vous pouvez me donner une bonne note parce que je parle en français! **VI.** Vous m'avez apporté une tasse de thé au lieu de café. J'ai demandé une tasse de café. Apportez-moi une tasse de café, s'il vous plaît. **VII.** 1. Ne vois-tu pas que je parle à quelqu'un? 2. Non. Je ne lui parle pas. 3. Je ne lui parle pas en ce moment. Je lui ai parlé hier. 4. Je ne leur parle pas maintenant (en ce moment). Je leur ai parlé ce matin. 5. Je te parle, à toi. Va-t'en!

TEST 3 (WORK UNITS 11–15)

Pages 248, 249, 250, 251

PART ONE: Speaking Proficiency. (NOTE TO TEACHER: The twelve situations given are a review of exercises in proficiency in speaking in Work Units 11 to 15. Your students will respond to you and you may guide them on this speaking test according to what they say in class or on a one-to-one basis at your desk.) **PART TWO: Listening Proficiency.** (NOTE TO TEACHER: Here are four short paragraphs that you will read aloud to your students. The directions are given in the test.) **Selection Number 1.** C'est quelque chose à boire. Il peut avoir le goût d'orange, ananas, pample-mouse, raisin, ou tomate. Il peut être en boîte ou en bouteille. C'est toujours délicieux. (Answer: **D**)

Selection Number 2. Hier soir la famille Paquet est allée à l'opéra. Ils ont vu la représentation de *Faust*. Ils ont quitté la maison à sept heures et demie et ils sont arrivés à l'opéra à huit heures. Ils sont entrés dans le théâtre et ils ont pris leurs places à huit heures et quart. La représentation a commencé à huit heures et demie. (Answer: **B**) **Selection Number 3.** Ce soir Pierre a servi le dîner pour la famille et les voisins, Monsieur et Madame Richy. Il a servi un ragoût à l'irlandaise. La recette pour le ragoût est sur la page d'en face. Madame Paquet a préparé le ragoût. (Answer: **B**) **Selection Number 4.** Janine a prêté ses CDs à son amie Suzanne au mois de septembre. C'est aujourd'hui le premier décembre. Janine veut reprendre ses CDs pour les écouter pendant les fêtes de Noël. Elle va voir son amie Suzanne qui dit qu'elle ne les a pas. (Answer: **C**) **PART THREE: Reading Proficiency** 1. **B** 2. **C** 3. **A** 4. **D** 5. **C** **PART FOUR: Writing Proficiency.** (NOTE TO TEACHER: Your students will respond in writing in different ways, depending on which ten situations they have chosen based on PART ONE: Speaking Proficiency in this test.)

WORK UNIT 16

Exercises, p. 255
I. 1. vrai. 2. vrai. 3. vrai. 4. faux. 5. faux. 6. faux. 7. faux. 8. vrai. **II.** 1. professeur, géographie. 2. Paris. 3. port. 4. fleuve. 5. dans, classe. 6. au, bureau. 7. continuer, leçon. 8. poser. **III.** 1. Elle est professeur de géographie. 2. La directrice (de l'école) entre dans la salle de classe. 3. Quand Madame Ravel quitte la salle, elle va dans le bureau de la directrice. 4. Robert a lancé un avion en papier contre l'horloge. 5. La leçon finit à trois heures.

Exercises, pp. 257–260
I. 5, 4, 2, 1, 3. **II.** Oui, cela est faux. 2. Oui, ceci est vrai. 3. Oui, c'est ça.

III. Word Hunt

IV. 1. C'est vrai. (NOTE TO TEACHER: You may want to remind your students that French people say *le foot* or *le football* for soccer; they say *le football américain* for football.) 2. C'est faux. 3. C'est vrai. 4. C'est vrai. 5. C'est faux. **VI.** 1. deux enfants 2. des robes d'été 3. des chemises à manches courtes 4. les chapeaux 5. (le) stationnement gratuit 6. (le) rabais de 20% 7. Annie est ma nièce. Demain c'est son anniversaire (de naissance)/birthday 8. Je vais lui donner un cadeau, une jolie robe d'été (un jouet, etc.) **V.** J'admire le tableau de Degas. C'est une répétition d'un ballet sur la scène. Les danseuses sont jolies. Leurs tutus sont beaux. Je vois le chorégraphe habillé en noir au milieu de la scène. Ce tableau exprime l'art des formes et du mouvement. C'est un tableau magnifique. Je l'aime beaucoup. La peinture est signée en haut, à gauche. Quel beau tableau! **VI.** Bonjour, madame/monsieur. Je suis (add your name). J'aimerais jouer un jeu de vrai ou faux comme dans cette leçon. Je vous assure que je ne vais pas lancer un avion en papier contre l'horloge comme a fait Robert dans l'histoire! **VII.** (NOTE TO TEACHER: There are many examples of this type of exercise in speaking proficiency in this work unit. Your students will respond in different ways.) **VIII.** 1. J'ai beaucoup parlé en français. 2. Quelques étudiants (élèves) ont parlé en français. Quelques étudiants n'ont rien dit. 3. Oui, j'ai écrit en français au tableau. 4. Moi! C'est moi qui ai gagné le grand prix aujourd'hui!

WORK UNIT 17

Exercises, pp. 263–264
I. Moi, je ne veux pas y aller (possibly: Je ne veux pas accepter leur invitation; Non, nous n'acceptons pas leur invitation—or any acceptable response)...MONSIEUR PAQUET: Ils m'ennuient

beaucoup. Je ne les aime pas. MONSIEUR PAQUET: (NOTE TO TEACHER: In this last réplique of Monsieur Paquet, the students may write any response that is acceptable from the dialogue on p. 236.) **II.** 1. entre eux et nous. 2. vous voir. 3. chez eux. 4. je ne les aime pas. 5. à l'invitation. **III.** 1. (d). 2. (d). 3. (a).

Exercises, pp. 265–267

I. 1. moi. 2. lui. 3. elle. 4. nous. 5. vous. 6. eux. **II.** 1. lui. 2. moi. 3. lui. 4. elle. 5. nous. 6. vous. 7. toi. 8. eux. 9. elles. 10. lui et moi. **III.** nous, moi, toi, vous, les, leur, les, les, les, moi, y. **IV.** 1. Le dîner que vous avez préparé est vraiment délicieux. 2. Je l'ai beaucoup aimé. 3. Merci pour l'invitation. Vous êtes très aimable et sympathique. **V.** 2. Bonjour, Janine. Salut! Comment vas-tu? 4. Merci, mais je ne peux pas. Mon père est malade et je dois rester à la maison avec lui. 6. Non, parce que ma mère est allée rendre visite à sa soeur en France. 8. Oui, tu peux venir chez moi. 10. Apporte un grand gâteau au chocolat avec toi. 12. Apporte, aussi, la musique et les paroles de la chanson *Sur le Pont d'Avignon*.

WORK UNIT 18

Exercises, pp. 270–271

I. 1. La famille Paquet a une belle voiture grise. 2. Non, les grosses voitures neuves ne sont pas meilleures que la voiture de Monsieur Paquet. 3. Pierre veut le tournevis pour régler le moteur. Il veut enlever la vis et l'écrou. 4. Pierre les met dans la poubelle. **II.** (NOTE TO TEACHER: There are personal questions asked of the students and they may respond in different ways.) **III. A.** 1. belle. 2. grise. 3. grande. 4. neuve. 5. chère. **B.** 1. grand. 2. blanc. 3. beau. 4. large (wide). 5 propre (clean).

Exercises, pp. 273–275

I. 1. Non, j'ai une maison grise. 2. Non, j'ai un mauvais ordinateur. 3. Non, j'ai une belle pomme. 4. Non, j'ai une pêche douce. 5. Non, j'ai un vieux chapeau. **II.** 1. Oui, elle est petite; il est petit aussi. 2. Oui, il est furieux; elle est furieuse aussi. 3. Oui, elle est gentille; il est gentil aussi. 4. Oui, elles sont belles; ils sont beaux aussi. 5. Oui, elle est neuve; elles sont neuves aussi. **III.** 1. Non, elle n'est pas petite; il n'est pas petit non plus. 2. Non, il n'est pas mauvais; il n'est pas mauvais non plus. 3. Non, il n'est pas gros; elle n'est pas grosse non plus. 4. Non, il n'est pas muet; elle n'est pas muette non plus. **IV.** 1. (d). 2. (c). 3. (c). 4. (b). 5. (b).

Exercises, pp. 276–280

I. 1. Oui, j'aime ma petite voiture neuve. 2. Oui, j'aime votre parapluie rouge. 3. Oui, j'aime votre maison blanche. 4. Oui, j'aime ton amie Monique. 5. Oui, j'aime mon petit frère. **II.** 1. Oui, c'est ma voiture. 2. Oui, c'est mon chapeau. 3. Oui, c'est son livre à lui. 4. Oui, c'est ma maîtresse de français. 5. Oui, c'est leur maison. **III.** 1. Oui, ce sont mes stylos. 2. Oui, ce sont leurs crayons. 3. Oui, ce sont mes gâteaux. 4. Oui, ce sont vos (or: tes) pommes. 5. Oui, ce sont nos (or: vos) pêches. **IV.** votre, ma, votre, votre, vos, sa, son, nos, leurs. **V.** 1. Je mange ma pêche. 2. Il mange son sandwich. 3. Ils mangent leur chocolat. 4. Elles mangent leur soupe. 5. Je mange mes petits fours. **VI. A.** Le garage est beau. J'aime beaucoup la couleur rouge. La jeune fille est belle. Elle a les cheveux noirs. Le petit garçon a les cheveux blonds. Le garçon répare la voiture blanche. Elle est grande et belle. La jeune fille lui dit: "Non! Non! Es-tu fou?" **B.** Ma maison est grande et belle. Elle est blanche. Elle est vieille mais confortable. **C.** Mon père est grand, intelligent, et sympathique. Ma mère est grande aussi et elle est intelligente et très aimable. Mon frère est beau et ma soeur est belle. Notre chien est grand et notre chat est petit. **VII.** Qu'est-ce que je fais? Mais tu vois, mon père, je vais engager le tournevis dans cette vis et je vais tourner. Maintenant je tourne le tournevis…là…là…là…J'enlève la vis et l'écrou. Ils ne sont pas utiles. Maintenant je les mets dans la poubelle. **VIII.** Un jeune homme marche sur le trottoir. Il passe par un vieux bâtiment en ruines (in ruins). Il couvre sa tête pour se protéger (to protect himself) parce qu'il y a des briques qui tombent. **IX.** 1. Les trois personnes jouent au foot. 2. Le jeune homme est le gardien de but. 3. Un garçon a envoyé le ballon au fond des filets et l'autre garçon reste surpris! **X.** 1. Oui, je l'aime beaucoup. 2. Je pense qu'elle attend un ami. 3. Oui, elles sont belles. J'aimerais aller à Tahiti.

WORK UNIT 19

Exercises, pp. 284–285

I. 1. lit, de l'horoscope, lui. 2. le meilleur. 3. plus forte. 4. le plus. 5. du moment, semaine, nouvelles. II. Chère amie Janine: Merci beaucoup pour ton invitation chez toi pour une soirée. Je ne peux pas accepter ton aimable invitation parce que je vais partir demain en avion pour la belle France! Je vais t'envoyer une carte postale de Paris! Grosses bises (Lots of big kisses), Ton amie Debbie (Ton ami Robert). III. 1. Pierre lit son horoscope. 2. Demain va être un jour parfait. 3. Une personne vous aime beaucoup. 4. Il y a un requin dans l'eau. 5. Le téléphone sonne.

Exercises, pp. 286–287

I. 1. Quel est votre (or: ton) nom? (possibly: Comment vous appelez-vous? or: Comment t'appelles-tu? or: Comment est-ce que vous vous appelez? or: Comment est-ce que tu t'appelles?). 2. Quelle est votre (or: ton) adresse? (NOTE TO TEACHER: Please see page 286 in book for the expected "Quelle est votre adresse?" and "Quel est votre nom?".) 3. Quel âge avez-vous? (or: Quel âge as-tu? or: Quel est votre âge? or: Quel est ton âge?). II. (NOTE TO TEACHER: These are personal questions and students may answer in different ways.) III. 1. Quel. 2. Quelles. 3. Quels. 4. Quelle. IV. 5, 3, 1, 4, 2. V. A. 1. beau. 2. grand. 3. intelligent. 4. sympathique. 5. aimable. B. 1. belles. 2. jolies. 3. intelligentes. 4. sympathiques. 5. aimables.

Exercises, pp. 288–290

I. A. 1. Je mange cette pêche. 2. Je mange ce gâteau. 3. Je mange ces petits fours. 4. Je mange cet ananas. 5. Je mange cette tomate. I. B. 1. Etudiez-vous cette leçon? 2. Etudiez-vous ce livre? 3. Etudiez-vous ces pages? 4. Etudiez-vous ces phrases? 5. Etudiez-vous ce poème? I. C. 1. Nous allons au cinéma avec ces jeunes filles. 2. Nous allons au cinéma avec cet ami. 3. Nous allons au cinéma avec cette amie. 4. Nous allons au cinéma avec ce jeune homme. 5. Nous allons au cinéma avec ces étudiants. II. 1. Bien! Je vous donne ce journal! 2. Bien! Je lui donne cette pomme! 3. Bien! Je leur donne ces pommes frites! III. 1. Je vais manger cet ananas et ces tomates. 2. Je vais écrire cette leçon et ces phrases. 3. Je vais boire ces vins et ces bières. 4. Je vais envoyer cette lettre. 5. Je vais acheter ce livre.

Exercises, pp. 292–297

I. 1. Non, il est moins grand que sa mère. 2. Non, elle est moins grande que son père. 3. Non, elle est moins intelligente que Janine. II. 1. Madame Paquet est plus grande que Janine. 2. Janine est moins grande que Pierre. 3. Mathilde est plus petite que Monique. 4. Suzanne est moins petite que Joseph. 5. Monsieur Richy est aussi grand que Monsieur Paquet. 6. Madame Paquet est aussi petite que Madame Banluc. III. 1. Non, ce n'est pas vrai. Janine est la plus intelligente du cours de mathématiques. 2. Non, ce n'est pas vrai. Suzanne est la plus grande du cours de français. 3. Non, ce n'est pas vrai. Simon est le moins grand de la famille. 4. Non, ce n'est pas vrai. Charles est le plus beau du groupe. 5. Non, ce n'est pas vrai. Hélène est la plus petite. IV. 1. Oui, cette phrase est moins facile que les autres; ces questions sont moins faciles que les autres aussi. 2. Oui, ce poème est plus difficile que les autres; cette leçon est plus difficile que les autres aussi. 3. Oui, cette voiture est plus belle que les autres; ces maisons sont plus belles que les autres aussi. 4. Oui, ce garçon est plus beau que les autres; ces jeunes filles sont plus belles que les autres aussi. 5. Oui, cette banane est plus délicieuse que les autres; ces gâteaux sont plus délicieux que les autres aussi. V. 1. plus. 2. grand. 3. aussi. 4. plus jolie. 5. le moins.

VI. Le Mot Mystère

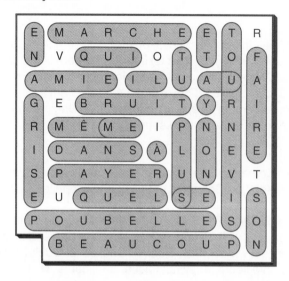

NOTE TO TEACHER: The mystery word is VOITURE; the scrambled letters that remain are, starting with the first line across: R, V, O, E, I, T, U.

VII. (NOTE TO TEACHER: A few lines of conversation are provided to get the students started. They can continue the conversation on their own. After you have corrected what they said, they may write it on a sheet of paper or on the chalkboard.) Bonjour! Vous désirez? Une chemise? Une cravate? Nous avons beaucoup de belles chemises. Voulez-vous regarder ces chaussettes? Elles sont vraiment jolies et elles ne coûtent pas beaucoup. C'est pour vous? Ou c'est pour une autre personne? C'est pour une soirée? Regardez! Vous avez choisi? C'est un grand plaisir de vous aider. **VIII.** 1. Il n'y a pas de problème. Dis-moi, est-ce qu'Anne est plus jolie que Monique? (OR: Dis-moi, Anne est-elle plus jolie que Monique?) 2. Dis-moi, mon père est-il plus grand que ton père? (OR: Dis-moi, est-ce que mon père est plus grand que ton père?) 3. Dis-moi, qui est le meilleur étudiant de notre classe de français? 4. Moi?! Tu penses que je suis le meilleur (la meilleure) étudiant(e) de notre classe de français?! 5. Merci! Maintenant, mangeons de la mousse au chocolat. C'est la meilleure. **IX.** À la plus sympa de toutes les mamans. Je te souhaite une joyeuse Fête des Mères. Je t'aime. Chez nous, j'ai appris la valeur de l'amour depuis mon enfance. De tout coeur.

WORK UNIT 20

Exercises, p. 301

I. Robert, arrête! Sois sage! Et toi, aussi, Debbie, arrête! Sois sage! Cela suffit! Robert, tu es capricieux. Et toi, aussi, Debbie, tu es capricieuse. Soyez sages, tous les deux! Robert, si tu continues, tu vas te coucher. Et toi, aussi, Debbie…Silence! Je vais changer le programme à la télé. Nous allons regarder un match de tennis. **II.** 1. (d) 2. (a). 3. (c). 4. (b). 5. (c). **III. A.** 1. distinctement. 2. constamment. 3. lentement. **B.** 1. beaucoup. 2. toujours. 3. vite. 4. bien.

Exercises, pp. 303–304

I. 1. distinctement. 2. seulement. 3. courageusement. 4. constamment. 5. patiemment. 6. fièrement. **II.** 1. Monsieur Richy aime beaucoup le ragoût brûlé. 2. Le professeur a bien parlé. 3. Janine a parlé constamment. 4. Elle est déjà partie. 5. Pierre a beaucoup mangé. **III.** 1. bien. 2. plus. 3. aussi . . . que. 4. plus . . . que. 5. moins.

IV. Le Mot Mystère

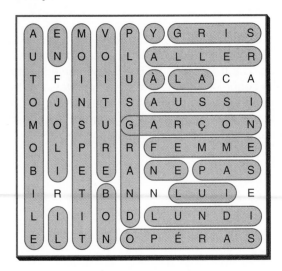

NOTE TO TEACHER: The mystery word is FRANCE; the scambled letters that remain are, starting with the third line across: F, C, A, R, N, E.

V. Catherine a sept ans. Elle est plus grande que son frère Joseph. Elle est toujours sage. Elle parle distinctement. Elle mange bien. Elle joue très bien avec son frère. Joseph a quatre ans. Il est sage aussi. Il est moins grand que sa soeur. Il parle lentement. Mais il parle aussi bien que sa soeur. Joseph mange beaucoup. Il mange plus vite que sa soeur. Catherine parle constamment.

TEST 4 (WORK UNITS 16–20)

Pages 305, 306, 307, 308
PART ONE: Speaking Proficiency. (NOTE TO TEACHER: The twelve situations given are a review of exercises in proficiency in speaking in Work Units 16 to 20. Your students will respond to you and you may grade them on this speaking test according to what they say in class or on a one-to-one basis at your desk.) **PART TWO: Listening Proficiency.** (NOTE TO TEACHER: Here are the four short paragraphs that you will read aloud to your students. The directions are given in the test.) **Selection Number 1.** Madame Ravel est professeur de géographie. Elle pose des questions aux étudiants. Après quelques minutes, la directrice de l'école entre dans la salle de classe pour lui dire que quelqu'un lui demande au téléphone. Les deux dames quittent la salle. (Answer: **B**) **Selection Number 2.** Claire et François ont accepté l'invitation à dîner chez leurs voisins, Monsieur et Madame Berger. Quand ils entrent dans le foyer, ils voient d'autres voisins chez eux. Tout le monde crie: Surprise! Surprise! (Answer: **D**) **Selection Number 3.** Quand Monsieur Paquet veut aller faire des courses dans sa voiture, il va au garage, monte dans sa voiture, et tourne la clef pour mettre le moteur en marche. Il entend un bruit et le moteur ne marche pas. Il appelle la station-service et le garagiste arrive. (Answer: **D**) **Selection Number 4.** Monique parle à Pierre au téléphone. Elle dit: Écoute, Pierre. Il y a une grande soirée chez moi ce soir. Nous allons danser et chanter. Ma mère a préparé un gâteau délicieux. Nous allons beaucoup nous amuser. Henri va venir, ainsi que Paul, Robert, Raymond, Suzanne, Hélène, ta soeur Janine, et d'autres amis. Veux-tu venir? (Answer: **D**) **PART THREE: Reading Proficiency** 1. **B** 2. **C** 3. **B** 4. **D** 5. **D** **PART FOUR: Writing Proficiency.** (NOTE TO TEACHER: Your students will respond in writing in different ways, depending on which ten situations they have chosen based on PART ONE: Speaking Proficiency in this test.)

WORK UNIT 21

Exercises, pp. 311–314

I. 1. Madame Paquet est malade. 2. Elle a mangé quelque chose qui lui a donné mal à l'estomac. 3. Elle est malade depuis hier. 4. Le docteur lui donne un médicament. 5. Il doit partir parce qu'il va dîner (or: il doit partir pour aller dîner) au Coq d'or. II. 1. Madame Paquet est malade depuis hier. 2. Absolument rien! 3. Pas même un oeuf à la coque! 4. Dis-moi ce que tu manges et je te dirai ce que tu es! (or: Dites-moi ce que vous mangez et je vous dirai ce que vous êtes!). 5. Prenez ce médicament et ne mangez rien. III. 1. Le docteur n'est pas arrivé. 2. Madame Paquet est malade depuis hier, n'est-ce pas? 3. Il est dans la chambre depuis quinze minutes.

IV. Mots-croisés

Exercises, pp. 317–325

I. 1. Non, je ne danse pas bien. 2. Non, mon père ne chante pas souvent. 3. Non, ma mère ne lit pas beaucoup. 4. Non, mes amis n'écrivent pas bien. 5. Non, je ne fume pas. II. 1. Non, je ne parle jamais beaucoup. 2. Non, mon père ne boit jamais beaucoup de lait. 3. Non, ma soeur ne travaille jamais beaucoup. 4. Non, mon ami n'étudie jamais beaucoup. 5. Non, je ne bois jamais beaucoup d'eau. III. 1. Non, Lucille ne mange rien. 2. Non, Guy n'écrit rien. 3. Non, je ne lis rien. 4. Non, Madame Paquet ne fait rien. 5. Non, je n'étudie rien. IV. A. 1. Non, je n'ai rien dit. 2. Non, elle n'a rien bu. 3. Non, mes amis n'ont rien étudié. 4. Non, je n'ai rien lu. 5. Non, je n'ai rien écrit. 6. Non, je n'ai rien bu. 7. Non, elles n'ont rien mangé. IV. B. 1. Non, je n'ai jamais voyagé en Angleterre. 2. Non, je ne suis jamais allé au Canada. 3. Non, je n'ai jamais vu un film français. 4. Non, elle n'est jamais allée à l'opéra. 5. Non, il n'a jamais lu un journal français. 6. Non, ils ne sont jamais allés en Espagne. 7. Non, elles n'ont jamais mangé un éclair. V. 1. Je sais que vous êtes malade. 2. Madame Paquet est dans son lit parce qu'elle est malade, n'est-ce pas? 3. Je mange quand j'ai faim (or possibly: Quand j'ai faim, je mange). 4. Le docteur va venir dans quelques minutes. 5. En une heure, le docteur est venu. VI. 1. être. 2. avoir. 3. aller. 4. attendre. 5. dire. 6. prendre. VII. 1. Il est absent depuis lundi. 2. Elle attend le docteur (or: Elle l'attend) depuis vingt minutes. 3. J'attends l'autobus (or: Je l'attends) depuis dix minutes. 4. Je travaille ici depuis le premier avril. 5. Je lis ce livre (or: Je le lis) depuis une heure. 6. Je lis ce livre (or: Je le lis) depuis ce matin. VIII. 1. Oui, il faut boire pour vivre. 2. Oui, il faut étudier pour apprendre. 3. Oui, il faut parler français dans la classe de français. 4. Oui, il faut parler espagnol dans la classe d'espagnol. 5. Oui, il faut faire les devoirs pour apprendre. IX. Merci, madame. 2. J'étudie le français depuis un an. 3. J'ai appris à parler français à l'école. 4. J'habite avec mes parents aux États-Unis. 5. J'étudie les mathématiques, les sciences, les langues, l'informatique, les ordinateurs, et d'autres matières. 6. J'aime votre pays, les Français, la culture, la musique, et l'art. 7. Je désire acheter un oreiller parce que je n'aime pas l'oreiller sur le lit dans ma chambre à l'hôtel. X. 1. Je désire acheter une plante. 2. Ce n'est pas pour moi. C'est pour offrir. 3. C'est pour un ami (une amie). C'est son anniversaire. 4. Oui, c'est très jolie. C'est combien? 5. Oui, je la prends. XI. 1. Madame Paquet est malade depuis hier. 2. Elle est dans son lit. 3. Elle a mangé quelque chose qui lui a donné mal à l'estomac. 4. Le docteur et son mari sont dans la chambre à côté d'elle. 5. Madame Paquet a envie de manger un oeuf à la coque et une tranche (a slice) de pain grillé. XII. Au plus sympa de tous les papas. Je te souhaite une joyeuse Fête des Pères. Je t'aime. Chez nous, j'ai appris la valeur de l'amour depuis mon enfance. De tout coeur. XIII. Mes amis, nous allons chanter en français. Catherine, veux-tu jouer du piano? Voici la musique et les paroles (spoken words) de la chanson *Frère Jacques*.

WORK UNIT 22

Exercises, pp. 328–329
I. 1. regarder les animaux. 2. acheter des choses. 3. manger. 4. boire. 5. consulter une chiroman-cienne. 6. m'amuser. II. (NOTE TO TEACHER: This is free composition and the students may write statements in French in different ways.) III. 1. Joseph et Joséphine sont allés (or: vont) au cinéma samedi. 2. Ils sont entrés (or: entrent) chez la chiromancienne. 3. Ils n'ont rien appris (or: n'ap-prennent rien) chez la chiromancienne. 4. François Paquet lui a payé (or: lui paye) dix euros pour les révélations.

Exercises, pp. 332–334
I. 1. Nous la changeons aussi. 2. Nous le corrigeons aussi. 3. Nous les appelons aussi. 4. Nous l'employons aussi. 5. Nous les achetons aussi. II. 1. Janine et Monique sont allées au cinéma. 2. Nous avons voyagé aux Etats-Unis. 3. Madame Sétou a regardé fixement la main de Madame Paquet. 4. Madame Sétou a révélé les secrets de votre main. 5. Claire et François Paquet ont acheté des souvenirs. III. 1. Nous arrangeons les fleurs. 2. Il achète une cravate. 3. Ils appellent la police. 4. Tu emploies le dictionnaire. 5. Nous prononçons le mot.

Exercises, pp. 336–339
I. 1. Oui, je vais faire un voyage au Canada. 2. Oui, elle va écrire une lettre. 3. Oui, il va jouer dans le parc. 4. Oui, ils vont voyager en Angleterre. 5. Oui, nous allons répondre à la question. II. 1. Non, je ne veux pas acheter une nouvelle voiture. 2. Non, il ne veut pas corriger les devoirs. 3. Non, il ne veut pas prononcer le mot. 4. Non, elle ne veut pas employer le dictionnaire. 5. Non, il ne veut pas fumer une cigarette. III. 4, 1, 3, 5, 2. IV. 1. Il n'y a pas un grand parc dans cette ville. 2. Il n'y a pas un arrêt d'autobus ici. 3. Il n'y a pas dix garçons dans la classe. V. 1. Oui, j'ai lu *Le livre de mon ami* d'Anatole France il y a trois mois. 2. Oui, il a vu Pierre il y a dix minutes. 3. Oui, je suis allé(e) en Californie il y a un an. 4. Oui, elles sont arrivées il y a une demi-heure. 5. Oui, elle est partie il y a une heure. VI. 1. Il y a trois enfants dans cette photo. 2. Ils sont dans un parc. 3. Ils jouent. 4. Il grimpe sur un arbre abattu. 5. Il est prêt à sauter. 6. Lui aussi, il grimpe sur un arbre abattu. VII. 1. Il fait très chaud aujourd'hui. Je suis très fatigué. Et toi? 2. Je suis très fatiguée aussi. Allons pren-dre une glace à la vanille!

WORK UNIT 23

Exercises, p. 342
I. 1. Il est allé acheter une chaîne stéréo. 2. Janine a préparé un grand déjeuner. 3. Madame Paquet est allée chez le coiffeur. 4. Pierre a acheté une boîte de chocolats. 5. Monsieur Paquet n'a pas branché la chaîne stéréo sur la prise de courant. II. A. Madame Paquet, Pierre, Janine, et Coco sont dans le salon. Monsieur Paquet est au téléphone. Pierre tient dans la main la corde électrique de la chaîne stéréo. La radio ne marche pas. La mère est inquiète. Janine sourit. Pierre dit: "Papa! Papa! Attends! Attends! Tu n'as pas branché la chaîne stéréo sur la prise de courant!" B. Mon ani-mal favori est le chien. J'aime aussi le chat, la girafe, la tortue, le cheval et le lapin. III. 1. Monsieur Paquet a acheté (or: achète) une chaîne stéréo. 2. Janine a préparé (or: prépare) le déjeuner. 3. Pierre est allé (or: va) chez un confiseur pour acheter une boîte de chocolats. 4. Madame Paquet est allée (or: va) chez le coiffeur pour une nouvelle coiffure. 5. Pierre est allé (or: va) chez un (or: une) fleuriste pour acheter des fleurs.

Exercises, pp. 346–349
I. 1. de. 2. à. 3. —. 4. de. 5. à. 6. —. 7. —. 8. à. 9. de 10. de. II. 1. Oui, j'ai envie d'aller au cinéma; ils ont envie d'aller au cinéma aussi. 2. Oui, elle a besoin d'aller au supermarché; elles ont besoin d'aller au supermarché aussi. 3. Oui, je suis sorti(e) sans dire un mot; elle est sortie sans dire un mot aussi. 4. Oui, j'apprends à lire en français; il apprend à lire en français aussi. 5. Oui, j'ai hor-reur de manger dans un restaurant sale; ils ont horreur de manger dans un restaurant sale aussi. III. 1. (c). 2. (d). 3. (d). IV. 3, 5, 1, 2, 4. V. 1. (d). 2. (c). 3. (c). VI. A. As-tu mal aux dents, Jean? As-

tu besoin d'aller chez le dentiste? Vas-tu chez le dentiste? Tu ne veux pas y aller? Pourquoi? As-tu peur des dentistes? Pourquoi? Je sais qu'il est désagréable d'aller chez le dentiste. **B.** Jean, mon ami, il faut aller chez le dentiste. Tu as tort d'avoir peur. Le dentiste va t'aider. La douleur va disparaître. **VII. A.** 1. la verrerie. 2. la porcelaine. 3. le linge de maison. **B.** 1. un tapis. 2. des meubles de cuisine. 3. une chaise. **VIII.** 1. Oui, il est superbe. La jeune fille lit un livre. C'est une liseuse. Quel livre lit-elle? 2. Elle est belle, n'est-ce pas? Ma maîtresse de français a la même coiffure. Je suppose qu'elle a vu ce tableau. 3. Oui, j'aime bien le noeud de ruban dans sa coiffure. C'est simple et joli. 4. N'oublie pas d'apporter un petit livre avec toi et un noeud de ruban!

WORK UNIT 24

Exercises, pp. 353–354

I. 1. Le chat parti, les souris dansent. 2. À bon chat, bon rat. 3. Mieux vaut tard que jamais. 4. Vouloir, c'est pouvoir. 5. À chacun son goût. **II.** 1. chat, dansent. 2. yeux, du. 3. père, fils. 4. mère, fille. **III.** 5, 1, 4, 2, 3. **IV.** Il y a trois souris dans cette photo. Elles jouent avec un ballon. Elles dansent aussi parce que le chat est parti. Dans l'autre photo, il y a un homme qui mange. Il est très gros. Il n'a pas de cheveux sur la tête. Il mange beaucoup parce qu'il a très faim. **V. A.** 1. jouer. 2. danser. **B.** 1. le poulet. 2. la purée de pommes de terre. 3. le maïs (corn). 4. le céleri.

Exercises, pp. 355–363

I. 1. Janine écrit la lettre. 2. Janine l'écrit. 3. Monique n'écrit pas la lettre. 4. Madame Richy me donne un cadeau. 5. Le professeur ne lui donne pas le stylo. 6. Il n'y a pas un bon restaurant près d'ici. 7. Il y a une mouche dans la soupe. 8. Il y en a beaucoup dans la soupe. 9. Je leur donne de l'argent. 10. Je ne vous donne pas l'éclair. **II.** 1. Louis a préparé le dîner. 2. Marie l'a préparé. 3. Il n'a pas préparé le dîner. 4. Janine n'a pas préparé la salade. 5. Robert a préparé les salades. 6. Jacques ne les a pas préparées. 7. Monique ne lui a pas donné les chocolats. 8. Raymond vous a donné les disques. 9. Madame Paquet ne leur a pas donné l'argent. 10. Je ne leur en ai pas donné. **III.** Ce café est très joli. Il se trouve près de l'**Arc de Triomphe**. Il y a beaucoup de personnes dans ce café. Les femmes et les hommes mangent, boivent et parlent. Je vois un homme qui sourit (is smiling). **IV.** 1. Moi! Moi! Je veux commencer un proverbe français. Tonya peut le finir. 2. Mieux vaut tard … 3. Je sais! C'est … que jamais. Mieux vaut tard que jamais! 4. Moi! Moi! Je veux commencer un proverbe français. 5. Tout est bien … 6. qui finit bien. 7. Qui a gagné le prix, Madame Marin? **V. A.** Mieux vaut tard que jamais. **B.** Le chat parti, les souris dansent. **C.** L'appétit vient en mangeant. **D.** Les murs ont des oreilles. **E.** Vouloir, c'est pouvoir. **VI.** (NOTE TO TEACHER: Your students may make a selection of proverbs at the beginning of this work unit.) **VII.** 1. Je pense qu'il est beau. Quel tableau! Je veux être artiste. 2. Je pense que c'est épatant! Quel artiste! Je veux être artiste aussi. 3. C'est merveilleux! Regardez la balustrade qui sépare la terrasse de la mer. 4. Si je pouvais peindre comme ça! 5. Vouloir, c'est pouvoir! 6. Regardez tous les bateaux à l'horizon! Mon Dieu! Et regardez le bateau à voiles près de la femme au parasol blanc. 7. Le jardin est beau. Je n'ai jamais vu un jardin si beau! 8. Le fanion à gauche est splendide. Le drapeau français à droite est impressionnant.

WORK UNIT 25

Exercises, pp. 367–368

I. 1. vrai. 2. vrai. 3. faux. 4. vrai. 5. vrai. 6. vrai. 7. vrai. 8. faux. 9. vrai. 10. vrai.

II. Fill in the Squares

1. LUI
2. DANSEZ
3. FAIM
4. MOUCHE
5. OU
6. GRAIN
7. MANGER
8. LACIGALE

III. 1. a chanté. 2. rien. 3. pas. 4. mouche. 5. va. 6. ne, jamais. 7. avez. 8. ai. 9. à. 10. avez, dansez. **IV.** 1. La cigale a chanté tout l'été. 2. Non, elle n'a pas travaillé. 3. Non, quand l'hiver arrive, la cigale n'a rien à manger. 4. La fourmi a travaillé tout l'été. 5. Non, la fourmi ne donne rien à manger à la cigale (or: Non, la fourmi ne lui donne rien à manger).

Exercises, p. 371

I. 1. Donnez-moi le livre! 2. Écrivez-lui la lettre! 3. Donnez-lui le gâteau! 4. Répondez-y! 5. Asseyez-vous et donnez-moi la main! **II.** 1. Ne l'apprenez pas! 2. Ne les étudiez pas! 3. Ne m'en donnez pas! 4. N'en mangez pas! 5. Ne leur parlez pas! **III.** Monique, il vient vers nous. Il va nous parler. Ne te lève pas. Ne lui parle pas. Ne lui réponds pas. Dis-lui, "Va-t'en!"

TEST 5 (WORK UNITS 21–25)

Pages 372, 373, 374, 375

PART ONE: Speaking Proficiency. (NOTE TO TEACHER: The eighteen situations given are a review of exercises in proficiency in speaking in Work Units 21 to 25. Your students will respond to you and you may grade them on this speaking test according to what they say in class or on a one-to-one basis at your desk.) **PART TWO: Listening Proficiency.** (NOTE TO TEACHER: Here are the four short paragraphs that you will read aloud to your students. The directions are given in the test.) **Selection Number 1.** Madame Paquet est malade depuis hier. Elle a mangé quelque chose qui lui a donné mal à l'estomac. Elle est souffrante dans son lit. Son mari a appelé le docteur pour lui donner un médicament. Le docteur va venir dans quelques minutes. (Answer: **D**) **Selection Number 2.** Claire et François sont allés à la foire samedi. Là, ils se sont bien amusés. Ils ont vu des expositions, ils ont acheté des souvenirs, et ils sont entrés chez une chiromancienne pour se faire lire les lignes de la main. (Answer: **C**) **Selection Number 3.** Monsieur Paquet est allé acheter une radio stéréophonique. Madame Paquet est allée chez le coiffeur. Janine a préparé un grand déjeuner, et Pierre est allé aux grands magasins acheter un petit cadeau pour sa mère. Il est allé, aussi, chez un confiseur pour acheter une boîte de chocolats. (Answer: **D**) **Selection Number 4.** La cigale a chanté tout l'été. Elle n'a pas travaillé. L'hiver arrive et elle n'a rien à manger. Elle va chez la fourmi, sa voisine, et elle lui dit: Ma chère amie, je n'ai rien à manger et j'ai faim. Pouvez-vous me prêter un grain de quelque chose jusqu'au printemps? (Answer: **D**) **PART THREE: Reading Proficiency** 1. **D** 2. **B** 3. **C** 4. **B** 5. **B** **PART FOUR: Writing Proficiency.** (NOTE TO TEACHER: Your students will respond in writing in different ways, depending on which fifteen situations they have chosen based on PART ONE: Speaking Proficiency in this test.)

PART 2: VOCABULARY

UNIT 1: **L'école**

Exercises, pp. 379–381

I. 1. (d). 2. (c). 3. (b). 4. (a). 5. (b). **II.** 1. (d). 2. (a). 3. (a). 4. (d). 5. (c). **III.** 1. (a). 2. (c). 3. (b). 4. (d). 5. (a). **IV.** 3, 5, 2, 1, 4. **V.** (Looking at the pictures across the page): le bureau, le cahier, le tableau noir, le stylo, le crayon. **VI. A.** 1. le livre. 2. le drapeau. 3. le pupitre. 4. le calendrier. 5. la carte de France. **B.** 1. le stylo. 2. le crayon. 3. le crayon feutre. 4. la craie.

UNIT 2: Les jours de la semaine, les mois de l'année, les saisons, et les jours de fête

Exercises, pp. 382–384
I. 1. (b). 2. (b). 3. (a). **II.** 1. (d). 2. (b). 3. (b). 4. (d). 5. (d). **III.** 1. (c). 2. (d). 3. (a). 4. (b). 5. (a). **IV.** (Looking at the pictures across the page): l'automne, l'hiver, l'été, le printemps. **V. A.** Je préfère Noël. Chez moi nous célébrons ce grand jour de fête. Nous avons un arbre de Noël qui est très beau. Nous mangeons, nous chantons, nous dansons, et nous échangeons des cadeaux. **B.** Pour moi, le mois favori de l'année est juillet. Il n'y a pas d'école. Je peux jouer dans le parc et je peux nager. J'aime beaucoup le soleil au mois de juillet parce qu'il fait chaud. **C.** Je préfère samedi. Il n'y a pas d'école. Le samedi je vais au cinéma avec mes amis.

UNIT 3: Les légumes, les poissons, les viandes, les produits laitiers, les desserts, les fromages, et les boissons

Exercises, pp. 385–387
I. 1. (d). 2. (a). 3. (d). 4. (d). 5. (a). **II.** 1. (b). 2. (c). 3. (c). 4. (d). 5. (c).

III. Word Search

V	O	C	A	F	E	L	V	S
I	E	V	E	A	U	A	I	O
A	U	B	E	R	G	I	N	E
L	F	J	A	M	H	T	U	I
I	S	J	A	M	B	O	N	L

IV. 1. (b). 2. (a). 3. (d). 4. (a). 5. (b). **V. A.** 1. des fruits. 2. des pâtisseries. 3. un grand gâteau. **B.** 1. du poulet. 2. des petits pois. 3. des pommes de terre. 4. des champignons. **VI.** (Looking at the pictures across the page): le beurre, l'oignon, le fromage, le gâteau, la pomme, les carottes, la viande, la glace, les petits pois, l'aubergine (that's what the drawing is supposed to look like!).

UNIT 4: Les animaux, les fleurs, les couleurs, les arbres, et les fruits

Exercises, pp. 388–391
I. 1. (c). 2. (d). 3. (d). 4. (b). 5. (d).

II. Un acrostiche

V	E	R	T					
O	E	I	L	L	E	T		
C	H	E	V	A	L			
A	U	B	E	R	G	I	N	E
B	A	N	A	N	E			
U	N	I	V	E	R	S	I	T	É
L	I	L	A	S				
A	N	N	É	E				
I	R	I	S					
R	A	I	S	I	N			
E	N	C	R	E				

III. 1. (c). 2. (b). 3. (b). **IV.** 1. (d). 2. (a). 3. (d). 4. (a). 5. (c). **V.** (Looking at the pictures across the page): un âne, un arbre, un oiseau, une fleur (or: une tulipe), une pêche, une poire, un cheval, une vache, une poule.

UNIT 5: **Le corps humain, les vêtements, la toilette**

Exercises, pp. 392–396

I. 1. (b). 2. (c). 3. (a). 4. (b). 5. (d). **II.** 1. (c). 2. (c). 3. (c). 4. (d). 5. (a). **III.** 1. (d). 2. (b). 3. (d). 4. (b). 5. (d). **IV.** 1. (d). 2. (b). 3. (a). 4. (c). 5. (b). 6. (c). 7. (d). 8. (b). 9. (b). 10. (b). **V.** 4, 3, 1, 2. **VI.** (Looking at the points of the arrows across the page, as in reading): la main, le bras, la tête (or: les cheveux), les cheveux (or: la tête), l'oreille, la bouche, le cou, l'épaule, le pied, le genou, la jambe. **VII.** (Looking at the pictures across the page): un chapeau, une robe, une chaussure (or: un soulier), un pullover (or: un chandail), un blouson, une jupe, un béret, une chemise, une écharpe, un gant, un veston, une cravate, un pantalon, une pantoufle, une chaussette.

UNIT 6: **La famille, la maison, les meubles**

Exercises, pp. 397–399

I. 1. (b). 2. (d). 3. (c). 4. (a). 5. (d). 6. (a). 7. (d). 8. (c). 9. (c). 10. (c). **II.** 1. (d). 2. (d). 3. (d). 4. (b). 5. (b). 6. (b). 7. (c). 8. (d). 9. (b). 10. (a). **III.** 1. (c). 2. (c). 3. (a). 4. (b). 5. (a). **IV.** 5, 4, 2, 3, 1. **V.** (Looking at the pictures across the page): la grand-mère, la fille, le grand-père, la fenêtre, le toit, la cuisine, l'escalier, la salle de bains.

UNIT 7: **La ville, les bâtiments, les magasins, les divers modes de transport**

Exercises, pp. 401–404

I. 1. (d). 2. (b). 3. (a). 4. (d). 5. (c). 6. (c). 7. (a). 8. (d). 9. (b). 10. (a). **II.** 1. boulangerie. 2. musée. 3. charcuterie. 4. bruit. 5. librairie. 6. voitures. 7. banque. 8. boucherie. 9. transatlantique. 10. gratte-ciel. **III.** 1. (b). 2. (d). 3. (b). 4. (c). 5. (b). **IV.** 1. (b). 2. (d). 3. (b). 4. (c). 5. (b). **V.** (Looking at the pictures across the page): un train, un parc, un bateau (or: un transatlantique), un autobus (a city bus; unless the picture looks like *un autocar* to some students; *un autocar* looks more like a tourist bus with a see-through roof made of glass or plastic, somewhat like a Greyhound bus; some French autocars look like extra long limousines, the type generally used to shuttle between airport and city), une bicyclette (or: un vélo), une moto (or: une motocyclette), une boîte aux lettres, une voiture de police. **VI.** (Looking at the pictures across the page): une voiture, un avion, un hôtel, un cinéma, une gare, un théâtre, une boucherie, une boulangerie, une pharmacie.

UNIT 8: **Les métiers et les professions, les langues, les pays, et la technologie**

Exercises, pp. 406–408

I. 1. (d). 2. (d). 3. (b). 4. (c). 5. (b). **II.** 1. l'allemand. 2. l'anglais. 3. le français. 4. l'espagnol. 5. l'italien. 6. l'espagnol. 7. le japonais. 8. le chinois. **III.** 1. Oui, on parle italien en Italie. 2. Oui, on parle anglais aux États-Unis. 3. Oui, on parle français et anglais au Canada. 4. Oui, on parle français en Belgique. 5. Oui, on parle français en France. 6. Oui, on parle espagnol en Espagne. 7. Oui, on parle français en Suisse. 8. Oui, on parle portugais au Portugal. 9. Oui, on parle espagnol au Mexique. 10. Oui, on parle grec en Grèce. **IV.** 1. une boulangère. 2. une bijoutière. 3. une serveuse. 4. une fermière. 5. une actrice. 6. une pharmacienne. 7. une maîtresse. 8. une épicière. 9. une coiffeuse. 10. une blanchisseuse. **V.** 1. une pâtisserie. 2. une pharmacie. 3. une librairie. 4. une charcuterie. 5. une bijouterie. 6. une blanchisserie. **VI.** 1. une librairie. 2. une pharmacie. 3. une crémerie. 4. un café. 5. une pâtisserie. 6. une boulangerie. **VII.** (Looking at the pictures across the page): un tailleur, une maîtresse, un coiffeur, une vendeuse, un fermier, un facteur, un dentiste, une boulangère, une fermière.

UNIT 9: **Poids, mesures, valeurs**

Exercise, pp. 409–410
I. 10, 5, 3, 6, 7, 1, 2, 4, 8, 9.

UNIT 10: **Antonymes et synonymes**

Exercises, pp. 412–414
I. 1. (c). 2. (a). 3. (a). 4. (b). 5. (d). **II.** 1. (a). 2. (c). 3. (d). 4. (b). 5. (d). **III.** 1. (b). 2. (a). 3. (c). 4. (c). 5. (a). **IV.** 1. (a). 2. (a). 3. (a). 4. (c). 5. (b). **V.** 1. UNE POMME. 2. UNE CHAISE. 3. UNE LAMPE. 4. UNE CHAUSSURE. 5. UN AVION. 6. UN LAPIN. 7. UN COCHON. 8. UN CHAPEAU. 9. UNE BROSSE À DENTS. 10. UN TÉLÉPHONE. 11. UNE VOITURE. 12. UN PARAPLUIE. 13. UN LIT.

PART THREE: IDIOMS, VERBAL EXPRESSIONS, AND DIALOGUES

UNIT 1: with **à**, with **au**

Exercises, pp. 418–419
I. 1. à propos. 2. à la maison. 3. à voix basse. 4. à mon avis. 5. au moins. 6. au revoir. **II.** au. 2. à. 3. à. 4. à. 5. à. 6. à. 7. au. 8. à. 9. à. 10. à. 11. au. 12. au. 13. à. 14. à. 15. à. **III.** (NOTE TO TEACHER: This is free composition and your students will respond in different ways.) **IV.** 2, 5, 3, 1, 4, 10, 6, 7, 8, 9.

UNIT 2: with **comment**, with **en**

Exercises, p. 421
I. A. 1. Comment allez-vous? 2. Comment vous portez-vous? 3. Comment ça va? **B.** 1. en bas. 2. en face de. 3. en retard. **II.** 1. en français, en anglais, en espagnol. 2. en automne, en hiver, en été. 3. C'est loin de l'école! 4. Je vous en prie! 5. Comment t'appelles-tu? (or: Comment vous appelez-vous?); je m'appelle Jacques.

UNIT 3: with **avoir**, with **être**

Exercises, pp. 423–424
I. 1. (NOTE TO TEACHER: This is free composition in the form of simple responses to general questions and your students will respond in different ways.) **II.** 1. Oui, j'ai l'intention d'aller au cinéma; il a l'intention d'aller au cinéma aussi (or: il a l'intention d'y aller aussi). 2. Oui, j'ai l'habitude d'étudier dans la bibliothèque; ils ont l'habitude d'étudier dans la bibliothèque aussi (or: ils ont l'habitude d'y étudier aussi). 3. Oui, j'ai chaud dans cette classe; ils ont chaud aussi. 4. Oui, j'ai faim en ce moment; elle a faim aussi. 5. Oui, j'ai soif en ce moment; ils ont soif aussi. **III.** (NOTE TO TEACHER: This is simple free composition and your students will respond in different ways.)

UNIT 4: with **de, du, d'**

Exercises, pp. 426–427
I. 1. Pierre a une nouvelle chemise. 2. Monsieur Paquet (or: Le père de Pierre) vient de peindre les murs de la cuisine. 3. Il y a un peu de vert, de bleu et de jaune sur la nouvelle chemise blanche de Pierre parce que son père (or: Monsieur Paquet) a peint les murs de la salle de bains en bleu et en vert et les murs de la cuisine en jaune, et il a employé sa chemise (or: la chemise de Pierre) pour nettoyer le pinceau! OR: Son père a employé sa chemise pour nettoyer le pinceau! (or any other acceptable response). **II.** (NOTE TO TEACHER: This is simple free composition).

III. Word Search

P	D	D	P	A	S	P	D	E	N	E	M	A	L
A	U	A	U	D	H	A	B	I	T	U	D	E	U
D	E	T	E	M	P	S	E	N	T	E	M	P	S
A	M	A	P	A	S	D	U	T	O	U	T	D	E
B	D	U	D	O	D	E	N	O	U	V	E	A	U
O	T	E	M	P	S	M	T	U	T	E	M	P	S
R	C	C	O	R	D	A	C	C	O	R	D	D	U
D	E	N	O	U	V	L	P	A	S	M	L	A	E

UNIT 5: with **par**, with **tout**, with **tous**, and miscellaneous

Exercises, pp. 429–430

I. 1. Ils sont dans un musée. 2. Ils veulent voir les dinosaures. 3. Non, il n'y a pas de dinosaures dans ce musée. 4. Non, Pierre n'a pas raison; il a tort. 5. Oui, Janine a tort aussi. 6. Oui, tous les deux ont tort. **II.** 1. par ici. 2. par là. 3. tous les jours. 4. de l'autre côté de la rue. **III.** 6, 4, 2, 5, 3, 1.

UNIT 6: with **faire**

Exercises, pp. 432–433

I. 1. Il fait beau aujourd'hui, n'est-ce pas? 2. Il fait du soleil aujourd'hui, n'est-ce pas? 3. Je veux faire une promenade. 4. Je veux faire une promenade en voiture (possibly: Je veux aller faire une promenade en voiture). 5. Tu vas (or: Vous allez) faire les bagages, je vais faire la malle, et nous allons faire un voyage. **II.** (NOTE TO TEACHER: This is simple free composition.)

III. Le Mot Mystère

A	M	N	O	N	À	N	U	I	T
T	I	F	A	I	R	E	M	E	O
T	E	M	A	U	V	A	I	S	U
E	U	C	H	A	U	D	Y	P	I
N	X	S	O	L	E	I	L	E	J
T	S	M	A	U	O	R	A	U	O
I	E	B	E	A	U	T	U	R	U
O	A	U	T	O	S	T	O	P	R
N	E	M	P	L	E	T	T	E	S

NOTE TO TEACHER: The mystery word is AMOUR. The scrambled letters that remain uncircled are in the sixth line across: MAUOR.

SCRIPTS

PART FOUR: SKILL IN LISTENING COMPREHENSION

I. Auditory-pictorial stimuli: pp. 436–441

Listen carefully to each question or statement that is read to you based on the pictures shown. Then choose the correct answer and write the letter on the blank line. Each statement or question will be read *twice.*

1. Combien de personnes y a-t-il dans cette photo? (b). 2. Où sont ces personnes? (b). 3. Qui est l'homme entre les deux personnes? (c). **Page 437:** 4. Combien d'enfants y a-t-il dans cette photo? (b). 5. Que font-ils? (b). 6. D'où viennent-ils? (d). 7. Où sont-ils? (d). **Page 438:** There are four pictures on this page. Under each picture there is a letter identifying it. Your teacher will read a series of four statements, numbered 8 to 11. Match each statement that you hear with the appropriate picture by writing the letter of the picture on the blank line. 8. Une mère tient son bébé sur les genoux (c). 9. Un enfant s'amuse sur une balançoire (b). 10. L'homme attrape l'enfant (a). 11. Une mère et son enfant sont dans le champ. Derrière elles, il y a une grande maison (d). **Page 439:** 12. Où se trouve ce monument? (a). 13. Qui a décrété l'érection de ce monument? (a). 14. Quelle avenue termine à cet endroit? (a). 15. Combien d'avenues rayonnent de cette place? (c). 16. Quel tombeau se trouve sous la grande arcade de ce monument? (c). **Page 440:** 17. Qu'est-ce que la jeune femme a dans la main? (b). 18. Et le professeur, qu'est-ce qu'il a dans la main? (b). 19. Qu'est-ce qu'il y a sur la table? (b). **Page 441:** 20. Dans cette photo il y a deux femmes et deux hommes (A). 21. Dans cette photo il y a trois hommes qui vous regardent (C). 22. Il y a des personnes qui vont monter dans un autobus (B). 23. Dans cette photo, vous voyez une dame qui a un menu à la main et un monsieur est assis à une table sur la terrasse d'un café-restaurant (D).

II. Differentiating sounds: p. 442

1. cure (d). 2. peur (d). 3. du (b). 4. vin (c). 5. Dieu (b). 6. ceci (a). 7. heureuse (c). 8. grande (c). 9. deux (c). 10. tu (d). (NOTE TO TEACHER: Here, you may want to choose other words in the groups to pronounce.)

III. Choosing the correct answer to a question: p. 442

Listen carefully to each question. Then choose the correct answer and write the letter on the blank line. Each will be read three times only. 1. Combien de jours y a-t-il dans une semaine? (a). 2. Combien de mois y a-t-il dans une année? (b). 3. Où se trouve l'Arc de Triomphe? (c). 4. Combien font trois et quatre? (b). 5. Quand on dit *merci,* que répond-on? (d). 6. Avec quoi mange-t-on de la soupe? (d). 7. Où Jeanne d'Arc est-elle née? (d). 8. Que fait-on quand on a faim? (d). 9. Quel est le premier mois de l'année? (c). 10. Que prend-on quand il pleut? (b).

IV. Pattern responses: p. 443

1. Janine va à la porte; et vous? (a). 2. Madame Richy lave les chemises; et les autres femmes? (b). 3. Je prends le petit déjeuner tous les matins; et vous? (c). 4. Pierre a peur des lions; de quoi a-t-il peur? (c). 5. J'ai étudié la leçon; et toi? (b). 6. J'ai lu un livre; et Marie? (d). 7. Louis étudie sa leçon; que fait-il? (d). 8. Cette maison est blanche; et le garage? (b).

V. Choosing rejoinders to statements or questions: p. 443

1. Bonjour, Janine. Comment allez-vous aujourd'hui? (c). 2. Je suis bien fatigué. (b). 3. Il fait bien froid aujourd'hui et je dois sortir. (a). 4. La femme refuse d'acheter les pommes; elle dit…(b). 5. Le maître de français dit: Pierre, dis-moi "bonjour"; Pierre répond… (c). 6. La maîtresse de français dit: André, dis "bonjour" à Suzanne; André dit…(d). 7. Quel temps fait-il? (d). 8. La maîtresse de français dit: Charles, demande-moi quel temps il fait; Charles dit…(c).

VI. Choosing the word or words whose meaning completes each statement: p. 444

1. Un bon enfant…(b). 2. Monsieur Bernard ne peut pas marcher parce qu'il est très…(d). 3. Le réveil a sonné et… (c). 4. Pauline ne peut pas ouvrir la porte parce qu'elle a perdu…(b). 5. Le train

va partir et si vous voulez l'attraper…(c). 6. Généralement, on se couche sur…(c). 7. Vous avez les mains sales; allez vous…(a). 8. Le soldat est allé à la guerre pour…(b).

VII. Choosing the word that belongs in the same class as the word that is read to you: p. 444
1. le tigre (c). 2. une fourchette (d). 3. un stylo (c). 4. une rose (c). 5. les oranges (b). 6. la tête (b). 7. une chaussure (c). 8. la cuisine (c).

VIII. Choosing the word that is defined: p. 445
1. La pièce où on prend une douche (d). 2. L'homme qui prépare des gâteaux (d). 3. Le frère de mon père (d). 4. Une personne qui étudie (d). 5. On emploie cette chose pour écrire au tableau noir (b). 6. Un animal qui donne du lait (c). 7. Où on va pour voir des objets d'art (c). 8. C'est un dessert (b).

IX. Choosing the synonym of the word which is pronounced: p. 445
1. le maître (c). 2. rester (a). 3. une faute (d). 4. finir (d). 5. habiter (b). 6. vouloir (c). 7. triste (d). 8. le visage (d).

X. Choosing the idiom or expression whose meaning completes each statement: p. 448
1. Je vais me coucher parce que…(c). 2. Jacques met son pardessus parce qu'il…(b). 3. Je vais ouvrir la fenêtre parce qu'il…(b). 4. Madame Duval ne peut pas entendre bien parce qu'on lui parle…(a). 5. Pierre a fait beaucoup de fautes dans ses devoirs et il va les…(a). 6. Je n'ai pas une voiture, alors je vais…(b). 7. Il n'y a pas de classes aujourd'hui parce que…(d). 8. Ce matin je n'ai pas pris mon petit déjeuner et maintenant…(b).

XI. Choosing the antonym of the word which is pronounced: p. 448
1. froid (d). 2. la beauté (b). 3. facile (b). 4. après (a). 5. la paix (c). 6. acheter (a). 7. faible (c). 8. le bruit (c).

XII. Choosing the word or words that are suggested by the situation described in a sentence: p. 449
1. On attend l'autobus (b). 2. Je vais à la gare maintenant (d). 3. J'ai une leçon de français (d). 4. Madame Ravel fait une promenade tous les jours (c). 5. Pierre Paquet va acheter du pain pour sa mère (b). 6. Madame Banluc est malade aujourd'hui (d). 7. Monsieur et Madame Paquet ont traversé La Manche (a). 8. Janine et Pierre vont s'asseoir sur la terrasse d'un café-restaurant (a).

XIII. True-False statements: p. 449
1. Une vache donne du lait (VRAI). 3. La cerise est un fruit (VRAI). 3. Quand on a soif, on mange (FAUX). 4. Le printemps est une saison (VRAI). 5. Il neige généralement en été (FAUX). 6. Le chat est un animal sauvage (FAUX). 7. Le boucher vend de la viande (VRAI). 8. Il y a soixante minutes dans une heure (VRAI). 9. Jeanne d'Arc est née à Domrémy (VRAI). 10. Six et deux font huit (VRAI).

XIV. Responding to statements on content: p. 449
1. Un jour, un enfant demande à son père de l'argent (a). 2. L'enfant désire donner l'argent à un pauvre homme (d). 3. Son père lui donne dix euros (a). 4. L'enfant est très heureux et il remercie son père (a). 5. L'enfant quitte la maison (b). 6. Il va chercher le pauvre homme pour lui donner les dix euros (b).

XV. Determining who the two speakers are in a short dialogue: p. 450
1. As-tu fait les devoirs pour aujourd'hui, Pierre? Non, monsieur, je n'ai rien fait (c). 2. J'ai mal aux dents, monsieur. Bien, madame, asseyez-vous ici et ouvrez la bouche (a). 3. J'aime beaucoup ta nouvelle robe, Janine. Merci, Monique, elle est jolie, n'est-ce pas? (a). 4. Pour combien vendez-vous ce vase, madame? Pour dix euros, monsieur (c).

PART FIVE: SKILL IN READING COMPREHENSION

I. True-False statements: p. 452
1. vrai. 2. faux. 3. vrai. 4. vrai. 5. faux. 6. faux. 7. faux. 8. faux. 9. vrai. 10. vrai. 11. vrai. 12. vrai. 13. faux. 14. vrai. 15. vrai. 16. faux. 17. faux. 18. vrai. 19. vrai. 20. vrai. 21. vrai. 22. faux. 23. vrai. 24. vrai. 25. vrai.

II. Pictorial stimuli: pp. 453–456
1. (a). 2. (c). 3. (b). 4. (a). 5. (b). 6. (c). 7. (a). 8. (c). 9. (b). 10. (c). 11. (b). 12. (c).

III. p. 457
3, 4, 8, 5, 2, 7, 6, 1, 10, 9.

IV. p. 458
1. oui. 2. non. 3. oui. 4. oui. 5. oui.

V. p. 458
1. (d). 2. (d). 3. (c). 4. (c). 5. (b).

VI. p. 459
1. A. 2. B. 3. A. 4. A. 5. B. 6. B.

VII. p. 460
1. (a). 2. (b). 3. (c). 4. (c). 5. (d). 6. (b). 7. (b). 8. (b). 9. (b). 10. (b).

VIII. Choosing rejoinders to statements or questions: pp. 460–461
1. (c). 2. (b). 3. (a). 4. (b). 5. (c). 6. (d). 7. (d). 8. (c). 9. (c). 10. (d). 11. (c). 12. (d). 13. (a). 14. (c).

IX. Choosing the word or words whose meaning completes a sentence: p. 462
1. (b). 2. (b). 3. (b). 4. (c). 5. (a). 6. (c). 7. (c). 8. (b). 9. (c). 10. (a).

X. Choosing the word that belongs in the same class as the italicized word: pp. 462–463
1. (c). 2. (d). 3. (d). 4. (d). 5. (c). 6. (b). 7. (a). 8. (b). 9. (a). 10. (b).

XI. Choosing the word that is defined or described: p. 463
1. (d). 2. (d). 3. (d). 4. (a). 5. (b). 6. (b). 7. (c). 8. (c). 9. (b). 10. (c).

XII. Choosing the synonym of the italicized word: p. 464
1. (c). 2. (a). 3. (d). 4. (b). 5. (b). 6. (c). 7. (d). 8. (c). 9. (a). 10. (d).

XIII. Choosing the idiom or expression whose meaning completes the sentence: pp. 464–465
1. (b). 2. (b). 3. (d). 4. (c). 5. (b). 6. (b). 7. (a). 8. (d). 9. (c). 10. (a).

XIV. Choosing the antonym of the italicized word: p. 465
1. (d). 2. (a). 3. (a). 4. (d). 5. (a). 6. (b). 7. (a). 8. (b).

XV. Choosing the missing word or words in each sentence that contains a particular structure or idiom: p. 466
1. (c). 2. (c). 3. (a). 4. (d). 5. (d). 6. (b). 7. (d). 8. (d). 9. (c). 10. (a).

XVI. Summarizing: pp. 466–467
1. (c). 2. (d).

XVII. Answering questions on content: pp. 467–468
I. 1. (a). 2. (b). 3. (c). II. 1. (a). 2. (d). 3. (c). 4. (b). III. 1. (c). 2. (d). 3. (a). 4. (b).

DICTÉES AND SCRIPTS

PART SIX: SKILL IN WRITING

I. Copying sentences: p. 470
(NOTE TO TEACHER: This exercise affords the students a chance to develop skill in writing accurately by practice in copying French correctly.)

II. Dictées: p. 470–471
1. Monsieur Paquet cherche son chapeau. Madame Paquet cherche le chapeau dans l'armoire, Janine cherche dans la commode, et Pierre cherche sous le lit. Le chien est sous la commode. **2.** Venez, tout le monde. Venez! Nous pouvons déjeuner sur l'herbe maintenant. Nous allons commencer avec les viandes. **3.** Janine et Pierre allument le téléviseur mais il ne marche pas. Tous les deux sont inquiets parce que l'émission ce soir est *La violence triomphe!* **4.** Pierre est en classe de mathématiques. Il lit un petit mot caché dans les pages de son livre. Il rougit. Il regarde la belle Anne-Marie et elle lui dit tendrement de ses beaux yeux bleus de ne pas révéler leur amour secret. **5.** Aujourd'hui Janine est au marché aux puces avec son amie Monique. Les deux jeunes filles passent la journée au marché parce que c'est très intéressant. (Teacher: These dictées are from the stories and dialogues in this book, starting from the beginning; if you like giving frequent short dictées (which I do), may I suggest—to make your work easier for you—to give short dictées from the other stories and dialogues, especially the proverbs, and guessing games, and riddles.)

III. Writing the word that your teacher reads to you; choosing the word that is the *antonym* of the word you write: p. 471
1. froid (d). 2. toujours (b). 3. tard (a). 4. malheureux (a). 5. vieux (a). 6. mensonge (b). 7. rire (a). 8. mourir (d). 9. finir (b). 10. silence (d).

IV. Combining short sentences into one sentence: pp. 471–472
1. J'ai soif et j'ai faim. 2. Je suis dans la maison parce que je suis malade. 3. La mère et l'enfant sont dans la cuisine. 4. Monsieur Christian est beau et grand. 5. Madame Bernard veut faire un voyage mais elle n'a pas d'argent.

V. Forming a sentence from word cues: p. 472
(NOTE TO TEACHER: This is simple free composition practice and your students will respond in different ways.)

VI. Writing the word that your teacher reads to you; choosing the word that is the *synonym* of the word you write: p. 473
1. vouloir (a). 2. certain (b). 3. heureux (b). 4. chaussure (a). 5. terminer (b). 6. médecin (d). 7. photo (a). 8. costume (a). 9. milieu (b). 10. préférer (b).

VII. Converting sentences: pp. 473–474
(a) 1. Ce livre est facile. 2. Elle est descendue vite. 3. Le garçon a bien mangé. 4. Il a écrit à son ami. 5. Elle a acheté un chapeau. **(b)** 1. Ces femmes sont heureuses. 2. Ces hommes sont beaux. 3. Ces jeunes filles sont jolies. 4. Les garçons ont joué avant d'étudier. 5. Les maîtresses ont corrigé les devoirs.

VIII. Parallel writing: p. 474
(NOTE TO TEACHER: This is simple free composition left to the imagination of the students.)

IX. Writing a substitute for a certain portion of a sentence: p. 475
(NOTE TO TEACHER: This is simple free composition left to the imagination of the students, but let me offer some samples): 1. J'ouvre la fenêtre. 2. Je ferme le livre. 3. Je vais au cinéma ce soir. 4. Mon ami raconte ses expériences dans la classe de français. 5. Il y a du thé dans la tasse. 6. Je

commence la leçon à six heures. 7. Ils écoutent la musique. 8. Mon père m'a donné un beau cadeau. 9. Madame Molet vient me voir demain. 10. Guy lève la chaise.

X. Building a sentence: pp. 475–476
(NOTE TO TEACHER: This is more simple free composition left to the imagination of the students, following the model.)

XI. Writing an appropriate response to one line of dialogue: p. 476
(NOTE TO TEACHER: More simple writing in French left to the imagination of the students, following the model.)
XII. Writing a response which would logically fit in with two lines of dialogue: p. 477
(NOTE TO TEACHER: More practice in writing simple French, following the model.)

XIII. Writing pattern responses: pp. 477–478
1. Je vais à la porte aussi. 2. Je m'assieds près de la fenêtre aussi. 3. Je prends le petit déjeuner tous les matins aussi. 4. J'ai peur des lions aussi. 5. J'ai étudié la leçon aussi. 6. Je lis un livre aussi. 7. Je suis bien fatigué(e) aussi. 8. Je sais jouer du piano aussi. 9. J'ai lu un livre aussi. 10. J'ai faim aussi.

XIV. Writing answers to written questions: p. 478
(NOTE TO TEACHER: More practice in simple French composition requiring personal answers.)

XV. Writing answers to oral questions: p. 478
1. Où êtes-vous allé(e) hier soir? 2. Qu'est-ce que vous avez mangé pour le petit déjeuner ce matin? 3. A quelle heure avez-vous quitté la maison ce matin pour aller à l'école? 4. Est-ce que vous êtes jamais allé(e) en France? 5. A quelle heure êtes-vous arrivé(e) à la maison hier après-midi?

XVI. Answering questions on content: pp. 479–480
(NOTE TO TEACHER: Here are some sample answers): I. 1. Ils vont au café qui se trouve en face du campus. 2. Ils prennent un café, un thé, ou un chocolat chaud. 3. Les amis parlent de leurs cours, de la politique, et de la musique. 4. Quand il fait beau, ils se promènent dans le parc. 5. Quand il fait mauvais, ils vont au cinéma. II. 1. Paul aime la petite rue parce qu'elle est charmante. 2. Quand Paul est en classe, c'est une rue tranquille. 3. Quand il sort de l'école, il y a beaucoup de bruit dans la rue. 4. Il aime bien voir les autos qui passent. 5. Il arrive à l'école en retard parce que souvent il va au grand garage près de sa maison pour regarder les autos. III. 1. Le ciel est bleu. 2. L'arbre berce sa palme. 3. La cloche tinte doucement. 4. L'oiseau chante sa plainte. 5. La paisible rumeur vient de la ville. 6. Non, je pense que le poète est triste.

XVII. Writing three simple sentences as directed: p. 481

XVIII. Writing a question, then answering it: p. 481

XIX. Writing two sentences based on an opening sentence: p. 482
(NOTE TO TEACHER: These last three exercises are practice in writing simple French left to the imagination of the students, following the models in the book.)

XX. Graphic stimuli: p. 482
1. Il est une heure. 2. Il est neuf heures vingt-cinq. 3. Il est trois heures moins un quart (or: moins le quart).

XXI. Pictorial stimuli: pp. 483–484
Sample composition: 1. Dans cette photo, il y a beaucoup de femmes qui dansent. Elles s'amusent beaucoup. Les femmes portent de jolies jupes. 2. Dans cette photo, je vois un homme. Il descend une échelle. Il est possible qu'il monte sur l'échelle. Il est sur le sol lunaire. Il s'appelle Edwin Aldrin, astronaute américain, photographié par Neil Armstrong.

CD Audio Script

INTRODUCTION

Whether you are a beginning student or have some knowledge of French, this program is designed to help you improve your proficiency in listening comprehension, fluency, and pronunciation. It will also increase your vocabulary by leaps and bounds because you will be able to use new words, phrases, and expressions in real-life situations.

Whenever possible, use this audio script with the CDs so you can see the French words you are hearing and saying. However, it is also feasible to listen to the CDs while driving, jogging, and at other times when you can't follow along with the script. If you listen to the CDs separately, read the audio script to preview or review conversations on the CDs, to become familiar with some of the more challenging exercises, and to study the English translations in the column next to the French dialogues, drills, and exercises.

This booklet contains everything you need while using the CDs—the complete audio script, English translations, and supplementary explanations. Ideally, the book and CDs should be used together because they reinforce each other. You will also enjoy and profit from using the book because you can see the illustrations and works of art as you practice speaking in French.

Originally designed for school use in a language laboratory, this is also an easy-to-use self-teaching program that helps you learn just by listening and imitating. All you need is your CD player and a desire to learn. So, enjoy yourself as you learn to speak French—now!

Christopher Kendris, Ph.D.
Theodore Kendris, Ph.D.

P.S. In these three CDs and in the audio script you are practicing over 8,000 French words.

WELCOME

Welcome to Barron's **French Now! Level 1, Fourth Edition,** copyright 2006 by Barron's Educational Series. This self-teaching course is based on selections of conversations and speaking proficiency activities in the 25 Work Units in Barron's book, **French Now! Level 1, Fourth Edition** that you are using. You will have a lot of practice in listening to authentic French and speaking the language you are learning during the pauses. In some units, you will also practice a few verb forms. At the end of each unit, you will hear a chime. This listening and speaking program will help you to improve your French fluency easily and naturally in a variety of situations. Just keep your book open, your CD player handy, and enjoy participating in **French Now! Level 1.**

UNIT 1

Let's begin by reviewing the present indicative tense of two commonly used verbs, **avoir** (to have) and **être** (to be). Let's use **avoir** in the affirmative and negative in simple sentences. Repeat during the pauses. If the pauses seem too short for you, stop your CD player for a longer pause as needed, then resume playing. You can always play the track again to listen to the French and repeat as many times as you wish.

J'ai une orange.	*I have an orange.*
Je n'ai pas une banane.	*I don't have a banana.*
Tu as la pomme.	*You have the apple.*
Tu n'as pas l'orange.	*You don't have the orange.*
Il a le crayon.	*He has the pencil.*
Il n'a pas le stylo.	*He doesn't have the pen.*
Elle a une table.	*She has a table.*
Elle n'a pas une lampe.	*She doesn't have a lamp.*
Nous avons une bicyclette.	*We have a bicycle.*
Nous n'avons pas une voiture.	*We don't have a car.*
Vous avez un téléviseur.	*You have a television.*
Vous n'avez pas une radio.	*You don't have a radio.*
Ils ont un appartement.	*They (masc.) have an apartment.*
Ils n'ont pas une maison.	*They (masc.) don't have a house.*
Elles ont un chat.	*They (fem.) have a cat.*
Elles n'ont pas un chien.	*They (fem.) don't have a dog.*

Now, let's use **être** (to be) in the affirmative and negative in simple sentences.

Je suis le père.	*I am the father.*
Je ne suis pas le fils.	*I am not the son.*
Tu es dans un cinéma.	*You are in a cinema.*
Tu n'es pas dans un théâtre.	*You are not in a theater.*
Il est en France.	*He is in France.*
Il n'est pas en Italie.	*He is not in Italy.*
Elle est dans le garage.	*She is in the garage.*
Elle n'est pas dans la maison.	*She is not in the house.*
Nous sommes dans la salle de classe.	*We are in the classroom.*
Nous ne sommes pas dans la rue.	*We are not in the street.*
Vous êtes dans le salon.	*You are in the living room.*

Vous n'êtes pas dans la salle à manger.	*You are not in the dining room.*
Ils sont petits.	*They (masc.) are short (small).*
Ils ne sont pas grands.	*They (masc.) are not tall (big).*
Elles sont grandes.	*They (fem.) are tall (big).*
Elles ne sont pas petites.	*They (fem.) are not short (small).*

Situation: You are at a table in a restaurant deciding what to eat and drink. You are talking with the server. First, listen to this conversation.

Bonjour! Vous désirez?	*Hello (Good day)! You desire? (You would like?)*
Je désire un sandwich.	*I'd like a sandwich.*
Un sandwich au jambon?	*A ham sandwich?*
Oui, un sandwich au jambon, s'il vous plaît.	*Yes, a ham sandwich, please.*
Et avec le sandwich?	*And with the sandwich?*
Une tasse de café? Avec crème? Sucre?	*A cup of coffee? With cream? Sugar?*
Et avec le sandwich au jambon, une tasse de café avec crème et sucre.	*And with the ham sandwich, a cup of coffee with cream and sugar.*
Vous désirez un fruit?	*Do you want a fruit?*
Je désire une pomme et une banane.	*I want an apple and a banana.*

Now, listen to the conversation again and repeat during the pauses.

Bonjour! Vous désirez? / Je désire un sandwich. / Un sandwich au jambon? / Oui, un sandwich au jambon, s'il vous plaît. / Et avec le sandwich? Une tasse de café? Avec crème? Sucre? / Et avec le sandwich au jambon, une tasse de café avec crème et sucre. / Vous désirez un fruit? / Je désire une pomme et une banane.

Now, during the pause, give an appropriate response in French when you hear the cue in English. After the pause, you will hear a confirmation so you can check what you said. During the second pause, correct yourself by repeating what you heard.

Bonjour! Vous désirez?	
Say that you want a sandwich.	Je désire un sandwich.
Un sandwich au jambon?	
Say: Yes, a ham sandwich, please.	Oui, un sandwich au jambon, s'il vous plaît.
Et avec le sandwich? Une tasse de café? Avec crème? Sucre?	
Say: And with the ham sandwich, a cup of coffee with cream and sugar.	Et avec le sandwich au jambon, une tasse de café avec crème et sucre.
Vous désirez un fruit?	
Say that you want an apple and a banana.	Je désire une pomme et une banane.

UNIT 2

During the pause, respond in French when you hear the cue in English. After the pause, you will hear a confirmation in French so you can check what you said. During the second pause, correct yourself by repeating what you heard.

Janine is going to the station.	Janine va à la gare.
Pierre is coming from the restaurant.	Pierre vient du restaurant.

Mrs. Paquet is coming from the department stores.	Madame Paquet vient des grands magasins.
Janine is coming from the library.	Janine vient de la bibliothèque.
Pierre is coming from the school.	Pierre vient de l'école.
Mrs. Paquet is giving a candy to the child.	Madame Paquet donne un bonbon à l'enfant.
Janine is going to the café.	Janine va au café.
Mrs. Paquet is going to the department stores.	Madame Paquet va aux grands magasins.

Situation: Your friend Janine is visiting you in your house. She is always asking questions. First, listen to this conversation.

Dis-moi, dans cette photo, qui est la femme qui mange?	*Tell me, in this photo, who is the woman who is eating?*
C'est ma tante Sophie. Elle mange tout le temps.	*It's my aunt Sophie. She eats all the time.*
Et ce parapluie sur le lit?	*And this umbrella on the bed?*
C'est le parapluie de ma mère.	*It's my mother's umbrella.*
Et les gants sous la chaise?	*And the gloves under the chair?*
Ce sont les gants de mon père.	*They are my father's gloves.*

Now, during the pause, give an appropriate response in French when you hear the question. After the pause, you will hear a confirmation so you can check what you said. During the second pause, correct yourself by repeating what you heard.

Dis-moi, dans cette photo, qui est la femme qui mange?
C'est ma tante Sophie. Elle mange tout le temps.
Et ce parapluie sur le lit?
C'est le parapluie de ma mère.
Et les gants sous la chaise?
Ce sont les gants de mon père.

UNIT 3

In this speaking exercise, you will practice the partitive. When you hear the English cue, say it in French. After you hear the confirmation, check what you said. During the second pause, correct yourself by repeating what you heard.

I have some coffee.	J'ai du café.
I have some meat.	J'ai de la viande.
Do you want some water?	Vous désirez de l'eau?
She doesn't have any coffee?	Elle n'a pas de café?
We don't have any meat?	Nous n'avons pas de viande?
You have some candies.	Vous avez des bonbons.
She doesn't have any candies.	Elle n'a pas de bonbons.
Suzanne has pretty hats.	Suzanne a de jolis chapeaux.
We have neither eclairs nor tarts.	Nous n'avons ni éclairs ni tartes.

Situation: You are at a party where there are five foreign exchange students. Janine and Pierre are there. You are introducing them to the new students. After you hear the statement in French, make your two statements during the first pause. During the second pause, correct yourself by repeating what you heard. Follow this model:

Jacques est de France.	*Jacques is from France.*
Il parle français.	*He speaks French.*
Il prononce bien le français.	*He pronounces French well.*
Louis est de France.	*Louis is from France.*
Il parle français.	*He speaks French.*
Il prononce bien le français.	*He pronounces French well.*
María est d'Espagne.	*María is from Spain.*
Elle parle espagnol.	*She speaks Spanish.*
Elle prononce bien l'espagnol.	*She pronounces Spanish well.*
Rosa est d'Italie.	*Rosa is from Italy.*
Elle parle italien.	*She speaks Italian.*
Elle prononce bien l'italien.	*She pronounces Italian well.*
Ian est d'Angleterre.	*Ian is from England.*
Il parle anglais.	*He speaks English.*
Il prononce bien l'anglais.	*He pronounces English well.*
Marlena est d'Allemagne.	*Marlena is from Germany.*
Elle parle allemand.	*She speaks German.*
Elle prononce bien l'allemand.	*She pronounces German well.*

Now, listen to this conversation between a clerk and a customer in a pastry shop, **dans une pâtisserie.**

Bonjour, monsieur. Vous désirez?	*Good day, sir. What would you like?*
Bonjour, madame. J'aimerais un grand gâteau au chocolat, s'il vous plaît.	*Good day, madam. I would like a big chocolate cake, please.*
Bien, monsieur. Et avec ceci?	*Okay, sir. And with this?*
Avec ceci, j'aimerais deux éclairs et deux tartes aux pommes.	*With this, I would like two eclairs and two apple tarts.*
Bien, monsieur. C'est tout?	*Okay, sir. Is that all?*
Oui, c'est tout, merci.	*Yes, that's all, thank you.*
Vous pouvez payer à la caisse. Merci, monsieur.	*You may pay at the cash register. Thank you, sir.*
Au revoir, monsieur!	*Good-bye, sir!*
Au revoir, madame!	*Good-bye, madam.*

Now, during the pause, give an appropriate response in French when you hear the question. After the pause, you will hear a confirmation so you can check what you said. During the second pause, correct yourself by repeating what you heard.

Bonjour, monsieur. Vous désirez?
Bonjour, madame. J'aimerais un grand gâteau au chocolat, s'il vous plaît.
Bien, monsieur. Et avec ceci?
Avec ceci, j'aimerais deux éclairs et deux tartes aux pommes.
Bien, monsieur. C'est tout?
Oui, c'est tout, merci.
Vous pouvez payer à la caisse. Merci, monsieur. Au revoir, monsieur!
Au revoir, madame!

UNIT 4

Let's practice the present indicative tense of a regular -er verb:

danser, *to dance*

After you hear the subject, there will be a short pause. During the pause, state the verb form. After the pause, you will hear a confirmation. During the second pause, repeat what you heard.

danser   *to dance*

je / je danse	*I / I dance, I am dancing, I do dance*
tu / tu danses	*you / you dance, you are dancing, you do dance*
il / il danse	*he / he dances, he is dancing, he does dance*
elle / elle danse	*she / she dances, she is dancing, she does dance*
nous / nous dansons	*we / we dance, we are dancing, we do dance*
vous / vous dansez	*you / you dance, you are dancing, you do dance*
ils / ils dansent	*they (masc.) / they dance, they are dancing, they do dance*
elles / elles dansent	*they (fem.) / they dance, they are dancing, they do dance*

Now, let's practice a few commonly used regular -er verbs in the present tense. Answer the following questions in the affirmative. During the first pause, answer the question. After the pause, you will hear a confirmation. During the second pause, repeat what you heard. Follow this model:

Chantez-vous?	*Do you sing?*
Oui, je chante.	*Yes, I sing.*
Et les enfants?	*And the children?*
Ils chantent aussi.	*They sing also.*
Dansez-vous?	*Do you dance?*
Oui, je danse.	*Yes, I dance.*
Et les enfants?	*And the children?*
Ils dansent aussi.	*They dance also.*
Pierre cherche-t-il le chapeau de son père?	*Is Pierre looking for his father's hat?*
Oui, il cherche le chapeau de son père.	*Yes, he's looking for his father's hat.*
Et Janine?	*And Janine?*
Elle cherche le chapeau de son père aussi.	*She's looking for her father's hat also.*
Hélène étudie-t-elle la leçon?	*Is Helen studying the lesson?*
Oui, elle étudie la leçon.	*Yes, she is studying the lesson.*
Et Robert?	*And Robert?*
Il étudie la leçon aussi.	*He is studying the lesson also.*
Écoutes-tu la musique?	*Are you listening to the music?*
Oui, j'écoute la musique.	*Yes, I'm listening to the music.*
Et les enfants?	*And the children?*
Ils écoutent la musique aussi.	*They are listening to the music also.*
Est-ce que vous fermez les fenêtres dans la maison?	*Are you closing the windows in the house?*
Oui, je ferme les fenêtres dans la maison.	*Yes, I'm closing the windows in the house.*
Et Suzanne?	*And Suzanne?*
Elle ferme les fenêtres dans la maison aussi.	*She is closing the windows in the house also.*

Now, let's look at the painting of Madame Georges Charpentier and her children by Renoir in your book. During the pause, answer the question. After the pause, you will hear a confirmation. During the second pause, repeat what you heard.

Qui est la femme?	*Who is the woman?*
C'est Madame Georges Charpentier. Elle est belle. Elle est heureuse.	*It's Mrs. George Charpentier. She is beautiful. She is happy.*
Combien d'enfants y a-t-il dans ce tableau?	*How many children are there in this painting?*
Il y a deux enfants dans ce tableau.	*There are two children in this painting.*
Est-ce que le chien est grand ou petit?	*Is the dog big or small?*
Le chien est grand.	*The dog is big.*
Aimez-vous ce tableau?	*Do you like this painting?*
Oui, j'aime beaucoup ce tableau.	*Yes, I like this painting a lot.*

UNIT 5

Let's practice the present indicative tense of a regular -ir verb:

finir, *to finish*

After you hear the subject, there will be a short pause. During the pause, state the verb form. After the pause, you will hear a confirmation. During the second pause, repeat what you heard. These verb forms are in your book.

finir   *to finish*

je / je finis	*I / I finish, I am finishing, I do finish*
tu / tu finis	*you / you finish, you are finishing, you do finish*
il / il finit	*he / he finishes, he is finishing, he does finish*
elle / elle finit	*she / she finishes, she is finishing, she does finish*
nous / nous finissons	*we / we finish, we are finishing, we do finish*
vous / vous finissez	*you / you finish, you are finishing, you do finish*
ils / ils finissent	*they (masc.) / they finish, they are finishing, they do finish*
elles / elles finissent	*they (fem.) / they finish, they are finishing, they do finish*

Now, let's practice a few commonly used regular -ir verbs in the present tense. They are in your book. Answer the following questions in the negative. They are in your book.

Est-ce que vous finissez la leçon?	*Are you finishing the lesson?*
Non, je ne finis pas la leçon.	*No, I am not finishing the lesson.*
Et Jacques?	*And Jacques?*
Il ne finit pas la leçon non plus.	*He is not finishing the lesson either.*
Est-ce qu'Henri désobéit?	*Does Henry disobey?*
Non, il ne désobéit pas.	*No, he does not disobey.*
Et les enfants?	*And the children?*
Ils ne désobéissent pas non plus.	*They do not disobey either.*
Est-ce que Monsieur Paquet choisit une auto?	*Is Mr. Paquet choosing a car?*
Non, il ne choisit pas une auto.	*No, he is not choosing a car.*
Et vous?	*And you?*
Je ne choisis pas une auto non plus.	*I am not choosing a car either.*

Rougissez-vous?	*Do you blush?*
Non, je ne rougis pas.	*No, I don't blush.*
Et les jeunes filles?	*And the girls?*
Elles ne rougissent pas non plus.	*They don't blush either.*

Now, let's look at the picture of the statue *Le Penseur* by Rodin in your book. When you hear the cue in English, say it in French during the pause. Then you will hear a confirmation. During the second pause, repeat what you heard.

It's a magnificent work of art.	C'est une oeuvre d'art magnifique.
I think that this statue is the most beautiful of all the works of Rodin.	Je pense que cette statue est la plus belle de toutes les oeuvres de Rodin.
It's a great joy to look at this statue.	C'est une grande joie de regarder cette statue.

Now, let's look at the young woman in the painting *Octobre* by Jean-Jacques Tissot. This practice is in your book. When you hear the cue in English, say it in French during the pause. Then you will hear a confirmation. During the second pause, repeat what you heard.

The painting by Tissot, French artist, is superb.	Le tableau de Tissot, artiste français, est superbe.
The young woman is beautiful.	La jeune femme est belle.
She has beautiful eyes.	Elle a de beaux yeux.
She is taking a walk.	Elle fait une promenade.

UNIT 6

CD 1
TRACK
7

Let's practice the present indicative tense of a regular **-re** verb:

vendre, *to sell*

After you hear the subject, there will be a short pause. During the pause, state the verb form. Then you will hear a confirmation. During the second pause, repeat what you heard. These verb forms are in your book.

vendre   *to sell*

je / je vends	*I / I sell, I am selling, I do sell*
tu / tu vends	*you / you sell, you are selling, you do sell*
il / il vend	*he / he sells, he is selling, he does sell*
elle / elle vend	*she / she sells, she is selling, she does sell*
Janine / Janine vend	*Janine sells, is selling, does sell*
nous / nous vendons	*we / we sell, we are selling, we do sell*
vous / vous vendez	*you / you sell, you are selling, you do sell*
ils / ils vendent	*they (masc.) / they sell, they are selling, they do sell*
elles / elles vendent	*they (fem.) / they sell, they are selling, they do sell*
Janine et Pierre vendent	*Janine and Pierre sell, are selling, do sell*

Now, let's practice a few commonly used regular **-re** verbs in the present tense. They are in your book. Answer the following questions in the affirmative.

La dame répond-elle au téléphone?	*Is the lady answering the telephone?*
Oui, elle répond au téléphone.	*Yes, she is answering the telephone.*
Et les dames?	*And the ladies?*

Elles répondent au téléphone aussi.	*They are answering the telephone also.*
Pierre répond-il à la lettre?	*Is Pierre answering the letter?*
Oui, il répond à la lettre.	*Yes, he is answering the letter.*
Et vous?	*And you?*
Je réponds à la lettre aussi.	*I am answering the letter also.*
Monsieur Coty vend-il la maison?	*Is Mr. Coty selling the house?*
Oui, il vend la maison.	*Yes, he is selling the house.*
Et Monsieur et Madame Dupont?	*And Mr. and Mrs. Dupont?*
Ils vendent la maison aussi.	*They are selling the house also.*

Now, here are a few questions that are not in your book. Try them for practice.

Attendez-vous l'autobus?	*Are you waiting for the bus?*
Oui, j'attends l'autobus.	*Yes, I am waiting for the bus.*
Et Caroline?	*And Caroline?*
Elle attend l'autobus aussi.	*She is waiting for the bus also.*
Les enfants entendent-ils la musique?	*Do the children hear the music?*
Oui, ils entendent la musique.	*Yes, they hear the music.*
Et vous?	*And you?*
J'entends la musique aussi.	*I hear the music also.*
Descendez-vous?	*Are you going down?*
Oui, je descends.	*Yes, I'm going down.*
Et les amis?	*And the friends?*
Ils descendent aussi.	*They are going down also.*

Situation: You are on an educational tour in Paris with a group of students from your school. Your guide is Madame Durand, who is a professor at the Université de Paris. You have been asking her questions about Paris. Now she has a few questions to ask you because she is impressed with your ability to speak French. First, listen to this conversation. It is also in your book.

Vous parlez français extraordinairement bien.	*You speak French extraordinarily well.*
Merci, madame.	*Thank you, madam.*
Depuis combien de temps étudiez-vous le français?	*How long have you been studying French?*
J'étudie le français depuis un an.	*I have been studying French for one year.*
Vous êtes extraordinaire! Où habitez-vous?	*You are extraordinary! Where do you live?*
J'habite aux États-Unis dans la ville de New York.	*I live in the United States in the city of New York.*
Aimez-vous mon pays?	*Do you like my country?*
J'aime beaucoup votre pays, la langue française, les Français, la culture française, la musique, et l'art français.	*I like your country a lot, the French language, the French people, French culture, music, and French art.*
Merci, Bon. Maintenant, nous allons au marché aux puces. Venez, tout le monde!	*Thank you. Good. Now, we are going to the flea market. Come along, everybody!*
Où allons-nous?	*Where are we going?*
Nous allons au marché aux puces?!	*We are going to the flea market?!*
C'est ça! Bravo!	*That's right! Bravo!*
Quel est le mot pour *flea* en français?	*What is the word for* flea *in French?*
Le mot est "la puce." Allons! Attention aux puces!	*The word is "la puce." Let's go! Watch out for the fleas!*

9

Now, listen to the conversation again. Answer these questions during the pause. Then you will hear a confirmation. During the second pause, repeat what you heard.

Vous parlez français extraordinairement bien.	*You speak French extraordinarily well.*
Merci, madame.	*Thank you, madam.*
Depuis combien de temps étudiez-vous le français?	*How long have you been studying French?*
J'étudie le français depuis un an.	*I have been studying French for one year.*
Vous êtes extraordinaire! Où habitez-vous?	*You are extraordinary! Where do you live?*
J'habite aux États-Unis dans la ville de New York.	*I live in the United States in the city of New York.*
Aimez-vous mon pays?	*Do you like my country?*
J'aime beaucoup votre pays,	*I like your country very much,*
la langue française,	*the French language,*
les Français,	*the French people,*
la culture française,	*French culture,*
la musique,	*music,*
et l'art français.	*and French art.*
Merci. Bon. Maintenant, nous allons au marché aux puces. Venez, tout le monde!	*Thank you. Good. Now, we are going to the flea market. Come along, everybody!*
Où allons-nous?	*Where are we going?*
Nous allons au marché aux puces?!	*We are going to the flea market?!*
C'est ça! Bravo!	*That's right! Bravo!*
Quel est le mot pour *flea* en français?	*What is the word for* flea *in French?*
Le mot est "la puce." Allons!	*The word is "la puce." Let's go!*
Attention aux puces!	*Watch out for the fleas!*

UNIT 7

This practice in listening and speaking is in your book. First, listen to the narration.

Pierre aime les sports. Son sport favori est le football. Il veut être toujours en forme parce qu'il est gardien de but dans son équipe à l'école. Il veut être toujours prêt à bien jouer. Il est au régime. Il mange seulement des aliments qui sont bons pour la santé. Pendant la saison de football, il évite les glaces, les pommes frites, et les pâtisseries. C'est un brave garçon! Pierre se couche de bonne heure. Il se lève avec le soleil. Il se lave soigneusement. Il s'habille vite. Et il prend le petit déjeuner.

Pierre likes sports. His favorite sport is soccer. He always wants to be in shape because he is the goalie for his team at school. He wants to be always ready to play well. He is on a diet. He eats only foods that are good for health. During soccer season, he avoids ice cream, French fries, and pastries. He's a fine boy! Pierre goes to bed early. He gets up with the sun. He washes himself carefully. He dresses himself quickly. And he has breakfast.

Listen to the narration again, paying special attention to the reflexive verbs. Now, listen to the narration again and repeat during the pauses.

Pierre aime les sports. / Son sport favori est le football. / Il veut être toujours en forme parce qu'il est gardien de but / dans son équipe / à l'école. / Il veut être toujours prêt / à bien jouer. / Il est au régime. / Il mange seulement des aliments / qui sont bons pour la santé. / Pendant la saison de football, / il évite les glaces, / les pommes frites, / et les pâtisseries. / C'est un brave garçon! / Pierre se couche de bonne heure. / Il se lève avec le soleil. / Il se lave soigneusement. / Il s'habille vite. / Et il prend le petit déjeuner.

Now, during the pause, answer these questions. Then you will hear a confirmation. During the second pause, correct yourself by repeating what you heard.

Quel est le sport favori de Pierre?	*What is Pierre's favorite sport?*
Le sport favori de Pierre est le football.	*Pierre's favorite sport is soccer.*
Pourquoi veut-il être toujours en forme?	*Why does he always want to be in shape?*
Il veut être toujours en forme parce qu'il est gardien de but dans son équipe à l'école.	*He always wants to be in shape because he is the goalie for his team at school.*
Quels aliments mange-t-il?	*What foods does he eat?*
Il mange seulement des aliments qui sont bons pour la santé.	*He eats only foods that are good for health.*
Se lève-t-il tard le matin?	*Does he get up late in the morning?*
Non. Il se lève avec le soleil.	*No. He gets up with the sun.*

Now, let's practice the present tense of the reflexive verb **se laver,** *to wash oneself.* After you hear the subject, there will be a short pause. During the pause, state the verb form with the subject in the affirmative and negative. Then you will hear a confirmation. During the second pause, correct yourself by repeating what you heard. These verb forms are in your book.

se laver	*to wash oneself*
je / je me lave; je ne me lave pas	*I / I wash myself; I don't wash myself*
tu / tu te laves; tu ne te laves pas	*you / you wash yourself; you don't wash yourself*
il / il se lave; il ne se lave pas	*he / he washes himself; he doesn't wash himself*
Pierre / Pierre se lave; Pierre ne se lave pas	*Pierre washes himself; Pierre doesn't wash himself*
elle / elle se lave; elle ne se lave pas	*she / she washes herself; she doesn't wash herself*
nous / nous nous lavons; nous ne nous lavons pas	*we / we wash ourselves; we don't wash ourselves*
vous / vous vous lavez; vous ne vous lavez pas	*you / you wash yourself; you don't wash yourself*
ils / ils se lavent; ils ne se lavent pas	*they (masc.) / they wash themselves; they don't wash themselves.*
elles / elles se lavent; elles ne se lavent pas	*they (fem.) / they wash themselves; they don't wash themselves*
les enfants / les enfants se lavent; les enfants ne se lavent pas	*the children wash themselves; the children don't wash themselves*

Now, let's practice a few irregular and regular reflexive verbs in the present tense. They are in your book. Answer these questions in the affirmative.

Vous asseyez-vous ici?	*Are you sitting here?*
Oui. Je m'assieds ici.	*Yes. I'm sitting here.*
T'endors-tu facilement?	*Do you fall asleep easily?*
Oui. Je m'endors facilement.	*Yes. I fall asleep easily.*
Vous amusez-vous dans la classe de français?	*Do you have fun (do you amuse yourself) in French class?*
Oui. Je m'amuse dans la classe de français.	*Yes. I have fun (I amuse myself) in French class.*

UNIT 8

Let's practice some cardinal numbers. They are in your book. Repeat during the short pause.

zéro, un, deux, trois	*zero, one, two, three*
quatre, cinq, six	*four, five, six*
sept, huit, neuf, dix	*seven, eight, nine, ten*
onze, douze, treize	*eleven, twelve, thirteen*
quatorze, quinze, seize	*fourteen, fifteen, sixteen*
dix-sept, dix-huit	*seventeen, eighteen*
dix-neuf, vingt	*nineteen, twenty*
vingt et un, vingt-deux	*twenty-one, twenty-two*
trente, trente et un	*thirty, thirty-one*
trente-deux, quarante	*thirty-two, forty*
cinquante, soixante	*fifty, sixty*
soixante-dix	*seventy*
quatre-vingts	*eighty*
quatre-vingt-dix, cent	*ninety, one hundred*

Now, let's practice some simple arithmetical expressions in your book.

deux et deux font quatre	*two and two are (make) four*
trois fois cinq font quinze	*three times five are (make) fifteen*
douze moins dix font deux	*twelve minus ten are (make) two*
dix divisés par deux font cinq	*ten divided by two are (make) five*

And now, some fractions.

un demi	*a (one) half*
un tiers	*a (one) third*
un quart	*a (one) fourth*
un cinquième	*a (one) fifth*

Now, some approximate amounts.

une dizaine	*about ten*
une quinzaine	*about fifteen*
une vingtaine	*about twenty*
une trentaine	*about thirty*
une quarantaine	*about forty*

Let's practice some ordinal numbers.

premier, première	*first (masc.), first (fem.)*
deuxième	*second*
troisième, quatrième	*third, fourth*
cinquième, sixième	*fifth, sixth*
septième, huitième	*seventh, eighth*
neuvième, dixième	*ninth, tenth*

Situation: Catherine is with a friend at an auction salesroom because she wants to buy a small round table for her bedroom. First, listen to this conversation.

Aimes-tu la petite table ronde, Catherine?	*Do you like the little round table, Catherine?*
J'aime la petite table ronde mais je n'aime pas les mouches dans cette salle des ventes.	*I like the little round table but I don't like the flies in this salesroom.*
Oui. Les mouches dans cette salle des ventes sont terribles!	*Yes. The flies in this salesroom are terrible!*
Qui est la dame au premier rang qui offre soixante francs pour le fauteuil monstrueux?	*Who is the lady in the first row who is offering sixty francs for the monstrous armchair?*
Je ne sais pas. Elle doit être folle!	*I don't know. She must be crazy!*
Sûrement, elle doit être folle!	*Surely, she must be crazy!*
Alors, tu désires acheter la petite table ronde?	*Well, do you want to buy the little round table?*
Oui, elle est parfaite pour ma chambre.	*Yes, it is perfect for my room.*
As-tu assez d'argent, Catherine?	*Do you have enough money, Catherine?*
Oui, j'ai assez d'argent. Je vais offrir deux cents euros.	*Yes, I have enough money. I am going to offer two hundred euros.*
Tu vas offrir deux cents euros?! C'est trop!	*You're going to offer two hundred euros?! It's too much!*

(She raises her hand to shoo away the flies and the auctioneer thinks she's making a bid.)

Oh, ces mouches! Filez! Filez!	*Oh, these flies! Shoo! Shoo!*
Si tu offres deux cents euros, tu es folle aussi.	*If you offer two hundred euros, you're crazy, too!*
N'importe. La petite table ronde est parfaite pour ma chambre.	*It doesn't matter. The little round table is perfect for my room.*

Now, answer these questions during the pause. Then you will hear a confirmation. During the second pause, repeat what you heard. Before you answer these questions, you may want to listen to the conversation again.

Qui aime la petite table ronde?	*Who likes the little round table?*
Catherine aime la petite table ronde.	*Catherine likes the little round table.*
Est-ce qu'elle aime les mouches dans la salle des ventes?	*Does she like the flies in the salesroom?*
Non. Elle n'aime pas les mouches dans la salle des ventes.	*No. She doesn't like the flies in the salesroom.*
Pourquoi n'aime-t-elle pas les mouches?	*Why doesn't she like the flies?*
Elles sont terribles!	*They are terrible!*
Est-ce que Catherine désire acheter la petite table ronde?	*Does Catherine want to buy the little round table?*
Oui. Elle désire acheter la petite table ronde.	*Yes. She wants to buy the little round table.*
Pourquoi?	*Why?*
Elle est parfaite pour sa chambre.	*It is perfect for her room.*
A-t-elle assez d'argent?	*Does she have enough money?*
Oui. Elle a assez d'argent.	*Yes. She has enough money.*
Combien d'argent Catherine va-t-elle offrir pour la petite table?	*How much money is Catherine going to offer for the little table?*
Elle va offrir deux cents euros.	*She is going to offer two hundred euros.*

UNIT 9

This practice in listening and speaking is in your book. First, listen to the narration.

La famille Paquet fait des préparations pour un voyage en avion aux États-Unis. Madame Paquet a une soeur qui habite à La Nouvelle-Orléans avec son mari et ses trois enfants. Maintenant, ils font les valises et dans quelques minutes ils vont quitter la maison pour aller à l'aéroport Charles de Gaulle. Quelle heure est-il? Il est huit heures. Il faut se dépêcher. L'avion va partir dans deux heures. Madame Paquet est très heureuse parce qu'elle va revoir sa soeur. Janine et Pierre sont heureux aussi parce qu'ils vont voir leurs cousins pour la première fois. Monsieur Paquet est heureux parce qu'il va voir la Louisiane. Ils montent dans le taxi et dans quelques minutes ils arrivent à l'aéroport.

The Paquet family is making preparations for a trip by airplane to the United States. Mrs. Paquet has a sister who lives in New Orleans with her husband and her three children. Now, they are packing the suitcases and in a few minutes they are going to leave the house to go to the Charles de Gaulle Airport. What time is it? It is eight o'clock. We have to hurry. The plane is going to leave in two hours. Mrs. Paquet is very happy because she's going to see her sister again. Janine and Pierre are happy too because they're going to see their cousins for the first time. Mr. Paquet is happy because he's going to see Louisiana. They get into the taxi and in a few minutes they arrive at the airport.

Now, listen to the narration again and repeat during the pauses.

La famille Paquet fait des préparations / pour un voyage en avion aux États-Unis./ Madame Paquet a une soeur / qui habite à La Nouvelle-Orléans / avec son mari et ses trois enfants. / Maintenant, ils font les valises / et dans quelques minutes / ils vont quitter la maison / pour aller à l'aéroport Charles de Gaulle. / Quelle heure est-il? / Il est huit heures. / Il faut se dépêcher. / L'avion va partir dans deux heures. / Madame Paquet est très heureuse / parce qu'elle va revoir sa soeur. / Janine et Pierre sont heureux aussi / parce qu'ils vont voir leurs cousins / pour la première fois. / Monsieur Paquet est heureux / parce qu'il va voir la Louisiane. / Ils montent dans le taxi / et dans quelques minutes / ils arrivent à l'aéroport.

Now, during the pause, answer these questions. After the pause you will hear a confirmation. During the second pause, correct yourself by repeating what you heard.

Est-ce que la famille va faire un voyage aux États-Unis en avion?

Is the Paquet family going to take a trip to the United States by plane?

Oui. La famille va faire un voyage aux États-Unis en avion.

Yes. The family is going to take a trip to the United States by plane.

Où habite la soeur de Madame Paquet?

Where does Mrs. Paquet's sister live?

Elle habite à La Nouvelle-Orléans.

She lives in New Orleans.

Comment s'appelle l'aéroport?

What is the name of the airport?

L'aéroport s'appelle Charles de Gaulle.

The name of the airport is Charles de Gaulle.

Quelle heure est-il?

What time is it?

Il est huit heures.

It is eight o'clock.

Pourquoi faut-il se dépêcher?

Why is it necessary to hurry?

Il faut se dépêcher parce que l'avion va partir dans deux heures.

It's necessary to hurry because the plane is going to leave in two hours.

Pourquoi Madame Paquet est-elle très heureuse?

Why is Mrs. Paquet very happy?

Elle est très heureuse parce qu'elle va revoir sa soeur.	*She is very happy because she is going to see her sister again.*
Et Janine et Pierre? Pourquoi sont-ils heureux aussi?	*And Janine and Pierre? Why are they happy also?*
Ils sont heureux parce qu'ils vont voir leurs cousins.	*They are happy because they are going to see their cousins.*
Et Monsieur Paquet? Pourquoi est-il heureux?	*And Mr. Paquet? Why is he happy?*
Il est heureux parce qu'il va voir la Louisiane.	*He is happy because he is going to see Louisiana.*

Now, let's practice telling time. When you hear the cue in English, say it in French during the pause. Then you will hear a confirmation. During the second pause, repeat what you heard.

What time is it?	Quelle heure est-il?
It is one o'clock.	Il est une heure.
It is ten minutes after one.	Il est une heure dix.
It is a quarter after one.	Il est une heure et quart.
It is half past two.	Il est deux heures et demie.
At what time?	À quelle heure?
At nine in the morning.	À neuf heures du matin.

Now, let's practice dates, ages, months of the year, days of the week, and seasons of the year.

What's the date today?	Quelle est la date aujourd'hui?
Today is May first.	C'est aujourd'hui le premier mai.
Today is June second.	C'est aujourd'hui le deux juin.
How old are you?	Quel âge avez-vous?
I am twenty-five years old.	J'ai vingt-cinq ans.

Here, repeat the French during the pause.

Les mois de l'année sont	*The months of the year are*
janvier, février, mars,	*January, February, March,*
avril, mai, juin,	*April, May, June,*
juillet, août, septembre,	*July, August, September,*
octobre, novembre,	*October, November,*
décembre.	*December.*
Les jours de la semaine sont	*The days of the week are*
dimanche, lundi,	*Sunday, Monday,*
mardi, mercredi,	*Tuesday, Wednesday,*
jeudi, vendredi,	*Thursday, Friday,*
samedi.	*Saturday.*
Les saisons de l'année sont	*The seasons of the year are*
le printemps, l'été,	*spring, summer,*
l'automne, l'hiver.	*autumn, winter.*

Situation: Your friend and her family are planning a trip to France. This practice in speaking is a variation of the conversation in your book. When you hear the cue in English, say it in French during the pause. After the pause, you will hear a confirmation so you can check what you said. During the second pause, correct yourself by repeating what you heard.

Hi, Luc! How are you?	Salut, Luc! Comment vas-tu?
Not bad. And you? What's new?	Pas mal. Et toi? Quoi de neuf?
Very well, thank you. I'm going to take a trip to France with my family.	Très bien, merci. Je vais faire un voyage en France avec ma famille.
That's great!	C'est formidable!
When are you going to leave?	Quand allez-vous partir?
We are going to leave Thursday, April fourth.	Nous allons partir jeudi, le quatre avril.
Are you going to leave by plane or by boat?	Allez-vous partir en avion ou en bateau?
We are going to leave by plane. On AIR FRANCE.	Nous allons partir en avion. Sur AIR FRANCE.
At what time are you going to leave?	À quelle heure allez-vous partir?
We are going to leave at 11 o'clock in the evening.	Nous allons partir à onze heures du soir.
You're lucky! Have a good trip!	Tu as de la chance! Bon voyage!

UNIT 10

This episode of the talent show at school is in your book. First, listen to the narration.

C'est aujourd'hui vendredi. C'est le grand jour du concours de talents dans la grande salle de l'école. Il y a des étudiants qui vont chanter, danser, faire des tours de force et des tours de main, jouer d'un instrument de musique, et raconter des contes drôles. Janine et Pierre sont dans le concours de talents, aussi. Pierre est le magicien et Janine est l'assistante. Ils préparent leur représentation. Donne-moi mon chapeau haut de forme, Janine. Je n'ai pas ton chapeau haut de forme, Pierre. Apporte-moi mon bâton. Je n'ai pas ton bâton. Donne-moi ma cape. Je n'ai pas ta cape. Apporte-moi le lapin. Je n'ai pas le lapin. En ce moment, quelques spectateurs dans la grande salle crient: Dansez! Chantez! Faites quelque chose! Ce sont les étudiants, les maîtres, et les maîtresses qui crient. Zut, alors! Ne finissons pas, Janine. Nous n'avons pas le chapeau haut de forme, le bâton, la cape, et le lapin. Ne choisis pas cette alternative, Pierre. Alors, restons-nous ou partons-nous? Il faut faire quelque chose! Allez-vous faire quelque chose, enfin?! demandent tous les spectateurs. Ne réponds pas, Janine. Tout d'un coup, Coco arrive en courant dans la grande salle. Sur la tête il a le chapeau haut de forme, dans la gueule le bâton et la cape, et sur le dos le lapin. Viens ici, Coco! Assieds-toi, Coco! C'est merveilleux! Maintenant, finissons la représentation. Janine et Pierre finissent leur représentation. Les autres étudiants finissent leurs représentations, aussi. Et qui gagne le grand prix? Coco, naturellement! Parce qu'il a beaucoup de talent!

Today is Friday. It's the big day of the talent show in the school auditorium. There are students who are going to sing, dance, do feats of strength and hand tricks, play a musical instrument, and tell funny stories. Janine and Pierre are in the talent show, also. Pierre is the magician and Janine is the assistant. They are preparing their presentation. Give me my top hat, Janine. I don't have your top hat, Pierre. Bring me my baton. I don't have your baton. Give me my cape. I don't have your cape. Bring me the rabbit. I don't have the rabbit. At that moment, some spectators in the auditorium shout: Dance! Sing! Do something! They are the students, men teachers, and women teachers who are shouting. Shoot! Let's not finish, Janine. We don't have the top hat, the baton, the cape, and the rabbit. Don't choose that alternative, Pierre. Well, do we stay or do we leave? We must do something! Are you going to do something, after all?! all the spectators ask. Don't answer, Janine. All of a sudden, Coco arrives running in the auditorium. On his head he has the top hat, in his mouth the baton and the cape, and on his back the rabbit. Come here, Coco! Sit down, Coco! It's wonderful! Now, let's finish the presentation. Janine and Pierre finish their presentation. The other students finish their presentations, too. And who wins the grand prize? Coco, naturally! Because he has a lot of talent!

Listen to the narration again.

Now, answer these questions during the pause. After the pause, you will hear a confirmation to check what you said. During the second pause, correct yourself by repeating what you heard.

Quel jour est-ce aujourd'hui?	*What day is it today?*
C'est aujourd'hui vendredi.	*Today is Friday.*
Or: C'est vendredi.	Or: *It's Friday.*
Pourquoi y a-t-il beaucoup de personnes dans la grande salle de l'école?	*Why are there many people in the school auditorium?*
C'est le grand jour du concours de talents.	*It's the big day of the talent show.*
Qui est le magicien?	*Who is the magician?*
Pierre est le magicien.	*Pierre is the magician.*
Qui est l'assistante?	*Who is the assistant?*
Janine est l'assistante.	*Janine is the assistant.*
Est-ce que Pierre et Janine ont le chapeau haut de forme, le bâton, la cape, et le lapin?	*Do Pierre and Janine have the top hat, the baton, the cape, and the rabbit?*
Non. Ils n'ont pas le chapeau haut de forme, le bâton, la cape, et le lapin.	*No. They don't have the top hat, the baton, the cape, and the rabbit.*
Tout d'un coup, qui arrive en courant dans la grande salle?	*All of a sudden, who arrives running in the auditorium?*
Tout d'un coup, Coco arrive en courant dans la grande salle.	*All of a sudden, Coco arrives running in the auditorium.*
Qui gagne le grand prix?	*Who wins the grand prize?*
Coco gagne le grand prix!	*Coco wins the grand prize!*
Pourquoi gagne-t-il le grand prix?	*Why does he win the grand prize?*
Il gagne le grand prix parce qu'il a beaucoup de talent!	*He wins the grand prize because he has a lot of talent!*

Now, let's practice the imperative form of three regular verbs—*to dance*, **danser**, *to finish*, **finir**, *to sell*, **vendre**. Repeat during the pause.

danse! dansez! dansons!	*dance! dance! let's dance!*
finis! finissez! finissons!	*finish! finish! let's finish!*
vends! vendez! vendons!	*sell! sell! let's sell!*

Now, let's practice the imperative of reflexive verbs in the affirmative and negative—*to sit down*, **s'asseoir**, *to get up*, **se lever**, *to wash oneself*, **se laver**. They are in your book.

In the affirmative. Repeat during the pause.

assieds-toi! asseyez-vous! asseyons-nous!	*sit down! sit down! let's sit down!*
lève-toi! levez-vous! levons-nous!	*get up! get up! let's get up!*
lave-toi! lavez-vous! lavons-nous!	*wash yourself! wash yourself! let's wash ourselves!*

In the negative. Repeat during the pause.

ne t'assieds pas! ne vous asseyez pas! ne nous asseyons pas!	*don't sit down! don't sit down! let's not sit down!*
ne te lève pas! ne vous levez pas! ne nous levons pas!	*don't get up! don't get up! let's not get up!*

ne te lave pas! ne vous lavez pas! ne
nous lavons pas!

*don't wash yourself! don't wash yourself! let's
not wash ourselves!*

Situation: Pretend that you are a dentist. In this exercise, use the polite form because you are telling your patient what to do. This practice in speaking is in your book.

When you hear the cue in English, say it in French during the pause. During the second pause, correct yourself by repeating what you heard.

Sit down, please.	Asseyez-vous, s'il vous plaît.
Open your mouth.	Ouvrez la bouche.
Close your eyes.	Fermez les yeux.
Close your mouth.	Fermez la bouche.
Open your eyes.	Ouvrez les yeux.
Get up, please.	Levez-vous, s'il vous plaît.

UNIT 11

In this exercise, which appears in your book, a brief description is given of something. Then you are asked, **Qu'est-ce que c'est?**/*What is it?* During the pause, tell us what is being described. Then you will hear a confirmation. During the second pause, correct yourself by repeating what you heard.

C'est quelque chose à boire. Il peut avoir le goût d'orange, ananas, pamplemousse, raisin, ou tomate. Il peut être en boîte ou en bouteille. C'est toujours délicieux. Qu'est-ce que c'est?

It is something to drink. It can have the taste of orange, pineapple, grapefruit, grape, or tomato. It can be in a can or in a bottle. It's always delicious. What is it?

C'est un jus de fruit.

It's a fruit juice.

C'est un meuble. Vous vous asseyez sur ce meuble.

It's furniture. You sit on this furniture.

Qu'est-ce que c'est?

What is it?

C'est une chaise.

It's a chair.

C'est un fruit. Il a la couleur rouge ou jaune ou verte. Qu'est-ce que c'est?

It's a fruit. It has the color of red or yellow or green. What is it?

C'est une pomme.

It's an apple.

C'est un animal qui a des plumes et des ailes. Il vole comme un avion. Qu'est-ce que c'est?

It's an animal that has feathers and wings. It flies like an airplane. What is it?

C'est un oiseau.

It's a bird.

Now, let's practice a few irregular verbs in the present indicative tense. These verbs are in your book.

After you hear the subject, there will be a short pause. During the pause, state the verb form with the subject. Then you will hear a confirmation. During the second pause, repeat what you heard.

aller *to go*

je / je vais	*I / I go, I am going, I do go*
tu / tu vas	*you / you go, you are going, you do go*

il / il va	*he / he goes, he is going, he does go*
elle / elle va	*she / she goes, she is going, she does go*
nous / nous allons	*we / we go, we are going, we do go*
vous / vous allez	*you / you go, you are going, you do go*
ils / ils vont	*they (masc.) / they go, they are going, they do go*
elles / elles vont	*they (fem.) / they go, they are going, they do go*

avoir   *to have*

je / j'ai	*I / I have, I am having, I do have*
tu / tu as	*you / you have, you are having, you do have*
il / il a	*he / he has, he is having, he does have*
Janine / Janine a	*Janine has, Janine is having, Janine does have*
nous / nous avons	*we / we have, we are having, we do have*
vous / vous avez	*you / you have, you are having, you do have*
ils / ils ont	*they (masc.) / they have, they are having, they do have*
elles / elles ont	*they (fem.) / they have, they are having, they do have*

apprendre   *to learn*

je / j'apprends	*I / I learn, I am learning, I do learn*
nous / nous apprenons	*we / we learn, we are learning, we do learn*
vous / vous apprenez	*you / you learn, you are learning, you do learn*

faire   *to do, to make*

je / je fais	*I / I make, I am making, I do make*
tu / tu fais	*you / you make, you are making, you do make*
elle / elle fait	*she / she makes, she is making, she does make*
nous / nous faisons	*we / we make, we are making, we do make*
vous / vous faites	*you / you make, you are making, you do make*
les enfants / les enfants font	*the children make, the children are making, do make*

Now, when you hear the cue in English, say it in French. This practice is based on the exercise in your book. The irregular verb forms are also in your book.

I want to buy a few presents.	Je veux acheter quelques cadeaux.
It's Christmas, you know!	C'est Noël, tu sais!
Do you have to buy some presents, too?	Est-ce que tu dois acheter quelques cadeaux, aussi?
We can go to the department stores together.	Nous pouvons aller aux grands magasins ensemble.
I have a lot of money!	J'ai beaucoup d'argent!
Do you want to take the subway or the bus?	Veux-tu prendre le métro ou le bus?
I want to take the bus.	Je veux prendre le bus.
Let's leave now!	Partons maintenant!

19

UNIT 12

The Passé Composé. First, listen carefully to the following narration. It is based on the story in your book. Later, you will answer questions about it.

Hier soir, la famille Paquet est allée à l'opéra. Ils ont vu la représentation de *Faust*. Ils ont quitté la maison à sept heures et demie et ils sont arrivés à l'opéra à huit heures. Ils sont entrés dans le théâtre et ils ont pris leurs places à huit heures et quart. La représentation a commencé à huit heures et demie. Pendant l'entracte, Madame Paquet est allée parler avec quelques dames. Monsieur Paquet est allé prendre un café. Pierre est allé acheter du chocolat, et Janine est allée boire un jus d'orange. Madame Paquet a parlé avec les dames et, puis, elle est retournée à sa place. Monsieur Paquet a pris son café et il est retourné à sa place aussi. Pierre a mangé son chocolat et il est retourné à sa place. Janine a bu son jus d'orange, mais avant de retourner à sa place elle a vu un homme et elle a parlé avec lui.

Yesterday evening, the Paquet family went to the opera. They saw the presentation of Faust. They left the house at seven thirty and they arrived at the opera at eight o'clock. They entered the theater and they took their seats at a quarter past eight. The presentation began at eight thirty. During intermission, Mrs. Paquet went to talk with some ladies. Mr. Paquet went to have coffee. Pierre went to buy some chocolate, and Janine went to drink an orange juice. Mrs. Paquet spoke with the ladies and, then, she returned to her seat. Mr. Paquet had his coffee and he returned to his seat also. Pierre ate his chocolate and he returned to his seat. Janine drank her orange juice, but before returning to her seat she saw a man and she talked with him.

Now, listen to the narration again. During the first pause, answer the following questions. During the second pause, repeat what you heard.

Qui est allé à l'opéra hier soir?

Who went to the opera last night?

La famille Paquet est allée à l'opéra hier soir.

The Paquet family went to the opera last night.

Qu'est-ce qu'ils ont vu?

What did they see?

Ils ont vu la représentation de *Faust*.

They saw the presentation of Faust.

À quelle heure ont-ils quitté la maison pour aller à l'opéra?

At what time did they leave the house to go to the opera?

Ils ont quitté la maison à sept heures et demie pour aller à l'opéra.

They left the house at seven thirty to go to the opera.

À quelle heure sont-ils arrivés à l'opéra?

At what time did they arrive at the opera?

Ils sont arrivés à huit heures à l'opéra.

They arrived at eight o'clock at the opera.

À quelle heure ont-ils pris leurs places dans le théâtre?

At what time did they take their seats in the theater?

Ils ont pris leurs places dans le théâtre à huit heures et quart.

They took their seats in the theater at a quarter past eight.

Pendant l'entracte, avec qui Madame Paquet a-t-elle parlé?

During intermission, with whom did Mrs. Paquet talk?

Pendant l'entracte, Madame Paquet a parlé avec quelques dames.

During intermission, Mrs. Paquet talked with some ladies.

Qu'est-ce que Pierre a mangé?

What did Pierre eat?

Il a mangé son chocolat.

He ate his chocolate.

Et Janine? Qu'a-t-elle bu?

And Janine? What did she drink?

Elle a bu un jus d'orange.

She drank an orange juice.

Avec qui Janine a-t-elle parlé?

With whom did Janine talk?

Elle a parlé avec un homme.

She talked with a man.

Now, let's practice some regular past participles of verbs that end in **-er, -ir,** and **-re.** You need to know them to form the passé composé. They are explained in your book. After you hear the verb, state the past participle. During the second pause, repeat what you heard.

danser / dansé	*to dance / danced*
apporter / apporté	*to bring / brought*
jouer / joué	*to play / played*
finir / fini	*to finish / finished*
choisir / choisi	*to choose / chosen*
rougir / rougi	*to blush / blushed*
vendre / vendu	*to sell / sold*
attendre / attendu	*to wait (for) / waited*
entendre / entendu	*to hear / heard*

Now, a few irregular past participles. They are in your book.

apprendre / appris	*to learn / learned*
prendre / pris	*to take / taken*
être / été	*to be / been*
faire / fait	*to do, to make / done, made*
boire / bu	*to drink / drunk*
dire / dit	*to say, to tell / said, told*
ouvrir / ouvert	*to open / opened*
rire / ri	*to laugh / laughed*
avoir / eu	*to have / had*
savoir / su	*to know (a fact) / known*
vouloir / voulu	*to want / wanted*

When you hear the verb, state it in the passé composé during the first pause. Use the subject that you are given. During the second pause, repeat.

danser / je	*to dance / I*
j'ai dansé	*I danced, I have danced, I did dance*
rester / tu	*to stay, to remain / you*
tu es resté	*you stayed, you have stayed, you did stay*
finir / vous	*to finish / you*
vous avez fini	*you finished, you have finished, you did finish*
arriver / Monsieur Paquet	*to arrive / Mr. Paquet*
Monsieur Paquet est arrivé	*Mr. Paquet arrived, has arrived, did arrive*
chanter / nous	*to sing / we*
nous avons chanté	*we sang, we have sung, we did sing*
aller / je	*to go / I*
je suis allé	*I went, I have gone, I did go*
partir / Janine	*to leave / Janine*
Janine est partie	*Janine left, Janine has left, Janine did leave*
venir / Pierre et Janine	*to come / Pierre and Janine*
Pierre et Janine sont venus	*Pierre and Janine came, have come, did come*
avoir / je	*to have / I*
j'ai eu	*I have had, I had, I did have*

être / je	*to be / I*
j'ai été	*I have been, I was*
faire / nous	*to do, to make / we*
nous avons fait	*we have done, we did, we did do or we have made, we made, we did make*

Now, in these statements, during the first pause, change the verb from the present tense to the passé composé. During the second pause, repeat.

Janine boit un jus d'orange.	*Janine is drinking an orange juice.*
Janine a bu un jus d'orange.	*Janine drank an orange juice.*
Monique va au cinéma.	*Monique is going to the cinema.*
Monique est allée au cinéma.	*Monique went to the cinema.*
Jean et Jeanne entrent dans le théâtre.	*Jean and Jeanne are entering the theater.*
Jean et Jeanne sont entrés dans le théâtre.	*Jean and Jeanne entered the theater.*

Situation: You are checking out of your hotel in Paris and you have been asked to comment on the services.

Answer the following questions in the affirmative in complete sentences. This practice is in your book.

Avez-vous été satisfait du service?	*Were you satisfied with the service?*
Oui, j'ai été satisfait du service.	*Yes, I was satisfied with the service.*
Avez-vous aimé votre chambre?	*Did you like your room?*
Oui, j'ai aimé ma chambre.	*Yes, I liked my room.*
Est-ce que les employés ont montré de la politesse?	*Did the employees show politeness?*
Oui, les employés ont montré de la politesse.	*Yes, the employees showed politeness.*

UNIT 13

Let's practice the direct object pronouns. They are in your book. Repeat during the pause.

me / *me;* te / *you (familiar);* le / *him, it (masc.);* la / *her, it (fem.);*
nous / *us;* vous / *you (singular polite or plural);* les / *them*

Now, let's use them in short sentences. You will hear a sentence with a direct object noun. During the first pause, change it to a direct object pronoun. During the second pause, repeat what you heard. This practice is in your book.

Follow this model.

Janine lit le poème.	*Janine is reading the poem.*
Janine le lit.	*Janine is reading it.*
Janine lit le livre.	*Janine is reading the book.*
Janine le lit.	*Janine is reading it.*
Pierre lit la lettre.	*Pierre is reading the letter.*
Pierre la lit.	*Pierre is reading it.*
Janine apprend le poème.	*Janine is learning the poem.*

Janine l'apprend.	*Janine is learning it.*
Pierre écrit la lettre.	*Pierre is writing the letter.*
Pierre l'écrit.	*Pierre is writing it.*
Janine apprend les poèmes.	*Janine is learning the poems.*
Janine les apprend.	*Janine is learning them.*

Now, when you hear the cue in English, say the statement in French. During the second pause, correct yourself by repeating what you heard.

Pierre knows me.	Pierre me connaît.
I love you (familiar te).	Je t'aime.
Janine knows him.	Janine le connaît.
The children see us.	Les enfants nous voient.
I understand you (polite vous).	Je vous comprends.
Janine and Pierre are eating them.	Janine et Pierre les mangent.

Now, you will hear a sentence with a direct object noun in the imperative. During the first pause, change it to a direct object pronoun. During the second pause, correct yourself by repeating what you heard. This practice is in your book.

Follow this model.

Écrivez la lettre!	*Write the letter!*
Écrivez-la!	*Write it!*
Apprenez le poème!	*Learn the poem!*
Apprenez-le!	*Learn it!*
Mangez la pomme!	*Eat the apple!*
Mangez-la!	*Eat it!*
Étudiez les leçons!	*Study the lessons!*
Étudiez-les!	*Study them!*

Now, let's use direct object pronouns in the negative imperative.

Follow this model.

Ne mangez pas les pommes!	*Don't eat the apples!*
Ne les mangez pas!	*Don't eat them!*
N'apprenez pas le poème!	*Don't learn the poem!*
Ne l'apprenez pas!	*Don't learn it!*
Ne buvez pas le jus!	*Don't drink the juice!*
Ne le buvez pas!	*Don't drink it!*
N'écrivez pas la lettre!	*Don't write the letter!*
Ne l'écrivez pas!	*Don't write it!*
Ne mangez pas les gâteaux!	*Don't eat the cakes!*
Ne les mangez pas!	*Don't eat them!*

Now, you will hear a sentence with a noun as direct object of an infinitive. During the first pause, change it to a direct object pronoun and place it in front of the infinitive. During the second pause, correct yourself by repeating what you heard. This practice is in your book.

Follow this model.

Monsieur Richy veut goûter le ragoût.	*Mr. Richy wants to taste the stew.*
Monsieur Richy veut le goûter.	*Mr. Richy wants to taste it.*
Pierre veut lire la lettre.	*Pierre wants to read the letter.*
Pierre veut la lire.	*Pierre wants to read it.*
Janine désire apprendre le poème.	*Janine wants to learn the poem.*
Janine désire l'apprendre.	*Janine wants to learn it.*
Pierre ne veut pas écrire la lettre.	*Pierre does not want to write the letter.*
Pierre ne veut pas l'écrire.	*Pierre does not want to write it.*

Let's practice using a direct object pronoun with a verb in the passé composé. During the first pause, change the direct object noun to a pronoun. During the second pause, correct yourself by repeating what you heard. This practice is in your book.

Follow this model.

Marie a préparé le dîner.	*Marie prepared the dinner.*
Marie l'a préparé.	*Marie prepared it.*
Robert a préparé la salade.	*Robert prepared the salad.*
Robert l'a préparée.	*Robert prepared it.*
Pierre et Janine ont préparé les dîners.	*Pierre and Janine prepared the dinners.*
Pierre et Janine les ont préparés.	*Pierre and Janine prepared them.*
Le chien a mangé les gâteaux.	*The dog ate the cakes.*
Le chien les a mangés.	*The dog ate them.*
J'ai fini le travail.	*I finished the work.*
Je l'ai fini.	*I finished it.*
Nous avons écrit les lettres.	*We have written the letters.*
Nous les avons écrites.	*We have written them.*

Situation: Catherine and Raymond are having something to eat in a cafeteria. This conversation is a variation of the one in your book.

When you hear the cue in English, say it in French during the pause. After the pause, you will hear a confirmation so you can check what you said. During the second pause, correct yourself by repeating what you heard.

Raymond, passe-moi la pizza, s'il te plaît.	*Raymond, pass me the pizza, please.*
La voici.	*Here it is.*
Tu n'en manges pas? Tu ne l'aimes pas?	*You aren't eating any of it? You don't like it?*
Non. Je ne l'aime pas.	*No. I don't like it.*
Pourquoi pas?	*Why not?*
C'est brûlé. Et le fromage est gommeux.	*It's burned. And the cheese is gummy.*
Dis-moi, Raymond, as-tu fait les devoirs de biologie pour demain?	*Tell me, Raymond, did you do the homework in biology for tomorrow?*
Non. Je ne les ai pas faits.	*No. I didn't do it.*
Passe-moi les hamburgers, s'il te plaît.	*Pass me the hamburgers, please.*
Tu manges beaucoup, Catherine.	*You eat a lot, Catherine.*
N'aimes-tu pas les hamburgers?	*Don't you like hamburgers?*
Non. Je ne les aime pas. Je ne les mange pas.	*No. I don't like them. I don't eat them.*

As-tu apporté les pâtisseries?	*Did you bring the pastries?*
Oui. Je les ai apportées.	*Yes. I brought them.*
Passe-moi une pâtisserie, s'il te plaît.	*Pass me a pastry, please.*
Non. Je vais les manger toutes.	*No. I'm going to eat them all.*

UNIT 14

Let's practice the indirect object pronouns. They are in your book. Repeat during the pause.

me / *to me;* te / *to you (familiar);* lui / *to him, to her, to it;* nous / *to us;*
vous / *to you (singular polite or plural);* leur / *to them*

Now, let's use them in short sentences. When you hear the cue in English, say it in French.

Pierre is giving me the cake.	Pierre me donne le gâteau.
Marie is giving the present to you (familiar te).	Marie te donne le cadeau.
Joseph is giving her the book.	Joseph lui donne le livre.
Catherine is talking to him now.	Catherine lui parle maintenant.
Madeleine is not writing to us.	Madeleine ne nous écrit pas.
I want to write to you (polite vous).	Je veux vous écrire.
She does not want to write to them.	Elle ne veut pas leur écrire.
Pass me the pastries, please (familiar form).	Passe-moi les pâtisseries, s'il te plaît.
Pierre is not giving me the cake.	Pierre ne me donne pas le gâteau.
Give him the cake!	Donnez-lui le gâteau!
Give me the money!	Donnez-moi l'argent!
Don't give her the money!	Ne lui donnez pas l'argent!
Janine wants to talk to them.	Janine veut leur parler.
I gave the cassettes to her.	Je lui ai donné les cassettes.

Now, let's practice the use of **y.** It is in your book. Answer the questions in the affirmative.

Follow this model.

Allez-vous à la bibliothèque?	*Are you going to the library?*
Oui, j'y vais.	*Yes. I'm going there.*
Les gants sont-ils dans le tiroir?	*Are the gloves in the drawer?*
Oui. Ils y sont.	*Yes. They are (there).*
Est-ce que le chapeau est sur la commode?	*Is the hat on the dresser?*
Oui. Il y est.	*Yes. It is (there).*
Aimez-vous aller au cinéma?	*Do you like going to the cinema?*
Oui. J'aime y aller.	*Yes. I like going there.*

Situation: You are talking to your friend Anne on the telephone. You are trying to obtain information about the whereabouts of the CDs you let her borrow in September.

Use the familiar form with Anne because she is your friend.

When you hear the cue in English, say it in French during the pause. After the pause, you will hear a confirmation so you can check what you said. During the second pause, correct yourself by repeating what you heard.

Anne, je t'ai prêté mes CDs au mois de septembre et aujourd'hui c'est le premier décembre.	*Anne, I lent you my CDs in the month of September and today is December first.*
Oui. Je sais. Je ne les ai pas.	*Yes. I know. I don't have them.*
Tu ne les as pas? Où sont-elles?	*You don't have them? Where are they?*
Je ne sais pas. Je les ai données à Suzanne. Va la voir.	*I don't know. I gave them to Suzanne. Go see her.*
Je ne peux pas aller la voir. Elle est en vacances en France.	*I can't go to see her. She is on vacation in France.*
Oh! Je sais maintenant! Suzanne les a données à Jacqueline. Elle les a.	*Oh! I know now! Suzanne gave them to Jacqueline. She has them.*
Non. Elle ne les a pas. Je lui ai parlé hier.	*No. She doesn't have them. I talked to her yesterday.*
Qu'est-ce qu'elle t'a dit?	*What did she say to you?*
Elle m'a dit que tu les as.	*She told me that you have them.*
Elle t'a dit que je les ai?? Impossible! Je ne les ai pas! Je te le dis!	*She told you that I have them?? Impossible! I don't have them! I'm telling you so!*
Et moi, je te dis que je ne les ai pas. Elle m'a dit que tu les as. Apparemment mes CDs sont perdues. Au revoir! Et passe une bonne journée!	*And me, I'm telling you that I don't have them. She told me that you have them. Apparently my CDs are lost. Good-bye! And have a nice day!*

UNIT 15

CD 2
TRACK
6

Let's practice using some interrogative pronouns in riddles. This practice is in your book. You will hear a brief statement. Then you are asked to solve the riddle by answering the question, *What am I?*/**Que suis-je?** or **Qu'est-ce que je suis?** or, *Who am I?*/ **Qui suis-je?**

During the first pause, answer the question. Then you will hear a confirmation. During the second pause, correct yourself by repeating what you heard.

Je porte toujours un chapeau mais je n'ai pas de tête. Que suis-je?	*I always wear a hat but I don't have a head. What am I?*
un champignon	*a mushroom*
Je vole comme un oiseau. Qu'est-ce que je suis?	*I fly like a bird. What am I?*
un avion	*an airplane*
J'habite dans l'eau. J'ai des yeux mais je n'ai pas de paupières. Qui suis-je?	*I live in water. I have eyes but I don't have eyelids. Who am I?*
un poisson	*a fish*
Je suis jaune dedans et blanc dessus. Qu'est-ce que je suis?	*I am yellow inside and white on top. What am I?*
un oeuf	*an egg*

Now, when you hear the cue in English, say it in French during the first pause. During the second pause, correct yourself by repeating what you heard. This practice is in your book.

Who is talking?	Qui parle?
Whom do you love?	Qui aimez-vous? *or* Qui aimes-tu?
To whom are you talking?	À qui parlez-vous? *or* À qui parles-tu?
About whom are you talking?	De qui parlez-vous? *or* De qui parles-tu?
What are you doing?	Que faites-vous? *or* Qu'est-ce que vous faites?

Situation: Janine has been on the phone for about an hour. Her brother Pierre wants to call some-one and he is pestering her by interrupting and asking her questions.

This practice is in your book. When you hear the cue in English, say it in French during the first pause. During the second pause, correct yourself by repeating what you heard. Use the familiar form because they are brother and sister.

I want to telephone a friend.	Je veux téléphoner à un ami.
Don't you see that I'm talking to someone?	Ne vois-tu pas que je parle à quelqu'un?
Yes, I see that you're talking to someone.	Oui, je vois que tu parles à quelqu'un.
To whom are you talking?	À qui parles-tu?
You're talking to Micheline?	Tu parles à Micheline?
No. I'm not talking to her.	Non. Je ne lui parle pas.
You're not talking to her?	Tu ne lui parles pas?
I'm not talking to her this minute.	Je ne lui parle pas en ce moment.
I talked to her yesterday.	Je lui ai parlé hier.
Are you talking to Marie and Monique?	Tu parles à Marie et à Monique?
I'm not talking to them now.	Je ne leur parle pas maintenant.
I talked to them this morning.	Je leur ai parlé ce matin.
To whom are you talking?	À qui parles-tu?
I'm talking to you, to YOU! Go away!	Je te parle, à TOI! Va-t'en!

UNIT 16

CD 2
TRACK 7

Now, let's practice a few true-false questions. When you hear the statement, respond in French with **Cela est vrai** if the statement is true. If it is false, say **Cela est faux.** During the second pause, correct yourself by repeating what you heard. These statements are based on the story in your book.

Paris est la capitale de la France.	*Paris is the capital of France.*
Cela est vrai.	*That is true.*
Marseille est un port sur la Méditerranée.	*Marseille is a port on the Mediterranean.*
Cela est vrai.	*That is true.*
La Seine est un fleuve.	*The Seine is a river.*
Cela est vrai.	*That is true.*
Madame Ravel est professeur de mathématiques.	*Mrs. Ravel is a professor of mathematics.*
Cela est faux.	*That is false.*
La directrice de l'école n'entre pas dans la classe.	*The school principal does not enter the class.*
Cela est faux.	*That is false.*
Suzanne est chargée de continuer la leçon.	*Suzanne is in charge of continuing the lesson.*
Cela est faux.	*That is false.*
Robert a lancé un avion en papier contre la fenêtre.	*Robert tossed a paper airplane against the window.*
Cela est faux.	*That is false.*
Il est trois heures, la leçon est finie, et Madame Ravel est heureuse.	*It is three o'clock, the lesson is finished, and Madame Ravel is happy.*
Cela est vrai.	*That is true.*

Situation: Your friend Richard did not go to school today because he is not feeling well. He has called you at home to find out what you did in French class.

This practice is in your book. When you hear the cue in English, say it in French during the first pause. During the second pause, correct yourself by repeating what you heard. Use the familiar form because you are friends.

Qu'est-ce que tu as fait dans la classe de français aujourd'hui?	*What did you do in French class today?*
J'ai beaucoup parlé en français.	*I talked a lot in French.*
Et les autres étudiants, aussi?	*And the other students, too?*
Quelques étudiants ont parlé en français. Quelques étudiants n'ont rien dit.	*Some students talked in French. Some students said nothing.*
Est-ce que tu as écrit en français au tableau?	*Did you write in French on the chalkboard?*
Oui, j'ai écrit en français au tableau.	*Yes, I wrote in French on the chalkboard.*
Qui a gagné le grand prix aujourd'hui dans la classe?	*Who won the first prize today in class?*
Moi! C'est moi qui ai gagné le grand prix aujourd'hui.	*Me! I won the first prize today.*
Félicitations!	*Congratulations!*
Merci!	*Thank you!*

UNIT 17

CD 3
TRACK
1

Let's practice the disjunctive pronouns. Disjunctive pronouns are also known as stressed or tonic pronouns. Repeat during the pause.

moi / *me or I;* toi / *you (familiar);* soi / *oneself;* lui / *him or he;* elle / *her or she;* nous / *us or we;* vous / *you (formal singular or plural);* eux / *them, they (masculine);* elles / *them, they (feminine)*

Now, let's use them in short sentences. When you hear the cue in English, say it in French during the first pause. During the second pause, correct yourself by repeating what you heard.

She is talking with me.	Elle parle avec moi.
I went to the movies with him.	Je suis allée au cinéma avec lui.
He is going to leave without her.	Il va partir sans elle.
Madeleine and he are intelligent.	Madeleine et lui sont intelligents.
The stew is for us.	Le ragoût est pour nous.
She is going to leave with you (formal singular).	Elle va partir avec vous.
We are going to go out with you (familiar singular).	Nous allons sortir avec toi.
This cake is for them (masculine).	Ce gâteau est pour eux.
These things are for them (feminine).	Ces choses sont pour elles.
He and I are going to the movies.	Lui et moi nous allons au cinéma.

Now, say the French words for the abbreviation **R.S.V.P.** It is the title of the story in your book.

Répondez, s'il vous plaît.   *Answer, please (or: Please reply).*

Situation: Janine has telephoned Robert to invite him to go to a dance with her this Saturday night.

When you hear the cue in English, say it in French during the first pause. During the second pause, correct yourself by repeating what you heard. This conversational practice is in your book. They are using the familiar form because they are friends.

Allô! Robert? C'est toi? C'est moi, Janine.	*Hello! Robert? Is that you? It's me, Janine.*
Salut, Janine! Comment vas-tu?	*Hi, Janine! How are you?*
Très bien, merci. Écoute. Je te téléphone pour te demander si tu veux aller à un bal ce samedi soir. Veux-tu y aller avec moi?	*Very well, thank you. Listen. I'm calling you to ask you if you want to go to a dance this Saturday night. Do you want to go (there) with me?*
Merci, mais je ne peux pas. Mon père est malade. Et je dois rester à la maison avec lui.	*Thank you, but I can't. My father is sick. And I have to stay home with him.*
C'est dommage. Ta mère ne peut pas rester chez toi avec lui?	*That's too bad. Your mother can't stay home with him?*
Non, parce que ma mère est allée rendre visite à sa soeur aux États-Unis.	*No, because my mother went to visit her sister in the United States.*
Est-ce que je peux venir chez toi pour regarder la télé avec toi?	*Can I come to your house to watch TV with you?*
Oui, tu peux venir chez moi.	*Yes, you can come to my place.*
D'accord. Je vais venir chez toi à huit heures.	*Okay. I'm going to come to your place at eight o'clock.*
Apporte un grand gâteau au chocolat avec toi.	*Bring a big chocolate cake with you.*
Un grand gâteau au chocolat? Avec moi? Okay. D'accord.	*A big chocolate cake? With me? Okay. Okay.*
Apporte, aussi, la musique et les paroles de la chanson *Sur le Pont d'Avignon.*	*Bring, also, the music and words of the song Sur le Pont d'Avignon.*
D'accord. Et nous allons chanter pour ton père qui est malade!	*Okay. And we are going to sing for your father who is sick!*
N'oublie pas le gâteau!	*Don't forget the cake!*

UNIT 18

Let's practice using descriptive adjectives. They are in your book. When you hear the cue in English, say it in French during the first pause. During the second pause, correct yourself by repeating what you heard.

a gray hat	un chapeau gris
a gray car	une voiture grise
gray hats	des chapeaux gris
gray cars	des voitures grises
a narrow passage	un passage étroit
a narrow street	une rue étroite
narrow passages	des passages étroits
narrow streets	des rues étroites

Now, when you hear the adjective in the masculine singular, change it to the feminine singular. These forms are in your book.

neuf / neuve	*new*
furieux / furieuse	*furious*

dernier / dernière	*last*
ancien / ancienne	*old*
bon / bonne	*good*
beau / belle	*handsome, beautiful*
frais / fraîche	*fresh*
sec / sèche	*dry*
long / longue	*long*
blanc / blanche	*white*

Now, when you answer these questions, change the descriptive adjective in the question to the one the speaker gives. Use **Non** in your reply but make your statement in the affirmative with the new adjective in the appropriate form. This practice is in your book.

Follow this model:

Avez-vous une voiture grise? (blanc)	*Do you have a gray car? (white)*
Non. J'ai une voiture blanche.	*No. I have a white car.*
Avez-vous une maison blanche? (gris)	*Do you have a white house? (gray)*
Non. J'ai une maison grise.	*No. I have a gray house.*
As-tu un bon stylo? (mauvais)	*Do you have a good pen? (bad)*
Non. J'ai un mauvais stylo.	*No. I have a bad pen.*
Est-ce que Pierre mange une mauvaise pomme? (bon)	*Is Pierre eating a bad apple? (good)*
Non. Il mange une bonne pomme.	*No. He is eating a good apple.*

Let's practice a few possessive adjectives. They are in your book. When you hear the cue in English, say it in French during the first pause. During the second pause, correct yourself by repeating what you hear.

my book	mon livre
my books	mes livres
your pen, familiar form	ton stylo
your pens, familiar form	tes stylos
her father	son père
his mother	sa mère
our house	notre maison
your umbrella, polite singular	votre parapluie
their sister	leur soeur
their sisters	leurs soeurs

Situation: You and your friend Debbie are at The Toledo Museum of Art in Toledo, Ohio, admiring the painting *Rue de Tahiti* / Street in Tahiti, by Paul Gauguin. Look at the picture in your book and participate in this conversation. When you hear the cue in English, say it in French during the first pause. During the second pause, correct yourself by repeating what you hear.

Quel beau tableau de Gauguin! L'aimes-tu?	*What a beautiful painting by Gauguin! Do you like it?*
Oui, je l'aime beaucoup.	*Yes, I like it very much.*
Cette femme à droite, que fait-elle? Est-ce qu'elle dort?	*That woman on the right, what is she doing? Is she sleeping?*
Je pense qu'elle attend un ami.	*I think she is waiting for a friend.*

Évidemment, cette rue de Tahiti est tranquille. Les montagnes au fond sont belles, n'est-ce pas?	*Evidently, this street in Tahiti is quiet. The mountains in the background are beautiful, aren't they?*
Oui, elles sont belles.	*Yes, they are beautiful.*
J'aimerais aller à Tahiti.	*I would like to go to Tahiti.*
Bon! Allons-y tout de suite!	*Good! Let's go there right away!*

UNIT 19

Let's practice using more adjectives in short sentences. They are in your book. When you hear the cue in English, say it in French during the first pause. During the second pause, correct yourself by repeating what you heard.

You are the best judge of your actions.	Vous êtes le meilleur juge de vos actions.
Your greatest quality is your patience.	Votre plus grande qualité c'est votre patience.
Beware of dangerous obstacles.	Méfiez-vous des obstacles dangereux.
Beware of small green automobiles!	Méfiez-vous des petites automobiles vertes!
What luck! You are going to see a big change!	Quelle chance! Vous allez voir un grand changement!
Your greatest quality is your imagination.	Votre plus grande qualité c'est votre imagination.
Don't go to the beach today. There is a starving shark in the water!	N'allez pas à la plage aujourd'hui. Il y a un requin affamé dans l'eau!

Now, let's practice the demonstrative adjectives. They are in your book. When you hear the cue in English, say it in French during the first pause. During the second pause, correct yourself by repeating what you heard.

this boy	ce garçon
this tree	cet arbre
this man	cet homme
this woman	cette femme
this church	cette église
these women	ces femmes
these men	ces hommes
these trees	ces arbres

Now, answer the following questions in complete sentences. In your answer, use the noun that is stated. Make all required changes in the forms of the adjectives. This practice is in your book.

Follow this model:

Qui est plus grand que Robert? (Janine)	*Who is taller than Robert? (Janine)*
Janine est plus grande que Robert.	*Janine is taller than Robert.*
Qui est plus grand que Janine? (Madame Paquet)	*Who is taller than Janine? (Mrs. Paquet)*
Madame Paquet est plus grande que Janine.	*Mrs. Paquet is taller than Janine.*
Qui est moins grand que Pierre? (Janine)	*Who is less tall than Pierre? (Janine)*
Janine est moins grande que Pierre.	*Janine is less tall than Pierre.*

Qui est aussi petit que Madame Banluc? (Madame Paquet)

Who is as short as Mrs. Banluc? (Mrs. Paquet)

Madame Paquet est aussi petite que Madame Banluc.

Mrs. Paquet is as short as Mrs. Banluc.

Situation: Françoise is the best student in her French class. François, a classmate, is having problems with adjectives and needs her help. Participate in this conversation.

Françoise, je ne comprends pas les adjectifs, les comparatifs, les superlatifs, et leur position. J'ai besoin de pratique.

Françoise, I don't understand adjectives, comparatives, superlatives, and their position. I need practice.

Il n'y a pas de problème, François.

There's no problem, François.

Dis-moi, François, est-ce qu'Anne est plus jolie que Monique?

Tell me, François, is Anne prettier than Monique?

Non. Anne n'est pas plus jolie que Monique. Monique est la plus jolie de la classe.

No. Anne is not prettier than Monique. Monique is the prettiest in the class.

Dis-moi, François, mon père est-il plus grand que ton père?

Tell me, François, is my father taller than your father?

Non. Ton père n'est pas plus grand que mon père.

No. Your father is not taller than my father.

Mais ta mère est plus grande que ma mère.

But your mother is taller than my mother.

Dis-moi, qui est le meilleur étudiant de notre classe de français.

Tell me, who is the best student in our French class?

C'est toi, Françoise. Tu es la meilleure étudiante de notre classe de français.

It's you, Françoise. You are the best student in our French class.

Moi? Tu penses que je suis la meilleure étudiante de notre classe de français?

Me? You think that I am the best student in our French class?

Oui, oui. Je t'assure!

Yes, yes. I assure you!

Merci! Maintenant, mangeons de la mousse au chocolat.

Thank you! Now, let's eat some chocolate mousse.

C'est la meilleure du monde!

It's the best in the world!

UNIT 20

CD 3
TRACK
4

Listen to the following monologue. It is Janine talking on the telephone with Madame Bédier, a neighbor. There are no pauses for repetition. Just listen carefully. Later, you will answer questions based on what you heard.

Allô! J'écoute. Ici Janine. Comment allez-vous, madame? Très bien, merci. Je ne fais rien ce soir. Vous allez au cinéma avec votre mari. Ah! Bon! D'accord. Oui, je peux venir chez vous ce soir et rester avec Renée. Oui, je sais. Oh, elle a déjà cinq ans! Oui, elle est grande pour son âge. Oui, je sais qu'elle est capricieuse. Qui, je sais qu'elle parle plus vite que les autres enfants. Oui, je sais qu'elle marche moins vite que les autres enfants. Bon! D'accord! À six heures et demie. A ce soir, madame.

Hello! I'm listening. Janine here. How are you, madam? Very well, thank you. I'm not doing anything this evening. You're going to the movies with your husband. Ah! Good! Okay. Yes, I can come to your house this evening and stay with Renée. Yes, I know. Oh, she is already five years old! Yes, she is big for her age. Yes, I know that she is capricious. Yes, I know that she talks faster than the other children. Yes, I know that she walks less quickly than the other children. Good! Okay! At six thirty. See you tonight, madam.

Listen again to what Janine says on the telephone.

Now, answer these questions during the first pause. During the second pause, correct yourself by repeating what you heard.

Avec qui Janine parle-t-elle au téléphone?	*With whom is Janine talking on the telephone?*
Janine parle au téléphone avec Madame Bédier.	*Janine is talking on the telephone with Mrs. Bédier.*
Est-ce que Janine fait quelque chose ce soir?	*Is Janine doing anything this evening?*
Non. Elle ne fait rien ce soir.	*No. She isn't doing anything this evening.*
Où va Madame Bédier ce soir?	*Where is Mrs. Bédier going this evening?*
Madame Bédier va au cinéma ce soir.	*Mrs. Bédier is going to the movies this evening.*
Avec qui va-t-elle au cinéma?	*With whom is she going to the movies?*
Elle va au cinéma avec son mari.	*She's going to the movies with her husband.*
Est-ce que Janine peut aller chez Madame Bédier ce soir?	*Can Janine go to Mrs. Bédier's house this evening?*
Oui. Elle peut aller chez Madame Bédier ce soir.	*Yes. She can go to Mrs. Bédier's house this evening.*
Avec qui Janine va-t-elle rester?	*With whom is Janine going to stay?*
Elle va rester avec Renée.	*She is going to stay with Renée.*
Est-ce que Renée est capricieuse?	*Is Renée capricious?*
Oui. Renée est capricieuse.	*Yes. Renée is capricious.*
Est-ce que Renée parle plus vite que les autres enfants?	*Does Renée talk faster than the other children?*
Oui. Elle parle plus vite que les autres enfants.	*Yes. She talks faster than the other children.*
Est-ce que Renée marche moins vite que les autres enfants?	*Does Renée walk less quickly than the other children?*
Oui. Elle marche moins vite que les autres enfants.	*Yes. She walks less quickly than the other children.*
À quelle heure Janine va-t-elle chez Madame Bédier?	*At what time is Janine going to Mrs. Bédier's house?*
Janine va chez Madame Bédier à six heures et demie.	*Janine is going to Mrs. Bédier's house at six thirty.*

Now, let's practice the pronunciation of some adverbs. They are in your book. Repeat during the pause.

beaucoup	*many, much, very much, a lot*
bien	*well*
déjà	*already*
encore	*still, yet, again*
mal	*badly*
mieux	*better*
souvent	*often*
distinctement	*distinctly*
seulement	*only*
furieusement	*furiously*
constamment	*constantly*
patiemment	*patiently*

The primary meaning of **n'est-ce pas?** is: *Is it not so?* But there are other English translations when it is tagged on to a statement; for example, it can mean: *isn't he? isn't she? aren't you? doesn't it?*

When you hear the cue in English, say it in French during the first pause. During the second pause, correct yourself by repeating what you heard.

Renée is five years old, isn't she?	Renée a cinq ans, n'est-ce pas?
You're going to the movies, aren't you?	Tu vas—*or*—Vous allez—au cinéma, n'est-ce pas?
It's beautiful weather today, isn't it?	Il fait beau aujourd'hui, n'est-ce pas?
It rains a lot here in April, doesn't it?	Il pleut beaucoup ici en avril, n'est-ce pas?
You have read the book, haven't you?	Tu as lu—*or*—Vous avez lu—le livre, n'est-ce pas?

UNIT 21

CD 3 TRACK 5

Listen to the following narration. It is in your book. There are no pauses for repetition. Just listen carefully. Later, you will answer questions based on what you heard.

Madame Paquet est malade depuis hier. Elle a mangé quelque chose qui lui a donné mal à l'estomac. Elle est souffrante dans son lit. Son mari a appelé le docteur pour lui donner un médicament. Le docteur va venir dans quelques minutes. Madame Paquet l'attend patiemment depuis vingt minutes. Le docteur est arrivé. Il est dans la chambre de Madame Paquet depuis quinze minutes. Il l'examine. Monsieur Paquet est avec eux. Dites-moi, docteur, faut-il appeler une ambulance pour transporter ma femme à l'hôpital? Non, monsieur. Il n'est pas nécessaire de la transporter à l'hôpital. Elle peut rester ici dans son lit. Elle n'est pas gravement malade. Les ambulances rendent grand service, mais dans ce cas votre femme peut rester où elle est. J'insiste, chère madame. Prenez ce médicament et ne mangez rien.

Mrs. Paquet has been sick since yesterday. She ate something that gave her a stomach-ache. She is sick in her bed. Her husband called the doctor to give her medicine. The doctor is going to come in a few minutes. Mrs. Paquet has been waiting for him patiently for twenty minutes. The doctor has arrived. He has been in Mrs. Paquet's room for twenty minutes. He is examining her. Mr. Paquet is with them. Tell me, doctor, is it necessary to call an ambulance to transport my wife to the hospital? No, sir. It is not necessary to transport her to the hospital. She can stay here in her bed. She is not seriously ill. Ambulances render a great service, but in this case your wife can stay where she is. I insist, dear madam. Take this medicine and don't eat anything.

Listen again to the narration.

Now, answer these questions during the first pause. During the second pause, correct yourself by repeating what you heard.

Qui est malade?	*Who is sick?*
Madame Paquet est malade.	*Mrs. Paquet is sick.*
Depuis quand est-elle malade?	*Since when has she been sick?*
Elle est malade depuis hier.	*She has been sick since yesterday.*
Qui a appelé le docteur?	*Who called the doctor?*
Son mari a appelé le docteur.	*Her husband called the doctor.*
Depuis combien de temps Madame Paquet attend-elle le docteur patiemment?	*How long has Mrs. Paquet been waiting for the doctor patiently?*
Elle l'attend depuis vingt minutes.	*She has been waiting for him for twenty minutes.*

Madame Paquet et le docteur sont dans la chambre. Qui est avec eux?	*Mrs. Paquet and the doctor are in the room. Who is with them?*
Monsieur Paquet est avec eux.	*Mr. Paquet is with them.*
Est-ce qu'elle est gravement malade?	*Is she seriously ill?*
Non. Elle n'est pas gravement malade.	*No. She is not seriously ill.*
Qu'est-ce que le docteur lui a donné?	*What did the doctor give her?*
Le docteur lui a donné un médicament.	*The doctor gave her a medicine.*

Now, let's practice a few negations. They are in your book. When you hear the cue in English, say it in French during the first pause. During the second pause, correct yourself by repeating what you heard.

I do not smoke.	Je ne fume pas.
I never smoke.	Je ne fume jamais.
I have never smoked.	Je n'ai jamais fumé.
Madame Paquet is eating nothing.	Madame Paquet ne mange rien.
She has not eaten anything today.	Elle n'a rien mangé aujourd'hui.

Now, let's practice using **faut-il?** and **il faut.** Answer the following questions in the affirmative during the first pause. During the second pause, correct yourself by repeating what you heard.

Faut-il boire pour vivre?	*Is it necessary to drink (in order) to live?*
Oui. Il faut boire pour vivre.	*Yes. It is necessary to drink to live.*
Faut-il étudier pour apprendre?	*Is it necessary to study to learn?*
Oui. Il faut étudier pour apprendre.	*Yes. It is necessary to study to learn.*
Faut-il parler français dans la classe de français?	*Is it necessary to speak French in French class?*
Oui. Il faut parler français dans la classe de français.	*Yes. It is necessary to speak French in French class.*

*Note that **il faut** in the *negative* means *one must not*. Examples:

Il ne faut pas dire de mensonges.	*One must not tell lies.*
Il ne faut pas voler.	*One must not steal.*

Situation: You have just arrived in Paris on an educational tour with a group of students. Your guide is Madame Simard. She is talking with you. This practice is in your book. When you hear the cue in English, say it in French during the first pause. During the second pause, correct yourself by repeating what you heard.

Vous parlez français extraordinairement bien.	*You speak French extraordinarily well.*
Merci, madame.	*Thank you, madam.*
Depuis combien de temps étudiez-vous le français?	*How long have you been studying French?*
J'étudie le français depuis un an.	*I have been studying French for one year.*
Vous étudiez le français depuis un an? C'est tout? C'est extraordinaire! Où avez-vous appris à parler si bien le français?	*You've been studying French for one year? Is that all? It's extraordinary! Where did you learn to speak French so well?*
J'ai appris à parler français à l'école.	*I learned to speak French in school.*
Où habitez-vous? Avec qui? Dans quel pays?	*Where do you live? With whom? In what country?*

J'habite avec mes parents aux États-Unis.	*I live with my parents in the United States.*
Quelles matières étudiez-vous?	*What subjects are you studying?*
J'étudie les mathématiques, les sciences, les langues, l'informatique, les ordinateurs, et d'autres matières.	*I am studying mathematics, sciences, languages, computer science, computers, and other subjects.*
Aimez-vous mon pays?	*Do you like my country?*
J'aime votre pays, les Français, la culture française, la musique, et l'art.	*I like your country, the French people, French culture, music, and art.*
Merci bien. Maintenant, nous allons au marché aux puces.	*Thank you very much. Now, we are going to the flea market.*
Je désire acheter un oreiller parce que je n'aime pas l'oreiller sur le lit dans ma chambre à l'hôtel.	*I want to buy a pillow because I don't like the pillow on the bed in my room at the hotel.*
Attention aux puces!	*Watch out for the fleas!*

UNIT 22

Listen to the following narration. It is in your book. There are no pauses for repetition. Just listen carefully. Later, you will answer questions based on what you heard.

Claire et François sont allés à la foire samedi. Là, ils se sont bien amusés. Ils ont vu des expositions, ils ont acheté des souvenirs, et ils sont entrés chez une chiromancienne pour se faire lire les lignes de la main.	*Claire and François went to the fair Saturday. There, they had a good time. They saw exhibits, they bought souvenirs, and they went to a palm reader to have their palms read.*

Listen again to the narration.

Now, answer these questions during the first pause. During the second pause, correct yourself by repeating what you heard.

Où Claire et François sont-ils allés samedi?	*Where did Claire and François go Saturday?*
Ils sont allés à la foire samedi.	*They went to the fair Saturday.*
Est-ce qu'ils se sont bien amusés?	*Did they have a good time?*
Oui. Ils se sont bien amusés.	*Yes. They had a good time.*
Qu'est-ce qu'ils ont vu?	*What did they see?*
Ils ont vu des expositions.	*They saw exhibits.*
Qu'est-ce qu'ils ont acheté?	*What did they buy?*
Ils ont acheté des souvenirs.	*They bought souvenirs.*
Chez qui sont-ils entrés?	*To whose place did they go?*
Ils sont entrés chez une chiromancienne.	*They went to a palm reader's place.*
Pourquoi sont-ils entrés chez une chiromancienne?	*Why did they go to a palm reader?*
Pour se faire lire les lignes de la main.	*To have their palms read.*

Now, answer the following questions in complete sentences. In your answer, substitute an object pronoun for the noun direct object. Make your statement during the first pause. During the second pause, correct yourself by repeating what you heard.

Follow this model:

Bob arrange les fleurs. Et vous et votre soeur?	*Bob is arranging the flowers. And you and your sister?*
Nous les arrangeons aussi.	*We are arranging them also.*
Catherine arrange les livres. Et vous et votre frère?	*Catherine is arranging the books. And you and your brother?*
Nous les arrangeons aussi.	*We are arranging them also.*
Simone efface le tableau. Et vous et vos amis?	*Simone is erasing the chalkboard. And you and your friends?*
Nous l'effaçons aussi.	*We are erasing it also.*
Hélène prononce la phrase. Et les autres étudiants?	*Helen is pronouncing the sentence. And the other students?*
Ils la prononcent aussi.	*They are pronouncing it also.*
Janine achète les robes. Et les autres jeunes filles?	*Janine is buying the dresses. And the other girls?*
Elles les achètent aussi.	*They are buying them also.*

Now, let's practice the use of **il y a, y a-t-il ... ?, voici,** and **voilà.** When you hear the cue in English, say it in French during the first pause. During the second pause, correct yourself by repeating what you heard.

There is a good restaurant near here.	Il y a un bon restaurant près d'ici.
Is there a bus stop near here?	Y a-t-il un arrêt d'autobus près d'ici?
Are there any fruits on the table?	Y a-t-il des fruits sur la table?
Here is my mother and there's my father!	Voici ma mère et voilà mon père!
Here's a taxi!	Voici un taxi!
There's a taxi!	Voilà un taxi!
Here I am!	Me voici!
Here he is!	Le voici!
Here she is!	La voici!
Ah! There they are!	Ah! Les voilà!

UNIT 23

CD 3
TRACK
7

Let's practice some idiomatic expressions that take the preposition **de** with an infinitive. Repeat during the pause.

J'ai besoin d'aller chez le dentiste.	*I need to go to the dentist.*
Tu as envie de dormir?	*Do you feel like sleeping?*
Monsieur Paquet a horreur de réparer des radios.	*Mr. Paquet hates repairing radios.*
Nous avons peur de traverser le parc pendant la nuit.	*We are afraid to cross the park during the night.*
Vous avez raison d'avoir peur.	*You are right to be afraid.*
Ils ont tort de dire cela.	*They are wrong to say that.*

Now, the use of **il est** plus adjective plus **de** plus infinitive.

Il est agréable d'aller à un bal.	*It is pleasant to go to a dance.*
Il est amusant d'aller à un cirque.	*It's fun going to a circus.*
Il est désagréable d'aller chez le dentiste, n'est-ce pas?	*It's unpleasant going to the dentist, isn't it?*
Il est impossible de lire ce gros livre en une heure.	*It's impossible to read this big book within an hour.*
Il est intéressant d'aller à un musée, n'est-ce pas?	*It is interesting going to a museum, isn't it?*

And now, the use of the preposition **à** after certain verbs plus infinitive.

J'apprends à parler français.	*I am learning to speak French.*
J'apprends à lire en français.	*I am learning to read in French.*
Je commence à écrire en français.	*I am beginning to write in French.*
J'hésite à sortir parce qu'il pleut.	*I hesitate going out because it's raining.*

Let's practice the use of **pour, sans, avant de, au lieu de, afin de** plus infinitive.

Pierre est parti pour aller voir ses amis.	*Pierre left to go see his friends.*
Janine est sortie sans dire un mot.	*Janine went out without saying a word.*
Ils sont allés au cinéma avant de finir leurs devoirs.	*They went to the movies before finishing their homework.*
Elles sont sorties au lieu de rester à la maison.	*They went out instead of staying at home.*
Raymond est revenu afin de voir ses amis.	*Raymond returned in order to see his friends.*

Let's practice the use of no preposition after certain verbs plus infinitive.

J'aime aller au cinéma.	*I like going to the movies.*
Tu aimes mieux aller au théâtre, n'est-ce pas?	*You prefer going to the theater, don't you?*
Pierre déteste aller chez le dentiste.	*Pierre hates going to the dentist.*
Janine veut aller au Canada.	*Janine wants to go to Canada.*
Nous pensons aller en Angleterre.	*We intend to go to England.*
Pouvez-vous aller à l'Opéra avec moi ce soir?	*Can you go to the Opera with me tonight?*
Ils veulent aller en Australie.	*They want to go to Australia.*
Elles doivent aller à la bibliothèque.	*They have to go to the library.*

And, finally, let's practice the use of the preposition **de** after certain verbs plus infinitive.

J'ai oublié de fermer la fenêtre.	*I forgot to close the window.*
Je promets de venir chez vous.	*I promise to come to your place.*
Elle a refusé de sortir hier soir.	*She refused to go out last night.*
Je tâche de faire mes devoirs.	*I try to do my homework.*

Now, let's look at the French painting whose title is *La Liseuse* by Fragonard in your book and exercise eight on the facing page. During the first pause, answer the question. During the second pause, correct yourself by repeating what you heard.

Quel est le titre de ce tableau?	*What is the title of this painting?*
La Liseuse.	The Reader.

38

Quel est le nom de l'artiste?	*What is the name of the artist?*
Fragonard.	*Fragonard.*
Que fait la jeune fille?	*What is the girl doing?*
Elle lit un livre.	*She is reading a book.*
Est-elle jolie?	*Is she pretty?*
Oui. Elle est très jolie.	*Yes. She is very pretty.*
Que pensez-vous de sa coiffure?	*What do you think of her hair style?*
Je pense que sa coiffure est belle.	*I think that her hair style is beautiful.*

UNIT 24

CD 3
TRACK
8

Now, let's practice using a few popular French proverbs. During the first pause, say a proverb in French that would make a point in the following situations. During the second pause, correct yourself by repeating what you heard. This practice is in your book.

Situation: You just arrived twenty minutes late to French class for a big test. What might the teacher say to you?

Mieux vaut tard que jamais.	*Better late than never.*

Situation: Annie tells her mother that she doesn't feel like having dinner because she doesn't have an appetite. What might her mother say to her?

L'appétit vient en mangeant.	*Appetite comes while eating.*

Situation: Yvette is gossiping with Mimi about Julie. Mimi whispers to her that somebody might be listening in the next room. What proverb might she use?

Les murs ont des oreilles.	*Walls have ears.*

Situation: Robert is telling his friend Louis that he would like to have a summer job in the fast-food restaurant near his house but he doesn't know how to get the job he wants. What might Louis say to him?

Vouloir, c'est pouvoir.	*Where there's a will, there's a way. (To want is to be able.)*

Participate in this conversation about the French painting *Terrasse à Sainte-Adresse* by the artist Claude Monet. When you hear the cue in English, say it in French during the first pause. During the second pause, correct yourself by repeating what you heard.

Alors, aimez-vous ce tableau de Claude Monet?	*So, do you like this painting by Claude Monet?*
Je pense qu'il est beau. Quel tableau! Je veux être artiste.	*I think it's beautiful. What a painting! I want to be an artist.*
Je pense que c'est épatant. Quel artiste! Je veux être artiste, aussi.	*I think it's great. What an artist! I want to be an artist, too.*
Regardez la structure géométrique marquée par les deux mâts. C'est merveilleux.	*Look at the geometric structure marked by the two masts. It's marvelous.*
Si je pouvais peindre comme ça!	*If only I could paint like that!*
Vouloir, c'est pouvoir!	*Where there's a will, there's a way!*
Regardez tous les bateaux à l'horizon.	*Look at all the boats on the horizon.*

Le jardin est beau. Je n'ai jamais vu un jardin si beau.	*The garden is beautiful. I have never seen a garden so beautiful.*
Bon. Alors, maintenant que vous avez apprécié un tableau impressionniste, allons sur la terrasse pour un rafraîchissement!	*Good. So, now that you have appreciated an impressionist painting, let's go on the terrace for a refreshment!*
Bonne idée!	*Good idea!*

UNIT 25

Now, let's conclude our program of practice in speaking French with some listening comprehension.

Listen to the following ten true-false questions based on the poem in your book. After you hear a statement, say **vrai** if it is true, or **faux** if it is false.

La cigale a chanté tout l'été.	*The cicada sang all summer.*
Vrai.	*True.*
La cigale n'a pas travaillé pendant l'été.	*The cicada did not work during the summer.*
Vrai.	*True.*
La fourmi n'a pas travaillé.	*The ant did not work.*
Faux.	*False.*
La cigale n'a rien à manger.	*The cicada has nothing to eat.*
Vrai.	*True.*
La fourmi a beaucoup à manger.	*The ant has a lot to eat.*
Vrai.	*True.*
Quand l'hiver arrive, la cigale a besoin de nourriture.	*When winter comes, the cicada needs food.*
Vrai.	*True.*
La fourmi refuse de donner à manger à la cigale.	*The ant refuses to give (something) to eat to the cicada.*
Vrai.	*True.*
La fourmi a chanté tout l'été.	*The ant sang all summer.*
Faux.	*False.*
La cigale a faim.	*The cicada is hungry.*
Vrai.	*True.*
La fourmi dit à la cigale de danser.	*The ant tells the cicada to dance.*
Vrai.	*True.*

We hope you have improved your proficiency in listening comprehension and speaking French. If you think you need more practice, start all over again!

Au revoir! Au revoir!	*Good-bye! Good-bye!*